Bengal Secratariat Press

Report on the Condition of the Lower Classes in Bengal

Bengal Secratariat Press

Report on the Condition of the Lower Classes in Bengal

ISBN/EAN: 9783744763325

Printed in Europe, USA, Canada, Australia, Japan

Cover: Foto ©Suzi / pixelio.de

More available books at **www.hansebooks.com**

REPORT

ON THE

CONDITION OF THE LOWER CLASSES OF POPULATION

IN

BENGAL.

Calcutta:
PRINTED AT THE BENGAL SECRETARIAT PRESS.
1888.

Confidential.]

REVENUE DEPARTMENT.

AGRICULTURE—No. 87T—R.

DARJEELING, { DATED THE 30TH JUNE / ISSUED THE JULY } 1888.

FROM P. NOLAN, ESQ.,

Secretary to the Government of Bengal,

TO THE SECRETARY TO THE GOVERNMENT OF INDIA,

REVENUE AND AGRICULTURAL DEPARTMENT.

SIR,

I AM directed to acknowledge the receipt of your letter No. 44F—8—1, dated the 17th August 1887, requesting that some enquiry should, if practicable, be made into the actual condition of the lower classes of the population, especially in agricultural tracts, and that the information collected, with a concise summary of conclusions and results, should be submitted to the Government of India. The object of the enquiry is to ascertain whether there is any foundation for the assertion frequently repeated, that the greater part of the population of India suffers from a daily insufficiency of food; and if there is truth in the statement, in regard to any section of the people, to determine whether remedial measures can be devised. It is suggested in your letter that the enquiry might be made through the agency of the Agricultural Department.

Orders of the Government of India that an enquiry should be made as to the condition of the poorer classes.

2. In reply, I am directed to state that the Director of Agriculture and Land Records, having been consulted on the subject, expressed a decided opinion that, considering the limited establishment at his disposal, the proposed enquiry could not be completed by his department for many years to come. The District Officers were accordingly requested to make the required investigation during their cold weather tours, and such instructions as appeared to be

Agency by which the enquiry was made.

necessary were issued for their guidance. The opinion of Dr. Lethbridge, Inspector-General of Jails, was invited, as he has taken special means to ascertain the physical condition of prisoners on first admission to prison, and from his long experience is in a position to form an estimate of the degree to which they, and the classes to which they belong, obtain sufficient nourishment when pursuing their ordinary occupations. The Director of the Department of Land Records and Agriculture was also requested to conduct the enquiry with regard to tracts settled under his supervision, and districts of which his staff might undertake the analysis. The information obtained up to date is contained in the correspondence specified in the margin, of which a copy is annexed.

1. Commissioner of the Bhagulpore Division, No. 2, dated 9th April 1888, with enclosure.
2. Commissioner of the Bhagulpore Division, No. 3, dated 10th April 1888, with enclosures.
3. Commissioner of the Burdwan Division, No. 7RG, dated 16th April 1888, with enclosures.
4. Commissioner of the Bhagulpore Division, No. 4, dated 19th April 1888, with enclosure.
5. Commissioner of the Bhagulpore Division, No. 5, dated 23rd April 1888, with enclosure.
6. Director of the Department of Land Records and Agriculture, Bengal, No. 829Agri., dated 27th April 1888, with enclosures.
7. Commissioner of the Chittagong Division, No. 160GC—VII—3, with enclosures.
8. Commissioner of the Rajshahye Division, No. 109M, dated 30th April 1888.
9. Commissioner of the Bhagulpore Division, No. 7, dated 2nd May 1888, with enclosure.
10. Commissioner of the Chittagong Division, No. 160GC—VII—5, dated 3rd May 1888, with enclosure.
11. Director of the Department of Land Records and Agriculture, Bengal, No. 867, dated 5th May 1888, with enclosure.
12. Commissioner of the Bhagulpore Division, No. 8, dated 5th May 1888, with enclosure.
13. Commissioner of the Presidency Division, No. 1MA, dated 17th May 1888.
14. Commissioner of the Chittagong Division, No. 202GC—VII—6, dated 14th May 1888, with enclosure.
15. Commissioner of the Dacca Division, No. 712LR, dated 18th May 1888, with enclosure.
16. Inspector-General of Jails, Bengal, No. 3617, dated 20th May 1888, with enclosure.
17. Commissioner of the Chota Nagpore Division, No. 351R, dated 31st May 1888 (without enclosure).
18. Commissioner of the Patna Division, No. 286G, dated 2nd June 1888.
19. Commissioner of the Orissa Division, No. 20PG, dated 3rd June 1888.
20. Commissioner of the Burdwan Division, No. 13RA, dated 6th June 1888, with enclosure.

The scope of the enquiry limited by the time available for conducting it.

3. The Lieutenant-Governor must express his regret that it has not been found possible to lay the result of this enquiry before the Government of India by the 1st of May, the date originally specified in your letter No. 35F—6—2, dated the 21st March 1888. The Commissioners were unable to prepare their reports until some time after the end of the cold season: that of the Patna Division, which is of the greatest importance, as relating to the part of the province in respect of which most anxiety has been felt, was not received until the 7th June. On the other hand, Sir Steuart Bayley has much pleasure in acknowledging the care and ability shown by many of the officers consulted in dealing with one of the most difficult and important subjects which can engage the attention of a Government. Mr. Smith, Commissioner of the Presidency Division, and Mr. Lyall, Commissioner of Chittagong, have submitted reports of special value. Mr. Oldham, Collector of Burdwan, and Baboo Bissessur Banerjee, Settlement Officer, have made most careful enquiries.

Method of enquiry.

4. The question of the condition of the masses in Bengal has long occupied the attention of Government, but such is the intrinsic difficulty of the subject, that no decisive result has been hitherto obtained. I may refer in particular to the correspondence ending with despatch No. 8, dated the 15th August 1871, in which the Secretary of State declared that the reports then available did not contain evidence on which any safe conclusion could be founded. In the present enquiry an attempt has been made to ascertain actual facts in limited areas, chosen as typical of the districts in which they are situated. In the selected villages the enquiries made have often been of a searching character, and have elicited interesting details as to the area of the holding of each ryot, the utensils which he uses, the extent to which he is indebted, the value of the ornaments worn by the females of his family, with estimates of the produce of the land, the cost of cultivation, of ordinary food, clothing, general subsistence, and of the social ceremonies which absorb so much of the income of natives of Bengal. Similar facts have been ascertained in regard to the wages of the labouring classes, the degree to which they are independent, and the expenditure they have to incur.

5. All the officers of Government consulted, without a single exception, bear witness to the fact that the industrial classes are far more prosperous in the eastern than in the western districts of the province. In the Chittagong Division the cultivators and agricultural labourers are described as being in a state of at least comparative comfort. In favour of this view Mr. Lyall, the present Commissioner, quotes the annual reports of the last fifteen years, extracts from which are given at the end of his letter. He also cites the opinion of Babu Shambhu Chandra Mookerjee, the editor of a well-known journal, who writes in his book *Travels in Bengal*, page 14:—"I am infinitely delighted to observe the evidence of comfort and comparative civilization in the peasantry of these parts. It is something that so many about here are well protected in the cold weather by the cheap cottons and woollens of Europe. The women have all more costly ornaments, if less heavy and numerous, than their mothers or grand-mothers could boast of. We rarely come across the old abomination of the twisted leg cuff (*bank mal*), as it deserves to be called, rather than anklet. Shell bracelets are few and far between, but of a more manageable description than the manacles used of yore. Silver clearly predominates; brass is nowhere. At Dacca we saw the Hindustani women had replaced by smaller and lighter silver jewellery their heavy pewter bracelets. Here, on the banks of the Megna, we found all the women display silver; some in profusion. It was all due to jute." The only allegation of actual deficiency in this division of the amount of food required for the support of healthy life is made by a native official as regards what he describes as the middle class; that is, those who consider themselves above manual work. The local rate of money wages is four annas a day, employment appears to be steady, and larger wages are earned by those who go in search of temporary work to Arracan.

Comparative prosperity of the eastern divisions.

Chittagong.

6. The report made by the Commissioner of Dacca as to his division is even more reassuring. Mr. Larminie goes so far as to state that, looking to their needs, the peasantry are about the most prosperous in the world. The cultivators are well off, and their condition has been improved in recent years by the extension of the cultivation of jute. Labourers in the Backergunge district receive four to six annas a day; elsewhere their wages are probably somewhat lower than in Chittagong. The enquiry has, however, been less searching in the Dacca Division than elsewhere, and probably a careful investigation in selected villages would have resulted in a somewhat more qualified statement as to the degree of prosperity enjoyed. It will be understood that in all districts of Bengal, as indeed in most parts of the old world, there are many poor persons who, by reason of the failure of their trade, temporary cessation of employment, or sickness, suffer much distress. The weavers, potters, and some other castes or classes, who cling to an hereditary employment in places where it has ceased to be remunerative, or in numbers exceeding the demand, are in a bad condition. The ryots, even where most prosperous in the Backergunge district, where it is said that each holding averages 9 acres, producing 13 maunds of cleaned rice an acre, are said to be very generally in debt, at least from the sowing time till harvest.

Dacca.

7. A portion of the Presidency Division partakes of the character of Eastern Bengal, including, as it does, the partly-reclaimed tracts of the Sunderbuns, which afford some outlet for an increasing population. It is, moreover, in this division, that the influence of an extending foreign trade, and of the development of manufactures on European models, has been most completely felt. In the Rajshahye Division there is a considerable amount of waste land in Julpigoree and Darjeeling, while in the five remaining districts the increase of population, as shown in the census returns, has not been such as to press unduly on the resources of the land. In Rungpore, which is stated to be in a very prosperous state, there has been an actual decrease of 2·58 per cent. In that district, as also in Dinagepore, Purneah, and Maldah, the climate is unfavourable, but, perhaps on account of this disadvantage, rents are easy, reclaimable waste exists, and the demand for labour is in excess of the local supply. Thus in the central districts the working classes are prosperous, though not quite to the same extent as Eastern Bengal. The agricultural

Presidency and Rajshahye Divisions, with Purneah and Maldah, constituting Central Bengal.

labourer gets from three to four annas a day, and there is a greater demand than elsewhere for skilled labour. The substantial ryots appear to be very well off, as indeed they are everywhere, but we hear more of under-ryots cultivating on the *bhauli* system, according to which the landlord receives half the crop as rent. Such ryots are never in good circumstances. In the Moorshedabad district, on the extreme west, the conditions are somewhat less favourable than in the rest of the divisions, and the wages of agricultural labour occasionally fall to the rate of two annas a day, which may be considered the minimum consistent with the unstinted supply of food to ordinary families. In Dinagepore the labouring classes are frequently weighted by debt, and continue in many cases servants for life to their creditors. This servitude is sometimes even hereditary, the son accepting as his own the father's debts. But, with the possible exception of parts of the Moorshedabad district, it may be said that in Central Bengal the question of a deficiency of food does not arise.

Burdwan Division, Hooghly and Burdwan districts.

8. The metropolitan district of Hooghly, with its dependent district of Howrah, has the full benefit of the neighbourhood of Calcutta, and has also been affected by the Burdwan fever, which greatly reduced its population. The Collector, Mr. Toynbee, takes a very favourable view of the situation, observing, as stated in the Commissioner's report:—"The condition of the poorer classes in this district, compared with that of the same classes in England, may unhesitatingly be described as superior in every respect. There is no such thing as want or starvation among them, and not one individual who does not know, when he rises in the morning, how or where he will procure food for the day. Their wants are few and easily satisfied. The climate in which they live and all their surroundings are enervating and, to our view, demoralizing; ambition they have none, beyond the immediate wants and wishes of the day; but judged from their own point of view, and by their own standard, they are prosperous and contented, and I doubt not that there are thousands upon thousands of the English poor who will gladly change their places with them." Mr. Oldham, the Collector of Burdwan, ascertained by a very careful enquiry that the inhabitants of his district have ample means of subsistence. The evidence collected as to their freedom from debt, and the disappearance of the rural money-lenders, is novel and interesting. The facts reported can scarcely be explained merely by a reference to the improved condition of the cultivators and labourers, as the business of money-lending is found to flourish in districts where these classes are certainly more prosperous than in Burdwan. Mr. Oldham writes:—

"Referring to the poorer cultivators and field-labourers, the result of my enquiries may be set forth in the following propositions:—

"(1) In a purely agricultural area they, with their families, form about 75 per cent. of the population.

"(2) In the Burdwan district they all bear traces of disease. They may all be said to be enfeebled by disease; that is, by fever and its consequences. Among some castes leprosy is terribly common.

"(3) They bear the burden of their helpless and sick relatives, who are about 5 per cent. of them.

"(4) The rates of their remuneration have risen considerably within the last 20 years, and above the proportion of the increased dearness of provisions.

"(5) There is no indebtedness among them, and the indebtedness which used to exist has disappeared.

"(6) The wives and elder children of a poor cultivator or labourer who is in ordinary health are not forced to resort to out-door labour, and are employed solely on domestic duties.

"(7) An adult male, even though in poor physical condition, receives, at the lowest calculation, one and a half times as much as will support a working man's life and supply clothing and lodging, and the average is higher. The proportion of surplus for a woman is much lower; not reaching to as much again.

"(8) Finally, taking the rates of food which have prevailed for the last 13 years, they have enough with which to procure, and they do procure, a sufficiency of wholesome food, enough to support their wives, children, and dependent relatives on; to bestow on their universal charity; to expend on festivals and celebrations, and to enable them to meet at least the approaches of a time of scarcity. They are much better off than I, on a superficial view of their circumstances, or than their own fellow-residents of superior station, suppose them to be; and the only individuals among them who have no margin, or but the slenderest margin, are their dependent relatives, the most numerous of whom are old widows and others disabled by sickness, age, or some bodily or mental infirmity."

The census returns of 1881 show a diminution since 1872 of six per cent. in the population of Burdwan, and it is believed that even greater desolation was caused by the fatal Burdwan fever during the previous decade. The total mortality from this cause is estimated in the last census report at no less than 700,000, and since then this fatal disease was very active in the years 1881 to 1884. Thus Burdwan and Hooghly, where the diminution in population amounted to twelve and a half per cent., show an economical aspect the reverse of that presented by the rest of these provinces, inasmuch as the population is failing, while the demand for labour increases, and the supply of land for cultivation remains undiminished. Under such conditions it appears that a sufficient maintenance may be earned even by a people debilitated by recurring illness.

Bankoorah and Midnapore present the first symptoms of failing prosperity.

9. In reviewing the condition of the Lower Provinces from east to west, the first symptoms of chronic poverty appear in the districts of Bankoorah and Midnapore. As to Bankoorah, the only district in the Burdwan Division which at the last census showed an increase of population, while the report is not on the whole unfavourable, it is said that the labourers are not fully employed at certain seasons, when they are reduced to one meal a day and suffer much. The emigrants to Assam show, to the eyes of the Civil Surgeon, no sign of being affected by want of due nourishment, but the majority of those admitted to jail are said to suffer from scorbutic diathesis. In Midnapore the enquiry has not, in the opinion of the Commissioner, been very satisfactorily supervised, and the diminutive size of the holdings of cultivators reported in the villages examined can hardly be reconciled with the easy proportion of population to area, as shown by the census, if the villages are to be considered typical. The rate of daily wages is said to be three annas, employment being locally available for six months of the year only. At other times labourers have ready access to Calcutta. It is stated that about 10 per cent. of the population have only one meal a day, and although no great reliance can be placed on this estimate, it is probable that the condition of the people is decidedly inferior to that of Bengalis generally.

In Behar the working classes are, comparatively speaking, in bad circumstances.

10. In regard to the physical condition of the people, the province of Behar, which includes the districts of Monghyr and Bhagulpore, as well as the Patna Division, has unfortunately a distinctive character. For the present purpose Chumparun may be excluded from consideration, that district containing much land still imperfectly reclaimed, and perhaps also Shahabad. The tract remaining consists of seven adjoining districts—Patna, Gya, Mozufferpore, Durbhunga, Sarun, Bhagulpore and Monghyr—with a population of 15,313,359, according to the last census. There is no doubt that in this part of Behar, while the upper and middle classes are prosperous, the ordinary labourers, and the smaller cultivators, amounting, according to the estimate of the Commissioner of Patna, to some forty per cent. of the population, are much worse off than the corresponding classes in Bengal. Daily wages in these districts are nowhere estimated at more than two annas, and in many cases do not exceed five or six pice a day. Even the lowest rate of wages quoted will suffice in ordinary times to supply food and necessary clothing for the individual worker; and as payments are generally made partly or entirely in grain, there is some allowance for periods of scarcity. But it would appear that wages less than two annas a day in money value cannot supply the wants of the number of persons ordinarily dependent on the bread-winner. There is not employment for all the local labourers available, and a considerable

Howrah is entered in the census returns as a district in Burdwan wherein population increased; but Howrah is really only a subdivision of Hooghly.

number seek work in other districts. The smaller cultivators have not sufficient land to support them in comfort; and though this is a statement applicable to every part of Bengal, the evil is felt most in Behar, because remunerative employment is not readily found there for the time the ryots can spare from their own fields. The rents also are comparatively high, and ryots enjoy, or at least have enjoyed in former times, less security of tenure.

Opinions as to the sufficiency of their nourishment.

11. It is in these districts that we must look for evidence of the poorer classes suffering from an insufficient diet. The Collector of Bhagulpore writes:—"Directly a crop shows signs of failing, the ryot husbands his store; and in such years as we had before 1885, both the smaller ryot and the labourers were undoubtedly under-fed. Generally, however, I agree with the majority of those whom I have consulted that in years of ordinary prosperity the labourer gets enough food for himself and his family, except for perhaps one or two months in the year, when he is on short commons." The Settlement Officer, Mr. Collin, writing with special reference to two villages examined by him in the district, observes:—"From the foregoing description of the condition of the agricultural classes in this pergunnah (Daphor), it appears that they need not at present cause any apprehension, and that in ordinary years they have sufficient means of subsistence. The picture which I have drawn does not, however, show any great prosperity, and shows that the lower classes, which, including the weaving class, amounting to 25 per cent. of the population, have little chance of improving their position, and that they would have no resources to fall back upon in time of scarcity." The nominal list of the inhabitants of mouzah Paharpore, submitted by the Assistant Settlement Officer of the same estate, gives a somewhat less favourable impression. The Collector of Monghyr's report is very brief, but with regard to three out of ten villages statistically examined he remarks that he has come across many inhabitants who were thin and apparently in want of due nourishment. The Collector of Patna writes of ryots holding less than four local bighas, or two and a half acres:—"Their fare is of the very coarsest, consisting to a great extent of *khesari dál*, and the quantity is insufficient during a considerable part of the year. They can only take one full meal instead of two. They are badly housed, and in the cold weather insufficiently clothed." As to labourers, he adds that their condition is rather worse. "They are almost always paid in kind, the usual allowance of a grown man being 2 to 2½ seers of the coarsest and cheapest grain, value about 1¼ annas. Women receive about half this rate, but their employment is less regular. Ordinarily, male labourers do not find employment for more than eight months of the year.

"A wage of 1¼ annas per day would be about Rs. 2-6 per mensem; but taking an average of Rs. 2 per mensem throughout the year, the annual earnings of an adult would be about Rs. 24; his wife's earnings might be Rs. 6; total Rs. 30, which is not enough to give two adults and two children a full supply of the coarsest food, with sufficient clothing and a hut to shelter them. The Subdivisional Officer of Behar estimates the earnings of a labourer at 2 annas per diem, or Rs. 4 per mensem; but even this rate, which I think an over-estimate, would only yield Rs. 32 for the eight months during which labour is generally to be had.

"The conclusion to be drawn is that of the agricultural population a large proportion, say 40 per cent., are insufficiently fed, to say nothing of clothing and housing. They have enough food to support life and to enable them to work, but they have to undergo long fasts, having for a considerable part of the year to satisfy themselves with one full meal in the day."

In Durbhunga the Collector states that, in the villages examined by him, 60 per cent. of the ryots held less than four Behar bighas of land, and adds "there is no doubt that the bulk of the cultivating population are occupiers of small holdings, and it is very probable that the holdings of 2 bighas or less are more numerous than those of between 2 and 4 bighas. A small holding may, however, be sufficient by itself for the entire maintenance of its tenant and his family, if the lands are suitable for the most remunerative crops, such as tobacco, sugarcane and opium; and the smallness of the holding is not therefore always evidence of the tenant's poverty. Still, as a very general rule, the tenants of small holdings of less than 4 bighas are badly off, and it is necessary, where their families are of the usual size, that they should supplement cultivation by labour. This labour they obtain generally by assisting the more independent tenants in the cultivation of their holdings or harvesting of their crops, or by temporarily emigrating into neighbouring districts to help in gathering in the harvests." With regard to Gya, the Commissioner accepts a statement made by the Collector that forty per cent. of the population are insufficiently fed. The information given in the Commissioner's report as to Mozufferpore is not precise, while from Sarun no reply has as yet been received; but it is known from other sources that these districts, though better off than Gya and Patna, partake generally of the character of the tract referred to. It is to be noticed, as evidence of importance, that Dr. Lethbridge, the Inspector-General of Jails, concurs with the Superintendents of the jails of Mozufferpore, Gya, Sarun and Monghyr in considering that the poorer classes admitted suffer from previous insufficiency of food. The Superintendents of jails in the other five districts of Behar do not offer any opinion upon the subject. Dr. Lethbridge adds:—

"Having for ten years paid a yearly visit to nearly every district in Bengal, His Honor the Lieutenant-Governor may wish to have my opinion as to the general condition of the poorer classes in Bengal. The only parts of the province in which there need be an anxiety on this score are Behar and Chota Nagpore. In Behar, the districts of Mozufferpore and Sarun, and parts of Durbhunga and Chumparun, are the worst, and there is almost constant insufficiency of food among those who earn their living by daily labour."

This lowness of wages in Behar has long been noticed.

12. The comparatively low rate at which labour is remunerated in Behar has long been the subject of comment, and is referred to in almost every annual report from the Patna Division. In the Commissioner's report for the year 1874-75, in which special attention had been drawn to the question by the measures taken for the relief of scarcity, Sir Steuart (then Mr.) Bayley quoted the following statements of the Deputy Magistrate of Behar:—" 'It is a matter of wonder for what small wages the coolies labour here. For what we pay 6 annas in Eastern Bengal, 8 annas in Calcutta, for that we pay 3 to 4 pice in Behar. Then the amount of work a cooly in this part of the country performs is something wonderful when compared with that in Lower Bengal.' Again, carpenters, masons, weavers are paid at equally cheap rates. A carpenter who gets 2 annas here per day is sure to get 6 annas in Calcutta, Burdwan, or Dacca; a mason who gets here 4 annas per day, gets 12 annas in Calcutta for work of equal excellence; so do the weavers, potters, &c. The lower classes of labourers, as coolies ploughing in the fields, digging earth, carrying grain, are paid not more than 3 to 4 pice, or 2½ seers of paddy or *janara* when they are paid in kind, which is generally done." In a minute prefixed to the Bengal Administration Report for that year, Sir Richard Temple observed that the poverty of the labourers was such as to induce a low and weak physique.

Inferiority not due to soil, climate, or want of employment.

13. The marked inferiority of Behar in regard to the prosperity of the labouring classes is not attributable to want of fertility in the soil, to an enervating climate, to any weakness or idleness in the people themselves, to defects in communications, or to the absence of such industries as elsewhere afford employment. On the contrary, it may be said that the soil of Behar is of average quality, while in all the other matters indicated that province possesses a distinct superiority over most parts of Bengal. The inhabitants are comparatively healthy, strong and industrious; the communications by rail, road, and river are fairly good; the opium and indigo operations and sugar mills employ an exceptionally large number of the rural population.

But to the greater supply of labourers.

14. With regard to the cause of the comparative poverty of the labouring classes of Behar, Sir Steuart Bayley wrote in 1875:—" Over the culturable area of the division, with the single exception of North Chumparun (and putting aside certain *quasi*-culturable* tracts in Shahabad and Gya), there is hardly any waste land, and the pressure of the population per square mile is excessive, ranging in cultivated tracts between 500 and 750 per square mile—a population, too, almost wholly agricultural. Rents, including therein the innumerable cesses by which they are supplemented, are limited in the case of the lower and better class of agriculturists by little else than their inability to pay more.

* "By *quasi*-culturable land, I mean land which, without capital or expensive means of irrigation, cannot be made available for cultivation."

"So long as the existing competition for land exists, it must always have its natural effect in the depressed and impoverished condition of the cultivating class."

The view that wages are lower in Behar than elsewhere, and rents are higher, simply because labourers and competitors for land are more numerous, may now be somewhat extended, as it appears from the present correspondence that the pressure of population on natural resources has a decisive influence on the rate at which labour is remunerated throughout the Lower Provinces generally. In the extreme east, where labour is most scarce, wages are highest, and the rate decreases almost proportionately as we travel towards the west. The only exception to the uniformity in the rate of improvement in the position of the labouring classes as we travel eastward is to be found in the districts which are particularly unhealthy—in Hooghly and Burdwan, where there has been an actual decrease of population owing to epidemic fever; in Rungpore, Dinagepore and Purneah, where fever is endemic. In these districts, though the people are enfeebled by sickness, and their labour is therefore less efficient, they find no difficulty in obtaining a maintenance, because their numbers are not permitted to rise to the point at which they would press unduly on the resources of the country.

Increasing density of population in Behar.

15. The rapid increase shown in the population of Behar was considered at the time to be the most surprising feature of the census of 1881. As the compiler of the report observes:—"When the census of 1872 was taken, the density of the population which covered this area was the subject of frequent comment, and it has received the continuous attention of Government ever since. In that year the average number of persons to the square mile in the Patna Division was 553, distributed as follows:—

Sarun	.. 778	Gya	.. 413
Patna	.. 742	Chumparun	.. 408
Tirhoot	.. 691	Shahabad	.. 393

It has frequently been asserted that it was impossible for the soil to support any further increase in a population most of whom depend on agriculture for their livelihood, yet the figures now returned seem to show that a large increase was not only possible, but that it has actually taken place in every district of the division. Thus the Durbhunga district, which was formerly the north-eastern portion of the district of Tirhoot, shows an advance of 23·09 per cent., Chumparun follows with 19·48 per cent., Mozufferpore (the other portion of the old Tirhoot district) with 14·99 per cent., Shahabad with 13·97 per cent., Patna with 12·64 per cent., Sarun with 10·49 per cent., and Gya closes the list with 9·07 per cent. In density of population the districts have increased in a different degree, but, with the single exception that the pressure of population on the soil is now higher in Chumparun than in Gya, their order is the same as it was in 1872, viz.—

	Persons per square mile.		Persons per square mile.
Sarun	869·71	Chumparun	487·57
Patna	845·05	Gya	450·91
Mozufferpore & Durbhunga ..	824·73	Shahabad	450·15

giving an average for the division of 637·03 per cent. per square mile."

The increase in the district of Monghyr was 8·55 per cent., in Bhagulpore 7·75 per cent.; the density per square mile being—Monghyr 502·37, Bhagulpore 460·67. In considering the density of the population as an index to its pressure on the means of subsistence, it is necessary to remember that Bhagulpore, Monghyr, Gya and Shahabad contain large tracts of comparatively barren mountains.

Effect of low wages on the condition of the cultivators.

16. In addition to the rapid increase of the population, the high rates of rent in force in Behar, and the arbitrary methods of enhancement have been quoted as causes of the poverty of the ryots. The abundance of cheap and efficient labour is in itself an advantage to farmers, and, taken apart from certain indirect effects, could never account for their inferior condition. These indirect effects are the readiness of ryots, holding at rates much below those

which may be obtained by competition, to under-let at a rack-rent, leaving the actual cultivation to a class of paupers; the disposition to subdivide where the younger members of the family cannot obtain a decent subsistence by labour; and the tendency of landowners to enhance rents held, without direct and efficient legal sanction, at privileged rates. Such tendencies may, to some extent, be counteracted, and it is possible that, had their rights been ascertained and upheld at an early period, the ryots might now form a privileged class, raised above the surrounding poverty, as they do in the Bhojpore pergunnah of Shahabad, and as many of them do elsewhere, having preserved holdings of adequate size, held on a secure tenure, at fair rents. It is also probable that the Bengal Tenancy Act, which has for the first time rendered it possible for the majority of ryots to prove occupancy rights, may do much to promote the growth of such a privileged class, particularly if its provisions be brought home to every cultivator by a survey and record of rights in the manner recommended in my letter No. 283—116LR, dated the 25th January 1888. But such measures cannot permanently alter the condition of the landless labourers, or of those having holdings too small for subsistence—in fact of the 40 per cent. of the population of certain districts, about whom anxiety is expressed by the Commissioner. And while these continue to multiply beyond the means of subsistence, their number must create a demand for land on any terms, which will always be a source of danger to the superior cultivators. The economical rent, the margin of profit between the wages of the labour necessary to raise the produce, and the price at which that produce will sell, must under such conditions remain high; and where under-letting is permitted, or landholders are allowed to let vacant holdings at discretionary rents, there must always be a tendency towards an approximation between the actual and the economic rent.

Emigration recognized as a means of raising wages in Behar.

17. Sir Steuart Bayley observed in 1875, agreeing in this with Mr. MacDonnell, then Collector of Durbhunga, that if the idea of emigration could be once popularised, so as to take such a hold of the people as it did of the Irish twenty-five years ago, it would be the best thing that could happen to these districts. The introduction of manufactures, he added, was another possible remedy; but neither with regard to the one or the other did he venture to entertain any great hopes. Emigration is to some extent practised—to the colonies, to the tea plantations in Assam, and, with far greater effect, to the eastern districts generally, where up-countrymen are to be found in considerable numbers, both as temporary sojourners and as permanent settlers.

Lines of emigration opened.

18. Much stress was laid by all authorities at the time on the importance of facilitating this emigration from the east to the west by the construction of railways, and the work since done in that direction has not been inconsiderable. Since 1874 the Tirhoot State Railway (224 miles), the Patna-Gya Railway (57 miles), the Bengal and North-Western Railway (portion in Bengal 92½ miles), all converging at Patna on the internal line of the East Indian Railway, have been constructed. The Assam-Behar Railway, from Sahebgunge on the Ganges to Parbuttipore on the Northern Bengal line and the Brahmaputra, will be completed next year, and will shortly afterwards be connected with the Tirhoot State Railway. These lines are connected with the Northern Bengal Railway (249 miles) and its continuation to Darjeeling (50 miles), also constructed since 1874. A great improvement has similarly been effected in the steamer communication with Assam and Cachar, by which emigrants travel in considerable numbers.

Reasons why emigration has been limited.

19. The extent to which this emigration from west to east is now carried on is illustrated by the statements showing that at the census of 1881 there were in Bengal Proper 47,548 persons born in Sarun, 38,220 from Shahabad, 40,536 from Patna, 25,481 from Mozufferpore, 18,167 from Monghyr, 36,235 from Gya, 12,958 from Bhagulpore. That the movement has not assumed larger dimensions is partly accounted for by the fact that the work which would find the most suitable employment for emigrants, the reclamation of waste land from jungle, seems to be peculiarly injurious to the health of up-countrymen. It involves an exposure to malarious fever, to which their constitutions have not become accustomed. This is the real obstacle to all comprehensive projects for settling the superfluous population of Behar on the extensive wastes of Assam and

Burmah. It may be that such emigrants, acting together in large bodies, could eradicate the jungle, if organized with care and supported by capital, due provision being made for their sanitary protection; but they seem quite incapable of reclaiming jungle as such work is generally done in Chittagong and the Sunderbuns, that is, by the efforts of individual cultivators. In addition to climatic influence, the difference of language between Behar and Bengal offers an obstacle to free emigration. And the reluctance of the labouring classes to leave their homes, even where no barrier of this kind exists, is always considerable. In England it is understood that where a Wiltshire labourer some years ago received nine shillings a week, in Yorkshire he might have obtained thirteen shillings for the same hours and the same work. The difference between wages prevalent in Ireland and England, England and the Colonies, has always been very great, and has not been effaced by emigration.

Popular education considered as a remedy for low wages.

20. Even emigration can be regarded only as a temporary remedy for an excess in the supply of labour, where the latter is due to causes so permanent as the marriage customs of the people and the salubrity of the climate. The ultimate conditions of prosperity for the lowest class in the community appear to be the establishment of a standard of comfort, below which they will not consent to sink. And this can probably be brought about only by the diffusion of education among the masses—a subject which has long occupied the attention of this Government. The census of 1881 showed 95·52 per cent. of the population of these provinces as illiterate; or, if attention be confined to the male population above the age of five years, and all learners be classified as literate, 90 per cent. The proportion of these male illiterates at the date of the census was greatest in the Chota Nagpore and Bhagulpore Divisions, where it was 95 per cent.; and it was 94 per cent. in the Patna Division, against 86 per cent. in Bengal Proper. The last report of the Director of Public Instruction shows that Durbhunga and Mozufferpore are, after the Chittagong Hill Tracts, the most backward districts from an educational point of view. It seems certain that the forty per cent. of the population of these districts and of Patna, referred to by the Commissioner as insufficiently nourished, must be wholly illiterate. Expenditure on primary education, which in 1887-88 exceeded seven lakhs of rupees, is the creation of recent years, and it is matter of great regret that the state of the finances does not permit of a further effort being made to benefit the working classes in this direction. There can be little doubt that popular education, could it be made a reality for the poorest class, as it has been for those somewhat higher in the social scale, would have a beneficial influence on their physical condition, by facilitating emigration, increasing the efficiency of their labour, and also ultimately, though perhaps not until after a very long interval, raising the standard of living below which they will not consent to fall, even under the influence of time-honoured marriage customs.

Chota Nagpore district.

21. In the above review no reference has been made to the two divisions of Chota Nagpore and Orissa, each of which represents a nationality distinguished by language and customs—in the case of Chota Nagpore by economic conditions also—from the rest of the Lower Provinces. In Chota Nagpore wages are even lower than in Behar, but grain is cheaper, and the primitive inhabitants resort largely to the jungle produce of the country in order to eke out their means of subsistence. Mr. Baker, Deputy Commissioner of Manbhoom, writes:—"Turning now to the agricultural labourers, we find that in 157 households there are 355 earning members, of whom 240 are males and 115 are females. In other words, in this class there is one working woman for every two working men. It is satisfactory to find that more than three-fourths of these labourers usually obtain employment for the greater part of the year, thus:—

Number employed for less than three months in the year ..	43
Number employed for more than three months and less than six months	49
Number employed for more than six months	263
	355

The earnings of these 355 labourers during the year amount to 2,785 maunds of paddy, valued at Rs. 1,740, together with Rs. 2,122 in cash. Their total earnings thus amount to rather less than Rs. 11 per head per annum. The total income of an average family of this class from all sources is—

	Rs.
For labour	24·6
„ cultivation (net)	4·48
„ miscellaneous	·73
	29·81

The Commissioner considers these estimates of income too low. His own opinion as to the division generally is expressed as follows:—

"The following, however, may be taken as the opinion which I have formed on certain points. The number of persons living on charity only is very small indeed. The great majority of the people are sure of two meals at least in the day in an ordinary season, and of the remainder most, if not all, are sure of two meals a day in an ordinary year, with the exception of the latter part of the hot weather. Rice is not by any means the only food, though it is the most important article. It is largely supplemented by vegetables, maizes and other crops grown in the rains, by *mahua*, and in a large portion of the division by numerous jungle products. Further, there is some fish, though not much in comparison with Lower Bengal, and animal food, both wild and tame, is occasionally procurable. There are few, if any, animals which are not accepted as food by some caste or tribe. Emigration has been of great advantage, especially to Chota Nagpore Proper. It has been the means of relieving the pressure which exists in some places on the land, it has brought much money into the division, and has afforded to some extent a check on the rapacity of money-lenders and landlords. Probably at least half the cultivators are in debt, but the amount of debt is generally small. It is usually incurred for the purpose of paying rent or performing some social ceremony. In some places seed-grain is borrowed; in others each ryot saves his own. The cultivators as a class are better off than the village artizans or mere labourers, but in towns the artizans are very well paid. The artizans and labourers are far less in debt than the cultivators, because they have less to offer as security. The rates of wages are certainly rising. In the parts most inhabited by aboriginals, they are still very low, and often the wages of one or two members of the family are regarded merely as supplementing the general resources. The effect of European enterprise, in the matter of tea cultivation, the collection of tussar cocoons, and other produce, has been to throw large sums of money into the country; and the construction of the Bengal-Nagpore Railway, now in progress, and the feeder roads will have the same results. Upon the whole, though beyond any doubt there are very many poor people in the division, whose livelihood, especially when there are partial failures of crops, is precarious, there seems to be no doubt that the great majority are not ordinarily severely pressed. The physique of different classes, and castes, and tribes varies very much, but generally speaking it is fairly good."

Orissa.

22. It so happens that in Orissa the Officiating Commissioner and the Officiating Collectors of the three districts have little experience of the division, and the report cannot therefore be regarded as of great value. It is on the whole of a reassuring tendency.

Comparative prosperity of the different classes of the population.

Cultivators.

23. The condition of the cultivators who possess sufficient land to afford full occupation for their families appears to be everywhere superior to that of labourers and the majority of artizans. None of the reports indicate any very severe incidence of rent on farmers holding considerable areas, or even on cottier cultivators, provided they hold more than four acres. A large proportion of such ryots appear to be in debt everywhere, except in Burdwan, but this does not prevent their subsistence in a certain degree of comfort. Ryots holding less than four acres seem, as a rule, to supplement their cultivation by labour, although many of them find adequate employment on very small holdings by raising the more valuable crops, such as opium.

Where a ryot has to work for hire, his condition seems to differ but little from that of other agricultural labourers; but it is probably somewhat better. The labourer who also holds land can always change position with the labourer who holds none; and if he does not do so, it must generally be because the change would be disadvantageous.

24. The artizans of Bengal, as goldsmiths, carpenters, and blacksmiths, are generally much better off than the unskilled labourers. But as their occupations are hereditary, and are changed with difficulty, they suffer much when any alteration in trade renders their particular handicrafts unremunerative. Such a change occurred when native cotton stuffs were generally superseded by English goods, with results very injurious to the weavers. The depression of this industry has, however, been very gradual, and the artizans have to a great extent taken to other employments. In the Presidency Division many of the weavers have land and money also; some have sent members of their families to work in the mills on good wages. As to the Dacca Division, the Commissioner states that some of the Tipperah weavers have refused to take to other work, but that this is not generally the case. In Burdwan they have taken to agriculture and to service in the mills, at least as a means of supplementing their ordinary trade.

Artizans.

25. The condition of agricultural labourers has been described above as varying with the locality. It may be remarked here that the present enquiry, wherever it has been carried out in detail, has shown that such labourers are numerous. They are not recognized as a distinct class in the census returns, and the information as to their numbers is very deficient. The statement frequently made in official reports, and repeated in the present correspondence by the Commissioner of Chittagong and Collector of Noakholly, that there are very few landless workers in Bengal generally or in particular districts, appear to rest on no sufficient foundation. Thus, notwithstanding the general assertion of the Commissioner, in the villages examined in Salkawa, khas tehsil, Chittagong, 290 out of 887 families are classified as labourers; in Cox's Bazar 1,724 out of 4,405. They constitute a large body, probably a fourth of the whole population, and their numbers are everywhere recruited by cultivators having holdings too small for their support. The rate of the agricultural labourer's wages is always an index to the degree of prosperity enjoyed by the working classes in a Bengal district.

Agricultural labourers.

26. The returns give considerable information, often of a very definite character, as to the proportion of the population in debt in some of the villages examined and the extent of the obligations. Of Burdwan alone is it reported that the custom of borrowing does not prevail among the ryots. The subject has been treated with care in the report of Mr. Smith, Commissioner of the Presidency Division, who states that of 158 families of cultivators in two villages examined in the 24-Pergunnahs, "as many as 116 were found to be in debt. Thirty-one families owe sums from Rs. 25 downwards, 35 owe from Rs. 26 to Rs. 50, 30 from Rs. 51 to Rs. 100, 9 from Rs. 101 to Rs. 150, 4 from Rs. 151 to Rs. 200, and 7 owe from Rs. 200 to Rs. 400. The debts amount in all to Rs. 8,387, or Rs. 53 per family, taking all 158 families. Taking indebted families only, each one's debt amounts to Rs. 72, or nearly the selling value of one year's crop. It does not, however, follow from this that the cultivating class is generally steeped in penury. There is scarcely a person among them with any credit who will not make use of it to its full extent, and it is quite possible that some of the remaining 42 families are not in debt, because they have not sufficient credit to justify the *mahajan* allowing them advances.

Indebtedness of the poorer classes.

"Of 145 labouring families in the two selected villages, 95 are in debt to the extent of Rs. 3,990, or Rs. 42 per family, while 50 are free from debt. As with ordinary cultivators, so also in the case of labourers, these debts are contracted and wiped off in whole or part year by year. During the three or four harvest months in ordinary years, the circumstances of both classes are fairly easy, and the mahajan's account is settled so far as means and inclination permit. During the remaining months those who run through their stocks owing to bad seasons or extravagance have to turn to him again and borrow, as they also occasionally do when they are in need of marriage and *sradh* expenses, and their credit justifies the loan.

"With both classes (cultivators and labourers) good seasons go to balance bad seasons in the matter of the mahajan's bill. During times of scarcity heavier debts are incurred, which are paid off in years of plenty. In ordinary years balance of accounts is fairly maintained. It is in the nature of a native of the lower classes, and for that matter often of higher classes as well, to accept advances whenever he can get them. Indebtedness seldom means starvation, but usually quite the reverse."

On this point, Mr. Boxwell, Officiating Commissioner of Patna, states:—"General indebtedness of a poor agricultural community is not like, and is much less bad than, the common indebtedness of an extravagant man. It means nothing more than that in the tight season—that is, the season of ploughing and sowing—the mahajan advances what he recovers with interest in the harvest. The strange notion that borrowing makes a permanent addition to a cultivator's income, and the common view that a peasantry in debt is on its way to ruin, seem to be equally wrong and almost equally paradoxical. In a low state of civilization people are unable to do their own saving. Their mahajans do it for them, and make them pay well for it; but in an ordinary year the produce of the soil, including of course pasture and jungle, supports the cultivator, the labourer, the mahajan, and the landlord."

Similarly it is stated with regard to a village in the Nuddea district, where the number of cultivators is 44, that "3 do not borrow, but can afford to lend money and paddy to their neighbours; 9 have no necessity to borrow; 15 are too poor to get credit, and 17 families borrow: that is, about 38 per cent. of the cultivators borrow. Some of these 17 ryots borrow food for one month, some for three months, and a few for five months. These borrow paddy in May or June and repay in August or September with 37½ per cent. interest in kind for the few months intervening between the taking of the loan and the repayment. Many ryots have to borrow money for a short time for payment of rent, and these debts are contracted at the rate of 24 or 30 per cent. per annum. These are in the nature of temporary accommodations contracted when the crops are ready, but have not been actually sold. With a view to sell the crop to the best advantage, but at the same time to meet the pressing demand of the landlord, this money debt is contracted, but repaid within a short time. Money debts for marriages and other social ceremonies are contracted occasionally; that is, twice or thrice during the lifetime of a man. But many make wrong starts with a debt contracted for their marriages either by themselves or their fathers, and remain handicapped with it all their lives. To this must be added the debt they are obliged to incur in bad seasons, and the high rate of interest. In spite of this, owing to the removal of restrictions on the cultivation of lucrative crops, the opening out of the country by rail and other roads, and the numerous other advantages brought about by the English rule, the material condition of the ryots and of all classes connected with agriculture has greatly improved, and is improving every day. Ryots with 25, 20, 15 bighas, or less, usually borrow. We have seen that they require about 50 or 60 maunds of paddy a year. The largest borrower, therefore, does not borrow more than 20 or 25 maunds of paddy, the value of which is as many rupees. It is admitted by all the ryots that the wife of the poorest ryot has more than that amount in silver and gold on her person; and if the ryot felt the burden of the debt very heavily, he could at once pay off by selling the jewels. The debt is kept on partly from habit and partly, it is said, to keep up a connection with the mahajan, whose assistance may be needed when crops have seriously failed, and when there is a litigation. The mahajan is an institution which the ryots think it worth while to support, even at the sacrifice of a certain quantity of paddy in the shape of interest. The mahajan himself occasionally oppresses his debtors, but protects him from the oppression of the zemindar or others, and saves him from starvation in seasons of scarcity.

"In E (another village where enquiries were hold), where there are 60 cultivators, 30 do not borrow, and the remaining 30 borrow to the following extent: 15 borrow paddy for five months' consumption, 12 borrow paddy for three months' consumption, 3 borrow for a month or less. The rate of interest is 25 or 37½ per cent., according as the ryot is solvent or poor. The poorer and the less punctual debtors have to pay the higher rate of interest."

In Angurea village, Midnapore, the average debt of a family was found to be Rs. 84.

27. It is sometimes alleged that many members of the classes considered to be above manual labour suffer very real distress, their numbers being in excess of the employment afforded by the occupations open to them. The only allegation of general want in Chittagong Division is made by a Subdivisional Officer with reference to this class. The Commissioner of the Presidency Division remarks with regard to two selected villages:—"Those in indifferent circumstances belong to the decayed class of *bhodro lok*, who will not accept labourer's work, and will not stoop to beg openly. Extravagance, litigation, and apathy have combined to reduce them to a condition which, whatever their faults may be, must excite our sympathy. Many of them practically subsist on the charity of their well-to-do kinsfolk and caste-fellows, removed only by the less ostentatious manner of giving and receiving alms from the class of professional beggars."

Poverty among the superior classes.

28. The Native States on the confines of Bengal occupy the elevated tracts of the Himalayas, or jungle-covered hills, and the circumstances of their inhabitants scarcely admit of comparison with those of the cultivators of the plains in British territory. The Commissioner of Chittagong observes:—"I do not think a comparison with Hill Tipperah is fair, unless it be between the people of Hill Tipperah and the Chittagong Hill Tracts. The conditions of life in the hills and in the plains are so different that a comparison is impossible. The mode of cultivation differs, the people are of a different race and have different wants, but in their way the hill people too are well off. The people of the Hill Tracts have fewer taxes than those of Hill Tipperah, but there is more strictness of rule to compensate for this. If emigration be taken as the test, then the Hill Tracts are more popular, the balance of emigration being of late years decidedly in favour of the British district. The hillman, however, is essentially a man who takes no thought for the morrow. If he has a good rice crop, he brews more beer, and what he cannot eat or drink he leaves to rot. He makes a good deal of money by his cotton and *til*, but this too he spends, and is therefore entirely dependent on his crop, and suffers severely when there is a bad one. He is also a confirmed gambler, and will play for his last cowrie."

Comparative prosperity of lower orders in British and Native States.

Mr. Wace, Collector of Bhagulpore, writes:—"Of one thing I am sure, viz. that our poorer cultivators are better off than their neighbours in Nepal. My last district before this, viz. Darjeeling, bordered on Nepal, and there was a steady flow of immigration across the border to the tea gardens and to our khas mehals. In this district there is nothing of this kind to tempt the Nepalese labourer, and there is but little immigration from Nepal. Considering, however, the pressure on the land here and in Nepal, one would expect emigration to the Terai. This does not occur: we exchange bad characters and insolvents occasionally, and a few of our substantial ryots do a little cultivation across the border, but there is nothing to tempt the poor man."

The Commissioner of Patna offers no decisive opinion on the subject. The Commissioner of Chota Nagpore observes:—"My own opinion is that, on the whole, the inhabitants of the States are nearly as well fed and clothed as those of the British districts, but their houses are certainly not so good. This probably arises from their being less secure and more autocratically governed. I have been told, I can hardly say with what truth, that in the Tributary States generally it is very difficult for a subject to grow rich. The people of Gangpore seem to me to be generally better off than others. Many of them wear gold ornaments, and seem to have a comparatively high standard of living. I do not think that there is very much emigration either from or to the States. The Rajahs are fully alive to the importance of attracting population, and grant lands on very easy terms. The Rajah of Jushpore told me last year that a good many people from Burway (a wild and backward zemindari in the west of Lohardugga) have come into his State to avoid exactions from the family of the Rajah of Burway. On the other hand, the Rajah of Gangpore complained to me that he was much cheated by immigrants from the Lohardugga district, who took lands from him and cleared them, and occupied them only during the period when little or no rent was being levied. The Chiefs are all anxious to receive new-comers and to prevent the emigration of their own people."

29. The example of the Native States seems at least to show that the existence of an abundant supply of waste land, such as was at one time available in most parts of Bengal, is compatible with great poverty among cultivators and agricultural

Improvement in the condition of the masses.

labourers. The Lieutenant-Governor is inclined to believe that at the commencement of British rule these classes were almost everywhere as badly off as they are now in the worst districts, and that the degree of prosperity they at present enjoy in Bengal Proper is the result of gradual improvement. The agricultural labourers in former times were certainly held in bondage, receiving only a subsistence, a state of things of which many traces still remain, and are disclosed by the present reports. The Commissioner of Rajshahye observes that wages have doubled within the last twenty years, and that there has been a perceptible rise in the standard of comfort as regards dress. Nearly all the reports from Bengal Proper indicate the substitution of brass for earthenware cooking vessels, a change now almost completely effected, and of female ornaments of gold and silver for those of brass. The general use of umbrellas by the working classes, proved by the importation at Calcutta of two millions a year, is also a novelty, introduced within the last few years. In South Behar, and perhaps in Chota Nagpore, the improvement has been confined to the more substantial cultivators and the upper classes, the actual labourers, though to some degree emancipated, experiencing little amelioration. There would seem to have been at all times great pressure on the land in actual cultivation in South Behar, as shown by the almost universal prevalence of the *bhaoli* system, under which the landlord takes as much as half the produce of the soil. These districts were the highway from Upper India to Bengal; they are most popular as a place of residence; and they appear always to have been fully peopled, except immediately after severe famine or destructive war. North Behar has apparently passed through a period of partial reclamation of waste and jungle under British rule, and while the process was in progress the working classes there, and the smaller cultivators, probably enjoyed better circumstances than they do at present. They were in the position now occupied by the ryots of North Chumparun.

Summary of facts and inferences.

30. The general result of the enquiry is that, in the greater part of the Lower Provinces, the industrious classes find no difficulty in supplying their primary wants, and are as a rule well nourished. Their prosperity is greatest in the eastern districts, and gradually diminishes as we carry the survey towards the west. It is not impaired by endemic disease, even where this has reduced the population, and left the survivors to some extent emaciated or enfeebled. On the contrary, the reports from districts so afflicted show that the inhabitants are somewhat better off than in the neighbouring tracts. But the signs indicating prosperity cease when we reach Behar, where, though the cultivators having holdings of a size sufficient to afford full occupation to their families are well-to-do, and the middle class enjoys exceptional comfort, wages are very low, so that those who depend for their living entirely or mainly on their daily labour earn a very scanty subsistence. The number of these labourers, including those who hold some land, is estimated at about forty per cent. of a population of over fifteen millions. The cause of the lowness of wages appears to be the multiplication of the labourers in a healthy climate, and under a social system founded on early marriages, up to the point at which employment can be found on the lowest terms consistent with the continued maintenance of families. This cause is of a permanent nature, existing social and climatic conditions remaining unchanged. Its effects would not be counteracted by any conceivable development of local industry, as such development could hardly progress in geometric ratio with the increase of population. Emigration can afford a sufficient and lasting remedy only if it be conducted on a large scale and continuously. If, after a system of emigration had been established, its operation were to be checked by the occupation of lands now waste, the existing difficulty would arise again. It is possible that popular education, which has hardly as yet touched this part of the population, might, in the course of many years, effect a permanent change for the better, by altering the views and habits of the people. In the meanwhile it would greatly facilitate the application of partial and temporary remedies, such as the introduction of new industries and emigration.

I have the honour to be,

Sir,

Your most obedient servant,

P. NOLAN,

Secretary to the Government of Bengal.

W. J.—Reg. 76T—136—1-7-88.

CONFIDENTIAL.

No. 2, dated Bhagulpore, the 9th April 1888.

From—JOHN BEAMES, ESQ., Commissioner of the Bhagulpore Division and Sonthal Pergunnahs,

To—The Secretary to the Government of Bengal, Revenue Department.

REFERRING to your confidential letter No. 35Agri., dated the 9th December 1887, I have the honour to submit herewith copy of the Deputy Commissioner, Sonthal Pergunnah's confidential report, without number, dated the 6th instant, received to-day. The other district reports will follow as soon as received. I adopt this course as, in a matter of this sort, Government will probably prefer to have the actual reports of the district officers.

2. I will submit my own opinion, if required, after reading the reports of all the district officers, as my acquaintance with this Division is not as yet sufficient to enable me to express a definite opinion on a subject which can only be adequately treated by officers who have long experience of the districts under discussion.

Dated Doomka, the 6th April 1888.

From—R. CARSTAIRS, ESQ., Offg. Deputy Commr., Sonthal Pergunnahs,

To—The Commissioner of the Bhagulpore Division and Sonthal Pergunnahs.

IN reply to your confidential letter No. 1 of the 3rd instant, calling for an immediate report on the condition of the people, I beg to say that the subject has had my careful attention, and I have set on foot enquiries, such as those recommended by Mr. Finucane, in various parts of the district. Of most of these the results are not yet to hand, and will be submitted on receipt.

2. Meantime I submit a short report dealing with the general condition of the district so far as I have been able to learn it.

3. This district is chiefly agricultural. There are no large communities of decayed artisans such as the weavers of Chandrakona.

4. As the district has been recently cleared from jungle, there has been nearly all over the district a rapid expansion of the area under cultivation. Although there has been considerable immigration, this expansion has been such as to give comparative ease to the cultivating classes. The district has now been filled up, and is overflowing into Maldah. Symptoms of pressure are appearing as inferior land is being taken up, and the country is now cleared in many parts. But on the whole there is no severe pressure.

5. There is one exception to this state of things. The paharias of the western hills especially are in a state of great poverty. They live from hand to mouth. Mr. Grant, Sub-divisional Officer of Godda, told me he once searched 50 paharia houses, and did not find so much as the food for the evening meal of that day. They were waiting for the return of the women who had carried firewood for sale to the market, and would bring back food. I have recently reported on them in my No. 86Ct. of the 17th February 1888.

6. The problem how to deal with the paharias is difficult. We cannot remit any taxes for they pay none. I think their condition is due to their drunken habits and idleness, but these again no doubt have causes. The story is shortly this. The paharias were a hunting people and used to enjoy the jungles of the plains around their hills by hunting and taking the forest produce. The Government long tried to get them to clear and cultivate the plains, but failing let in the Sonthals, who cleared and occupied the plains. The paharias were driven back up the hills and penned in there. Now in many parts they have not enough to live on, and the little they have they waste in drink. What to do is at present under consideration.

7. The part of the district known as the Damin-i-Koh, about 1,300 square miles in area, is that part which was occupied by the paharias. The northern paharias or Malé cultivate with the spade. The southern or Mal paharias cultivate largely with the plough. The plains are occupied nearly exclusively by Sonthals, who are low rented, and as a rule well off. They have good houses, pigs, poultry, sheep and goats, besides buffalo and cattle. Besides the field grain they eat all sorts of birds and animals and the fruit of the mohua, sâl, and kend (ebony) trees.

8. Outside the Damin (which was not brought under the Permanent Settlement) is the permanently settled tract. The rents here are higher than in the Damin, but low compared with the neighbouring districts. Two great advantages are enjoyed by the ryots throughout the district: the first, that their rents have all been settled by a Government officer; and the second, that they pay their rents through a headman who is removable by the Deputy

Commissioner for misconduct. The headman has his faults, but is a distinct improvement on the village gomasta. The chief grain crops are Indian-corn and rice, and the double staple reduces the risk of famine.

9. There is no large means of irrigation, but the undulating nature of the country affords great facilities for local protective works. The land is on the whole too high for rice, except in the low belt on the north, east and south, but is intersected with beds of streams. Rice land is made—

(1) by reclaiming beds of streams issuing from springs which are terraced off;
(2) by forming a reservoir at the top of hollows which have been scoured by the flood water, and levelling up the land protected;
(3) by forming a reservoir on the side of a slope and cultivating the land below it. The reservoir is made by simply raising a bank to retain the water, the natural slope forming the bank on the upper side;
(4) by means of "daurs" or small channels led out of a river bed at a high level and conducting water into fields lower down. In Godda sub-division particularly these abound and are often several miles long.

10. Besides protected rice land, much is left unprotected. In a year like that just past, the crops on such land fail and there is distress. The failure will probably give a stimulus to protective works which are well understood. Zemindars make large "bands," as the reservoirs are called, and "daurs," while village headmen and ryots commonly make small ones. Government has for some years back, owing to misunderstandings, set a bad example by spending almost no money even on repairs of existing works. This, I believe, is now set right. In all Wards' estates officers have done much in making such works, and I cannot refrain from mentioning in particular the late Mr. Jones, who took immense trouble in the Wards' estates of Deoghur.

11. The chief bar in the way of improvement of the ryot in this district is the money-lender. I would distinguish between him and the legitimate trader by saying that, while the latter strives to establish dealings for mutual advantage, the former's chief object is to established a row. To meet the money-lender the usuary clause of Regulation III of 1872 was introduced. This is not the place to discuss that clause, which I look on as most useful and wholesome. The evil cannot be met by legislation, but by administrative action. Unless Government is willing to become mahajan to the ryots, which I do not look upon as a proper function of Government, mahajans must continue to be, because the ryots cannot do without them.

12. The true power of the mahajan is, I think, his monopoly, and the only way to break that is to open up the country by means of good roads passable all the year round. These would serve many purposes, and among others this: When produce has to be rushed out of the country before the rains, and nothing more can be brought in during the rains on account of want of communication, the mahajan can make his own terms with his debtors for food and seed grain. He need not go to law to enforce his illegal claims. It is enough if he does as the small London shop-keeper does—stop their credit. Most small debt suits are the last squeeze of many applied by the creditor. Now I do not say that roads will cure this: but they give a good chance to the ryot who now has none.

13. The importance of the subject will be my excuse for reiterating what I have often said before, that I think the Government is not doing its full duty in the matter of roads. We only look at what is before our nose, and the roads that are made and alone are kept up in most districts are simply such as are suitable for the needs of district officers at the seasons when those officers need them. I admit that many of the roads have much traffic, but that is just because district officers go to important places, and also because if you have a road traffic will grow on it. I have tried to understand by experience the needs of those, the vast majority of people in the district, who live at a distance from our district roads, and have partly realised, I think, how hard is their case. This deficiency of roads exists not merely in this district, but in every district of Bengal. Not to travel away from my subject, it deprives every ryot of a large proportion of the fruits of his labour, because he is forced to sell in a hurry when produce is cheap, and even then does not get the full benefit of the market owing to the cost of transport. I have seen bullock carts struggling over steep hills covered with bolders, so great is the effort to reach the market.

14. I have already stated frequently how I think the road policy should be shaped. I am willing to admit that I may be wrong in the method proposed, but seeing that bad roads are throttling industry and trade, and inflicting great annual loss on the country, I urge that this work, which is peculiarly one that Government alone can do, be taken up without delay.

15. Artisans are, as a rule, fully employed. Day labourers are chiefly agricultural labourers. They are engaged as a sort of voluntary bondsmen by employers, whose object it is to have cheap labour available whenever required. This relation, which had a suspicious likeness to slavery, formed the subject of an enquiry last year, but was considered to be practically safe, as the bond is voluntary and the labourer can always emigrate. The advantage to him is that he is sure of support in the off season. Generally speaking, people that are unable to get

steady employment at home go abroad to the Railway or the Calcutta districts or the tea districts to labour, or to Maldah as colonists. Emigrants are chiefly Sonthals.

16. The other chief evil that I think should be met is the invasion of common rights which is going on everywhere. Members of communities are everywhere invading the common rights, their immediate private gain outweighing their share of the common loss. I think, seeing the ineffectual way in which private landlords or villagers protect those common rights, it is time for Government to step in and mark off the common lands, whether village forest, grazing ground, road, water reservoirs, &c., and declare who is responsible for their being safeguarded. It would be a matter of much time and difficulty to ascertain these according to varying circumstances, but I think it is time to consider the best and easiest means of doing this.

17. I shall lose no time in sending on the details of villages when received.

C. E. G.—Reg. No. 546C—37—14-4-88.

[CONFIDENTIAL.]

No. 3, dated Bhagulpore, the 10th April 1888.

From—JOHN BEAMES, ESQ., Commissioner of the Bhagulpore Division and Sonthal Pergunnahs,

To—The Secretary to the Government of Bengal, Revenue Department.

IN continuation of my confidential letter No. 2 of yesterday's date, I beg to submit herewith copies of the reports received to-day from the Collectors of Bhagulpore and Maldah.

The Collectors of Monghyr and Purneah have not yet submitted their reports, but urgent reminders have been sent to them.

Dated Bhagulpore, the 7th April 1888.

From—A. A. WACE, ESQ., C.S., Collector of Bhagulpore,

To—The Commissioner of the Bhagulpore Division.

I HAVE the honour to submit the report called for by the Government circular No. 35, dated 9th December, forwarded with your confidential No. 1, dated 19th December 1887, on the condition of the lower classes of the population in agricultural tracts.

2. On receipt of your orders I addressed a confidential letter demi-officially to my three sub-divisional officers, to the Sub-Deputy Collector in charge of Government estates in the Sudder, and to the managers of each of the Wards' estates in the district, calling on each to collect personally, in the ordinary course of his tour and without rousing either suspicion or undue hopes, certain figures and answers to questions formulated by me. Two of my sub-divisional officers, one of the managers, and my Sub-Deputy Collector have replied to my call to date. Some of the statistics furnished are, I fear, worthless; but I submit some of them below for consideration, without, however, much confidence that they will offer a "solid foundation for general conclusions."

3. My instructions to each officer were to select six villages in the tract in his charge—two always prosperous and safe from calamity, two known to have been of late years more or less distressed, and two of average prosperity; then to subdivide the families of each into certain classes of which I need for the purposes of this report only quote the following:—

A. Those living entirely on the proceeds of land cultivated either by the members of the family or by hired labour.

B. Those living chiefly as above, but occasionally hiring themselves out as labourers.

D. Those entirely dependent on wages of agricultural labour.

E. and F. Those living entirely or chiefly by skilled labour, *e.g.* weavers, carpenters, potters, &c.

4. The results are as follows. The numbers against each class represent the percentage of each class:—

In villages the condition of which is ordinarily—

	Good.	Fair.	Bad.
Class A	50	48	55
„ B	14	19	19
„ D	36	33	26

P. S.—Since these averages were struck, the Madhepura sub-divisional officer's figures have come in, showing:—

In villages—

	Good.	Fair.	Bad.
Class A	28	46	24
„ B	46	27	30
„ D	26	27	46

Each of the tracts reported on comes from a different sub-division.

5. The proportion of those living wholly or partly by skilled labour to agriculturists is as—

12 to 88	... ...	in good villages.
6 to 94	... ...	in fair ditto.
13 to 87	... ...	in bad ditto.

With reference to these figures it must be remembered that large villages have been chiefly dealt with, and these always contain a few members of each profession. Smaller villages are more entirely agricultural, and indent on the potter, the carpenter, the weaver, &c., of their larger neighbours.

6. The figures above given, if fairly reliable, will, when read with what I have to say about each of the three main classes,—

Cultivating ryots,
Labourers, and
Artisans,

indicate the general condition of the rural population as a whole.

7. Before dealing with each separately, I may as well summarize the replies to some of my enquiries as they affect the population generally, and as answered, not in respect to the particular villages analysed, but to the officer's charge generally.

8. The mass of the ryots are not under-fed; but there are everywhere a few who, not being able-bodied themselves and being too poor to command labour when most in request, get a poor outturn off their land, and so are more pinched sometimes than even a good labourer. The majority of my informants consider the labourer to be under-fed for about a fourth of the year. My reports show this to be truer of the south than the north. The labourer as a rule gets two meals, that of the midday being generally, except in harvest, uncooked. The full meal is put at about eight chittacks for an adult. Artisans generally get two cooked meals, except the weavers, who, like the labourers, with whom they too often rank, now have to put up with one of the meals dry.

9. There is no tendency to substitute brass for earthen vessels, but no importance is attached to the continued use of the latter. Religious and social ceremonies will, happily for the potter, long give a preference to them and to the iron pan which is largely used for cooking rice. The sub-divisional officer of Soopole, who writes more hopefully of his people than other officers, observes, however, that the leaf is giving way to the earthen vessel.

10. There is a consensus of opinion that a goldsmith gets less to do in a rural village than his father did. There is less spare cash among the ryots than there was.

11. My instructions were to distribute the cultivators of classes A and B into four sub-divisions—

a.—Those paying more than Rs. 20 rent a year.
b.—Rs. 20—Rs. 10.
c.— „ 10— „ 5.
d.—Less than Rs. 5.

The statistics of four reports give the following percentage for class A, viz. those living entirely by cultivation in the three classes of villages :—

			Good.	Fair.	Bad.
Sub-division *A*	...	...	39	33	32
Ditto *B*	...	...	31	27	25
Ditto *C*	...	...	18	19	22
Ditto *D*	...	...	12	21	21

In class B, living partly by cultivation and partly by labour,—

36 per cent. in good villages,
58 „ in fair ditto,
30 „ in bad ditto,

pay less than Rs. 5 rent.

The above figures justify Mr. Finucane's criticism of Mr. Justice Cunningham's figures, and, compared with the average rent per acre of the district, come nearer to the former's estimate struck in Durbhunga.

12. I do not think that the above figures suggest that the cultivators of this district are as a class in a condition which renders the future of agriculture precarious. Even though, however, the mass of them generally get a full diet throughout years of average prosperity, the large majority of them live in debt and have practically mortgaged most of their crop before it is harvested. My subordinates were instructed to try and get statistics as to the proportion in classes A and B in the selected villages who were in debt—

(*a*). To the extent of more than one year's yield of their land.
(*b*). Less than one year's yield.
(*c*). Not at all.

In Banka the sub-divisional officer's figures divide nearly the whole population between A and B, and put a few more under head (*b*) than (*a*). In a Ward's estate in Madhepura the manager puts only 12 per cent. in each of the first two classes, while the sub-divisional officer gives the average as follows in villages—

				Good.	Fair.	Bad.
A	...	...	...	9	9	34
B	...	...	...	77	36	42
C	...	...	...	14	55	24

In Soopole the percentages run thus—

A	...	...	...	...	...	37
B	...	...	...	...	...	39
C	...	...	...	...	...	24

The collection of these statistics has been of course more difficult than those classifying the holdings of ryots which have been got chiefly from putwaries' papers. Enquiries about debt in a village always challenge concealment to whichever party you may go, for the mahajan at once suspects taxation. But figures were perhaps scarcely necessary to prove the melancholy fact, which any one acquainted with the mofussil knows, that the majority of our ryots live in debt and only pay off one year in order to begin borrowing for the next.

13. In a year of prosperity the labourer is not badly off, and his condition has, if anything, improved within the last decade. There is a general consensus of opinion that he is more independent than he was. He is less of a serf and more free to offer his labour to the man who will pay best for it. Large cultivators have often spoken to me of the way the old rule of buying a man's exclusive services for the year is going out. This was done by a lump payment of anything from Rs. 10 to Rs. 30 at the beginning of the year, no interest being charged, but the advance being worked off by labour, the master finding always one and sometimes two meals a day. I called on my subordinates to ascertain, in returning the total number of labourers in the villages analysed, what number always worked for one ryot. The figures are as follows:—

50 per cent. in Banka.
60 „ in Madhepura.
42 „ in Soopole.

The proportion in the Sudder sub-division is very much less, but hardly as low as my Sub-Deputy Collector, in the particular tract he took, makes out.

14. The labourer's wage as quoted in cash still remains miserably low, and varies from five pice in the south and extreme north to six pice over most of the district. The chief reason, however, why this rate is still quoted is that cash payments are rare, and in this way the labourer has benefited to a small degree by the rise of prices, viz. to the extent that his wage in grain exceeds his actual consumption thereof. The balance goes further in purchasing his few other wants at the village shop. The ordinary wage in grain varies from 4 seers of coarse grain like the millets to 2½ seers of rice. Part of this is paid by a midday meal in the field and part in grain at the end of the day. In harvest time the labourer gets a proportion of what is brought to the threshing-ground. This varies in the rice harvest from one sheaf in 16 to one in 12, the former being the more general rate; and labourers engaged by the year get rather more liberal treatment, viz. one in eight or one in ten; but then while the daily labourer's work ends at the threshing-ground, the regular servant has work to do there too. This wage is equivalent to about 5 seers of husked grain, and thus rice harvest wages are about double those of other times. On the bhadoi crop a labourer gets one-sixteenth of the grain; but in the rubbee harvest the payment is by the sheaf, the outturn being here again about double the general wage. These harvest seasons cover perhaps two or three months of the year, and it is at intervals between them that the labourer is said to be under-fed. In tracts yielding only one crop there is more fear of this than in tracts with varied crops coming in three times a year; for though the labourer in the former is better off when the one rice harvest is going on, that very condition blinds him to the necessity of providing for the slack time before him.

15. These grain payments, though they suit the rural economy of the country, are of course the real danger to the population. Directly a crop shows signs of failing, the ryot husbands his store, and in such years as we had before 1885 both the smaller ryots and the labourers were undoubtedly under-fed. Generally, however, I agree with the majority of those whom I have consulted that in years of ordinary prosperity the labourer gets enough food for himself and his family except for perhaps one or two months in the year, when he is on short commons. The fact, however, remains that serfdom is on the decrease, and the growing independence of labour can only arise from a feeling that the labourer is bettering himself by choosing his own master. The less he is tied to one man, the more free he is to go abroad and seek labour when it is slack in and around his village.

16. I now come to consider the artisan, the carpenter, blacksmith, potter, weaver, &c. All these are as a rule paid in grain also, and in this way have, like the labourer, benefited by the rise of prices. The opening of the railway in the north has brought this fact home to the village community, and I heard of a case lately where a ryot was trying to make the carpenter keep his plough in order for the year for a smaller dole of grain because the former dole was worth more in the bazars tapped by the railway than the carpenter used to get. The payment is usually made on the plough, and for this all agricultural implements are kept in order for the year. An ordinary village carpenter makes his three or four annas a day at this rate, and gets two cooked meals. The potter earns only about half as much, but then his women and children help him. The only artisan about whom there need be any anxiety is the weaver. Imported cloth has ruined this industry, and the answers to my enquiries go to show that about half of this class have taken to field labour. The falling off in this industry is particularly marked among the tusser weavers in Bhagulpore, where the number of looms is only one-half of what it was ten years ago. The result has been to concentrate the industry in the hands of those most well-to-do, and the poor weavers have taken to daily labour, many turning masons. Generally I may say that the weaver is the worst fed man now in the village community; but as he is adapting himself to the times, his children will be no worse off than the day-labourer.

17. My enquiries also were directed to ascertain the proportion of the population living on charity. The returns show uniformly that in the villages tested the number is not worth considering. The fact is that those who have no family to hang on to gravitate towards the larger centres of the population. The few who do live by begging appear to be about as well off as the labourer.

18. The above summarizes the information I have collected. On the statistics by themselves I should be afraid to found theories. I can only hope that, compared with figures from other districts, they may help other people to form them.

19. Of one thing I am sure, viz. that our poorer cultivators are better off than their nieghbours in Nepal. My last district before this, viz. Darjeeling, bordered on Nepal, and there was a steady flow of immigration across the border to the tea-gardens and to our khas mehals. In this district there is nothing of this kind to tempt the Nepalese labourer, and there is but little immigration from Nepal. Considering, however, the pressure on the land here and in Nepal, one would expect emigration to the Terai. This does not occur: we exchange bad characters and insolvents occasionally, and a few of our substantial ryots do a little cultivation across the border, but there is nothing to tempt the poor man. I attach a statement comparing the rates for cultivated lands believed to prevail in Nepal with those of the adjoining pergunnah of this district belonging to the Maharajah of Durbhunga. This shows our rates to be slightly lower than those of Nepal, and the pergunnah quoted is rated high for the district. For orchard and grass lands our rates are much higher. The real difference on cultivated lands is believed to be still more in our favour, for the exactions of Nepalese officials are proverbial. A little ryot would not willingly expose himself to these; and although a substantial ryot can, by currying favour with the officials, avoid some of these for a long time, he occasionally loses everything by one false step. There is thus less security of property, and generally speaking our population, even in hard times, sticks to British territory.

Statement showing the different rates of culturable lands in Pergunnah Naraidigar and Nepal Terai.

Pergunnah Naraidigar standard Lugga 7½ cubits.			Terai standard Lugga 9 cubits.		
Description of lands.	Quantity of lands.	Rates.	Description of lands.	Quantity of lands.	Rates.
		Rs. A. P.			Rs. A. P.
Dhan	1st class ...	5 0 0	Dhan ...	1st class ...	6 6 0
Do.	2nd „ ...	4 4 0	Do. ...	2nd „ ...	5 6 0
Do.	3rd „ ...	1 8 0 to 3 13 0	Do. ...	3rd „ ...	3 8 0 to 4 4 0
Bheet	1st „ ...	4 0 0	Bheet ...	1st „ ...	4 8 0
Do.	2nd „ ...	3 0 0 to 3 12 0	Do. ...	2nd „ ...	3 4 0 to 4 0 0

A. A. Wace,
Collector.

No. A, dated Maldah, the 7th April 1888.

From—H. G. Sharp, Esq., Collector of Maldah,

To—The Commissioner of the Bhagulpore Division.

With reference to your endorsements No. 1, dated 19th December 1887, and No. 1, dated 3rd instant, on Government agricultural circulars No. 35, dated 9th December 1887, and No. 16, dated 2nd instant, I have the honour to submit the following report on the condition of the lower classes of the population of this agricultural district.

2. In pursuance of the suggestions made in the side noted parts of the correspondence, three "tarafs" or groups of villages (small as nearly all in this district are) were selected, with careful consideration of their conditions, as being, when taken together, typical of nearly half of the district. The tarafs are several miles apart, in two different pergunnahs, and in making the selection the aim was at getting fair specimens of all the more prominent features, some in one group, some in another. The points in which the statistics of these groups are similar are a fair measure of the similarity of the whole of this part of the country, and the points in which they differ include most of those which would be found in a more extensive range. For instance in taraf Malatipore, of the labouring classes there are Beldars but no Shudris, in Nabagram there are Shudris but no Beldars, and in Singhiya alone are there Patnis, Telis, Rishis (cobblers), and fishermen. In Malatipore alone are there potters and goldsmiths; in Singbyia alone, weavers;

Sir E. Buck's letter dated 17th August 1887, paragraph 2.—"A quantity of vague......statements afford no basis for any definite conclusions ...... Evidence should be of a positive and trustworthy character."

Sir E. Buck's letter dated 2nd September 1887, paragraph—1. "At present all that is desired is a further accumulation of evidence." Paragraph 2.—"A clear summary of facts."

Mr. Finucane's letter dated 27th September 1887, paragraph 5.—"There is no trustworthy statistical information," Paragraph 6.—"District officers should take one or more typical village and......ascertain the actual facts .... If actual facts were collected in this way even for one village in each district, they would.........afford a more solid basis......than any number of opinions based upon general impressions and unsupported by facts."

Government of Bengal Circular dated 9th December 1887, paragraph 1.—"There can be no doubt that a report of actual facts, even for a limited area, judiciously selected as typical, would be of much use as offering a solid, though narrow, foundation for general conclusions." Also paragraphs 7 and 8 of the same Circular.

and in Nabagram alone, carpenters. The area and rental of the holdings, as will be seen in the tables, are also different, and give fair instances of the different pergunnahs.

3. All the villages hitherto selected belong to the Chanchal estate; but lest it should at first sight seem that the estate represents a too limited area, it may be noted that the property is scattered over more than half the district from north to south. The village of Chanchal itself, and those near the principal house, were excluded because in such villages of a wealthy zemindari unusual conditions are generally found. There are several advantages on this estate which cannot be secured elsewhere. In the extracts just quoted, accuracy and completeness are the foremost demands. On estates in the possession of private owners it is practically impossible to get such complete details as have now been got. The necessary records do not exist; the local agents are not trained in the way of preparing them; and public officers could not act thoroughly without inquisition to an inconvenient degree. There are in this district no such Government estates of the kind mentioned in paragraph 1 of Mr. Nolan's letter, managed by a strong staff which could collect the particulars of itself. But it was my intention next to visit one or two of the largest Government estates in the south of the district and to collect similar statistics there. My successor will perhaps be able to carry out this plan, and the collection of the details there obtained with those which are now submitted would probably give a fair and comprehensive account of the actual condition of the district. Meanwhile, this first instalment is presented under the orders contained in the last sentence of the Government of India's circular dated 17th August.

4. The Chanchal estate has been under the Courts of Wards for upwards of 15 years; there has always been a strong establishment, trained like other establishments under Government and possessing besides information and practice in matters of the kind now under consideration, which scarcely any other Government establishments possess, save such as are kept for the sole purpose of administering a few large estates in certain districts; and the accuracy and completeness of the records* of the Chanchal estate are such as are never found except on estates of one of these classes. Much of the information is ready to hand which could in other circumstances be collected only with great labour and after all with uncertainty, and there is an agency fitted to collect the other subsidiary details needed in the course of the enquiries.

* Paragraph 4 of Mr. Nolan's letter. "Settlement and partition papers will always give the required data for particular villages."
Paragraph 6 of Mr. Finucane's letter. "With the help of the existing rent-rolls ascertain the actual facts."

5. I first drew up a set of tables and notes, assigning a few papers to each of a very few selected officers, comprising such particulars as concerned their ordinary work and were in their hands not at all likely to excite suspicion or uneasiness. All the notes were written with my own hand, and the tables, &c., were designed with much care and trouble so as to comprise all material facts. The original papers have never left my own custody. Clerks have been specially chosen for intelligence and trustworthiness to copy this report and to fill up statements. After drawing up the notes and tables, I consulted the manager of the Chanchal estate, Baboo Kali Narayan Ray, on several consecutive days, amending the notes as occasion required. After the first one or two consultations we went to the selected villages and questioned the people and made various observations. This was repeated both at the villages and at Chanchal (for the purpose of checking the inquiries by reference to records) on several days. I also visited the villages alone; and altogether every opportunity has been taken for collecting trustworthy information. The village headmen were generally intelligent and willing, and care was taken, in questioning them as well as in all other respects, to avoid the appearance of prying and the raising of alarm. Being pretty familiar with the vernacular, I had no difficulty in taking up the matter in the way of easy and friendly conversation, making notes from time to time. Baboo Kali Narayan Ray has most ably and zealously co-operated throughout, and has supplied a large quantity of details and much valuable information. I have great pleasure in adding another to my previous testimonies to the work of this excellent officer. In accordance with paragraph 2 of Sir E. Buck's letter, dated 2nd September, abstracts are submitted herewith of the fuller statements retained in this office.

6. The whole of the details* has been digested with the help of my general knowledge of the district, which is now considerable, of several records and files bearing on the subject, and of the experience collected in the famines of 1873-74 and of 1877 (during which I was for about seven months in two of the worst districts of Madras), and in the distress of 1884-85 in this district. Care has been taken to describe so far as possible the normal and permanent condition of the people† and of their affairs, without much comparison of former times or of transient circumstances.

* Paragraph 6 Mr. Finucane's letter.—"The conclusions......would, as a matter of course, have to be tested and perhaps modified by the personal impressions formed on general considerations."

† Paragraph 3 of Sir E. Buck's circular, dated 17th August.
Paragraph 5 of Mr. Finucane's letter.
Paragraph 2 of Mr. Nolan's letter.

7. As no Native State approaches the boundary of this district, no remarks can be made on that portion of the correspondence in which these States are mentioned.

8. In table I will be found an exact census of the selected groups, which consist respectively of three, nine and four villages. The census was taken separately for each village of which all the details have been recorded in this office. The population has been shown under the four prescribed orders—

(*a*) Cultivator,
(*b*) Agricultural labourers,
(*c*) Artisans, and
(*d*) Those who subsist on charity.

To get the correct total, a fifth heading,

(*e*) Others,

has been added, and the comparison of the numbers under (*e*) with each of the other numbers, and with their total, is useful as showing the proportions between those whose condition may cause anxiety and those who are above that level. The number of households has been shown for each order; and for the four prescribed orders the separate numbers also of men, boys, women and girls, to allow criticism of the comparisons of wages, food, &c. These sub-divisions are unnecessary under the head (*e*) others.

9. The following are the percentages on the total population—

(*a*) Cultivators	... ...	(1,496) :	43
(*b*) Labourers	... ...	(1,156) :	33
(*c*) Artizans	... ...	(162) :	4
(*d*) Beggars	... ...	(88) :	4
(*e*) Others	... ...	(598) :	17
	Total ...	(3,500) :	100

10. In table II will be found first the details and then the abstract of the areas of the holdings and of the average rental. The areas are divided thus:—

(i) Not more than 1 acre.
(ii) More than 1 acre and not more than 2 acres.
(iii) Ditto 2 acres ditto 3 ,,
(iv) Ditto 3 ,, ditto 5 ,,
(v) Ditto 5 ,, ditto 10 ,,
(vi) Ditto 10 ,, ditto 20 ,,
(vii) Ditto 20 acres.

The average rental per acre, and on the whole holding for each class, and in each village of all the groups, has been accurately calculated, and the following are among the principal results. Mr. Finucane quotes Mr. Cunningham's figures to the effect that "66 per cent. of the ryots of the province pay a rental of less than Rs. 5, which it is said implies a holding of two or three acres." The present exact enquiry shows that in these villages the number of holdings not exceeding 3 acres is 110, or 53 per cent. of the total number 206, while the number of holdings which pay rent not exceeding Rs. 5 is 54, or 26 per cent. The implication just mentioned fails in these villages, and if Mr. Cunningham's figures are correct (which Mr. Finucane doubts), the average rental here (Rs. 3-1-6 per acre) is higher than in the province as a whole.

11. The following tables give different views of the condition of the land and of the holdings:—

A

[The areas are in standard bighas.]

Taraf.	Total area.	Deduct area of lakhiraj or rent-free lands.				Remainder.	Details of column 7.	
		Debattar.	Piran.	Jagir.	Total.		Cultivated or rent-paying lands.	Uncultivated or waste land.
1	2	3	4	5	6	7	8	9
	Bighas.	bighas.	Bighas.	Bighas.	Bighas.	Bighas.	Bighas.	Bighas.
Malatipore	2,451	104	2	73	179	2,272	1,491	781
Singbiya	3,693	323	......	133	456	3,237	2,517	720
Nabagram	2,989	206	......	119	324	2,665	2,191	474
Total ...	9,133	633	2	325	959	8,174	6,199	1,975

The proportion of uncultivated land (here 1,975 bighas) to the total (9,133 bighas) is being reduced every year in the north and east of the district by the immigration of Sonthals, the increase of the population, and the improvement of the means of communication and of the other conditions of the district.

12. B.

Taraf.	Number of Khudkasht or resident cultivators' holdings.						Number of Paikast or non-resident cultivators' holdings.					Total number of holdings.					
	Cultivated by the ryots themselves.	Sublet to under-ryots for half the produce.	Cultivated by servants.	Garden.	Homestead and lands in the vicinity thereof.	Total.	Cultivated by the ryots themselves.	Sublet to under-ryots for half the produce.	Cultivated by servants.	Garden.	Total.	Cultivated by the ryots themselves.	Sublet to under-ryots for half the produce.	Cultivated by servants, column 4 + column 10.	Garden, column 5 + column 11.	Homestead and lands in the vicinity thereof, column 6.	Total of columns 7 and 12.
1	2	3	4	5	6	7	8	9	10	11	12	13	14	15	16	17	18
Malatipore	59	46	4	2	76	187	45	18	2	1	66	104	64	6	3	76	253
Singhiya	70	45	67	...	42	224	61	25	65	...	151	131	70	132	...	42	375
Nabagram	77	39	53	...	14	183	37	14	13	...	64	114	53	66	...	14	247
Total ...	206	130	124	2	132	594	143	57	80	1	281	340	187	204	3	132	875

The number of holdings cultivated by resident sub-tenants who give half the produce instead of rent is 130 among a grand total of 875, and the number cultivated by resident ryots themselves is 206.

13. Tables III, III*a*, III*b* and VI are the most important of all, and a very large number of details have been collected and examined, and very many calculations have been made towards preparing them. To get the average rental the total area of the two pergunnahs Hatinda and Gourhand, 51,236 acres, has been taken, of which the rent-roll (*minus* the rent of jalkars) is Rs. 1,24,739, giving the average of Rs. 2-6-7½ per acre. In table A in paragraph 11 it will be seen that the total area of rent-paying cultivated land is 6,199 bighas or 2,046 acres. The average area of a holding is thus nearly 10 acres; but the holder of such an area would be a rather well-to-do man. A holding of five acres has been taken as typical for the purposes of this enquiry about the poorer classes. The average rental for a holding of five acres is thus Rs. 12-1-2, which, with the cess, amounts to Rs. 12-7-2 as shown in table IIIA.

14. All the supplementary items (straw, livestock, &c.) enumerated in paragraph 4 of Mr. Nolan's letter have been considered, and several others besides. The custom of the district does not permit the cultivators to make any profit out of hides, and fish have been taken in reduction of the household expenses. In addition to the crops, &c., named in table III enquiries and notes have been made about several others, and kept in this office under the instructions already quoted.

15. Table VI shows the average produce of various crops per acre and the rates at which the cultivator can himself dispose of the produce to merchants, hucksters or other distributors. The entries have been made after very careful and prolonged enquiry and discussion in the manner described in paragraph 5; the difficulties were great owing to the variety of the statements made and the strong tendency of agriculturists to represent the produce and price as less than the reality.

16. The following abstract of table III represents the crops grown during the summer and autumn on a typical holding of five acres—

	Proportionate area. In parts of a rupee. A.	P.	In land measure. A.	R.	P.
(*a*) winter rice	10	0	3	0	20
2, summer 1-16 } Autumn 15-16 }	4	0	1	1	0
3, Jute	1	0	0	1	10
(*b*) 4, Indian-corn, turmeric, large vegetables, cucumbers, &c.	0	3	0	0	12·5
(*c*) 5, Homestead and land close to the homestead	0	6	0	0	25
(*d*) 6, Garden	0	3	0	0	12·5
	16	0	5	0	0

17. Another point on which close enquiry has been made with considerable difficulty is the average proportion of land which is cropped twice a year, and after full consideration this has been estimated at about 1¼ (or, on the calculations, more exactly 1 acre 1 rood 9·375 poles) in 5 acres. I was at first inclined to think that this proportion was too low; but it seems after all as nearly correct as may be. Certainly a large area which might be made to grow two crops is allowed to lie fallow in rotation, as the constant crops would exhaust its

fertility. The yearly area of crops on an average holding of 5 acres will accordingly be 6 acres 1 rood 9·375 poles, the excess being cultivated for spring as well as for rain crops; and the produce and its value, and the expenses of cultivating this gross area, have been shown in tables III, III*a* and III*b*. The expenses have been duly reduced, as shown in the tables, from the rates at which the cost of separately cultivating a very small holding would have to be taken.

18. Some of the crops of which all or nearly all the produce has been shown as consumed at home are of course grown in large quantities by certain cultivators, *e.g.* bamboos or cucumbers, and other garden stuff. But the holdings of such persons are not typical, and if much of such produce were sold, other crops would be reduced. Straw, too, is largely sold by some; but such persons cannot make any considerable profit out of cattle, and in this typical case the cultivator is taken as using almost all his own straw, but on the other hand as selling young livestock to advantage. Bamboos on such a holding (not a jungly one) are all wanted at home for fencing, wicker-work, and fifty other purposes. In some parts of this district mangoes are a well-known source of profit; but if the cultivator of a small area has much of an orchard, he has so much less arable land, and would not be one of the typical agriculturists whose family consumes nearly all their fruit. These notes will show that the various kinds of produce and sources of miscellaneous profit have not been overlooked, and that the quantities entered in table III for home consumption and for sale respectively have been adjusted with due regard to fact and practical business.

19. Home consumption has been calculated for a family of five, at 33⅓ seers of rice and other grains a head a month. These grains comprise cheena, kowen, wheat, barley &c. The members of such family are estimated to consume on the average one-eighth seer of pulse daily. After deducting these quantities for home use and the costs shown in the tables, it is calculated that the holder of five acres has in an average year a little more than Rs. 12 in ready cash. Nor has account been taken of the cost, among other matters, of ceremonies and festivities, of ornaments, of possible school fees (except Rs. 3 for petty expenses), and specially of interest on debts. To meet these charges Rs. 12 is a very slight fund. On the other hand the quantities entered as reserved for home use are large enough to imply comfort, and, in my opinion, larger than in practice are so reserved in an ordinary year. They have been entered in defference to the opinions of competent advisers; but I suspect that they represent the case of a good year, and that with average seasons they are generally less without stint. The expenses of transplanting, weeding, &c., seem to me also too high, but have been entered for the same reasons. When a family of the lower middle class, consisting on the hypothesis of five members, keeps am ample share of the produce for home use, they would probably do all or nearly all the work on a holding of five acres, or they could at the worst reduce the external expenses of the field without much trouble; and again in a year of drought or of flood there are two things to set off against bad outturn—the higher prices got for whatever is harvested, and the much reduced cost of weeding and reaping.

20. On the whole the results of the enquiry in this direction go to show that cultivators with holdings less than the average have in ordinary years more than enough to live upon in a way that implies the best physical condition of which the climate and their habits admit, and with a margin to provide against an occasional bad season.

21. The wages and other income of agricultural labourers are described in tables IV and IV*a* on two principal systems of daily and of yearly contract. Those who take daily wages get regular employment during hardly more than half the year, and during the rest they do odds and ends of very various kinds, such as bamboo-work, making ploughs, baskets, fishing tackle, string, &c., collecting and selling wood, "*ber*" fruit, honey and other jungle produce, snails, shells and limestone, husking and parching rice, and gleaning. The income of men, boys, women and girls is separately shown, and the totals assume that one of each of these four is pretty constantly at work. There may be the usually quoted number of five in the family, of whom four might work. The women, however, in many households do not work, so the totals are shown slightly higher than the real average. When they do they work from about 9 A.M. to 4. P.M. for about two months, and the wages of only two months are entered in column 3 of table IVA.

22. Men and boys get from the employer a morning meal of dried paddy, and the principal midday meal of rice, with fish or pulse, &c. When a Hindu works for a Mahomedan, or *vice versa*, the labourer gets, instead of cooked food, the raw grain, oil, &c., and fuel, or sometimes the money value on the following scale:—

	Rs.	A.	P.
Men, at 9 pies a day for 6 months	8	7	0
Boys, at 6 ditto ditto	5	10	0

23. Weekly payments seem to be unknown. Monthly payments are apparently never during more than two months of the year. The rates are shown in Table IV, and are in addition to the value of two meals a day, as above. The monthly rates are naturally higher than the yearly; but besides the irregularity a monthly labourer has to work much harder while he is at it than a yearly servant. The former gets very little time for his meals.

24. Yearly servants get three or four pieces of thin cloth and one coarse thicker cloth for winter. Wages to this class are sometimes paid in advance for two or three years, and the debtor has to serve out his time on a bond, of which examples are from time to time

quoted in the report of the Registration Department. The value of their food is taken as Rs. 24 and Rs. 16 for men and boys respectively, and the entries in column 6 of table IVA are thus calculated:—

	Men. Rs. A.	Boys. Rs. A.
3 pieces of cloth	1 2	0 12
1 " washing	0 5	0 4
1 " winter	1 4	0 12
Occasional presents on holidays	0 3	0 3
Total ...	2 14	1 15

At harvest one-sixth of the crop is distributed among the reapers, and the value of this is shown in column 5. Yearly labourers seem to have leisure and opportunity to make a little extra money for themselves in the ways described in paragraph 21.

25. The Beldars, as is well known, earn more than most other labourers. They do earthwork generally during five months, ordinarily agricultural work on daily wages during two months, and miscellaneous jobs during the rest of the year. They are prone to periods of idleness, which reduce the yearly total from what it would be at the rates they command when they choose.

26. Agricultural labourers here never get land rent-free, or any interest in land. They pay rent for their homesteads. Their remuneration is calculated quite independently of such privileges, which are granted in some other districts.

27. The aggregate value of wages, food and other contributions during a whole year, received respectively by individuals and by a family of four working members as described, is shown in table IVA. The average is generally upwards of Rs. 75, and this is sufficient for their livelihood and for such social expenses of ceremonies, cheap ornaments, &c., as they are forced to meet. They are often in debt, and then they have to make their wages meet the interest too, or to work out a bond in the manner already mentioned.

28. The number, earnings and expenses of the inhabitants of orders (*c*) artisans and (*d*) beggars are shown in tables V and VII.

29. The civil medical officer states his opinion of the physique, &c., of the poorer classes of the district thus:—"They are well-fed, and they are better off than those in Behar and southern Bengal. As regards their physical condition, I think they are weaker, especially those living in the Barindra tract (the eastern half of the district), than the people (lower class) in other parts of Bengal, owing, I believe, to their habits of using opium and to long-standing unhealthiness of the place from malaria. The condition of the poorer classes in eastern Bengal is much better than that of this district."

30. This opinion agrees with my own formed after nearly three years' residence, with long tours, in this district, after experience in seven of the nine divisions of the province, and tours in almost all parts except Orissa and Chota Nagpore. In the section on the "condition of the people" in my General Administration Report for 1884-85, somewhat full descriptions and comparisons were given, of which the outline is that as this district lies midway between the poverty-stricken districts of Behar and the prosperous Dacca Division, so does the condition of its poorer classes. The weavers are badly off, and it can only be hoped that they will gradually take to other employments. But the rest of the artisans are fairly well off, and the labourers, though living poorly and from hand-to-mouth, are not on the verge of destitution, as so many are in the western districts. A large proportion of them undergo suffering in bad years and need urgent relief in times of severe drought or flood. Of the beggars little can be said but that their numbers are not excessive; they get on fairly well at ordinary times, but so long as they exist their supplies must, when their supporters are in need, be cut so short as to leave them in real distress.

TABLE I.

MES OF THE ARAFS OR GROUPS OF VILLAGES.	ORDER (*a*) CULTIVATORS. Number of						(*b*) AGRICULTURAL LABOURERS. Number of						(*c*) ARTISANS. Number of						(*d*) THOSE WHO SUBSIST ON CHARITY. Number of						(*e*) OTHERS.		(*f*) TOTAL. Number of						Grand total of population.
	Households.	Men.	Boys.	Women.	Girls.	Total inmates.	Households.	Men.	Boys.	Women.	Girls.	Total inmates.	Households.	Men.	Boys.	Women.	Girls.	Total inmates.	Households.	Men.	Boys.	Women.	Girls.	Total inmates.	Households.	Total inmates.	Households, total of columns 2, 8, 14, 20, 26.	Men.	Boys.	Women.	Girls.	Inmates.	
1	2	3	4	5	6	7	8	9	10	11	12	13	14	15	16	17	18	19	20	21	22	23	24	25	26	27	28	29	30	31	32	33	34
Jatiporo ...	59	92	56	107	45	300	48	65	36	67	27	195	13	23	25	28	14	90	10	7	2	12	1	22	86	485	216	187	119	214	87	485	1,092
ghiya ...	70	168	150	172	92	582	141	182	142	209	124	657	9	13	13	16	10	52	12	17	7	20	9	53	11	67	243	380	312	427	235	67	1,421
bagrain ...	77	160	137	196	121	614	70	79	58	109	58	304	2	6	4	6	4	20	1	1	1	1		3	10	40	160	246	200	312	183	46	987
Total ...	206	420	343	475	258	1,496	259	326	236	385	209	1,156	24	42	42	50	28	162	23	25	10	33	10	78	107	592	619	813	631	953	505	598	3,500

Table II.

Taraf Malatipur.

Serial number.	Names of villages.	Particulars of holdings. — Area. — From	Particulars of holdings. — Area. — To	Particulars of holdings. — Number of holdings.	Average rental. — Per acre.	Average rental. — On the whole holding.	Remarks.
1	2	3	4	5	6	7	8
		Acres.	Acres.		Rs. A. P.	Rs. A. P.	
1	Malatipur ...	...	1	1	5 6 9	3 10 0	
2	Ditto ...	1	2	8	3 1 0	4 12 0	
3	Ditto ...	2	3	1	2 5 0	5 5 0	
4	Ditto ...	3	5	2	2 8 0	7 14 11½	
5	Ditto ...	5	10	1	2 2 0	20 7 9	
6	Ditto ...	20	30	...	......	......	
	Total ...	...	...	13	2 10 0	6 10 0	Average rates and rental of the mouzah.
1	Lalganj ...	1	1	2	3 1 0	2 6 3	
2	Ditto ...	1	2	10	3 1 0	4 11 0	
3	Ditto ...	2	3	9	2 6 9	5 8 0	
4	Ditto ...	3	5	7	2 7 6	9 6 3	
5	Ditto ...	5	10	1	2 2 8	20 12 3	
6	Ditto ...	10	20	2	2 5 0	31 8 0	
7	Ditto ...	20	30	1	2 0 0	41 2 3	
	Total ...	...	...	32	2 5 2	9 2 0	Ditto ditto.
1	Gobindpara ...	1	1	1	2 1 0	1 6 0	
2	Ditto ...	1	2	7	2 12 0	4 7 9	
3	Ditto ...	2	3	1	1 11 0	4 7 3	
4	Ditto ...	3	5	2	2 12 0	11 10 0	
5	Ditto ...	5	10	2	2 6 0	19 0 10½	
6	Ditto ...	10	20	1	2 9 9	26 0 6	
	Total ...	...	...	14	2 9 0	9 0 0	Ditto ditto.
	Grand Total ...	...	...	59	2 7 0	8 8 0	

Table II.

Taraf Singhia.

Serial number.	Names of villages.	From	To	Number of holdings.	Per acre.	On the whole holding.	Remarks.
		Acres.	Acres.		Rs. A. P.	Rs. A. P.	
1	Singhia ...	...	1	1	3 5 8	2 9 1½	
2	Ditto ...	1	2	1	3 13 9	6 0 10½	
3	Ditto ...	2	3	1	3 14 9	11 0 4½	
	Total ...	...	...	3	3 13 0	6 8 9	Average rates and rental.
1	Dakshin Singhia	1	2	1	6 5 3	7 9 0	
2	Ditto ...	2	3	3	4 10 8	10 3 9	
3	Ditto ...	3	5	5	3 4 0	12 9 3	
4	Ditto ...	5	10	2	2 12 0	22 0 0	
	Total ...	...	...	11	3 5 6	13 3 0	Ditto ditto.
1	Bargachhia ...	...	1	1	3 7 3	2 4 10½	
2	Ditto ...	1	2	2	3 10 5	6 0 9	
3	Ditto ...	2	3	1	4 0 7	8 14 1½	
4	Ditto ...	3	5	2	3 3 4	10 11 3	
5	Ditto ...	5	10	1	3 2 6	20 4 6	
6	Ditto ...	10	20	1	2 8 3	26 10 10½	
7	Ditto ...	20	...	1	2 7 0	51 6 4½	
	Total ...	...	...	9	2 13 4	15 9 0	Ditto ditto.
1	Amirpur ...	1	2	1	4 5 5	7 15 3	
2	Ditto ...	2	3	1	3 9 0	9 7 10½	
3	Ditto ...	3	5	2	3 12 6	13 2 9	
4	Ditto ...	10	20	2	2 15 3	39 2 0	
	Total ...	...	...	6	2 15 0	20 5 6	Ditto ditto.
1	Ramnagur ...	1	2	2	4 1 0	7 5 0	
2	Ditto ...	2	3	3	2 11 9	7 0 0	
	Total ...	...	...	5	3 2 0	7 1 6	Ditto ditto.

Table II.

Taraf Singhia.

Serial number.	Names of villages.	Particulars of holdings. Area. From	To	Number of holdings.	Average Rental. Per acre.	On the whole holding.	Remarks.
1	2	3	4	5	6	7	8
		Acres.	Acres.		Rs. A. P.	Rs. A. P.	
1	Kamargunge ...	1	2	1	3 2 3	4 10 1½	
2	Ditto ...	2	3	1	3 0 9	7 2 3	
3	Ditto ...	3	5	2	3 9 6	15 0 0	
4	Ditto ...	5	10	1	2 8 6	14 3 10½	
	Total ...	...	—	5	3 0 10½	11 3 0	Average rates and rental.
1	Sujagunge ...	...	1	5	5 0 9	1 12 9	
2	Ditto ...	1	2	9	3 15 0	5 0 9	
3	Ditto ...	2	3	6	2 9 0	9 5 9	
4	Ditto ...	3	5	4	3 6 3	18 7 7½	
5	Ditto ...	5	10	5	4 8 3	23 0 0	
6	Ditto ...	10	20	2	2 10 6	27 8 9	
	Total ...	...	...	31	3 10 9	7 8 9	Ditto ditto.
	Grand Total ...	...	...	70	3 3 10	10 11 10	

Table II.

Taraf Nabagram.

Serial number.	Names of villages.	From	To	Number of holdings.	Per acre.	On the whole holding.	Remarks.
		Acres.	Acres.		Rs. A. P.	Rs. A. P.	
1	Duliabarhi ...	...	1	1	7 8 0	3 1 9	
2	Ditto ...	1	2	7	3 4 6	4 14 6	
3	Ditto ...	2	3	3	3 4 3	8 4 9	
4	Ditto ...	3	5	3	3 0 0	11 9 6	
5	Ditto ...	5	10	8	3 1 10½	3 14 0	
6	Ditto ...	20	...	1	2 4 8	54 8 9	
	Total ...	...	...	23	2 15 7	14 14 7	Average rates and rental.
1	Chandigachi ...	...	1	1	5 15 8	3 1 0	
2	Ditto ...	1	2	2	3 8 0	6 1 3	
3	Ditto ...	2	3	3	3 9 6	8 2 4	
4	Ditto ...	3	5	10	2 15 7	11 7 6	
5	Ditto ...	10	20	1	2 13 5	29 9 0	
	Total ...	...	...	17	3 1 0	10 13 2	Ditto ditto.
1	Darkinara ...	...	1	4	4 13 7	2 13 3	
2	Ditto ...	2	3	2	3 0 0	8 10 3	
3	Ditto ...	3	5	2	3 7 0	13 1 3	
4	Ditto ...	5	10	12	3 1 6	20 5 9	
5	Ditto ...	10	20	1	2 8 3	33 8 9	
	Total ...	...	...	21	3 1 0	15 13 5	Ditto ditto.
1	Shahaghati ...	...	1	3	6 15 3	3 1 9	
2	Ditto ...	2	3	4	3 12 6	9 2 3	
3	Ditto ...	3	5	6	3 10 0	14 11 6	
4	Ditto ...	5	10	3	2 12 9	17 1 0	
	Total ...	...	...	16	3 6 0	11 9 5	Ditto ditto.
	Grand Total ...	...	...	77	3 1 6	13 9 0	

TABLE II.

Abstract.

Serial number.	Names of tarafs and pergunnahs.	Particulars of holdings. Area. From	To	Number of holdings.	Average rental. Per acre.	On the whole holding.	Remarks.
1	2	3	4	5	6	7	8
1	Pergunnah Gourhand— Taraf Malatipur.	...	...	59	2 7 0	8 8 0	
2	Pergunnah Hatindah— Taraf Singhia.	...	...	70	3 3 10	10 11 10	
3	Pergunnah Hatindah— Taraf Nabagram.	...	...	77	3 1 6	13 9 0	
	Total ...	...	...	206	3 1 6	11 2 6	

TABLE III.

	1	2	3	4	5	6	7	8
	Crops, &c.	Area cultivated under each crop. (The total of this column exceeds the 5 acres because part of the 5 acres is cultivated under two crops at different seasons, see paragraph 17.)	Produce of grain or other principal matter, e.g. canes, sugar, &c., excluding the straw, &c., detailed below. Per acre.	Of the area entered in column 2.	Consumed at home.	Sold (column 4 minus column 5).	Rate at which the quantity entered in column 6 is sold per maund by the cultivator.	Money got by sale in columns 6 and 7.
		A. R. P.	M. S.	M. S. C.	M. S. C.	M. S. C.	Rs. A. P.	Rs. A. P.
(a)	Winter rice	3 0 20	18 0	56 10 0	36 0 0	20 10 0	1 0 0	20 6 0
	Autumn rice boro (coarse) summer rice	1 1 0	18 0	23 20 0	13 0 0	10 20 0	1 0 0	10 8 0
	Wheat and barley	0 0 25	15 0	2 13 12	1 13 12	1 0 0	2 8 0	2 0 0
	Khesari (pulse)	0 0 25	9 0	1 16 4	0 31 4	0 25 0	0 14 0	0 8 9
	Musuri (do.)	0 0 6·25	9 0	0 14 1	0 6 9	0 7 8	0 12 0	0 2 3
	Bút or gram	0 0 6·25	9 0	0 14 1	0 4 1	0 10 0	2 0 0	0 8 0
	Linseed	0 0 12·5	4 20	0 14 1	0 1 1	0 13 0	4 0 0	1 4 9
	Peas	0 0 12·5	6 0	0 18 12	0 13 12	0 5 0	1 0 0	0 2 0
	Mugh	0 0 6·25	2 20	0 3 14½	0 2 10½	0 1 4	2 0 0	0 1 0
	Mustard	0 1 25	6 0	2 32 8	0 7 8	2 25 0	3 4 0	8 8 6
	Jute	0 1 10	12 0	3 30 0	0 10 0	3 20 0	3 4 0	11 6 0
	Flax	0 0 3·125	6 0	0 4 11	0 0 11	0 4 0	4 8 0	0 7 2
	Pepper	0 0 3·125	12 0	0 9 6	0 4 6	0 5 0	7 8 0	0 15 0
	Potatoes	0 0 3·125	12 0	0 9 6	0 4 6	0 5 0	1 8 0	0 3 0
	Dhunia (spice)	0 0 3·125	4 20	0 3 8½	0 1 8½	0 2 0	2 8 0	0 2 0
	Bara kalai (pulse)	0 0 3·125	6 0	0 4 11	0 2 11	0 2 0	2 0 0	0 1 7
	Cheena	0 0 6·25	9 0	0 14 1	0 10 1	0 4 0	1 0 0	0 1 7
	Kowan	0 0 6·25	9 0	0 14 1	0 10 1	0 4 0	1 0 0	0 1 7
	Kheri	0 0 3·125	6 0	0 4 11	0 4 11	......	1 0 0	......
	Til (oil-seed)	0 0 3·125	4 20	0 3 8½	0 0 8½	0 3 0	7 8 0	0 9 0
	Onions	0 0 3·125	15 0	0 11 11½	0 5 11½	0 6 0	1 4 0	0 3 0
	Kala jira (spice)	0 0 3·125	4 20	0 3 8½	0 0 8½	0 3 0	3 0 0	0 3 7
	Total ...	5 3 39·375	197 20	92 30 8½	52 15 12½	40 14 12	......	58 4 9
(b)	Straw	0 0 3·125	......	......	......	......	......	......
	Makai	0 0 1·5625	9 0	0 3 8½	0 3 8½	......	......	......
	Melons, &c.	0 0 3·125	......	......	......	......	......	1 0 0
	Uchha (cereal crop)...	0 0 1·5625	16 0	0 5 13½	0 2 13½	0 3 0	1 4 0	0 1 6
	Parbal (ditto)	0 0 1·5625	16 0	0 5 13½	0 2 13½	0 3 0	1 4 0	0 1 6
	Turmeric	0 0 1·5625	12 0	0 4 11	0 1 11	0 3 0	5 0 0	0 6 0
		0 0 12·5	51 0	0 19 14½	0 10 14½	0 9 0	......	1 9 0
(c)	Various vegetables and garden produce	0 0 25	......	......	......	......	......	3 0 0
	Total ...	6 0 36·875	248 20	93 10 7½	52 26 11½	40 23 12	......	62 13 9
	Fruits.							
(d)	Mangoes and other fruits and bamboos	0 0 12·5	......	......	......	......	......	3 0 0
	Total ...	6 1 9·375	248 20	93 10 7½	52 26 11½	40 23 12	......	65 13 9
(e)	Canes, grass, charcoal and miscellaneous	......	......	......	......	......	......	1 0 0
	Live-stock, &c.							
(f)	Cows and oxen	......	......	......	......	......	......	5 0 0
	Goats, sheep and ponies	......	......	......	......	......	......	2 0 0
	Poultry and eggs	......	......	......	......	......	......	1 0 0
	Milk	......	......	......	......	......	......	5 0 0
	Total ...	......	......	......	......	......	......	13 0 0
	GRAND TOTAL ...	6 1 9·375	248 20	93 10 7½	52 26 11½	40 23 12	......	79 13 9

Table IIIA.

Details of lands comprised in the holding of 5 acres. Kind of land.	Area. A.	R.	P.	Rate per acre. Rs.	A.	P.	Rental. Rs.	A.	P.	Total amount.
1. Homestead	0	0	9·375	9	0	0	0	8	5¼	
2. Lands closely adjoining the homestead	0	0	15·625	4	8	0	0	7	0	
3. Garden	0	0	12·5	4	8	0	0	5	7½	
4. Paddy land, first class	2	0	0	3	0	0	6	0	0	
5. Ditto, second class	2	0	0	1	14	0	3	12	0	
6. Ditto	0	2	39·375	1	5	0	0	15	8	
7. Straw	0	0	3·125	1	8	0	0	0	5¼	
Total ...	5	0	0	......			12	1	2	
Cess ...	......			......			0	6	0	
Total ...	5	0	0	......			12	7	2	12 7 2

CULTIVATION EXPENSES.

As part of the 5 acres is cultivated under two or more crops at different seasons, the expenses are shown for 6 acres 1 rood 9·375 poles.

Details.	Amount. Rs.	A.	P.	Total amount.
1. Cost of plough, &c.	1	8	0	
2. Cost of first breaking up the soil	0	12	0	
3. Cost of seed, at Rs. 1-4 for 30 seers	0	15	0	
4. Weeding	3	0	0	
5. Thinning, transplanting, &c.	0	6	0	
Total cost per acre ...	6	9	0	
Taking Rs. 6-9 as the cost of cultivating 1 acre, the cost for cultivating 6 acres 1 rood 9·375 poles would come to Rs. 41-6-4½. The cost, however, of cultivating 6 acres and odd collectively would be somewhat less than when the same amount of land is cultivated separately. Thus ⅙th of the total expenditure may be deducted, as the 6 acres is contained in one plot. On deducting Rs. 6-14-4¾, or ⅙th, from the total, the net expenses would accordingly be	34	7	11¾	34 7 11¾
Grand Total ...	......			46 15 1¾

Table IIIB.

Table showing total receipts and disbursements.

Receipts.

Description.	Amount. Rs.	A.	P.
Column 8—			
Heading (*a*), Table III ...	58	4	9
(*b*) ...	1	9	0
(*c*) ...	3	0	0
(*d*) ...	3	0	0
(*f*) ...	1	0	0
(*g*) ...	13	0	0
Total ...	79	13	9

Disbursements.

Description.	Rs.	A.	P.	Amount. Rs.	A.	P.
Rent and cesses				12	7	2
Cultivation expenses				34	7	11¾
Household expenses of a family of five—						
Cloth ...	7	0	0			
Bedding, &c. ...	3	0	0			
Oil ...	4	8	0			
Earthen pots ...	0	8	0			
Other utensils ...	1	0	0			
Fish ...	0	12	0			
Petty expenses ...	3	0	0			
Total ...	......			20	12	0
Grand total ...	......			67	11	1¾
Balance in hand ...	......			12	2	7¼
Total ...	......			79	13	9

Table IV.

Castes.		Number of householders.	Number of inmates. Men.	Boys.	Women.	Girls.	Total.	Rates of wages. Men.	Boys.	Women.	Girls	Yearly value of food when supplied by the employer.	Yearly value of any other contributions made by the employer.	Remarks.
1		2	3	4	5	6	7	8	9	10	11	12	13	14
Turnf Malatipora.														
								Rs. A. P.	Rs. A. P.	Rs. A. P.	Rs. A. P.	Rs. A. P.	Rs. A. P.	
Mahomedans ...	...	26	39	16	24	15	104	0 2 0 3 0 0 21 0 0	0 1 0 1 8 0 9 0 0	0 0 9	0 0 6	Men 8 7 0 Boys 5 10 0 Men 4 0 9 Boys 3 0 0 Men 24 0 0 Boys 18 0 0	.... 2 14 0 1 15 0	Daily wages. Monthly. Yearly.
Hindus—														
Koch ...	...	7	8	8	12	3	31	0 2 0 3 0 0 21 0 0	0 1 0 1 8 0 9 6 0	0 0 9	0 0 6	Ditto ...	Ditto ...	Daily. Monthly. Yearly.
Ganesh ...	...	2	2	...	3	1	6							
Hurbi ...	...	3	6	2	5	1	14	0 2 0 3 0 0 21 0 0	0 1 0 1 8 0 9 0 0	0 0 9	0 0 6	Ditto ...	Ditto ...	Daily. Monthly. Yearly.
Beldar ...	...	10	10	10	13	7	40	0 2 6 0 3 0	0 1 3 0 1 6	0 1 6 0 2 0	0 0 9 0 1 0	....	....	Daily. Contract.
Total	...	48	65	36	67	27	196	......	......	......	......	......	......	
Taraf Singhiga.														
Mahomedans ...	...	54	68	53	88	50	269	As above.						
Hindus—														
Koch ...	...	1	4	4	1	...	9							
Ganesh ...	...	12	16	8	17	4	44							
Harhi ...	...	3	3	4	3	1	10							
Beldar ...	...	54	66	60	77	52	255							
Patni ...	...	8	15	6	15	11	47							
Teli ...	...	1	1	...	...	...	1							
Shudri ...	...	5	8	2	7	3	20							
Rishi ...	...	2	2	4	1	2	10							
Fishermen ...	...	1	...	1	1	...	3							
Total	...	141	188	143	209	124	667							
Taraf Nabagram.														
Mahomedans ...	...	54	53	41	80	38	212	As above.						
Hindus—														
Ganesh ...	...	3	7	3	5	6	21							
Sudri ...	...	7	10	6	12	8	36							
Hurbi ...	...	6	9	8	12	6	35							
Total	...	70	79	58	109	58	304							

Table IVA.

Statement showing the various sources and values of the yearly income of labourers.

1	2	3					4					5					6					7				
Castes.	Classification of wages.	Total sum got in wages during a whole year.					Yearly value of food, &c., column 18 of Table IV.					Yearly value of grain, &c., given at harvest or on other special occasions.					Yearly value of any other contributions by the employer, column 13 of Table IV.					Total yearly income.				
		Men.	Boys.	Women.	Girls.	Total.	Men.	Boys.	Women.	Girls.	Total.	Men.	Boys.	Women.	Girls.	Total.	Men.	Boys.	Women.	Girls.	Total.	Men.	Boys.	Women.	Girls.	Total.
		Rs. A. P.	Rs. A. P.	Rs. A. P.	Rs. A. P.	Rs. A. P.	Rs. A. P.	Rs. A. P.	Rs. A. P.	Rs. A. P.	Rs. A. P.	Rs. A. P.	Rs. A. P.	Rs. A. P.	Rs. A. P.	Rs. A. P.	Rs. A. P.	Rs. A. P.	Rs. A. P.	Rs. A. P.	Rs. A. P.	Rs. A. P.	Rs. A. P.	Rs. A. P.	Rs. A. P.	Rs. A. P.
Beldars ...	Contract wages ...	28 2 0	14 1 0	18 12 0	9 6 0	70 5 0	......	......	......	......	......	5 0 0	......	2 0 0	0 8 0	7 8 0	......	......	......	......	......	33 2 0	14 1 0	20 12 0	9 14 0	77 13 0
Harhis ...	Daily " ...	22 8 0	11 4 0	4 3 6	2 13 0	40 12 6	8 7 0	5 10 0	......	......	14 1 0	18 0 0	0 8 0	4 8 0	1 0 0	24 0 0	......	......	......	......	......	48 15 0	17 6 0	8 11 6	3 13 0	78 13 6
	Yearly " ...	21 0 0	9 0 0	......	......	30 0 0	24 0 0	18 0 0	......	......	42 0 0	......	......	......	......	......	2 14 0	1 15 0	......	......	4 13 0	47 14 0	28 15 0	......	......	76 13 0
Fishermen ...	Daily " ...	22 8 0	11 4 0	4 3 6	2 13 0	40 12 6	8 7 0	5 10 0	......	......	14 1 0	5 0 0	......	2 0 0	......	7 0 0	......	......	......	......	......	35 15 0	16 14 0	6 3 6	2 13 0	61 13 6
	Yearly " ...	21 0 0	9 0 0	......	......	30 0 0	24 0 0	18 0 0	......	......	42 0 0	......	......	......	......	......	2 14 0	1 15 0	......	......	4 13 0	47 14 0	28 15 0	......	......	76 13 0
Wood-cutters	Daily " ...	22 8 0	11 4 0	4 3 6	2 13 0	40 12 6	8 7 0	5 10 0	......	......	14 1 0	15 0 0	......	5 0 0	0 8 0	20 8 0	......	......	......	......	......	45 15 0	16 14 0	9 3 6	3 5 0	75 5 6
	Yearly " ...	21 0 0	9 0 0	......	......	30 0 0	24 0 0	18 0 0	......	......	42 0 0	......	......	......	......	......	2 14 0	1 15 0	......	......	4 13 0	47 14 0	28 15 0	......	......	76 13 0
Others—																										
Hindus ...	Daily " ...	22 8 0	11 4 0	4 3 6	2 13 0	40 12 6	8 7 0	5 10 0	......	......	14 1 0	8 0 0	2 0 0	20 8 0	2 0 0	32 8 0	......	......	......	......	......	38 15 0	18 14 0	24 11 6	4 13 0	87 5 6
	Yearly " ...	21 0 0	9 0 0	......	......	30 0 0	24 0 0	18 0 0	......	......	42 0 0	......	......	......	......	......	2 14 0	1 15 0	......	......	4 13 0	47 14 0	28 15 0	......	......	76 13 0
Mahomedans	Daily " ...	22 8 0	11 4 0	4 3 6	2 13 0	40 12 6	8 7 0	5 10 0	......	......	14 1 0	8 0 0	2 0 0	14 8 0	2 0 0	26 8 0	......	......	......	......	......	38 15 0	18 14 0	18 11 6	4 13 0	81 5 6
	Yearly " ...	21 0 0	9 0 0	......	......	30 0 0	24 0 0	18 0 0	......	......	42 0 0	......	......	......	......	......	2 14 0	1 15 0	......	......	4 13 0	47 14 0	28 15 0	......	......	76 13 0

Table V.

Details of Table I, Order C, Artisans.

Caste and occupation.	Number of households.	Number of Inmates.					Average Income.					
							Monthly.			Yearly.		
		Men.	Boys.	Women.	Girls.	Total.	Men.			Men.		
Malatipore.							Rs.	A.	P.	Rs.	A.	P.
Potters (kumhars)	5	7	12	12	3	34	8	5	4	100	0	0
Blacksmiths	2	4	5	5	4	18	10	13	4	130	6	0
Goldsmiths (patnis) ...	6	12	8	11	7	38	5	4	0	63	0	0
Total ...	13	23	25	28	14	90	24	6	8	293	0	0
Singhiya.												
Blacksmiths (Karmakars) ...	1	3	1	5	3	12	9	14	4	118	12	0
Weavers	8	10	12	11	7	40	4	0	0	48	0	0
Total ...	9	13	13	16	10	52	13	14	4	166	12	0
Nabagram.												
Carpenters	2	6	4	6	4	20	12	0	0	144	0	0
Grand Total ...	24	42	42	50	28	162	50	5	0	603	12	0

Table VI.

Showing the average produce per acre, and the rates at which the cultivator can himself sell the produce.

Crops.	Produce per acre.			Rate per maund of [illegible] lbs.			Value of produce per acre.		
1	2			3			4		
	Mds.	S.	C.	Rs.	A.	P.	Rs.	A.	P.
Winter (haimanta) rice	18	0	0	1	0	0	18	0	0
Autumn (bhado) rice	......			......			......		
Coarse summer (boro) rice	18	0	0	1	0	0	18	0	0
Wheat	......			......			......		
Barley	15	0	0		0	0	30	0	0
Khesari (pulse)	9	0	0	0	14	0	7	14	0
Musur („)	9	0	0	0	12	0	6	12	0
Gram	9	0	0	2	0	0	18	0	0
Linseed	4	20	0	4	0	0	18	0	0
Peas	6	0	0	1	0	0	6	0	0
Mugh pulse	2	20	0	2	0	0	5	0	0
Mustard	6	0	0	3	4	0	19	8	0
Jute	12	0	0	3	4	0	39	0	0
Flax	6	0	0	4	8	0	27	0	0
Chilies	12	0	0	7	8	0	90	0	0
Potatoes	12	0	0	1	8	0	18	0	0
Dhania (spice)	4	20	0	2	8	0	11	4	0
Bara kalai	6	0	0	2	0	0	12	0	0
Cheena	9	0	0	1	0	0	9	0	0
Kowen	9	0	0	1	0	0	9	0	0
Khiri	6	0	0	1	0	0	6	0	0
Oil-seeds	4	20	0	7	8	0	33	12	0
Onions	15	0	0	1	4	0	18	12	0
Kala jira (spice)	4	20	0	3	0	0	13	8	0
Makai (Indian-corn)	9	0	0	1	4	0	11	4	0
Uchha, Patal, &c., vegetables	15	0	0	1	4	0	18	12	0
Turmeric	12	0	0	5	0	0	60	0	0

Table VII.

Details of Table I.—Order d.—Beggars.

Caste, &c.	Number of households.	Number of Inmates.					Practice and Habits.	Yearly earnings and expenses.			Remarks.
		Men.	Boys.	Women.	Girls.	Total.		Gross yearly earnings of each individual.	Gross yearly earnings of the total in column 7.	Expenses of the total in column 7.	
1	2	3	4	5	6	7	8	9	10	11	12
								Rs. A. P.	Rs. A. P.	Rs. A. P.	
Village Malatipore.							*Taraf Malatipur.*				
Mahomedans	1	...	2	1	...	3	Beg from door to door and receive alms in the shape of rice, pulse, oil, salt, vegetables, &c.	7 12 0	23 4 0	23 4 0	
Brahmins	1	1	...	...	...	1	Beg and receive money alms at the hands of well-to-do persons living in and out of the village.	24 0 0	24 0 0	24 0 0	
Village Lalgunge.											
Bairagis	8	6	...	11	1	1	Beg from door to door and receive alms in the shape of rice.	18 0 0	306 0 0*	306 0 0	* No earnings have been attributed to the girls.
Total ...	10	7	2	12	1	22		......	......	......	
							Taraf Singhiya.				
Village Singhiya.											
Bairagis	11	17	6	29	9	61	Beg from door to door and receive alms in the shape of rice, &c.	......	......	......	
Village Bujaganj.											
Bairagis	1	...	1	1	...	2					
Total ...	12	17	7	30	9	63		18 0 0	846 0 0†	846 0 0	† The earnings of the boys and girls (shewn in columns 4 and 6) have been excluded.
Village Chandigachhi.							*Taraf Nabagram.*				
Bairagis	1	1	1	1	...	3	Ditto ...	18 0 0	36 0 0†	36 0 0	

Maldah,

The 7th April 1888.

H. G. Sharp,

Collector.

H. P.—Reg. No. 6560—137—17-4-88.

CONFIDENTIAL.]

No. 7RG, dated Burdwan, the 16th April 1888.

From—N. S. ALEXANDER, ESQ., Commissioner of the Burdwan Division,
To—The Secretary to the Government of Bengal, Revenue Department.

WITH reference to your No. 36Agri., dated 9th December 1887, I have the honour to submit the following report.

2. A copy of your circular was sent to each Collector in this division, with a request that, if possible, a few typical villages or parts of villages should be taken in various parts of the district and enquiries made in a quiet and unostentatious manner. I have received reports from the Collectors of Burdwan, Hooghly, Bankoora, and Midnapore, and the Covenanted Deputy Collector of Howrah, extracts from which I give in this report. Full enquiries could not be made, as the report was called for when the cold season, during which this sort of enquiry can best be made, had nearly half expired; and the time during which the enquiry was to be made has been shortened by your urgent call for the submission of the report. The statistics elicited show, I think, however, that in this division, in the districts from which reports have been received, the classes concerning whom enquiry has been made have most of their physical wants supplied. There are perhaps a few who are reduced to one meal a day, but such is the exception and not the rule. The fact that the people in the villages in which enquiries were held had all of them brass utensils, and that the women wore ornaments of some kind or other, speaks for itself, and shows that the mass of the population must be in a position that precludes the idea of their being under-fed. When the physique and general appearance of the people is below par, it is not due to under-feeding, but to the malarious atmosphere of the country in which they live and the external squalor of their surroundings. The disrepair and untidiness of their houses are due more to their lack of knowing anything better than to their extreme poverty. I am not personally well acquainted with this part of the country, having only spent a few weeks in each district during the past cold season; but from what I have seen, I am inclined to agree with Messrs. Toynbee and Oldham, the Collectors of Hooghly and Burdwan, in their estimates of the general condition of the people. The chief cause of debt is of course the expenditure on social ceremonies, marriages, &c.

3. I regret no report has yet been received from the district of Beerbhoom, as it would be well to know the condition of the people of that district, who are mostly Sonthals or Bauris, or people of an aboriginal or semi-aboriginal class.

4. It will be seen that most of the weaver class supplement their earnings from their trade as weavers by working as agriculturists or agricultural day-labourers when they cannot get work to do in their trade as weavers.

5. With reference to paragraph 4 of your circular, there have been no settlements or partitions in this division in recent times of sufficient magnitude to furnish statistics; nor do there appear to have been any revisions of the cess valuations under Act (IX B.C.) of 1880, except in the small district of Bankoora.

6. Where the wages of day-labourers are paid in kind, it has been taken into account in the villages in which enquiries were made, and the number of persons subsisting entirely on charity have been shown by those Collectors. Most are, I think, either professional beggars or religious mendicants, Baishnabs, Faquirs, &c.

7. It is rare to find females tending cattle in the fields and forests; but I noticed several cases in the districts of Midnapore and Bankoora where the people are of a semi-aboriginal origin. Women in general are employed in such work as husking paddy, pounding soorkee, carrying in the harvest, and such like occupations; but they do not, as far as my experience goes, ever work in the fields regularly as day-labourers. Women working as day-labourers will almost invariably be found to be Nagpore Kols, Dhangars, and, in a few cases, Sonthals. No women of the ordinary cultivator class in Bengal would work in the fields for hire except under the pressure of dire necessity.

BURDWAN DISTRICT.

8. Concerning this district, Mr. Oldham, the Collector, has submitted a report, from which the following extracts are given. Mr. Oldham has had some experience of the district ; he is an officer of some standing, who has had considerable experience of work as a Settlement Officer and a Famine Relief Officer, and is therefore likely to have formed an accurate opinion of the facts enquired into by him. He personally conducted the enquiry held in one large typical village :—

9. " There are no recent road cess papers or settlements or partitions in progress in this district, from the papers of which any useful analysis could be made. Owing, too, to the peculiar circumstances preceding and attending the creation of the patni system, there is an almost entire absence of zemindari papers bearing on the subject. I therefore had to select a typical area ; and, after holding a census, which, though intended to be rough, was really accurate, of the adult inhabitants whose monthly income was indubitably less than Rs. 7, or the equivalent of Rs. 7, I proceeded to enquire into their individual circumstances. The area selected was the cluster of two villages grouped round the side called Kaksa. This place contained by the census of 1881, 1,120 houses with 5,655 inhabitants. It is situated on the junction of the laterite country with the deltaic soil, partly on the former and partly on the latter. It contains a Musulman quarter and a fair sprinkling of artizans, and is as representative an area for the Burdwan district as could possibly be found. It is the home of Moulvi Syed Nijabut Hossain, General Manager of Wards' Estates in the Sonthal Pergunnahs, who is an aymadar, and has a number of tenants in the place, every resident inhabitant of which he personally knows. I have known him intimately for many years, and have reason to hold the highest opinion of his integrity. I sent for him and he remained with me while I held my enquiries, and gave great assistance to me in doing so.

10. " I lay particular stress on my mention of Moulvi Nijabut Hossain as a reference for the facts and conclusions which I am about to detail. Not only is he a resident of position, a person of proved integrity, and himself a landlord in the area in which my specific enquiries were held, but his experience has, in a peculiar degree, qualified him to be a judge of the matter under enquiry. He was my assistant in Chumparun in the relief operations of 1874, and in Madras in the famine of 1877. While there, he had charge of the house relief system. He was a license-tax assessor in Midnapore for the next three years, and since 1881 has been the very successful Manager of of Wards' Estates under a ryotwari system in Deoghur and Jamtara. Like most natives of his class, I find him at first to be an extreme pessimist, and he pronounced the condition of the poor of Kaksa to be deplorably bad. Like others, he had taken no relative view of the case. He had never calculated the exact difference between what a labourer could live on and what he actually received, and never dreamed of taking into account anything but the direct income in cash or kind, and, finally, was more surprised at the facts actually elicited than I was myself.

11. " My enquiries at Kaksa occupied the end of December and the first few days in January. I then visited almost every part of the rest of the district, and throughout my tour compared at each opportunity the salient points ascertained to exist at Kaksa with similar conditions elsewhere; while I took note of all differing conditions. The result confirmed my general impressions originally formed that nowhere in the district is there a lower rate of income, a lower standard of ease, a narrower margin for subsistence, or a greater prevalence of poverty among the agricultural and labouring classes than at Kaksa.

II. Results : cultivators and agricultural labourers.

12. " In the Burdwan district it is impossible to separate these two divisions among the poorer classes. While there is no cultivator with an holding of less than 4 acres who does not supplement his earnings from it by working as a labourer, there are scarcely any agricultural labourers who do not hold land from a garden patch of 10 cottahs to a share in rice fields. Even the non-agricultural labourers very often hold patches of cultivation, and it is here worth while to glance at and dismiss this class. They fall roughly into divisions, viz., coal mine coolies and labourers engaged at molasses manufactures, at railway

yards and grain stores, in driving carts, as boatmen, and on piece work of all kinds. The labour of the coal mine coolies is always at a premium; and though their circumstances and surroundings look squalid and wretched in the extreme, their bodies are invariably well-nourished, and they get quite enough to eat and far more than enough to drink. The other special labourers are all men for this district, of exceptional physique, and their average earnings are not less than Rs. 8 a month all the year round. For some months they are much higher.

13. " Referring to the poorer cultivators and field labourers, the result of my enquiries may be set forth in the following propositions:—

(1). " In a purely agricultural area, they, with their families, form about 75 per cent. of the population.

(2). " In the Burdwan district they all bear traces of disease. They may all be said to be enfeebled by disease, that is, by fever and its consequences. Among some castes leprosy is terribly common.

(3). " They bear the burden of their helpless and sick relatives who are about 5 per cent. of them.

(4). " The rates of their remuneration have risen considerably within the last 20 years, and above the proportion of the increased dearness of provisions.

(5). " There is no indebtedness among them, and the indebtedness which used to exist has disappeared.

(6). " The wives and elder children of a poor cultivator or labourer who is in ordinary health are not forced to resort to out-door labour, and are employed solely on domestic duties.

(7). " An adult male, even though in poor physical condition, receives, at the lowest calculation, one-and-a-half times as much as will support a working man's life and supply clothing and lodging, and the average is higher. The proportion of surplus for a woman is much lower, not reaching to as much again."

(8). " Finally, taking the rates of food which have prevailed for the last thirteen years, they have enough with which to procure, and they do procure, a sufficiency of wholesome food enough to support their wives, children, and dependent relatives on, to bestow on their universal charity, to expend on festivals and celebrations, and to enable them to meet at least the approaches of a time of scarcity. They are much better off than I, on a superficial view of their circumstances, or than their own fellow residents of superior station, supposed them to be; and the only individuals among them who have no margin, or but the slenderest margin, are their dependent relatives, the most numerous of whom are old widows and others disabled by sickness, age, or some bodily or mental infirmity.

14. " I now proceed to an analysis of the foregoing statements. Of the prevalence of disease, I had painful testimony in my census. I had with me the enumerators who had taken that of 1881, and examined their methods and was satisfied of their care and accuracy. In 1881 the Kaksa area had 1,120 houses with 5,655 people. In my census 698 houses with 3,730 people were counted. The decrease is attributable to the malaria which, in the west of the district, was most violent in the years 1881 to 1884. The ruined houses and abandoned sites were everywhere visible. The people's physique was poor and fever-striken, and throughout the district they present the same appearance. In fact, the sickly physique is now the ordinary physique, and commands the ordinary labour rates. The healthy physique is the exceptional one, and commands special and very high rates.

Dependents.

15. " Old women are by far the most numerous of these, and some of them were distant relatives of the persons who supported them. Nearly all were able to earn a trifle by *dhan* husking, and I did not see one who had not one or more brass utensils in her hut or room. Their food was sufficient, and their extreme poverty was most manifested in the flimsy rags with which they were dressed. Other dependents were cripples and imbeciles. At Kaksa these dependents were just under 5 per cent. of the poorer classes. As long as common rice sells for 20 seers for the rupee, their daily food in full sufficiency is not precarious.

16. "Twenty years ago as said, though probably thirty years were meant (and whatever the period, it was one within the memory of the people), the rate used to be for reaper or ordinary field labourer his food and four seers of *dhan* each day. The rates are now his food and five seers of *dhan* per diem. The price of *dhan* has nearly doubled in the period. Moreover, in the height of the field season (from August to December), labour is at a premium and special rates have to be given.

Increased wages.

17. "The disappearance of indebtedness, which was general in 1872 (*vide* Hunter's Statistical Account), is a remarkable circumstance. The rural mahajans, to whom the poor cultivators and labourers were practically bound as serfs, have also disappeared. The present class of mahajans only deals with the middle class on the security of landed property, which is nearly always rent-free. Most of the people whom I questioned owed nothing at all; others owed a rupee or two to a fellow labourer, or a rupee or two to their permanent employer. These employers still retain their field labourers by lending grain to them in the slack season without interest. These transactions are not regarded as loans, still less as mahajani.

Indebtedness.

18. "The only women and children whom I found employed on out-door labour for hire belonged to the poor relation and semi-dependent class—widows and orphans. The poorest Bauri labourer did not let his wife work for any one but himself.

Employment of wives and children.

19. "I give the following sample cases—one of an ordinary labourer of poor physique, another of a leper, and the third of a young woman dependent, which I applied and tested in many similar instances. These cases were picked at random and pronounced by Moulvi Nijabut Hossain to be excellent samples. With the average price of common rice, about 20 seers per rupee, as it has been for many years past, an adult male or female can support a working life and pay for lodging and clothing on Rs. 2 a month, and can do so with a margin of Rs. 2-8:—

Actual earnings of a labourer.

(1). "Kali Bauri, an attenuated little man of 30, under five feet in height, and 90lbs in weight, has had fever repeatedly; has a wife and one child. He is (as are all the male Bauris in the same *busti*) a permanent farm labourer (*lag paita*), and is paid all the year round, whether he works or not, as long as he is in employment. He holds his house rent-free, and has also 10 cottahs of cultivation rent-free from his employer. I calculate his income as follows:—

	Per diem.	Per mensem. Rs.	A.	P.
1. Daily wages in cash	2 annas	3	12	0
2. Daily food, which consists of boiled rice, parched rice, oil, tobacco, condiments given by his employer, at a low calculation	8 pie	1	4	0
3. House rent (free)	......	0	3	0
4. Miscellaneous receipts, viz., thatching materials free from his employer, produce of his land, produce of his fowls (he had three broods of chickens, and eggs sell for one pice a piece), at a low calculation	......	0	5	0
		5	8	0
Value of his wife's services to him—she does all his household work; she, moreover, partakes of his free food and is fed for nothing—Nijabut Hossain's appraisement	......	2	0	0
Total ...		7	8	0

The total monthly income of his family might be fairly valued at Rs. 7-8. At the rates now prevalent, and which have prevailed for food for many years past, Rs. 4-8 a month or its equivalent would be sufficient for their support. Kali Bauri's habitation was a tiny hut. It was quite weather-tight and very clean inside, and contained, besides, brass utensils, clothes and bedding, and a store of rice. It was exactly typical of the other Bauri huts in the place.

"His wife works for him alone. He said his marriage cost him Rs. 20, and that he will spend Rs. 30 on his daughter's marriage. The bystanders jeered at this and said it was exaggerated and unnecessary.

"It is to be remembered that Kali Bauri's daily two annas represent the five seers of *dhan* which are the ordinary rates in which the people generally expressed wages, whether so given or given in cash, as in Kali Bauri's case.

(2). "The next case is that of one of the leper Bauri partially isolated and certainly segregated from his fellows because of his leprosy. His household consisted of his wife, his mother and himself, and all were lepers. He was a casual labourer.

"He had received the previous day, which was in the slack season, his food and four seers of *dhan* for casual work. His mother was a faggot gatherer. His wife worked only for him in the house. He had spent Rs. 5 or Rs. 6 on his marriage. He owed nothing to anyone. His house was much the same as Kali Bauri's but, rather better, and it had a garden patch. This was a thoroughly typical case, as Nijabut Hossain admitted, of the leper labourers. The disease was appallingly common. It is widespread among the Bauris, who will eat more carrion than any other caste.

(3). "The third case was of a Bauri widow, a girl of about 20, with no relatives living. She was pointed out to me by Nijabut Hossain as an instance of absolute pauperism, just short of mendicancy. She lived by the charity of the Bauris for whom she did odd jobs. But this girl refused to work for Nijabut Hossain at his house, which is close by, that is, on his premises, for less than 7 pice a day without food, or 4 pice a day with food; and I was assured that no labourer of her stamp, and, indeed, no woman labourer of any kind, could be got for a lower rate.

III. Artizans.

20. "These may be divided into the ordinary artizans, such as carpenters, blacksmiths, and potters, who are necessary for every community, and the artizans engaged on special industries in particular centres, such as the weavers and braziers or workers at other hardware in this district. The former may be dismissed at once. Their average incomes are higher far than those of the labourers; and if sometimes they are not really so well off, it is solely because their standard and status are higher. Thus, at Kaksa the carpenter was pointed out to me by Nijabut Hossain as one of the paupers in particularly indigent circumstances. I found him inhabiting a comparatively fine house, and he refused to take employment under the Burdwan Raj as a permanency for less than Rs. 12 a month. His earnings used to average about Rs. 30 a month. The rates for all ordinary artizan labour are exceptionally high here, while the class is far from numerous.

21. "Coming to the special handicraftsmen, it is much more difficult to give anything like statistical information. If their trade is brisk, they flourish. When it is slack they suffer, and suffer the more because they cling to it notwithstanding its decay, and refuse to seek the more remunerative occupations open to them. The brass and hardware trade after many vicissitudes is at present fairly brisk, and the artizans who pursue it are well off and earning none less than an average of Rs. 6 a month, or its equivalent. A weaver in full work could earn the same, but few weavers are in full work; and I find it impossible to estimate what their actual earnings are. But the labour market, with its minimum rate of 10 pice a day all the year round, is open to them.

IV. Mendicants.

22. "The condition of no class varies so much as that of the mendicants. The houses of some professional Mahomedan beggars which I visited at Kaksa showed a high standard of comfort, and, comparatively speaking, of luxury. But there were also the homeless beggars, nearly all cripples or diseased persons, who derived a bare subsistence from charity. At Kaksa there were 20 of these people, or over ½ per cent. of the population; but my observation elsewhere showed that the number at Kaksa, probably because of its situation on the Grand Trunk Road, was unusually large, and that nowhere else, except at Burdwan, was there so high a proportion of mendicants.

23. "It has been noticed in the foregoing paragraphs that the material surroundings of the poorer classes, their houses, clothes, utensils and ornaments often indicate a very different position from that in which an examination into their incomes shows them to be. The plainest case is that of the colliery coolies whose earnings are the highest of any ordinary labourers, and whose huts, clothes, and surroundings are sordid in the extreme. The state of these externals much depends on the race to which the people belong, and the social position which they hold and feel themselves bound to maintain. The Bauris and Sonthals care for brass ornaments only. Brass utensils are everywhere now in use, and the adoption of the umbrella even by coolies is as universal.

24. "The chief varying conditions which I noticed at other places than Kaksa were a smaller proportion of mendicants, a slighter prevalence of leprosy, and the extent to which the food-supply was supplemented by fishing. But at no other place in the district does a lower rate of wages prevail; nor is there a caste of lower status and in poorer circumstances than the Bauris.

25. "Appended I beg to give the Civil Surgeon's opinion on the points on which he was consulted. He has furnished me with a copy of his report on the subject to the Inspector-General of Jails, which I also beg to append, chiefly in order to point to the errors contained in it regarding rates of wages. There is also no class of artizans or labourers in this district which earns less than a total income of Rs. 3, or, indeed, of Rs. 5 per month. In the case of the 48 persons so shown in the Civil Surgeon's report, only the wages actually paid in cash can have been taken into account.

BANKOORA DISTRICT.

26. Mr. Tayler, the Collector of Bankoora, has submitted a report from which the following extracts are given. Mr. Tayler has had considerable experience of Bankoora:—

27. "With a view to ascertain the actual facts relating to the condition of the lower classes of the population, I caused enquiries to be made in two villages, one in the Sudder, thana Bankoora, and the other in thana Bishenpore, each being as much typical as possible of the various parts of the sub-division to which it appertains.

28. "In reporting the result of the enquiries, I would presume that these people do not keep any account of their income and expenditure, as almost all of them are illiterate. The facts and figures given by themselves were not always correct; but before adopting anything, statement made have been duly tested by actual observation of the manner in which they live and the furniture and utensils they use. In fact, every endeavour has been made to base the conclusions arrived at on sufficient and reliable data.

29. "In accordance with the instruction contained in paragraph 3 of the Government circular, the lower classes were divided into the following order:—

"(*a*). Cultivators.
"(*b*). Agricultural and other labourers.
"(*c*). Artizans (weavers, black and gold smiths, carpenters, potters, &c.).
"(*d*). Beggars, or those who subsist on charity.

30(*a*). "The name of the village selected for the Sudder sub-division is Narra. There are ten families of cultivators in it, each consisting of eight members on the average, of whom two are adult males, two adult females and four children. The average area cultivated by the cultivator is five acres, which in ordinary years produce 230 maunds of grain, or 46 maunds per acre and 16 kahans of straw. The value of this outturn at the prevailing rate of 10 annas per maund and 2 *pans* of straw per rupee comes to Rs. 156. The outturn in grain is seldom supplemented by fodder and live-stock which he keeps for his own use. Carcasses of cattle are thrown away, the *Muchis* taking the hides free of cost, as the religious prejudices of the Hindus, who form the great majority of the population of this district, prevent them selling hides. None of the cultivators found in the village have tanks or ponds as a depository for fish. Jungles are owned by the upper classes from whom they get firewood or wood for house building. The only other means of supplementing the income from cultivation is by husking the rice of the upper classes—a work which is performed by the female members of the house, and is paid for invariably in grain, of which the estimated value is Rs. 12 in a year. The cultivators have cows, but the milk they produce is consumed by the children. The female members, though they do not actually work with the males in the field, give the latter material assistance in the threshing, cleaning, and storing of the grain, besides doing the work of house-keeping, cooking, and even that of cowherd when the services of a boy are not available. The estimated income of a cultivator is therefore Rs. 168 a year from all sources. The following are his outgoings:—

	Rs.
"Food—	
Two meals a day, including fuel, dâl, oil and salt, &c. ...	120
Clothing	15
Rent of land	15
Wages of labourers employed in emergent or critical times of the agricultural operations	5
	155
Other expenses—	
Repair of implements, trinkets for women, tiffin for children, social and religious ceremonies	10
Total ...	165

"In average years his receipts are just enough to make both ends meet. It is only on such extraordinary occasions as marriage, purchase of live-stock, or failure of crop that he gets involved in accounts and debts from which he experiences considerable difficulty in extricating himself. As a matter of fact, there is scarcely one among the ten families which has not at least a debt of Rs. 10 to pay. On the whole, however, they now show signs of comparative prosperity.

31(*b*). "There are 19 labourers in the village; each has a family of five members on the average, including himself, to support. They hold no land. The daily wages of a labourer are 2 annas, and those of the females, two of whom are usually present in the family at 1½ annas each a day, are annas 3. They are for the most part paid in grain. At the seasons of sowing, transplanting, and cutting paddy they are fully employed, but at other times they suffer much for want of employment and are reduced to one meal a day. In years of drought or short crop, they migrate to the eastern districts in quest of labour and return home as soon as the paddy-cutting season is over. The Bauris, Domes, and Bagdis are the poorest of this lot. They labour under the cultivator, build mud walls, and make bamboo baskets. The females bring firewood from the jungle and sell it to the nearest market. Coolies for emigration to Assam are for the most part recruited from these aboriginal tribes.

32(*c*). "There are 11 artizans in the village, of whom four are weavers, two blacksmiths, one gold and silver smith, two carpenters, one barber and one malakar.

33. "The number of members is ordinarily five in a family of weavers; each has a handloom on which they work for themselves; about a third of the labour is shared by the female members. The outturn of a weaver's loom in a month is Rs. 5 net; he holds an acre of land besides. The total receipts from all sources are estimated to be Rs. 80 net annually (after deducting rent of land and cost of cultivation), which is sufficient to support him with his family and children. If the import of piece-goods from Manchester has caused distress to weavers in the more advanced districts, it has but slightly affected the condition of those living in the rural tracts in this district where cotton is grown which is spun into thread and a coarse sort of cloth is made. The rural population prefers this to Europe cloth on account of its durability.

34. "Two families of blacksmiths reside in the village, and each consists of ten members. They carry on their hereditary calling, and at the same time

cultivate about four bigahs of land. The net income from each source is Rs. 50 a year. They are as a class well off. So also are the two carpenters and the one goldsmith in this village. The barber and the malakar (dealer in flowers and sola toys) are not, however, so well off; they sometimes suffer for want of sufficient work and get into debt.

35(*d*). "This class is represented chiefly by the *Baishnabs.* There are eight beggars in the village who subsist on charity, each has a house of his own; and the reverence in which their sect is held by the lower classes enables them to eke out a tolerable means of livelihood. These are all religious mendicants.

36. "The food of the lower classes consists of coarse rice and *dâl* with vegetables occasionally. The average quantity consumed daily is one seer for an adult man, ¾ths seer for an adult woman, and ½ a seer for a boy or girl. This is divided into two meals, taken at midday and evening respectively. In the morning a moderate quantity of *moori* or parched rice is taken. They dwell in huts with mud walls usually 12 by 8 feet and 12 feet high, thatched with straw. The cultivators and artizans have generally two such huts furnished with wooden doors and windows. The ornaments worn by the women are brass or bell-metal bracelets, armlets, and anklets, a complete set of which costs about 8 annas. A brass *lota* (water pot), a few bowls or cups of the same metal or stone, and a stone or bell-metal plate constitute the utensils of a family, the aggregate value of which is Rs. 2 or so.

37. "There are about 150 cultivators, 40 labourers, and 25 artizans (carpenters, blacksmiths, weavers, &c.) in the village of Radhanagore in thana Bishenpore. The cultivators hold about 2 acres of land each on an average, which consists of several kinds of land as a rule, and whose average yield of different kind of food-grains is about 20 maunds pucca per acre. The major portion of the produce is consumed at home, and the rest goes partly to the market and partly to the money or grain-lenders, but the quantity or its price cannot be ascertained with any amount of correctness, as no proper account book is kept. The cultivators generally get loans of money or grain which they repay after the harvest, or as soon after it as they can, and sell the unconsumed portion of the produce in small quantities as occasion requires. This accounts for the absence of an account book. Of the other sources of income, hides of dead cattle are disposed of in the manner stated above. Straw and milk are sold to a large extent, but the amount they fetch cannot be accurately known for want of accounts. Approximately it is something like Rs. 7 per annum as regards each family, considering that these articles are sold only when not wanted at home.

38. "There are no regular dealers in live-stock, and the cultivators seldom sell their cattle. Live-stock cannot therefore be taken as a regular source of income. There is a jungle close to the village, but it belongs not to them, but to their zemindar, who is paid for any jungle produce that is taken by them.

39. "Regarding the expenses of cultivation and indebtedness of the cultivators, the average expense per acre is about Rs. 12 (average rent Rs. 4-8 and average household expenses Rs. 7-8). It is difficult to speak of indebtedness, for, as stated above, there is no account of the amount borrowed and repaid; but looking at the external condition of the cultivators and other people, including labourers, I think they are generally beyond the power of the heartless money-lenders, and live more comfortably off than their forefathers. The mode in which they live does not cost as much as to drain their purse; but the expensive system of marriage and other ceremonies, which is general among all sections of the people, oblige them to incur debts which often take them years to repay.

40. "Agricultural labourers are not a class of men distinguished from other labourers, the same set doing all sorts of manual work, such as house-building, earth-cutting, &c. There are different rates of wages for different kinds of work, and persons of different ages; and every person on an average get 2½ annas a day, which is barely sufficient to meet his daily expenses. When a man has sufficient stock of grain, he pays his workmen in kind worth the amount mentioned above. Labourers do not get food or food and lodging, and none of them have land. There is, however, no want of work for them.

41. "The artizans (weavers, blacksmiths, goldsmiths, carpenters, &c., are not paid by the day, and it is therefore difficult to estimate their earnings; but it appears, with the exception of weavers, that all are better off than formerly, and earn sufficient for their subsistence all the year round. In the case of potters and weavers only women work at home, assisting their male relatives in their business. The average number of members in a family of any of these classes is 2 males, 1 female, and 3 children.

42. "The estimated number of beggars in the village is 20, who live entirely on the charity of the people.

43. "In conclusion, I beg to state that Dr. Wilson, the Civil Surgeon of the district, says, from his own experience of the coolies proceeding to Assam, that the physique of the class from which they are drawn is not affected by want of due nourishment. But his experience is different in the jail, the majority of admissions into which show indication of scorbutic diathesis, the result of insufficient and poor diet."

MIDNAPORE DISTRICT.

44. Mr. Vowell, the Collector of Midnapore, has not given much personal attention to the subject. The extracts given have been made by me from reports submitted by the Sub-divisional Officers of Ghattal and Tumlook in the district of Midnapore which I had to put into readable English. These subdivisions are on the eastern or Calcutta side of the district; many of the poorer people get work in and about Calcutta or its suburbs during about six months of the year, and so supplement the family earnings got from the home bit of land—

45. "Three villages were visited by the Sub-divisional Officer of Ghattal viz., (1) Aguria, situated on the western part of thana Daspore, which is exposed to floods but not always, (2) Naihati, situated on the eastern part of that thana, which is always exposed to floods, (3) Bonpore, situated on the northern part of thana Chandrakona, which is always free from floods.

46. "The Sub-divisional Officer of Ghattal visited the above villages and held a personal enquiry into the condition of the residents. The following figures have been submitted by him as the result of his enquiry, which he writes he made carefully and unobtrusively. The villages visited are situated in agricultural tracts and are inhabited by the poorest classes. The statements are marked A, B, C, D, and E. A gives the statistics as to cultivation; B, those as to agricultural labour; C, artizans; D, persons living by charity; and E, others.

47. "The first three headings in all the statements give the number of males, number of females, and number of children in a family. Besides these particulars, Statement A gives the following information, viz., the number of working males, area of cultivation, description of the different sorts of crops, quantity of each crop, average outturn per bigah, the number of plough bullocks in a family, quantity of straw obtained from each bigah, quantity of grain which a family can sell after consumption, average selling rate of paddy, rate of annual rent and cesses, amount of debt, if any, number of milch cows in each family and whether they sell any milk, if so, what is the monthly earning therefrom, value of ornaments, if any, in the family, quantity of brass utensils possessed by the family, and other means of earning. From the statement it will appear that *no females or children have ordinarily to work as field labourers*, though they may perhaps be employed during harvest time to aid in getting in the crop. Statement B, besides the information given in Statement A, shows the rates of wages of day-labourers, the estimated amount of time they get during a year, other professions, if any, they follow, and the monthly income they derive from day-labour exclusive of cultivation. Statement C shows the artizans who do not cultivate any land; those who do have been shown in Statement B. In Statement C have been shown only the *bastu* or homestead lands held by them, and the amount of rent and cesses paid. Besides these particulars, the following statistics have been given in this form, viz., the average amount earned monthly by potters and weavers, the number of looms each family of weavers work, the amount of cloth they turn out monthly, the average rate earned monthly by carpenters and others, the number of milch cows each family keeps and the income derived from them, the amount

of debt, if any, the value of gold and silver ornaments in each family, the quantity of brass utensils, and, lastly, any other sources of income. Statement D gives statistics as to persons living on charity. These are for the most part poor and helpless widows. Statement E has been prepared only for village Naihati. This statement gives the same statistics as Statement C. In this those persons only have been shown who live only by service or day-labour.

48. "It will be seen that in village Aguria there are 171 families or houses, and its population consists of 292 males, 365 females, and 326 children—total population 983. Of these belonging to the actual cultivator class are 60 males, 89 females, and 59 children, who form 22 per cent. of the entire population of the village. Of the day-labourer class there are 83 males, 101 females, and 72 children, or 26·5 per cent. of the whole population. Of the artizan class are 148 males, 165 females, and 191 children, or 50 per cent. of the population. Of persons living on charity there are one male, 10 females, and four children, or 1·5 per cent. of the whole population. As to Statement A, it is noted that the chief crop is rice. The average quantity of land, both culturable and homestead, held by each family is 4 bigahs 15 cottahs (nearly 1½ acres), or about 12 cottahs or ⅗ths of a bigah per head. Out of the 27 families of cultivators in the village, 14, or nearly half, hold amounts of land less than 3 bigahs or 1 acre in extent. Those 27 families contain 208 souls, of whom 54 males work. The latter have, therefore, each to support four souls. The average outturn of crop which each individual of the cultivating population gets annually is 2 maunds 11 seers and 2 chittacks. At the rate of Re. 1-5 a maund of paddy, the average annual income per head of this class of the population averages about Rs. 3 annually. The incidence of the average annual rental per head is Re. 1-4-10. Thus, the net annual income from cultivation amounts to about Re. 1-12 per head. The average debt per family is Rs. 84, or nearly Rs. 11 per head. The average outturn of crop per bigah is 6 maunds. The average annual net income per head, as above stated, appears absurdly low. The fact is that this is supplemented by the sale of straw, by fishing, by the collection and sale of firewood, and by the males going to Calcutta for employment as coolies or domestic servants.

B.—"The class of labourers hold on an average 2½ bigahs of land, both culturable and homestead, per family. Out of the 40 families, 23 held amounts of land of less than 3 bigahs in extent. These 40 families number 256 souls, of whom 77 are males, who are the earning members. They have each to support 3·3 heads including himself. The average outturn of rice is about 6 maunds per bigah. The average quantity of crop per head of population is 2¼ maunds, and at the rate of Re. 1-5 per maund it would give about Rs. 3 as in the case of cultivators as stated above. Their rent is Re. 1-6-6 per head. Their net annual income from cultivation would be nearly Re. 1-10 per head. For a certain portion of the year, not less than six months, all the working males get employment as day-labourers. The average daily rate is annas 3. The thatchers and others get 3½ annas to 4 annas a day. Income from labour per head of population, including females and children, is Rs. 10 annually; so their total income from labour and cultivation is nearly Rs. 12 per annum, or Re. 1 monthly. Like the purely cultivating classes, the income is supplemented by the sale of straw, by fishing, by the collection of firewood, &c. The average amount of debt is Rs. 2-11-6; so that this class is better off in this respect than the cultivating class.

C. *Artizans.*—"The potters and weavers have been shown separately in this class. The total artizan population of the village consists of 96 families, with 504 souls. Of these, 75 are potters, 23 weavers, and 406 goldsmiths, carpenters, confectioners and others. Of these, 145 males, 52 females, and 1 child, or a total of 198 persons, are working members. Each of these has to support 2·5 souls, including himself. The monthly rate of earning per head of the potters is Re. 1-13, of weavers Re. 1-8, and of the rest Re. 1-6: so the potters are the best to do of all classes. The average monthly rate of the earnings of the entire artizan population is Re. 1-7 per head. The average debt per head of the entire population of this class is Rs. 4. They hold only a few cottahs of homestead land in each family.

D. " *Persons living on charity.*—The total population of this class in the village is 15, of whom only one is a male, 10 females, who are all widows and four children. The male, two females, and the four children belong to a family of the Baishnabs, who are beggars by profession. None of these have any source of income besides begging.

49. "The next village is Naihati. It has 79 families or houses. The total population is 439, of whom 136 are males, 173 females and 130 children. The cultivator class shows a population of 10 males, 19 females, and 16 children, or 11 per cent. of the entire population. The artizans number 24 males, 28 females, and 23 children, or 17 per cent. of the population. Those who live by charity are three males, three females and one child, or 1·5 per cent. of the population. "Others" are 29 males, 31 females, and 21 children, or 19·5 per cent. of the population. Thus, in this village the B class or agricultural labourers preponderate. The percentage of D class is the same in this village as in the village of Aguria. From Statements A and B, it would appear that the only crop grown in this village is rice, while at Aguria mulberry and other cereals are grown by the people besides rice, which is, however, the staple crop. (A.) This statement shows a total population of 11 families and 47 souls, the total area under cultivation 62 bigahs, the total outturn of the crop 412 maunds, the total amount of rent and cesses paid by the villages Rs. 142, and the total amount of debt Rs. 406. Of the total population of 47 souls, 19 males and three females, or a total of 22, are the working members; each of these has to support two souls. The average per head of population is $1\frac{3}{10}$ bigahs of land with an outturn of 8 maunds of paddy annually, Rs. 3 rent and cesses, and Rs. 8 of debt. The average yield of paddy per bigah is 6 maunds as in Aguria. At the rate of Re. 1-5 per maund, the annual income per head of population would be Rs. 10-8. Deducting the annual amount of rent and cesses per head as above stated, the annual net income of a person in this village would be Rs. 7-8. This class of people in this village appear to be better off than their fellows in Aguria. The reason of the difference is not far to seek. In this village the average quantity of land held by each head of population is $1\frac{3}{10}$ bigahs, while in Aguria the proportion is only $\frac{4}{5}$ths of a bigah per head. As this village is always subject to floods, the population is scantier than at Aguria, the amount of land held by each person in the latter village being larger than in the former. The net income at Rs. 7-8 annually per head from cultivation is supplemented in the same way as in Aguria. (B.) This statement shows a total population of 36 families, comprising 223 souls, total quantity of land 129 bigahs, outturn of paddy 804 maunds, the total amount of rent and cesses Rs. 332, total amount of debt Rs. 2,312, and the total monthly income from daily wages Rs. 227. Of the 223 souls in the village, 64 males, four females, and one child are earning members. Each of them supports on the average 2·25 persons, including himself. The average per head of population is 11 cottahs of land, 4 maunds of paddy, Re. 1-7 of rents and cesses, Rs. 100 of debt, and Re. 1 per month from daily wages. Taking the selling price of paddy at Re. 1-5 per maund, and deducting the amount of rent and cesses, it gives a net annual income of Rs. 3-13 per head from cultivation. The annual income from wages is Rs. 12 : the total net income from the two sources comes therefore to Rs. 16 per head annually, or Re. 1-5 monthly; while at Aguria it is Re. 1 only. The reason of the difference is that in this village there are several holders of service lands whose names have been included in the statement, and who earn much more than a day-labourer. Otherwise the circumstances and the rates of wages of day-labourers are the same in both villages.

(C.)—" There are not many artizans in this village. There are only 11 families with a total population of 75 souls. If these, 23 males and 17 females work and support on the average two souls. One is a goldsmith, three are Sows or Soondees, and the rest weavers. The average rate of the monthly earnings is Re. 1-5 per head; while in Aguria it is Re. 1-8. Some of them hold small quantities of land in the village, and the abovementioned income of them is supplemented by the earnings from cultivation. The debt per head is Rs. 10. (D.)—The population under this head is only seven in this village. They do not require any particular mention. (E.)—In this statement have been shown people who live solely by service, fishing, and widows who live by paddy-husking. Their total number is 87 and comprise 18 families. Of these, 24 males and seven females are working members, and they each support three souls on the average. The monthly earnings from paddy-husking of each widow is Re. 1-4. The average monthly earnings per head of the entire population under this statement is Rs. 2-4. But as several service-holders, some of whom earn Rs. 50 or so monthly, have been included in this statement, the abovementioned average monthly income appears to be much larger than those of the people of other classes. Debt her head is Rs. 8.

50. " The next village is Banpore. It is a part of the town of Ramjibanpore, but it is an agricultural village. There are 94 houses or families in the village. Its total population is 360, of whom 110 are males, 137 females, and 113 children. The agriculturists are 118 of all sexes, or 32·8 per cent. of the population ; the agricultural day-labourers are 222, or 61·7 per cent.; the artizans 17, or 4 7 per cent.; and persons living on charity are only 3, or ·8 per cent. of the population. The class of agricultural labourers is predominant in this village.

A.—" This statement shows a total number of families 31, with 118 members, of whom 33 males and 9 females work, and have to support each three souls ; total area under cultivation 200 bigahs of land, including homestead; 1,668 maunds as the total outturn of crops (paddy, including sugarcane and cereals); the total amount of rent and cesses paid is Rs. 1,020 and the total amount of debt is Rs. 1,336, excluding quantities of paddy which several of the families owe. The above would give the following average per head of population, viz , $1\frac{7}{10}$ of a bigah of land, 14 maunds of crop, Rs. 8-10 of rent and cesses, and Rs. 11 of debt. Calculating the value of the average quantity of paddy per head of population at Re. 1-10 a maund, and deducting the amount of rent and cesses per head from it, the net income from cultivation per head would be Rs. 9-12 annually. This calculation is based on the outturn of paddy only, but in this village, as would appear from the statement, almost every cultivator grows sugarcane, pulses, &c., which are more valuable crops than paddy and which fetch higher price. So the average net income per head of population may be safely calculated at Rs. 12 per annum from cultivation. Thus it would appear that this class of the population in this village is much better off than in either of the aforementioned two villages. This is on account of the lands in the village being much superior in quality and giving more than 8 maunds as the average yield of crop per bigah annually. Besides cultivation, several persons under this statement follow professions, such as rice-dealers, weavers, priests, &c., which supplement the income from their cultivation. It is also supplemented by the sale of straw, collection of firewood, &c. Thus the net monthly income of the cultivating class in this village may be put down at Rs. 2 per head.

B.—" This statement shows a total number of families 55, and a population of 222 souls. Of these, 68 males, 34 females, and 17 children work and have to support two souls each. The total land under cultivation is 252 bigahs, including the *bastu* lands. The total annual outturn of crop is 1,308 maunds. The total amount of annual rent and cesses is Rs. 879. The total amount of debt is Rs. 1,529. The total monthly income from wages of day-labourers is Rs. 2-8. The above figures would give the following proportions per head of population :—Land $1\frac{1}{10}$th bigah, crop 6 maunds, rent and cesses Rs. 4, debt Rs. 7, income from day-labour 15 annas monthly. The average outturn per bigah of land is 6 maunds. Taking the selling price of paddy at Re. 1-15 a maund, and deducting the amount of annual rent and cesses, the net income from cultivation would be Rs. 4 annually per head under this statement. Adding it to the amount of annual income from wages, &c., the total net income of each head of agricultural labourer would be Rs. 16 annually, or Re. 1-5 monthly. This income corresponds with the income of the same class of people in village Naihati. Nineteen families of fishermen have been included in this statement. The rates of daily wages range from 1 anna to 3 annas in this village. The women get 1 anna to 1 anna and a half a day.

C.—" Only six families of artizans, with a total population of 17 souls, have been shown in this statement. One of them is an oilman, 3 weavers and 2 blacksmiths. Besides these, one family of weavers has been included in Statement A and one in Statement B. Of the total population, 7 males and 3 females are working members, and they have to support two souls on the average. The average income per head of the artizans would be Re. 1-10 monthly, or Rs. 20 annually, and debt Rs. 8. The average earnings of weavers are Re. 1-5 monthly, or about equal to those of the weavers of village Naihati.

D.—" There are only two families or three persons who live on charity in this village. They do not require any particular notice.

51. " Thus, from the above facts and figures, it would appear that the agricultural labourers are in a better condition in this sub-division than the purely cultivating classes, and the artizan classes again are much better off than the agricultural labourers. The average income of a purely cultivating male, female, or child is Re. 1 a month, that of an agricultural labourer is Re. 1-5, and of an artizan is Re. 1-8, excluding the average rents and cesses which they pay. The average debt per head is Rs. 8. Almost every family of all classes has got a certain amount of debt, which is chiefly incurred on marriage or other social ceremonies. The average yield of crop per bigah is 6 maunds and per acre 18 maunds. The above monthly incomes are supplemented by the sale of straw, milk, collection of fire-wood, and the sale of cowdung cakes. These transactions are chiefly managed by the women of the family. The females and grown up children of the artizan classes help the heads of the family in their respective professions. The wages of the day-labourers in this sub-division are paid only in money, and not partly or entirely in kind, food, or lodging. They do not get work throughout the year, but are employed chiefly during the cultivating, harvesting, and thatching seasons. The cost of cultivation in the sub-division is nearly Rs. 4 per bigah, including the hire of plough bullocks and wages of labourers. The hire of a plough and pair of bullocks, including the driver, is annas 4 a day, and they work only from early morning till noon. Almost every family has a quantity of brass utensils and a quantity, though very small, of silver, and, in some cases, gold ornaments. The dress of an ordinary peasant is a *dhooti*, a cloth worn round the waist and reaching down to the knee, and a piece of smaller cloth called a *gamcha* (a scarf). This piece is ordinarily used as a towel at bathing time, and as a head-dress or turban when they work in the fields. Those in a better position can afford the luxury of a *piran* or shirt, a *chadar* or long scarf worn on the upper part of the body, a pair of slippers or country-made shoes and an umbrella. These things are used by *bhadra loke* or the higher class of people. A Manchester-made *dhooti*, which is mostly used, costs about 12 annas, a scarf or *gamcha* costs about annas 4, a *piran* costs about Re. 1. A Manchester-made *chadar* costs annas 8, a pair of slippers annas 12 to Re. 1-8, and an umbrella about Re. 1-4; so a *bhadra loke* can ordinarily be fully dressed and equipped at a cost of Rs. 4. The dress of a woman consists of a single *dhooti* or *sari* (Manchester or Bombay made), which is wrapped or worn round the person from the head to the ankles. An ordinary *dhooti* or *sari* costs about a rupee. She has no other dress, whether a peasant woman or a *bhadra loke*, but generally she wears some sort of ornaments, silver or gold, which every one of her sex is fond of. The physique of the people, if not affected by any disease, is healthy and strong. This shows that they do not generally suffer from privation of food. In several of the poorest cultivating families, and those who live on charity only, the people have generally only one meal a day. Their percentage can be taken as 10 of the entire agricultural population. The people live in thatched huts mostly in a very miserable state of repairs. The houses of well-to-do classes, though thatched, are very neat and tastefully built.

52. " The figures are, I believe, incredibly low. If any class or classes of people lived long on such incomes, they not only would not possess any property, such as brass utensils and silver ornaments, but these persons would show a certain degree of emaciation, and marked degeneration would be observed in the physique of the people generally. The statistics given have not been tested by the Collector in any way, and on the face of them appear unreliable. The Sub-divisional Officer is obliged to admit this, and falls back on supposing that the people make a good thing of it by supplementing their apparent income, which it is quite evident they *must do*.

Village of Suadighi, in the Tumlook sub-division, district of Midnapore.

53. "This village is situated in pergunnah Tumlook on the northern border of the pergunnah, at a distance of about six miles from the town of Tumlook. It was inundated during the flood which overtook this sub-division in 1865, the disastrous results of which have made such an impression on the minds of the people that they often date the events of their life from a time anterior or posterior to the flood of 1572 (*i.e.*, 1272 amli). The village, however, is not liable to inundation at the time of ordinary floods. It is within the Tumlook zemindari, half of which is owned by the Sooltangacha Estate, which was but recently under the management of the Court of Wards, and the remaining half is held partly as proprietors and partly as putnidars by the Mysadal zemindars.

54. "The population of the village is about 370. The people are generally agricultural cultivators, many of whom, however, supplement their income by the wages they earn by working occasionally as labourers. In fact, most of the cultivators with small holdings have to do so, as the produce of their cultivation is not sufficient to maintain them and the persons depending on them. There are only two families of artizans (weavers) in this village. I subjoin an analysis of the population of this village divided into the four classes of—

" I. Agricultural cultivators.
" II. Labourers.
" III. Artizans.
" IV. Beggars.

"With the quantity of lands cultivated by each cultivator reduced to the standard bigah, and the number of mouths each has to feed, so far as I could ascertain, I should state here that while a standard bigah consists of 14,400 square feet, the pergunnah bigah consists of 22,500 square feet, *i.e.*, the latter is a little over 1½ times as large as the standard bigah. The average rate of rent for each pergunnah bigah of paddy land varies between Rs. 3 and Rs. 4 per bigah; but there are patches of land bearing a much lower rate of rent due to the badness of the soil, which is unfavourable to their proper cultivation.

I.—Cultivators.

Number.	Name.	Quantity of land held in standard bigahs.	Number of persons each has to feed.	Remarks.
		Bgs.		
1	Madhusudon Chuckerbutty ...	18	7	
2	Lukhi Narain Chuckerbutty ...	19	11	Has got also small dealings in paddy.
3	Ramtaran Chuckerbutty	22	15	Also begs and occasionally earns money as a member of a jatra troupe
4	Ram Churn Mulliok	1½	3	Has got a son who goes to Calcutta for work.
5	Modhusudon Mondle	9	5	
6	Poran Bhuia	7	5	Occasionally lends out small sums of money on interest.
7	Durpa Narayan Mondle	7	4	
8	Koylash Mondle (junior)	7	3	
9	Sagor Chandra Shi	24	9	Ditto ditto.
10	Gobinda Shi	24	5	Ditto ditto.
11	Prem Chand Mundle	10	3	Ditto ditto.
12	Srimonta Bera	7	4	Gets also a pay of Re. 1 per month as the zemindari chatial.
13	Tara Chand Das	9	7	Has got a brother, Hara Chund Das, who gets a pay of Rs. 4 per month as the village chowkidar.
14	Denoo Matta	7	5	
15	Chintamoni Matta	7	3	
16	Modon Matta	13	6	
17	Mohesh Panja	6	5	
18	Banoo Panja	3	8	
19	Tarini Mundle	5	8	
20	Matiram Mundle	6	5	
21	Gora Chand Mundle... ...	6	5	
22	Bipro Mundle	6	5	
23	Hari Das	3	5	
24	Giridhar Manna	7	2	Gets also a pay of Rs. 4 per month as a bungalow chowkidar.

Number.	Names.	Quantity of land held in standard bighas.	Number of persons each has to feed.	Remarks.
		Bgs.		
25	Hari Matta	7	6	
26	Thakur Das Mundle...	12	7	
27	Natai Mundle	10	5	
28	Halodhar Mundle	12	9	
29	Koilash Mundle (senior)	9	6	
30	Kali Mundle	6	7	
31	Bestuhari Matta	24	10	Also lends out small sums of money on interest.
32	Lalchund Mundle	9	3	
33	Tetu Maiti	9	4	
34	Keenoo Sant	3	4	
35	Gopi Mundle	10	7	
36	Madhub Chundra Mundle	19	8	Ditto ditto.
37	Komal Bera	4	3	
38	Chintamoni Saute	12	5	
39	Gour Jasoo	7	3	Also breeds cocoons.
40	Gurai Manji	10	5	Ditto.
41	Bhogi Jana	15	6	Ditto.
42	Akhoy Manji	7	5	
43	Bikram Manji	19	6	
44	Prem Chand Manji	7	4	
45	Sonatun Manji	7	5	
46	Srinath Manji	6	3	
47	Srimonta Palui	2	3	
48	Khaira (senior)	3	4	
49	Sheik Maijuddin	18	10	His nephew works in Calcutta.
50	Dasu Mistri	3	5	
51	Korim Mistri	2	2	
52	Jamir Khan	3	4	
53	Sheik Akbar	18	10	
54	Khaira (junior)	2	3	
55	Sheik Ghasi	3	5	
56	Sheik Nocouri	7	7	He and his brother work in Calcutta.
57	Sheik Ali	12	6	
58	Haru Tanti	2	4	Is a weaver by trade, and has also got a cloth shop.
59	Surat Khan	3	4	
60	Morad Khan	3	4	
61	Lal Khan	3	3	
62	Gopi Das	3	3	He and his brother also beg.
63	Keloo Ghora	4	4	A brother works in Calcutta.
64	Needhu Ghara	3	3	
65	Sanyasi Hait	6	7	
66	Gora Chand Pal	6	5	
67	Bekram Guchait			
68	Srinath Guchait			
69	Prosad Guchait			
70	Jogonnath Mondle			
71	Keenoo Mondle			These men cultivate lands on the Suadighi chur, varying in quantity from 6 to 7 bighas. Their permanent residence is elsewhere, but they live here in what are called *chas-ghorse* (agricultural huts).
72	Jonardan Mondle			
73	Gobordhun Dahiri			
74	Denoo Mundle			
75	Bindabun Dora			

55. "Most of the cultivators named above hold land, not only in the village of Suadighi, but also in the Suadighi chur, which is a large cultivated chur on the river to the west of the village.

56. "II.—*Labourers*—

"(1). Radhu Bera.

"(2). Renoo Sha (is also a weaver by profession).

"The two persons named above cultivate no lands of their own, but are employed as labourers by others. As I have already stated, the greater number of agriculturists often work as labourers, and in this way supplement the income they derive from their own cultivation. Sometimes they work on the *budlee* principle, *i.e.*, exchange labour, without receiving any money wages. During the agricultural seasons, when the labourers are employed in field work, either in ploughing lands, sowing or transplanting paddy, or harvesting the produce, they are remunerated at rates varying from 10 to 14 pice per head for a day's work. At other times they are paid at the rate of 8 pice per head. Besides this, they get one meal on each day that they labour. Some of the well-to-do agriculturists have in their permanent employ labourers whose wages vary from Rs. 24 to Rs. 36 per annum.

When these are boys, they get considerably less, often Rs. 12 only per annum. These labourers board in the house of their employers, but they are very few in number.

57. "*III. Artisans*—There are only two artizans named in the margin in this village. Both of them are weavers. The first, Hari Tanti, has got some small cultivation of about two bigahs of his own, and also keeps a cloth shop. Both he and his mother weave. Their income from weaving would be about Rs. 3 or Rs. 4 per month. The other, Renoo Sha, has got no land, but, in addition to weaving cloth, also works as a labourer. His income as a weaver would be about Rs. 3 per month. These weavers charge generally 8 pice for a piece of *gamcha* (kind of coarse towel), and from 6 annas to 10 annas for a piece of cloth. In case the materials are supplied by the customers, they do not get more than 8 pice for a piece of cloth.

(1). Hari Tanti.
(2). Renoo Sha.

58. "*IV.—Beggars*—

(1). Doya Boistabi.
(2). Khudi Boistabi.
(3). Parbati Boistabi.
(4). Gopi Das (son of the above).
(5). Situ Boistabi.
(6). Ramcoomar Chuckerbutty (who lives with Situ Boistabi as his wife and has become a professional beggar, though a Brahmin).
(7). Ramtonu Chuckerbutty.

"Of the persons named above, Gopi Das, with his mother, Parbati Boistabi, and Ramtonu Chuckerbutty, have also got some cultivation of their own. Doya Boistabi has got some fruit-trees and plants, which go some way in contributing to her maintenance.

59. "On enquiry, I found that the average yield per standard bigah of cultivated land in fairly good years is about 4 kuries of paddy, that is, about 11 maunds, taking 1 kurie of paddy to be equal to 1 maund 30 seers. One kurie of paddy does not yield, when husked, much over 1 maund of rice; so the average yield per standard bigah of cultivated land would be a little over 4 maunds of grain. This calculation does not seem to differ much from that of one of the Famine Commissioners, who estimated the yield by acre to be 13 bushels of grain, or 12$\frac{2}{3}$ maunds. It should be here stated that the agriculturists derive some profit from the straw also, selling, as they do, what remains after thatching their huts and serving as fodder for their cattle. The average yield of straw per standard bigah is 1$\frac{1}{2}$ kahans.

60. "I find that most of the agriculturists of this village possess a considerable number of cattle that pasture on the Suadighi *chur*, which has been brought under cultivation within the last seven years.

61. "Paddy is now being sold in these parts at the rate of 2 *máns* per rupee, 1 kurie being equal to 4 *máns*. One kahan straw fetches about Re. 1-8. Now, taking the average yield of paddy per bigah to be about 4 *kuries*, and the average yield of straw to be 1$\frac{1}{2}$ *kahans*, it will be found that the cultivator would get about Rs. 10-4 if he could sell all the paddy and the straw which he grows on one bigah of land. But of course he actually sells a portion only of the paddy and the straw, keeping the rest for his own consumption, for the fodder of his cattle, and for thatching his house.

62. "The daily food of the people is, of course, boiled rice, which they eat twice daily. The rice they have not to buy, but they have to buy oil, salt, and other condiments, the cost of which would come up to about 8 annas per head for each adult male. As more than three-fourths of the people cultivate 5 bigahs of land and upwards, and as those who hold smaller jotes almost invariably supplement their income by their earnings as labourers, I think it can be fairly concluded that all the people have a sufficiency of food.

63. "As has been stated above, the rent of land per each pergunnah bigah is between Rs. 3 and Rs. 4 per bigah. The actual expenses of cultivation incurred by the cultivators, who employ their own labour and have not to buy the seedlings which they plant, do not come up to more than Re. 1 per

bigah; so it will be seen that the expenses of cultivation are not more than Rs. 3 per standard bigah. Thus, it will be seen that the agriculturists derive a fair net profit from their lands, which, added to their earnings as labourers, is sufficient to enable them to have a sufficiency of food. The labourers are in much request during the agricultural seasons, at the time of ploughing their lands or sowing or transplanting paddy, as well as gathering the harvest. At other times also, those who are willing do not find much difficulty in getting work.

64. "We should not, however, leave from the account the indebtedness of many of the cultivators. I found on enquiry that the debts were very often incurred not to procure food for the debtors, but to enable them to marry, as among the lower classes of the people the intending bridegroom has to pay a pretty considerable sum to the father of the bride. For example, Chintamony Matta, a man about 50 years old, who holds some seven bigahs of land, is indebted to the extent of about Rs. 250. He explained the fact of his indebtedness by stating that he had to pay a *pon* or portion of Rs. 56 to the father of his second wife and of Rs. 72 to that of his third wife, whom he married about a year ago. His age, of course, made the father of the girl demand a higher *pon* than he would have otherwise done. The poor man has not been able to pay off his debt, which, with interest, now amounts to a pretty large amount. This man's cousin, Madan Matta, is indebted for a similar reason. But in general people are not greatly indebted.

65. "The people did not appear to possess strong physique, but their general health was not bad, nor did they present an emaciated appearance. Their clothes are always scanty, not so much from poverty as from the fact that they are not used to wearing much clothes. Many of the women, however, use gay coloured *saries* on gala days and at village festivals. The houses are always thatched, with generally mud walls. The interior of the huts is almost always very dark, as the people do not generally keep any aperture for ventilation or light. A person curious to see the inside would have to take a light with him, even in day time. The people generally sleep on the *dabas* or verandahs of their huts, which are simply used as the receptacle of whatever property they may possess. The use of brass utensils has generally superseded that of clay pottery, and *thalies* and *baties* are to be found in almost every house. The ornaments worn by the women are generally of silver, the *madulies* (armlets) and *nuths* (nose rings) only being of gold. The silver ornaments in general use are *balas*, *churis* for the wrists, and *chandrahar* for the waist.

66. "In conclusion, I beg to point out the fact that as Calcutta is easily accessible, there are many families in this village, one or two members of which regularly work in Calcutta for some months every year. Their wages are often considerable, Rs. 8 or more per month, and many of them work on the brick-kilns, so there is no dearth of work for those who are willing to work and whose holdings may be too small to maintain their owners by agriculture alone. The number of artizans in this village is, as I have already stated, small, there being only two families of weavers; one of these weavers has also got some cultivation of his own, while the other has to work as a labourer, which would establish the fact that the income they derive from weaving is not sufficient to maintain them. The beggars are for the most part old women of the Baishnab sect, the members, of which are professional beggars. They are not large in member, and have other means of living besides begging. On the whole, I think the residents of this village do not suffer from an insufficiency of food."

67. The only contribution to the report made by Mr. Vowell, the Collector of Midnapore, is given by me in the following extract:—

68. "The circumstances of the west of the district are very different to those of the riverface. The population is more scanty, and there is a large admixture of aborigines whose standard of comfort is low, and who do not hesitate to go to a great distance for labour when pressure comes.

69. "On the other hand the distance from markets makes grain and labour much cheaper. A typical village situated in the Kesiari Estate has been examined by the Deputy Collector, Baboo Bissessur Banerjee.

70. "In this the land is of more medium quality, and is dependent on rainfall; only one crop is grown and but little garden produce.

71 "There are 117 families with holdings ranging from 2 to 30 bigahs. The average yield is 8 or 8½ maunds of paddy, cost of cultivation Rs. 2-13-3 a bigah. The wages of the daily labourer is 1 anna 6 pie with 3 pie for oil, tobacco and fried rice. The Deputy Collector puts down the net profit, after including Re. 1 for straw, as a little over Rs. 2 a bigah, and the keep of cattle, price of plough, &c., has to be deducted from this. The ryots whose holdings are less than five bigahs supplement their income by trade or other occupation. There are 30 families living thus, partly by agriculture and partly by some other occupation. As regards their style of living he says two full meals of coarse rice are a luxury. Salt is their ordinary condiment, and *kalmi*, a tank plant, and bringal, their vegetable food. Fish and *dál* they do not get more than once a week for dinner.

72. "There are 81 families of tusser weavers in the village. The cost of a piece of tusser is now Rs. 6-6 against Rs. 4-12, and it sells for Rs. 8. A weaver can make three pieces in the month, and therefore earns Rs. 4-14.

73. "For a family of four persons the cost of living is estimated at 6 annas 6 pie per diem as against 3 annas 6 pie 20 years ago.

74. "The weavers smoke opium extensively, so that they evidently have a little surplus to spend on luxuries; but it is also considered a preventive against fever. About 20 of the weavers have taken to agriculture to eke out their trade, and some 10 more are engaged in service at Rs. 2 or Rs. 2-8 a month.

75. "There are 10 families who live by begging. The villagers are very liberal to them during the harvest time, but in Jeyt and Assar the Deputy Collector says they have little to give, and the beggars are then very badly off. He thinks, too, that the number of people reduced to this state is shown to have increased in the village, partly owing to the evil effects of malarious fever and partly to those of opium.

HOOGHLY DISTRICT.

76. Mr. Toynbee, the Collector of Hooghly, who has had a long experience of that district, has submitted a report, from which the following extracts are given:—

77. "The Government circular referred to above was received somewhat late in the tour season, so that the enquiries made were not so extended as they might otherwise have been. This was, however, so far as this district is concerned, of little importance, as the condition of the people is so prosperous and well to do that the enquiry itself might well have been dispensed with altogether.

78. "Enquiries were made by the Collector in the following Government estates selected as typical examples of certain tracts of country, viz.:—

(*a*) "*Belcooli.*—Typical of the semi-suburban villages lying on either side of the East Indian Railway between Hooghly and Bali.

(*b*) "*Nobinaprojapatipur.*—A specimen of a village which some 8 or 10 years ago had been brought to a very low condition by the rack-renting of a farmer, but now reviving under a liberal system of Government khas management. It is also typical of the *poorest* villages on the eastern bank of the Damudar river, and protected from its floods by the Government embankments.

(*c*) "*Mujpur and Peasura.*—Typical of the richest villages in the same tracts.

(*d*) "*Rajpur, Gopaldaha, Tantisali, Majpur and Bahukhadali*—Government estates and typical villages of that tract of the country west of the Damudar which is yearly washed by the spill floods of that river. The rice crop on these lands is very precarious, and they grow chiefly *rubbi.* The Government assessment has been recently greatly reduced and the inhabitants are about as well off as their neighbours.

79. "The Joint-Magistrate, Mr. D. J. Macpherson, when on tour, made a full enquiry into a typical zemindari village in the Dhaniskhali thana.

80. "The Sub-divisional Officer of Serampore made a similar enquiry into the condition of the weavers of *Kharsarai,* whose occupation has been so injuriously affected by the competition of Manchester goods.

81. "The Superintendent of the Jail has also made enquiries in the jail in accordance with the Government orders.

82. "The Covenanted Deputy Collector of Howrah has made similar enquiries within his jurisdiction, similar to those made in Hooghly proper, but his report has not yet reached the Collector. As Howrah is even more prosperous than Hooghly proper, the omission is of little importance.

83. "The general result of the enquiries made is to show conclusively that in this district all the classes referred to in the Government circular eat twice a day, and enjoy a full meal on each occasion. Here and there a poor widow or beggar may be found who does not *always* get two meals a day; but, as a rule, even they, the poorest of the poor, do so. No single instance of emaciation or disease, due to want of food, came to light during any of the enquiries. As regards clothing, the wants of the poorer classes are very limited and are sufficiently provided for. In the cold weather no doubt a little extra and warmer clothing would be acceptable, especially to their children. But as soon as the sun is up, they bask in its rays and are content. Few, if any, of the classes referred to in the Government circular have any idea of thrift or of saving money for a rainy day, and they are most of them in debt to their mahajan; but this impecuniosity and indebtedness are due not to their poverty but to their extravagance and imprudence. They spend far more on social and religious ceremonies than they can afford I think: little of a lifelong debt, so long as they can secure the gratification of the moment. Labour is abundant and wages are high, and if any man, woman, or child does not get all material wants fully satisfied, it is their own fault. Perhaps the poorest class in the district is the weaver class, whose trade has suffered so severely from the competition of Manchester goods. Mr. Duke, the Sub-divisional Officer of Serampore, says of them that they 'eat twice a day pretty regularly, but in some cases with considerable difficulty.' The chief effect on them seems to be that they have to eat a coarser kind of rice than they used to eat, and that they are more hopelessly indebted to their mahajans than before; in fact they are 'little more than half as well off as they used to be.' Many of them find work in the European jute mills in the Serampore sub-division, and there earn high wages; but the majority are too fond of their homes to leave them and seek employment elsewhere; they struggle on and exist, and are therewith content. The enquiries made in the jail by the Civil Surgeon support the general result of the local mofussil enquiries, the conclusion arrived at being that the physical condition of the artizan group was the worst; the general health of cultivators and labourers appeared about equal. The condition of the poorer classes in this district, compared with that of the same classes in England, may unhesitatingly be described as superior in every respect. There is no such thing as want or starvation among them, and not one individual who does not know when he rises in the morning how or where he will procure food for the day. Their wants are few and easily satisfied. The climate in which they live and all their surroundings are enervating and, to our view, demoralizing: ambition they have none beyond the immediate wants and wishes of the day; but judged from their own point of view, and by their own standard, they are prosperous and contented, and the Collector doubts not that there are thousands upon thousands of the English poor who will gladly change their places with them. The Collector has not considered it necessary to give any figures in support of a conclusion which is so patent to every observer, and which has year by year impressed itself more and more on his (Collector's) mind since he came to the district nearly five years ago."

HOWRAH DISTRICT.

84. A report has been submitted by Mr. Ritchie, the Magistrate of Howrah, from which the following extracts are given. Mr. Ritchie appears to have given considerable attention to the subject, and to have made personal enquiries into the matter under report:—

85. "The portion of the Howrah district lying in the immediate vicinity of Calcutta and Howrah town is so largely affected by its nearness to that great labour market that it cannot be regarded as in any way typical of rural Bengal. Any able-bodied man can at once find employment and

earn Rs. 7 a month; and, indeed, this continuous demand for labour affects the whole district. As an instance of the excellent wages that may be earned, I may mention the Boureah Cotton Mills. The Manager, Mr. Downs, tells me that, taking the wages all round, from children on Rs. 2-8 to vice-men on Rs. 30 a month, the monthly wages of his hands average from Rs. 9 to Rs. 9-9. Any unskilled coolie can earn Rs. 7 a month. Many hands who come in from neighbouring villages are content to do 21 days' work only in the month, saying that they can earn quite sufficient in that time, and do not care to labour on the remaining days.

86. "To show how little distress there is in the district in an ordinary year like the present, and how fully labour finds employment, it may be noted that in February this year the excavation of the new drainage canal from the Rajapore jheel was begun; it was important to push on the work as quickly as possible, and many contracts were given out. Although 5 and 6 annas a day could easily be earned by earthwork, it was found among several hundred coolies engaged that nearly all of them were Dhangars from Chota Nagpore and other outsiders brought to the spot at much expense. The contractors told the Covenanted Deputy Collector it was almost impossible to get local coolies. It is true that the season was a busy one, as paddy-threshing was going on. Allowing, however, for this, it seems to be a very significant fact that in the midst of a rural population averaging in density over 1,100 to the square mile, labour was already so fully occupied that it was difficult to attract anybody to a new work like the Rajapore Canal.

87. "For the purposes of this report, the Covenanted Deputy Collector abstained therefore from enquiries in the tracts where the conditions may be called abnormal, and selected the most outlying part of the district, namely, the portions between the Roopnarayan and Damudar rivers. He proceeds to give the result of a detailed enquiry into the condition of village Shyampore, which is very typical of the whole thanna of that name forming the southernmost portion of the tract between the two rivers mentioned. Shyampore village is in the zemindari of the wealthy Sil family, who are absolutely unknown to the villagers personally, and of whose influence as proprietors there are no traces in the shape of tanks, roads, or otherwise. The village has been leased in putni to a well-to-do resident tenant of the Kaibarta caste. There are altogether 192 households in the village; most of these are Kaibartas, who are, beyond comparison, the best cultivators and the most industrious and thrifty class in this district; but of the 192 households, 110 find place on the putnidar's rent-roll. The remaining 82 consist chiefly of houses of widows (12), priests (14), persons in service such as washermen, &c., labourers (35). The area of the mâl land or land yielding rent to the zemindar is 998 bigahs, with an annual rental of Rs. 2,985, giving an average rent of Rs. 3-1 per bigah and 9 bigahs as the average size of a holding, including bastu or homestead land. There are, however, also 200 or 300 bigahs of rent-free land in the village not shown in the rent-roll. The cultivated land is all low rice land, from which is also obtained a crop of khasari kalai.

Rates of wages—
Ordinary 2½ annas per day for sowing; 3½ annas per day for thatching a house; building 3½ to 4 annas per day.

88. "A constant interchange of labour, which is regularly paid for in cash at the rates marginally noted, goes on between the various households at the seasons of ploughing, sowing, reaping, and threshing. To form a judgment on the prosperity of a given household, it is not sufficient to know the land occupied and the rate of rent; an equally important factor in the matter is the number of able-bodied hands who earn wages or save the necessity of employing hired labour. Part of the holding, too, is usually sublet where the family is a small one, and they have not the means of employing labour. To take concrete instances. Thakur Das Sant, a ryot, had a holding of only 1¾ bigahs. There were, however, four stalwart brothers who were always earning wages, besides 3 women and 3 children. The family had also 5 bigahs in *bhag* or sublet by another ryot on the condition of an equal division of outturn. The houses and granary in their homestead were substantial; they kept 3 plough-bullocks, 3 cows, and 2 sheep. The whole family have as much rice as they can eat and the stalwart brothers have something to spare for the country liquor shop. Close by lives Shyam Mullik who has 5 bigahs on the

rent-roll, but is old and decrepit with no family, and finds it difficult to get always his two meals a day.

89. "Ishwar Chunder Boistob has 15 bigahs, and there are three men in the household. Notwithstanding, he supplements his income by leaving the village annually for 3 or 4 months to earn wages in a jute mill.

90. "These instances are given to show that it is fallacious and delusive to expect statistics to present a true picture of the ryot class. There is a number of minute considerations to be taken into account in every individual case. Although the rents of this village are undoubtedly high, being from Rs. 3 to Rs. 4 for rice land, said not to yield not more than from 7 to 10 maunds for bigah, the ryots as a body are undoubtedly prosperous. Silver ornaments abound, the houses are particularly substantially built, and the physique of the people is very good. It is asked sometimes as a test what number of ryots are independent of external employment, *i.e.*, confine themselves to the cultivation of their own holdings with a family of 4 or 5 members; it is probably necessary to have 15 bigahs to be independent. In Shyampore there are only 32 out of the 110 jotedars who have as much land as this.

91. "A ryot's income is eked out in many ways. His women are always busy husking rice. The mahajans advance paddy to the ryot. The ryot, after husking it, carries the husked rice to market (at Shyampore he carries it on his head to Kharberya, 2 miles distant), and sells it, and then repays the mahajan. From 2 annas to 4 annas profit in the rupee was the rate obtaining when I visited Shyampore. When it is remembered what a large amount of paddy comes into the mahajan's hand, nearly equivalent in value to the rental of the village, and that in the well-to-do households the paddy for family consumption is given out to be husked, it will be perceived that an important part in the village economy is played by rice-husking. Then, there are the fish which are often caught for nothing in pools and streams, the vegetable cultivation near the houses, the produce of fruit-trees, all of which contribute to the ryot's income. Women have been seen in the dry paddy fields grubbing up a little bitter weed which grows in the cracks of the soil in the stubble, which would be taken to market and sold. This exemplifies the extremely thrifty way in which the ryots live. The impressions left on the Covenanted Deputy Collector's mind, after going minutely into the circumstances of the Shyampore ryots, was that the industrious households live very comfortably. Although it was difficult to see by the method of calculating household expenses and comparing them with the produce of the holdings and the wages earned how ends were made to meet, yet it was evident that there was free circulation of the wealth of the village, which caused it ultimately to be very evenly distributed among all members of the community. From what the Collector saw elsewhere, he thinks that the condition of this village may be taken as very typical of that of other parts of thanna Shyampore.

92. "In the neighbouring thanna of Bagnan, he selected a poor village on the left bank of the Damudar, Madhabpore. The villagers are nearly all of the low Chandal caste. The rent of 306 bigahs of land is Rs. 1,078, giving Rs. 3-8 as the average rate per bigah. The land is only ordinary rice land. Out of 48 holdings, in the case of three only did the area of the holding exceed 15 bigahs. The village had been flooded in 1885, and rents in consequence had fallen into arrear. The villagers were not so well off as in Shyampore. Even in a village like this, there is no appearance of poverty. A common labourer has his brass utensils, and his single hut is a picture of neatness."

93. The Covenanted Deputy Collector thinks that he has reported sufficiently for the purpose of the present enquiry, for which there is small occasion in such a district as Howrah.

A.

Statement showing the particulars of Families in the Mousah of Banpore living solely on Cultivation, in Thana Chandracona, Sub-division Ghatal, District of Midnapore.

Consecutive number.	Name of the head of the family.	Number of males.	Number of females.	Number of children.	Number of working males.	Number of working females.	Number of working children.	Area of cultivation.	Description of different sorts of crops.	Quantity of each crop.	Average outturn per bigah.	How many plough bullocks.	Quantity of straw per bigah.	Quantity of grain the family can sell after consumption.	Average selling rate of paddy per maund.	Average sellin rate of pulse.	Amount of rents and cesses.	Amount of debt, if any.	Number of milch cows in each family, and whether they sell any milk, and what the monthly earnings.	Price of ornaments, if any.	Utensils.
								B. K. CH.		MDS. S. CH.	MDS. S. CH.		K. P. G.	MDS. S. CH.	RS. A. P.		RS. A. P.	RS. A. P.		RS. A. P.	MDS. S. CH.
1	Ananta Ghose	2	2	...	2	...	...	8 10 0	Paddy ... Pulses ...	58 0 0 0 20 0	7 0 0	2	0 8 0	31 35 0	1 5 0	......	24 0 0	70 0 0	......	... ...	0 6 0
2	Petamber Ghose	1	1	2	1	...	...	8 0 0	Paddy ...	48 0 0	6 0 0	1	0 8 0	13 0 0	1 5 0	......	24 0 0	40 0 0	......	16 14 0	0 12 0
3	Kali Ghose	1	3	2	1	...	...	30 0 0	Paddy ... Rubbi ... Sugarcane ...	200 0 0 4 0 0 5 0 0	6 29 0	6	0 7 0	......	......	......	20 10 8	50 0 0	1	163 0 0	0 20 0
4	Nibaran Mandal	1	2	...	1	...	...	8 5 0	Paddy ...	40 0 0	4 30 0	2	0 7 0	21 0 0	1 5 0	......	20 0 0	130 0 0	......	......	0 8 0
5	Nobin Chandra Ghose	1	1	3	1	...	1	12 0 0	Paddy ... Pulses ...	72 0 0 0 15 0	6 0 0	2	0 6 0	40 0 0	1 5 0	......	38 5 0	30 0 0	......	......	0 7 0
6	Srimanta Ghose	1	1	3	1	...	1	13 0 0	Paddy ... Pulses ... Sugarcane ...	72 0 0 0 20 0 5 0 0	6 0 0	2	0 6 0	45 0 0	1 5 0	......	40 0 0	43 0 0	......	......	0 10 0
7	Nilmohan Ghose	1	1	2	1	...	1	9 0 0	Paddy ... Pulses ... Sugarcane ...	60 0 0 0 20 0 4 0 0	7 0 0	2	0 6 0	45 0 0	1 5 0	......	33 0 0	30 0 0	......	......	0 10 0
8	Charan Sircar	1	2	1	1	...	...	22 0 0	Paddy ... Pulses ...	100 0 0 0 15 0	4 17 0	1	0 6 0	73 0 0	1 5 0	......	53 12 0	40 0 0	......	......	0 8 0
9	Srinath Roy	1	3	1	1	2	...	10 0 0	Paddy ... Pulses ...	56 0 0 0 15 0	5 24 0	2	0 6 0	31 0 0	1 5 0	......	28 0 0	......	1	10 0 0	0 10 0
10	Dayal Ghose	1	1	1	1	...	...	10 0 0	Paddy ... Sugarcane ...	48 0 0 5 0 0	5 12 0	2	0 9 0	46 0 0	1 5 0	......	40 0 0	40 0 0	......	......	0 6 0
11	Lausen Ghose	1	3	1	1	3	1	12 0 0	Paddy ... Pulses ...	64 0 0 0 30 0	5 13 0	2	0 8 0	64 0 0	1 5 0	......	40 0 0	30 0 0	......	......	0 15 0
12	Hriday Neogi	1	1	2	1	...	2	8 0 0	Paddy ... Pulses ...	40 0 0 0 10 0	5 0 0	2	0 10 0	40 0 0	1 5 0	......	34 1 0	10 0 0	......	......	0 4 0
13	Krithbas Neogi	2	...	1	2	...	...	16 0 0	Paddy ... Pulses ...	80 0 0 0 7 0	5 0 0	5	0 8 0	76 0 3 Paddy 33 30 0 Pulses 1 0 0	1 5 0	......	68 2 0	......	1	......	0 10 0
14	Mahes Ghose	1	2	1	1	...	...	13 15 0	Paddy ... Rubbi crop ... Sugarcane ...	60 0 0 1 18 0 1 0 0	5 0 0	2	0 8 0	34 30 0	1 5 0	At 20 seers per rupee.	40 9 0	20 0 0	......	......	0 4 0
15	Kali Bagh	...	1	1	...	1	1	7 10 0	Paddy ...	20 0 0	2 20 0	1	0 8 0	23 0 0	1 5 0	......	21 0 0	10 0 0	......	......	0 3 0
16	Prem Chand Tanti	1	1	...	1	1	...	5 10 0	Do. ...	24 0 0	4 30 0	2	0 7 0	34 0 0	1 5 0	......	22 0 0	12 0 0	......	......	0 6 0
17	Gobordhun Pandit	1	1	...	1	...	...	6 0 0	Do. ...	24 0 0	4 0 0	1	0 7 0	34 0 0	1 5 0	......	15 1 0	8 0 0	......	4 0 0	0 10 0
18	Arjun Pandit	1	1	1	1	...	...	2 0 0	Do. ...	12 0 0	4 0 0	1	0 8 0	12 0 0	1 5 0	......	4 0 0	10 0 0	......	......	0 8 0
19	Hriday Pandit	2	1	...	1	...	...	3 0 0	Do. ...	13 0 0	4 0 0	2	0 8 0	12 0 0	1 5 0	......	4 0 0	10 0 0	......	......	0 10 0
20	Uday Pandit	2	1	...	2	...	...	4 0 0	Do. ...	20 0 0	5 0 0	2	0 7 0	20 0 0	1 5 0	......	16 8 0	60 0 0	......	12 0 0	0 6 0
21	Lakhi Narain Chakravarti	1	1	1	1	...	...	3 0 0	Do. ...	12 0 0	4 0 0	...	0 6 0	......	......	......	11 0 0	6 0 0	1	25 0 0	0 15 0
22	Pratap Chakravarti	1	1	...	1	...	...	0 7 0	Do. ...	2 0 0	5 27 0	...	0 6 0	......	......	......	2 8 0	12 0 0	1	......	0 10 0
23	Sib Narayan Chakravarti	2	2	...	2	...	...	6 2 0	Do. ...	24 0 0	4 0 0	2	0 8 0	......	......	......	26 0 0	100 0 0	1	12 0 0	0 24 0
24	Nafar Bag	2	3	4	2	...	...	23 0 0	Paddy ... Sugarcane ... Pulses ...	140 0 0 6 0 0 1 0 0	6 11 0	7	0 8 0	100 0 0	1 5 0	......	84 0 0	60 0 0	1	60 0 0	1 0 0
25	Akhil Pal	...	1	1	...	...	1	7 0 0	Paddy ...	26 0 0	5 5 10	2	0 8 0	......	......	......	30 0 0	40 0 0	1	30 0 0	30 0 0
26	Ram Charan Bandopadhya ...	1	2	1	1	...	1	16 0 0	Do. ...	60 0 0	5 0 0	2	0 8 0	45 0 0	1 5 0	......	53 14 0	28 0 0	1	30 0 0	0 15 0
27	Guru Dasi Debi	...	1	...	...	1	...	7 0 0	Do. ...	36 0 0	5 5 10	...	0 6 0	36 0 0	1 5 0	......	32 0 0	150 0 0	......	......	0 10 0
28	Chandi Charan Ghose	1	1	...	1	...	...	18 0 0	Do. ...	80 0 0	6 25 10	2	0 8 0	80 0 0	1 5 0	......	40 0 0	150 0 0	......	......	0 7 0
29	Syama Charan Ghose	1	1	3	1	...	1	19 0 0	Do. ...	30 0 0	6 26 10	2	0 8 0	80 0 0	1 5 0	......	40 0 0	150 0 0	1	......	0 6 0
30	Gadadhar Kamar	1	2	2	1	...	...	2 15 0	Do. ...	30 0 0	6 28 0	2	0 7 0	......	......	......	7 0 0	......	1	25 0 0	0 20 0
31	Sibu Ghose	1	1	3	1	...	1	6 0 0	Do. ...	72 0 0	5 13 5	2	0 6 0	30 0 0	1 5 0	......	18 8 0	20 0 0	......	......	0 7 0
	Total ...	34	47	37	33	9	11	199 14 0	....	1,668 7 0	......	...	......	......	......	......	190 11 0	1,836 0 0	......	......	......

B.

Statement showing the particulars of Families living on Agriculture and Labour of Mousah Banpore.

Consecutive number.	Name of the head of the family.	Number of males.	Number of females.	Number of children.	Number of working males.	Number of working females.	Number of working children.	Area of cultivation.	Particulars of different sorts of crops produced annually.	Quantity of each crop.	Average outturn per bighah.	Number of plough bullocks.	Quantity of straw per bighah.	Quantity of grain the family can sell after consumption.	Average selling rate of paddy.	Amount of annual rent and cesses paid.	Rate of wages of day-labourers.	Estimated amount of time they get work during the year.	Average income per month during the whole year of 12 months calculated on the number of working males in a family.	Amount of debt, if any.	Number of milch cows in each family, whether they sell any milk, and what their monthly earnings.	Approximate value of ornaments.	Utensils.
								B. K. CH.		Mds. s. ch.	Mds. s. ch.		K. P. G.	Mds. s. ch.	Rs. A. P.	Rs. A. P.	Rs. A. P.	Months.	Rs. A. P.	Rs. A. P.		Rs. A. P.	Mds. s. ch.
1	Isvar Chandra Ghose...	5	3	3	3	...	...	17 0 0	Paddy ... Pulses ... Sugarcane ...	100 0 0 1 0 0 3 0 0	5 23 14	2	0 5 0	65 0 0	1 5 0	60 4 0	0 2 6	1	1 2 9	125 0 0	......	23 0 0	0 8 0
2	Ram Sasui	1	2	...	1	...	1	8 0 0	Paddy ... Pulses ...	48 0 0 1 0 0	4 15 0	2	0 8 0	35 0 0	1 5 0	37 0 0	0 2 6	4	1 9 0	30 0 0	......	7 0 0	0 12 0
3	Hriday Ghose ...	1	2	...	1	...	...	8 10 0	Paddy ... Pulses ...	44 0 0 0 15 0	5 7 0	2	0 10 0	35 0 0	1 5 0	38 0 0	0 2 6	8	0 12 6	30 0 0	......	......	0 30 0
4	Petambar Ghose (senior)	2	...	1	2	...	...	4 10 0	Paddy ... Pulses ...	18 0 0 0 15 0	4 0 0	2	0 7 0	18 0 0	1 5 0	18 0 0	0 2 6	8	6 4 0	18 0 0	......	......	0 6 0
5	Adhar Kanga	1	1	1	1	...	1	9 0 0	Paddy ... Pulses ...	48 0 0 0 15 0	5 15 0	2	0 8 0	31 0 0	1 5 0	28 0 0	0 2 6	4	1 9 0	18 0 0	......	......	0 10 0
6	Sanatan Neogi	1	2	...	1	1	...	4 10 0	Paddy ... Pulses ...	12 0 0 0 10 0	2 30 0	...	0 8 0	13 30 0	1 5 0	14 0 0	0 1 8	10	2 0 6	13 0 0	......	......	0 3 0
7	Ramchand Ghose ...	1	...	...	1	...	...	6 0 0	Paddy ... Pulses ...	24 0 0 0 15 0	6 3 8	...	0 0 0	27 0 0	1 5 0	24 0 0	0 3 0	10	4 11 0	5 0 0	......	......	0 3 0
8	Gour Ghose	1	1	...	1	...	...	6 0 0	Paddy ... Pulses ...	24 0 0 0 10 0	4 2 8	1	0 6 0	27 0 0	1 5 0	24 0 0	0 3 0	4	1 14 0	100 0 0	......	......	0 3 0
9	Natabar Neogi	1	1	...	1	...	...	8 0 0	Paddy ... Pulses ...	40 0 0 0 10 0	5 1 4	1	0 6 0	40 0 0	1 5 0	34 1 0	0 3 0	1	0 7 6	60 0 0	......	......	0 5 0
10	Gopal Kabi	1	1	2	1	1	...	5 0 0	Paddy ... Pulses ...	20 0 0 0 5 0	4 1 0	1	0 7 0	20 0 0	1 5 0	20 4 0	0 1 6	9	2 1 9	10 0 0	......	......	0 3 0
11	Amanda Kabi	1	1	2	1	...	...	0 10 0	......	......	......	...	......	......	......	5 4 0	0 3 0	11	5 2 6	30 0 0	......	......	0 3 0
12	Hriday Ghose	1	1	...	1	...	...	3 0 0	Paddy ... Pulses ...	20 0 0 0 15 0	6 31 11	1	0 6 0	20 0 0	1 5 0	9 5 0	0 3 0	9	4 3 6	16 0 0	......	......	0 4 0
13	Fakir Mandal	1	1	2	1	...	...	2 10 0	Paddy ...	16 0 0	6 16 0	...	0 8 0	12 0 0	1 5 0	11 0 0	0 1 0	11	1 11 6	20 0 0	......	......	0 8 0
14	Ganes Mandal	2	2	...	2	...	...	6 0 0	Paddy ... Pulses ...	40 0 0 0 16 0	6 27 10	2	0 10 0	25 0 0	1 5 0	25 0 0	0 1 6	10	4 11 0	15 0 0	......	5 0 0	0 10 0
15	Potambar Neogi (junior)	1	...	1	1	...	1	8 0 0	Paddy ... Pulses ...	44 0 0 0 15 0	5 21 14	2	0 9 0	15 30 0	1 5 0	25 12 0	0 3 0	8	0 15 0	......	......	......	0 15 0
16	Advaita Chackravarti...	1	1	...	1	...	...	0 3 0	......	......	......	...	......	......	......	......	......	......	......	......	......	......	0 10 0
17	Kunja Mandal ...	1	2	...	1	...	...	3 10 0	Paddy ...	18 0 0	6 24 0	...	0 8 0	8 0 0	1 5 0	11 0 0	0 3 0	6	3 15 0	40 0 0	......	......	0 5 0
18	Amrit Roy	1	2	1	1	3	...	8 0 0	Paddy ... Pulses ...	48 0 0 0 15 0	6 3 6	2	0 8 0	30 0 0	1 5 0	26 8 0	0 2 6	5	1 15 3	15 0 0	1	......	0 15 0
19	Tara Chand Chakravarti	2	2	1	2	...	...	7 0 0	Paddy ...	36 0 0	5 5 11	2	0 8 0	......	......	31 5 0	......	......	30 0 0	20 0 0	1	20 0 0	0 15 0
20	Raghav Mandal ...	3	3	...	3	...	...	7 0 0	Do. ...	36 0 0	5 5 11	2	0 8 0	36 0 0	1 5 0	*28 0 0	0 3 6	4	5 2 9	34 0 0	......	15 0 0	0 5 0
21	Tara Chand Ghose ...	1	1	1	1	...	1	10 0 0	Do. ...	53 0 0	5 8 0	2	0 8 0	53 0 0	1 5 0	27 0 0	0 3 6	5	1 15 3	12 0 0	1	......	0 6 0
22	Rami Bewa	...	1	...	...	1	...	0 2 0	......	......	......	...	......	......	......	0 5 0	0 1 8	9	1 12 3	......	......	......	0 7 0
23	Srimanta Mandal ...	1	1	1	1	...	...	0 1½ 0	......	......	......	...	......	......	......	0 5 0	0 3 0	11	5 2 6	10 0 0	......	......	0 5 0
24	Haris Ghose	1	1	...	1	...	...	0 1 0	......	......	......	...	......	......	......	0 3 0	0 5 0	11	5 2 6	5 0 0	1	......	0 7 0*

* He earns nearly Rs. 7 by selling milk.

B.—*Continued.*

Consecutive number.	NAME OF THE HEAD OF THE FAMILY.	Number of males.	Number of females.	Number of children.	Number of working males.	Number of working females.	Number of working children.	Area of cultivation.	Particulars of different sorts of crops produced annually.	Quantity of each crop.	Average outturn per bigah.	Number of plough bullocks.	Quantity of straw per bigah.	Quantity of grain the family can sell after consumption.	Average selling rate of paddy.	Amount of annual rent and cesses paid.	Rate of wages of day-labourers.	Estimated amount of time they get work during the year.	Average income per month during the whole year of 12 months calculation on the number of working males in a family.	Amount of debt, if any.	Number of milch cows in each family, whether they sell any milk, and what their monthly earnings.	Approximate value of ornaments.	Utensils.
								B. K. CH.		Mds. S. CH.	Mds. S. CH.		K. P. G.	Mds. S. CH.	Rs. A. P.	Rs. A. P.	Rs. A. P.	Months.	Rs. A. P.	Rs. A. P.		Rs. A. P.	Mds. S. CH.
25	Dinu Khan	3	3	1	3	...	...	25 0 0	Paddy ... Sugarcane ... Pulse ...	140 0 0 1 20 0 1 0 0	5 32 0	4	6 7 0	Paddy 140 0 0 Sugar 1 20 0	1 5 0	85 0 0	0 3 0	8	4 3 8	800 0 0	1	10 0 0	1 0 0
26	Kailas Khan	1	1	...	1	...	...	9 0 0	Paddy ...	48 0 0	5 13 5	2	0 7 0	48 0 0	1 5 0	87 0 0	0 3 0	4	1 14 0	100 0 0	......	......	0 10 0
27	Nidhiram Samui ...	1	2	...	1	...	...	8 0 0	Paddy ...	30 0 0	4 0 0	4	0 8 0	24 0 0	1 5 0	22 0 0	0 3 0	6	2 3 6	28 0 0	......	10 0 0	0 13 0
28	Haradhan Ghose ...	1	3	...	1	...	...	7 0 0	Paddy ...	28 0 0	5 5 11	2	0 6 0	28 0 0	1 5 0	30 0 0	0 3 0	3	1 6 6	20 0 0	1	12 0 0	0 13 0
29	Tarak Neogi	1	3	3	1	...	1	5 0 0	Paddy ... Pulses ...	30 0 0 1 0 0	6 6 0	2	0 8 0	25 0 0	1 8 0	24 8 0	0 3 0	3	0 15 0	20 0 0	......	12 0 0	0 12 0
30	Arun Neogi	1	1	3	1	...	...	5 0 0	Paddy ... Pulses ...	31 0 0 1 0 0	6 12 0	2	0 9 0	31 0 0	1 5 0	26 0 0	0 3 0	3	1 6 6	20 0 0	......	......	0 13 0
31	Uday Neogi	1	1	1	1	...	1	5 0 0	Paddy ... Pulses ...	31 0 0 0 30 0	6 14 0	2	0 9 0	31 0 0	1 5 0	26 0 0	0 3 0	2	0 15 0	24 0 0	......	......	0 7 0
32	Ramdhan Ghose ...	2	2	...	2	...	...	6 0 0	Paddy ...	32 0 0	5 13 5	2	0 10 0	30 0 0	1 5 0	18 8 0	0 3 0	3	2 13 0	20 0 0	......	20 0 0	0 12 0
33	Kailash Ghose	1	1	2	1	...	...	6 0 0	Do. ...	32 0 0	5 13 5	2	0 6 0	30 0 0	1 5 0	18 8 0	0 3 0	3	1 6 6	20 0 0	......	15 0 0	0 10 0
34	Prem Chand Ghose ...	1	1	4	1	...	1	6 0 0	Do. ...	32 0 0	5 13 5	2	0 8 0	32 0 0	1 5 0	18 8 0	0 3 0	3	1 6 6	20 0 0	......	7 0 0	0 11 0
35	Becharam Ghose ...	1	2	1	1	...	...	6 0 0	Do. ...	32 0 0	5 13 5	2	0 8 0	33 0 0	1 5 0	18 8 0	0 5 0	4	1 14 0	20 0 0	......	10 0 0	0 15 0
36	Muchiram Dule ...	1	2	1	1	...	...	2 1 0	Do. ...	12 0 0	5 20 0	...	0 7 0	......	......	5 5 9	0 3 0	9	4 3 8	8 0 0	......	7 0 0	0 6 0
37	Chintamani Dule ...	1	3	3	1	2	...	2 15 0	Do. ...	15 0 0	5 0 0	...	0 8 0	......	......	7 12 0	0 3 0	9	4 3 6	10 0 0	......	......	0 7 0
38	Dwarika Nath Dule ...	1	1	3	1	1	...	2 16 0	Do. ...	12 0 0	4 20 0	...	0 9 0	......	......	8 0 0	0 3 0	9	4 3 6	5 0 0	......	......	0 4 0
39	Fakir Dule	1	...	...	1	...	...	0 2 8	......	......	......	...	......	......	......	0 4 0	0 3 0	9	4 3 6	4 0 0	......	......	0 3 0
40	Al·ram Dule	2	2	1	2	2	...	2 2 0	Paddy ...	10 0 0	4 21 0	...	0 10 0	......	......	5 4 0	0 3 0	8	7 8 0	12 0 0	1	......	0 2 0
41	Kartick Dule	3	2	1	3	2	...	1 3 0	Do. ...	8 0 0	5 8 0	...	0 8 0	......	......	2 14 0	0 3 0	9	12 10 6	5 0 0	......	......	0 4 0
42	Kariram Dule	1	1	4	1	1	1	0 3 0	......	......	......	...	......	......	......	0 2 0	0 3 0	9	4 3 6	10 0 0	......	......	0 2 0
43	Sasthi Dule	2	2	5	2	3	1	1 2 0	Paddy ...	5 0 0	5 4 0	...	0 6 0	......	......	2 14 0	0 3 0	9	8 7 0	12 0 0	......	3 0 0	0 3 0
44	Haradhan Dule (senior)	3	2	4	2	2	..	1 13 0	Do. ...	8 0 0	5 0 0	1	0 7 0	......	......	4 2 0	0 3 0	9	8 7 0	5 0 0	......	......	0 5 0
45	G..bardhan Dule ...	1	1	...	1	1	...	2 1 0	Do. ...	9 0 0	4 20 0	...	0 8 0	......	......	5 2 0	0 3 0	9	4 3 6	2 0 0	......	......	0 4 0
46	Golami Dule	1	1	3	1	1	1	0 2 0	......	......	......	...	......	......	......	0 6 0	0 3 0	9	4 3 6	3 0 0	......	......	0 3 0
47	Rama Nath Dule... ...	1	1	4	1	1	2	0 1 0	......	......	......	...	......	......	......	0 2 0	0 1 6	11	2 9 3	15 0 0	......	......	0 3 0
48	Tarishi Dubni	...	1	5	...	1	3	0 5 0	......	......	......	...	......	......	......	1 4 0	0 1 6	12	2 13 0	10 0 0	......	......	0 2 0
49	Srimanta Dule ...	1	1	1	1	1	1	3 3 0	Paddy ...	16 0 0	5 1 8	1	0 8 0	4 0 0	1 5 0	10 8 0	0 3 0	9	4 3 8	5 0 0	......	15 0 0	0 9 0
50	Bhola Nath Dule ...	1	1	4	1	1	1	0 3 0	......	......	......	...	......	......	......	0 6 0	0 3 0	9	4 3 6	6 0 0	......	......	0 4 0
51	Rakhale Dule ...	1	1	2	1	1	...	18 0 0	Paddy ...	29 0 0	8 0 0	2	0 7 0	10 0 0	1 5 0	7 5 0	......	12	......	......	......	16 0 0	0 10 0
52	Bhuban Dule ...	1	2	3	1	2	...	0 2 0	......	......	......	...	......	......	......	0 4 0	0 3 0	9	4 3 6	12 0 0	......	......	0 3 0
53	Bhajahari Dule ...	1	1	2	1	1	...	0 3 0	......	......	......	...	......	......	......	0 4 0	0 3 0	9	4 3 6	10 0 0	......	......	0 2 0
54	Nanda Dule	1	1	...	1	1	...	1 0 0	Paddy ...	5 0 0	5 0 0	...	0 8 0	......	......	2 8 0	0 3 0	9	4 3 6	10 0 0	......	......	0 8 0
55	Sabu Dule	2	3	...	2	3	...	1 5 0	Do. ...	6 0 0	5 10 0	...	0 8 0	......	......	2 15 0	0 3 0	9	8 7 0	5 0 0	......	......	0 5 0
	Total ...	65	50	74	68	34	17	251 10 0	......	1,308 6 0	......	...	......	......	......	579 2 9	......	......	213 1 0	1,539 6 0	......	......	......

C.

Statement showing the particulars of Families of Artizans living in the Village of Banpore, Thana Chandracona.

…e of the head of the family.	Number of males.	Number of females.	Number of children.	Number of working males.	Number of working females.	Number of working children.	Quantity of bastu land.	Amount of rent paid annually.	Monthly rate of earnings of potters.	Monthly rate of earnings of weavers.	Number of looms in each house.	Number of cloths they can turn out a month.	Daily rate of wages of carpenters.	Monthly rate of earnings of oilmen and others.	Number of milch cows and the amount of income derived therefrom, if any.	Amount of debt, if any.	Value of ornaments.	Utensils.
							B. K. CH.	Rs. A. P.		Rs. A. P.				Rs. A. P.		Rs. A. P.	Rs. A. P.	Seer
…dhan Kalu …	1	1	—	1	1	…	0 5 0	2 4 0	…	……	…	……	…	6 0 0	…	25 0 0	……	4
…ihan Tanti …	1	2	…	1	1	…	1 0 0	5 2 0	…	4 0 0	1	10 pairs	…	……	1	38 0 0	……	5
…Chand Tanti …	1	1	1	1	1	…	0 2 0	2 0 0	…	8 0 0	1	4 "	…	……	…	……	30 0 0	15
…Chand Tanti …	2	1	…	2	…	…	0 2 0	1 4 0	…	5 0 0	1	12 ,,	…	……	…	12 0 0	12 0 0	10
…rdhan Kamar …	1	2	…	1	…	…	0 10 0	5 14 0	…	……	…	……	…	6 0 0	1	60 0 0	……	10
…adhar Kamar …	1	1	1	1	…	…	0 4 0	0 10 0	…	……	…	……	…	5 0 0	1	……	60 0 0	20
Total …	7	8	2	7	3	…	2 3 0	……	…	18 0 0	3	26 pairs	…	16 0 0	…	133 0 0	……	…

D.

Statement showing particulars of Families living on Charity in Village Banpore, Thana Chandracona.

Consecutive number.	Name of the head of the family.	Number of males.	Number of females.	Number of children.	Number of working males.	Number of working females.	Number of working children.	Quantity of bastu land.	Annual amount of rent.	Means of earning.	Number of milch cows.	Value of ornaments.	Utensils.
								B. K. CH.	Rs. A. P.				Seers.
1	Madhav Sircar … …	1	1	…	1	1	…	0 2 0	1 0 0	Paddy-grinding	…	……	2
2	Bhabamati Bewa … …	…	1	…	…	…	…	0 2 0	0 8 0	Charity …	…	……	1
	Total …	1	2	…	1	1	…	0 4 0	……	……	…	……	…

A.

Statement showing the particulars of Families in Mousah Aguria living solely on Cultivation.

Consecutive number.	NAME OF THE HEAD OF THE FAMILY.	Number of males.	Number of females.	Number of children.	Number of working males.	Number of working females.	Number of working children.	Area of cultivation.	Description of the different sorts of crops.	Quantity of each crop.	Average outturn per bigah.	How many plough bullocks.	Quantity of straw per bigah.	Quantity of grain the family can sell after consumption.	Average selling rate of paddy.	Amount of annual rent and cesses.	Amount of debt, if any.	Number of milch cows in each family, and whether they sell any milk, and what is the monthly income.	Value of ornaments.	Utensils.	Other means of earning.
								B. K. CH.		MDS. S. CH.	MDS. S. CH.		K. P. G.			RS. A. P.	RS. A. P.	RS. A. P.	RS.	MDS. S. CH.	
1	Udaya Mana	1	4	2	1	...	...	4 0 0	Soorgunga ... Paddy ...	1 0 0 28 0 0	1 0 0 7 0 0	...	......	...	...	10 8 0	50 0 0	2 at 1 8 0	36	0 20 0	
2	Rama Nath Charan	4	5	5	4	...	...	5 10 0	Paddy ... Soorgunga ...	23 0 0 6 20 0	4 0 0	...	0 10 0	...	...	20 0 0	1,000 0 0	4	400	5 20 0	
	Baikantha Sasmal	3	4	2	2	...	...	5 0 0	Paddy ... Soorgunga ...	23 0 0 1 0 0	8 0 0	...	0 8 0	...	...	18 8 0	......	3	128	1 0 0	Paddy transaction.
4	Chota Baikantha Surmal	2	3	...	2	...	...	5 0 0	Paddy ...	37 0 0	7 8 0	1	0 10 0	...	...	14 0 0	50 0 0	......	10	0 8 0	
5	Hari Das Maiti	1	1	1	1	...	...	1 10 0	Do. ...	9 0 0	6 0 0	...	0 12 0	...	...	8 0 0	20 0 0	......	5	0 2 8	
6	Mohendra Maiti	1	1	2	1	...	...	1 10 0	Do. ...	9 0 0	6 0 0	...	0 12 0	...	...	8 0 0	25 0 0	1 at 1 8 0	6	0 5 0	
7	Gayaram Maiti	2	3	2	2	...	...	1 10 0	Do. ...	9 0 0	6 0 0	...	0 12 0	...	...	8 0 0	40 0 0	1	86	0 20 0	Ditto.
8	Khetra Mohan Maiti...	1	1	3	1	...	...	1 10 0	Do. ...	9 0 0	6 0 0	...	0 12 0	...	...	5 0 0	28 0 0	1	10	0 6 0	Ditto.
9	Sridhar Dhara	5	8	6	5	...	...	6 0 0	Soorgunga ... Paddy ...	1 0 0 56 0 0	6 0 0	...	0 10 0	...	...	21 8 0	......	4	40	0 20 0	Ditto.
10	Behari Maiti	1	1	2	1	...	...	1 10 0	Paddy ...	12 0 0	8 0 0	...	0 10 0	...	...	9 0 0	20 0 0	1	15	0 15 0	Transaction in brass.
11	Dinu Paramanik	1	1	3	1	...	...	1 10 0	Do. ...	12 0 0	8 0 0	...	0 10 0	...	...	9 0 0	......	1	15	0 5 0	Paddy transaction.
12	Uma Charan Paramanik	3	3	...	3	...	...	2 0 0	Do. ...	15 0 0	7 20 0	...	0 10 0	...	...	8 8 0	100 0 0	1 at 1 8 0	8	0 12 0	Service.
13	Bisva Nath Sasmal	4	5	2	4	...	...	5 0 0	Do. ...	56 0 0	7 0 0	1	0 10 0	...	...	18 10 0	......	2	5	0 15 0	Do.
14	Hari Das Sasmal	2	5	3	2	...	...	5 0 0	Do. ...	40 0 0	0 8 0	...	0 10 0	...	...	19 12 0	......	2 at 2 12 0	33	0 15 0	Do.
15	Syam Dian	2	2	4	1	...	...	6 0 0	Do. ...	24 0 0	4 0 0	3	0 10 0	...	...	27 0 0	......	1	200	0 25 0	Bhusi shop.
16	Sibu Dian	1	3	2	1	...	...	5 8 0	Do. ...	24 0 0	8 0 0	...	0 10 0	...	...	16 0 0	......	......	100	0 16 0	Dealing in milk.
17	Kenaram Sasmal	3	5	...	3	...	...	6 0 0	Do. ...	48 0 0	8 0 0	1	0 10 0	...	...	18 8 0	100 0 0	......	7	0 6 0	Service.
18	Ramkumar Chowdhuri	8	8	4	4	...	...	10 0 0	Do. ...	78 0 0	10 20 0	...	0 12 0	...	...	8 0 0	......	4	50	1 0 0	Bhusi shop.
19	Durga Das Ghosal	1	1	...	1	...	...	1 12 0	Do. ...	12 0 0	7 0 0	...	0 5 0	...	...	......	100 0 0	......	......	0 4 0	
20	Kedar	1	3	...	1	...	...	0 10 0	Do. ...	5 0 0	10 0 0	...	0 8 0	...	...	......	100 0 0	2	5	0 10 0	
21	Priya Nath Mahapatra	3	4	2	3	...	...	1 10 0	Do. ...	12 0 0	8 0 0	...	0 10 0	...	...	1 2 0	500 0 0	3	20	0 15 0	Service.
22	Krista Das Ghose	1	1	...	1	...	...	......	......	......	......	...	......	...	...	......	......	......	......	......	Do.
23	Parmesvar Acharjia	3	5	5	3	...	...	1 0 0	Paddy ...	8 0 0	8 0 0	...	0 10 0	...	...	......	......	......	5	0 6 0	
24	Ram Saday Chakravarti	3	6	4	2	...	...	1 10 0	Do. ...	12 0 0	8 0 0	...	0 10 0	...	...	......	20 0 0	1	10	0 10 0	
25	Kali Das Chakravarti	1	3	1	1	...	...	4 0 0	Soorgunga ... Paddy ...	8 0 0	2 0 0	...	......	...	...	......	100 0 0	1	......	0 5 0	
26	Uma Charan Chakravarti	1	1	...	1	...	...	0 10 0	......	......	......	...	......	...	...	......	......	......	......	0 5 0	
27	Durga Das Chakravarti	2	4	3	2	...	...	1 0 0	Soorgunga ...	2 0 0	2 0 0	...	......	...	...	1 12 0	......	1	35	0 11 0	
	Total ...	60	69	59	54	...	...	120 19 0	......	531 20 0	......	...	......	...	...	245 5 0	2,263 0 0	......	......	......	

Statement showing the particulars of Agricultural Labourers in Village Aguria in Thana Daspore, Sub-division Ghatal.

Number of working children.	Area of cultivation.	Description of crops they get annually.	Quantity of each crop.	Average outturn per bigah.	Number of plough bullocks.	Quantity of straw per bigah.	Quantity of grain the family can sell after consumption.	Average selling rate of paddy.	Amount of annual rent and cesses paid.	Rate of wages of day-labourer.	Estimated amount of time they get work during the year.	Average income per month during the whole year of 12 months calculated on the number of working males in a family.	Amount of debt, if any.	Number of milch cows in each family, whether they sell any milk, and what the monthly earnings.	Approximate value of ornaments.	Utensils.	REMARKS.
	B. K. CH.		Mds. s. CH.	Mds. s. CH.		P. K. G.			Rs. A. P.	Rs. A. P.	Months.	Rs. A. P.	Rs. A. P.	Rs. A. P.	Rs. A. P.	Mds. s. CH.	
......	6 0 0	Paddy ... Soorgunga ...	58 0 0 0 20 0	6 0 0	2	0 12 0	......	......	21 15 0	0 8 0	9	8 7 0	......	2 at 3 0 0	15 0 0	0 10 0	
......	3 0 0	Paddy ... Mulberry ...	18 0 0 1 0 0	6 0 0	...	0 12 0	1 md. of mulberry leaves.	......	12 0 0	0 8 0	8	3 12 0	25 0 0	1 at 1 0 0	5 0 0	0 8 0	
......	2 0 0	Paddy ...	14 0 0	7 0 0	1	0 12 0	......	......	7 8 0	0 8 0	8	7 8 0	30 0 0	1 at 1 4 0	10 0 0	0 7 0	
......	1 10 0	Paddy ... Mulberry ...	12 0 0 2 0 0	8 0 0	...	0 12 0	2 mds. of mulberry leaves.	......	19 10 0	0 4 0	9	11 4 0	......	2 at 2 4 0	16 0 0	0 5 0	
......	1 0 0	Paddy ...	7 0 0	7 0 0	...	0 12 0	......	......	7 2 0	......	......	......	70 0	1 at 1 4 0	8 0 0	0 8 0	Barber.
......	2 0 0	Do. ...	14 0 0	7 0 0	...	0 14 0	......	......	11 0 0	......	......	......	......	......	......	0 2½ 0	Do.
......	1 0 0	Do. ...	7 8 0	7 0 0	...	0 12 0	......	......	18 8 0	......	......	......	20 0 0	1 at 1 8 4	4 0 0	0 6 0	Dealing in brass.
......	2 10 0	Do. ...	16 0 0	6 20 0	...	0 10 0	......	......	15 0 0	0 2 6	4	8 2 0	......	......	8 0 0	0 4 0	
......	4 0 0	Do. ...	38 0 0	8 0 0	...	0 10 0	......	......	21 8 0	0 8 0	10	18 12 0	30 0 0	2 at 2 8 0	20 0 0	0 9 0	
......	2 0 0	Do. ...	16 0 0	8 0 0	...	0 10 0	......	......	11 4 0	0 8 0	8	8 12 0	20 0 0	1 at 1 4 0	6 0 0	0 4 0	
......	3 0 0	Do. ...	24 0 0	8 0 0	1	0 10 0	......	......	18 0 0	0 3 0	6	5 10 0	......	1 at 1 12 0	10 0 0	0 11 0	
......	1 10 0	Do. ...	9 0 0	6 0 0	...	0 9 0	......	......	13 4 0	0 8 3	4	3 1 0	......	1 at 1 8 0	7 0 0	0 8 0	
......	8 10 0	Do. ...	66 0 0	8 0 0	2	0 12 0	......	......	Jaghir.	......	......	......	25 0 0	......	7 0 0	0 6 0	Simandar.
......	1 0 0	Do. ...	6 0 0	6 0 0	...	0 10 0	......	......	6 4 0	0 5 0	8	4 11 0	30 0 0	......	5 0 0	0 4 0	
......	5 0 0	Paddy ... Soorgunga ...	35 0 0 1 0 0	7 0 0	2	0 12 0	......	......	19 0 0	0 4 0	8	0 10 0	......	2 at 2 12 0	20 0 0	0 12 0	
......	3 0 0	Paddy ... Soorgunga ...	24 0 0 2 0	8 0 0	2	0 12 0	......	......	16 0 0	0 5 0	6	0 4 0	40 0 0	1 at 1 8 0	......	0 2½ 0	
......	2 0 0	Paddy ...	10 0 0	5 0 0	...	0 9 0	......	......	9 8 0	0 5 0	6	5 10 0	40 0 0	......	4 0 0	0 5 0	
......	......	......	......	......	...	......	......	......	3 8 0	0 3 0	5	3 12 0	25 0 0	......	8 0 0	0 4 0	
......	2 10 0	Paddy ... Soorgunga ...	18 0 0 0 24 0	6 20 0	1	0 10 0	......	......	9 4 0	0 3 0	6	5 10 0	......	......	4 0 0	0 5 0	
......	3 0 0	Paddy ...	17 0 0	6 20 0	3	0 12 0	......	......	8 0 0	0 3 0	9	8 7 0	50 0 0	......	4 0 0	0 5 0	
......	4 0 0	Paddy ... Soorgunga ...	24 0 0 2 0 0	8 0 0	2	0 12 0	......	......	21 0 0	0 8 0	8	15 0 0	......	......	15 0 0	0 12 0	
......	3 0 0	Paddy ...	24 0 0	8 0 0	...	0 12 0	......	......	14 4 0	......	......	......	......	1	50 0 0	0 20 0	Ganja shop.
......	4 0 0	Do. ...	24 0 0	8 0 0	2	0 12 0	......	......	26 0 0	0 4 0	6	7 8 0	50 0 0	2 at 2 0 0	6 0 0	0 6 0	
......	3 0 0	Do. ...	24 0 0	8 0 0	...	0 12 0	......	......	13 8 0	0 3 6	9	14 12 3	50 0 0	1 at 1 8 0	10 0 0	0 5 0	
......	1 10 0	Do. ...	12 0 0	8 0 0	2	0 11 0	......	......	9 1 0	0 3 0	8	7 8 0	......	......	12 0 0	0 5 0	
......	0 12 0	Do. ...	4 20 0	7 20 0	...	0 10 0	......	......	6 4 0	0 3 0	9	8 7 0	50 0 0	......	4 0 0	0 2½ 0	
......	1 10 0	Do. ...	12 0 0	8 0 0	...	0 11 0	......	......	9 0 0	0 2 3	9	4 10 3	......	1 at 1 8 0	6 0 0	0 5 0	
......	1 5 0	Do. ...	10 0 0	8 0 0	...	0 12 0	......	......	5 0 0	......	......	......	40 0 0	2 at 5 0 0	15 0 0	0 13 0	Dealing in brass.
......	4 0 0	Do. ...	32 0 0	8 0 0	...	0 12 0	......	......	14 0 0	0 3 0	9	8 7 0	15 0 0	1 at 1 8 0	4 0 0	0 5 0	
......	1 10 0	Do. ...	12 0 0	8 0 0	...	0 11 0	......	......	4 5 0	0 3 0	8	3 12 0	......	1 at 1 12 0	4 0 0	0 3 0	
......	......	......	......	......	...	......	......	......	6 6 0	0 3 0	8	5 12 0	25 0 0	......	5 0 0	0 8 0	
......	0 2 0	......	......	......	...	......	......	......	0 6 6	0 3 0	7	6 9 0	5 0 0	......	......	0 1 0	
......	0 1 0	......	......	......	...	......	......	......	0 3 0	0 8 0	8	3 12 0	......	......	......	0 3 0	
......	0 10 0	......	......	......	...	......	......	......	1 12 0	Chowkidar	......	......	50 0 0	......	......	0 4 0	Chowkidar.
......	0 5 0	......	......	......	...	......	......	......	1 0 0	......	......	......	......	1 at 1 8 0	100 0 0	0 10 0	Dealing in molasses.
......	0 2 0	......	......	......	...	......	......	......	0 8 0	......	......	......	......	......	20 0 0	0 4 0	Ditto.
......	0 4 0	......	......	......	...	......	......	......	0 12 0	......	......	......	......	......	50 0 0	0 10 0	Ditto.
......	0 5 0	......	......	......	...	......	......	......	1 0 0	......	......	......	......	......	10 0 0	0 5 0	Ditto.
......	0 4 0	......	......	......	...	......	......	......	1 0 0	......	......	......	......	......	60 0 0	0 12 0	Bhusi shop.
......	0 10 0	Paddy ...	4 0 0	8 0 0	...	0 10 0	......	......	3 0 0	0 5 0	9	21 1 6	......	1 at 1 8 0	12 0 0	0 5 0	

C.

Statement showing the particulars of Artisans in Village Aguria, Thana Daspore, Sub-division Ghatal.

Consecutive number.	Name of the head of the family.	Number of males.	Number of females.	Number of children.	Number of working males.	Number of working females.	Number of working children.	Quantity of bastu land.	Amount of annual rent.	Monthly rate of earnings of potters.	Monthly rate of earnings of weavers.	Number of looms in each family.	Number of cloths they can turn out.	Monthly rate of carpenters and others.	Number of milch cows and the earnings thereby.	Amount of debt, if any.	Value of ornaments.	Utensils.	Other means of earnings.
								B. K. CH.	Rs. A. P.	R. A. P.	Rs. A. P.			Rs. A. P.		Rs. A. P.	Rs. A. P.	Mds. S. CH.	
1	Pancharam Kumar	2	6	1	2	2	...	0 10 0	1 8 0	12 0 0	......	...	...	......	1	......	8 0 0	0 5 0	
2	Sibu Kumar	3	3	2	3	3	...	1 12 0	3 10 6	15 0 0	......	...	...	......	1	......	16 0 0	0 6 0	
3	Bhagbut Kumar	4	0	0	4	0	...	1 5 0	3 0 0	24 0 0	......	...	...	......	2	40 0 0	24 0 0	0 12 0	
4	Romanath Kumar	1	1	...	1	1	...	0 6 0	1 4 0	6 0 0	......	...	...	......	...	......	5 0 0	0 2 0	
5	Gorachand Kumar	3	3	4	3	3	...	0 10 0	1 12 0	21 0 0	......	...	...	......	...	......	15 0 0	0 8 0	
6	Srimunta Kumar	1	1	3	1	1	...	0 4 0	1 0 0	7 0 0	......	...	...	......	1	......	5 0 0	0 2 0	
7	Govinda Kumar	3	1	3	3	1	...	0 10 0	2 8 0	16 0 0	......	...	...	......	1	......	16 0 0	0 7 0	
8	Sundar Kumar	2	2	2	2	2	...	0 5 0	1 4 0	12 0 0	......	...	...	......	...	......	6 0 0	0 5 0	
9	Bhagbut Kumar	2	3	2	2	3	...	0 8 0	1 8 0	18 0 0	......	...	...	......	1	......	8 0 0	0 4 0	
10	Khettra Kumar	2	3	...	2	1	...	0 3 0	0 6 0	11 0 0	......	...	...	......	2	......	8 0 0	0 5 0	
11	Chintamani Tanti	1	3	2	1	1	...	0 5 0	1 0 0	......	8 0 0	2	12	......	...	......	......	0 2 0	
12	Hari Mandal	1	3	...	1	1	...	0 14 0	3 0 0	......	8 0 0	1	13	......	1	100 0 0	12 0 0	0 10 0	Cloth shop.
13	Nobin Tanti	1	1	3	1	1	...	0 4 0	1 0 0	......	8 0 0	1	14	......	...	......	4 0 0	0 4 0	Ditto.
14	Behari Tanti	1	1	2	1	1	...	0 12 0	1 14 0	......	5 0 0	1	12	......	1	25 0 0	10 0 0	0 10 0	
15	Ajodhya Tanti	1	1	2	1	1	...	0 12 0	1 14 0	......	7 0 0	1	10	......	1	15 0 0	10 0 0	0 8 0	
16	Sidesvar Das	1	1	4	1	...	...	0 2 0	0 10 0	......	......	...	...	8 0 0	...	......	16 0 0	0 6 0	Trade in twist.
17	Sitaram Poddar	1	2	...	1	...	...	0 1 0	0 5 0	......	......	...	...	8 0 0	1	......	40 0 0	0 8 0	Ditto.
18	Bisu Poddar	2	3	...	2	...	...	0 2 0	0 15 0	......	......	...	...	10 0 0	1	50 0 0	25 0 0	16 0 0	Trade and goldsmith.
19	Sidhesvar Poddar	2	2	3	2	...	...	0 3 0	1 0 0	......	......	...	...	10 0 0	...	......	60 0 0	0 20 0	Ditto.
20	Srinath Nandi	1	1	3	1	...	...	0 5 0	1 8 0	......	......	...	...	4 0 0	...	25 0 0	......	0 3 0	Ditto.
21	Tarachand Dutt	2	2	...	2	...	...	0 6 0	1 8 0	......	......	...	...	9 0 0	...	......	100 0 0	0 10 0	Pharidar.
22	Baikuntha De	1	2	1	1	...	...	0 2 0	0 10 0	......	......	...	...	8 0 0	...	......	75 0 0	0 20 0	Goldsmith.
23	Sitaram Poddar	1	1	1	1	...	...	0 16 8	4 13 0	......	......	...	...	5 0 0	...	30 0 0	32 0 0	0 10 0	Trade in twist.
24	Bhosi Poddar	2	2	3	2	...	...	0 10 0	2 2 0	......	......	...	...	10 0 0	2	50 0 0	40 0 0	0 20 0	Ditto
25	Trailokhya Poddar	2	1	1	2	...	...	0 1 0	0 8 0	......	......	...	...	6 0 0	...	15 0 0	......	0 3 0	Ditto.
26	Rakhal Poddar	1	1	3	1	...	...	0 2 0	0 8 0	......	......	...	...	7 0 0	...	40 0 0	30 0 0	0 10 0	Goldsmith.
27	Dayal Poddar	1	1	3	1	...	...	0 2 0	0 12 0	......	......	...	...	10 0 0	...	......	50 0 0	0 20 0	Trade in twist.
28	Govinda Poddar	1	1	2	1	...	...	0 1 0	0 6 0	......	......	...	...	8 0 0	...	......	50 0 0	0 20 0	Ditto.
29	Guru Charan Poddar	1	1	4	1	...	...	0 2 0	0 10 0	......	......	...	...	7 0 0	...	15 0 0	......	0 5 0	Ditto.
30	Hari Poddar	1	1	...	1	...	...	0 2 0	0 14 0	......	......	...	...	5 0 0	...	......	......	0 2 8	Goldsmith.
31	Gopal Adhya	1	2	...	1	...	...	0 9 0	Rent free.	......	......	...	...	8 0 0	1	......	40 0 0	0 20 0	Trade in twist.
32	Rama Nath Poddar	1	1	2	1	...	...	2 0	0 10 0	......	......	...	...	7 8 0	...	......	10 0 0	0 10 0	Goldsmith.
33	Gobordhan Dom	1	4	3	1	4	...	0 2 0	0 7 0	......	......	...	...	9 0 0	...	15 0 0	8 0 0	0 5 0	Wicker-work.
34	Kartick Dom	2	3	3	2	3	...	0 4 0	0 9 0	......	......	...	...	8 0 0	...	10 0 0	8 0 0	0 6 0	Ditto.
35	Rama Nath Dom	1	2	2	1	2	...	0 1 0	0 4 0	......	......	...	...	7 0 0	...	......	......	0 2 0	Ditto.
36	Nimai Dom	1	1	2	1	1	...	0 2 0	0 9 0	......	......	...	...	6 8 0	...	......	......	0 2 0	Ditto.
37	Chandra Dom	1	1	...	1	1	...	0 3 0	0 10 0	......	......	...	...	6 0 0	...	......	......	......	Wicker and chowkidar.
38	Domi Dom	2	1	3	2	1	...	0 1 0	0 5 0	......	......	...	...	5 0 0	...	......	12 0 0	0 6 0	Chowkidar.
39	Haru Dom	1	1	1	1	1	...	0 2 0	0 8 0	......	......	...	...	5 0 0	...	......	......	0 5 0	Ditto.
40	Akhaya Dom	1	1	2	1	1	1	0 1 0	0 6 0	......	......	...	...	6 0 0	...	......	......	0 4 0	Ditto.
41	Bhajahari Konanga	2	2	3	2	...	...	0 4 0	1 4 0	......	......	...	...	8 0 0	...	......	3 0 0	0 6 0	Trade of cows.
42	Gopal Sarnakar	2	3	3	2	...	...	0 10 0	2 0 0	......	......	...	...	14 0 0	1	40 0 0	100 0 0	1 0 0	
43	Aghore Sarnakar	2	1	1	2	...	...	0 10 0	2 0 0	......	......	...	...	14 0 0	1	25 0 0	75 0 0	0 30 0	
44	Arun Sarnakar	2	1	1	2	...	...	0 10 0	2 4 0	......	......	...	...	10 0 0	...	80 0 0	......	0 10 0	
45	Akhil Sarkar	1	2	2	1	...	...	1 5 0	3 12 0	......	......	...	...	7 0 0	1	70 0 0	25 0 0	0 5 0	
46	Baikantha Sarnakar	1	2	4	1	...	...	0 9 0	3 0 0	......	......	...	...	8 0 0	1	36 0 0	......	0 10 0	
47	Chaitan Sani	1	2	1	1	...	...	0 2 0	0 12 0	......	......	...	...	10 0 0	1	......	50 0 0	0 20 0	Trade in hair combs.
48	Subal Sani	1	1	1	1	...	...	0 3 0	0 10 0	......	......	...	...	7 0 0	...	......	36 0 0	0 16 0	Ditto.
49	Gopal Dutt	1	2	3	1	...	...	0 2 0	0 10 0	......	......	...	...	13 0 0	...	......	30 0 0	0 20 0	
50	Pitambar Sani	4	3	3	3	...	...	0 4 0	1 4 0	......	......	...	...	18 0 0	...	107 0 0	50 0 0	0 20 0	Trade in hair combs.
51	Hriday Sani	3	3	2	3	...	...	0 10 0	1 4 0	......	......	...	...	18 0 0	...	25 0 0	100 0 0	0 15 0	Trade and masonry.
52	Dwari Sani	2	2	3	2	...	...	0 5 0	1 12 0	......	......	...	...	8 0 0	...	128 0 0	80 0 0	0 20 0	Trade in hair combs.
53	Chintamani Sani	1	2	4	1	...	...	0 3 0	1 7 0	......	......	...	...	7 0 0	...	80 0 0	80 0 0	0 20 0	Ditto.
54	Gopi Nath Sani	3	3	5	3	...	...	0 7 0	2 15 0	......	......	...	...	18 0 0	2	100 0 0	100 0 0	1 0 0	Confectioner.
55	Ratan Sani	1	2	3	1	...	...	0 5 0	0 12 0	......	7 0 0	...	...	......	1	50 0 0	80 0 0	0 20 0	

56	Makund Sani	1	1	...	1	...	...	0 15 0	3 11 0	......	7 8 0	...	...	......	...	......	40 0 0	0 15 0	
57	Boikuntha Pal	1	1	3	1	...	...	0 2 0	0 6 0	......	5 0 0	...	...	......	2	......	50 0 0	1 0 0	Selling fried grains.
58	Uday Pal	2	2	3	2	3	...	0 15 0	4 8 0	......	15 0 0	...	...	......	5	......	500 0 0	1 0 0	Ditto.
59	Jadu Chandra	2	3	6	2	2	...	0 13 0	3 0 0	......	13 0 0	...	...	......	2	......	100 0 0	1 0 0	Ditto.
60	Beni Chandra	1	2	1	1	2	...	0 3 0	0 11 0	......	9 0 0	...	...	......	1	90 0 0	7 0 0	0 4 0	Ditto.
61	Mahendra Chandra	1	1	3	1	1	...	0 2 0	0 11 0	......	8 0 0	...	...	......	1	......	166 0 0	0 15 0	Ditto.
62	Gopal Pain	1	1	...	1	1	...	0 2 0	0 11 0	......	7 0 0	...	...	......	...	25 0 0	25 0 0	0 8 0	Ditto.
63	Jagannath Kamar	1	2	1	1	...	...	0 2 0	0 11 0	......	8 0 0	...	...	......	1	......	25 0 0	0 8 0	
64	Chaitan Kamar	2	2	...	2	...	...	0 2 0	0 10 0	......	11 0 0	...	...	......	1	......	10 0 0	0 6 0	
65	Kali Kamar	2	2	9	2	...	...	0 3 0	0 12 0	......	10 0 0	...	...	......	1	33 0 0	......	0 5 0	
66	Radha Nath Kamar	2	2	...	2	...	...	0 2 0	0 12 0	......	10 0 0	...	...	......	...	100 0 0	......	0 2 0	
67	Prem Chand Kamar	2	1	4	2	...	...	0 2 0	3 10 0	......	6 0 0	...	...	......	...	50 0 0	6 0 0	0 3 0	Trade in goats.
68	Chintamani Baishnav	1	1	2	1	...	...	0 3 0	0 8 0	......	5 0 0	...	...	......	...	......	......	0 5 0	Cloth shop.
69	Isvar Kamar	2	2	...	2	...	...	0 12 0	2 4 0	......	10 0 0	...	...	......	1	......	25 0 0	0 10 0	
70	Nayan Kamar	2	1	...	2	...	...	1 7 0	5 13 0	......	9 0 0	...	...	......	...	100 0 0	......	0 5 0	
71	Baikuntha Kamar	2	2	5	2	...	...	1 8 0	7 12 0	......	8 0 0	...	...	......	...	125 0 0	6 0 0	0 10 0	
72	Antaram Kamar	2	1	3	2	...	...	0 2 0	0 6 0	......	8 0 0	...	...	......	...	50 0 0	......	0 5 0	
73	Srirup Kamar	2	1	...	3	...	...	1 18 0	10 0 0	......	9 0 0	...	...	......	...	50 0 0	4 0 0	0 4 0	
74	Sitaram Kamar	2	2	3	2	...	...	0 4 0	0 8 0	......	12 0 0	...	...	......	...	......	100 0 0	1 0 0	
75	Kali Kamar	2	2	2	3	...	...	0 5 0	0 13 0	......	16 0 0	...	...	......	...	......	150 0 0	1 10 0	
76	Trailokya Kamar	1	1	4	1	...	...	0 4 0	3 10 0	......	10 0 0	...	...	......	...	......	100 0 0	2 0 0	
77	Srikantha Kamar	2	...	...	2	...	...	0 4 0	0 8 0	......	4 0 0	...	...	......	...	25 0 0	......	0 3 0	
78	Kali Mandul Jele	1	1	1	1	...	...	0 4 0	3 10 0	......	5 0 0	...	...	......	1	......	15 0 0	0 6 0	
79	Gora Chand Jele	1	1	1	1	...	...	0 5 0	1 12 0	......	5 0 0	...	...	......	...	22 0 0	......	0 4 0	
80	Chintamani Jele	2	2	...	3	...	...	0 2 0	0 8 0	......	10 0 0	...	...	......	1	50 0 0	10 0 0	0 3 0	
81	Thakur Das Jele	2	2	...	2	...	...	0 8 0	1 0 0	......	10 0 0	...	...	......	...	8 0 0	10 0 0	0 8 0	
82	Kali Mandul	5	4	12	4	...	...	1 0 0	4 0 0	......	20 0 0	...	...	......	3	......	50 0 0	1 5 0	
83	Chota Gorachand Mandul	1	...	...	1	...	...	0 4 0	1 4 0	......	5 0 0	...	...	......	...	......	10 0 0	0 3 0	
84	Rama Nath Mandul	1	1	3	1	...	...	0 5 0	1 0 0	......	5 0 0	...	...	......	3	10 0 0	......	0 4 0	
85	Gopal Mandul	1	2	1	1	...	...	0 5 0	1 5 0	......	5 0 0	...	...	......	...	25 0 0	......	0 2 0	
86	Sristidhar Barik	2	5	2	2	...	...	0 12 0	3 0 0	......	16 0 0	...	...	......	3	100 0 0	100 0 0	0 10 0	
87	Sribas Mandul	2	3	1	2	...	...	0 4 0	1 0 0	......	10 0 0	...	...	......	...	......	5 0 0	0 4 0	
88	Radhakrishna Mandul	3	2	...	3	...	...	0 6 0	1 8 0	......	8 0 0	...	...	......	...	60 0 0	34 0 0	0 6 0	
89	Chaitan Jele	1	1	2	1	...	...	0 3 0	1 4 0	......	5 0 0	...	...	......	1	......	5 0 0	0 4 0	
90	Nitai Jele	1	1	2	1	...	...	0 3 0	1 4 0	......	6 0 0	...	...	......	1	......	......	0 3 0	
	Total ...	148	165	191	146	53	1	81 1 0	......	......	633 8 0	...	...	......	...	3,050 0 0	......	......	

D.

Statement showing the particulars of those who live on charity in Village Aguria.

Consecutive number.	Name of the head of the family.	Number of males.	Number of females.	Number of children.	Number of working males.	Number of working females.	Number of working children.	Quantity of bastu land.	Amount of annual rate.	Means of earnings.	Number of milch cows.	Value of ornaments.	Utensils.
								B. K. CH.	Rs. A. P.			Rs. A. P.	Mds. S. CH.
1	Nalim Das	1	2	4	1	...	...	0 7 0	1 6 0	Begging	2 at Rs. 2-4	10 0 0	0 5 0
2	Peli Bewa	...	1	...	...	1	...	......	......	Ditto	......	......	0 1 0
3	Ditto	...	1	...	...	1	...	0 1 0	......	Ditto	......	......	......
4	Bisasti Boistabi... ...	...	1	...	...	1	...	0 1 0	......	Ditto	......	......	0 1 8
5	Tari Bewa	...	1	...	...	1	...	0 1 8	......	Ditto	......	......	0 3 0
6	Degami Bewa	...	1	...	...	1	...	0 1 0	......	Ditto	......	......	0 2 0
7	Karuna Bewa	...	1	...	...	1	...	......	......	Ditto	......	......	......
8	Rebati Bewa	...	2	...	...	2	...	0 2 0	......	Ditto	......	......	......
	Total ...	1	10	4	1	8	...	0 13 8	......	......	......	......	......

A.

Statement showing the particulars of Families in Mousah Naihati living solely on Cultivation.

Consecutive number.	Name of the head of the family.	Number of males.	Number of females.	Number of children.	Number of working males.	Number of working females.	Number of working children.	Area of cultivation.	Description of the different sorts of crop.	Quantity of each kind of crop.	Average outturn per bigah.	Number of plough bullocks.	Quantity of straw per bigah.	Quantity of grain the family can sell after consumption.	Average selling rate of paddy.	Rate of annual rent and cesses.	Amount of debt, if any.	Number of milch cows in each family, and whether they sell any milk, and what the monthly earnings.	Price of ornaments, if any.	Utensils.
								B. K. CH.		M. S. CH.	M. S. CH.		P. K. G.		Rs. A. P.	Rs. A. P.	Rs.	Rs. A. P.	Rs.	[illegible]
1	Akhay Kumar Mandal...	2	1	4	2	...	...	16 0 0	Paddy.	96 0 0	6 0 0	2	0 10 0	...	1 5 0	36 0 0	100	1	36	[illegible]
2	Chintamoni Mandal ...	1	2	1	1	...	...	1 0 0	Do.	4 0 0	4 0 0	1	0 10 0	...	1 5 0	6 0 0	4	1 at 1 4 0	18	[illegible]
3	Kakil Mandal	...	3	1	...	1	...	9 0 0	Do.	50 0 0	6 0 0	2	0 10 0	...	1 5 0	29 0 0	25	1 at 1 4 0	15	[illegible]
4	Girish Chundra Mandal	...	1	1	...	1	...	1 10 0	Do.	12 0 0	8 0 0	...	0 10 0	...	1 5 0	4 0 0	5	......	...	[illegible]
5	Kenaram Dutt	2	3	3	1	...	...	8 0 0	Do.	48 0 0	6 0 0	...	0 10 0	...	1 5 0	Rent-free.	150	3	70	[illegible]
6	Mihir Chandra Dutt ...	1	2	1	1	...	...	12 0 0	Do.	96 0 0	8 0 0	1	0 16 0	...	1 5 0	Ditto.	...	1	200	[illegible]
7	Arun Chandra Bera ...	1	1	3	1	...	...	3 5 0	Do.	21 0 0	6 20 0	1	0 10 0	...	1 5 0	12 8 0	...	......	5	[illegible]
8	Jadu Maiti	1	2	2	1	...	...	3 5 0	Do.	21 0 0	6 26 0	2	0 10 0	...	1 5 0	12 8 0	40	......	3	[illegible]
9	Advaita Saw	1	3	5	1	...	...	3 0 0	Do.	16 0 0	5 0 0	1	0 10 0	...	1 5 0	14 8 0	50	2 at 1 8 0	14	[illegible]
10	Satrughan Maji	1	2	...	1	...	...	1 5 0	Do.	10 0 0	8 0 0	2	0 10 0	...	1 5 0	16 0 0	32	2 at 3 0 0	9	[illegible]
11	Rai Mani Bewa	...	1	...	...	1	...	5 0 0	Do.	33 0 0	0 0 0	...	0 16 0	...	1 5 0	13 0 0	...	1 at 0 12 0	8	[illegible]
	Total ...	10	10	18	9	3	...	62 5 0	... ..	412 0 0	......	...	.....	...	......	142 8 0	406	......	...	—

B.

Statement showing the particulars of Agricultural Labourers of Village Naihati, Thana Daspore, Sub-division Ghatal, District Midnapore.

Consecutive number.	Name of the head of the family.	Number of males.	Number of females.	Number of children.	Number of working males.	Number of working females.	Number of working children.	Area of cultivation.	Description of crops they get annually.	Quantity of each crop.	Average outturn per bigah.	Number of plough bullocks.	Quantity of straw per bigah.	Quantity of grain the family can sell after consumption.	Average selling rate of paddy.	Amount of annual rent and cesses paid.	Rate of wages of day-labourer.	Estimated amount of time they get work during the year.	Average income per month during the whole year of 12 months, calculated on the number of working males in a family.	Amount of debt, if any.	Number of milch cows in each family, whether they sell any milk, and what is the monthly earnings.	Approximate value of ornaments.	Utensils.	Other professions, if any.	Remarks.
								B. K. Ch.		Mds. S. Ch.	Mds. S. Ch.		K. P. G.			Rs. A. P.	Rs. A. P.	Months.	Rs. A. P.	Rs. A. P.	Rs. A. P.	Rs. A. P.	Mds. S. Ch.		
1	Kailas Chandra Ghose	2	2	...	1	...	...	22 0 0	Paddy...	176 0 0	8 0 0	1	0 10 0	...	...	50 0 0	......	......	13 0 0	280 0 0	1	300 0 0	1 20 0	Service.	
2	Prasanna Kumar Dutt ...	2	3	4	1	...	...	2 5 0	Do. ...	18 0 0	8 0 0	...	0 10 0	...	...	......	......	......	12 0 0	300 0 0	1	150 0 0	1 4 0	Ditto.	
3	Bhut Nath Dutt	3	2	3	2	...	...	3 0 0	Do. ...	20 0 0	8 0 0	...	0 10 0	...	...	......	......	......	10 0 0	150 0 0	2	100 0 0	0 20 0	Ditto.	
4	Upendra Nath Dutt	1	1	3	1	...	...	4 10 0	Do. ...	35 0 0	8 0 0	...	0 10 0	...	...	5 2 0	......	......	8 0 0	200 0 0	......	100 0 0	1 0 0	Ditto.	
5	Joggannath Mandul	2	2	4	2	...	...	7 0 0	Do. ...	40 0 0	8 0 0	...	0 10 0	...	...	20 0 0	......	......	5 0 0	100 0 0	1	100 0 0	0 30 0	Ditto.	
6	Kartick Chandra Mandul ...	2	2	1	2	...	...	3 0 0	Do. ...	16 0 0	8 0 0	2	0 10 0	...	...	10 0 0	0 3 0	5	2 5 6	22 0 0	1 at 1 4 0	15 0 0	0 5 0		
7	Fakir Chandra Mandul ...	1	2	...	1	...	...	3 0 0	Do. ...	16 0 0	8 0 0	...	0 10 0	...	...	10 0 0	0 2 0	4	1 14 0	25 0 0	......	12 0 0	0 4 0		
8	Madhu Sudan Manna	3	3	3	3	...	...	3 0 0	Do. ...	12 0 0	8 0 0	2	0 10 0	...	...	16 0 0	......	......	8 0 0	50 0 0	1 at 1 0 0	25 0 0	0 6 0	Service.	
9	Lakhi Narayan Manna ...	2	1	...	2	...	...	1 10 0	Do. ...	11 0 0	8 0 0	...	0 10 0	...	...	7 0 0	......	......	8 0 0	25 0 0	1 at 1 0 0	10 0 0	0 2 0	Ditto.	
10	Sarup Mandul	1	2	2	1	...	...	1 5 0	Do. ...	8 0 0	8 0 0	...	0 10 0	...	...	7 0 0	......	......	7 0 0	72 0 0	2 at 2 0 0	......	0 4 0	Petty shop.	
11	Jogonnath Bera	5	4	5	3	...	...	10 0 0	Do. ...	60 0 0	8 0 0	2	0 10 0	...	...	58 0 0	......	......	12 0 0	100 0 0	1	60 0 0	0 20 0	Service.	
12	Srimanta Kole	1	1	4	1	...	...	0 15 0	Do. ...	2 20 0	7 0 0	...	0 8 0	...	...	5 0 0	0 3 0	4	1 14 0	15 0 0	1 at 1 0 0	......	0 2 0		
13	Isvar Kole	1	2	...	1	...	...	0 15 0	Do. ...	3 20 0	7 0 0	...	0 8 0	...	...	5 0 0	0 3 0	5	1 6 2	30 0 0	......	......	0 2 0		
14	Gora Chand Kole	4	3	2	3	...	...	6 0 0	Do. ...	46 0 0	7 0 0	3	0 8 0	...	...	24 0 0	......	......	10 0 0	......	2	40 0 0	0 12 0	Petty shop.	
15	Dhorma Das Kole	2	2	1	2	...	...	0 10 0	Do. ...	4 0 0	8 0 0	...	0 10 0	...	...	6 0 0	......	......	6 8 0	20 0 0	......	......	0 7 0	Service.	
16	Advaita Manna	2	3	...	2	...	...	1 5 0	Do. ...	10 0 0	8 0 0	...	0 10 0	...	...	8 0 0	......	......	7 0 0	8 0 0	1 at 1 0 0	14 0 0	0 5 0	Barber.	
17	Narayan Chandra Manna ...	2	2	4	2	...	...	1 10 0	Do. ...	6 0 0	8 0 0	1	0 10 0	...	...	18 0 0	0 2 0	5	2 5 6	50 0 0	1 at 0 12 0	......	0 5 0		
18	Srinath Chandra Padikar ...	4	4	...	3	...	...	2 8 0	Do. ...	8 0 0	4 0 0	1	0 10 0	...	...	9 0 0	......	......	10 0 0	60 0 0	2 at 1 8 0	40 0 0	0 12 0	Boatman.	
19	Haradhan Das	2	2	2	2	...	...	1 8 0	Do. ...	6 0 0	4 0 0	1	0 10 0	...	...	6 8 0	0 2 0	6	2 13 0	......	......	20 0 0	0 8 0		
20	Nobin Chandra Saw ...	2	3	6	2	...	...	2 0 0	Do. ...	7 20 0	6 0 0	1	0 7 0	...	...	7 0 0	......	......	7 0 0	60 0 0	1 at 1 0 0	......	0 4 0	Service.	
21	Dinabandhu Santra	1	2	...	1	...	...	1 14 0	Do. ...	6 0 0	7 0 0	2	0 8 0	...	...	6 0 0	......	......	6 0 0	25 0 0	......	5 0 0	0 6 0	Boatman.	
22	Srinath Chandra Santra ...	1	2	...	1	...	...	1 15 0	Do. ...	6 0 0	7 0 0	2	0 8 0	...	...	6 0 0	......	......	6 0 0	40 0 0	1 at 1 0 0	5 0 0	0 6 0	Ditto.	
23	Srinath Chandra Patra ...	4	2	...	3	...	...	3 10 0	Do. ...	17 20 0	7 0 0	1	0 8 0	...	...	21 0 0	0 3 0	4	1 14 0	100 0 0	......	12 0 0	0 4 0		
24	Ram Chand Maji	3	4	1	3	...	...	1 5 0	Do. ...	10 0 0	8 0 0	...	0 10 0	...	...	16 0 0	0 2 0	5	2 5 6	50 0 0	2 at 2 0 0	......	0 4 0		
25	Advaita Paro	2	2	4	2	...	...	4 0 0	Do. ...	32 0 0	8 0 0	2	0 10 0	...	...	16 0 0	......	......	4 0 0	36 0 0	1 at 1 4 0	25 0 0	0 8 0	Boatman.	
26	Kailas Chandra Dian	2	4	3	2	...	...	8 0 0	Do. ...	46 0 0	7 0 0	3	0 8 0	...	...	28 0 0	......	......	18 0 0	128 0 0	2 at 4 0 0	75 0 0	0 10 0	Milkman.	
27	Baburam Dian	1	2	...	1	...	...	0 10 0	Do. ...	4 0 0	8 0 0	...	0 10 0	...	...	4 0 0	......	......	5 0 0	16 0 0	1 at 1 0 0	6 0 0	0 2 0	Service.	
28	Sibu Ghose	2	3	...	2	...	...	3 0 0	Do. ...	16 0 0	8 0 0	...	0 10 0	...	...	11 0 0	......	......	10 8 0	164 0 0	2 at 3 0 0	50 0 0	0 7 0	Milkman.	
29	Akbay Palla	1	2	2	1	...	1	16 0 0	Do. ...	88 0 0	8 0 0	2	0 10 0	...	...	12 0 0	......	......	16 0 0	120 0 0	1 at 1 4 0	75 0 0	0 15 0	Ditto.	
30	Gopal Samanta	1	3	1	1	1	...	0 8 0	Do. ...	2 20 0	8 0 0	...	0 10 0	...	...	5 0 0	......	......	4 0 0	60 0 0	1 at 0 12 0	......	0 2 0	Service.	
31	Gopal Sing	1	5	4	1	2	...	5 0 0	Do. ...	16 0 0	6 0 0	2	0 7 0	...	...	11 0 0	......	......	8 0 0	40 0 0	1	6 0 0	0 5 0	Ditto and paddy-husking.	
32	Sibu Manna	1	2	...	1	...	...	0 10 0	Do. ...	4 0 0	8 0 0	...	0 10 0	...	...	5 0 0	0 3 0	4	4 0 0	25 0 0	......	10 0 0	0 7 0	Barber.	
33	Advaita Samanta ...	2	1	4	2	...	...	3 0 0	Do. ...	20 0 0	8 0 0	2	0 10 0	...	...	12 0 0	......	......	3 0 0	25 0 0	1 at 1 0 0	8 0 0	0 5 0	Service.	
34	Isvar Chandra Santra ...	2	2	4	2	...	...	1 0 0	Do. ...	8 0 0	8 0 0	3	0 10 0	...	...	9 0 0	......	......	5 0 0	25 0 0	......	5 0 0	0 4 0	Boatman.	
35	Brindaban Samanta ...	1	1	...	1	...	...	0 15 0	Do. ...	6 0 0	8 0 0	...	0 10 0	...	...	6 0 0	0 2 0	5	2 5 6	10 0 0	......	......	0 2 0		
36	Guru Das Jelia	1	1	...	1	1	...	0 15 0	Do. ...	6 0 0	8 0 0	...	0 10 0	...	...	0 6 0	......	......	3 0 0	8 0 0	1 at 1 0 0	......	0 5 0	Fisherman.	
	Total ...	70	86	67	64	4	1	128 19 0	......	804 20 0	......	...	......	...	...	333 0 0	......	......	327 3 3	2,612 0 0	......	......	......		

C.

Statement showing Families of Artisans in the Village of Naihati.

Consecutive number.	Name of the head of the family.	Number of males.	Number of females.	Number of children.	Number of working males.	Number of working females.	Number of working children.	Quantity of bastu lands.	Amount of annual rent.	Monthly rate of earnings of potter.	Monthly rate of earnings of weavers.	Number of looms in each weaver's house.	Number of cloths they turn out.	Daily rate of carpenters and their monthly earnings.	Monthly earnings of oilmen.	Monthly earnings of goldsmiths.	Number of milch cows and earnings thereby.	Amount of debt, if any.	Value of ornaments.	Utensils.
								B. C.	Rs. A.		Rs. A.		Pairs.		Rs.	Rs.	Rs. A.	Rs.	Rs. A.	Rs. A.
1	Govachand Sarnakar	1	3	4	1	1	...	1 1	6 0	...	......	...	......	...	...	18	1 at 1 0	60	50 0	0 7
2	Sekh Amdu Tanti	2	2	...	2	2	...	0 10	......	...	5 0	1	12	...	...	...	......	40	5 0	0 2
3	Sekh Dhanu Tanti	2	2	...	2	2	...	0 10	2 0	...	3 0	1	6	...	...	...	1 at 1 4	20	9 0	0 3
4	Sekh Tincauri Tanti	4	4	4	3	4	...	1 0	2 0	...	8 8	2	22	...	...	...	1 at 1 12	20	2 0	0 4
5	Sekh Hara Tanti	1	1	1	1	1	...	0 8	0 11	...	4 0	1	10	...	...	...	......	16	1 4	0 2
6	Sekh Halim Tanti	1	2	1	1	1	...	0 8	0 12	...	4 0	1	10	...	...	...	......	14	......	0 1
7	Sekh Chowdhuri Tanti	5	4	2	5	4	...	0 6	1 0	...	28 0	3	30	...	...	...	1 at 0 12	15	15 0	0 5
8	Sekh Bara Harra Tanti	2	1	2	2	1	...	0 11	1 8	...	6 0	1	10	...	...	...	......	8	......	0 1
9	Srinath Chundra Saw	1	3	3	1	1	...	0 8	10 0	...	......	...	......	...	8	...	......	50	8 0	0 7
10	Nabakumar Saw	2	3	1	2	...	...	0 8	10 0	...	......	...	......	...	9	...	......	100	12 0	0 8
11	Ganadhar Saw	3	3	3	3	...	...	0 16	18 0	...	......	...	......	...	14	...	2	100	16 0	0 10
	Total ...	24	28	23	23	17	...	......	......	...	56 8	10	......	...	31	18	......	503	......	......

D.

Statement showing the particulars of those who live on Charity in Village Naihati.

Consecutive number.	Name of the head of the family.	Number of males.	Number of females.	Number of children.	Number of working males.	Number of working females.	Number of working children.	Quantity of basta land.	Amount of annual rent.	Means of earnings.	Number of milch cows.	Value of ornaments.	Utensils.
								B. K. CH.	Rs. A. P.			Rs. A. P.	Mds. s. ch.
1	Alaka Bewa	...	1	...	1	...	...	......	......	Begging	...	... ..	......
2	Hari Charan Das	1	2	...	2	...	...	1 0 0	0 4 0	Do.	...	8 0 0	0 2 0
3	Balai Jelea	2	...	1	...	...	...	0 5 0	1 4 0	Do.	...	......	0 3 8
	Total ...	3	3	1	3	...	...	......	......	......	...	......	......

E.

Consecutive number.	Name of the head of the family.	Number of males.	Number of females.	Number of children.	Number of working males.	Number of working females.	Number of working children.	Quantity of basta land.	Annual rent.	Amount of debt, if any.	Monthly rate of earnings.	Number of milch cows.	Other means of earnings.	Value of ornaments.	Utensils.
								B. K. CH.	Rs. A. P.	Rs. A. P.	Rs. A. P.			Rs. A. P.	Mds. s. ch.
1	Srinath Chandra Dutta ...	2	2	4	1	...	...	1 0 0	Rent-free	......	50 0 0	1	Service ...	200 0 0	0 3 0
2	Khira Chandra Mitra ...	2	2	2	1	...	...	1 0 0	Ditto.	50 0 0	6 0 0	...	Do. ...	50 0 0	0 2 0
3	Haradhan Ghorue	2	3	...	2	...	...	0 2 0	0 8 0	32 0 0	6 0 0	1	......	8 0 0	0 3 0
4	Adari Bewa	...	1	...	...	1	...	......	......	......	1 4 0	...	Paddy-husking.	......	0 1 0
5	Abinash Chandra Mookerjee.	1	1	...	1	...	...	2 0 0	Rent-free	25 0 0	5 0 0	1	Service ...	40 0 0	0 5 0
6	Ganga Narain Sen	5	5	3	4	...	...	1 16 0	Ditto.	250 0 0	63 0 0	2	Do. ...	500 0 0	2 0 0
7	Bamacharan Dutta	2	3	2	1	...	...	1 0 0	Ditto.	150 0 0	10 0 0	1	Do. ...	25 0 0	0 20 0
8	Moti Lall Dutta	5	3	2	4	...	...	1 0 0	Ditto.	125 0 0	10 0 0	1	Do. ...	100 0 0	0 20 0
9	Sular Sasmal	1	2	1	1	...	...	1 0 0	0 4 0	2 0 0	6 0 0	...	......	......	0 5 0
10	Gopal Chandra Dhuba ...	1	3	1	1	...	...	0 7 0	1 0 0	......	6 0 0	1	......	16 0 0	0 7 0
11	Dayamoi Bewa	...	1	...	...	1	...	0 5 0	Rent-free	......	1 4 0	...	Paddy-husking.	......	0 1 0
12	Tetu Bera	1	1	...	1	...	...	0 5 0	1 8 0	25 0 0	6 0 0	1	......	......	0 5 0
13	Fakir Chand Bera	2	3	...	2	...	...	0 5 0	1 8 0	40 0 0	6 0 0	...	Service ...	......	0 2 0
14	Lakhi Narain Samanta ...	1	2	4	1	...	...	1 0 0	6 0 0	12 0 0	6 0 0	...	......	10 0 0	0 5 0
15	Tara Chand Jelea	2	2	...	2	2	...	0 5 0	1 4 0	25 0 0	6 0 0	...	Fisherman.	......	0 5 0
16	Godadhar Jelea	1	1	...	1	1	...	0 13 0	2 0 0	10 0 0	4 0 0	...	Ditto.	......	0 2 0
17	Haradhan Jelea	1	2	1	1	1	...	......	......	5 0 0	4 0 0	...	Ditto.	......	0 2 0
18	Mati Bewa	...	1	1	...	1	...	0 5 0	1 8 0	......	1 4 0	...	Paddy-husking.	......	0 2 0
	Total ...	29	37	21	24	7	...	......	......	751 0 0	197 13 0	...	......	......	......

KOOMUD NATH MOOKERJEE,
Sub-divisional Officer.

W. LeB.—Reg. No 7920—137—21-4-88.

[CONFIDENTIAL.]

No. 4, dated Bhagulpore, the 19th April 1888.

From—JOHN BEAMES, ESQ., Commissioner of the Bhagulpore Division and Sonthal Pergunnahs,

To—The Secretary to the Government of Bengal, Revenue Department.

IN continuation of my confidential letter No. 3 of the 10th instant, I have the honour to submit herewith copy of a report received from the Deputy Commissioner, Sonthal Pergunnahs, giving the result of enquiries made into the condition of the residents in Dhanakpaja, pergunnah Ambar, sub-division Pakour.

Enquiry into the condition of the residen

Number.	Names of residents.	Number of dependents below age of sixteen years.	Number of dependents above age of sixteen years.	Number in the family who work for wages.	Rates of wages earned.	Amount of annual wages earned.	Area of cultivable holdings. Dhan.	Area of cultivable holdings. Bari.	Average yield per bigha.	The price for which unconsumed produce sold.	Expense of cultiv including rent
						Rs. A. P.	B. c.	B. c.	Mds. s.	Rs.	
1	Baigal Manjhi, headman.	5, including one infant.	9	4	Male as. 3. Female as. 1-6 daily.	19 12 0	15 0	26 0	Dhan. 12 0 Bari. 3 0	100	Rs. 20 + rent Rs. 1 = Rs. 35-8.
2	Dato Santal ...	3	6	3	Ditto ...	29 8 0	20 0	17 0	11 10 3 0	70	Rs. 16+15 rent Rs. 31.
3	Harma " ...	4, including one infant.	3	1	Rs. 3-8 per month for 11 months.	38 8 0	6 0	9 0	11 0 3 0	17	Rs. 3+6 rent Rs. 9.
4	Bikram " ...	3	3	2	As. 2 and as. 1-3	16 4 0	20 0	9 5	10 0 3 0	80	Rs. 10+9 rent Rs. 19.
5	Bagtoe " ...	6 ... ... 3 young children.	5	2	Ditto	18 4 0	25 0	8 0	12 0 3 0	90	Rs. 16+18 rent Rs. 43.
6	Fagu " ...	3, including one infant and two young children.	6	4	Rs. 4, Rs. 3-12, Rs. 2-15 per month.	83 1 0	10 10	6 10	10 0 3 0	20	Rs. 5+6-6 rent Rs. 11-6.
7	Surbu " ...	4 young children ...	1	1	Rs. 3-12	11 4 0	5 10	3 10	10 0 3 0	16	Rs. 2+3-3 rent Rs. 5-3.
8	Mongla " ...	2, including one infant.	2	1	" 3-12	11 4 0	9 10	6 15	10 0 3 0	20	Rs. 6+5-6 rent Rs. 11-6.
9	Hari " ...	2 young children ...	1	2	" 3-12 and Rs. 2-5 ...	19 4 6	5 0 3 Bhag.	1 0	10 0 5 6½ for his share 3 Bari.	20	Rs. 2+3 rent...
10	Parao " ...	2 Ditto ...	2	2	" 3-12 and " 2-5 ...	72 12 0	3 0	3 10	10 0 3 0	......	Rs. 2-3 rent ...
11	Karu " ...	2 Ditto ...	4	3	" 3-12 and " 2-5 ...	100 8 0	2 0	3 0	10 0 3 0	......	Works himself; rent Rs. 1-4.
12	Sango Santalin ...	....	...	1	" 2-13 or as. 1-5 ...	33 12 0	2 0	2 0	6 0 3 0	......	Rs. 2+1-4 rent
13	Kambo "	3	...	1	" 2-13 or " 1-6 ...	33 12 0	10 10	5 0	10 0 3 0	20	Rs. 7 rent ...
14	Balia Santal ...	4, including one infant.	4	3	" 3-8 per month for seven months and Rs. 2-12 for whole year.	58 4 0	Cultivates his mother Kambo Santalin's lands, and gets half produce.				
15	Surja " ...	1 infant	1	2	As. 3, as. 1-6, as. 1-3 daily.	72 12 0	......	......	......	......	......
16	Burhan " ...	....	1	2	Ditto	72 12 0	......	......	......	......	......
17	Lakhiram " ...	2 young children ..	1	2	Ditto	72 12 0	......	......	......	......	......
18	Man Singh " ...	2 Ditto ...	1	2	Rs. 3-12 and Rs. 2-13 ...	78 12 0	......	1 10	0 0 3 0	......	Annas 6+10=Rs. 1-'
19	Chamru " ...	....	2	3	Rs. 2-13 per month by each of the women and by Chamru himself. Rs. 1-4 cash monthly, Rs. 13 for all and dal monthly, 2 mds. dhan monthly, 1 chittack oil daily, 6 pieces of cloth yearly and cooked food at festival.	67 8 0 and 5 mds. besides amount in preceding column.	......	1 10	0 0 3 0	......	" 3 rent

hanakpaja, Pergunnah, Ambar, Sub-division Pakour.

rtent to hich in-lebted.	Number of live stock.	Number of utensils used.	Costs for ornaments.	Amount expended yearly on clothes.	Amount expended on social ceremonies (annually.)	Amount expended on marriages when necessary for males and females.	Amount expended on salt and oil for family use (annually.)	Amount expended on ingredients and spices (annually).	Amount expended on tobacco (annually).	Value of liquor consumed (yearly).	Number of meals eaten per day.	REMARKS.
Rs. A. P.				Rs. A. P.	Rs. A. P.		Rs. A. P.	Rs. A. P.	Rs. A. P.	Rs. A. P.		
29 0 0	3 Buffaloes. 5 Cattle. 5 Goats and sheep. 1 Pig.	Thalees ... 4 Batis ... 5	For newest brass ornaments Rs. 3-8 and for renewals Rs. 1-12 (not yearly.)	20 0 0	16 0 0	For sons, cash Rs. 15. Feast Rs. 20. He gets Rs. 8 for daughters and expends Rs. 5.	Salt 6 0 0 Oil 5 0 0	3 0 0	2 8 0	17 0 0	Three meals.	Most of the women have special costume for festivals; it costs from Rs. 2-8 to Rs. 3, and lasts for about eight years.
35 0 0	2 Buffaloes. 1 Bullock. 5 Goats. 1 Pig.	Thalees ... 3 Batis ... 4 Ghoti ... 1	Ditto ...	20 0 0	5 0 0	Ditto ...	Salt 4 0 0 Oil 4 8 0	2 0 0	3 0 0	9 0 0	Ditto.	
8 0 0	2 Buffaloes. 4 Oxen. 2 Pigs.	Thalees ... 4 Batis ... 4	Ditto ...	6 0 0	3 0 0	Ditto ...	Salt 2 8 0 Oil 2 8 0	0 8 0	2 13 0	2 0 0	Ditto.	
11 0 0	3 Sheep. 4 Pigs.	Thalees ... 2 Batis ... 4	Ditto ...	9 0 0	5 0 0	Ditto ...	Salt 2 0 0 Oil 3 8 0	2 0 0	3 0 0	5 0 0	Ditto.	
16 0 0	3 Buffaloes. 8 Oxen. 2 Sheep. 1 Pig.	Thalees ... 4 Batis ... 5	Ditto ...	20 0 0	6 0 0	Ditto ...	Salt 5 0 0 Oil 5 0 0	2 0 0	2 0 0	11 0 0	Ditto.	
6 0 0	5 Buffaloes. 6 Oxen. 8 Goats. 2 Pigs.	Thalees ... 3 Batis ... 2	Ditto ...	20 0 0	5 0 0	Ditto ...	Salt 4 0 0 Oil 5 0 0	2 8 0	1 0 0	9 0 0	Ditto.	
2 0 0	2 Buffaloes.	Bati ... 0	Ditto ...	5 0 0	1 0 0	Ditto ...	Salt 2 8 0 Oil 3 0 0	1 8 0	1 0 0 besides home plant.	4 0 0	Ditto.	
2 8 0	2 Buffaloes. 6 Oxen. 1 sheep.	Batis ... 2 Thaleo ... 1	Ditto ...	6 0 0	3 0 0	Ditto ...	Salt 2 8 0 Oil 8 0 0	1 0 0	1 0 0	2 0 0	Ditto.	
3 0 0	4 Oxen. 8 Pigs.	Batis ... 2 Thalees ... 2	Ditto ...	3 0 0	1 8 0	Ditto ...	Salt 1 0 0 Oil 0 9 0	0 12 0	0 12 0	3 0 0	Ditto.	
4 0 0	3 Oxen. 2 Goats.	Bati ... 1	Ditto ...	5 0 0	2 0 0	Ditto ...	Salt 2 8 0 Oil 3 0 0	1 0 0	1 0 0	2 0 0	Ditto.	
7 0 0	5 Oxen. 8 Goats. 1 Sheep.	Batis ... 2	Ditto ...	7 0 0	2 0 0	Ditto ...	Salt 8 0 0 Oil 3 0 0	1 0 0	......	2 0 0	Ditto.	
......	......	Bati ... 1 Thaleo ... 1	Ditto ...	3 0 0	......	Ditto ...	Salt 1 0 8 Oil 2 8 0	1 0 0	......	1 0 0	Ditto.	
5 0 6	1 Cow.	Batis ... 4	Ditto ...	6 0 0	4 0 0	Ditto ...	Salt 2 8 0 Oil 3 0 0	0 12 0	......	8 0 0	Ditto.	
2 0 0	6 Oxen belongs to his sister.	" ... 3 Thalee ... 1	Ditto ...	16 0 0	4 0 0	Ditto ...	Salt 3 0 0 Oil 3 8 0	2 0 0	1 0 0	4 0 0	Ditto.	
......	1 Cow and calf.	Batis ... 2	Ditto ...	4 8 0	......	Ditto ...	Salt 1 0 0 Oil 1 0 0	0 8 0	0 8 0	......	Ditto.	
......	1 Bullock.	Batis ... 2 Thalee ... 1	Ditto ...	4 8 0	......	Ditto ...	Salt 1 0 0 Oil 1 0 0	0 8 0	0 8 0	......	Ditto.	
......	1 Heifer.	Bati ... 1	Ditto ...	4 8 0	......	Ditto ...	Salt 1 0 0 Oil 1 0 0	0 8 0	0 8 0	......	Ditto.	
......	......	Batis ... 4	Ditto ...	6 0 0	......	Ditto ...	Salt 2 0 0 Oil 2 0 0	0 8 0	1 0 0	2 0 0	Ditto.	
......	2 Bullocks.	" ... 2	Ditto ...	6 0 0	5 0 0	Ditto ...	Salt 3 0 0 Oil see col. 6.	1 0 0	1 0 0	3 0 0	Ditto. Says his family eats three times and he twice, as he does not like eating in the morning.	

REPORT.

The residents of this village may be divided into three classes, viz., (1) rayats dependent principally on the profits of cultivation; (2) those relying partly on cultivation and partly on wages of labour; and (3) others depending wholly on wages.

The number in class (1) is 8, out of 19 residents or heads of families.

The average number of dependents below the age of 16, including infants and young children, is three, and above that age three. The average number who add to the income by labour is two, and the amount thus earned is Rs. 31-8-7 per house.

The quantity of land possessed is 16 bighas 1 cotta paddy, and 10 bighas 5 cottas bari per house, giving an yield of 10 maunds 31 seers per bigha of paddy, and 3 maunds per bigha of bari.

The total amount incurred in cultivation is Rs. 10-6 + Rs. 8-4-6 payable as rent per each house, and the extent of this indebtedness is Rs. 13-2-5 per house.

The average number of live-stock possessed is as follows :—

2 Buffaloes,
3 Oxen,
3 Goats and sheep, and
1 Pig ;

and the number of brass utensils used is two plates and three cups per house.

The amount expended annually per each house for clothes is Rs. 13-6 ; on social ceremonies is nearly Rs. 6; salt Rs. 3-11; oil Rs. 3-15; ingredient and spices Rs. 1-9-6; tobacco Rs. 1-14-7, and liquor Rs. 7-2.

The number in class (2) is five. The average number of dependents is two below 16 years, and one above that age.

The number per each house earning Rs. 47-8 by labour is nearly two. The area possessed by each house is 3 bighas 16 cottas paddy, and 2 bighas 12 cottas bari, which give an average outturn of 9 maunds 22 seers of the former and 3 maunds of the latter.

The cost for cultivation is Rs. 1-3-2+2-2-9 on account of rent.

The average amount of their debts is Rs. 3-3-2. The number of buffaloes and oxen possessed is three; goats and pigs 3; and brass utensils two. Amount expended annually per each house on clothes is Rs. 5-3-2; social ceremonies Rs. 2-1-7; salt Rs. 2-4-9; oil Rs. 2-8; ingredients and spices Re. 1; tobacco 8 annas 9 pie, and liquor Rs. 2-9-7.

There are six of the third class having on an average three dependents; two per house earn by labour Rs. 78-7-2 yearly. They have no debts, possess two heads of oxen and nearly three brass vessels per each house; they expend annually Rs. 6-14-8 on clothes; Re. 1 on social ceremonies, and Rs. 7-9-4 on salt, tobacco, oil, ingredients and spices, and liquor per each house.

All classes eat three meals a day: the morning meal being composed of stale rice and salt or vegetables, and midday and night meals consisting of a plate of rice, dal and vegetables; also sometimes flesh or fish. After the janera and kodo harvests these are frequently used as a change, besides jungle fruits and vegetables; occasionally fruits such as mangoes, jack, custard-apple and melons are eaten as a luxury.

The exact quantity of rice eaten cannot be stated, but, as far as ascertained, about one and a half seer per each adult, and from half to three-fourth seer of rice per child is used daily; and from the appearance of the people it is evident they do not stint themselves. The clothes worn is mostly English and Bombay made dhuti and markin.

The last class appeared better clothed, and the reason given was they had often ready money in their hands.

Their houses, of course, though no longer composed of wattle and mud, but of strong mud walls, was less substantial than the dwellings of the first two classes. On the whole I think the people are fairly well off and are not suffering from insufficiency of food. These remarks apply more or less to all Sonthal villages. Where there is a deficiency of land, there is a movement among the people to emigrate, but there is no real suffering from insufficiency of food.

The 14th April 1888. E. McL. Smith.

Dated Doomka, the 17th April 1888.

Memo. by—R. Carstairs, Esq., Offg. Deputy Commissioner.

Copy forwarded to the Commissioner, Sonthal Pergunnahs, Bhagulpore, in continuation of my confidential letter of the instant. This gives a fair description of a typical Sonthal village on the east side of the district. There is a movement from that side towards Maldah.

C. E. G. - Reg. No. 10810—137-24-.-88.

CONFIDENTIAL.

No. 5, dated Bhagulpore, the 23rd April 1888.

From—JOHN BEAMES, Esq., Commissioner of the Bhagulpore Division and Sonthal Pergunnahs,

To—The Secretary to the Government of Bengal, Revenue Department.

IN continuation of my confidential letter No. 4 of the 19th instant, I have the honour to submit herewith copy of a report received to-day from the Collector of Purneah regarding the condition of the lower classes of the people of his district.

2. The statements appended to the Collector's letter requiring correction have been returned to him for revision. They will be submitted shortly.

Dated Purneah, the 21st April 1888.

From—H. G. COOKE, Esq., Collector of Purneah,

To—The Commissioner of the Bhagulpore Division.

WITH reference to your order contained in confidential No. 1 of the 19th December 1887, it is to be regretted that the order did not reach the districts earlier in the cold weather.

2. My enquiries, which were necessarily personal ones, are confined to one portion of the district; that portion, inasmuch as it is neither the most nor the least prosperous, may be regarded as typical.

3. I may premise my report by certain facts of general application which are not mere general impressions.

4. Indigenous beggars outside the towns and business centres are unknown. They are to be found in Purneah town, and doubtless in Kissengunge, Kasba and Saifgunge, and possibly in one or two other trade centres. The power and inclination to give may account for their existence at such places.

5. Outside the above places the only beggars met with are wandering vagabonds, chiefly from the west.

6. Fact No. 2. When it is necessary to obtain unskilled labour for the roads or for railway operations, such labour has to be imported from the west.

7. This I know from my connection with the district roads and my observations on the railway work. I have enquired of contractors the reason for this, and the answer has always been that the local men have their land, and they do not care to take up work on the line.

8. The people of Purneah are for the most part wanting in effort or desire to improve themselves. They have learnt to be content with such things as they have; they will not even, when in want, accept good wages if it involves their leaving their homes and working a little more than they are accustomed to; hence their unwillingness to take work on the line, or to enter domestic service, or to emigrate to Darjeeling.

9. This is commonly attributed to their prosperity: I fear this is not always the case. I think that the debility produced by the deadly climate of the place assists to make the people indolent and spiritless.

10 I have noticed a mental paralysis among the European and Eurasian residents, which I attribute to the same cause. European officers feel the tendency and overcome it for a season, but I am inclined to think that in the long run succumb to it.

11. The early stages of disorder are indolence and listlessness, which manifest themselves during periods of malarious fevers only, but undoubtedly become chronic in time.

12. Hence we find the Purneah acclimatized European or Eurasian a man of conspicuously weak mental fibre, frequently also physically slothful; but it is remarkable that this condition of partially suspended vitality is consistent with length of days—a befagged existence appears in some cases to be indefinitely protracted.

13. If such be the case with a stock originally vigorous and hardy, the influence of the climate on the weaker native population must be still more marked. I may be excused for this digression, as my contention as to climatic influences affecting the economic condition of the population will account for facts which I shall comment on, and what is more important is the deplorable result of paralysing the vigor and enterprise of the race will ever be found a huge obstacle to any efforts made by Government to improve the condition of the people.

14. A third fact refers to emigration. Though the Chota Nagpore or Dhangar coolies pass through the district in hundreds every year, voluntarily going to Darjeeling in search of employment, no Purneah cooly was ever known to do so.

15. I must again digress. Some of these same Dhangars have settled in the south and west of the district, and either find the place a land of Goshen, as it is the practice to describe the district, or become fever-stricken and indolent like the rest.

16. Fifthly, it is a fact that the people of Purneah are not litigious. They are mild, docile and long-suffering. To what is this fact to be attributed? I think, first, to their easy rates of rent, which do not provoke litigation; and secondly, to the indolence aforesaid.

17. As a sixth fact, I may mention, without going into details, that the rents here are low, sometimes nominal, and always light in relation to the capabilities of the land.

18. As a seventh, I never saw a worse housed population, though I have camped in many districts; this I attribute to constitutional indolence. All the above facts apply to cultivators, labourers and village craftsmen.

19. They indicate that, if the condition of the people is not better, it is not due to their wanting opportunity, but rather to their wanting inclination to improvement. This will complicate the question of providing a remedy should one appear necessary, even if it does not frustrate any effort in that direction.

20. The above facts also show that nothing can be charged to rack-renting, which does not exist in the district, owing to the vast area of cultivable soil that is still available for settlement.

21. I shall pass now to the consideration, first, of the state of cultivators in the village of Khanwah, in pergunnah Dharampore, thannah Dhamdaha, in the estate of the Maharaja of Durbhanga. The statistics were prepared with the aid of a very experienced officer of the Raj.

22. I send it on as I received it with the following remarks :—

(1) The bigha in this pergunnah is nearly an acre in extent, viz., 4,011½ square yards; the ratio of an acre to a bigha is 1·206 to 1.

(2) I note that in Statement A each holding is divided into a certain portion exclusively devoted to early rice, and the remainder devoted exclusively to winter crops. This is notoriously not generally the case. The *bhadoi* land is almost invariably productive of both these crops, but as the effect of correcting the estimate according to the above general law would be to show the ryot's position to be far better than it is, I prefer to let it pass with the above comment, the result shown being, as it is, very favourable to the ryot.

(3). The cold-weather crop, which appears to have been cultivated in some cases, was *kesari*, the most valueless of all crops. Similarly, as in the last note, it would be possible for me to remark that land that will grow *kesari* would grow wheat, oats and other far more valuable crops, and that the statement furnished shows an exceptionally unfavourable state of things for the ryot: but for the same reason that I have already given, I refrain from correcting the figures by multiplying the produce by three to give the value of some of the better crops that might and do in most cases take the place of *kesari*.

(4). On the other hand, I think that the home consumption under all heads—food, clothing, religious observances, &c.—is not covered by a little over one seer a day or 10 maunds, worth about Rs. 10 per head a year including children, or much less than the earning of a day labourer. Allowing for the cheapness that is due to the cultivator living on the produce of his own lands, I do not think that less than Rs. 2 for each adult and Re. 1 for each child should be allowed for all expenses of living. There remains the cost of cultivation, which appears under-estimated. From enquiries I have made elsewhere, Rs. 2 a bigha for each crop is not an excessive estimate, and that Re. 1 as per statement is undoubtedly defective. Enough has been said, I think, to show that in this by no means specially favoured village the cultivators are in ordinary years extremely comfortably off.

23. The next village I dealt with was composed entirely of labourers; the statistics of this were compiled with the aid of Mr. Wodschow, an indigo planter of great experience of the district, with every inclination to represent facts as they are. The statement marked B gives a list of the inhabitants with details as to their means of livelihood. I have added a footnote showing certain other sources of gain that exist, and an explanatory note as to the hired servant who receives only 8 annas a month as ploughman.

24. This is a form of slavery; for an advance of Rs. 15 or Rs. 20 a man becomes the servant of another on nominal pay.

25. It was impossible to follow each individual of this village through his various forms of labour throughout the year.

26. To illustrate this, I, in consultation with Mr. Wodschow, prepared a statement showing the usual occupations, month by month, of men in that village, which I append in form C.

27. From this it appears that, taking the year round, the labourers can make both ends meet, and even become possessed of cattle, swine and carts, which must be the outcome of thrift.

28. There are two periods of slack work—the first about June, and perhaps to some extent before that; the second in October. Against this must be set off the fact that about ten months of the year admit of savings, which enable the labourer to tide over the slack periods.

29. I do not think that the state of labourers is such as to call for Government interference, especially for the reason I have given in my preliminary remarks, that the people would not avail themselves of an opportunity to get better pay if it involved their leaving their homes.

30. Mr. Taylor, another planter, assures me that the above is an unfavourable picture of the condition of labourers as compared with what exists in the neighbourhood of the railway.

31. Finally as to handicrafts. Artizans in towns are extremely well off and independent, and form so very small an unit of the population that I think it unnecessary to go into their case.

32. In the country the village barhi or carpenter receives an allowance of 15 to 20 seers per plough at each harvest, of which there are generally two in this district ; for this he keeps the plough in repairs. He also makes ploughs, boats, chests and other rough carpentry.

33. The napit or barber receives 10 seers of the crop at each harvest from each homestead, besides presents at sradhs and marriages, and sundry other emoluments for offices performed by him according to custom. He may also hold lands.

34. The dhobi or washerman receives 5 to 10 seers according to the size of the family from each household at each harvest.

35. The chamar or cobbler has a right to the skins of all cattle dying in the village. These he sells, and he does a little rough cobbling if needs be. His wife, the chamarin, is the hereditary midwife of the village and is paid by presents.

36. The above form all the crafts generally found in a Purneah village. Blacksmith's work is done by carpenters.

37. There is no want, so far as I can learn, in any of these classes. They are necessities to the village, and the villagers arrange that they shall live in reasonable comfort.

38. Weavers are not a conspicuous class in this district. They do not, so far as I can learn, exist in the part where my enquiries were made.

39. In the north they do exist and find a good sale for their coarse cloths and their colored cloths for the use of females. Some gunny cloth is also produced by this class.

40. If they do not find work they take to agriculture : lands are plentiful in this district.

41. My examples have been selected from a by no means specially prosperous part of the district. I am inclined to think below the average.

42. My general conclusion is that no class of the community stands in need of special measures for their relief.

C. E. G.—Reg. No. 12670—137—26-4-88.

CONFIDENTIAL.]

No. 829Agri., dated Calcutta, the 27th April 1888.

From—M. FINUCANE, Esq., C.S., Director of the Department of Land Records and Agriculture, Bengal,

To—The Secretary to the Government of Bengal, Revenue Department.

I HAVE the honour to acknowledge the receipt of your letter No. 3695—652Agri., dated the 9th December last, requesting that enquiries into the condition of the lower classes of the population be conducted by the Agricultural Department only (1) as regard the districts of which analysis may be undertaken, and (2) as regards the areas surveyed under my direction.

2. In reply I have the honour to report that there having been no agency available for the purpose, it has not been found possible to undertake the analysis of any district during the current year; and the areas under survey, except in Mozufferpore, in Srinagar, in Bhagulpore, and in Angul in Orissa, are so limited that no conclusions can be based on the results of enquiries instituted in them.

3. Without a comprehensive enquiry, and without reports for the various districts of Bengal, I do not therefore feel in a position to offer, and do not understand that I am called upon to express, an opinion generally on the questions raised in the Government of India's circular which forms an enclosure of your letter under reply.

4. As regards the special tracts of considerable extent which have been brought under survey, special reports have been received which are submitted in original. A special report on Mozufferpore has already been submitted to Government with my remarks, and need not be further referred to here. It shows that the condition of the agricultural classes in that part of the country is at present far from satisfactory, and would appear to have much deteriorated as compared with past times.

5. The conclusions of Mr. Collin, settlement officer of Srinagar, regarding the condition of the agricultural classes in north Bhagulpore, is that in ordinary years they have sufficient means of subsistence; but he adds that the facts elicited in the course of his enquiries do not indicate any great prosperity, and they show that the lower classes, amounting to 25 per cent. of the population, would have nothing to fall back upon in a year of scarcity.

1. Settlement Officer of Dubalhati, Rajshahye.
2. Settlement Officer of Bogri and Kesiari, Midnapore.
3. Settlement Officer of Bhetia, Midnapore.
4. Settlement Officer of Baluakandi, Tipperah.
5. Settlement Officer of Nalchera, Noakhally.
6. Settlement Officer of Maldwar Estate, Dinagepore.
7. Settlement Officer of Sunkerpore Estate, Dinagepore.
8. Settlement Officer of Churamon Estate, Dinagepore.
9. Settlement Officer of Bamunghati in Mhurbhunj.
10. Settlement Officer of Angul, Cuttack.
11. Settlement Officer of Srinagar and Banaili Estate, Bhagulpore.

6. The reports of the officers noted in the margin are herewith submitted in original. It would serve no useful purpose to examine these reports in detail, as no general conclusion can be based upon them without the reports from other officers in the same or neighbouring districts.

7. My personal opinion is that the condition of the agricultural classes in Behar, including parts of Bhagulpore Division, has deteriorated within the period of British rule, and that it is now deteriorating, while that of the population of the greater part of Bengal Proper has improved; that no appreciable portion of the rural classes in Bengal Proper as distinguished from Behar is suffering from want of food; but, as already remarked, the reports now submitted, though some of them are valuable so far as they go, do not afford grounds for forming any general conclusions.

Dated Bhagulpore, the 20th April 1888.

Demi-official from—A. A. WACE, Esq., C.S.,

To—M. FINUCANE, Esq., C.S.,

I SEND you on Collin's report in original, and with it a note comparing some of the statistics with what I collected for my report. Collin has gone to work in a different way to that on which I told my sub-divisional officers to work, and so further comparison of figures is almost impossible. In this note I have cut out the Srinugger Manager's figures because they are so inconsistent with everything else that I will not use them unless they tally with Barun Deo Narain's figures more than they do with others I have. Dopahar is scarcely a typical pergunnah of this district, but the general conclusions Collin has arrived at agree fairly with mine. I think he has made a little too much perhaps of the continuousness of labour. These are slack times, and I doubt if the wage earned in good times is sufficient to give them all a *full* meal in the slack times. You would not thank me, I fear, for sending you my draft report to read; but when Beames has done with it I daresay he would lend it you if you want to check your settlement officers' reports by Collectors' information.

CONFIDENTIAL.]

No. 17, dated Noagan, the 13th April 1888.

From—MOONSHI NUNDJEE, Settlement Officer, Dubalhati Estates,
To—The Collector of Rajshahye.

WITH reference to your memorandum No. 75G, dated the 10th instant, giving cover to a letter No. 706—721Agri., from the Director of the Agricultural Department, Bengal, I have the honour to state that I have also received a copy of the letter direct from the Director, directing me to submit the report through you not later than the 15th instant. The report is ready, but the figured statement, I regret to say, cannot be ready before this evening; and as the report will be of little use without the statement, I do not find myself in a position to submit the report by return of post. I will despatch it by tomorrow's post, and it will reach you on the 15th, and I beg you will be kind enough to excuse me for one day's delay.

I need hardly explain here the difficulty which I have experienced in preparing a report of this nature within six weeks of my joining my appointment here. But as the matter is urgent I propose to submit a copy of the report direct to the Director, and beg that your remarks thereon may be communicated to him as soon after the 15th as possible. This arrangement will save time and I hope you will be pleased to approve of it.

No. 19, dated Noagan, the 14th April 1888.

Memo. by—MOONSHI NUNDJEE, Settlement Officer, Dubalhati Estates.

COPY, with copy of report No. 18, dated the 13th instant, forwarded to the Director of the Department of Land Records and Agriculture for information.

No. 18, dated Camp Noagan, the April 1888.

From—MOONSHI NUNDJEE, Settlement Officer, Dubalhati Estates,
To—The Collector of Rajshahye.

WITH reference to your memorandum No. 1684G., dated the 5th March 1888, giving cover to a letter No. 113Agri., dated the 23rd January 1888, from the Director of the Department of Land Records and Agriculture, I have the honour to submit the following report regarding the actual condition of the lower classes of the population of the Dubalhati estates.

2. *Operations under the Bengal Tenancy Act.*—The survey operations of the Dubalhati estates could not be commenced until the 3rd March last, on which date I joined my appointment here, having finished my duties in connection with the settlement of the Government estate of Chur Nulchira in the district of Noakhally.

3. During the short period of six weeks that I have been in charge of the work, it has been difficult for me to collect, in the ordinary course of my duty, accurate statistics on, the subject in the manner suggested. I hope, however, that although the information which I have been able to gather during the short time at my disposal is not the result of detailed enquiries, it may be accepted as sufficiently correct for our present purposes.

4. The Government notification directing that a survey and record of rights of the estates be made under sub-section 2 (*a*), section 101 of the Bengal Tenancy Act, was published in the *Calcutta Gazette* of the 21st December last. The estates are situated in pergunnah Barbakpore, and consist of 198 villages containing an area of 31,870 acres. They contain many marshes and swamps (*bils*) which dry up during the hot weather, but which expand into broad sheets of water during the rainy season. A sort of coarse rice called *boro*, or spring crop, is grown along the edges of the *bils*. The *boro* land forms a hot-bed of dispute between the Rajah and his tenants, the former claiming it to be *khamar* and the latter to be a part of their occupancy holding.

5. *Description of the tract.*—The whole tract appears to be fortunate in its natural configuration. It has a good proportion of high as well as low land, and the result is that the injury caused to low land crops by flood or heavy rainfall is to a considerable extent counterbalanced by a good harvest in the high lands. Similarly in cases of drought the general harvest is not affected seriously, as the produce of low-lying lands is sufficient to avert any extreme distress.

6. *Uncertainty regarding rates of rent and area of holding.*—There being no settlement and partition papers of the estates, and the rates of rent and the area of ryoti holding being the real matter of dispute between the Rajah and his tenants, no reliable information regarding the area of a cultivator's holding and the rent payable by him can be obtained before the completion of the present survey and record of rights. And it was in consequence of this dispute between the parties that the Government, in its Resolution dated the 30th January 1888, was pleased to sanction, under section 56, clause 3 of the Tenancy Act, a modified form of receipt for use in the estate, in order that, pending such survey and settlement, the ryots might make lump payments of rents without the specification of details in the receipt.

7. An attempt was made by the Rajah, some years ago, to measure the ryoti lands and prepare a revised rent-roll. But the measurement was unproductive of any result, as the ryots did not agree to it.

8. The road cess returns filed on behalf of the Rajah under the Cess Act IX (B.C.) of 1880, and the old revenue survey records, do not give the required data for any villages. The returns do not show the area of the holding, and the annual rents entered therein are disputed by the ryots.

9. *Old revenue survey records.*—The revenue survey of the district was made between the years 1848 and 1856. The survey registers of the villages appertaining to the Dubalhati estates classify the village area into (1) cultivated, (2) site, and (3) uncultivated and waste. But there is nothing on record to show how much of the uncultivated area was capable of being brought under cultivation and how much was unfit for cultivation.

10. *Division of agricultural community according to present statistical information.*—I commenced enquiries in 10 typical villages of the estates to obtain some trustworthy statistical information on the subject under consideration. The figures of the 10 villages furnish sufficient data for a correct conclusion. The thanawar list of the Boundary Commissioner, showing the population of villages, &c., not being available, I have ascertained the number of persons in each village for the present purpose. I have divided the agricultural community into six classes, as will appear from Table I, and from the statistics of these villages it appears that 7·6 per cent. of the population employ hired labour for cultivating their land, 60·4 per cent. cultivate their land by their own labour, 24·6 per cent. depend on wages plus the profit of small holding, 5·1 per cent. depend on wages of labour only, 1·03 per cent. are dependent on charity, and 1·03 are dealers in hides, and that the density of population is 938·05 per square mile.

11. *Average area of holding and average rate per bigha.*—I have also compiled a statement (Table II) from the survey records and the cess returns, which shows that the average area of a holding is 11*b.* 9*k.* 9*c.*, or about 4 acres, and the average rent per bigha is 11 annas 11 pie. I have tested the figures by enquiry, and found them to be approximately correct.

12. Table II further shows that at the time of the revenue survey (1851-52) 48·6 per cent. of the whole area was cultivated, 5·02 site and 46·3 uncultivated and waste. But from what I have already seen of the estates, I can say that, with the exception of a few small areas occupied by roads, tanks, village sites, &c., the whole of the cultivated area is capable of yielding crops of some kind.

13. *Extent of cultivators' holdings.*—There is scarcely any cultivator holding more than 100 bighas. There are, however, cultivators who hold from 50 to 100 bighas. But the average size of the holding of a well-to-do cultivator varies from 30 to 12 bighas. A holding of 15 bighas is considered as sufficient to keep its holder in comfortable circumstances; but a holding containing less than 10 bighas is considered very small.

14. *Cereal crops.*—Besides rice the other cereal crops cultivated are ganja, jute, turmeric, chilly and sugarcane. But generally speaking a cultivator's entire holding is under rice and jute, with the exception of a small patch around the homestead in which he raises crops of vegetables.

15. *Cultivation of rice and jute and profit of cultivation.*—Rice and jute being the principal crops cultivated by the cultivator every year, I made some enquiries regarding his profit. I enquired of some trustworthy respectable men, who gave me the following figures :—

Crop.	Average produce per bigha.	Value (jute Rs. 3 per maund and paddy Rs. 1-8 per maund).	Average cost of cultivation.	Rent.	Net profit of the cultivator.
	Mds.	Rs.	Rs.	Rs A. P.	Rs. A. P.
Rice	12	8	2	1 8 0	4 8 0
Jute	10	30	8	2 0 0	20 0 0

Considering the fertility of the soil and the fact that paddy-fields produce crops of pulses or oilseeds, the above estimate may be considered fairly accurate. So a cultivator of 8 bighas of land may be considered as well off as a man earning money wages of Rs. 8 a month.

16. *Cost of living.*—The cost of living of a middle-sized family of the cultivating class, consisting of 5 persons, 3 adults and 2 children, may be safely estimated at Rs. 8-8-6, as under—

	Rs.	A.	P.
Rice, 3 maunds, value	5	0	0
Dall, 10 seers	0	12	6
Vegetables, chillies, spices, &c.	0	12	0
Oil	0	12	0
Salt	0	8	0
Fish	0	12	0
Total ...	8	8	6

17. But it must be remembered that the above expenses would be incurred if all the articles were purchased from the bazar. But as a matter of fact the cultivator obtains from his fields almost all the staple articles of food. The fish he requires is caught by himself, or by members of his family, in a neighbouring marsh or tank.

18. A cultivator of small holding, two or three bighas in area, supplements his ordinary means of livelihood by his wages of labour. Sometimes he receives a share of the crop in return for his labour. No cultivator would admit that he derived any income by the sale of straw, fodder, livestock, milk, &c.

19. *Old rates of rent.*—As for the rates of rent, the following extract from Dr. Hunter's Statistical Account of Rajshahye, page 78, is worthy of note here:—"Rates of rent have enormously increased during the present century, for the Collector states that prior to the decennial settlement in 1790 the rates current for ordinary land appear to have been about 2½ annas per bigha or under 1*s.* an acre." And it appears that since the permanent settlement the rates of rent in the estates have increased by 150 to 200 per cent.

20. *Wages.*—The rates of wages have also increased with the increase in prices of articles of food. The present rate of wages of an agricultural labourer is four annas per day without food or two annas per day in addition to food. But one-half of these is said to have been the rate 25 years ago. The women are generally employed in household work, but those of the poorer class occasionally work in the field. Children are employed in tending cattle.

21. *Condition of the cultivator.*—The cultivators are not continually in debt. Whenever they borrow money they do so for purchasing seed-grain or on the occasion of marriage or other religious ceremonies, the rate of interest being one anna per rupee, or 6-4 per cent. The debt is repaid with interest at the end of the harvest. The number of those seriously in debt is very small.

22. As far as I have been able to learn by enquiries, I have no doubt that the position of the cultivators and the labouring class is much better than it was 20 years ago. They are advancing in wealth and social self-respect. They no longer suffer their landlord to extort money from them in shape of salami or abwabs. Their easy circumstances enable them to resist all attempts of their landlord at enhancement of their rent. Those who used to do well with earthen pots and pans have now vessels of brass and copper. The improvement in houses, wages, dress and diet speak of their general prosperity. The women are more decently dressed than formerly; the women of a well-to-do cultivator no longer carry on their persons brass ornaments.

23. *Houses.*—The building materials used consist of bamboos, wooden posts, thatching-grass, cane and jute. Roofs are thatched with grass. The outer walls and inner partitions are made of bamboo mats or split bamboo, rough sticks or bamboos being used for rafters. Earth is but little used for building; houses with mud walls are not to be found except in some of the big villages. The house of the village mandal or head man is usually the best house in the village.

24. *Furniture.*—The brass utensils have to a very considerable extent superseded the cheap pottery formerly in use. We now find in the house of almost every cultivator a brass vessel (*gagra*) for carrying water, a brass jug (*lota*), a brass plate (*thala*), a brass cup (*bati*), not to speak of ordinary furniture such as a few cane baskets, some bamboo baskets, one or two quilts for use at night, and one or two mats, &c.

The agricultural implements, consisting of a plough (*nangal*), spade (*kodoli*), harrow (*beda*), reaping sickle (*kochi*), clod-crusher (*moi*), bill-hook (*dao*), &c., are of course in the house of every cultivator.

25. *Dress and ornaments.*—The dress of an ordinary cultivator is a *dhuti* and a *chudder*. Every well-to-do cultivator now uses an umbrella, a *piran* (shirt), and a pair of shoes, which was not the case some few years ago. The dress of the women is *sari*. The use of gold and silver ornaments has increased of late years, and even the poorest cultivator in the village is now ashamed to admit that brass ornaments are used by his women.

26. *Artizans, weavers, &c.*—Persons of these professions are few. The number of blacksmiths, goldsmiths and carpenters in the estates under survey may approximately be estimated at 5, 30 and 50 respectively. There are no brick-layers. There are two or three families of masons in village Dubalhati, which is the residence of the Rajah. The artizans either work at a fixed rate of wages varying from Rs. 10 to Rs. 15 per month, or carry on their work in their own houses, and occasionally sell their productions to merchants.

The few weavers that are to be met with in some of the villages work on their own account. The cultivators as a rule purchase cloth from the bazar for their own use.

27. *Conclusion.*—The day-labourer and persons living on charity obtain enough to supply their wants, and no portion of the population suffer from bad health by reason of poverty.

Table I.

Statement showing the classification of population in 10 villages appertaining to the Dubalhati Estates, pergunnah Barbakpore, district Rajshahye.

1	2	3	4	5	6																										7	8	9
Serial number.	Name of village.	Total area of village in standard bighas.	Total number of houses or families.	Total population.	Classification of Population.																										Average number of persons per house.	Average number of persons per square mile.	Remarks.
					a. Families employing hired servants for cultivating their land.					*b.* Families cultivating land by their own labour.					*b.* Families dependent on wages plus profit of small holdings.					*d.* Families dependent on wages of labour only.					*e.* Families dependent on charity.					*f.* Artisans, weavers, dealers in hides, etc.							
					A. Number of families.	B. Male.	C. Female.	D. Children.	E. Total.	A. Number of families.	B. Male.	C. Female.	D. Children.	E. Total.	A. Number of families.	B. Male.	C. Female.	D. Children.	E. Total.	A. Number of families.	B. Male.	C. Female.	D. Children.	E. Total.	A. Number of families.	B. Male.	C. Female.	D. Children.	E. Total.	A. Number of families.	B. Male.	C. Female.	D. Children.	E. Total.			
		Bgs.																																	
1	Kamaigari ...	932	62	347	6	15	21	32	68	36	65	91	89	245	...	...	...	...	...	9	10	10	9	29	1	3	2	...	5	...	...	...	...	...	...	...	
2	Chuk Bara ...	257	12	92	...	...	...	...	...	10	17	24	39	80	3	2	4	6	12	...	...	...	...	...	...	...	...	...	...	...	...	...	...	...	...	...	
3	Do. Fetullah ...	179	7	62	1	6	8	9	23	8	10	11	12	33	...	...	...	...	...	1	1	1	4	6	...	...	...	...	...	...	...	...	...	...	...	...	
4	Do. Joyhari ...	87	9	64	...	...	...	...	...	7	17	19	19	55	1	2	1	1	4	...	...	...	...	...	1	1	1	3	5	...	...	...	...	...	...	...	
5	Digha	211	21	134	2	7	12	17	36	10	13	23	22	58	5	8	10	5	23	4	4	6	7	17	...	...	...	...	...	...	...	...	...	...	...	...	
6	Chuk Ram Chandra ...	560	38	204	...	...	...	...	...	28	41	50	75	168	4	5	6	11	22	2	2	2	4	8	1	2	2	2	6	...	...	...	...	...	...	...	
7	Chuk Birahim ...	232	10	77	1	2	2	3	7	6	16	20	18	54	3	5	5	6	16	...	...	...	...	...	...	...	...	...	...	...	...	...	...	...	...	...	
8	Patakata	316	29	301	...	...	...	...	...	25	66	93	121	280	1	4	4	1	9	3	5	6	1	12	...	...	...	...	...	...	...	...	...	...	...	...	
9	Chuk Rampur ...	1,173	91	484	...	...	...	...	...	31	85	110	117	312	29	41	50	48	139	...	...	...	...	...	4	1	6	...	7	7	9	9	8	26*	...	...	* These are dealers in hides.
10	Hamigari	1,233	101	742	4	12	19	26	57	24	63	75	92	230	56	101	133	160	394	15†	18	24	16	58†	2	1	1	1	3	...	...	...	...	...	...	...	† These include 7 families (31 persons) who live by fishing.
	Total ...	5,173	367	2,507	14	42	62	87	191	202	394	516	606	1,516	101	168	218	238	619	34	38	49	43	130	9	7	13	6	26	7	9	9	8	26	6·8	938·08	

Noagon;
The 13th April 1888.

Moonshi Nundji,
Settlement Officer.

TABLE II.

Statement showing the classification of area of village and its annual value according to the revenue survey records and cess returns.

1	2	3				4		5	6	7
Serial number.	NAME OF VILLAGE.	AREA ACCORDING TO THE REVENUE SURVEY RECORDS.				NUMBER OF HOLDINGS AND AMOUNT OF RENT ACCORDING TO THE RETURN FILED BY THE RAJAH UNDER THE CESS ACT.		Average area of the holding.	Average rent per bigha.	REMARKS.
		Cultivated.	Bits.	Uncultivated and waste.	Total.	Number of ryoti holding.	Annual value of land, i.e. total rent payable to the zemindar.			
							Rs. A. P.	B. K. CH.	Rs. A. P.	
1	Kamaigari	500	45	387	932	66	463 0 6	14 2 6	0 8 0	The villages of Patakata and Chuk Ramper do not appear in the road cess return, and so they have been omitted from this statement.
2	Chuk Bara	150	11	96	257	28	247 5 6	9 3 9	0 15 4	
3	Do. Fatehullah ...	100	7	65	172	18	178 13 7	9 11 0	1 0 7	
4	Do. Jayhari	48	14	25	87	20	117 10 9	4 7 0	1 5 7	
5	Disha	110	16	85	211	29	234 11 3	7 5 6	1 1 7	
6	Chuk Ram Chandra ...	284	30	246	560	35	545 5 9	16 0 0	0 15 5	
7	Birahim...	100	18	120	238	13	157 3 5	17 16 14	0 10 10	
8	Hamigari	500	50	683	1,233	112	738 13 6	11 0 2	0 9 6	
	Total ...	1,792	185	1,707	3,684	321	2,747 15 5	11 9 9*	0 11 11*	* These figures have been arrived at, not by adding the figures in the column, but by finding out the averages in the total area and the total rent.

MUNSHI NUNDJI,
Settlement Officer.

NOAGON,
The 13th April 1888.

H. P.—Reg. No. 1867C—187—7-5-88.

CONFIDENTIAL.]

Dated Midnapore, the 13th April 1888.

From—BABU BISSESSAR BANERJEE, Settlement Officer of Bogri and Kesiari,
To—The Director of Land Records and Agriculture (through the Collector of Midnapore.

WITH reference to your Nos. 115 and 116, dated the 23rd January, I have the honour to submit herewith my notes on the condition of the agricultural classes in estate Kesiari and Bogri.

My enquiries, it will be seen, were confined to one mouzah in each estate, the mouzahs to which my notes refer being typical in many respects of the other villages comprised in the estates.

THE following note embodies the result of the enquiries made by me regarding the material condition of the ryots of mouzah Hasimpur comprised in estate Kesiari.

I confined my enquiries to this village alone, as it is in many respects typical of the other villages appertaining to the estate, and as the settlement of this village, undertaken on the application of the proprietors of the estate under the Tenancy Act, having been brought to completion, I am in a position, so far as the condition of its inhabitants is concerned, to adduce actual facts in support of my conclusions.

The culturable area of this village consists for the most part of single-cropped land, nothing but the *aman* or late paddy crop being grown thereon.

The soil is not of the best quality, and there being no facilities for irrigation, a river or a khal, the ryots are wholly dependent on rain-water for a good crop. They live in constant dread of a drought or of excessive rainfall, especially of the former.

Having nothing but single-cropped lands to depend upon, the failure of the winter paddy crop means heavy distress to the ryots.

In other parts of the country the failure of one crop is made up for by growing other crops on the same land. This is not possible here.

No kind of garden produce is grown in this part of the district, the soil being not suited for them. There are a few patches of garden produce here and there in the mouzah; but owing to the ravages of monkeys there is nothing like a systematic attempt to grow them on a larger scale. The Hindu ryots never think of killing these monkeys.

In the village of Hasimpur there are 117 families of cultivators, the area of their holdings ranging from 2 to 30 bighas. The average yield per bigha is 8 or 8½ maunds of paddy, each member of a family consuming 1¼ maunds a month.

The cost of cultivation per bigha is as follows:—

	Rs.	A.	P.
Seed-grains	0	6	0
Labour for ploughing	1	0	0
Manure	0	5	0
Labour for reaping and harvesting	1	10	6
Rent and cesses	1	6	9
	4	12	3

This cost is incurred when everything is done by hired labour. But cultivators do not always hire labourers for cultivating their fields. In most cases they do the work themselves, and the money which they have to pay in hard cash is the rent, the cesses and the wages of labourers; but the cost of their own labour and the keep of necessary cattle would bring up the total cost of cultivating a bigha of land to the amount given above.

The wages of daily labourers are 1 anna 6 pie per head per diem *plus* 3 pie for oil, tobacco and fried rice. Labourers are also hired for the year at Rs. 24 per head. This annual pay has to be paid in advance. Labourers engaged for the year are not allowed to board themselves at their employer's expense. Labourers generally allow themselves to be hired for the year in order to provide funds for emergent occasions, such as marriage of themselves or of their children, &c. They then shift for themselves as best they can for a whole year, and thus repay the amount advanced to them. The labourers who board themselves upon their employers cost the latter one anna per head daily.

One bigha of land, which is equal to 1¼ standard bigha, yields, as stated above, 8 or 8½ maunds of paddy, the money value of which is Rs. 6 at the rate of 12 annas per maund. The straw fetches one rupee, the total money value of the yield being Rs. 7. But the rent and cesses (Rs. 1-6-9) and cost of cultivation (Rs. 3-4-0) being deducted therefrom, the margin of profit left does not exceed Rs. 2 per bigha. But this, however, is not always their net profit, as it is subject to deduction on account of—

(1) Keep of cattle.
(2) Price of the plough and the cost of repairing it from time to time.
(3) Rent and cesses paid by ryots in bad year.

It appears that land and cattle are both deteriorating, the former from impoverishment caused by constant tillage, and the latter from want of fodder, there being no pasturage for them, and the straw of paddy being otherwise utilized, *i.e.* in thatching houses &c. Want of fodder for cattle is severely felt in the month of Cheyt, the cattle being then allowed to wander about in the neighbouring jungle in charge of a cowherd who is paid at the rate of one anna per head of cattle.

The absence of grazing-grounds is due to weavers and other castes who used to follow other professions before, having now taken to agriculture for their subsistence. The margin of cultivation has thus been extended far into the khas *palit* lands of the village.

The ryots whose holdings are less than five bighas supplement their income from agriculture by carrying on other business or trade. Similarly the weavers, who have suffered to a great extent owing to the importation of European piece-goods into the country, have, as stated above, taken to cultivation to eke out the very small income they derive from their professions. There are 30 or 32 families in this village who live partly by agriculture and partly by other trade or business.

The cost of maintenance per head is given below—

	A.	P.
Rice	2	0
Oil	0	9
Vegetable	0	6
Miscellaneous expenses	0	6

The ryots of this part of the district literally live from hand-to-mouth. Two full meals of coarse rice per day are a luxury to them. They cannot afford *dál* and vegetables daily; salt is their ordinary condiment, and *kalmi* (a kind of aquatic plant) and boiled *brinjal* form their daily vegetable diet. The increase of salt duty has been a great hardship to them. They think themselves fortunate when they get fish and *dál* at dinner; this they hardly do more than once a week.

They grow *kalmi* plants on the beds of old tanks in the village. The plants grown on the bed of a single tank are worth Rs. 40 or Rs. 50, one pice worth of these plants being not enough for even four men. The rent of a tank on the bed of which *kalmi* is grown is Rs. 8 or Rs. 10 per annum. If the water has to be baled out for preparing the bed for the cultivation of these plants, an additional cost of Rs. 10 or Rs. 12 is generally incurred.

The ryots in this part of the district cannot afford to save anything. Formerly many of them used to have enough paddy to last then throughout the year. This is not the case at present, it being due to a certain extent to the general rise in the price of the necessaries of life and also in the wages of labour. Their physique also has deteriorated from insufficient food and constant attacks of malarious fever.

BISSESSAR BANERJEE,
Settlement Officer.

Weavers.

THE importation of European piece-goods has impoverished the weavers. Many of them have given up their profession and now keep shops. Some are employed as servants. Most of them cannot afford to have two meals a day. The weavers who live at Hasimpur have not been so much impoverished as those in other places, for they do not weave cotton cloth, their principal business being the manufacture of *tasar* fabrics. There are 81 families of weavers in Hasimpur. Formerly the weaving of one *tasar* cloth would cost Rs. 5 as per details given below :—

	Rs.	A.	P.
Ten *pans* of cocoons	3	12	0
Spinning ditto into yarn	0	10	0
Labour	0	10	0
Total ...	5	0	0

Out of this amount, the weavers used to get four annas by selling the refuse *tasar* or shaddy; total net cost of a piece of *tasar* cloth was therefore Rs. 4-12.

Now a piece of *tasar* cloth costs Rs. 6-11, viz.—

	Rs.	A.	P.
Ten *pans* of cocoons	5	0	0
Spinning ditto into yarn	0	15	0
Labour	0	12	0
Total ...	6	11	0

Deducting the price of refuse *tasar*, which amounts to five annas, the net cost comes to Rs. 6-6; but a piece of *tasar* cloth sells at Rs. 8 at most, and so weavers get a profit of Rs. 1-10 per piece. Formerly a piece used to sell at Rs. 7, and the cost of manufacture being Rs. 4-12 only, the weavers used to get a profit of Rs. 2-4.

Formerly they used to pay Rs. 3-12 and now Rs. 5 for cocoons for a piece of cloth. This amount they have to pay in cash. They have to pay nothing for labour, they doing the work assisted by the women and children of their family. A weaver cannot weave more than three pieces a month; if these pieces sell at Rs. 8 each, the weaver's profit amounts to Rs. 9 a month, it being the outcome of the united labour of two men. One-third of this profit is due to the members of the family who assist in the work, and two-thirds to the man who works at the loom. This profit does not compare unfavourably with that earned by the weavers before; but their capacity for labour has been much reduced owing to the prevalence of epidemic fever among them. Two men now earn what one man earned before. The decrease of profit has been much aggravated by the general rise in the price of the necessaries of life and an additional item of expenditure, *i.e.* medical treatment. Formerly rice used to sell at 10 or 15 annas a maund; now it sells at Rs. 1-4, Rs. 1-12, and in some years at Rs. 2-8 a maund.

The European piece-goods have also to a certain extent affected the sale of *tasar* cloth. The following table compares the cost of living as it was 20 years ago with what it is now. The cost given is for a family consisting of four members only—

	Cost of living 20 years ago.			Cost of living as it is now.		
	Rs.	A.	P.	Rs.	A.	P.
Rice for 4 persons at 1 seer per head ...	0	1	0	0	2	0
Fire-wood	0	0	3	0	0	6
Oil, salt, tobacco, spices, betels ...	0	0	9	0	1	6
Fish and vegetables	0	1	0	0	1	6
Miscellaneous	0	0	6	0	1	0
	0	3	6	0	6	6

The cost is nearly double what it was 20 years ago.

The people of this place have been much enfeebled by smoking opium, to which they are very much addicated. Most of the weavers here smoke opium. They are gradually becoming weak and indolent. Of the 81 families of weavers living in this village, 50 live by their profession, 20 or 22 partly by their profession and partly by agriculture, eight or nine men work as paid servants of other weavers. They are paid at the rate of Rs 2 or Rs. 2-8 a month Their wives and daughters spin *tasar* yarn and earn on an average almost as much as their husbands and fathers. The weavers cannot save anything; they generally have to borrow when they marry themselves and on other similar occasions. Having no capital, they borrow Rs. 20 or Rs. 25 at a time from their mahajans, and by selling cloths repay them gradually.

Bissessar Banerjee,
Settlement Officer.

Beggars.

There are 10 families in Hasimpur who live by begging. Alms are given to them in the shape of handeful of rice; but they do not get alms in this shape all the year round, for most of the inhabitants of this village live by agriculture, and they are generally very liberal to the beggars at the harvest season when they have enough rice at home It is in Jeyat or Ashar, when the ryots have paid up their debts to their mahajans and zemindars, that the beggars cease to receive alms from the villagers. This is the worst part of the year so far as the beggars are concerned; for the ryots, having not enough for their own maintenance at that time of the year, can give them no alms.

The number of beggars are increasing. The cause of this increase of poverty among the people of Hasimpur is (1st) epidemic fever and (2nd) opium-smoking, which has reduced many a well-to-do family to poverty. The people here believe that opium-smoking is a preventive against fever, and under this belief they seldom give up the habit.

Under the influence of this drug they gradually get enfeebled and poor, become indebted to their mahajans and zemindars who, in course of time, repay themselves by selling off their tenures and houses under decrees obtained in the Civil Court, and then their debtors become paupers. Many ryots become beggars by being extravagant on the occasion of marriages, &c.

Bissessar Banerjee,
Settlement Officer.

Note on mouzah Sandhipur, pergunnah Bogri.

There are 90 families in this village.

Seventeen families of these families are Brahmins, all the remaining families being Sudras.

Forty-three families live by agriculture and partly by working as labourers.

The area of holdings of 20 families ranges from two to six bighas.

Of 26 families from two to five bighas.

Of eight families from five to 10 bighas.

The cost of cultivation per bigha is as follows :—

	Rs.	A.	P.
Price of seed-grains	0	4	0
Hire of a plough for eight days	1	8	0
Price of manure including cost of conveyance	1	8	0
Sowing and transplanting	0	8	0
Turning the sods with a spade	0	4	0
Reaping and conveying sheaves to threshing-ground	0	8	0
Threshing or shaking the grains off the sheaves	0	4	0
Rent and road cess	2	4	0
	7	0	0

The average-yield per bigha is $2\frac{1}{2}$ *aras*=10 maunds. An *ara* sells at Rs. $3\frac{1}{2}$, the price of the whole yield being Rs. 8-12. The price of the straw is Rs. 1-8. Total income per bigha being Rs. 10-4.

The net profit, deducting cost of cultivation as shown above, is Rs. 3-4.

The cultivators have to pay the rent and road cess in cash, and in some places the price of manure also. The other items of expenditure do not represent so much money paid, but simply the estimated cost of their personal labour or that of their neighbours who help them in the work, they being repaid by being similarly helped by those they help. This system of mutual help which obtains among cultivators is called *gantu*.

In this mouzah there is very little land of the first quality, most of the lands being of the second or third quality. They depend entirely on rainfall, and if there is a drought or scarcity of rainfall the ryots get little or no crop. A drought is more injurious to the crops here than heavy rainfall.

Patches of sugarcane, mustard, and different kinds of pulses and also of wheat and barley are seen near the homesteads of the ryots, but the land (*kula*) suited for their cultivation is not available in sufficient quantity.

The cultivation of sugarcane is very expensive, and requires a large quantity of manure, the cost being Rs. 40 per bigha; the yield does not fetch more than Rs. 50 or Rs. 52.

The ryots wholly dependent on cultivation for their subsistence are by no means well off, the cultivable land being not available in sufficient quantity. Their income from cultivation is usually supplemented by what they get from selling firewood, which they bring from the neighbouring *sál* jungle.

Each family of ryots consists of five members, including adults and children.

Before the Orissa famine, when living was very cheap here, a family of five or six members could maintain itself at Rs. 8 or Rs. 9 a month, at Rs. 1-8 per head. But this is no longer possible, living being much dearer now. Now each member costs Rs. 2 or Rs. 2-4 a month.

It will be seen that the cost of living has increased almost twofold.

The marriage expenses also have increased. Rs. 30 or Rs. 40 was the total expenditure formerly incurred at a marriage. Bracelets made of conch-shells and a few other trinkets were the ornaments given to a bride in those days. Now silver and gold ornaments are demanded and given, and this forms the heaviest item of expenditure of a marriage. Most of the ryots in this village are of the Sadgop caste. There are many rajahs and zemindars of this district who belong to this caste, and it is said that their example has made marriage very expensive among the poorer Sadgops also. This is one of the causes of their indebtedness.

They use brass and other metal utensils, which are getting more and more into use among them.

There are ten families of labourers in this village. Their wages are Rs. 2 each per mensem for those who are proficient in their work, and those who are less proficient get Rs. 1-8. In addition to their wages they are supplied with food, cloth, oil and fried rice by their employers. Formerly the wages of labourers was 12 annas or 1 rupee each. Day labourers get $1\frac{1}{2}$ annas per diem and one meal and oil and fried rice which are worth three pice: total nine pice per diem. These men are constantly employed at the harvest time and at the time when the people repair or construct their houses. At other times their services are seldom in demand.

There are four families in this village who live by begging and by selling firewood which they bring from the jungle.

There are no artizans in this village.

The remaining five families* in the village follow other occupations than agriculture.

* 2 Napits (barbers).
2 Malakars (who make tinsel ornaments for idols).
1 Bania (keeps shop).

BISSESSAR BANERJEE,
Settlement Officer.

H. P.—Reg. No. 18590- 137—7-5-88.

CONFIDENTIAL.]

Dated Midnapore, the 18th April 1888.

From—The Settlement Officer of Bhita, Midnapore (through the Collector of Midnapore),

To—The Director of the Department of Land Records and Agriculture, Bengal.

WITH reference to your letter No. 116Agri., dated 23rd January 1888, I have the honour to report as follows.

In Bhita I selected mouzah Bhita, as it is an important village and typical in many respects of the others.

General condition.—The entire area of the village is 1,375 bigahs (according to 8 feet 2½ inch nal), of which the culturable area consists of single cropped lands, nothing but *amun* or late paddy crop being grown thereon. The quality of the soil is good. Facilities for irrigation are afforded by the Kalighai river which passes near the village and by means of a *bund*.

In other parts the failure of one crop is made up by growing other crops on the same lands but it is not practicable here. The failure of the single crop means heavy distress to the ryots.

The soil here is not fitted to grow any kind of garden produce. The ryots occasionally make attempts to grow bringals and other vegetables on lands adjoining their homesteads, but the outturn is not at all promising.

Cultivators.—There are 152 families in the village, of whom 126 are cultivators. The verage yield per bigah is 8 or 8½ maunds of paddy, each member of a family consuming 1½ maund a month.

Cost of cultivation per bigah is as follows :—

	Rs.	A.	P.
Seed grain	0	6	0
Labour for ploughing	1	0	0
Manure	0	12	0
Labour for reaping and harvesting	0	10	6
Rent, &c.	1	1	0
Total ...	3	13	6

The above cost is incurred when the ryot employs hired labour. But generally the ryots do the work themselves, and save the cost. The ryot engages other assistance temporarily when there is a great despatch, or he is prevented by illness or accident. It is usual for the ryot to pay in cash the rent and cesses : as he engages labour he repays it by his own labour. The manure he gets from his own cattle, and it is only when his own stock is wasted away that he purchases from those who can spare.

Daily labourers are employed at 5 pice per idem with 2 pice more for tobacco, &c., as refreshments. Labourers are also employed for the month on Re. 1 in cash and by giving them two meals per day and lodging, but this happens only in harvest time, when men from other villages sojourn on purpose: or, as in the case of the villagers, when in debt or in urgent need of money.

Produce of a bigah.—It has been stated above that the yield per bigah is 8 or 8½ maunds, which, counting at the present rate, is equivalent to Rs. 6 : add to this the price of straw Re. 1, or in all Rs. 7. The cost has been stated as Rs. 3-13-6, of which the ryot actually spends Rs. 2. Taking in all, I think the ryot's profit may be shown as Rs. 5 per bigah. But it is a rough approximate ; in times of scarcity the ryot's profit may be little or nothing.

Formerly it was a rule almost with all villagers to set apart a particular piece of ground as grazing ground for the cattle. But now, on account of the great demand for land, all bits are utilized and nothing left out. The cattle are not sufficiently fed ; the ryots pay them little or no attention. A great deterioration has taken place in the cattle.

There are 70 families in the village who till 1 to 2 bigahs of land, 23 who till 2 to 5 bigahs, 20 who till 5 to 10 bigahs, 13 who till 10 bigahs and upwards.

The ryots who cultivate less than 5 bigahs resort to various modes in raising their income. When the harvest period is over, the able-bodied visit distant places and villages and hire themselves as labourers. The general state of the peasantry is not very bad. It is true their diet is not very nourishing, but they can afford to have two meals a day. Generally they partake of boiled rice with salt to season it. They do not purchase fish, but the women of the family net in the Kalighai river, and thus try to enrich their repast.

The ryots who hold lands more than 5 bigahs comparatively live better, and can afford to pay for some of the necessaries of life.

Professional classes.—Ten families of manjis who live by fishing only.

Four families of weavers have small holdings of land.

Three families of barbers, in addition to shaving, cultivate small holdings.

Four families of dhobis, in addition to washing clothes, hire as labourers and cultivate small holdings.

The diet of the mangis is superior to the others; the men fish, while the women sell in the markets.

Weavers.—The weavers now attach only a secondary importance to weaving. Formerly they considered weaving their principal means of subsistence, and therefore devoted the best part of their time to it. Now they find only a limited number of customers for their goods after the importation of European piece-goods. Accordingly, they now try to find out some other employment which will prove more profitable. With the decline of their trade, they have taken to cultivating small areas. They weave in their spare moments. A weaver by working can thus earn Re. 1 per month. The women of the family do not weave, but they assist the male members in their weaving by preparing thread and keeping everything ready for them. The weavers now weave a very coarse kind of cloth, commonly worn by the poor people, as they find it cheaper and at the same time very lasting.

Beggars.—There are four families of Boisnabs in the village. They are idle people who resort to this mode of living, as it is the easiest, by taking advantage of the caste superstitions of the common men. Generally they receive handfuls of rice from the families they visit, but occasionally on festive and other occasions they receive more. They are not an unmixed evil, as their name implies they are Boisnabs, a sort of holy men. They perform the minstrelsy of the village, and try to instil into the villagers religious and moral teaching.

No. 234G, dated Midnapore, the 18th April 1888.

Memo by—C. Vowell, Esq., Collector of Midnapore.

Forwarded to the Director of the Department of Land Records and Agriculture, Bengal.

W. LeB.—Reg. No. 1860C—137—3-5-88.

CONFIDENTIAL.]

Dated Comillah, the 24th March 1888.

From—The Settlement Deputy Collector of Jawar Balnakandi, Tipperah,

To—The Director of the Department of Land Records and Agriculture, Calcutta (through the Collector of Tipperah).

WITH reference to your letter No. 119, dated 23rd July 1887, calling on me to make certain enquiries in the manner suggested by you regarding the actual condition of the lower classes of the population, especially in the agricultural tracts, I have the honour to submit the following report on the result of my enquiries.

2. As Jawar Balnakandi is in the district of Mymensing, I selected Nabipur Hossentala, a village in pergunnah Bardakhat, thana Muradnagar, as the typical village to be reported about. I have been engaged on settlement duties under the Tenancy Act in this village, and thus I have been able to collect the necessary statistical information without attracting any special attention of the villagers or the public in general as desired by Government.

3. There are 213 families, consisting of 1,035 persons, in Nabipur Hossentala. I have divided these families into 8 classes according to their conditions and circumstances as shown in a tabular statement marked A hereto annexed.

4. The persons shown in classes III and VI, or 9·8 per cent. of the population of the village, are in a prosperous condition. What I mean to say is that these persons, after defraying all expenses, including those attendant on marriage and other social ceremonies, have it in their power to lay by some money. This I say from my personal observation.

5. Class I includes the persons who live entirely on cultivation. Their aggregate income is sufficient to meet their requirements. They can also make some saving out of their agricultural profits. Hence I do not enter into the details of the income and expenditure of this class of people. The mode of living and expenditure, &c., described at length below with regard to class II apply in respect of this class.

6. Class II shows 44 families, consisting of 206 persons, or about 20 per cent. of the entire population, who are supported by the wages of labour and small profits of their holdings. Each family holds on an average 1 acre 1 rood 5 poles and 23 yards of land, including homestead, one acre producing on an average 18 maunds of paddy or about 13 maunds of rice; some of the arable lands in this village yield two crops, viz. *aus* or *amun* and winter crops. The earning of each working member in this class is Rs. 4-4 a month; sometimes they get their food from those they serve, but the money payment in such case is proportionately small. They do not work for the whole month together, as they have to look after their own cultivation and other business. On an average they work on wages for 17 days in a month. Their wages on labour, together with their produce of small holdings, can support a family consisting on the average of five persons including boys and girls. Their arable lands generally produce food-grains, chillies and pulses, which this class of people can hardly sell, but which they keep for their own consumption. The rice produced in their own land can meet their requirements for about 4½ months of a year on the average.

(*a*). The homestead lands supply their vegetables, fruits and spices, such as onions, garlic and coriander, &c., which they partly sell. The income on this account can be estimated at Rs. 3 a year. They also sell milk, except on the occasion of marriage or other social ceremonies, or when they like to indulge in the luxury of a dish made by it. The major portion of this class of people are Mahomedans, who keep poultry, which they partly sell and partly consume in their own kitchen, generally on the occasion of social ceremonies. This I have not taken into account, as there are some *Hindu* families in this class. These persons do not generally purchase fish, which are almost always caught in the neighbouring bheels, rivers, canals and tanks. They also do not purchase pulses, chillies, tamarind, vegetables and fruits. They also do not purchase firewood. They generally grow jungly trees, specially *mandars*, round about their homestead. This, together with the straw they get, serves as fuel. When firewood can be had from the neighbouring jungles, they sell the straw. They are also not required to pay anything for washing their clothes, which duty devolves on the women of the family. They are not to pay wages of labour for erecting or repairing their houses. This they perform themselves with the labour of their neighbour in exchange.

(*b*). Several persons of this class go in a company to the neighbouring hills, wherefrom they get the sunngrass, bamboos, and canes at a nominal cost for erection or repairs of their houses. The excess quantity of materials is sometimes sold by them to meet the expenditure incurred by them on this or any other account. The well-to-do cultivator has generally four huts, viz., one dwelling-house with one roofed shed attached to it for husking grains, one cookshed, one cowshed, and to the south an extra spare house to receive guests and relations. The poor family holds only one dwelling-house and a cowshed.

(*c*). They are only to pay rents at an average of Rs. 2 per acre of arable land, and to purchase food-grains for about 7½ months a year, as well as their clothes, oil and salt, betel, betelnuts and gur; besides these, they are to incur the expenses of marriage and other social ceremonies.

(*d*). This class of people use very small quantity of oil for lighting; they manufacture oil at home from castor and other seeds. The expenditure therefore on this item is very insignificant. Their expenses under the item of clothes are not much, because they use country made clothes which are more lasting. The Manchester or Bombay machine-made *dhuties* and *saries* are a luxury to them. In social ceremonies they incur small additional expenditure, because they are not required to purchase either milk, meat or fish as stated above. The expenditure of their marriage does not exceed from Rs. 20 to Rs. 26; on an occasion like this, they generally borrow money to meet the expenses. This they gradually liquidate from the savings they make; frequently they offer their services to their creditors in liquidation of their debts.

(*e*). The ornaments of the women of this class are very few, such as silver anklets, silver *balas* used on hands, silver *hasli* for the neck, *charies* made of earth mixed with lac, and golden nose-ring or *nackful*, golden *nath* being used very rarely. The aggregate expenditure on this item does not exceed Rs. 16; some of these ornaments, which are very lasting, are inherited and some are purchased. These ornaments they generally use on the occasion of social ceremonies and marriages as well as at the time of going to their relatives. They have no boxes or chests, but they keep their ornaments and money in earthen handies.

(*f*). It is only in the years of drought, inundation, &c., that this class of people are required to borrow money and suffer from want of food. The duties of the women are to spin thread, to look after cattle, winnowing and husking paddy, washing clothes, preparing food for family, and also doing other indoor work. The boys and girls principally look after cattle and watch the crops of the fields to prevent the cattle trespassing upon them. All the members of the family more or less contribute towards their maintenance in the shape of wages, in cash or in labour. A Statement B, showing the estimated annual receipt and expenditure of this class of people, is appended.

Class IV comprises the people who live on the wages of labour alone. They generally live from hand to mouth. Their earnings on the average amount from Rs. 5 to Rs. 6 a month. There are only nine families under this class, each consisting on an average 3·7 persons including boys and girls. They have no lands other than their homesteads, the advantages derived from which have been described above. The aggregate income of this class of people is altogether little less than that of class II. The expenditure and the mode of living of both the classes are equal, but they cannot make any saving. This class of people also suffer in abnormal years, when they do not get work.

I have shown such of the professional men in class VII who suffer from insufficiency of food. This class includes the barbers and the drummers, &c. There are 12 families of this class, consisting of 59 persons, including children, or 5·7 per cent. of the entire population.

In my capacity as Manager of Court of Wards and Government Estates, I have had ample opportunities of studying the condition of almost all orders of people. I can safely say that altogether 10 per cent. of the entire population suffer from the insufficiency of food. My views have been corroborated by the enquiries I have made on this occasion.

I have generally remarked that, firstly, a few professional men, specially the barbers, weavers, washermen, fishermen, and sweepers, and, secondly, the beggars, are the greater sufferers. The principal reason of their suffering is that they stick to the income of their own profession only and feel it a degradation to accept service or follow any other business. The caste prejudice is at the bottom. This cannot be remedied by legislation, as long as the social status of the country is not improved.

Class VIII.—The beggars as a class must exist in the country, but there is no reason why the professional beggars stick to begging instead of entering into business.

No. 66G—XIV-3, dated Comillah, the 14th April 1888.

Memo.—By the Collector of Tipperah.

This has been prepared under my superintendence; the form of figurative statement was supplied by me, and I concur generally in the conclusions arrived at by the Settlement Deputy Collector. The foundation, confined as it is to a single village, is, however, in my opinion, not broad enough to have any absolutely reliable conclusions based on it.

Statement A.

Mouzah Nabipur Hussentala, Pergunnah Bardakhat.

Class of people.	Applicable to all classes. Number of families. (1)	Population. (2)	Average number in each family. (3)	Aggregate number of working members in population. (4)	Average number of working members in each family. (5)	Applicable to first three classes. Aggregate area of holdings sub-divided into (6) Rice land.	Betel garden.	Jute land.	Other kind of land.	Total.	Average area of each holding sub-divided into (7) Rice.	Betel.	Jute.	Other kinds.	Total.	Aggregate quantity of produce of holdings from (8) Rice.	Betel.	Jute.
						Acres.				Acres.						Mds.		
1. Cultivators, pure and simple.	115	574	4·9	151	1·3	374	...	...	...	374	3·2	...	...	...	3·2	5,006	...	...
2. People supported partly by agriculture and partly by wages of labour.	44	206	4·6	54	1·2	41	...	...	...	41	·93	...	...	...	·93	571	...	...
3. People supported partly by agriculture and partly by trade or profession.	17	97	5·7	29	1·7	17	...	...	...	17	1	...	...	...	1	259	...	...
4. Day labourers for hire only who have no land	9	34	3·7	9	1	......	...	...	...	......	...	...	...	...	...	...	...	...
5. Artisans, pure and simple, who have no land.	...	...	...		...	......	...	...	...	......	...	...	...	...	...	...	...	...
6. People who subsist only by trade or profession (except artizans, barbers, &c.)	1	5	5	1	1	......	...	...	...	......	...	...	...	...	...	...	...	...
7. Barbers, washermen, drummers and other such classes who have no land.	12	59	4·9	16	1·3	......	...	...	...	......	...	...	...	...	...	...	...	...
8. Beggars	15	60	4	...	...	......		...	...	......	...	...	...	...	...	...	...	...
	213	1,035																

Class of people.	Average produce per holding in rice, betel, jute, &c., in a year. (9)	Value of produce per holding in a year. (10)	Cost of production per holding. (11)	Annual rent of land, including homestead. (12)	Balance available per family for support for a year. (13)	Balance available per head for support for a year. (14)	Applicable to classes 2, 3, 4, 5 and 7. Aggregate earnings per year. (15)	Average earnings per family per year. (16)	Earnings available per head for a year. (17)	Total of columns 14 and 17. (18)	Remarks. Adult males.	Adult females.	Boys.	Girl.	Total.
	Mds	Rs. A.	Rs. A. P.	Rs. A. P.	Rs. A. P.	Rs. A. P.	Rs. A.	Rs. A. P.	Rs. A. P.	Rs. A. P.					
1. Cultivators, pure and simple.	44·3 of rice.	Rice ... 66 0 Other produce, 80 0 146 0	22 0 0	7 9 2	116 6 10	23 13 2	......	......	......	23 12 2	151	183	124	116	575
2. People supported partly by agriculture and partly by wages of labour.	12·9 of rice.	Rice ... 16 0 Other produce, 44 0 62 0	Hire of cattle and plough Rs. 8.	5 14 7	52 1 8	11 5 2	2,831 3	64 12 9	14 1 4	25 6 6	54	63	51	38	206
3. People supported partly by agriculture and partly by trade or profession.	15·2 of rice.	Rice ... 22 8 Other produce, 7 8 30 0	6 6 0	5 10 0	20 6 0	5 9 2	7,950 0	467 10 4	52 0 6	85 10 10	29	33	20	15	97
4. Day labourers for hire only who have no land	......	......	......	......	......	......	594 0	66 0 0	17 12 4	......	7	15	5	7	34
5. Artisans, pure and simple, who have no land.	......	......	......	......	......	......	......	......	......	......	......	......	...	...	...
6. People who subsist only by trade or profession (except artizans, barbers, &c.)	......	......	......	......	......	......	300 0	300 0 0	60 0 0	60 0 0	1	2	2	...	5
7. Barbers, washermen, drummers and other such classes who have no land.	......		......	......	......	......	768 0	64 0 0	13 1 0	13 1 0	16	17	11	15	59
8. Beggars	......	......	......	......	......	......	......	......	......	......	11	22	14	13	60
											269	335	277	204	1,035

KALI SANKER SEN,
Settlement Deputy Collector.

Explanatory notes on the Statement marked A.

(*a*).—The figures in column 6(*a*) include the lands which yield two crops.

(*b*).—The homestead lands have not been shown in this statement: all the residents, including beggars, have homestead lands more or less. Each family holds one-third of an acre on the average.

(*c*).—The figures shown against heading "other produce" in column 10 represent the value of winter crops as well as of the vegetables, fruits, and other products grown in the homestead and the adjoining lands or *virat bhiti*.

(*d*).—*Column* 11.—In calculating the cost of production, the labour of the cultivators themselves has not been taken into consideration, but the cost of hired labour and the wear and tear of agricultural implements of cattle have been taken into account.

(*e*).—*Column* 11, *Heading* 3.—This class of people have no cattle or agricultural implement, for they do not cultivate their lands themselves, but let them out on the barga system, that is, for half the produce of the lands; hence the value of the cultivator's share of the produce has been shown as cost of production.

(*f*).—*Column* 12.—The rents shown here also include the jama of homestead lands.

(*g*).—*Column* 15, *Headings* 3 *and* 6.—The figures in this column represent the profits of trade, the interest derived from money lent, and the salaries or part profit awarded as remuneration for conducting commercial business.

KALI SANKER SEN,
Deputy Collector.

The 10*th April* 1888.

B.

Statement showing the details of estimated receipt and expenditure of the family in Class II consisting on the average of 4·6 persons, including children, for 1 year.

RECEIPT.

	Rs.	A.	P.	
Wages of earning member per family amount to Rs. 4-4 a month, or annually	64	12	9	
18 Maunds paddy producing 12 maunds of rice, at Rs. 1-8 per maund ...	18	0	0	
Vegetables	24	0	0	Other produce as shown in column 10, heading 2.
Pulses	6	0	0	
Fruits, viz., plantains, jack, &c.	5	0	0	
Straw	4	0	0	
Chillies	2	0	0	
Spices, including onions ...	1	0	0	
Fish	6	0	0	
Milk	12	0	0	
Firewood and cow-dung ...	10	0	0	
Sale proceeds of live-stock	5	0	0	
Bamboos, canes, &c. ...	10	0	0	
	167	12	9	

EXPENDITURE.

	Rs.	A.	P.
Rice 2 maunds 30 seers per month, at Rs. 1-8 per maund for 12 months ...	49	8	0
Fish	12	0	0
Vegetables	10	0	0
Fruits	1	0	0
Milk	6	0	0
Pulses	8	0	0
Oil	1	0	0
Salt	3	0	0
Tobacco	3	0	0
Betel	2	0	0
Chillies	2	4	0
Tamarind	0	4	0
Spices	1	0	0
Firewood	10	0	0
Gur	1	8	0
Earthen plates, &c. ...	1	0	0
Brass utensils	2	0	0
Cloth	15	0	0
Bedding	1	0	0
Rent and cess	8	0	9
Cost of productions ...	6	0	0
Cost of ornaments based on the average of 8 years ...	2	0	0
Cost of marriage based on the average of 10 years ...	6	0	0
Repairing houses ...	10	0	0
Medicine and diet of patients	1	0	0
Miscellaneous expenses, consisting of looking-glass, comb, red-powder, &c. ...	1	0	0
Annual festivals ...	3	0	0
	157	1	0

KALI SANKER SEN,
Deputy Collector.

W. LeB.—Reg. No. 1861C—137—8-5-88.

CONFIDENTIAL.]

No. 57—VII-1G, dated Noakhally, the 14th April 1888.

From—ANUNDORAM BOROOAH, Esq., Offg. Collector of Noakhally,
To—The Commissioner of the Chittagong Division.

WITH reference to your No. 794GC—VII-56, dated 20th December 1887, I have the honour to state that the people of this district are mainly, probably 90 per cent., agriculturists, and their condition appears to me to be much better than the condition of the same class in Behar and Western Bengal. Any casual observer will notice that they are comparatively well-fed, well-dressed, and well-housed. Land is very fertile, producing from 15 to 16 maunds per *kani*. Munshi Nandji puts the average produce of Nulchira at 45 maunds, but the ryots there often get as much as 60 maunds. The demand for land is not great, as outsiders have a dread of this district and immigration is unknown. The cost of production is small. Munshi Nandji puts it down at Rs. 17 per *kani*, and my enquiries elsewhere showed he was right. It, however, includes labour, which in the case of the poorer ryots is done by themselves. There is, therefore, a very large margin of profit for ryots, specially where they do not sublet. At Badoo, a Government estate, the rate is 10 annas per bigah, but I find that some of the actual cultivators pay to howladars as much as Rs. 12 per *kani*, and yet there is a net profit of Rs. 16 per year in paddy alone, taking the average yield as 45 maunds.

2. Agricultural labourers do not exist as a separate class; but the poorer ryots work for others during the two agricultural seasons, lasting about four months in all. They earn 4 to 5 annas in this work per day, besides a rich meal at mid-day. This is the custom of the district, and men will not work if they are not well-fed on thire. This also goes to show that the condition of the ryots is not at all bad.

3. The number of beggars does not seem to exceed 500 in the whole district. The men, women, and children who regularly come to take alms from me number about 150. In the mofussil, in my various camps, they seldom exceed 20. Some of these, however, have their own lands and come to beg, because they are professional *Fakirs* and *Bairagees*. The Bairagees by birth, however, include some well-to-do men, such as money-lenders and rich priests who never beg.

4. The condition of weavers has much deteriorated. But most of them have taken to cultivation, and their physique compares favourably with that of the same class in Burdwan and Moorshedabad.

5. It is difficult to ascertain how far the ryots are indebted, as they do not like to disclose their affairs. The number of simple bonds registered during the last five years are as follows:—

1883-84	1,530
1884-85	1,796
1885-86	2,735
1886-87	2,795
1887-88	2,680

But it is not known how many of these refer to ryots and how many to other classes.

6. I may, however, note that during my whole service in this district, comprising a period of about three years, I have noticed only two cases where men have gone to jail in default of payment of fine where fine was alone inflicted.

7. The Superintendent of the Jail gives as opinion that convicts gain in weight after admission. This is, however, not quite correct. There are at present 56 convicts in the jail, and the jailor reports that 28 only have gained some weight.

8. Copies of reports received from the Nulchira Officer, the Sub-divisional Magistrate, the Ward's Manager, and the Jail Superintendent are submitted for your information.

No. 58VII—1G, dated Noakhally, the 14th April 1888.

Memo. by—ANUNDORAM BOROOAH, Esq., Officiating Collector of Noakhally.

COPY, with copy of the report of Munshi Nandji, forwarded to the Director of Land Records, with reference to his No. 729Agri., dated 5th April 1888.

Dated Camp Noagan, the 3rd April 1888.

From—MUNSHI NANDJI, Settlement Officer, Nulchira Estate,
To—The Collector of Noakhally.

WITH reference to the Director of the Department of Land Records and Agricultures' No. 108, dated the 23rd January 1888, received with your No. 75A, dated the 23rd February 1888, I have the honour to submit the report therein called for, regarding the actual condition of the lower classes of the population of the Government Estate of Chur Nulchira, of which the settlement was completed by me under Chapter X of the Bengal Tenancy Act in February last.

2. *Preliminary.*—The letter under reply having reached me after I had left your district to join my present appointment as Settlement Officer of Dubalhati Estates in Rajshahye, I have

had no opportunity afforded me to make the requisite enquiries in the manner suggested. I had, however, compiled the necessary information from my settlement completion report, upplemented with such facts as came within my knowledge during the course of the settlement operations.

3. *General description of the tract.*—Nulchira contains an area of 18,211 acres, and a total population as ascertained by the census of 1881 of 3,500 souls. It is some 10 miles to the north of the Bay of Bengal, and presents a flat and open surface. It is laid out for the most part in well cultivated rice fields.

4. *Settlement.*—Nulchira became the property of Government in 1837 under the operation of Regulation XI of 1825. It was settled in two halves with two *meadi* talukdars for a term of 30 years. The settlement fell in 1869 and the re-settlement becoming necessary, the chur was measured under Regulation VII of 1822. But owing to a variety of causes, which need not be noticed here, the re-settlement could not have been brought to a close. It was therefore decided to bring this long-pending settlement to a conclusion according to the new procedure introduced by the Bengal Tenancy Act. Accordingly a survey has been made and a record of rights of the tenants prepared and fair rent settled under that Act.

5. According to the present measurement 72 per cent. of the whole chur is cultivated and 11 per cent. is unfit for cultivation. The density of population being 125 per square mile, there is still much more for extension of cultivation.

6. *Classification of tenants.*—At the time of preparation of the record of rights it was found that there were four classes of tenants, viz. howladars, nim-howladars, ryots and jotedars. The howladars held transferable tenures under the settlement-holders and the nim-howladars held transferable tenures under the howladars. Under the last-mentioned two classes, there were ryots and jotedars.

7. The settlement-holders had created howlas covering the whole area of the chur. The number of such howlas was 335, of which 169 were recorded as tenures and 166 as the holdings of privileged ryots. The number of nim-howlas were 93, of which eight were recorded as under-tenures and the rest as ryoti holdings.

8. The 169 howla tenures, comprising an area of 43,080 bigahs, were held by 1,409 howladars, the average area of the tenure of each howladar being 31 bigahs. The following is the classification of holdings of subordinate tenants under the howla tenures :—

Number.	Classification of tenants.	Number of tenants.	Number of holdings.	Area of holdings in bigahs.	Average area of the holding of each tenant.
1	Under-tenure holder	22	8	1,094	50 bigahs.
2	Settled ryot	366	260	5,027	14 „
3	Non-occupancy ryot	612	516	7,543	12 „

9. The number of howladars who were recorded as privileged ryots was 529, of whom 501 were possessed of right of occupancy and 28 had not acquired such right. The number of their holdings was 155 and 11 respectively, the average area of the holding of a ryot howladar being 15 bigahs.

10. The number of under-ryots in Nulchira was 149, of whom 126 cultivated land under the ryot howladar and 23 under ordinary ryots. The number of their holdings was 108, containing an area of 1,204 bigahs ; so the average area of an under-ryot's holding amounted to 8 bigahs.

11. The jotedars had no right to record. They held land from year to year at a rent varying according to the prospect of the season. The jotedars are in fact for the most part nomads, who are in the land one year and away the next. Their cultivation expands and contracts with the rise and fall of the price of rice. Such of the jotedars, however, as had settled on the land had their holdings and the rents recorded in the settlement proceedings.

12. *Local standard of measurement.*—The local measure by which rent is paid is the *kani*. But the size of the *kani* varies according to the number of inches in the cubit. The *kani* is measured by a *nul* of 16 cubits, the sides of the *kani* being 12 *nuls* and the ends 10. The ryoti *kani* is equal to 69,120 square feet or 4-16 standard bigahs when the length of the cubit is 18 inches. But the howladar in Nulchira is allowed a cubit of 20¾ inches, and this increase in the cubit makes the *kani* 91,632 square feet or 6-7-9 standard bigahs.

13. *Existing rent as ascertained by the Settlement Officer.*—The howladars held under leases from the settlement-holders at a uniform rate of Rs. 4-2 per *kani* or 9·3 annas per standard bigah after certain deduction on account of *matton* and *ailaton*. The nim-howladars' rates varied from Rs. 5 to Rs. 4-8 per *kani*, the average rate per bigah being 12 annas. The rate payable by the cultivating ryots was Rs. 6 per *kani* or Rs. 1-4 per standard bigah. But these rates, it must be remembered, were for cultivated or *hasil* land only, the culturable and unculturable land being held by the howladars and their subordinate tenants without payment of any rent.

14. *Fair rent fixed by the Settement Officer.*—But in settling fair and equitable rent under section 104, clause (2) of the Tenancy Act, not only the above rates were raised but a

fair and equitable rent was assessed on the culturable land, the *nalaik* or land unfit for cultivation being only exempted from assessment.

15. The lands in possession of those howldars who are recognised as tenure-holders were assessed at the full cultivating rates, *i.e.*, Rs. 1-4 per bigah for *hasil* land, 4 annas per bigah for culturable land known as *laikabad*, *sanat patit* and *jungle*, and 1 anna per bigah for *molongchur* or salted land and included in the gross rents. They were allowed a profit of 40 per cent. on the balance which remained after deducting from the gross rents collection expenses at 10 per cent.; or in other words, they were allowed 46 per cent. on the gross rents. To put the case more clearly, the howladari rate was raised from 9·3 annas to 10·9¾ annas per standard bigah, and a fair and equitable rent at the rates abovementioned was assessed on the culturable area which the howladars claimed to hold rent-free.

16. The rent of the howladar reduced to the status of a privileged ryot was raised from 9·3 annas to 12 annas per standard bigah, and the culturable land was assessed at the rates before mentioned.

17. The rent of the nim-howladars recognized as under-tenure holders was settled in the same way as the rent of the howladars, except that the former was allowed a profit of 25 per cent. besides 5 per cent. as collection expenses, or 28¾ per cent. on the gross rents. Thus the rent of the nim-howladar under-tenure holder was raised from 12 annas to 14¾ annas per bigah for *hasil* land, the culturable land being assessed at the said rates.

18. The present rent paid by the occupancy and non-occupancy ryots at the rate of Rs. 6 per *kani* or Rs. 1-4 per bigah for *hasil* land was held to be fair and equitable, as there was no grounds for its enhancement. But the culturable lands were assessed at the same rates as those abovementioned.

19. Information regarding the expenses of cultivation, average produce per bigah, price of food-grains, &c., has been given in my completion report.

20. *Cost of cultivation.*—As might be expected, the tenants of the estates would not give correct information on the above points lest it would lead to an enhancement of their rent. The most intelligent of them would give figures which were misleading. But during my long stay there, I took every opportunity to question such of the illiterate and ignorant peasants as would give an unvarnished statement of facts. It was from the statement of such persons, and from my personal enquiry into the soil and capabilities of the land, that the total cost of cultivation of one howladari *kani* was ascertained as follows:—

	Rs.	A.	P.
10 Ploughings, at 2 ploughs per rupee	5	0	0
1 Maund of seed	1	0	0
10 Labourers, at 3 per rupee for transplanting... ...	3	5	3
Diet for ditto	1	4	0
3 Labourers, at 3 per rupee for weeding	1	0	0
Diet for ditto	0	4	6
10 Labourers, at 3 per rupee for cutting	3	5	3
Diet for ditto	1	0	0
2 Labourers for thrashing, with diet	0	13	0
Total	17	0	0

21. The process of weeding is nominally resorted to in Nulchira, and therefore Rs. 1-4 is quite sufficient for the weeding of one *kani* of land.

22. The difference of diet between the labourers employed in transplanting paddy and those employed in weeding, cutting, &c., is due to the fact that the price of paddy rises as usual during the transplanting season and falls as soon as *aus* paddy is in the market when labour is required for weeding, cutting, &c. The labour becomes very cheap during the harvesting time when four or five coolies can be had for a rupee. So Rs. 17 is the maximum cost of cultivation for one howladari *kani*. But as the howladari *kani* is equal to 6*b.* 7*k.* 9*ch.*, the cost of cultivation of one standard bigah is Rs. 2-10-8. Accordingly the cost of cultivation of one ryoti *kani* which contains 4-16 standard bigahs is Rs. 12-12-9.

23. *Average produce.*—The average produce of one howladari *kani* in Nulchira may be safely estimated at 45 maunds, or 7 maunds (fraction omitted) per standard bigah, the average produce per ryoti *kani* being 34 maunds.

24. *Price of paddy.*—As regards the prevailing market value of paddy for the last 20 years, there are no reliable data upon which to base a correct conclusion. It is certain, however, that within the last 20 years the maximum value of a maund of paddy was not above Rs. 2 and the minimum value below Re. 1; so taking the average price to be the mean of the two, Rs. 1-8 would appear to be the market value of 1 maund of paddy. But to make the calculation indisputably accurate, I would take the lowest market value, *i. e.*, Re. 1 per maund. So the price of the average produce of one ryoti *kani* (34 maunds) amounts to Rs. 34. Deducting from this sum Rs. 12-12-9 on account of the cost of cultivation and Rs. 6 as rent, the balance is Rs. 15-3-3, which would be the net profit of the cultivator.

25. *Natural calamities.*—But the tenants contended that they were entitled to some consideration on account of the damage caused to the crops by blight, flood, &c. Although the crops in some places are sometimes attacked and injured by insects, but the injury caused does not affect the general harvest and may be left out of account. But the lands

are flooded by salt water inflicting sometimes considerable damage to the crops. I made particular enquiry into this matter and ascertained that such inundations as caused damage to crops were few and far between. Of course at every full and new moon, especially at the time of equinox, there is a tidal wave (*juar*) for successive days, which causes no damage to crops except in exceptional years when the south-west gale blows strongly.

26. During the late cyclone in the Bay (26th of May) a portion of Nulchira was submerged. I was in camp at Nulchira at that time, and I sailed over a portion of the chur in a boat to form an idea of the damage complained of. It appeared that the *aus* crop was damaged to some extent. But a heavy shower soon improved the prospect and the *amun* crop has been a bumper one this year.

27. It is true that the storm-wave of 1876 was very disastrous in its effects and caused much loss to life and property. But it is admitted that such a cyclone has not occurred within the last 50 years. It appeared, however, from enquiry that such salt water inundation as caused damage to the crops occurred at an interval of five or six years, and that the cultivators were entitled to some consideration on that account. Assuming therefore that the cultivators lose one year's crops every six years, they are entitled to a remission of one year's rent, *i. e.*, Rs. 6, and to recover Rs. 12-12-9, the cost of cultivation, total Rs. 18-12-9, which being divided by 6, the quotient is Rs. 3-2-1½, which represents approximately the annual loss sustained by them. This amount should be set off against the estimated annual profit of Rs. 15-3-3; the balance is Rs. 12-1-2½ or 12 in round number.

28. *Profit.*—It will be thus seen that the margin of profit left to the ryots is double the amount of rent they pay to their landlords, and this is no doubt a very fair remuneration for their toil, trouble and outlay. But their profit does not end here. Besides the paddy, the ryots obtain from the low lands a rotation of crop of pulses (*khesari, moong* and *kalai*) and from high lands linseed and chillies, not to speak of the country vegetables, such as *begoon*, gourds, pumpkins, cucumbers, &c., which are brought for sale in the local market. Then, both the ryots and howladars have another source of income from cocoanuts, tal-palms, date-palms, plantains, &c., which are grown around the homestead of every tenant, and which supply the local demand.

29. *Soil.*—The rich alluvial soils of Nulchira are cultivated with much less labour than stiffer soils of the plain, and yield a bumper crop except in exceptional years. Irrigation is not generally practised, and the rains which begin early in May and last till about October provide all the water that the crops need.

30. *Condition of the cultivators.*—The condition of the tenants is now prosperous. They are seldom in debt. The majority of them are resident cultivators and every one, even the poorest, possesses some land. A howladar with a farm of 31 bigahs (10 acres) is regarded as a substantial man, and there can be no doubt that this area would be sufficient for the comfortable maintenance of a cultivator with a small family. The average size of a holding is not smaller than 8 bigahs (about 3 acres), as shown in paragraph 10 above, and a peasant with this area is, no doubt, well off. The rent is low, the soil is rich, and the outturn far exceeds the local consumption.

31. The area under rice crop according to the recent measurement is 36,844 bigahs. Taking the average produce of 1 bigah to be 7 maunds as stated in paragraph 23, the total yield of paddy would be 2,57,908 maunds. After making deduction on account of wastage and for seed grain, there remains 2,42,000 maunds for food. The population according to the census of 1881 being 3,500 persons, a local consumption at the rate of 12 maunds per head would amount to 42,000 maunds, leaving a surplus of 2,00,000 maunds of paddy (or 1,00,000 maunds of rice) for export.

32. As a rule the tenant obtains from his field almost all that he requires. The food of an ordinary cultivator is composed of rice, *khisari dál*, vegetables and fish, and these he has not to import from other places.

33. Then the houses of the tenants, their clothing and their general unwillingness to work as day labourers in spite of the high wages offered, speak of their general prosperity.

34. *Houses.*—They live in hamlets, each hamlet consisting of two or more houses which are built (thatch and matting) on a slightly raised platform composed of earth thrown up from the surrounding ditches. Each hamlet is surrounded by trees and undergrowth. The number of houses according to the census returns of 1881 is 700, or 25 houses per square mile.

35. *Dress and ornament.*—The dress of a well-to-do tenant consists of a *dhuti*, a *chadar*, and a skull cap. The clothing of the poorer class is of a coarse description. The Mahomedans seldom use *chadar* and their *dhuti* is of a small size. Both the Hindus and Mahomedan women wear *saries* or large cloths covering the whole body. The ornaments worn by the women of well-to-do cultivators are silver bracelets, silver anklets, gold ear-rings and silver necklace.

36. *Furniture.*—The furniture in the house of an ordinary cultivator consists of a *lota* (brass jug), a *thala* (brass plate), a *budna* (copper water-pot used especially by Mahomedans), a *bati* (brass cup), a mat or two (*hugla*), some baskets and stools (made of bamboo), some coarse quilts for night covering, one or two earthen pots (*kulsis*) and a few earthen cooking vessels.

37. *Day labourers.*—There are no landless day labourers in Nulchira. As I have stated above, every man holds or possesses a share in a piece of land sufficient to prevent his being compelled to work as a day labourer for daily wages. The women and children are seldom employed in the fields. The women do all the household work, and the children of petty cultivators are employed in tending cattle.

38. *Wages.*—The cultivators employ during the cultivating season a considerable number of coolies who go there from Noakhally, Chittagong, and other places to labour for daily wages. Wages have doubled during the last 25 years, and the present wages range from 4 annas to 5 annas each per day.

39. *Weavers and artisans.*—There are no weavers. But there are goldsmiths and black-smiths who do not cultivate land, but who earn enough from their trade for support. Their average daily wage is 8 annas each. There is no other class of skilled labourers.

40. *Persons dependant on charity.*—The few Bairagees (about 10 in number) that are to be found in Nulchira fall within the category of persons who depend upon charity. But some of them have an additional source of income from the cultivation of small holdings, while others who have no connection with land obtain enough by begging to supply their wants. In fact, they have all their daily requirements supplied, and look as healthy as a well-to-do cultivator. But their number is so small that they may be left out of account.

41. *Conclusion.*—From the statistics given above, it may be said that no proportion of the agricultural population of Nulchira is dependant on charity, or on wages of labour, and that no body suffers from a daily insufficiency of food at present.

CONFIDENTIAL.]

No. 84G, dated Dinagpore, the 22nd April 1888.

From—C. R. MARINDIN, Esq., Collector of Dinagepore,
To—The Director of Land Records and Agriculture, Bengal.

WITH reference to your No. 129Agri, dated the 23rd January 1888, I have the honour to forward the reports received from the Settlement Officers in original. A copy of my report to the Commissioner will follow. The return of the reports is requested when done with.

No. 8, dated Camp Ranisankail, the 7th April 1888.

From—BABOO HARIS CHUNDER RAI, Settlement Officer, Maldwar Estate,
To—The Collector of Dinagepore.

WITH reference to No. 110, dated the 23rd January 1888, from the Director of Land Records and Agriculture, Bengal, and your No. 1129C.R.G., dated 24th February last, on the subject of the lower classes of population, I have the honour to submit the following report regarding pergunnah Maldwar, within the jurisdiction of thana Ranisankail.

2. Agreeably to your requisition, I have made detailed enquiries in some villages and sporadic ones in others, in the manner suggested by you, and have embodied the result thereof in the form of a tabular statement, which I beg to submit herewith.

3. Statement I contains the result of the detailed enquiries in villages Shial Losh and Suagram. In village Shial Losh there are altogether 62 inhabitants, of which 35 are male adults and 19 female adults, and 8 minors under 12 years of age. All these adults are capable of work.

4. Of the male adults 4 are khodkasht ryots, and 9 under-ryots. There are no agricultural labourers, artizans, or professional beggars in the village. The khodkasht ryots have each of them adequate lands for cultivation, and being the original settlers of the soil, and having had the pick of the lands, are in a well-to-do position now. They take meal thrice a day, and, like other well-to-do ryots, eat rice, dal (pulse), vegetable, fish, &c. They have brass utensils in addition to earthen pots. They dress themselves with *dhuties* and *chuddurs*. Their females wear a sort of country-made coarse cloth of thicker stuff called *kapa*, *nimshati*, *choutara* and *dhrua*. Some of them have silver and gold ornaments of small value. They have good and neat small houses of thatching-grass and bamboo. Almost all of them have cattle. Their females do not work for their livelihood, but for their own household and cultivation work. Except for debt, which they incur to meet their marriage expenses, which, under the social custom, include a capital sum paid by the bridegroom or his guardian to the bride's father and mother, they would have been in a very well-to-do condition.

5. These remarks, *mutatis mutandis*, apply to the ryots of Suagram, where there are 14 male adults, 13 female adults, and 13 children. These villages become unhealthy during Bhadra, corresponding with September and October, from the effects of the incessant rains, and the people fall victims to a sort of fever peculiar to this part of the district. The men do not relish English medicine, but, out of ignorance and credulity, rely on the supposed physical powers, called *mahiti*, of a sort of people acquainted with the mysteries of the thing. They would not go to consult a physician until and unless the *mahiti* fails. They have to expend a small sum in invoking *mahitis*.

6. Next to the cultivators come in social condition the agricultural labourers, who are paid in money and partly in kind. Sometimes they are allowed food, clothes and lodging. When paid in money only, an agricultural labourer will get three annas a day; but when supplied with food, lodging, and clothes, will be paid at the rate of one anna three pies per diem. Peculiar to this part of the country, the agricultural labourers do frequently hold a certain area of land, which is always reserved for staple crops—here the paddy.

7. It is true that, unlike the cultivators, this class of people cannot afford to use brass utensils instead of cheap pottery, or buy ornaments for their wives. But the food they eat, the clothes they wear, the houses in which they live, are similar to those of the cultivators. They do also undergo the same sort of expenses on account of marriage and other social ceremonies: *e.g.*, funeral expenses as their fellow brethren. The only prominent distinction observable is their large indebtedness to mahajans, who advance money on an exorbitant rate of interest, and realise the amount with interest in cash and grain generally after the harvest is gathered, thus bringing them back to their former state of misery and indebtedness. The females of these people are not allowed to work for hire; but they may be said to eke out to a certain extent their means by working at home. During the leisure hours they prepare rice from paddy which the males sell in the bazar, deriving as profit three annas in the rupee. One adult female on the average will, besides attending to household expenses, gain more than a rupee in a month. In 9 cases out of 10 the labourers contract debts to meet marriage expenses.

8. Among the artizans may be mentioned the weavers, who colonise between Ranigunge and Ranisankail on the main road. Statement II will show that these men hold no lands, but depend entirely on their profession. I have not been able, in spite of my endeavours, to arrive at a standard whereby their income can be correctly estimated. The hand-to-mouth way of living to which they are subject can be understood at a glance at the figures shown in the statement.

As a rule an adult female weaver will, in addition to her household work, earn about a third part of what an adult male will earn.

9. The statistics collected will show that the weavers are largely indebted to mahajans. Their indebtedness appears to be always the same. These people appear to be considerably poor, and their poverty is the more enhanced owing to their indolent habit of being unoccupied unless pressed hard by the necessities of life. In slack seasons they, as would be supposed, suffer a great deal more. They have very little to afford too in the direction of ornaments for the females, who wear nothing but plain shells at a nominal cost. They could dispense with the use of these even, if they were only allowed by the Hindu society to do so. The use of brass utensils is also limited. One can scarcely afford to display more than the very ordinary utensils returned as per margin. It will appear from the column of remarks that the debts of these people are in consequence of marriage expenses.

Glass	...	...	1
Thali	...	..	1
Ghoti	...	...	1
Batis	...	...	2

10. I have not yet come across any professional beggars here. I am certainly doubtful of their existence. But if there are such men, their number is very limited.

11. I have been in the course of my duties to several villages, and personally carefully observed the manner in which the lower classes of population subsist on the food they eat, the houses in which they live, the clothes they wear, the ornaments they can afford to buy, and the extent to which the cheap pottery formerly in use has been superseded by brass utensils. But I have nowhere found that the physique of labourers in this part of the district is affected by due nourishment.

12. Speaking generally, the above report applies throughout the whole of the pergunnah except in the number of inhabitants, which are in some villages more and in some less.

vege-table.															
Do. ...	0	4	0	0	0	2	0	0	2	0	0	4	3	3	4	(II) Contracted to meet marriage expenses.
Do. ...	0	5	0	0	0	3	0	0	3	0	0	5	3	3	4	
Do. ...	0	6	0	0	0	3	0	0	3	0	0	6	3	3	4	
Do. ...	0	7	0	0	0	4	0	0	4	0	0	6	3	3	4	
Do. ...	0	4	0	0	0	2	0	0	2	0	0	4	3	3	4	(III) Incurred to meet marriage expenses.
Do. ...	0	5	0	0	0	3	0	0	3	0	0	5	3	3	4	
Do. ...	0	6	0	0	0	4	0	0	3	0	0	6	3	3	4	
Do. ...	0	5	8	0	0	3	0	0	2	0	0	6	3	3	4	*One member of the family is employed as servant, whose wages are appropriated to defray the household expenses.
Do. ...	0	6	0	0	0	4	0	0	2	0	0	6	3	3	4	
Do. ...	0	1	8	0	0	1	0	0	1	0	0	2	3	3	4	
Do. ...	0	7	8	0	0	4	0	0	3	0	0	8	3	3	4	
Do. ...	0	6	0	0	0	4	0	0	2	0	0	6	3	3	4	
	1	27	6	0	2	7	0	1	15	0	4	4	39	39	52	
Do. ...	0	5	0	0	0	3	0	0	3	0	0	6	3	3	4	† One member employed as servant, whose wages defray a portion of the household expenses.
Do. ...	0	8	0	0	0	5	0	0	4	0	0	8	3	3	4	(IV) Incurred to meet marriage expenses.
Do. ...	0	4	0	0	0	4	0	0	2	0	0	6	3	3	4	(a) One member employed as servant, whose wages defray a portion of the household expenses.
Do. ...	0	5	0	0	0	3	0	0	2	0	0	5	3	3	4	(b) Do. do.
Do. ...	0	3	8	0	0	2	0	0	1	0	0	4	3	3	4	(c) Two members employed as servants, whose wages defray a large portion of the household expenses.
Do. ...	0	12	8	0	0	8	0	0	6	0	0	8	3	3	4	(V) Incurred to meet marriage expenses.

HARIS CHUNDRA RAI,
Settlement Officer.

Expenses annually.								How many meals a day.				
Ornaments.	Utensils.	Marriage.	Feasts.	Any other sorts.	Total expenditure.	Nature of food in daily consumption.	Quantity used daily.	By adult male.	By adult female.	By children.	Debt.	Remarks.
Rs. A. P.	Rs. A. P.	Rs.	Rs. A. P.	Rs.	Rs. A. P.		S. C.				Rs.	
6 0 0	0 8 0	10	2 0 0	1	179 6 0	Rice, dal, fish, vegetable, chirs, muri.	8 0	2	2	2	150*	* This debt was contracted to make up the loss incurred in trade in cloth.
4 0 0	1 0 0	12	3 0 0	8	200 0 0	Ditto ...	9 0	2	2	3	100	Incurred to meet the expenses on account of marriage.
1 0 0	0 8 0	...	1 0 0	6	58 8 0	Ditto ...	4 0	2	2	3	...	
0 8 0	0 8 0	6	1 0 0	4	125 0 0	Ditto ...	6 8	2	2	3	800	Ditto ditto.
......	0 8 0	2	1 0 0	3	105 6 0	Ditto ...	8 0	2	2	3	80	Ditto ditto.
1 0 0	1 0 0	4	1 8 0	7	164 8 0	Ditto ...	8 0	2	2	3	60	Ditto ditto.
1 0 0	0 8 0	2	1 0 0	2	73 8 0	Ditto ...	7 0	2	2	3	25	Ditto ditto.
1 0 0	1 0 0	3	0 8 0	6	133 8 0	Ditto ...	6 0	2	2	3	100	Ditto ditto.
1 0 0	0 8 0	4	0 8 0	6	109 0 0	Ditto ...	8 0	2	2	3	40	Ditto ditto.
3 0 0	1 0 0	4	2 0 0	6	161 0 0	Ditto ...	6 0	2	2	3	50	Ditto ditto.
2 0 0	0 8 0	1	0 8 0	4	120 0 0	Ditto ...	8 0	2	2	3	250	Ditto ditto.
1 0 0	0 8 0	...	0 8 0	4	108 8 0	Ditto ...	7 0	2	2	3	80	Ditto ditto.
3 0 0	1 0 0	1	1 0 0	7	157 0 0	Ditto ...	0 12	2	2	3	60	Ditto ditto.
......	......	...	......	1	81 0 0	Ditto ...	3 0	2	2	3	...	
......	0 8 0	...	0 8 0	2	55 0 0	Ditto ...	3 8	2	2	3	76	Ditto ditto.
1 0 0	1 0 0	4	1 0 0	4	103 0 0	Ditto ...	8 0	2	2	3	400	Ditto ditto.
......	0 4 0	1	......	2	75 12 0	Ditto ...	1 0	2	2	3	14	Ditto ditto.
......	......	...	......	1	27 0 0	Ditto ...	4 0	2	2	3	...	
0 8 0	1 0 0	4	0 8 0	4	107 0 0	Ditto ...	3 0	2	2	3	70	Ditto ditto.
0 4 0	......	...	0 8 0	2	67 12 0	Ditto ...	4 8	2	2	3	20	Ditto ditto.
2 0 0	1 0 0	2	1 0 0	3	89 8 0	Ditto ...		2	2	3	25	Ditto ditto.
0 4 0	......	...	......	1	54 4 0	Ditto ...	2 8	3	3	4	300†	† Incurred to defray marriage expenses.

No. 12, dated Baloorghat, the 14th April 1888.

From—BABOO SASI BHUSAN DUTTA, Settlement Officer, Sunkerpore Estate,
To—The Collector of Dinagepore.

IN compliance with Director's confidential letter No. 109, dated 23rd January 1888, and to your subsequent instruction laid down in letter No. 1129G, dated 24th February 1888, I have the honour to submit the following report and statement regarding the condition of the lower classes of people in the villages which were selected for the required information.

2. The villages selected for the purposes are Hushinpore, Khanpore and Bad Banqi Roynagore, and my enquiry was confined only to the tenants who were found to lead their lives miserably. The area, by present survey of the aforesaid villages, is found to be 1,566 acres 2 roods, and the number of resident ryots to be 85, out of which tenants were found worth to be noticed here. In my opinion this will give a rough idea of a certain per cent. of the poorer class in this quarter ; of course in every village the proportion of such class of people is not the same.

3. The areas shewn in the statement were all put down in village bighas, which vary from the English bigha in proportion of nearly 2 to 3, and the quantity of produce of paddy was shewn in maunds measuring 60 tolas, which is prevalent in this part of the district, consequently in making. Comparison of the produce per village in the statement with that of standard maunds of 80 tolas per English bigha, the quantity shall have to be reduced to half. The vast difference of produce per bigha is owing to situation of lands. The lands producing 5 or 4 maunds per bigha are high and low lands ; the former retains no rain water, and the latter are subject to inundation during high flood. But in the level plain in the Khior produce of paddy per bigha being 8 to 9 maunds, and this produce would be considered maximum rates founded upon the best harvest of this year.

4. The accompanying statement will show that it has touched upon cultivators agricultural labourers, weavers, and those who subsist on charity. Among the four orders of tenants, the weavers are the poorest possible. The scarcity of rain in 1290 and 1291 (Bengali year) has reduced the condition of tenants in general to a great extent. The amount of debt shewn in the statement against each tenant partly resulted from the famine which appeared in the aforesaid years, and partly from the heavy charges upon marriage, especially among the Kaiborths and weavers. The payment of these debts by instalments, together with its interest at a higher rate, falls heavily upon them ; that it drains off annually nearly one-fourth of the resources of each family.

5. It will appear from the statement that the wages of male members of a family, supplemented by the profits of small holdings, are not sufficient to meet the household expenses ; hence to remove their wants the females of poorer classes of cultivators are often found to be employed in threshing rice of the neighbouring people on the receipt of wages at the rate of one seer in every ten ; the proceeds were therefore taken into account in calculating the total income of every family.

6. The nature of food these poorer classes used to take daily is of the very poorest sort, consisting of cooked rice, dal, curry and fish ; the last one is easily available free of cost from the tanks and nallas, which are found to be numerous in this district. Among the Mahomedans, both female and male take three meals a day, and children four meals ; and among Hindoos, the adult males are in the habit of taking three meals, but females never take more than twice a day. The morning meals are taken only with salt, onion and capsicum ; and the noon and night meals with curries or fish to the smallest quantity possible.

7. The dress generally worn by the males of the lower class of people is a narrow piece of cloth which is locally known by *lengti*, and one coarse sheet for protection from cold in winter season ; of course the females use what is required to secure their self-respect in a poor style.

8. The number of people who subsist upon charity was found to be in village Hushinpore. From the mode of their living, they did not seem to have been suffering from insufficiency of food, but some of them continue to save something monthly, but it is very difficult to get out their actual income.

9. One principal point which is worth to be noticed here as to the cause of the miserable state of these people is that they are in general very slack in physical labour in comparison to those of Dacca and Furreedpore districts, where the agricultural labourers and cultivators work hard even in the midsummer day, whereas the people of these quarters are very seldom found to reap the corn with their own hands during winter season.

1	2	3	4	5	6	7	8	9						10	11		
								Income from sale of—							Expenses of Cultivation annually.		
Name.	Whether ryot or under-ryot.	Area of land under cultivation.	Produce annually per bigha.	Quantity of produce sold.	Money value of produce sold.	Quantity kept for food.	Money value of special crops, such as chillies, mangoes, &c.	Straw.	Live stock.	Milk and ghee.	Hide.	Jungli produce.	Any other source.	Total income (plus columns 6, 8, 9, and 7 including price of paddy kept for food.)	Rent.	Plough.	Bullock.
		B. K. C.	Mds.	Mds.	Rs. A. P.	Mds.	Rs. A. P.	Rs.	Rs.	Rs.	Rs.	Rs.	Rs.	Rs. A. P.	Rs. A. P.	Rs. A. P.	Rs. A. P.
Dino Bandhu Das	Ryot	19 0 0	5	70	47 0 0	25	......	...	...	...	48	...	...	112 0 0	16 8 0	3 0 0	18 0 0
Sooku Poli	Do.	13 0 0	5	...	......	65	......	...	...	...	...	...	...	43 0 0	10 0 0	5 0 0	9 0 0
Ramkumar Poli	Do.	20 0 0	5	...	......	104	......	...	...	...	...	...	...	68 0 0	21 0 0	3 0 0	16 0 0
Nobin Poli	Do.	10 0 0	5	...	......	50	......	...	...	...	...	...	...	84 0 0	9 0 0	4 0 0	9 0 0
Noyhul Nasya	Do.	14 0 0	5	35	24 0 0	35	......	...	...	...	...	...	...	48 0 0	10 12 0	1 4 0	8 0 0
Gangakanta Pator	Do.	19 0 0	5	48	32 0 0	48	......	...	...	5	...	...	...	71 0 0	11 0 0	1 4 0	4 8 0
Kookra Mandal	Do.	48 0 0	5	120	80 0 0	12	......	...	...	...	...	...	...	160 0 0	30 0 0	3 8 0	15 0 0
Joykam Boona	Do.	8 0 0	5	4	2 0 0	36	......	...	...	...	...	...	...	26 0 0	6 0 0	1 4 0	5 0 0
Lakhikanta Das	Do.	6 0 0	5	4	2 8 0	26	......	...	...	...	...	...	...	18 0 0	3 8 0	1 4 0	22 8 0
Palu Kasya	Do.	9 0 0	9	60	40 0 0	21	......	...	...	...	...	...	61	115 0 0	11 0 0	1 4 0	13 0 0
Rama Boona	Do.	10 0 0	9	...	......	40	......	...	...	...	...	...	...	27 0 0	8 0 0	1 4 0	8 0 0
Kartic Kasya	Do.	16 0 0	5	40	27 0 0	40	......	...	...	...	...	...	...	54 0 0	7 0 0	3 0 0	10 0 0
Gonesh Kasya	Do.	26 0 0	5	78	52 0 0	32	......	...	...	...	...	...	...	87 0 0	17 8 0	6 0 0	10 0 0
Sookdeb Das	Do.	12 0 0	6	36	24 0 0	38	......	...	...	...	...	...	...	48 0 0	13 0 0	1 4 0	16 0 0
Keshob Das	Do.	22 0 0	6	66	44 0 0	66	......	...	...	...	...	...	...	88 0 0	22 0 0	2 8 0	13 4 0
Gopal Boona	Do.	25 0 0	9	30	20 0 0	70	......	...	...	...	...	...	...	67 0 0	20 0 0	0 8 0	—
Maloo Mandal	Do.	29 0 0	9	171	100 0 0	117	12 0 0	...	...	...	...	...	...	190 0 0	25 8 0	1 8 0	12 0 0
Panawoolah	Do.	18 0 0	9	72	48 0 0	95	4 6 0	...	...	...	...	...	...	116 8 0	27 0 0	1 0 0	—
Hagroo Nasya	Do.	19 0 0	8½	67	44 12 0	53	6 0 0	...	...	...	...	...	...	85 12 0	17 0 0	1 0 0	8 0 0
Balkanta Das	Do.	20 10 0	8	86	45 0 0	58	......	...	...	18	...	...	...	101 8 0	13 8 0	1 0 0	—
Shook Charn Chak	Do.	39 16 0	9½	172	114 0 0	152	......	...	...	13	...	...	...	226 0 0	83 4 0	1 8 0	—
Sreekanto Das	Do.	18 0 0	9	54	36 0 0	54	......	...	...	...	...	...	...	72 0 0	16 0 0	1 0 0	19 0 0
Sreedhur Das	Do.	9 0 0	7	15	10 0 0	40	......	...	...	...	25	6	...	73 0 0	23 0 0	1 0 0	12 0 0
Ishan Chandra Das	Do.	9 0 0	12½	48	32 0 0	65	......	...	...	...	...	...	...	75 0 0	10 0 0	1 0 0	5 0 0
Madhob Chandra Das ...	Do.	21 0 0	11½	120	80 0 0	122	......	...	...	20	...	...	...	181 0 0	24 0 0	3 0 0	9 0 0
Joynal Nasya	Do.	17 0 0	9	78	52 0 0	75	......	...	...	...	...	4	6	112 0 0	20 0 0	1 0 0	8 0 0
Manggon	Do.	32 0 0	11½	216	144 0 0	144	......	...	...	...	...	...	...	240 0 0	40 0 0	2 0 0	18 0 0
Ramtanu Das	Do.	23 0 0	8	88	60 0 0	88	......	...	...	...	...	...	...	120 0 0	24 0 0	2 8 0	22 0 0
Doulat Nasya	Do.	26 0 0	8	104	70 0 0	104	......	...	...	...	...	...	...	140 0 0	30 0 0	2 8 0	6 0 0
Gana Nasya	Do.	9 0 0	8	36	24 0 0	36	......	...	...	...	...	...	...	48 0 0	9 4 0	2 8 0	6 0 0
Mamu Nasya	Do.	25 0 0	7	60	40 0 0	115	......	...	...	...	...	...	...	117 0 0	50 0 0	2 0 0	12 0 0
Hari Das	Do.	15 0 0	8	60	40 0 0	60	......	...	...	...	...	...	...	80 0 0	16 0 0	1 0 0	14 0 0
Ram Chand Das	Do.	28 0 0	8	112	75 0 0	112	......	...	...	...	...	...	...	150 0 0	31 0 0	2 0 0	12 0 0
Lochmon Boona	Do.	25 0 0	4	40	27 0 0	60	......	...	...	...	...	...	...	67 0 0	29 0 0	2 0 0	6 0 0
Budhoo Boona	Do.	24 0 0	4	86	57 0 0	14	......	...	...	...	...	...	...	86 0 0	18 0 0	3 0 0	12 0 0
Brishu Mandal...	Do.	12 0 0	5	50	33 0 0	10	......	...	...	...	...	...	...	40 0 0	11 0 0	3 14 0	22 0 0
Jadab Das	Do.	26 0 0	7½	72	50 0 0	63	8 0 0	...	...	...	...	...	22	117 0 0	24 0 0	......	8 0 0
Pabon Nasya	Do.	14 0 0	8	32	22 0 0	76	......	...	...	...	...	...	12	84 0 0	20 0 0	15 0 0	—

BALOOGHAT,

The 14th April 1888.

I.

vators.

12									13	14	15	16	17				18			19
Household expenses (annual).													Quantity used daily.				How many meals are taken.			
Food.	Lodging.	Servants.	Clothes.	Ornaments.	Marriage.	Feasts.	Utensils.	Any other sorts.	Total of column 12.	Extent of debt at present to mahajans.	Number of persons in family.	Nature of food in daily consumption.	Of cooked rice.	Of other grains.	Of fish, &c.	Of anything else.	By adult male.	By adult female.	By children.	Remarks.
Rs.	Rs.	Rs.	Rs.	Rs.	Rs.	Rs.	Rs.	Rs.	Rs.	Rs.	No.		Srs.	Srs.	Srs.					
204	5	51	15	...	...	...	...	...	275	60	7	Rice, curry, fish, &c.	...	2	½	...	Twice	Twice	Four times.	Debt for marriage and household expenses.
144	5	...	10	...	...	...	...	...	159	30	5	Ditto ...	7½	2	½	...	Do. ...	Do. ...	Do. ...	Debt for household expenses only.
192	5	...	10	...	...	...	...	...	107	100	7	Ditto ...	8	2	½	...	Do. ...	Do. ...	Do. ...	Debt for marriage ceremonies.
108	5	...	5	...	...	...	...	...	118	100	4	Ditto ...	6	1½	½	...	Do. ...	Do. ...	Do. ...	Ditto.
300	16	27	12	...	...	...	...	...	339	390	12	Ditto ...	12	3	½	...	Thrice	Thrice	Do. ...	Out of total debts, Rs. 150 is for marriage expenses and others for household expenses.
84	10	40	6	...	...	...	...	...	140	24	3	Ditto ...	4½	1	½	...	Twice	Twice	Do. ...	For household expenses only.
300	12	...	20	...	...	...	...	...	322	20	12	Ditto ...	12	3	½	...	Do. ...	Do. ...	Do. ...	Ditto.
60	5	...	5	...	...	...	...	...	70	...	3	Ditto ...	3	1	½	...	Do. ...	Do. ...	Do.	
60	3	...	5	...	...	...	...	...	68	22	3	Ditto ...	3	½	½	...	Do. ...	Do. ...	Do. ...	Debt for purchasing bullock.
150	4	...	10	...	...	...	...	...	170	25	6	Ditto ...	8	2	1	...	Do. ...	Do. ...	Do. ...	Ditto for household expense only.
210	5	...	5	...	...	...	...	...	220	...	8	Ditto ...	15	3½	2	...	Do. ...	Do. ...	Do.	
220	4	...	16	...	...	...	...	...	249	14	8	Ditto ...	8	2	1	...	Do. ...	Do.	Do. ...	Debt for household expenses.
300	10	...	18	...	...	...	...	...	328	...	11	Ditto ...	11	2	1	...	Do ...	Do. ...	Do.	
156	10	...	12	...	...	...	...	...	178	30	6	Ditto ...	7	1½	½	...	Do. ...	Do. ...	Do. ...	Ditto.
240	12	38	15	...	...	...	...	...	305	100	9	Ditto ...	10	2½	1	...	Do. ...	Do. ...	Do. ...	Ditto.
180	...	...	6	...	...	...	...	...	180	...	7	Ditto ...	7	1	...	...	Do. ...	Do. ...	Do.	
180	...	41	6	...	...	5	...	...	232	...	7	Ditto ...	8	1	1½	...	Do. ...	Do. ...	Do.	
168	...	11	8	...	...	5	...	...	198	40	6	Ditto ...	6½	½	½	...	Do. ...	Do. ...	Do. ...	Debt for household expenses.
84	...	7	4	...	...	2	...	...	97	40	3	Ditto ...	4	½	½	...	Do. ...	Do. ...	Do. ...	Ditto.
115	3	24	7	...	...	7	...	...	156	...	4	Ditto ...	4	½	...	...	Do. ...	Do. ...	Do.	
240	...	10	16	...	...	5	...	...	271	180	8	Ditto ...	8	2	½	...	Do. ...	Do. ...	Do. ...	Debt for marriage and purchase of bullocks.
156	3	...	9	...	...	...	...	...	168	125	6	Ditto ...	5	1	½	...	Thrice	Do. ...	Do. ...	Debt for marriage and purchasing bullocks.
80	2	15	5	...	...	...	...	...	102	45	3	Ditto ...	3	1	½	...	Do. ...	Do. ...	Do. ...	Ditto.
84	2	...	6	...	...	...	...	...	92	...	3	Ditto ...	4	1	½	...	Do. ...	Do ...	Do.	
196	5	45	16	...	...	...	...	...	264	150	8	Ditto ...	8	1½	½	...	Do. ...	Do. ...	Do. ...	Debts for marriage and household expenses.
108	8	14	5	...	...	...	...	...	135	150	4	Ditto ...	4	1	½	...	Do. ...	Do. ...	Do. ...	Ditto.
336	8	...	16	...	...	...	...	...	360	150	12	Ditto ...	12	2½	½	...	Do. ...	Do. ...	Do. ...	Ditto.
168	5	...	16	...	...	...	...	...	189	250	6	Ditto ...	6	1	½	...	Do. ...	Do. ...	Do. ...	Ditto.
336	6	...	14	...	...	...	...	...	356	40	14	Ditto ...	12	2½	1	...	Do. ...	Do. ...	Do. ...	Ditto.
96	8	...	7	...	...	...	...	...	111	69	4	Ditto ...	5	1½	1	...	Do. ...	Do. ...	Do. ...	Ditto.
115	5	...	8	...	...	...	...	...	128	100	4	Ditto ...	6	1½	1	...	Do. ...	Do. ...	Do. ...	Ditto.
144	3	10	13	...	...	...	...	...	170	500	5	Ditto ...	5	1½	1	...	Do. ...	Do. ...	Do. ...	Ditto.
240	5	20	16	...	...	...	...	...	280	120	9	Ditto ...	8	2	1	...	Do. ...	Do. ...	Do. ...	Ditto.
384	5	...	25	...	...	...	...	...	414	20	16	Ditto ...	36	4	1	...	Do. ...	Do. ...	Do. ...	Ditto.
432	8	...	32	...	...	...	...	...	475	26	18	Ditto ...	30	4	2	...	Do. ...	Do. ...	Do. ...	Ditto.
240	5	...	20	...	...	...	...	...	265	...	9	Ditto ...	10	2	1	...	Do. ...	Do. ...	Do. ...	
120	5	...	10	...	...	...	...	12	147	40	4	Ditto ...	6	1	½	...	Do. ...	Do. ...	Do. ...	Debt for household expenses.
156	...	...	5	...	...	6	...	...	167	9	6	Ditto ...	6	1	½	...	Do. ...	Do. ...	Do. ...	Ditto.

SASI BHUSHUN DUTT,
Settlement Officer, Sunkerpore Estate.

1	2	3	4	5		6	
				Area under each kind of crops.		Produce of each sort per bigha.	
Name.	Caste.	How employed.	Area of holding, if any.	Paddy.	Mustard, kalai, &c.	Paddy.	Mustard, kalai, &c.
			B. K. C.	B. K. C.	B. K. C.	Mds. s. c.	Mds. s. c.
Prankisto Das	Kaibortha	Agricultural labourer.	3 10 0	......	3 10 0	......	1 10 0
Hanroo Poll	Poll	Ditto	22 0 0	16 0 0	6 0 0	5 0 0	0 25 0
Nara Hari Poll	Do.	Ditto	7 0 0	3 10 0	3 10 0	6 0 0	0 20 0
Giri Poll	Do.	Ditto	7 0 0	6 0 0	1 0 0	6 0 0	0 20 0
Chiroo Das	Kaibortha	Ditto	......	......	......	......	......
Srudhur Nasya	Koch	Ditto	......	......	......	......	......
Shanja Nasya	Do.	Ditto	16 0 0	16 0 0	......	5 0 0	......
Amir Nasya	Musalman	Ditto	10 0 0	10 0 0	......	13 0 0	......
Kheist Nasya	Ditto	Ditto	10 12 15	10 0 0	0 12 15	7 0 0	0 20 0
Nakari Nasya	Ditto	Ditto	14 8 3	14 8 3	......	9 0 0	......
Darbaree Mandal	Ditto	Ditto	10 9 11	10 8 0	0 1 11	8 0 0	0 28 0
Karim Ullah	Ditto	Ditto	14 0 0	14 0 0	......	8 20 0	......
Diloo Nasya	Ditto	Ditto	17 0 0	17 0 0	......	5 0 0	......
Tinkaree Nasya	Ditto	Ditto	9 16 0	9 3 0	0 13 0	9 0 0	0 20 0
Shona Nasya	Ditto	Ditto	23 0 0	19 0 0	4 0 0	9 0 0	0 30 0
Ekharee Nasya	Ditto	Ditto	13 3 0	12 0 0	1 3 0	8 0 0	0 30 0
Mochen Nasya	Ditto	Ditto	14 0 0	12 0 0	2 0 0	10 0 0	......
Rahut Seik	Ditto	Ditto	......	......	......	......	......
Chajiton Seik	Ditto	Ditto	0 15 0	0 15 0	......	4 0 0	......
Kooraoo Nasya	Ditto	Ditto	......	......	......	......	......
Chona Jog	Jugi	Ditto	......	......	......	......	......
Ghunta Jog	Do.	Weaver	......	......	......	......	......
Ishawer Jog	Do.	Agricultural labourer.	......	......	......	......	......
Bhubon Jog	Do.	Ditto	......	......	......	......	......
Huri Charon Jog	Do.	Ditto	......	......	......	......	......
Kungalu Jog	Do.	Ditto	5 10 0	5 10 0	......	6 0 0	......
Nafor Jog	Do.	Weaver	6 0 0	6 0 0	......	7 0 0	......
Koita Jog	Do.	Ditto	8 0 0	8 0 0	......	7 0 0	......
Chuncha Jog	Do.	Ditto	24 0 0	24 0 0	......	7 0 0	......
Beneswer Baboo	Mochi	Fisherman	17 0 0	17 0 0	......	4 0 0	......
Dino Bundhu Das	Bairage	Professional beggar.	......	......	......	......	......
Banqu Das	Ditto	Ditto	......	......	......	......	......
Joydebi Das	Ditto	Ditto	......	......	......	......	......
Tinkari Das	Ditto	Ditto	......	......	......	......	......
Hari Das	Ditto	Ditto	......	......	......	......	......
Rash Behari Das	Ditto	Ditto	......	......	......	......	......
Modhu Das	Ditto	......	......	......	......	......	......
Dina Bundhu Das	Ditto	Professional beggar.	10 0 0	10 0 0	......	8 0 0	......

Baloorghat,
The 19th April 1888.

II.

11				12	13	14	15								16	17	18	19			20	
Wages of self and family.				Total income (plus columns 8, 10, 11 and 9 including prices of quantities unfit for food.)	Number of persons in family.	Cost of cultivation, if any.	Household expenses (annual).								Total expenditure (plus columns 14 and 15).	Nature of food in daily consumption.	Quantity used daily.	How many meals a day.			Debts.	Remarks.
Money.	Food.	Clothes.	Lodgings.				Food.	Lodgings.	Utensils.	Clothes.	Ornaments.	Marriage.	Feasts.	Any other sorts.				By adult male.	By adult female.	By children.		
Rs.	Rs.	Rs.	Rs.	Rs. A. P.	No.	Rs. A. P.	Rs.	Rs.	Rs.	Rs.	Rs.	Rs.	Rs.	Rs.	Rs. A. P.		Mds. S. C.				Rs.	
24	15	...	...	65 8 0	5	7 0 0	84	5	...	9	...	...	...	...	105 0 0	Rice, curry, dâl, fish, &c.	0 4 0	Twice	Thrice	Four times	40	Debt for household expenses.
60	70	...	...	205 0 0	7	31 0 0	192	10	...	20	...	...	...	...	253 0 0	Ditto ...	0 7 0	Do.	Do. ...	Do.	200	Ditto ditto.
38	36	...	...	94 0 0	5	15 0 0	144	2	...	15	...	...	...	...	176 0 0	Ditto ...	0 6 0	Do.	Do. ..	Do.	20	Ditto ditto.
40	36	...	...	90 0 0	5	15 0 0	120	3	...	8	...	...	...	...	143 0 0	Ditto ...	0 5 0	Do.	Do. ...	Do.	32	Ditto ditto.
30	30	...	...	65 0 0	4	......	120	...	...	5	...	...	...	...	125 0 0	Ditto ...	0 6 0	Do.	Do. ...	Do.	31	Ditto and for the funeral ceremonies of his deceased wife.
72	36	...	...	108 0 0	6	......	156	5	...	15	...	...	...	...	176 0 0	Ditto ...	0 7 0	Do.	Do. ...	Do.	50	For household expenses only.
36	36	...	...	125 0 0	5	20 0 0	144	5	...	10	...	...	...	...	179 0 0	Ditto ...	0 7 0	Do.	Do. ...	Do.	12	Ditto ditto.
88	24	...	...	147 0 0	6	9 0 0	150	...	...	10	...	...	...	...	169 0 0	Ditto ...	0 7 0	Do.	Do. ...	Do.	10	Ditto ditto.
70	7	...	...	74 0 0	4	27 0 0	120	...	...	5	...	...	...	...	152 0 0	Ditto ...	0 4 0	Do.	Do. ...	Do.	20	Ditto ditto.
11	...	...	...	94 0 0	6	33 8 0	156	...	...	6	...	...	7	...	202 8 0	Ditto ...	0 6 0	Do.	Do. ...	Do.	100	Ditto and for purchasing bullocks.
26	...	...	...	86 8 0	5	18 0 0	144	...	...	6	...	...	7	...	170 0 0	Ditto ...	0 6 0	Do.	Do. ...	Do.	54	Ditto ditto.
40	12	...	...	183 0 0	7	37 0 0	192	...	...	6	...	...	6	...	241 0 0	Ditto ...	0 6 0	Do.	Do. ...	Do.	19	Ditto ditto.
60	20	...	...	116 0 0	6	15 0 0	156	...	...	12	...	...	5	...	188 0 0	Ditto ...	0 6 0	Do.	Do. ...	Do.	...	
48	18	...	...	118 4 0	6	31 8 0	156	...	...	8	...	...	7	...	202 8 0	Ditto ...	0 5 0	Do.	Do. ...	Do.	20	The debt is owing to marriage of his daughter.
8	...	...	...	129 0 0	4	64 0 0	120	...	...	5	...	...	7	...	196 0 0	Ditto ...	0 5 0	Do.	Do. ...	Do.	50	Debt for purchasing bullocks and for household expenses.
12	12	...	...	96 4 0	5	26 8 0	84	...	...	4	...	...	3	...	117 8 0	Ditto ...	0 5 0	Do.	Do. ...	Do.	57	Ditto ditto.
35	18	...	...	134 8 0	5	33 0 0	144	...	...	5	...	...	3	...	185 0 0	Ditto ...	0 5 0	Do.	Do. ...	Do.	68	For arrears of rent and for household expenses.
48	24	...	...	72 0 0	3	......	84	...	...	5	...	...	3	...	93 0 0	Ditto ...	0 3 4	Do.	Do. ..	Do.	10	Debt for household expenses.
48	24	...	...	74 0 0	4	3 0 0	120	...	...	4	...	...	2	...	129 0 0	Ditto ...	0 4 0	Do.	Do. ...	Do.	...	
30	18	...	...	48 0 0	3	......	84	...	...	4	...	...	4	...	92 0 0	Ditto ...	0 3 0	Do.	Do. ...	Do.	100	Debt for purchasing bullocks and for household expenses.
36	30	...	...	66 0 0	5	......	84	2	...	6	...	...	...	...	92 0 0	Ditto ...	0 3 0	Do.	Do. ...	Do.	50	For household expenses only.
108	60	...	...	169 0 0	13	......	350	5	...	30	...	...	...	...	385 0 0	Ditto ...	0 11 0	Do.	Do. ...	Do.	50	Ditto ditto.
36	30	...	...	66 0 0	4	......	120	2	...	10	...	...	...	...	132 0 0	Ditto ...	0 4 8	Do.	Do. ...	Do.	60	Ditto ditto.
50	30	...	...	80 0 0	3	......	84	3	...	8	...	...	...	...	95 0 0	Ditto ...	0 3 8	Do.	Do. ...	Do.	50	Ditto ditto.
40	30	...	...	70 0 0	6	......	156	2	...	8	...	...	...	...	166 0 0	Ditto ...	0 6 0	Do.	Do. ...	Do.	50	Ditto ditto.
5	...	...	...	27 0 0	3	14 0 0	84	...	...	5	...	...	...	...	89 0 0	Ditto ...	0 2 0	Do.	Do. ...	Do.	60	Debt for marriage ceremonies.
36	...	...	...	64 0 0	7	19 0 0	168	...	...	6	...	...	...	...	193 0 0	Ditto ...	0 6 0	Do.	Do. ...	Do.	33	Debt for household expenses.
36	...	...	...	73 0 0	5	21 0 0	120	2	...	7	...	...	...	...	150 0 0	Ditto ...	0 6 0	Do.	Do. ...	Do.	40	Ditto ditto.
36	...	...	...	142 0 0	8	42 0 0	204	...	...	20	...	...	...	...	206 0 0	Ditto ...	0 3 0	Do.	Do. ...	Do.	150	Debt for marriage.
15	5	...	...	65 0 0	9	50 0 0	240	10	...	10	...	...	...	...	310 0 0	Ditto ...	0 8 0	Do.	Do. ...	Do.	...	
...	...	...	...	......	5	......	...	...	...	...	...	...	...	...	......	Ditto ...	......	...	......	...	...	
48	72	...	...	120 0 0	10	......	240	...	...	...	...	...	...	...	240 0 0	Ditto ...	0 15 0	Twice	Twice	...	56	He has two brothers who are in service as cooks. Very poor.
...	...	...	...	......	3	......	...	...	...	...	...	...	...	...	......	Ditto ...	......	...	......	...	...	
...	...	...	...	......	4	......	...	...	...	...	...	...	...	...	......	Ditto ...	......	...	......	...	...	
...	...	...	...	......	4	......	...	...	...	...	...	...	...	...	......	Ditto ...	......	...	......	...	...	
...	...	...	...	......	4	......	...	...	...	...	...	...	...	...	......	Ditto ...	......	...	......	...	...	
16	36	...	...	52 0 0	3	......	84	4	...	9	...	...	...	...	97 0 0	Ditto ...	0 3 0	Twice	Twice	...	...	His younger earns Rs. (16+36) by his services as cook.
...	...	...	...	54 0 0	2	10 0 0	60	5	...	5	...	...	...	...	80 0 0	Ditto ...	0 2 8	Do.	Do. ...	Four times	...	

Sasi Bhushun Dutt,

Settlement Officer, Sunkerpore Estate.

No. 3, dated Camp Patiraj, the 15th April 1888.

From—BABOO NABIN CHUNDRA ROY, Settlement Officer, Churamon Estate,
To—The Collector of Dinagepore.

WITH reference to your circular No. 1129G, dated the 24th February 1888, and the Director of Land Records and Agriculture's letter No. 111Agri., dated the 23rd January 1888, I have the honour to submit herewith, in tabular statements A and B prescribed in your letter quoted above, the enquiries made by me in connection with the condition of the poorer classes of the people.

2. The enquiries have been made in five villages. The villages are not large ones, but the whole villages have been done. The total number of families is 41. One of the villages consists entirely of Mussulmans, and the remaining four entirely of Hindus of Desi and Pali caste, who form the bulk of the agricultural population. The villages are agricultural ones, and contain no artizans or beggars. Of the total 41 inhabitants, 29 are cultivators, and 12 agricultural labourers. Twenty-two of the cultivators are Hindus, and 7 Mussulmans. Of the labourers 10 are Hindus and 2 Mussulmans.

3. The average holding of cultivating ryots is 6 acres, excluding the holding of Peeru Mondal of mouzah Beranni, who, as Mondal, holds 38 acres. Of the 12 agricultural labourers 6 hold no land, and 6 hold altogether very nearly 10½ acres, or on an average 1⅓ acres. The area of the holdings and the rents paid have been compared with the measurement papers.

4. The average produce of dhan is 18 maunds per acre, that of rabi, which is principally mustard seed, is 5 maunds per acre. The value of the produce has been taken at the prevailing market price—dhan at Re. 1 a maund, and sarso at Rs. 2-8. The special crops sold are brinjals and chillies. Income from other sources is derived principally from sale of gunny cloth, which is woven by the women.

The wages received by agricultural labourers are generally Rs. 2 a month, besides food and cloth given them.

5. *Column* 12 *of the Statement A.*—The expenses incurred for food are the prices of salt, mustard oil, spices and dal. The cost on these items for one person is usually Rs. 5 a year as shown below :—

Articles.	Quantity per year.		Value.		
	Srs.	ch.	Rs.	A.	P.
Salt, at 2¾ kachas (1⅜ oz) daily ...	... 15	8	1	15	0
Mustard oil, at 1¼ kachas (10 drams) daily	... 7	0	2	3	0
Spices	... .		0	5	0
Dal, at 1 chittack daily (3 days a week)	... 9	0	0	9	0
Total			5	0	0

Vegetables are grown on the lands adjoining homesteads, and fish, which is taken during four months in the year, from February to May, is caught by the villagers in the *bils* and *jheels*.

Hardly any expenses are incurred annually for repairs of houses. The houses are thatched with the stalks of dhan plants grown in the fields, and bamboos which are plenty in this part of the country, and of which almost every one has some clumps, are obtained without cost.

Ornaments and brass utensils are purchased once for all or at long intervals.

The principal feast is the *nahanno* ceremony, or the taking of new rice in December. Hardly any other feast is given. The usual cost incurred on this head is Rs. 2.

Column 14.—Of the 41 families, 23 are indebted—15 for marriage, and the remaining 8 for other causes.

Column 15.—The total population in the five villages is 285, of which 89 are adult males, 90 adult females, and 106 children. The average number of persons in a family is—

Adult male.	Adult female.	Children.	Total.
2·1	2·1	2·5	6·7

Column 16.—The staple food of the people is rice, which is taken usually with *sak* cooked edible leaves. Dal is taken 2 or 3 days in a week. In winter, brinjals and pumpkins (*lau*) are taken. Fish is taken during 4 months from February to May. It is caught by the villagers in the *bils* and *jheels*.

Columns 17 *and* 18.—Every adult male and female take two meals a day, and breakfast in the morning, which is either *julpan* (*chura* or *muri*) or rice of the preceding night kept soaked in water. The children take *julpan* twice and rice twice.

The quantity of rice consumed by each adult, male and female, in two meals is 12 chittacks a day, besides 4 chittacks of *chura* or *muri* as julpan. In place of *julpan* the Mussulmans take cold rice of the preceding night as breakfast. Altogether a person consumes one seer of rice a day. The children take about one-half the quantity in julpan and cooked rice.

The quantity taken is sufficient. Dal, which is a principal article of food of the natives, is, however, very sparingly taken. *Sak*, edible leaves, especially of jute plants, is taken rather largely.

In place of salt, alkali is occasionally used as condiment for fish and vegetables.

It is obtained by burning stalks of mustard seed plants or of plantain leaves. The ashes are mixed with water to a certain consistence, and an alkaline liquor is strained out of it through a cloth. Vegetables and fish cooked with this liquid are taken with relish.

Column 19.—The clothing used by the people is very scanty. A *lengti*, which consists of a cloth 1½ yards long and 9 inches broad, is the ordinary clothing used to cover the body. Besides the *lengti* a *gamcha*, which is a cloth 2 yards long and 1 yard broad is used; it is tied round the head or carried on the shoulder.

The clothing of the females consists of a *siota* or a cloth 1¾ yards long and 1 yard broad. It is worn by tieing round the chest, and reaches to the knees. It is either of cotton or of jute. When going out to marketing, &c., another similar cloth is used as upper garment; this is tied across the shoulder and back.

The child or the marketing articles are often carried tied with this cloth on the back.

Column 20.—Brass utensils are to a great extent used by the people.

Column 21.—A pair of *sankha* or bracelet of conch shells is the ordinary ornament used. The price is about Rs. 2, and a pair would last life long. Silver and gold are also used in addition by many of value from Rs. 4 to Rs. 36.

Column 22.—Besides household work and husking of rice, the women weave gunny cloth and make marketing. Many help in the weeding and cutting of crops. The Mussulman women do not weave gunny, and few do out-door works.

6. The general condition of the lower classes is much inferior to that of the similar class of people in the districts of 24-Pergunnahs, Pubna and Rajshahye, of which I have experience. This is chiefly due, I think, to the sparseness of population and to the general backwardness of this district. The people are timid, indolent and very superstitious. The women are, however, laborious and courageous.

Statement A

1	2	3		4		5	6	7	8		Inco		
Name.	Whether ryot or under-ryot.	Area of land under cultivation.		Produce annually per bigha.		Quantity of produce sold.	Money value of produce sold.	Quantity kept for food.	Money value of special crops, such as chillies, mangoes, brinjals, &c.		Straw.	Live stock.	Milk and ...
			Bgs.		Mds.	Mds.	Rs. A. P.	Mds.		Rs. A. P.	Rs.	Rs.	R
*Village Itakhari.**													
Ranjit Desi	Ryot	Aghani ...	20	At 6 maunds per bigha ...	120	42	42 0 0	78	Brinjals ...	6 0 0	...	...	..
		Bhadoi ...	2	Ditto ...	12	......	......	12					
		Rabi ...	3	At 1½ maunds per bigha ...	4½	4½	11 4 0	......					
		Total ...	25		136½	46½	53 4 0	90					
2. Thakura Desi	Do. ...	Aghani ...	9	At 6 maunds per bigha ...	54	......	......	54	Ditto ...	5 0 0	3	...	..
		Bhadoi ...	1	Ditto ...	6	......	......	6					
		Rabi ...	2	At 1½ maunds per bigha ...	3	3	7 8 0	......					
		Total ...	12		63			60					
3. Jhubra Desi	Do. ...	Aghani ...	17	At 6 maunds per bigha ...	102	30	30 0 0	72	Ditto ...	5 0 0	...	...	..
		Bhadoi ...	2	Ditto ...	12	......	......	12					
		Rabi ...	2	At 1½ maunds per bigha ...	3	3	7 8 0	......					
		Total ...	21		117	33	37 8 0	84					
4. Gopal Desi	Do. ...	Aghani ...	14	At 6 maunds per bigha ...	84	40	40 0 0	44	Ditto ...	5 0 0	...	...	..
		Bhadoi ...	2	Ditto ...	12	......	... ..	12					
		Rabi ...	2	At 1½ maunds per bigha ...	3	3	7 8 0	......					
		Total ...	18		99	43	47 8 0	56					
5. Bhadu Desi	Do. ...	Aghani ...	17	At 6 maunds per bigha ...	102	30	30 0 0	72	Ditto ...	6 0 0	...	...	..
		Bhadoi ...	2	Ditto ...	12	......	......	12					
		Rabi ...	2	Ditto ...	3	3	8 0 0	......					
		Total ...	21		117	33	38 0 0	84					
6. Matru Desi	Do. ...	Aghani ...	24	At 6 maunds per bigha...	144	58	58 0 0	86	Ditto ...	8 0 0	...	..	
		Bhadoi ...	4	Ditto ...	24	......	......	24					
		Rabi ...	3	Ditto ...	4½	4½	11 4 0	......					
		Total ...	31		172½	62½	69 4 0	110					
7. Cheharu Desi	Do. ...	Aghani ...	9	At 6 maunds per bigha...	54	6	6 0 0	48	Ditto ...	4 0 0	...	...	..
		Bhadoi ...	2	Ditto ...	12	......	......	12					
		Total ...	11		66	6		60					

* Number of cultivators ... -
Ditto of agricultural labourers -

Total number of famil

ultivators.

9			10	11				12					23
rom sale of—				Expenses of cultivation.				Household expenses (annually).					
Hides.	Jungle produce.	Any other source.	Total income.	Rent.	Plough.	Bullock.	Any other sort.	Food.	Lodging.	Servants.	Clothes.	Ornaments.	Remarks.
Rs.	Rs.	Rs. A. P.	Rs. A. P.	Rs. A. P.	Rs. A. P.	Rs. A. P.	Rs. A. P.	Rs. A. P.	Rs. A. P.	Rs. A. P.	Rs. A. P.	Rs. A. P.	
...	...	Gunny cloth. 12 0 0	71 4 0	11 7 0	2 0 0	8 0 0	9 0 0 Servant.	25 0 0 excluding rice.	...... Paddy straw is used for thatching, bamboos from own clumps, labour of self helped by neighbours.	......	4 0 0	Purchased once for all.	
...	...	Ditto 12 0 0	27 8 0	4 0 0	1 0 0	4 0 0	......	13 0 0 excluding rice.	Ditto ...	......	3 0 0	Ditto ...	
...	...	Ditto 12 0 0	54 8 0	7 0 0	1 0 0	4 0 0	......	30 0 0 excluding rice.	Ditto ...	......	6 0 0	......	
...	...		52 8 0	13 0 0	1 0 0	4 0 0	......	18 0 0 excluding rice.		......	4 0 0	Purchased once for all.	
...	...	Gunny cloth. 24 0 0	68 0 0	8 12 0	2 0 0	8 0 0	......	30 0 0 excluding rice.		......	8 0 0	Purchased once for all or at long intervals.	
...	...	Ditto ... 24 0 0	99 4 0	4 0 0	3 0 0	12 0 0	......	30 0 0 excluding rice.		......	9 0 0	Ditto ...	
...	...	Ditto ... 12 0 0	23 0 0	4 0 0	1 0 0	2 0 0	......	10 0 0 excluding rice.		......	4 0 0	Ditto ...	

... 7
... 1
... 8

Statement A.—

1	2	3	4		5	6	7	8			
									Income		
Name.	Whether ryot or under-ryot.	Area of land under cultivation.	Produce annually per bigha.		Quantity of produce sold.	Money value of produce sold.	Quantity kept for food.	Money value of special crops, such as chillies, mangoes, brinjals, &c.	Straw.	Live stock.	Milk and ghee.
		Bgs.		Mds.	Mds.	Rs. A. P.	Mds.	Rs. A. P.	Rs.	Rs.	Rs.
*Village Biranol.**											
1. Chepa Desi	Ryot ...	Aghani ... 8½ Bhadoi ... ½ Rabi ... 1	At 6 maunds per bigha ... Ditto ... At 1½ maunds per bigha ...	51 3 1½	.... 1½	.... 3 12 0	51 3	Brinjal ... 6 0 0	—	...	—
		Total ... 10		55½			54				
2. Pohato Desi	Do. ...	Aghani ... 15 Bhadoi ... 3 Rabi ... 2	At 6 maunds per bigha ... Ditto ... At 2 maunds per bigha ...	90 18 4	Aghani ... 10 ...... Rabi ... 4	10 0 0 ...... Rabi ... 14 0 0	80 18	Ditto ... 7 0 0	...	...	...
		Total ... 20		112	14	24 0 0	98				
3. Bijal Pali	Do. ...	Aghani ... 4½ Rabi ... 1½	At 6 maunds per bigha ... At 1 maund per bigha ...	27 1½	...... 1½	...... 3 12 0	Aghani ... 27	......	...	...	...
		Total ... 8		28½							
4. Piru Mandal	Do. ...	Aghani ... 95½ Bhadoi ... 5 Rabi ... 13	At 6 maunds per bigha ... At 6 maunds per bigha bhadoi ... At 2 maunds per bigha ...	573 30 26	390 16	390 0 0 ...... 46 0 0	183 30 10		...	...	...
		Total ... 113½		629	406	435 0 0	223				
Village Jugduba.†											
1. Dundi Desi (senior) ...	Do. ...	Aghani ... 5¼ Rabi ... 1	At 6 maunds per bigha ... At 1½ maunds per bigha ...	31½ 1½	16 1½	16 0 0 3 12 0	15½		—	...	—
		6¼		33	17½	19 12 0					
2. Dundi Desi (junior) ...	Do. ...	Aghani ... 10 Bhadoi ... 2 Rabi ... 4	At 9 maunds per bigha ... At 6 maunds per bigha ... At 1 maund per bigha ...	90 12 4	32 2	32 0 0 ...... 5 0 0	Aghani ... 58 12 2		...	...	—
		16		106	34	37 0 0	72				
3. Khamdru Desi ...	Do. ...	Aghani ... 14 Bhadoi ... 2 Rabi ... 3	At 6 maunds per bigha ... Ditto ... Rabi ...	84 12 4½	24 3	24 0 0 ...... 7 8 0	Aghani ... 60 Bhadoi ... 12 Rabi ... 1½	......	...	...	—
		19		100½	27	31 8 0	73½				
Chak Buri Pukhar.‡											
1. Yetuha Paramanik ...	Do. ...	Aghani ... 21½ Bhadoi ... 1 Rabi (onion). ... 1	At 6 maunds per bigha ... At 4 maunds per bigha ... At 6 maunds per bigha ...	129 4 6	Aghani ... 69 ...... Rabi ... 3	Aghani ... 69 0 0 ...... Rabi ... 1 14 0	Aghani ... 60 Bhadoi ... 4 Rabi ... 3		...	...	—
		23½		139	72	70 14 0	67				
2. Galti Mullah	Do. ...	Aghani ... 27¼ Bhadoi ... 3 Rabi ... ½	At 5¼ maunds per bigha ... At 5½ maunds per bigha ... At 4 maunds per bigha ...	143 16½ 2	Aghani ... 61 ...... Rabi ... 1	Aghani ... 61 0 0 ...... Rabi ... 0 10 0	Aghani ... 82 Bhadoi ... 16½ Rabi ... 1		...	...	—
		30¾		161½	62	61 10 0	99½				
3. Gulbar Paramanik ...	Do. ...	Aghani ... 23 Bhadoi ... 2 Rabi (onion). ... 1	At 7½ maunds per bigha ... Ditto ... At 10 maunds per bigha (onion) ...	172½ 15 10	Aghani ... 41 ...... Rabi ... 6	Aghani ... 41 0 0 ...... Rabi ... 3 12 0	Aghani ... 131½ Bhadoi ... 15 Rabi ... 4		—	...	—
		26		197½	47	44 12 0	150½				

* Number of cultivators 4
Ditto of agricultural labourers ... 6
Total number of families ... 10

† Number of cultivators ... ...
Ditto of agricultural labourers
Total number of families ...

Cultivators.—continued.

9			10	11				12					13
OM SALE OF—				EXPENSES OF CULTIVATION.				HOUSEHOLD EXPENSES (ANNUALLY).					
...ities.	Jungle produce.	Any other source.	Total income.	Rent.	Plough.	Bullock.	Any other sort.	Food.	Lodging.	Servants.	Clothes.	Ornaments.	REMARKS.
Rs.	Rs.	Rs. A. P.	Rs. A. P.	Rs. A. P.	Rs. A. P.	Rs. A. P.	Rs. A. P.	Rs. A. P.	Rs. A. P.	Rs. A. P.	Rs. A. P.	Rs. A. P.	
—	—	Gunny cloth. 50 0 0	61 12 0	4 10 0	2 0 0	8 0 0	......	38 0 0	......	......	5 6 0	......	
—	—	Ditto ... 31 0 0	62 0 0	14 0 0	2 0 0	4 0 0	......	30 0 0		......	7 0 0	......	
—	...	Sale proceeds of oil ... 24 0 0	37 12 0	2 12 0	1 0 0	5 0 0	......	15 0 0	......	......	3 0 0	......	
...	...	Gunny cloth. 24 0 0 Sale proceeds of molasses (*goor*) 20 0 0 Rent of service lands ... 25 0 0 69 0 0	507 0 0	80 0 0	7 0 0	28 0 0	Servants wages. 144 0 0	60 0 0		......	40 0 0	3 0 0	
...	...	Wages of labour on the average 2 months in year 6 0 0	25 12 0	2 9 6	1 0 0	6 0 0	......	5 0 0		......	2 0 0	......	
...	...	Gunny cloth ... 24 0 0	61 0 0	14 6 0	1 0 0	4 0 0	......	24 0 0	......	......	5 0 0	......	
...	...	Ditto ... 30 0 0	61 6 0	17 0 0	3 0 0	8 0 0	......	28 0 0		......	6 0 0	......	
...	...	Profit in dealing of rice 23 0 0	98 14 0	13 9 0	1 0 0	4 0 0	Servant 19 0 0	25 0 0	......	......	5 0 0	1 0 0 for churies of shell lac and lead bracelets.	
...	...	Ditto ... 14 8 0	78 2 0	19 8 0	1 0 0	4 0 0	13 0 0	30 0 0	——	——	6 0 0	......	
...	...	Ditto ... 23 0 0 Sale of kids ... 2 0 0 25 0 0	69 12 0	14 6 0	1 6 0	4 6 0	......	30 0 0	3 0 0	......	12 0 0	......	

... ... 3
... ... 1
... ... 4

Number of cultivators 7
Ditto of agricultural labourers ... 2
Total number of families ... 9

Statement A.—

1	2	3	4	5	6	7	8	9		
								Income		
Name.	Whether raiyat or under-raiyat.	Area of land under cultivation.	Produce annually per bigha.	Quantity of produce sold.	Money value of produce sold.	Quantity kept for food.	Money value of special crops, such as chillies, mangoes, brinjals, &c.	Straw.	Live-stock.	Milk and ghee.
Chak Buri Pukhar—concluded.		Bgs.	Mds.	Mds.	Rs. a. p.	Mds.	Rs. a. p.	Rs.	Rs.	Rs.
4. Hamid Mullah	Raiyat	Aghani ... 31 Bhadoi ... 2 Rabi ... 1 34	At 7 maunds per bigha 217 At 7½ maunds per bigha ... 15 (Onion) ... 10 242	Aghani ... 77 ...... Rabi ... 6 83	Aghani ... 77 0 0 ...... Rabi ... 5 12 0 80 12 0	Aghani ... 140 Bhadoi ... 15 Rabi ... 4 159	......	...	...	...
5. Kalu Mundal	Do. ..	Aghani ... 12½ Rabi (onion) ... ½ Adhi aghru 12 Total ... 25	At 7½ maunds per bigha ... 93 At 10 maunds per bigha ... 5 At 7½ maunds per bigha ... 45 143	Aghani ... 32 Rabi ... 2 34	Aghani ... 33 0 0 Rabi ... 1 4 0 33 4 0	Aghani ... 106 Rabi ... 3 109		...	...	...
6. Bhilsha Nasya	Do. ...	Aghani ... 8½ Rabi (onion) ... ½ Total ... 9	At 7½ maunds per bigha ... 63 At 10 maunds per bigha ... 5 68	Aghani ... 33 Rabi ... 3 36	Aghani ... 33 0 0 Rabi ... 1 14 0 34 14 0	Aghani ... 30 Rabi ... 2 32		...	...	...
7. Kadu Nasya ...	Do. ...	Aghani ... 17 Rabi (onion) ... 1 Total ... 18	At 7 maunds per bigha ... 119 At 10 maunds per bigha ... 10 129	Aghani ... 19 Rabi ... 7 26	Aghani ... 19 0 0 Rabi ... 4 6 0 23 6 0	Aghani .. 100 Rabi ... 3 103		...	...	...
Village Baje Kokua.										
1. Kuar Deshi	Do. ...	Aghani ... 9 Bhadoi ... 2 Rabi ... 3 14	At 6 maunds per bigha ... 54 At 4 maunds per bigha ... 8 At 2 maunds per bigha ... 6 68	.... Rabi ... 6	.... Rabi ... 15 0 0	Aghani ... 54 Bhadoi ... 8 62	Chillies and brinjal ... 18 0 0	...	...	...
2. Shadhu Deshi	Do. ...	Aghani ... 6½ Bhadoi ... ... Rabi ... 2½ 9	At 7 maunds per bigha ... 45 ...... At 2 maunds per bigha ... 5 50	.... Rabi ... 2½	.... Rabi ... 6 4 0	Aghani ... 45 ...... Rabi ... 2½ 47½	Jute and brinjal ... 9 0 0	...	...	...
3. Kadua Deshi ...	Do. ...	Aghani ... 7 Rabi ... 1 8	At 5 maunds per bigha... 35 At 2 maunds 2 37	Rabi ... 2	Rabi ... 5 0 0	Aghani ... 35 Rabi	Chillies, jute and brinjal 18 0 0	...	...	...
4. Jhabu Deshi ...	Do. ...	Aghani ... 16 Bhadoi ... 2 Rabi ... 4 22	At 4 maunds per bigha ... 64 At 4 maunds per bigha ... 8 At 1¼ maunds per bigha ... 5 77	...... Bhadoi ... 8 Rabi ... 5 13	...... Bhadoi ... 8 0 0 Rabi ... 15 0 0 23 0 0	Ahgani ... 64	Chillies and brinjal, &c. 32 0 0	...	...	...
5 Darbaru Deshi	Do. ...	Aghani ... 9 Bhadoi ... 1 Rabi ... 3 13	At 4 maunds per bigha ... 36 ...... 3½ At 1½ maunds per bigha ... 4½ 44	.... Rabi ... 4½	.... Rabi ... 11 4 0	Aghani ... 36 Rabi ... 3½ 30½	Chillies and brinjal ... 6 8 0	...	...	...
6. Mathur Deshi	Do. ...	Aghani ... 10 Bhadoi ... 2 Rabi ... 3 15	At 6½ maunds per bigha... 65 At 6 maunds per bigha... 12 At 2 maunds per bigha... 6 83	.... Rabi ... 6	.... Rabi ... 15 0 0	Aghani ... 65 Rabi ... 12 77	Chillies and brinjal ... 12 8 0	...	...	...

Cultivators — Continued.

9			10	11				12					13
rom sale of—				Expenses of Cultivation.				Household expenses (annually).					
Hides.	Jungle produce.	Any other source.	Total income.	Rent.	Plough.	Bullock.	Any other sort.	Food.	Lodging.	Servants.	Clothes.	Ornaments.	Remarks.
Rs.	Rs.	Rs. A. P.	Rs. A. P.	Rs. A. P.	Rs. A. P.	Rs. A. P.	Rs. A. P.	Rs. A. P.	Rs. A. P.	Rs. A. P.	Rs. A. P.	Rs. A. P.	
...	...	Profit including rice ... 40 0 0 Price of goat ... 5 0 0 45 0 0	125 13 0	16 0 0	1 0 0	4 0 0	......	40 0 0	3 0 0	......	10 0 0	1 0 0 For churies of shell-lac and leaden bracelets.	
...	...	Profit in dealing of rice ... 40 0 0	73 4 0	6 0 0	1 0 0	4 0 0	Servant. 12 0 0	33 0 0	1 0 0	......	7 0 0	1 0 0	
...	...		34 14 0	4 8 0	4 0 0	......	......	6 0 0	3 0 0	......	4 0 0	1 0 0	
...	...	Profit in dealing of rice ... 36 0 0 Sale of kid ... 4 0 0 Wages of occasional labour 15 0 0 55 0 0	78 6 0	5 8 0	1 0 0	4 0 0	......	30 0 0	2 0 0	......	7 0 0	1 0 0	
...	...	Gunny-cloth ... 18 0 0	51 0 0	10 0 0	1 0 0	4 0 0	......	29 0 0		......	6 0 0	1 0 0	
...	...	Gunny-cloth ... 24 0 0	29 4 0	5 8 0	......	......	......	29 8 0	......	......	4 0 0		
...	...	Gunny-cloth ... 19 0 0	35 8 0	6 0 0	8 0 0	3 0 0	......	15 0 0		......	5 0 0	1 0 0	
...	...	Gunny-cloth ... 3 0 0	55 0 0	19 8 0	1 0 0	4 0 0	......	17 0 0		6 0 0	5 0 0		
...	...	Gunny-cloth ... 13 0 0	29 12 0	11 0 0	0 8 0	3 0 0	......	12 0 0	......	......	8 0 0	......	
...	...	Gunny-cloth ... 24 0 0	51 8 0	17 0 0	1 0 0	4 0 0	......	24 0 0	......	......	4 0 0		

STATEMENT

1	2	3	4	5	6	7	8		
NAME	Whether raiyat or under-raiyat.	Area of land under cultivation.	Produce annually per bigha.	Quantity of produce sold.	Money value of produce sold.	Quantity kept for food.	Money value of special crops, such as chillies, mangoes, brinjals, &c.	Straw.	Live-stock.
			MDS.	MDS.	RS. A. P.	MDS.	RS. A. P.	RS.	RS.
7. Lal Das Deshi	Raiyat	Aghani ... 11 Bhadoi ... 1 Rabi ... 3 15	At 6 maunds per bigha .. 66 ... . 4 At 1½ maunds per bigha ... 4½ 74½	.... Rabi ... 4½	.... Rabi ... 11 4 0	Aghani ... 66 Bhadoi ... 4 70	Chillies, jute and brinjal 13 0 0	...	...
8. Hadu Deshi	Under-raiyat	Aghani ... 5 Bhadoi ... 2 Rabi ... 4 11	At 6 maunds per bigha .. 30 At 4 maunds per bigha ... 8 At 2 maunds per bigha ... 8 46	.... Rabi ... 8	.... Rabi ... 24 0 0	Aghani ... 30 Bhadoi ... 8 38	Chillies, jute &c., ... 23 0 0	...	...
		823	3,323	1,135	1,277	2,260	182	3	
		B. K. CH. = 21 9 10	MDS. S. CH. = 114 23 7	MDS. S. CH. = 20 5 8	RS. A. P. = 44 0 6	Mds. S. CH. = 77 37 3	RS. A. P. = 6 4 4	0 1 7	

Number of cultivators ...
Ditto of agricultural labourers

Total

CAMP PATIRAJ,
The 15*th April* 1888.

Cultivators—Concluded.

9			10	11				12					23
[F]ROM SALE OF—				EXPENSES OF CULTIVATION.				HOUSEHOLD EXPENSES (ANNUALLY).					
Hides.	Jungle produce.	Any other source.	Total income.	Rent.	Plough.	Bullock.	Any other sort.	Food.	Lodging.	Servants.	Clothes.	Ornaments.	REMARKS.
Rs.	Rs.	Rs. A. P.	Rs. A. P.	Rs. A. P.	Rs. A. P.	Rs. A. P.	Rs. A. P.	Rs. A. P.	Rs. A. P.	Rs. A. P.	Rs. A. P.	Rs. A. P.	
...	...	Gunny-cloth ... 24 0 0	47 4 0	18 0 0	1 0 0	4 0 0	......	16 0 0	......	......	5 0 0	......	
...	...	Do. ... 40 0 0 Profit from mustard seed ... 35 0 0 75 0 0	121 0 0	15 0 0	1 0 0	4 0 0	......	88 0 0 Including rice.	......	......	7 0 0	......	
		723 82	2,185 9 0	370 5 6	43 0 0	153 0 0	197 0 0	765 8 0	10 0 0	8 0 0	195 0 0	8 0 0	
		=24 15 2	=75 5 9	=12 12 3	=1 7 8	=5 4 4	=6 12 8	=26 6 0	=0 5 6	0 3 9	=6 11 7	=0 4 4	

7
2
—
9
—

LALIN CHANDRA RAY,
Settlement Officer Churamon Estate.

STATEMENT B.—

1	2	3	4	5	6	7	8	
NAMES.	Castes.	How employed.	Area of holding, if any.	Area under each kind of crop.	Produce of each sort per bigha.	Quantity of each sort sold.	Money value of column 7.	Quantity of each sort kept for food.
Village Itakhuri.			Bigha.	Bgs.	Mds.	Mds.	Rs. A. P.	Mds.
(1.) Ghatu Deshi ...	Deshi ...	Agricultural labourer.	1	Aghani ... 1	Adhi Aghani 2	......	......	2
Village Biranoi.								
(1.) Kanai Deshi ...	Deshi ...	Ditto ...	......	......	......			
(2.) Pach Katu ...	Pali ...	Ditto ...	7½	Aghani ... 6½ Rabi 1 7½	At 4 maunds per bigha. 26 Ditto ... 1½	Aghani ... 12 Rabi 1½	Aghani 12 0 0 Rabi 3 12 0 15 12 0	Aghani... 14
(3.) Abhoy Pali ...	Do. ...	Ditto ...	......	......	......	......	......	......
(4.) Nambhari Pali ...	Do. ...	Ditto ...	......	......	......		......	......
(5.) Karib Deshi ...	Deshi ...	Ditto ...	6	Adhi Aghani 6	18	......		18

Agricultural Labourer.

10	11				12	13	14	15
Money value of any special crops, such as chillies and mangoes, &c.	Wages of self and family.				Total income.	Number of persons in family.	Cost of cultivation, if any.	Remarks.
	Money.	Food.	Clothes.	Lodging.				
Rs.	Rs. A. P.	Rs. A. P.	Rs. A. P.		Rs. A. P.		Rs. A. P.	
Gunny cloth 12	Self ... 36 0 0	Self ... 16 0 0	Self ... 2 0 0	...	66 0 0	Adults— Male ... 2 Female ... 1 Child ... 1 (Infant) 4	Rent— 0 4 0	
Ditto ... 24	Wages of self and nephew. 72 0 0	Food of self and nephew. 30 0 0	Cloth of self and nephew. 3 0 0	...	129 0 0	Adults— Male ... 2 Female ... 3 Children 6 11	......	
Price of mustard oil prepared. 12	Wages of self. 24 0 0	Self ... 18 8 0	Self ... 2 0 0	...	69 12 0	Adults— Male ... 1 Female ... 1 2	8 6 0	
......	Self and brother. 38 0 0	Self and brother. 30 0 0	Self and brother. 3 0 0	...	71 0 0	Adults— Male ... 2 Female ... 1 3	......	
......	Self and 3 other adults. 57 0 0	Self and 3 other adults. 30 0 0	Self and 3 other adults. 3 0 0	...	90 0 0	Adults— Male ... 2 Female ... 2 Children 8 12	......	
Price of gunny cloth. 54	Self ... 34 0 0	Self ... 16 8 0	Self ... 2 0 0	...	96 0 0	Adults— Male ... 2 Female ... 3 Children 5 10	4 8 0	

STATEMENT B.—

1	2	3	4	5	6	7	8	9
NAMES.	Castes.	How employed.	Area of holding, if any.	Area under each kind of crop.	Produce of each sort per bigha.	Quantity of each sort sold.	Money value of column 7.	Quantity of each sort kept for food.
			Bigha.	Bgs.	Mds.	Mds.	Rs. A. P.	Mds.
(6.) Juranu Deshi ...	Deshi ...	Agricultural labourer.	8	Aghani ... 7 Rabi ... 1	Aghani at 6 maunds per bigha ... 42 Rabi ... 2½	Rabi ... 2	Rabi ... 5 0 0	Aghani... 42 Rabi ... ½
Village Jag Daba.								
(1.) Ananda Deshi ...	Do. ...	Ditto ...	3	Aghani ... 3	18	......	......	Aghani... 18
Village Buripakar Chak.								
(1.) Amiat Nasya ...	Musulman	Ditto ...	......	......	......	......	......	......
(2.) Hagru Nasya ...	Ditto ...	Ditto ...	......	......	......	......	......	......
Village Bage Kokno.								
(1.) Bataahu Deshi ...	Deshi ...	Ditto ...	6	Aghani ... 3½ Bhadoi ... 1 Rabi ... 1½ — 6 —	Aghani at 6 maunds per bigha ... 21 Bhadoi at 6 maunds per bigha ... 6 Rabi at 2½ maunds per bigha ... 2½	Rabi ... 2½	Rabi ... 5 10 0	Aghani... 21 Bhadoi... 6 — 26 —
(1.) Gyan Deshi ...	Do. ...	Ditto ...	......	......	......	......	......	......

C. E. G. & W. LeB.—Reg. No. 18642—137—12-5-88.

Agricultural Labour.—concluded.

10	11				12	13	14	15
Money value of any special crops, such as chillies and mangoes, &c.	Wages of self and family.				Total income.	Number of persons in family.	Cost of cultivation, if any.	Remarks.
	Money.	Food.	Clothes.	Lodging.				
Rs.	Rs. A. P.	Rs. A. P.	Rs. A. P.		Rs. A. P.	6	Rs. A. P.	
Brinjals ... 8	Self and son. 50 0 0	Self and son. 30 0 0	Self and son. 4 0 0	...	97 0 0	Adults— Male ... 3; Female ... 2; Children 4; — 9	8 0 0	
Gunny cloth 16	Self ... 36 0 0	Self ... 16 0 0	Self ... 2 0 0	...	72 0 0	Adults— Male ... 2; Female ... 1; Children 2; — 5	4 0 0	
......	Self ... 24 0 0; And wife by husking rice ... 7 8 0; 31 8 0	Self ... 16 0 0	Self ... 2 0 0	...	49 8 0	Adults— Male ... 1; Female ... 1; Child ... 1 (Infant). — 3		
......	Self ... 30 0 0; Females by husking rice ... 17 0 0; 47 0 0	Self ... 16 0 0	Self ... 2 0 0	...	65 0 0	Adults— Male ... 1; Female 2; Children 2; — 5	......	
Brinjal ... 6; Gunny cloth 12; — 18	Self ... 12 0 0; And 2 sons at Rs. 13 each = 26 0 0; 38 0 0	Self and sons. 48 0 0	Self and sons. 6 0 0	...	109 10 0	Adults— Male ... 3; Female ... 2; — 5	8 12 0	
Gunny cloth 12	Self ... 20 0 0			...	32 0 0	Adults— Male ... 1; Female ... 1; Child ... 1 (infant). — 3	......	

CONFIDENTIAL.]

No. 4, dated Bamunghattee, the 11th April 1888.

From—S. DATTA, ESQ., Settlement Officer, Bamunghattee, Mourbhunj Raj,
To—The Director of Land Records and Agriculture, Bengal (submitted through the Superintendent of Orissa Tributary Mehals).

I HAVE the honour to acknowledge the receipt of your letter No. 709 of 5th instant, ordering me to submit, through the Collector of my district, the report called for by your Nos. 104-119Agri. of 23rd January.

2. I have been ordered by the Superintendent of the Tributary Mehals of Orissa to submit the report through him; so it cannot possibly reach you on 18th or 19th instant.

3. The agricultural classes do not form necessarily the lower classes of the people of Bamunghattee. The sirdars (indigenous police officers) and pradhans, who are all cultivators, form the highest class; the ryots holding lands of about seven acres and over form the middle class; the cultivators whose holdings are not so large, or who make subsistence partly by cultivation and partly by other means, are considered the lower classes.

4. The papers of all the villages of the pergunnah are not fully prepared as yet, but the following figures are taken from 30 villages of a large *pirh* (Jamda).

The average area of holdings, viz.—

	Acres.
Paddy land	6·3
Dohi land	3·1
Total ...	9·4

The holdings are large, and most of the ryots maintain themselves comfortably by agriculture.

5. But as this is a newly opened out country, and as all the culturable lands have been brought under the plough, this state of things will not continue for more than 20 or 25 years as population increases, unless the neighbouring sub-division named Simlipal Hills be brought afresh under cultivation.

6. The following table will show the percentage of holdings—I, over eight acres; II, between 8 acres and 4 acres; and III, under 4 acres, in eight large villages:—

	I	II	III.
Bahalda	37	35	69
Bodkeram	40	43	61
Badra	12	27	25
Bhagat Mohalpani	6	14	10
Malikram	11	30	24
Gamhoria	22	14	19
Paborpur	13	14	11
Tarna	9	37	38
Total percentage ...	24·2	34·4	41·4

If I could get the figures of all the villages (700) of Bamunghattee, I think the percentage of the second class holdings would be found larger.

7. Those who can get little or no maintenance by cultivation have recourse to cocoon-rearing and lac-growing, which (though uncertain) are both very lucrative. Something like 2,500 *kahans*, valued at Rs. 20,000, were grown in the sub-division last year; and the value of the lac grown could not have been less.

8. Cocoon-rearing and lac-growing have so sensibly improved the position of the hiring classes that large cultivators cannot readily get labourers now at the old customary rate, which in some places has been slightly increased.

9. The position of the *pànas* or weavers is hopelessly bad. With the introduction of cheap but rotten Manchester goods, their trade is becoming worse every year. A fair portion of them have taken to agriculture, but the position of the rent is really painful.

10. By the census there were—

(i.)	Aboriginal tribes	69,551
(ii.)	Semi-aboriginal tribes (including Kormis)	11,334
(iii.)	Hindus of all descriptions	12,653
(iv.)	Non-Hindus	499
(v.)	Mahomedans	479
		94,516

These figures will show that this is a truly and strictly aboriginal country, not Hinduised as yet.

11. If it is wanted, I may submit a fuller report on the subject at the end of the settlement work. I have hitherto abstained from making those enquiries which are necessary for information required for this report, lest I should rouse the suspicion of the people; so cannot embody in this report anything more than my general impression that, excepting the weavers, the Bamunghattee people are the happiest people in Bengal, Assam and Orissa.

W. LeB.—Reg. No. 1865C—137—8-5-88.

CONFIDENTIAL.]

No. 4T, dated Uugul, the 12th April 1888.

From—BABOO A. K. ROY, Joint Settlement Officer,
To—The Director of Land Records, Bengal (through the Superintendent, Tributary Mehals, Cuttack).

WITH reference to your letter No. 105Agri., dated 23rd January last, I have the honour to submit a report on the condition of the poorer classes in the Angul estate.

2. Both the tehsildar and Sub-Deputy Collector, to each of whom I forwarded a copy of your letter, were asked for their views on the subject. It is to be regretted that their reports have not been received.

3. In the pergunnah of which the records furnished by the survey were in my charge, statistics have been collected in a few mouzahs on the lines indicated by you in the extract from your letter No. 102T, forwarded to this office. These statistics are embodied in statement I, herewith enclosed. The villages in pergunnah Panchgarh, of which these (rather incomplete) statistics are given, may be taken as specimen villages for the whole pergunnah. If these statements are read in connection with my letter No. 331, dated 15th March 1888, enclosed with my rate report, a pretty correct idea may, it is hoped, be formed of the real condition of the lower classes in the pergunnah. Barring individual mouzahs with peculiar surroundings, such as those bordering upon forest reserves, it may be broadly stated that the condition of life amongst ryots does not differ much in the different pergunnahs of the estate, and the following general observations may be taken to apply to the whole of the estate.

4. *General observations.*—The population of the estate* may be divided into (I) those who live by cultivation, (II) those who live otherwise.

* *Vide* abstract from census schedule herewith enclosed.

In division I are the following classes arranged according to their state of prosperity :—

1. Sarbarakars.
2. Thani (resident, occupancy or settled) ryots.
3. Pahi (non-occupancy) ryots.
4. Shikmis.

It is to be regretted that there is no reliable information regarding the proportion the Thani and Pahi ryots respectively bear to the total population; but without pretending to statistical accuracy, it may be roughly said that with their families "Thani" ryots form about 40 per cent., Pahi 30 per cent., Shikmi or Korfa ryots about 15 or 20 per cent. of the total population. The number of sarbarakars is less than 400 in the whole estate. The remainder of the population come under Division II.

They consist of the Chandua ryots (who hold no land for cultivating purposes) and their relatives.

They are divisible into—

1. (*a*).—*Agricultural labourers*
   (*b*).—*Non-agricultural labourers.*
2. *Beggars.*
3. *Artisans.*—They are—
   (*a*). Weavers.
   (*b*). Dyers.
   (*c*). Potters.
   (*d*). Iron manufacturers.
   (*e*). Barbers.
   (*f*). Blacksmiths.
   (*g*). Washermen.
   (*h*). Rearers of silk-cocoons.
   (*i*). Dealers in silk.

DIVISION I.

5. *Sarbarakars.*—Sarbarakars are as a rule prosperous, though seldom wealthy. Their prosperity is due to the following causes :—

(1).—They receive liberal allowances from Government for the collection of land revenue in their respective mouzahs. The allowances are as high as 15, 20 and 25 per cent. on the gross jummahs.

(2).—They have been allowed, since the last settlement (1855), to take out at a nominal rent junglebooree and moat kabuliyat sarbarakari leases of large areas of cultivable waste and jungle lands, to settle ryots on them, or otherwise cause their cultivation and to enjoy the entire profits of such cultivation, which are often very large.

(3).—They have been allowed during the least 33 years to evict and enhance the rents of the Pahi ryots at pleasure without being themselves liable to pay enhanced revenue.

(4).—They have held and cultivated, by right of priority of occupation as well as by might, the very best lands of the village. Instances of sarbarakars being found in occupation of lakhiraj and jajir lands granted rent free to other parties are not very uncommon.

(5).—Lastly, being usually men of property, position, intelligence and influence, they cultivate their lands better and receive a larger outturn of crops than others. Some of them also sell off their surplus produce to bunniahs at an advantage.

Sarbarakars are seldom found to be indebted. Their houses are large with several farm-yards and idol houses attached to the homestead; their granaries are spacious and well stored; their homestead lands are well cultivated, and their idols are well kept and worshipped. They are themselves well clad, sometimes even showing a gaudy exterior. and so are their families and children, both the latter being adorned generally with silver and gold ornaments, rarely with brass or bronze; and they perform their marriage and religious ceremonies with *eclat*. On such occasions they feed their kith and kim sumptuously with sweets and cakes in addition to the proverbial "ten curries" added to rice and *dâl*. Even the poorer classes of sarbarakars must have, on such occasions, a dozen drums and tom-toms beating all round the village for several days.

Their ordinary diet consists of rice, pulses and vegetables, cooked with mustard oil, salt and spices, ghee often replacing oil. Some of them take daily milk and sweets in addition. Two fresh-cooked meals a day is the usual rule, but three meals are indulged in by some, and four meals (rarely) by others. Each meal usually consists of the following articles:—

Rice	1 lb (half a seer).
Dal (kulthi, biri, moong or ararh)	$\frac{1}{4}$ lb.
Vegetables (brinjal, sag, plantain yams, rarely potatoes) ...	$\frac{1}{8}$ lb.
Salt	$\frac{1}{8}$—$\frac{1}{16}$ of a chittack.

Onions and garlic are not prohibited food to the Gurjat Hindoos, and many sarbarakars have their homestead lands well cultivated with them. Since the reclamation of jungle lands, game has become rather scarce, but the Gurjati has not lost his taste for flesh; the better classes of sarbarakars still indulge in goat's flesh at least once a month. Though the humble *handi* retains its place, brass *gurras*, *cheraga* and *cherag* stands are generally found in sarbarakars' houses, and the brass, *lota* of all sizes invariably so. Iron utensils are to some extent used in their kitchen, but earthen pots very nearly hold their own place. Brass and copper vessels have not as yet been introduced.

The sarbarakars preferring Manchester goods, have for the most part rejected country-made fabrics. These, though certainly more durable, are more expensive. On the other hand, their women as yet show no preference to machine-made cloths, and the chief reason is that they find their dimensions unsuited to their mode of dressing. The length of the cloth used by them varies between 12 and 14 hands.

The more respectable sarbarakars wear jackets and sometimes country-made slippers; but their children have all learnt (since the survey training class came into existence) the use of the coat and boots.

Sarbarakars generally keep in their house a cot or *charpay*, and have both a quilt and a pillow for their bedding. Mats and blankets (sometimes carpets) are also used by them.

Here and there, amongst Pans, exceptional cases of needy sarbarakars are to be met with; but their indigence is not due to a want of income, but to extravagance and drunkenness.

6. *Thani ryots.*—Thani ryots, too, are seldom needy. This is due to the fact that they were allowed, under the terms of the pottahs granted to them at the last settlement, to reclaim from the jungle, and cultivate without paying any additional rent, as much land as the quantity they severally engaged for at the last settlement. It is true the sarbarakars have in many cases deprived them of their rights, and exacted from them rent for land which they were entitled to hold rent-free during the term of the last settlement But I have as yet come across no case in which a Thani ryot has been deprived of this right wholesale.

The condition of the Thani ryot differs of course according to the area and class of his holding, just as much as the condition of the sarbarakar differs according to the area and class of his mouzah. But while it can be said that no sarbarakars are in absolute want, it cannot be said that all Thani ryots enjoy that sort of immunity from poverty. The lesser Thani ryots gradually merge into the poverty-stricken class of Pahi ryots.

7. *Pahi ryots.*—Thani ryots holding land in non-occupancy rights are called Pahi in respect of such lands. But these ryots enjoy, as a fact, occupancy rights on these lands, and they cannot properly be included in the class "Pahi." It is also well to exclude from this category ryots who, owning land in any of the neighbouring estates, hold in addition some lands in this estate as Pahi ryots. By the term "Pahi." I wish to signify all ryots who hold land exclusively in the Pahi interest. Very few, if indeed any, of such ryots appear to be well off. They have hitherto been at the mercy of the sarbarakar, who has been allowed to eject them with impunity as soon as he got his lands reclaimed and prepared by them at their cost and expense.

8. *Shikmis.*—There is not much to choose between Pahi ryots and Shikmis; but while the one class hold land on their own account, and continue to hold on in spite of enhanced rents, in hope of securing occupancy rights and having these rights recognised by Government, the other class give up their cultivation of their superior ryots' lands as soon as they find the rent too heavy.

9. Leaving out the Pans and Haris, who are undoubtedly the poorest, as they are the most wicked and criminal of all the ryots of the estate, whether they are Thani or Pahi (even amongst them the relative condition of the Thani ryot is certainly superior to that of the Pahi, there is not much difference in the mode of living between the poorest class of Thani ryots and the

poor Pahi and Chandua ryots. They live in huts that are no better than hovels, and seldom have any stored grain as a "reserve" against scarcity. They possess but little "Harmasúl" lands, and have therefore to go for the greater part of the year without sufficient vegetables in their meals. Their diet usually consists of from two to three pounds or more of rice and a quarter of a chittack of salt; *dál* (moong, biri or kulthi), though greatly wished for, is not always obtained. *Ság* or green leaves plucked from wild plants is added to their meal whenever they can be had. Green mangoes, the mohun fruit, the fruit of the kendoo (*diospyros*), yams (*dioscorea*), and the roots or fruits of other wild plants are added to their daily food whenever these are available. But it has to be observed that although these things are had recourse to as additional articles of diet, these ryots never subsist on them exclusively. They have always a stock of rice at home sufficient or nearly sufficient to last them during the year, and these additional articles serve merely as auxiliaries both to prolong the lasting of their stores of rice and to add body and flavour to their daily diet. When their stock of rice gets exhausted, or when they perceive such exhaustion to be imminent, they would agree to serve as agricultural labourers; but it is considered a great humiliation. It is on this account that the number of labourers having profits of small holdings is very small in this estate.

Ryots of this class are generally economical, and they content themselves with cooking their vegetables (whenever these can be had) with salt and castor or mustard oil, which they also rub on their body before bathing (and those who can afford, before going to bed). Milk, ghee, cakes, and sweets are things which are almost as good as unknown to them, milk being given only to infants and new-born babes.

Even the lowest and poorest amongst this class of ryots cannot, in my opinion, be said to suffer in physique from an insufficiency of food; but an insufficiency of salt and vegetables in their diet is noticeable.

The better amongst this class of ryots use brass utensils; but while the poorer sarbarakars and Thani ryots each have several brass *gurras* and *lotas*, the very best amongst these would seldom have more than a couple of *gurras* and *lotas* each, while the poorer amongst them would share one *gurra* and one *lota* between three or four of them. Earthen pots still predominate amongst this class of ryots. They sleep on the floor of their huts on a *chatai patia* (made out of the leaf of the date palm), *masina* or *masuni* (made out of the leaf of a species of cypress), with a piece of wood (*pudu*) serving as a pillow. Carpets, blankets, beds and bedsteads, which are rare even amongst Thani ryots, may be said to be absent in the houses of Pahi ryots.

10. The ornaments worn and cost of marriage ceremonies amongst the several classes of inhabitants of the estate may be roughly estimated as follows:—

I.—*The average sarbarakars.*—(*a*) Ornaments for men—

	Rs.	A.	P.
Loory (earrings, golden), two to each ear	6	10	0
Mala (for the neck, golden), one	10	15	0
Total ...	16	15	0

(*b*) For women—

		Rupees.	
Nakchana	for the nose ...	10—20	or more.
Fully			
Dandy			
Loory (earring)	" ear ...	15—30	"
Phasia			
Chaurimundi	" head ...	5— 6	"
Necklace (gold) ...	...	20—50	"
Finger rings, four or five ...	... ...	10—20	"
Gajra ...	For the arm (of silver or gold)	20—40	"
Churi ...			
Tara (for arm)	... ...	5—20	
Bechaha, jhuntia, bala, habula (of silver for the ankle or foot)		15—50	
	Total ...	100 (to 236 up to Rs. 500)	

(*c*) For children—

	Rupees.
Kharoo (silver) bracelet	4— 6
Loory (earrings)	6—10
Konthi (neck)	4— 6
Total ...	14—22

And often the following:—

Finger rings	2— 5
Silver waistband	10—15
Total	26—42

The dowry given to the bride at marriage varies amongst respectable sarbarakars from Rs. 50 to Rs. 100, and the total cost of a marriage ceremony amongst them is roughly estimated as between Rs. 100 to Rs. 500.

II.—*The average Thani ryot.*—Amongst Paiks and high castes, men do not wear ornaments, but amongst Gouras and others, men do.

	Rupees.
(*a*) Men—	
Silver kharoo	6 to 10
Loory, four	12 to 15
Total	18 to 25
(*b*) Women—	
Kharoo (brass), 10 or 12 pieces	3 to 6
Loory (gold), two or four	6 to 10
Nose ornaments, fully, dandy, nackchana, &c. ...	10 to 20
Tara (brass or silver)	2 to 10
Bala (bell-metal)	1-8 to 4
Total ...	22-8 to 50
(*c*) Children—	
Kharoo	2 to 4
Loory	6 to 8
Kanthi	4 to 10
Total	12 to 22

The dowry of the bride at marriage costs from Rs. 10 to Rs. 50. The minimum cost of marriage is Rs. 15, the maximum Rs. 100.

III.—*The average Pahi ryot.*

Ornaments for women—		
Brass kharoo	Rs.	2 to 5
Fully	As.	1 to 2
Mudu	,,	1 to 2
Kansa bala	Rs.	2 to 3
Brass tara (silver)	,,	1-8 to 6-12
Total ...	Rs.	5-10 to 15

The cost of marriage with the average Pahi ryot varies from Rs. 10 to Rs. 25.

11. For an account of the Pans and Haris—the lowest and poorest by far of the Gurjati ryots—I would solicit a reference to my letter No. 331 (enclosed with late report). Some of the poor Pans literally subsist for some months on the fruits of trees and bulbs or roots of wild plants. The following are amongst the plants which supply the Pans, Haris, and other poor people with food:—

Kendoo (Diospyros)	Fruit.
Anaba (Mangifera indica)	,,
Mohala (Bassia latipolea)	,,
Kaitha (Feronia elephanti)	,,
Jamboo (Engina Jambolum)	,,
Chara	,,
Boonra	,,
Dhirai Kulee	,,
Khur Kulee	,,
Khejar (Phœnix dactylifera)	,,
Tala (Borassus flabelli formis)	,,
Kaina (Tentuli) (Tamarindus indica)	,,
Salu Sarki (Shorea robusta)	Flower.
Kanter Thulkur.	
Kusum	Fruit.
Panioloo.	
Pitu.	
Kalian (œ).	
Kabara.	
Ghorooroo.	
Karauj.	

With the reclamation of jungle lands, these trees are becoming scarce, and barring the reserved and unreserved forests none of them is to be found in large numbers except the mango and the mohua and the tal palm.

12. Abject poverty, though rare, is still not altogether absent. I have come across starving women and children with nothing but the remnants of tattered rags round their waists—undeveloped urchins and thin—lean, wasted skeleton-like old men—all looking like famine-stricken people—poverty and misery both. This is, I believe, only possible amongst Pans and Haris, and rarely perhaps amongst one or two Khoina and Kond families.

13. Women of the better classes of ryots earn no money and do no field work. Their chief duty consists in cooking the daily meals of the family and looking after other household duties. Women of the poorer classes, specially amongst the lower castes, such as Gouras, Tantis, Khorias, Pans, and Haris, collect cowdung and fuel, and add to their husbands' income by spinning cotton and sundry other work. The Goura women are by both caste and profession good dairy maids. Women of all classes and castes husk paddy.

14. The agricultural resources of the country are large, but it will be long before they are properly utilized. There can be no doubt that the country is rapidly advancing under British rule; but its agricultural condition is yet very backward. and no wonder. Wild or semi-wild people, who have hitherto received an abundance of food-supply from nature, with little on no labour, can hardly be expected, under the influence of a short period of British rule, to develop industrious habits and take great pains or devote great labour for the production of food.

It will be some time before they are fully educated to their wants and needs, and it will require a longer time before they evolve the requisite faculties of industry and assiduity in the production of their food. It is for this reason that agriculture is yet scarcely out of its rudimentary state in the Gurjats, and amongst Pans and Haris in particular. No doubt also for this reason the supply of labour of all kinds is still very limited. Until lately wild fruits and edible roots were to be found in abundance in this estate, and the Pans and Haris could with impunity steal their neighbour's property. Life was easy. Now things are changed. The old trees and roots have either vanished or are vanishing rapidly, and there is competition for culturable waste and jungle lands. There is besides the hard grip of the law, which destroys personal liberty the moment a neighbour's estate is encroached upon or his property is stolen. The more intelligent classes have fully realized all this, and have adapted themselves to the times: the less intelligent classes are following in their wake, and are gradually evolving faculties required to cope with the situation; while the least intelligent classes find it still very difficult to realize their condition; and, like the majority of the Pans and the Haris, now take to leading a nomad life in the jungles. now to emigration, and now to theft and robbery, to escape from what they consider as a very severe struggle for existence.

15. The sense of security that has been generated amongst the respectable classes of people by the administration of law and order could not fail to be an attraction to respectable residents of the neighbouring tributary states. The result is seen in emigration of such people from these states into Angul. Nearly all the small mouzahs of pergunnah Panchgar are inhabited by emigrants from Dhenkanal, Talchar, and Hindol.

DIVISION II. *Chandua Ryots.*

16. (*a*) *Agricultural Labourers.*—These are (1) ploughmen and (2) shepherds and cow-boys. Both are generally engaged by the year, seldom by the season, never by the month or by the week. During the harvesting season, they are sometimes employed by the day.

The wages of a ploughman generally are as follows:—

	Money value. Rs.	A.	P.
6 Khandis of paddy per month for eight months of the year* ...	8	0	0
60 „ again for the whole year	10	0	0
10 „ in advance	1	10	6
One pair of clothes	1	0	0
Cash	1	0	0
Mahfi, or estimated produce of a bit of land given rent free ...	1	0	0
Total ...	22	10	6

Where the twelve-month payment of paddy is made, the wages come up to Rs. 25-10-6.

In addition to this, the ploughman gets his lodging free and also receives perquisites on ceremonious occasions.

These wages are uniform, or nearly uniform, all over the estate.

The ploughman usually does the work of both shepherd and cow-boy. Those who keep a lot of cattle entertain in addition one to two cow-boys. One boy is supposed to be capable of keeping only 10 bullocks in his charge. His wages are 60 mans of paddy per year per pair. His earnings come therefore to be about 25 mans of paddy per month. This is often supplemented by presents from the employer on festive occasions. Practically a boy of from 12 to 16 years of age is found to be in charge of nearly double the number of cattle, and his earnings, though not quite doubled, are at any rate near one and a half times as much. A boy of the same age would be found in charge of six pairs (*hals*) of buffaloes, although three pairs is considered to be a good number. For tending three pairs of buffaloes, he would receive three khandis (equal to sixty mans or nearly eighteen seers) of paddy per month.

* Occasionally for twelve months.

Boys in this estate begin to tend sheep and gather cowdung and firewood at the age of six or seven. Three or four such boys are often found in charge of about twenty sheep and a herd of cattle numbering 20 or 30 heads. Women of the labouring class do not, as a rule, get work all the year round. During the rains and the harvesting season they are employed in the paddy fields, but their chief work is husking paddy. When working by the day in the fields, they would get from five to ten mans of paddy daily as their wages, according as they work for five or ten hours a day (male labourers employed by the day would also get the same wages). When employed in husking paddy, women receive one man of rice (not unhusked) for each khandi of paddy husked. If fully employed during the day, they would earn about six to eight mans of rice, but as a rule their daily earnings do not exceed four mans and are often less, because people do not like to get more than three or four khandis of paddy husked at a time. In addition to the rice, they get the bran (but not the chaff), a little salt, oil and turmeric as perquisites.

Many of the labourers of the Pan caste can weave. When manual labour is not in demand and rice is scanty, as during the hot-weather months, they eke out a rather precarious livelihood by weaving coarse cloths. Their women, too, turn out a little money by spinning cotton.

The average annual income of the family of an agricultural labourer, consisting of man, wife and one child (one boy of 12 years of age), would be approximately as follows:—

	Rice.	Perquisites.			Total money value.		
	Khandis.	Rs.	A.	P.	Rs.	A.	P.
Man	144	6	0	0	30	0	0
Woman	72	3	0	0	15	0	0
Boy (10 to 12 years of age) ...	18	2	0	0	5	0	0
Total	234	10	0	0	50	0	0

Their average annual expenditure would be approximately as under—

I.—For food.

	Rice.	Other articles, such as salt, spices, oil, vegetables, &c.			Total.		
	Khandis.	Rs.	A.	P.	Rs.	A.	P.
Man ...	54	3	0	0	12	0	0
Woman ...	54	5	0	0	14	0	0
Boy ...	36	2	0	0	8	0	0
Total ...	144	10	0	0	34	0	0
II.—For ornaments, clothing, and sundry other things ...	...	...			10	0	0
In all					44	0	0

This would leave a balance of Rs. 6 in the hands of the labourer at the end of the year. It is possible for a prudent man to lay it by and in a few years to buy a pair of bullocks, and gradually pass on from the position of labourer to that of cultivator. Cases of such transition, though not unknown, are yet few.

The higher castes, such as Paiks, Sudas, Chasas, &c., look down upon the labouring class with contempt. Only Gourus, Khoiras, Toouras, Konds, Pans and Haris are found willing to work as labourers.

17. (*b*). *Non-agricultural labourers.*—These consists of the Koras of Sanbalpore. There are about 100 of them here, and they are employed on the roads. Their wages vary from two to four annas a day.

18. *Beggars.*—In this estate professional beggars are very few in number. As far as my information goes, there are only three families of beggars—one family at Kosla, a second at Khalasi, and a third at Bagdia, three villages in three different pergunnahs. They number in all about thirty persons. They are locally known as "Yoges," but are not in any sense renowned for their asceticism.

Boys and girls of the lower castes, such as Toouras, Khoiras, Lobons, &c., are sometimes seen begging in the streets, but they do not practise begging as a profession.

19. 3. *Artizans.* (*a*) *Weavers.*—Within the last twenty years the weaving industry has, it is said, greatly declined. The weaver caste no longer depend, as they did twenty years ago, on weaving as their only means of livelihood, but have betaken themselves to agricultural pursuits. Although the poorer classes of people still prefer the durability of the coarse native cloth to the fineness of Manchester fabric, yet the handlooms do not pay, and they are used more with a view to supply domestic needs than to supply the local demand for cloth.

The parts and price of an ordinary handloom such as is generally used by the poorer classes of Pans and weavers are as follows :—

Number.	Local name of parts of a handloom.	Value.		
		Rs.	A.	P.
1	Pania	0	4	9
1	Tanta	0	12	0
1	Toora	0	8	0
4	Baws	0	3	0
2	Chakis	0	2	0
2	Maruni	0	4	0
1	Rope	0	4	0
1	Nalee or danya made of deer horn (or buffaloes' horn) ...	1	0	0
1	Arta	0	4	0
1	Asari	0	1	0
1	Small charpi	0	0	6
1	Kancha	1	0	0
1	Maria	0	3	0
1	Kondakatee	0	0	6
	Masuli, wooden pegs, &c. &c.	0	5	9
	Total cost ...	5	8	0

An ordinary loom lasts for about thirty years. The depreciation with cost of repairs and interest on capital would together be about Rs. 1-8 per year.

The market price of a piece of cloth turned out by the loom, and measuring 16 hands long and two hands broad, is Rs. 1-8. For each such piece cotton of the value of Rs. 1-2 has to be exchanged by the weaver for the quantity of thread required. One man takes about four days to make such a piece, so that his daily earnings are not higher than one anna six pies.

A family of weavers consisting of man, wife and child (say about twelve years of age) will turn out about 100 to 120 pieces of cloth in the year, if employed on no other work. The receipts and expenditure of the most laborious family would be—

Receipts.	Rs.	A.	P.	Expenditure.	Rs.	A.	P.
120 pieces of cloth at Rs. 1-8 each ...	180	0	0	Thread at Rs. 1-2 per piece	135	0	0
				Depreciation of implements and interest on capital...	1	8	0
				Sundries ...	0	8	0
Total ...	180	0	0	Total ...	137	0	0

The balance of income over expenditure is thus Rs. 43 only. It is to be observed that this is less by Rs. 7 than that of an agricultural labourer.

20. (*b*). *Dyres*.—There are no professional dyers in the estate.

21. (*c*). *Potters*.—The potting industry has had encouragement from both the late Chief of Angul and the British Raj. Many potters have still some lands awarded to them as rent-free jagir, yet it has perceptibly declined, everybody says, within the last few years, the one great reason being the increased demand for brass vessels. But the potters have more or less concentrated themselves in one or two villages in each pergunnah of the estate. This fact, the formation of something like a co-operative society, has helped a good deal in keeping up the profession as a paying concern.

A family of potters consisting of man, wife and child (above ten years of age) would turn out in the year, if constantly employed—and the potters are as a rule constantly employed—earthen pots to the value of about Rs. 60 in the year). The cost of production would be about Rs. 5 including the value of the fuel consumed, depreciation of implements, and interest on capital. They are better off than both agricultural labourers and weavers, but there is the risk of fire in their godowns, which they say occurs every five or six years and causes damages amounting to Rs. 20 at the least.

22. (*d*). *Iron manufacturers*.—With all the hard work for which the iron manufacturers are famous, these people are in a bad way. They work, it is said, men, women and children, for ten to fourteen hours a day (the two cases I have seen corroborate this view), and yet cannot eke out a decent livelihood, in spite of the fact that they pay nothing for the native ore. The largest number of these is in pergunnah Uperbis, but their actual number is not known. It is said, but I have had no opportunity of testing it, that two able-bodied persons, say man and woman, working all day long, cannot earn more than one anna a day. I have

seen a dozen of these people who came a-begging to Ungul turn about a couple of months ago, and they did really look famished.

23. (e). *Rearers of silk cocoons and dealers in silk.*—The reclamation of jungle land has very nearly exterpated both these classes from the estate. In pergunnah Tindes near the Almallik boundary, the rearers still survive in small numbers. Formerly the Pans and Haris used to depend largely on this industry for their livelihood. But the asan tree (*Terminalia tomentosa*), on the leaves of which the silkworms feed, and upon which chiefly are silkworms reared in this estate, has been all but driven into the reserved forest by the denuding axe of the cultivator, and the silkworm rearers have necessarily dwindled down to a very small number. But the few that survive are said to be not very badly off. According to the account given me by two Pans, they still seem to make each a clear profit of from Rs. 40 to Rs. 60 within the three months of the rearing season.

24. Blacksmiths, washermen and village barbers enjoy the profits of small holdings rent free in addition to their ordinary wages, which in no case have I found to be less than four mans of paddy per diem on the average. These wages are gradually increasing, but still with this increase these people cannot to said to be above poverty. They appear, however, to be better off than agricultural labourers, and so are braziers and goldsmiths.

25. To sum up my own general impressions regarding the condition of the population of this estate—

(1). As to the cultivating classes—

(*i*). The sarbarakars with their relations, numbering no less than 2,500 to 3,000 persons, are well-to-do, though not affluent.

(*ii*). The Thani ryots would not come to be included in the poorer classes of the population.

(*iii*). Of the Pahi ryots, those having a holding of, say, three acres and under are certainly very poor. Their income from land does not exceed Rs. 30 in average years, while their cost of cultivation in seldom less than Rs. 10. Naturally they have to borrow rice for their subsistence, and are therefore the class of people mostly indebted. They are worse off than labourers and artizans, and have to look to the produce of the jungle, more than any other class of people, as an additional means of living.

2. As to the non-cultivating classes—

(*i*). Agricultural labourers seldom starve.

(*ii*). The weavers are worse off than agricultural labourers, *i.e.* those few of them who hold no land.

(*iii*). Potters are better off than agricultural labourers.

(*iv*). The iron manufacturers are the worst of all.

The typical mouzahs selected in pergunnahs Panchgar would give a very fair idea, in my opinion, of the general condition of the population as far as the several classes are represented in them. But the numerical values of the several classes in these villages afford no criterion for the whole estate. Statistical information regarding each separate class is not available. But if I were to make a guess, I would say that the total of all classes, Pahi ryots, Shikmis, labourers, weavers, iron manufacturers and others, who may be considered as suffering in physique from an insufficiency of food, would not in any case exceed five per cent. of the total population of the estate.

The actual condition of the tenantry of this estate appears to me to compare unfavourably with that of Raipur in the Central Provinces, and much more so with that of Bengal proper.

Statement I.—Population, &c., of a few typical villages of Pergunnah Panchyar.

Name of village.	Total number of				Beggars.				Labourers who have no land for cultivation.				Number of non-working persons in labourers' families.				Labourers having small holding.*				Non-working number in family of column 5.				Description of food consumed by the adult—			Description of food consumed by the non-adult—			Remarks.
	Men.		Women.		Men.		Women.		Men.		Women.		Men.		Women.		Men.		Women.		Men.		Women.		Man or women.			Boy or girl.			
	Adult.	Non-adult.	Adult.	Non-adult.	Adult.	Non-adult.	Adult.	Non-adult.	Adult.	Non-adult.	Adult.	Non-adult.	Adult.	Non-adult.	Adult.	Non-adult.	Adult.	Non-adult.	Adult.	Non-adult.	Adult.	Non-adult.	Adult.	Non adult.	Kind of food.	Quantity.	Price.	Kind of food.	Quantity.	Price.	
Golmara	217	129	235	142	...	...	...	...	36	32	36	53	1	12	1	14	...	...	...	...	...	...	...	...	Rice, salt and vegetables with *dâl* (occasionally).	Given under the head of agricultural labour in the body of the accompanying report.					Old mouzah (large).
Apurtipur	16	14	18	8	...	...	...	...	...	...	...	...	...	...	...	...	...	...	...	...	...	...	...	...							New " (small).
Achaipur	6	1	6	2	...	...	...	...	...	...	...	...	...	...	...	...	...	...	...	...	...	...	...	...							Just reclaimed mouzah.
Majbeka	9	11	7	3	...	...	...	...	...	...	...	...	...	...	...	...	...	...	...	...	...	...	...	...							Pan mouzah.
Tantelihata	23	21	38	19	...	...	...	...	4	2	3	5	...	...	...	...	...	...	...	...	...	...	...	...							Ditto.
Barachur	12	10	12	15	...	...	...	...	1	...	1	...	...	...	...	...	...	...	...	...	...	...	...	...							Ditto.
Budapank	244	169	261	186	1	...	2	...	13	12	15	14	1	3	2	4	1	2	1	1	5	2	5	3							Typical old mouzah.
Panarahkarani	24	17	19	23	...	...	...	...	1	...	1	3	...	...	...	...	...	...	...	...	...	...	...	...							Pan mouzah.

* Ryots with small holdings would occasionally work as labourers; but it is difficult to make them confess it. The total number of such ryots in mouzah Budapank is, according to the sarbarakar, 88 out of a total population of 880, *i.e.*, just 10 per cent. The total number of persons these 80 men have to support (besides themselves) is 73.

A. K. Roy,

Joint Settlement Officer.

Statement showing the outturn and consumption of crops in pergunnah Punchgar.

(Excluding two mouzahs as not yet measured.)

Particulars.		Amount.		
OUTTURN, &c.		Rs.	A.	P.
I.—Saradh—	Bharans.			
First class 1,460 acres at 3 bharans per acre ...	4,380			
Second class 2,025 acres at 2½ bharans per acre ...	5,062			
Third class 3,350 acres at 1½ bharans per acre ...	5,025			
Total ...	14,467			
Paddy 14,467 bharans at Rs. 5 per bharan ...		72,335	0	0
II.—Taila—	Rs.			
First class—*Bealidhan*, acres 195=195 bharan (minimum yield), at Rs. 3 per bharan ...	585			
Ditto. —Kothi, 195 acres = 48 = 195 bharans (minimum yield), at Rs. 8 per bharan ...	384			
		969	0	0
Second class—Rase 1,935·5 acres = 19.350 khandis (minimum yield) at Re. 1 per 4 khandis		4,837	8	0
Third class—Rase 32,508 khandis at Re. 1 per 4 khandis ...		81,271	0	0
Total ...		86,268	8	0
*Total consumption in the year as detailed below		50,000	0	0
Money value of surplus price		36,268	8	0
Amount Government jummah at proposed rates		11,500	0	0
Balance ...		24,768	8	0

POPULATION.†

			Seers.
Men and women	3,955	at 12 chittacks per head per day ...	2,966½
Children ...	3,954	at 8 ditto ditto ...	1,477
Total ...	6,909		4,443

* 4,443 seers of rice = 8,886 seers of paddy = 22,216 mans = 27·77 bharans = 138·85 rupees per day = 138·85 × 12 × 30 per year = 1,666·20 × 30 per year = 49,986 rupees, say = 50,000 rupees.

† Excluding the two mouzahs not yet measured.

Existing classification of ryots into Thani, Pahi and Chandua in a few Mouzahs of Pergunnah Panchgar.

Number.	NAME OF MOUZAH.	Thani ryots of last settlement.	Pahi ryots.	Chandua ryots.	Total ryots.	Ryots with holdings of three acres and under.	Ryots with rentals of Rs. 5 and under.	REMARKS.
1	Golmarah ...	81	100	30	211	65	......	
2	Majhika ...	......	13	......	13	10	3	According to statements of ryots.
3	Tentelihatata ...	......	18	......	18	8	......	
4	Bagachur ...	1	14	......	15	8	3	Ditto.
5	Budupank ...	104	78	2	184	49	71	Ditto.
6	Panarahkarani ...	1	10	3	14	5	6	Ditto.

Explanation.—This list includes only those who have their names entered in the khasras. Other members of their family are excluded. Out of a total population of 880 in Budapank, only 184 are ryots, of whom 12 per cent. are Thani and 9 per cent. are Pahi.

Abstract from the census returns, 1881.

No.	NAME OF KILLAH.	Occupied houses.	Unoccupied houses.	Male.	Female.	Total.	Resident population.	REMARKS.
1	Uperbis	4,107	1	11,619	11,132	22,751	22,145	The census papers were burnt up, and these figures are not supposed to be very accurate, but they would clearly show the relative values of the pergunnahs.
2	Tainsilis	410	......	1,059	942	2,001	2,000	
3	Panchgar	1,244	......	3,775	3,797	7,572	7,458	
4	Khambakalinga ...	2,244	9	6,672	6,545	13,217	12,847	
5	Poornaghur	660	......	1,724	1,598	3,322	3,120	
6	Tikerpara	611	......	1,600	1,444	3,044	2,870	
7	Taras	2,529	5	7,159	7,081	14,240	13,989	
8	Talmul	2,704	3	8,997	8,827	17,824	17,286	
9	Tindes	1,821	......	4,363	4,312	8,639	8,527	
10	Gondibeah	1,589	......	4,635	4,404	9,075	8,781	
	Total ...	17,719	18	51,403	50,082	1,01,425	99,032	

	Cattle.														Sheep.				Goats.		Fowls.						
	Bulls.		Bullocks.		Cows.		Calves.		Bull buffaloes.				She buffaloes.		Rams.		Ewes.										
	Number.	Length and height.	Number.	Length and height.	Number.	Length and height.	Male number.	Female length and height.	Number.	Length and height.	Number.	Length and height.	Number.	Length and height.	Number.	Length and height.	Number.	Length and height.	He goats.	She goats.	Cocks.	Hens.	Number of ploughs.	Number of carts and gotias.	Number of wells.	Number of tanks.	Number of horses.
Golmarah	1	6×4	211	6×4	254	6×4	84	87	10	6×4	72	7×5	40	7×5	12	3×3	85	3×2	15	40	17	30	136	71	25	30	...
Apartipur	...	...	19	6×4	18	6×4	9	4	...	...	2	7×5	...	...	4	3×2	15	3×2	1	4	5	6	12	3	...	1	...
Achalpur	...	...	12	6×4	...	...	...	...	...	...	2	7×5	...	...	...	...	2	3×2	...	2	3	1	6	3	...	3	...
Majheka	...	...	14	6×4	...	...	...	...	...	...	...	...	...	...	...	...	...	...	3	7	5	10	7	1	...	1	...
Tentalihata	2	6×4	19	6×4	34	6×4	15	5	...	...	16	7×5	12	7×5	4	3×2	12	3×2	4	20	3	5	20	3	...	3	...
Bagachur	...	...	11	6×4	3	6×4	1	2	...	...	...	...	...	...	...	...	...	...	1	4	3	4	6	...	...	2	...
Budupank	6	6×4	223	6×4	229	6×4	77	80	6	6×4	94	7×5	140	7×5	16	3×2	88	3×2	17	93	54	60	171	68	5	23	2
Panarahkarani	...	...	37	6×7	46	6×4	6	5	...	...	4	7×5	...	...	...	...	5	3×2	1	12	3	11	19	10	...	2	...

A. K. Roy,
Joint Settlement Officer.

H. P.—Reg. No. 1862C—137—9-5-68.

CONFIDENTIAL.]

No. 233, dated Camp Buloah, the 13th April 1888.

From—E. W. COLLIN, ESQ., C.S., Settlement Officer, Raj Banaili and Srinagar Estate,
To—The Collector of Bhagulpore.

WITH reference to the circular letter No. 35Agri., dated 9th December, from the Secretary to the Government of Bengal, Revenue Department, calling for an enquiry as to the condition of the lower classes in Bengal, I have the honour to submit the following report in accordance with instructions from the Director of Land Records, Bengal (No. 714, dated 5th April 1888).

2. I have, as suggested in the letter from the Government of Bengal, made detailed enquiries in regard to two villages in the Duphar pergunnah of Bhagulpore where settlement operations are going on. Baboo Burhandeo Narain, First Assistant Settlement Officer, has made similar enquiries in pergunnah Khulekhund, and has been directed to submit his report to you direct.

3. I have submitted the results of my enquiries in an appendix (in original), and I beg to make the following remarks upon the facts there given.

4. I understand that the enquiry is intended to determine whether the lower classes of the population have sufficient means of subsistence. The first point, therefore, to determine is what is sufficient for subsistence. It may be presumed that the wealthier raiyats have a sufficiency, and the amount of food consumed by the poorer classes may be taken as a test. It appears that in this pergunnah a raiyat dependent on labour consumes a little less than a seer of either rice or bread made of *merua* or such pulses. The amount of food is varied, according as the staple food is supplemented by dâl, vegetables, &c. This amount is consumed in two meals, and is presumably sufficient.

5. The next question is whether the poorest class can always obtain this daily supply of food. Those dependent on agriculture must be first considered. A family in the two villages, where enquiries were made, averages six persons, of whom two are able-bodied males, two able-bodied females, and two infants, or men and women unable to work. They do not all eat so much as an able-bodied man, and an allowance of four seers per day is considered sufficient for a family. This makes a total requirement of 36 maunds a year. Now, it will be seen from the figures given in the appendix that a holding of 2½ acres will supply this amount of grain, after deducting all expenses of cultivation and rent. In addition to the produce of the land, it appears that the raiyats of the two villages have other means of subsistence from cattle, with which the villages are well stocked. I conclude, therefore, that a raiyat holding over 3 acres is well off for all ordinary contingencies, allowing for his expenditure on clothes about Rs. 4 per year at the lowest calculation per family. It remains to consdier the condition of those who hold less than 3 acres.

6. It should be first pointed out that it is almost impossible to ascertain the area held by each raiyat. They cultivate lands in more villages than one, and any conclusions drawn from the examination of the rent-roll of a single village is sure to be fallacious. In the Mozufferpore settlement proceedings, the area of a raiyat in any particular village had to be increased by 33 per cent. to ascertain the total area cultivated by him in all villages. For this reason any conclusions drawn from road cess returns are unsatisfactory. The number of raiyats in Rughunathpur holding under 3 acres is 50 per cent. of the whole number, but it is known that a large number of these hold lands in the surrounding villages, and also cultivate rice lands on produce-rents. The village of Rughunathpur is situated on high ground surrounded by low-lying villages where rice is grown, and where the inhabitants are few. The raiyats of Rughunathpur therefore hold lands in those villages. In Sitapur the number of raiyats holding under 3 acres is 26 per cent. of the total number, and of these some hold lands in other villages, and others hold as sub-tenants on produce-rents. I estimate therefore that the number of raiyats holding under 2½ acres does not exceed 20 per cent. of the total number. For most of these, there is probably some special reason for their holding such a small amount of land, as they have other means of subsistence. Thus, Jogrup Sahu in Rughunathpur holds 1½ acres, and has besides 6 cows, 4 bullocks, 2 buffaloes, 2 goats, 1 plough, and an oil-mill. Purae Mandal holds 2½ acres, and has 7 cows, 2 bullocks, 2 goats, and a plough. Other raiyats are known to work as labourers besides being cultivators. Further, in considering the statistics of population, I have calculated the average family at six persons; but some families of course exceed this number, while others are less, and it is probable that the small families have small holdings. Considering that the rent of land is very low in this pergunnah, the highest rate being not more than Rs. 3 per acre, and waste land is fairly plentiful, it is not probable that any raiyat holds less than he requires for the support of his family.

7. The next class of persons to be considered are those dependent upon labour. The number of these amount to about 35 per cent. in the two villages, of whom about half are dependent upon the proceeds of their various occupations, such as weaving and the like. The remaining 17 per cent. are dependent on field labour, and it is to be considered whether they get sufficient to support themselves and their families. This 17 per cent. represents about 102 persons, of whom 32 will be able-bodied men, 32 able-bodied females, and 38 infants or sick persons. Now the daily wage paid in kind is four pucca seers of unhusked rice, which, when husked, will make 3 seers of rice. Assuming that labour is continuous, each family will have two members earning daily 6 seers of rice, whereas the total requirement of a family is four seers. It appears therefore that, assuming that labour is continuous, there is a sufficient

margin after providing for the daily food of the family. It remains to be seen if the labour is continuous. According to the figures for the two villages under report, there are in Rughunathpur 34 labourers and in Sitapur 56 labourers. The amount of arable lands in the former village is 434 acres and in Sitapur 1,264 acres. Rughunathpur is a residential village, and the labourers there work in the neighbouring villages. Thus, taking the average, there is one labourer to every 20 acres of land. Considering that, especially in Rughunathpur, there are many large holdings, and that the land is rice land requiring considerable cultivation, there can be little doubt that there is a sufficient demand for labour. Besides labour in the field, there is labour connected with the cattle of the village, which employs the children as well as the men, repairs of houses, cleaning out tanks, attendance on marriage and other ceremonies, and menial employments in the houses of wealthy raiyats. Added to this, are the amounts earned at harvest time, where wages are paid at the rate of one-eighth of the produce, and where the whole family are engaged in the harvest.

8. The calculations which I have made are for an average year. They would of course not apply to a year of scarcity. They show that in average years the condition of the agricultural classes is such that they can always depend upon a sufficient supply of food, with a margin for clothing.

9. The next point is the condition of those dependent on resources other than agricultural. These amount to about 15 per cent. of the population, and the principal occupations in the villages under report are weaving, fishing, and shepherding. Weavers do not work on their own account, but work up the cotton supplied by others at the usual daily wage. Fishermen supply the bazars with fish, and shepherds tend their own flocks, and make blankets of the wool. They have no resources from land, and, so far as I can ascertain, have sufficient to support themselves. Considering that, out of a population of over 2,000, only 2 per cent. are weavers, it is probable that they get sufficient work. The shepherds are undoubtedly well off; one of the number is a mahajan.

10. The general condition of the people may be tested in other ways. It will be observed that they hold considerable stocks of cattle, and the produce of the buffaloes is sold as *ghee*. There is only one beggar, an old woman, in the two villages. The number reported incapable from sickness is about 3 per cent. of the population; women do not, as a rule, work in the fields. Each family has on an average three separate houses. The indebtedness of the villagers is not serious, viz., in Rughunathpur 42 raiyats out of 70 owe Rs. 671. The people live in grass and bamboo houses, only because the soil is not suitable for building mud walls. There is not much sickness, except at the close of the rains, which is due to the bad subsoil drainage. Although the majority of the raiyats still use earthen vessels for cooking, yet the wealthier have brass utensils, and nearly all have a brass drinking vessel and dish.

11. I have not thought it worth while to calculate the profits of the cultivation of land beyond showing the net profits in money or in grain after deducting the cost of cultivation and the rent, and assuming that the grain is sold at the time of harvest in the village. It is of course often stored and sold or lent at such time as the market has risen. Assuming, however, that a raiyat holds four acres, of which two are rice land, one acre double cropped on which *merua* and other pulses are grown in the rains and mustard seed in the cold weather, half an acre wheat land and half an acre *kurthi* land, he will have the following account after paying the cost of cultivation and rent :—

	Maunds.		Maunds.
Rice	27	Wheat	2½
Rain crop	12	Linseed	1
Mustard crop	4	*Kurthi*	4

He will require for the support for himself and family all the rice and the rain crop, and will be able to sell the rest, the value of which will be Rs. 16, besides the value of the straw and chaff for his cattle, from which other profits from calves and *ghee* will be obtained.

12. From the foregoing description of the condition of the agricultural classes in this pergunnah, it appears that they need not at present cause any apprehension, and that in ordinary years they have sufficient means of subsistence. The picture which I have drawn does not, however, show any great prosperity, and shows that the lower classes which, including the weaving class, amount to about 25 per cent. of the population, have little chance of improving their position, and that they would have no resources to fall back upon in time of scarcity.

I. *Rughunathpur.*—Pergunnah Duphar, district Bhagulpore.

Area.—The total cultivated area of the village is 434 acres, which is divided among 70 raiyats—

Of these	1 raiyat holds over	50	acres.
„	10 raiyats hold over	15	„
„	8 do.	8	„
„	16 do.	3	„
„	35 raiyats hold under	3	„

In addition, these raiyats hold land in surrounding villages which probably raise their holdings by at least one-third.

Population—

The total population in 607, divided as follows :—

Grown up men	... ...	171
Ditto women	... ...	194
Boys over 12 years	... ...	22
Girls over do.	... ...	28
Boys under do.	... ...	100
Girls do. do.	... ...	92
		607

Of the children, 61 boys are unmarried and 43 girls. There are 23 widowers and 46 widows.

There are 106 families, and the average number of a family is a little less than six persons. Of the total population of the village, 70 per cent. are able-bodied and capable of working. The number incapable are 192, of whom 169 are infants and 16 aged, five ill and two blind.

Castes.—There are the following castes :—

Hulwayes	22	Koeri	19
Telis	49	Dosadhs	71
Gareris or shepherds ...	106	Chamars	33
Barbers	19	Weavers	29
Blacksmiths	11	Dhanuks	17
Fishermen	7	Dhunniahs	84
Cowherds	20		

Occupations—

64 per cent. of the population are cultivators.
2 " are cultivators and labourers.
34 " are labourers and artizans.

There is only one beggar woman in the village. Of the labourers, above 17 per cent. are employed as follows, viz.:—

7 per cent. are weavers. They work up cotton supplied by others at a daily wage.
6 " Gareris or shepherds who keep sheep and make blankets.
2 " Mullahs who live by fishing.
2 " Telis or oil-pressers.

These men hold no land in the village, but work, in the case of the first class, for daily wage and in the case of the others for profit. The remainder of the labourers work in the fields.

Cattle.—There are the following cattle in the village :—

226 cows distributed among 53 persons.
165 bullocks diaributed among 48 persons.
65 buffaloes distributed among 21 persons.
69 goats distributed among 40 persons.
476 sheep distributed among 9 persons.
4 horses or ponies.
8 carts.
53 ploughs.
13 oil-mills.

Houses.—The population of 607 persons is divided into 106 families, who live in 377 separate houses or huts. There are no mud, hut, or pucca houses. The huts are made of bamboo and grass with thatched roofs. The character of the soil is such that mud walls cannot be built.

Indebtedness of the population.—There are five mahajans for the village, and the total amount of cash debt is said to be Rs. 761 divided among 42 persons. Besides this, there are considerable amounts of grain lent not every year. The rate for cash loans is 6 pies in the rupee per month. The rate for grain lending is 50 per cent. to be paid at the time of harvest. If the principal is not then repaid, one-third is added to this total. Thus, if one maund is borrowed, 1½ maunds are repaid, or in default 2¼ maunds next year.

(II). *Sitapur* village, pergunnah Duphar, Bhagulpoore.

Area.—The total cultivated area is 1,264 acres held by 126 raiyats, or an average of 10 acres each—

34 raiyats hold under 3 acres.

There are 35 tenants in the village who hold no land, and are distributed a follows :—

5 Gareris or shepherds.
20 Mullahs or fishermen (the village is near the Kosi).
8 Kumars or potters.
1 Weaver.
1 Priest.

Population.—The total population in 1,577, divided as follows :—

Men	492
Women	524
Boys under 12	283
Girls under 12	278
Total ...	1,577

There are incapable of work besides infants 561, as follows :—

3 Men too old.
25 Men diseased.
12 Women do.
There are 153 widows.
47 widowers.

There are 268 families, and the average number in a family is (as in Rughunathpur) a little less than six persons.

Occupation.—One half of the population are returned as cultivators; the other half as labourers. A few women work as labourers. There are no persons subsistent on public charity.

Regarding the occupations, I think that the number returned as labourers must include a number of raiyats who hold as sub-tenants of other raiyats, this being a common form of tenure in this pergunnah. About 13 per cent. depend on their occupation as fishermen (8 per cent.), Telis or oil-presses (1 per cent.), shepherds (2 per cent.), weavers and priests (2 per cent).

Cattle.—There are the following cattle in the village :—

Cows	566
Bullocks	274
Buffaloes	163
Sheep	246
Ponies	24
Country carts	17

Houses.—As in Rughunathpur, the houses are all of bamboo and grass and are thatched with grass. There are 268 families living in 845 separate huts.

Indebtedness of the people.—There are five mahajans who lend at 4½ pice in the rupee per month. All but about 15 of the raiyats are indebted to them, but I have not been able to ascertain the amounts.

The foregoing facts are special to the two villages.

The following facts apply equally to the two villages of Sitapur and Rughunathpur.

Crops and cost and profits of cultivation.—The following are the rates of rent in Rughunathpur :—

	Per acre.		
	Rs.	A.	P.
Rice land	1	12	0
Upland (double cropped), at	1	9	0
Single-cropped lands, at	1	7	0
Land left fallow for wheat, at	1	2	0
Land on which *kurthi* only grows	0	9	0
Grazing ground	0	4	0

The following are the rates in Sitapur :—

	Per acre.		
	Rs.	A.	P.
Rice land	1	6	0
Single-cropped land, at	1	2	0
Wheat land	0	9	0
Kurthi „	0	8	0
Grazing „	0	4	0

The land in Rughunathpur is chiefly upland; that in Sitapur chiefly rice land. With regard to the costs and profits of cultivation, it is almost impossible to give any exact statement. The cost varies according to the position of the cultivator. If he can cultivate all his land by his own effort or his family, his cost is nothing. A raiyat often exchanges services with others, and so has not to provide for labourers.

If a cultivator employs coolies, the cost incurred depends upon his position. Generally speaking, he has a certain number of dependents who work his ploughs; they get the use of the ploughs in exchange for their own lands. The cost of the bullocks is nothing on the same principle. They are fed with rice straw or are grazed by the abovementioned dependents. There is some expense in the seed, and in weeding, but it is paid for in *dhan*. The expense of cutting the grain is paid in kind, and the amount so given away is not calculated in the gross yield. Thus, if a man says that his field yields 20 maunds per acre, he has deducted the cost of cutting, viz., one-eighth. The real produce has been 22½ maunds. Similarly, it is impossible to calculate the profits exactly. The quality of the soil varies. Some men whom I have questioned put the produce at 45 maunds per bigah (=1·67 of an acre)|: others at 20 maunds. There is an authenticated instance of eight cottahs (about ⅓ acre) producing 48 maunds of *dhan*. Again, in calculating the produce of different crops, it must be remembered that crops are mixed or are sown separately, or two crops are sown in the rains and in the cold weather. These facts affect the produce, and any calculation of a particular crop is apt to be misleading.

Lastly, in calculating the value of the produce, it must be remembered that it varies at different times of the year. Thus *dhan* when first cut sells at about two maunds to the rupee and afterwards sells at under one maund. These prices are the prices in the village. In other cases the produce is not sold at all, and thus the value can only be calculated with reference to the amount of food required by its possession.

The following are the best figures which I have been able to procure regarding the cost of cultivation of the usual crops and the profits—

		Rs.	A.	
Dhan—Cost of cultivation and rent	...	5	7	per acre.

		Rs.	A.
Produce 23 maunds per acre—			
Grain	... ...	18	0
Straw	... ...	1	8
Total	...	19	8

The price of *dhan* is here calculated at 50 seers to the rupee.

Rain crops.—Such as *bhadoi, dhan, merua, sama, kalai, kaoni, kurthi*, &c.

Cost of cultivation ... ... Rs. 2-8 per acre.

		Rs.	A.
Produce 12 maunds per acre	...	12	0
Straw	...	0	8
Total	...	12	8

The produce is calculated at one maund per rupee.

This class of land produces a cold weather crop, generally mustard seed.

Cost of cultivation, Rs. 2-8

Produce 5½ maunds per acre = Rs. 14, at 16 seers to the rupee.

Thus the total cost of cultivating double-cropped upland is Rs. 5 per acre, add for rental Rs. 1-10 per acre—total Rs. 6-10 per acre—profits Rs. 26-8 per acre.

If the land is fertile, linseed will also be sown. The cost of cultivation will not be increased, and the produce will be about 2 maunds per acre, value at Rs. 2-8 per maund= Rs. 5.

In some cases another crop, such as *masuri*, is sown, producing about 1½ maunds at 1 maund per rupee= Rs. 1-8. Thus the total produce will, in exceptional lands, be Rs. 33 against an expenditure of about Rs. 7 per acre.

Wheat—Is either grown on ordinary upland or on land left fallow during the rains. The latter is the ordinary practice.

The cost of cultivation is Rs. 4-6 per acre—

		Rs.	A.	P.
The produce is 7 maunds per acre, the value of which at 30 seers to the rupee	... =	9	4	0
Value of chaff	...	2	0	0
Total	...	11	4	0

If other crops are sown in the field, the produce is proportionately reduced. Linseed is often sown with wheat, producing about two maunds per acre, of which the value is Rs. 5, making a total gross produce of Rs. 16-4.

Single-cropped lands are grown with such crops as *rahar* or other pulse.

The price of cultivation of *rahar* is Rs. 5-12, per acre, and the produce is about 12 maunds, of which the value is at Rs. 2 the maund Rs. 24, and the value of the wood is about a rupee.

Wheat lands and single-cropped lands are rare. The more common class of soil is locally known as jungle, on which *kurthi* only grows.

Kurthi.—The cost of cultivating *kurthi* is Rs. 3-1 per acre, and the produce per acre is 9 maunds; value at 1 maund to the rupee, Rs. 9.

The following are the net profits of cultivation of the different crops on an average, expressed in rupees and in grain:—

	Net profit. Rs. A. P.		
1. Rice	12 1 0	per acre,	or 13½ maunds, plus the straw.
2. Double-cropped lands—			
Ram crop ...	10 0 0	„	or 12 maunds of grain.
Cold weather crop, such as mustard seed ...	9 8 0	„	or 4 „
Total ...	19 8 0	„	or 16 „
If other crops are grown—			
Add for linseed ...	5 0 0	„	or 2 „
Musuri	2 0 0	„	or 2 „
Total ...	26 8 0	„	or 20 „
3. *Wheat*	6 4 0	„	or 5 „
If other crops are sown, add for linseed ...	5 0 0	„	or 2 „
Total ...	11 0 0	„	or 7 „
4. *Rabar* or *ek-fasala* crop—			
Net profit ...	17 0 0		or 9 maund per acre.
5. *Kurthi*.—Net profit ...	6 0 0		or 8 „

* *N. B.*—The amount of profit in grain is the amount of grain left after deducting cost of cultivation. It does not necessarily bear any proportion to the net profit in money.

Food of the people.—Well-to-do raiyats have two meals, and eat during the day about ½ seer of rice supplemented with *dâl*, *ghee*, *dahi* or (curds), vegetables, milk, &c.

The lower class of raiyats eat rice, or bread made of *merua*, and such grains, and coarse vegetable, such as *sâg*, *kuddu*, &c. They eat twice a day and eat about a cutcha seer or 14 chittacks during the day. The amount of the staple food eaten depends on the other articles with which it is supplemented.

Food of the cattle.—The cattle are fed on rice staw, which is plentiful, and on the chaff of other crops. During the hot weather they are grazed in the rice lands, and at other times fed with grass scraped from the fields. No food is bought for them.

Wages.—Wages are generally paid in kind, and are 5 cutcha seers or 4 pucca seers of unhusked rice per day, or one seer less, and one meal. This amounts to about one anna six pie per day. If a stranger hired labour he would pay two annas. When ploughs are hired they are paid two annas a day. But generally the ploughs belongs to a big raiyat who lends them to smaller raiyats in exchange for their services in driving them.

Cart-hire is 6 annas a day, but they are often let at 4 annas per day.

Implements.—The implements used for agriculture are—

(1) The plough (*hâl*.)
(2) The harrow (*chouki*).
(3) The mattock (*kodali*).
(4) Kachya (sickle).
(5) Smooth sickle (*hassua*).
(6) Kurpi for cutting grass.
(7) Axe (*basala*).

Utensils.—Nearly all the raiyats of these two villages cook their food in earthern vessels. The richer raiyats have brass utensils in their houses, which they use on great occasions. Nearly all raiyats have a brass *lota* and a brass dish.

Ornaments.—Nearly every family has some ornaments. The total value of ornaments in Rughunathpur is Rs. 793 divided among 22 raiyats, and in addition to this there are 246 ornaments, such as necklaces, armlets, &c., divided among about 160 people.

Dress.—The weathier raiyats wear English cotton goods, and sometimes silk clothes and renew them every six months. In winter they have a *rejai* which costs Rs. 2. The poorer classes wear English cotton stuff at Re. 1 and Re. 1-2 a piece, which lasts a year, and in winter a blanket, cost Rs. 2-8, lasting four years, or a thick sheet, country-made, cost Re. 1-8, which lasts two years.

Water-supply.—All water is supplied from wells. The water is only a few feet below the surface, and not very good.

Sickness.—The chief period of sickness is from August to November when fever and throat complaints prevail.

The two villages taken by Mr. Collin for his enquiries are Rughunathpur and Sitapur, both in pergunnah Duphar.

I. RUGHUNATHPUR.

The following are the statistics of tenures :—

1 of over 50 acres.
10 of over 15 acres.
8 of over 8 acres.
16 of over 3 acres.
35 of less than 3 acres.

It is stated that in this pergunnah rent is never above Rs. 3; so we may take Rs. 2 as an average, or say Rs. 2-4.

We can then reduce these holdings to classes A, B, C, D, of the former reports thus :—

a.	Raiyats paying over Rs. 20 rent 1+10+8=	19
b.	" " from Rs. 10 to Rs. 20 rent, say 10 out of 16 who hold from 3 to 8 acres=	10
c.	" " from Rs. 5 to Rs. 10 rent, the remaining 6 of holders of 3 to 8 acres, and Rs. 20 out of 35 who hold under 3 acres=	26
d.	" " less than Rs. 5 rent, the other 15=	15

This reduced to percentages gives :—

a. 16, *b.* 26, *c.* 23, *d.* 37.
[*a.* 27, *b.* 14, *c.* 37, *d.* 22.]

It appears for another part of the report that the highest rent in the village is Rs. 1-12 and most is Rs. 1-9. Thus the percentages will have to be altered thus :—

a. 11, *b.* 18, *c.* 16, *d.* 25

as against *a.* 35, *b.* 28, *c.* 20, *d.* 18, of all the other reports for all villages.

II. Of Sitapur, the only information is that the average holding is 10 acres, and 34 out of 126 raiyats hold less than 3 acres. Of these, we may put 14 or 12 per cent. of the whole in class *d.*

Highest rate in Sitapur, Rs. 1-6.

The only other point on which Mr. Collin's figures can be tabulated side by side with former statistics is the division of the people into classes according to their work.

For Rughunathpur the following figures are given :—

(*i.*) Cultivators, 64 per cent.
(*ii.*) Cultivators and labourers, 2 per cent.
(*iii.*) Labourers and artizans, 34 per cent.

Of (*iii.*) 7 per cent. are weavers, 6 per cent. shepherds (also make blankets), 2 per cent. are fishermen, 2 per cent. are Telis or oil-pressers	17	per cent.
Adding barbers, blacksmiths, and potters, say, another 23 per cent. (Mr. Collin gives a list of all the castes, but the numbers given, being individuals, not householders, are not of much help)	23	"
Total ...	40	"

Thus of class (*iii*) we may make a division thus :—

(*iiia.*) Labourers only 60 per cent. of 34 per cent.=20 per cent. of whole.
(*iiib.*) Artizans (some of whom labour also) 40 per cent. of 34 per cent.=14 per cent. of whole.

Then putting A for *i*, B for *ii*, D for *iiia*, and E and F for *iiib*—
We thus get A75; B2; D 23 per cent.
Total A + B + D to E+F 86 to 14
against 90 to 10 of all other tables.
And A51; B, 17; D, 31 per cent. (all other tables).

The list of castes given by Mr. Collin for Raghunathpur is as follows :—

Hulwais	22	Koeris	19
Telis	47	Dosadhs	71
Gareris	106	Chamars	33
Barbers	19	Weavers	29
Blacksmiths	11	Dhanuks	17
Fishermen	7	Dhaunniahs ...	84
Cowherds	20		

W. LeB.—Reg. No. 1866C—137—9-5-88.

CONFIDENTIAL.]

CONDITION OF THE MASSES.

No. 160GC—VII-3, dated Chittagong, the 28th April 1888.

From—D. R. Lyall, Esq., Commissioner of the Chittagong Division,

To—The Secretary to the Government of Bengal, Revenue Department.

I have the honour to submit the report called for in your No. 35Agri., dated 9th December 1887. The report of the Collector of Chittagong was only received on the 18th, and I have had several annual reports to get off which has delayed the submission of this report.

2. Before entering into district details, I think it well to make a few general remarks on the condition of the masses in this division as compared with those of other parts. It is an admitted fact that the ryot of Bengal is better off than the ryot of Behar. What the ryot of Bengal is to the ryot of Behar, that is the ryot of the greater part of this division to the ryot of Bengal. He is infinitely better off, lives better, dresses better, and altogether is more comfortably off than the ryot of Central Bengal or even of Dacca and Furreedpore. The Backergunge ryot alone can be compared with the ryots of this division generally in his standard of comfort.

3. The class of agricultural labourer as distinguished from the cultivator may be said not to exist here; though a very large number of cultivators also work as agricultural labourers, and even go as far as Arracan for labour, whence they come back with Rs. 20 to Rs. 40 cash after two months' work. Those shown as having no fixed holdings in the Chittagong returns ordinarily cultivate as under-tenants from year to year, but without fixed holdings.

4. The family system is also an important factor in determining the degree of comfort of the people at large.

The people of Chittagong and Noakholly add to their income very greatly by service at sea as lascars and firemen, and by acting as traders in Burmah. In Chittagong also a large number of men go yearly to the Government kheddas on high pay. All these men are drawn from the cultivating class, and the family income is largely increased by their earnings.

5. Yet another source of income which affects a large number in Chittagong and Tipperah, and a smaller number in Noakholly, is the trade in hill produce. The number of men who make money out of this is very large, and they too belong to the cultivating class.

6. From the above it is clear that if the produce of soil is anything like sufficient to feed the people, the bare means of subsistence is supplemented by a every large amount of solid cash earned in other ways. Export statistics, however, show that there is a very large surplus of rice which finds its way to Chittagong and is exported from there. The average exports are about 1½ million maunds.

This rice is almost entirely the produce of the division. Very little comes from the parts of Backergunge which lie on the Megna, but the bulk of the Backergunge surplus goes to Calcutta.

All reports show that no ryot sells rice unless he has enough for his own and his family food, and ordinarily a surplus to provide against a bad season.

From Chittagong itself the surplus is not very large. Noakholly gives the greatest part and Tipperah a large proportion. In addition to the rice thus sold, the ryots of the whole of the northern part of the Tipperah district have a great stand-by in jute, the well-known marts of Bakrabad and Kurrimgunge taking their names from places in this district; while the southern parts of Tipperah and Noakholly supplement their rice crops by their plantations of betel-nut.

7. In paragraph 2 of the letter under reply a line is drawn between the normal or permanent condition of the masses and their condition from year to year. The normal state is practically determined by the degree of prosperity enjoyed by the people for a succession of years, and the reports of this division show a very large balance in favour of prosperity.

I annex extracts from the divisional reports for the last 15 years which show this conclusively. These reports show that the people have the means to tide over bad years without extraneous help, and that they have a large surplus to fall back on.

8. It may be said these are official reports; but the evidence of others is the same. On his way to Agartollah in 1878, while passing through Tipperah, Baboo Shambhu Chandra Mukerjea writes thus of the people (page 14 of his book):—"I am infinitely delighted to observe the evidence of "comfort and comparative civilization in the peasantry of these parts.

"It is something that so many about here are well protected in the cold "weather by the cheap cottons and woollens of Europe. The women have all "more costly ornaments, if less heavy and numerous, than their mothers or "grand-mothers could boast of.........Shell bracelets are few and far between. ".........Silver clearly predominates. Brass is nowhere..........Here on the "banks of the Megna we found all the women display silver—some in pro- "fusion. It was all due to jute."

Again on page 38 he says that the ryots "not only pay down their rents "in money, but often do not know what to do with the balance in hand."

In both these cases he draws attention to the improvement as compared with a few years before.

His remarks on the boatmen of East Bengal, pages 17 and 25-26, though written of the Dacca boatmen, also apply equally to the boatmen of this division.

This is a purely non-official testimony in support of the consensus of official evidence, and these extracts show how the prosperous state of the people of Tipperah struck an observant fellow countryman of Central Bengal.

The extract from the report of 1886-87, paragraph 21, shows how the same thing struck an official fresh from Behar.

9. The combined result of all the abovementioned sources of income is that the people have a fund of accumulations to fall back on, which the ryots of Behar have not.

A part of Tipperah has for three years had excessively scanty crops, and there were at one time grave doubts as to last year's crop, in which case the people would have required some assistance; but the accumulations of previous years were sufficient to tide them over the bad year, and there was sufficient purchasing power left in the people at large to enable them to support even the beggars, only a few hundred rupees having been disbursed in public charity.

10. Referring to paragraph 8 of the letter, I say generally that the poorer classes in this division have ample to eat. On this point the evidence of Baboo Shambhu Chandra Mukerjea above quoted may be considered valuable, and all the district officers are at one on this point.

The houses of the people are generally substantial and comfortable.

They are well clothed—the people of Tipperah and Noakholly generally in English cloth; while the Chittagong men wear, as a rule, country-woven clothes. Brass utensils are common, and the women wear silver ornaments.

11. I do not think a comparison with Hill Tipperah is fair, unless it be between the people of Hill Tipperah and the Chittagong Hill Tracts.

The conditions of life in the hills and in the plains are so different that a comparison is impossible.

The mode of cultivation differs; the people are of a different race and have different wants, but in their way the hill people too are well off.

The people of the Hill Tracts have fewer taxes than those of Hill Tipperah, but there is more strictness of rule to compensate for this.

If emigration be taken as the test, then the Hill Tracts are more popular, the balance of emigration being of late years decidedly in favour of the British district.

The hillman, however, is essentially a man who takes no thought for the morrow. If he has a good rice crop he brews more beer, and what he cannot eat or drink he leaves to rot. He makes a good deal of money by his cotton and til, but this too he spends, and is therefore entirely dependent on his crop, and suffers severely when there is a bad one. He is also a confirmed gambler, and will play for his last cowrie.

12. The natural question that arises in any one's mind who reads what I have written above is—why then are the people as a rule in debt although they are so prosperous?

The causes are—first, litigation, and next expensive marriage and funeral ceremonies.

The litigiousness of the people of this division is notorious, and a very large quantity of their surplus money is expended in this way.

The cost of marriages has also increased among the lower classes of late years, owing to their increased ability to spend.

Not only among the lower classes, but even much higher up it is considered, I might almost say, a duty to get into debt on the occasion of a marriage or *shradh*, and a man who spends only what he can afford runs the risk of being considered mean.

This is no exaggeration, but a fact, and it accounts for much of the indebtedness of the people.

13. The Collector of Chittagong has only submitted figured statements for the south part of his district, *i.e.*, the part south of the Sungoo. These are marked A and B. He promises similar statements for the north part of the district shortly. I extract the following remarks from the covering report regarding the food of the people of these parts:—

"The cultivators (Hindus and Mahomedans) while employed in the fields "and *katurias* generally take three meals a day, some rice at all meals, and some "chillies instead of curry in one, and in two others sometimes a little vegetables "(শাক) and dry fish, and at other times only one of them. Those who have "got children cannot indulge in three meals, as the children must be fed. Poor "men scarcely take two meals a day, and if they can get some rice to satisfy their "appetite, they will remain content. The greater part of the Mahomedans "take three meals a day, and the Hindus in general "take twice only. The Mahomedan women take "but twice daily. Generally the diet of the Maho-"medans is poor, and is hardly sufficient; but they "are still satisfied with it, and all are healthy."

Note—I do not agree with this last assertion. The ordinary Mahomedan of this district consumes a good deal of animal food, and altogether lives wells.

D. R. LYALL.

14. The Collector of Tipperah, too, only submits detailed statements regarding two villages. These are sent marked D and E; also a consolidated Statement C. I may note that the villages reported on both lie in the tract which has suffered severely from inundation for three years, and that the figures may be taken as showing the state of the people of that part at their very worst after a succession of bad years. The figures are all, I consider, unduly low. I quote the Collector's remarks regarding each of the classes:—

"5. Column 18, against heading 1, shows the means of support available "for each member of this class. But this 'means' is greatly supplemented by "the personal exertions of individual members of the family, who go and fish "in the neighbouring bheels, keep poultry, cows and goats, and make some "profit by selling live-stock, and also eggs and milk. The male members "of a family go once a year into Hill Tipperah, and bring their building "materials, such as thatching-grass bamboos, wooden posts, and other forest "produce, for example ratans and canes. They use what they require for "the construction of their own houses, and sell the rest with considerable "profit to themselves. The female members of the family wash the clothes, "spin thread, husk the grains, cook the food, and contribute materially "towards the support of the household. The cost "of feeding each prisoner in the jail last year "amounted to Rs. 19-2-9, with a net income of "Rs. 21-9-9 per head, as shown in the statement, "I conclude that class I is fairly well off and cannot "suffer from an insufficiency of food; a considerable "surplus must be left* after reserving a sufficient "portion of the produce for home consumption, "which can be sold, and the proceeds spent in pur-"chase of clothes and other necessaries. This is "the only class that has any superfluous produce "left for sale; it has not to buy rice and most "other edible commodities. All the other classes "must purchase more or less of the principal articles of food. I may say "here that by reducing the produce of cultivation to a money value, I think "I am restricting the estimate of the ryot's means of support to the narrowest

If a prisoner with all the intermediate profits can be fed on Rs. 19-2-9, a ryot could feed equally well on Rs. 12. The margin is therefore much larger than that assumed by the Collector.

The Sub-divisional Officer of Brahmunberiah estimates the value of food that a ryot with a family of six has to buy at Rs. 30 a year, excluding what he produces.

The Sub-divisional Officer of Chandpore says it costs a man Rs. 25 a year for food, buying everything.

D. R. LYALL.

* This is true.

D. R. LYALL.

"limits; the ryot has many sources for eking out his subsistence, which I "cannot appreciate by any money value, but which nevertheless are very "elastic, and ought to be taken into account.

"6. In respect of class II also, the remarks made in paragraphs 3, 4, "and 5 above apply generally. They may be said to be quite as well off, if "not better, than class I; and they certainly do not suffer from an insufficiency "of food.

"7. With regard to class III, I am quite satisfied that they are very "well off; and are the most prosperous of the community. They do not "generally cultivate their lands themselves, but let it out on the *barga* "system, according to which they receive half the produce, the cultivator "keeping for himself the other half. Hence the costs of production are "calculated against this class in the statement at half the value of the "produce."

"8. In respect of class IV, I must say that, in my opinion, they live "as a rule from hand to mouth. In a year of bad harvests they suffer con- "siderably, and whenever from any other cause they cannot be provided with "sufficient labour. In calculating their earnings, I have taken into considera- "tion the time they must remain idle, owing to illness and other unavoidable "causes: notwithstanding all this, they do not generally suffer from insuffi- "ciency of food, though occasionally, doubtless, they find themselves in very "straitened circumstances.

"9. Some of the members of class V are in a very bad state. This class "comprises principally weavers, blacksmiths: also carpenters. The last two "constituents of this class are, however, well off. "Weavers suffer much, because they are so conser- "vative, and will not betake themselves to modes "of getting a livelihood other than those that have "come down to them from father to son, though they have been driven out of "the market by the importation of English piece-goods.

Some of the Tipperah weavers have refused to take to any other occupation, but this is not generally the case.

D. B. LYALL.

"10. With regard to class VI, no remark seems to be necessary.

"11. Class VII, comprising drummers, barbers, and washermen are "almost equally badly off with the weavers of class V.

"12. Beggars do not suffer in a year of good crops; they must suffer "when the outturn of harvest is insufficient."

The following facts regarding wages of labourers are given by the Sarail Manager:—"The rates of wages paid to agricultural labourers vary according "to circumstances. If a man is employed for a whole year under contract, "he would get Rs. 30 on the average for the whole year, besides food at the "house of his employer. During February, March, April and May, when the "land is ploughed, the rate is Rs. 11 for four months; in August and Septem- "ber, when the jute and *aus* harvests are reaped, he gets Rs. 4-8 a month; "and in November and December, when *amun* is harvested, the rates rise to "Rs. 7-8 per month. In all these cases the labourer gets food, and the "rate of wages of the daily labourer is always 4 annas a day. The whole "of the Sarail pergunnah being agricultural, a labourer gets work in the fields "for about eight months in a year on an average pay of Rs. 3, besides food "for himself. His annual earning, therefore, is Rs. 24 in cash, besides food for "himself, and with which he can maintain a wife and a child. His wife "would separately husk grain for wages; and the boy, if 10 years old or more, "would tend cattle of others on Re. 1 per month, besides food. The labourers "generally have a robust and healthy appearance, and there does not appear "anything in them which indicates under-feeding or want of due nourish- "ment."

I also extract the summing up of the Collector of Tipperah:—

"18. *General conclusions.*—I will sum up by expressing my opinion that "classes III and VI practically never suffer from insufficiency of food. Class "II is, though not so respectable, really better off than class I, and both can "suffer from insufficiency of food only after a succession of bad harvests. One "bad season only will not greatly affect the supply of food so far as these "two classes are concerned. Class IV, landless labourers, must suffer, if not "generally, at any rate in the case of individuals, whenever there is a really "bad season. Classes V and VII are practically always in straitened circum-"stances; and beggars are of course in a still worse plight. Altogether it is my "belief that at least 10 per cent. of the population "suffer from a chronic insufficiency of food, be the "harvest good or bad. By insufficiency of food I "mean anything less than the usual three full meals "a days, the first eaten cold, and the other two hot"

: This is a very high standard. It is only of late that two full meals and a cold one have become common, and there is no doubt that men can live and thrive on one full meal and one cold meal, and that this was formerly the usual number.

D. R. LYALL.

15. As I have noted, I think he assumes a very high standard.

16. The Collector of Noakholly has submitted statistics of only one village which is sent, marked F. He has been directed to submit more.

He considers that 90 per cent. of his district are agriculturists, and that their condition is "much better" than that of the same class in Behar and West Bengal. They are "comparatively well fed, well dressed, and well housed."

Regarding agricultural labourers he says: "Agricultural labourers do not "exist as a separate class. But the poorer ryots work for others during the "two agricultural seasons lasting about four months in all. They earn 4 to "5 annas in this work per day, besides a rich meal at mid-day. This is the "custom of the district, and men will not work if they are not well-fed on "hire. This also goes to show that the condition of the ryots is not at all "bad."

Of real beggars, *i.e.*, those who beg from poverty, he does not think there are 500 in the district. The professional and hereditary beggars are, he states, often well-to-do men, though they continue to beg and are ranked as beggars.

Weavers in Noakholly have generally taken to agriculture.

The late Settlement Officer of Nulchira considers that the cost of cultivation is Rs. 2-10-8 a bigha on that island, and the value of the crop (7 maunds) from Rs. 7 to Rs. 14, or, say, an average of Rs. 10-8.

The Sub-divisional Officer of Fenny alone reports that the state of the people is bad. He says: "My impression is that fully one-third of the popu-"lation, consisting chiefly of what is known as the middle class, suffers from "daily insufficiency of food, and the struggle with all, excepting a few territorial "lords and holders of high Government situations, is becoming harder every "day."

He considers that population is increasing faster than the means of feeding that population, and that the rise in wages has been more than counter-balanced by a rise in the price of provisions. He looks on the exportation of rice as an evil.

He laments the closing of the salt works, and ends his report as follows:—"Indeed, as was remarked by a late Magistrate of Furreedpore, with whom it "was my painful lot to inspect a scarcity-stricken locality, people would formerly "be killed in numbers by plagues and famines, but those who would survive "them would live in affluence. Now the civilized resources of our Government "have checked the death-rate on the one hand and killed the local trade and "industries on the other; and the result is that those who live suffer from a "chronic scarcity of food."

This is the pessimist's view, and is utterly opposed to the opinion of all other officers in the division, and is not shared by the many officers whose opinions are given in the appendix to this report.

Copies of paragraphs 64 to 72 from the General Administration Report for the year 1872-73.

MATERIAL CONDITION OF THE PEOPLE.

PARA. 64. I quote at length the remarks of the several Magistrates regarding this important and interesting subject. The Magistrate of Chittagong says:—"As regards material well-being, the people of Chittagong have generally nothing to complain of, and the past year has been no exception to the rule. They are mostly agriculturists; and even day-labourers, domestic servants, &c., have their patch of land, which is cultivated by them or their families. That the people are well off is obvious from their independence. Tea-planters complain that they sometimes find it difficult to get labourers even at a fair rate of wages. During the field season local labour is especially deficient, as the villagers then go to look after their own cultivation.

65. "The soil is productive, and yields an ample return for very little labour. Bamboos, canes, thatching-grass and firewood are plentiful, and on unoccupied waste lands may for be had for the cutting. Provisions are abundant and generally cheap. The neighbouring province of Arracan affords a remunerative field for the surplus labour of the district, and coolies working in the Port of Chittagong or Akyab can earn, I am told, as much as eight annas a day. There has been no famine, pestilence, or other great public calamity during the year, and on the whole the material condition of the people may be said to have been prosperous.

66. "I fully agree with the Collector in his estimate of the general condition of the people. They are undoubtedly prosperous and well-to-do. I should describe their leading characteristics as independence, disrespect, and litigiousness. As a whole, I consider the demeanour of the people more wanting in respect than that of the people of any district within my experience.

67. "Their fondness for litigation is proverbial. Sir Henry Ricketts speaks of them as a 'people suffering from a litigious mania,' of the inclination of the people tending towards 'chicanery and fradulent dealings,' and again as being 'litigious, distrustful of each other, suspicious of our purposes and intentions, and prone to fraud.'"

These words, written as they were 25 years ago, are equally true of the character of the people to-day.

68. Mr. Park, of Tipperah, says:—"The people of this district would be exceedingly well off if their perverse tone of litigation and the eternal rent disputes did not stand in the way. The ryot has few wants, and the soil is splendidly fertile, and if he were a contented and peaceful man, he should be very happy. But much litigation is forced on him, and he loves it for its own sake." From the Sub-divisional Officer's description, I gather with a young Mahomedan is as proud of his first successful *makaddama* (for they are not law-suit) as the English youth who has won a great boat race or scored one hundred runs in a University cricket match.

69. It is not only that the ryots' zemindar is oppressive: the ryot himself is naturally recusant, and even this is not all. The absurd quarrels among each other, which result in the most wantonly false charges at the police-station, show they must take a positive pleasure in the progress of the case, quite apart from any idea of getting justice or obtaining any solid advantage. In short, they are as bad as the Mahomedans quoted in Mr. Welland's Jessore report, who, instead of speaking of 11 or 12 A.M., would say the "hour for making complaints" and so on. I can only suppose that the investigation of a case is a pleasurable break on the monotony of a dull life; but it is at least to be regretted that choice should be made of so extravagant a diversion: but the case is much the same with the zemindars and the intermediate holders. If they would each take a fair share of the goods the gods provide, there would be enough for all. But they all try to seize the ryot's share too, and he not unnaturally kicks against the pricks.

70. The Tipperah ryots are, in my estimation, a much pleasanter set of people than the Chittagonians, and there is a marked difference of demeanour, for they are much more respectful. They are equally fond of litigation, and indeed I have reason to think that this failure is very far from being confined to the districts of the division: it is a species of gambling and very fascinating. I should, however, be inclined to think that the litigiousness of the Tipperah people might be ascribed more to the force of custom, or at all events to some less wickedly evil cause than can be put down to Chittagong.

71. The force of custom is certainly a mighty power, as the following anecdote will show:—In riding through Jaffergunge, where is the cutcherry of Rajah Kamal Krishna Bahadoor, I got into conversation with the Manager, Rai Gopal Lochan Mitter, son of a rather distinguished father, who obtained the title of Rai Bahadoor for loyal service to the State. He informed me that he experienced the greatest difficulty in collecting his rents, but he nevertheless did not appear in the least disconcerted, for, says he, I am a new Manager; and in the experience of the estate similar difficulty has invariably occurred whenever there has been any change of management.

72. The Magistrate of Noakholly remarks as follows:—"The condition of the people has certainly improved of late years. This is seen both in their dress and in their dwellings. A peasant's dress formerly consisted of a piece of cloth round the loins worth not more than 6 or 8 annas.

"He now spends 4 or 5 rupees in clothes every half year, and wears a *dhuti*, *chudder* and cap. The introduction of English piece-goods has made these articles cheaper, and he is better able to pay for them. Houses which used to be built of straw, bamboos, and reed on low, marshy land are now constructed on well raised lands and of better and more durable materials. Each homestead is surrounded by a grove, which gives it a pleasing appearance, but scarcely promotes ventilation. The number of utensils in domestic use is much larger than formerly, and there is much more comfort. The cost of living has increased, say, for a cultivator from 6 pies to an anna per day, but the people are better off. Nearly every one has an acre or so of land in cultivation."

Copies of paragraphs 35 to 37 from the General Administration Report for the year 1873-74.

MATERIAL CONDITION OF THE PEOPLE.

PARA. 35. The condition of the people is said to be very good and improving. During the past year the cultivators and those connected with the land—and there are but few in the division who have not some land—have greatly benefited by the large demand for rice in the Western districts, and the high prices obtained for it. Food generally has risen in price owing to the large quantities of rice which were exported; but even among the poorest classes, there have been no traces of actual want, and beggars may be said to be almost unknown.

36. Generally speaking, the lower classes of people in this division are far better off than those in Western Bengal. Their houses are larger and better; they wear better clothes; they eat better food, not unfrequently flesh, and can afford to remain idle and to amuse themselves for days together. For instance, an ordinary ryot when his crops are planted but seldom thinks of working as a coolie. He usually passes his time in lazily watching his crops, or tending his six or eight cows and bullocks. At the same time he always considers it necessary to visit at least some two or three of the neighbouring weekly markets, in order ostensively to buy or sell, but really to meet his friends and to discuss the politics of the day.

37. For the general prosperity of the people, several reasons may be assigned. The following are the chief I think—*Firstly*, the land assessment is very low, and as a rule the ryots hold on easy terms; *secondly*, the principal crop, rice, rarely, if ever, fails from drought, and the soil is exceedingly fertile; *thirdly*, there is a ready market for rice, and water-carriage on every side provides easy access to traders. Within the last few years suits for the enhancements of rents have been largely instituted in the Tipperah and Noakholly districts. But nine years ago, when I was Collector of the former district, such suits were unknown. It should also be mentioned that the general prosperity of the people is, in a great measure, attributable to their peculiarly thrifty and careful habits. As a rule, the Mahomedans, who form the bulk of the population, are opposed to all extravagance and display, and seldom indulge in anything beyond an occasional feast to their friends. In some parts of Tipperah district, Mr. Alexander states the favourite motto is *mota bat, mota capar* (coarse food, coarse clothing).

Copies of paragraphs 25 to 28 from the General Administration Report for the year 1874-75.

MATERIAL CONDITION OF THE PEOPLE.

PARA. 25. The people of this division are as a whole in a most prosperous condition; they are nearly all agriculturists, and the high price lately commanded for rice, coupled with good harvest, has enriched them greatly. The vicinity of the hills always secures a more or less sufficient supply of rain: the crop therefore never seems to fail, and the enormous increase in trade and commerce during the last few years has not only raised prices, but afforded facilities for disposing of produce that were not enjoyed a few years ago. The people of Chittagong are all more or less connected with land, and are, moreover, a most enterprising race of people; they embark readily in trade, and do not object to crossing the sea if they can gain anything by doing so. Numbers go to Arracan for certain seasons of the year, where work is not only readily obtainable, but well paid. It is not to be supposed that in thus emigrating they abandon their connection with agriculture: some of the family always remain at home while others go for a time to distant places.

26. The inhabitants of Noakholly enrich themselves by exactly the same means, though not perhaps to the same extent as the Chittagonians; they have not the same facility of reaching British Burmah, but then they are not far from Calcutta, and many go to obtain temporary employment there.

27. In Tipperah there is no emigration, but the land rate appears to be low, and this coupled with good harvests and a ready market combine to increase the prosperity of the people. It is by no effort of their own that the people have attained this prosperity, but it has been caused by the rise in prices and the increased facilities of communication afforded them. The productive powers of the soil have not, I suspect, been increased by the agency or at the expense of the ryot, but he has found himself enriched by a combination of the circumstances over which he has had no control, and the burning question now is whethr a share of the profits, and if so what share, can be obtained by the landlord.

28. The inhabitants of this division are mostly agriculturists, and as such share in the general prosperity attaching to that class; some indulge in trade or are employed in manufacture, but not exclusively; few will be found who are not also interested in land. The rate of labour has within the last few years doubled, and it is yearly becoming more difficult to obtain workmen, as the people are becoming more and more independent and averse to seeking employment. A great change has of late years passed over the peasantry in this division, as well as over those in other parts of Lower Bengal: increased prosperity among members of the agricultural classes has brought with it a sense of their importance, and a wish to throw off all old feelings of feudal attachment, and set up their own interests in opposition to those of their landlords—a course in which they believe they have the support and sympathy of Government.

Extract paragraphs 17 to 31 from the General Administration Report for the year 1875-76, *Chittagong Division.*

MATERIAL CONDITION OF THE PEOPLE.

ONE remarkable feature in this division is that the interest in land and the wealth derived therefrom are more equally distributed among the people than in any other division of Lower Bengal. Chittagong especially is a land of substantial middlemen, who possess an influence often not wielded by the proprietor. Every man has land with which he is either directly or indirectly connected, which supplies him with food for the year, and respecting his right to which he is very sensitive, a feeling which makes the people litigious to a degree. The agricultural classes are very well off. A fertile soil, high wages both at home and in the neighbouring markets of British Burmah, and the increasing prosperity of the Chittagong port, render the condition of the cultivators and the lower orders of the people far more easy than the circumstances of such people in any other part of Bengal. The Collector of Chittagong reports that even the few beggars in the bazars have in most cases land of their own, and beg more by profession than from want.

"Nothing can afford more conclusive proof of the solvent and substantial condition of the people of this division than the events of the year that has just gone by. The year was not only marked by considerable failure of crops, but the market of Akyab, which during the harvesting and trading season draws nearly 60,000 people from the district of Chittagong, was unusually dull; the homesteads of the people were seriously damaged by the flood; while throughout the year cattle-disease did considerable havoc. Still there was no complaint of distress from any part of the country, and an exceptionally bad year has passed off without making any perceptible impression on the condition of the people.

"If petty litigation in the civil courts," writes the Collector of Chittagong, "is any clue to the prosperity of the lower orders, the year ended shows no signs of decadence. The rural post-offices show that 26,320 letters were posted in them, against 25,227 in the previous year. The majority of letters are connected with trade or remittances from the temporary emigrants to British Burma. Rangoon, Moulmein, Akyab, Calcutta, and Dacca are the stations for which correspondence is chiefly received.

"Notwithstanding the exceptionally unfavourable character of last year, the Collector of Noakholly reports that the condition of all classes, as regards prosperity, has been in most respects good. Most of the people have land, and cultivate all or some of it; and as there was a bumper crop in 1874, they have had sufficient stocks of rice to last them the year. It is customary with the people of Noakholly, as with those of Chittagong, to store up grain sufficient for the maintenance for one or two years, according to their circumstances, before they think of selling any portion of their harvest. They have also other resources than rice crops, such as the sale of betel-nuts and cocoanuts from the trees around their homesteads, which provides them with sufficient means for ordinary expenses.

"Immediately after the flood, there was a panic among the boatmen of Noakholly; rumours having reached them from Tipperah that, to avert the exigencies of the flood, boats were being seized there for compulsory service. This shut up the traders at home, and prevented the price of rice going up higher than it did during the immediate excitement on the occurrence of the flood. As it was, the price of ordinary rice rose from 20 seers to 16 seers a rupee, but with this the wages also rose, and the temporary rise in the price of rice was not so high as to put the day-labourers to any great strain or difficulty. Labour in the division can always command its own price in accordance with the general state of the food market."

"The generality of the lower class," the Collector thinks, "are relatively better off than the middle class, whose condition is becoming more and more deplorable every year. These are the people whose profession is the pen, and who, by their education and intelligence form the thoughtful portion of native society. To them manual labour is disgrace and degradation." The generality of them in this division no doubt hold land, but the income from it is far from being such as to enable them to provide for their wants. Having no capital at command, trade and commerce are beyond their reach, and their only hope is private or public service, the various avenues to which are being daily blocked up. The only independent professions open to them, law and medicine, are already crowded to excess, while the Calcutta University is unceasingly turning out every year a large number of half famished graduates into the field. The prospects of this class of people are certainly not hopeful; already the value of their service has fallen lower than the price of skilled labour (in not a few instances less than the wages of an ordinary day-labourer), and in a few years more, if no new openings can be afforded them, their existence may prove a matter of some embarrassment to the administration.

Copies of paragraphs 24 *and* 25 *from the General Administration Report for the year* 1876-77.

PARA. 24. I have on former occasions alluded to the substantial and thriving condition of the peasantry of this division. Their condition at the present moment is not so prosperous, but had it not been for their frugal habits, which enabled them to lay by something to meet an emergency like the present, their condition would have been worse than it is. In Chittagong two successive bad seasons have been experienced, and though prices are high and the times hard, the people manage to hold out without any Government interference. The condition of the people has been no doubt altered for the worse, but they have not lost confidence in themselves, and if they are only blessed with a good season or two, there is every hope of their retrieving the heavy losses which they have suffered.

25. Food-grains are selling just now at famine prices, and the lower orders, it has been reported, especially the beggar class, have been driven to extreme difficulty in getting their two meals a day. That these people should be able to get even one meal a day under existing

circumstances speaks well for the ability of the population generally to meet bad seasons, for there is no doubt that this continued loss has told on many persons who have been theretofore known as living in affluent circumstances; these latter have been known to sell their valuables at low prices or to raise money by pledging them. Indeed, the value of silver at one time fell to 6 annas a tolah, and that of gold to Rs. 13 a tolah. But this state of things is said to have now changed, and everything is by degrees returning to its normal condition.

Copies of paragraphs 15 *and* 16 *from the General Administration Report for the year* 1877-78.

PARA. 15. As to the material condition of the people there is little doubt that in the tracts devastated by the cyclone, the population has been slow in recovering. In Noakholly an impression that the fertility of the land had been destroyed by the salt water added to the difficulty of procuring seed grain and plough-cattle has led to a decrease on the cultivated area, and consequently to the amount of good stuff produced. As exportation still goes on, prices remain high and the lower classes are to a certain, extent distressed. The same tightness exists in Chittagong, though it has no doubt been greatly exaggerated. It may, however, be noted that the complaints have come chiefly from the zemindars; the actual cultivating classes have not complained much. This leads to the suspicion that the exaggeration was got up with a view to escape the road cess, public works cess and license-tax, all of which by an unfortunate coincidence came into operation at once. The following remarks by Mr. Veasey, the Collector of Chittagong, are worthy of attention, and to the best of my belief express accurately the real state of things:—

"16. The people are undoubtedly pinched in some places, more particularly in the littoral mouzahs, and nowhere have they quite recovered from the effects of the very serious losses they have sustained from the cyclone. Still I must record my dissent from the idea that there is any general distress, or that an indiscriminate remission of the public dues is either necessary or advisable. I write these lines at Banskhali, where, and in the adjacent sea-side mouzahs, the people have undoubtedly suffered more than in any other part of the district. Yet of the few women who have come to my camp to beg, several wore silver *kharus* showing that they at least have not reached their last resources. At the same time I find a lack of labourers for the road and embankment works now in progress, and the able-bodied men loafing about the villages tell me frankly that they have earned enough to keep them for a few days, and that until that is spent they have no intention of going back to work. It is just this apathetic improvidence, and this determination on the part of the Chittagong labourer to look upon his employer as an obliged person, which will lead to any privations he may have to undergo.

"In the institution of criminal charges which, frequently vexatious but seldom false, are so favourite an amusement in this district, I note but a slight falling off. Too much stress perhaps should not be laid upon this, as a Chittagonian, however poor, will never forego the luxury of a petition in support of which he has or thinks he can show that he has the slightest grounds.

"I am aware that the difficulty experienced in realizing road cess and the Government revenue may be thought to go against my views; but difficulty in the realisation of the public demands has always had to be encountered in this district, and there appears to prevail an unfortunate delusion that it is simply a question of time, and some at least of the collections must be abandoned. That the people generally have had to stint themselves in their daily meals, and that in many instances the poorer classes have been forced to dispose of their ornaments and of the brass and copper utensils acquired in more prosperous years, is undoubtedly a fact; but prices are already commencing to fall, and with seasonable weather during the next few months affairs will, I hope, soon be restored to their normal position.

Copy of paragraph 15 *from the General Administration Report for the year* 1878-79.

PARA. 15. The material condition of the people was everywhere prosperous. There are comparatively few rich people, but the masses are generally well-to-do, and severe poverty is almost unknown. It is stated by officers of all classes that the distress inflicted by the cyclone has, except in some few and narrow tracts, entirely disappeared. Cattle are also now in good condition. Indeed, the homestead of a Chittagong or Noakholly peasant is a picture of rural comfort and prosperity. The people everywhere are well clad, the local markets are well attended; and though there is still some difficulty in realizing Government dues, this arises not from inability, but from unwillingness to pay. There is apparently plenty of money for the favourite pursuit of litigation in the civil courts.

Copy of paragraph 13 *from the General Administration Report for the year* 1879-80.

PARA. 13. The condition of the people in both the districts is prosperous. As compared with that of the more westerly districts, it is exceptionally so. Mr. Fiddian remarks that "the season was a particularly unhealthy one in respect to fever, but cases of cholera were few, and there was nothing remarkable in other respects. The material condition of the great mass of the people left very little to be desired, being such as most other provinces and districts of India might envy. The people are well clothed and well fed; most of them have holdings of their own, which they cling to tenaciously, and possess a reserve fund of hard cash available whenever they want to carry on a law-suit or purchase permanent rights in a piece of land from the superior landholder. They are very little under the influence of zemindars, and have a considerable amount of independence about them. The women hold a good position and are not allowed to do any field work beyond the light task of gathering the *rabi* crops, now are they permitted to work on the road or any other public place or even to go to market. The rarity of suicides among them contrasts most favourably with the state of things in Hindu districts, and even in districts where Mahomedans of another sect are numerous." The above remarks apply equally to the people of Chittagong, no one can help being struck with the prosperous well-to-do condition of the peasantry in both districts.

Extract paragraph 16 *from the General Administration Report, Chittagong Division, for* 1880-81.

PARA. 16. The condition of the people in all the districts in this division has been one of great prosperity throughout the year. There is hardly anything to be added to what was reported last year under this head. The very abundance of the harvest has been a cause of complaint, for a plentiful supply has caused a great fall in prices, which has induced many villagers to hold back from selling. Stock being thus withheld or sold at low prices has resulted in an inability on the part of the ryots to pay their rents.

Extracts paragraphs 37 *to* 39 *from the General Administration Report, Chittagong Division, for* 1881-82.

PARA. 37. The condition of the people throughout the division has been one of unabated prosperity, except for those living along the eastern frontier of the Chittagong Hill Tracts, where, owing to the crops having been destroyed by rats, scarcity and distress prevailed. The crops in other parts of the division were good. In Chittagong there is no pauper class, and the class of people living entirely by labour is very small. Nearly all are cultivators in independent circumstances. The prices of produce have been considerably less than in several previous years; yet the trade of the districts has been brisk and increasing. Agriculturists generally have retained ample stock for their own use. In the Hill Tracts the condition of the people generally is reported to be very satisfactory, and the main crop was a bumper one.

Mr. Westmacott thus describes the daily life of the Noakholly people:—

"I observe that no one goes out to work till he has had a good meal, whereas elsewhere I have known the people fast till 11 o'clock. The days work, too, is a very short and easy one in Noakholly, and I think this may make the people stronger. The ordinary cultivators buy plenty of fish, flesh, and fowl, and live generously; they also wear good *dhuties*, long petticoats down to their heels, being considered due to decency by the Puritan Mahomedans. Women are rarely seen either at work or at the market, and on the whole the people are, as compared with ryots of the same class in the north, very comfortably off. The court amlahs and foreigners also are healthy compared with those north of the Ganges. Although the fall in the price of rice has seriously crippled the resources of the people and left them less cash to spend than they expected, it would be absurd to talk of distress. It is difficult to get a coolie for eight hours' work for 4 annas.

"The caste of weavers called Joogees is gradually taking to cultivation, their craft being ruined by the importation of cloth from Europe and America."

39. In Tipperah the people had abundance of cheap food during the year, but the fall in the price of rice seriously affected their pockets. Mr. Toynbee remarks:—"The greater part of the money savings and earnings of the people in this district appears to me to go into the pockets of pleaders, muktears, and hangers-on at the courts. They have taken the place once held by the amlah, and the expression 'ukil karaj' is something more than a mere figure of speech. Except in parts of South Sylhet, I have seen no ryots in India whose general material condition is better than that of the people of this district."

Extract paragraphs 27, 28, *and* 29 *from the General Administration Report for the year* 1883.

PARA. 27. *Hill Tracts.*—The condition of the people was far from satisfactory. The outturn of the jhooms being poor, the people had to live by cutting timber, bamboos, and forest produce.

28. *Tipperah.*—The material condition of the people continues good in spite of the glutted state of the rice market and the absence of the ready money in the ryots' hands. No labour can be procured locally. The railway survey parties had to pay at exorbitant rates.

29. *Noakholly.*—The condition of the people was prosperous.

Copies of paragraphs 21, 22, 23 *and* 24 *from the General Administration Report for the year* 1884.

PARA. 21. Regarding the condition of the people, the Magistrate of Chittagong observes briefly:—"The majority of the people in the district show undeniable marks of prosperity and independence."

22. The Magistrate of Tipperah writes:—"The people are well off. The absence of women from markets and the fields, showing that they are not required to work except for domestic purposes, is tolerable evidence of the fact that their husbands are able to earn enough for the support of their family. In most other districts, the females of the lower classes work in the fields, weeding and transplanting crops: they form the majority at markets and hâts, but in this district few seem to stir abroad beyond the precincts of their own villages,

"Rents are very low, and it would appear as if it were equally impossible for Government or for the zemindars to raise them. Village sites betoken ease and in some cases affluence. There is no labouring population, no large class which earns its daily bread by daily labour: it is perhaps hardly reasonable to expect that rents will rise until there is a surplus population compelled to earn its livelihood by daily labour for wages: petty cultivators by combination successfully resist any considerable rise."

23. The Magistrate of Noakholly writes to the same effect regarding the prosperous condition of the people of his district.

24. The material prosperity of the people of this division is indeed a fact which admits of no dispute. There are very few wealthy individuals; but on the other hand there are no paupers. The possession of wealth is widely diffused among all class of the community. I attribute this fortunate condition of things to the system of land tenures which prevails, under which almost every individual is the possessor of a small plot of land or interest in land and a fair rent: fixity of rates and free right of sale are almost universally claimed and recognized. Very few of the evils which are said to exist in other parts of these provinces, in consequence of the permanent settlement, exist in this division. Rack-renting is virtually unknown, and the only practical difficulty under the existing rent law which needs a remedy is the difficulty of realizing undisputed rents from under-tenants.

Copy of paragraph 28 from the General Administration Report for the year 1885.

PARA. 28. The reports are with one exception unanimous as to the material condition of the people being excellent, and even better than in the previous year, the cause being that they had excellent crops combined with high prices for the rice crop. The Magistrate of Chittagong considers that the extension of khas management, and the increase of leases to ryots direct from Government without the intervention of a middleman, has had much to do with the general prosperity. In Noakholly the Magistrate remarks that "the great bulk of the people are better off than in most parts of India," and but for their proneness to litigation, he considers they would be better off still. The Sub-divisional Officer of Fenny, while admitting the general outward prosperity, considers that parts of the country are rapidly becoming over-populated, and that even now the margin is not great owing to there being no outlet for the people except agriculture. Looking at the enormous food exports of the division, the time feared by this officer must be considered a long way off. It is undoubtedly unsatisfactory, as remarked by him, that so comparatively few of the people have any resource beyond their crops. This is, however, less the case in the two districts of Noakholly and Chittagong than in any part of Bengal with which I am acquainted, as these two districts furnish nearly all the lascars, who are now so largely employed in steamers, and thus add considerably to their gains. Another very large external source of gain will be dealt with under the next heading. This division has also fewer of the non-labouring middle class, who will not do manual labour than probably any other in Bengal. This is the class on whom a rise in the price of food tells severely, and who suffer when the ryot is most prosperous.

The single exception to the general prosperity was the Hill Tracts. The crops in the jhooms were by no means good, being dependent on the early rains, which were insufficient. Still until lately the local officers believed that there was enough to support the people till the Indian corn crop is got in July. In March it appeared that this was not the case, the crop, originally scanty, having been still further reduced by rats, and some help has had to be given in places. The value of the grain now being advanced will be recovered partly in cash and partly in labour.

Copy of paragraphs 21, 22, 23, 24 *and* 25 *from the General Administration Report for the year* 1886.

PARA. 21. The condition of the people of the division as a whole continued to be above average. They had rather above average rice crops, and high prices were obtained which is better for the ordinary ryot than bumper crops and low prices. The Collector of Chittagong notes that cultivating ryots are now applying for leases of Government lands direct, which are being freely given to the advantage of both Government and the ryot, as the rates taken by Government are lower than those charged by middlemen, while Government gets more by direct collection than the middlemen used to pay.

22. In Tipperah the crops were damaged in the lowlying lands of thanas Chandina, Muradnagar and of the Brahmonberiah sub-division, but the higher lands benefited, and the gain was probably quite as great on the whole as the loss. There was some individual suffering, and Mr. Skrine got a grant of Rs. 2,100 from the Central Inundation Committee in Calcutta and distributed it among some 300 families. There was no actual necessity for this, but I have no doubt the recipients were glad to get the money, and that it saved them from getting deeper into debt. The price of rice nowhere rose above 16 seers for the rupee.

23. In Noakholly the good harvest and high prices gave the people funds to indulge freely in litigation, which in all three districts is the favourite means of disposing of surplus cash. In one of the Ward's reports of the Noakholly district, the Manager (himself a Mahomedan) remarks on the large number of the ryots and tenureholders who have two wives (as sure sign of prosperity), and the way in which these women are supplied with jewellery, and remarks that, but for the money spent in litigation, these men would be very well-to-do indeed.

24. The Hill Tracts crops were better than in the previous year, and the people were, therefore better off; but all the advances given by Government in April were not repaid during the year.

25. As noted last year, the people of Chittagong and Noakholly are less entirely dependent on their crops than in any other part of Bengal. They get large sums for working in Burmah, and as lascars and firemen. A man working for six months as a fireman gets his food and Rs. 15 a month at least, of which he probably spends Rs. 2 or Rs. 3, and at the end of six months comes home with Rs. 70 or Rs. 80 in his pocket. The Boroouh Mugs of Chittagong too make large sums as cooks, and some 600 men go yearly on kheddah work, getting good pay and their food free.

Copy of paragraphs 20, 21, 22 *and* 23 *from the General Administration Report for the year* 1887.

PARA. 20. The agricultural population of the Chittagong district was prosperous. Crops were above average, and prices on the whole fair. The standard of comfort of the ordinary ryot is very high in Chittagong—quite as high as in any district in the province, Backergunge not excepted. The Collector says:—"The villages all over the district look prosperous. Every homestead has trees planted, golahs wherein paddy is stored, large stacks of straw covered with netting of straw rope and built on a platform. Buffaloes and cattle are numerous, and there are plenty of poultry and goats about. In Cox's Bazar carts have been introduced to fetch home the rice from the fields, which is a great step in advance. Wheeled traffic was quite unknown there within three or four years." The Burmese War had a bad effect on the trade with Burmah carried on by the Mug residents of Cox's Bazar, and several of the merchants suffered heavy losses. The Collector notes that, for the first time, he saw Mug women working on the roads, which indicates that the non-agricultural Mug population was not prosperous last year.

21. I have already indicated that the year has been a bad one in a large part of the Tipperah district. The present Collector has just joined from Durbhunga, and he thus contrasts the condition of the two districts:—"In Durbhunga a coolie is glad to earn 6 pice or at most 2 annas by a whole day's labour; for 4 or 6 annas he will go often so much as 30 miles in the day, carrying a box or package. In Tipperah a coolie labourer under any circumstances will not come to work for less than 5 or 6 annas a day, and he will charge a rupee if he has to walk anything like 20 miles. A labourer in Tipperah, it is said, must spend at least 10 pice in the day if he wishes to feed himself in a style suitable to his condition. The people in Tipperah fare better, and are more independent than those of Durbhunga, and they live in better houses, and are better clad; but yet they are not so well off as those of Dacca or Furreedpore or Mymensingh: at least such is my impression from my acquaintance with these districts. I think Tipperah is the poorest, or, perhaps I should say, the least well off of the Eastern Bengal districts, but this may be the result of the bad harvests that have been gathered in portions of the district of late years." Mr. Price has spent most of his time, since he joined, in Tipperah, in the parts where most damage was done, and where there has been a succession of three bad harvests, yet still he finds the people in better ease than in Durbhunga. In ordinary seasons the Tipperah ryot is better off than those of Furreedpore, Dacca and Mymensingh, and it is only the circumstances under which Mr. Price has seen the Tipperah ryot which has caused him to think his position worse than that of his fellows on the other bank of the Megna. When crops fail, the people of Brahmun-beriah and Kusba have two industries to fall back on, and thus procure money to purchase food. I mean the salting of fish and the cutting of jungle produce from the hills. Many have subsisted by these means during the past year, and none have been so distressed as to be compelled to fall back on road work. It is in fact the beggars, who always subsist on alms, who have suffered most, as people had less to give than usual.

22. The people of Noakholly benefited by the damages in Tipperah, and there was a steady flow of rice northward into the distressed parts. The year was thus a good one; but both the Collector and the Sub-divisional Officer of Fenny deplore the dependence of the people on agriculture and clerkships, and the want of any other trade or commerce. This is only partly true, as the people are largely employed in steamers and ships, but there is no doubt that the weaving industry has suffered severely.

The Sub-divisional Officer of Fenny writes very strongly regarding the harm he considers that the vernacular schools are doing. He expresses himself as follows:—"To throw adrift nto the world a cultivator's or an artisan's son as a vernacular scholar, hating his own profession, and finding no room for the use of his vernacular scholarship, except in writing anonymous petitions of a most disgraceful kind, is to ruin him body and soul." This is strong language, but there is some ground for it, and it is a matter of regret that even in a backward district like Noakholly the supply of men who refuse to do any work unconnected with writing should exceed the demand. It is such men who form the discontented and disloyal class, who are anxious for changes and what they call reforms, which they hope will give them employment.

23. The people of the Hill Tracts, who did not suffer from the depredations of rats, were well off. Plough cultivation is increasing, and the quantity of tobacco grown is larger every year.

From the nature of the country jhoming must always be the main occupation of the people, but there are large tracts of excellent soil in the valleys well fitted to grow profitable crops on. During the year under report 2,605 acres were settled after survey, and there are applications pending for 4,164 acres more. A very large number of these settlements are with hillmen.

Small cultivators, i.e., those who have fixed holdings of small size, even though they may also earn something by labour.	Labourers, i.e., those who have no fixed holdings of their own but live by labour.	Artisans, shop-keepers, boatmen, &c., who work for their living and own the implements of their trade.	Poor persons who are dependent on charity.	Males.	Females.	Total.	Number of families.	Number of families above manual labour of any kind.	Doing any cultivation, and at the same time also employing labourers or jotedars, i.e., higher sort of cultivators.	Small cultivators, i.e., those who have fixed holdings of small size, even though they may also earn some thing by labour.	Labourers, i.e., those who have no fixed holdings of their own but live by labour.	Artisans, shop-keepers, boatmen, &c., who work for their living and own the implements of their trade.	Poor persons who are dependent on charity.	Males.	Females.	Total.	Number of families.	Number of families above manual labour of any kind.	Doing any cultivation, and at the same time also employing labourers or jotedars, i.e., higher sort of cultivators.	Small cultivators, i.e., those who have fixed holdings of small size, even though they may also earn something by labour.	Labourers, i.e., those who have no fixed holdings of their own, but live by labour.	Artisans, shop-keepers, boatmen, &c., who work for their living, and own the implements of their trade.	Poor persons who are dependent on charity.	Males.	Females.	Total.	Grand total of population	REMARKS.
6	7	8	9	10	11	12	13	14	15	16	17	18	19	20	21	22	23	24	25	26	27	28	29	30	31	32	33	34
68	69	17	21	606	666	1,361	133	5	3	8	12	89	16	311	275	586	...	...	......	......	......	......	...	...	...	...	1,948	
19	17	4	...	112	113	225	...	...	......	......	......	......	...	...	...	...	...	...	......	......	......	......	...	...	...	...	225	
99	125	8	11	905	794	1,701	70	19	10	9	19	3	11	209	176	385	...	...	......	......	......	......	...	...	...	...	2,046	
40	49	1	10	534	510	1,044	6	...	1	1	......	4	...	26	17	43	...	...	......	......	......	......	...	...	...	...	1,087	
25	15	1	3	234	199	433	...	...	......	......	......	......	...	...	...	...	...	...	......	......	......	......	...	...	...	...	433	
18	6	4	1	112	98	210	...	...	......	......	......	......	...	...	...	...	...	...	......	......	......	......	...	...	...	...	210	
11	3	...	...	41	37	78	...	...	......	......	......	......	...	...	...		...	...	......	......	......	......	...	...	...	...	78	
37	7	...	6	157	160	317	...	...	......	......	......	......	...	...	...	...	...	...	......	......	......	......	...	...	...	...	317	
323	290	35	51	2,700	2,579	5,369	209	24	14	18	31	96	28	546	468	1,014	...	...	......	......	......	......	...	...	...	...	6,383	

B.

Result of Enquiries in Cox's Bazar Khas Thesil.

6	7	8	9	10	11	12	13	14	15	16	17	18	19	20	21	22	23	24	25	26	27	28	29	30	31	32	33	34
536	824	...	63	865	914	1,779	831	27	107	241	546	7	8	477	484	961	633	6	......	......	585	......	43	252	380	633	3,348	Total number of families of all classes is 845.
1,016	628	...	51	1,040	1,021	2,061	65	...	18	23	9	...	...	22	23	45	267	...	......	90	171	......	6	128	139	267	2,373	Total number of families of all classes is 465
25	180	...	...	93	118	211	...	...	......	......	......	...	...	...	...	...	...	...	......	......	......	......	...	...	...	...	211	Total number of families of all classes is 48.
165	91	23	7	176	178	354	...	...	......	......	......	...	...	...	...	...	...	...	......	......	......	......	...	...	...	...	354	Total number of families of all classes is 78.
1,742	1,734	23	121	2,174	2,231	4,405	976	27	120	264	555	7	8	499	477	976	899	6	......	90	756	......	49	380	519	899	6,159	

A. MANSON,

Magistrate.

C.

Consolidated Statement C prepared from Statements marked A and B.

APPLICABLE TO ALL CLASSES.					APPLICABLE TO FIRST THREE CLASSES.															
					AGGREGATE AREA OF HOLDINGS SUB-DIVIDED INTO—					AVERAGE AREAS OF EACH HOLDING SUB-DIVIDED INTO—					AGGREGATE QUANTITY OF PRODUCE OF HOLDINGS.					
					a	b	c	d	e	a	b	c	d	e	a	b	c			
Number of families.	Population.	Average number in each family.	Aggregate number of working members in population.	Average number of working members in each family.	Rice land.	Betel garden.	Jute land.	Other kind of land.	Total.	Rice.	Betel.	Jute.	Other kinds.	Total.	Rice.	Betel.	Jute.	Average produce per holding in rice, betel, jute, &c., in a year.	Value of produce per holding.	
1	2	3	4	5	6					7					8			9	10	
					Acres.		Acres.		Acres.	Acres.		Acres.		Acres.	Mds.		Mds.	Mds.	Mds. s. ch.	
192	1,051	5·4	301	1·5	575·8	...	67·3	...	643·1	3	...	·3	...	3·3	8,041	...	1,568	Rice ... 41·8 Jute ... 8·1	Rice ... 62 11 0 Jute ... 24 5 0 Other produce ., 63 8 0 150 6 0	Rice Jute
54	264	4·8	74	1·3	46·5	...	1·85	...	48·35	·8	...	·03	...	·83	653	...	31	Rice ... 12·8 Jute ... ·57	Rice ... 18 8 0 Jute ... 1 11 4 Other produce ... 27 0 0 46 13 4	Hire catt and plou
62	323	5·2	111	1·7	60	...	14·5	...	74·5	·9	...	......	...	1·1	869	...	189	Rice ... 14·1 Jute ... 3·1	Rice ... 22 0 0 Jute ... 10 0 0 Other produce ... 7 8 0 39 8 0	
25	101	4·04	35	1·4	......	...	......	...	......	......	...	......	...	......	...	...	...	......	......	
24	109	4·5	44	1·8	......	...	......	...	......	......	...	......	...	......	...	...	...	......		
1	5	5	1	1	......	...	......	...	......	......	...	......	...	......	...	...	...			
12	59	4·9	16	1·3	......	...	......	...	......	......	...	......	...	......	...	...	...			
18	63	3·5	...	...	......	...	......	...	......	......	...	......	...	......	...	...	...	......	......	

D.

Statement A.

Mouzah Nabipore Hoshentollah, Pergunnah Bardakhat.

LL	APPLICABLE TO FIRST THREE CLASSES.																			APPLICABLE TO CLASSES 2, 3, 4, 5 AND 7.			
Average number of working members in each family.	Aggregate area of holdings sub-divided into—					Average area of each holding sub-divided into—					Aggregate quantity of produce of holdings from			Average produce per holding in rice, betel, jute, &c., in a year.	Value of produce per holding.	Cost of production per holding.	Annual rent of land, including homestead.	Balance available per family for support for a year.	Balance available per head for support for a year.	Aggregate earnings per year.	Average earnings per family in a year.	Earnings available per head for a year.	Total of columns 14 and 17.
	a	b	c	d	e	a	b	c	d	e	a	b	c										
	Rice land.	Betel garden.	Jute land.	Other kind of land.	Total.	Rice.	Betel garden.	Jute.	Other kinds.	Total.	Rice.	Betel.	Jute.										
5	6					7					8			9	10	11	12	13	14	15	16	17	18
	Acres.		Acres.		Acres.	Acres.		Acres.		Acres.	Mds.		Mds.	Mds.	Mds. s. c.	Rs. A. P.	Rs. A. P.	Rs. A. P.	Rs. A. P.	Rs. A. P.	Rs. A. P.	Rs. A. P.	Rs. A. P.
1·3	374	...	......	...	374	3·2	...	......	...	3·2	5,099	...	...	44·3 of rice ...	Rice ... 66 0 0 Other produce ... 80 0 0 Total ... 146 0 0	22 0 0	7 9 2	116 6 10	23 12 2	......	......	......	23 12 2
1·2	41	...	... ...	...	41	·99	..	......	...	·99	371	...	...	12·9 of rice ...	Rice ... 18 0 0 Other ... 44 0 0 Total ... 62 0 0	Hire of cattle and plough 6 0 0	3 14 7	33 1 5	11 5 2	2,851 8 0	34 12 9	14 1 4	25 6 6
1·7	17	...	......	...	17	1	...	......	...	1	259	...	...	15·2 of rice ...	Rice ... 22 8 0 Other ... 7 8 0 Total ... 30 0 0	6 0 0	3 10 0	20 6 0	3 9 2	7,950 0 0	467 10 4	33 0 8	35 10 10
·1	......	...	......	...	......	......	...	......	...	......	...	...	...		....		......	......	......	594 0 0	66 0 0	17 13 4	......
...	......	...	......	...	......	......	...	......	...	......	...	...	...				......	......	......	......	......	......	......
1	......	...	......	...	......	......	...	......	...	......	...	...	...				......	......	......	300 0 0	300 0 0	60 0 0	60 0 0
1·3	......	...	......	...	......	......	...	......	...	......	...	...	...	......		......	......	......	......	768 0 0	64 0 0	13 1 0	13 1 0
...	......	...	......	...	......	......	...	......	...	......	...	...	...	......	....	......	......	......	......	......	......	......	......

KALISANKER SEN,
Settlement Deputy Collector.

Average number in each family.	Aggregate number of working members in population.	Average number of working members in each family.	Aggregate area of holdings sub-divided into— a Rice land.	b Betel garden.	c Jute land.	d Other kind of land.	e Total.	Average area of each holding sub-divided into— a Rice.	b Betel.	c Jute.	d Other kinds.	e Total.	Aggregate quantity of produce of holdings from a Rice.	b Betel.	c Jute.	Average produce per holding in rice, betel, jute, &c., in a year.	Value of produce per holding in a year.	Cost of production per holding.	Annual rent of land, including homestead.	Balance available per family for support for a year.	Balance available per head for support for a year.	Aggregate earnings per year.	Average earnings per family in a year.	Earnings available per head for a year.	Total of columns 14 and 17.
3	4	5	6					7					8			9	10	11	12	13	14	15	16	17	18
			Acres.		Acres.		Acres.	Acres.		Acres.		Acres.	Mds.		Mds.	Mds.	Rs. A. P.	Rs. A.	Rs. A. P.	Rs. A. P.	Rs. A. P.	Rs. A. P.	Rs. A. P.	Rs. A. P.	Rs. A. P.
6·8	151	2	201·8	...	67·3	...	269·1	2·6	...	·8	...	3·4	2,945	...	1,568	Rice ... 58·3 Jute ... 20·3	Rice ... 57 0 0 Jute ... 61 0 0 Other produce ... 47 0 0 165 0 0	Rice ... 7 0 Jute ... 10 0 17 0	15 0 0	133 0 0	21 7 0	......	......	......	21 7 0
5·8	20	3	5·5	...	1·85	...	7·35	·5	...	·2	...	·7	83	...	31	Rice.. 8·2 Jute... 3·1	Rice ... 11 0 0 Jute ... 10 0 0 Other produce ... 10 0 0 31 0 0	Hire of cattle and plough 3 0	4 0 0	25 0 0	3 0 0	1,200 0 0	120 0 0	20 11 0	23 8 0
5	33	1·3	43	...	14·5	...	57·5	1	...	·3	...	1·3	650	...	169	Rice... 14 Jute... 3·7	Rice ... 21 0 0 Jute ... 12 0 0 33 0 0	16 8	7 0 0	9 8 0	1 14 4	5,850 0 0	130 0 0	26 0 0	27 14 4
4·2	28	1·5	......	...	......	...	......	......	...	......	...	......	...	...	...		......	......	......	......	......	1,380 0 0	81 4 0	19 8 9	19 8 9
4·5	44	1·9	......	...	......	...	......	......	...	......	...	......	...	...	...		......	......	......	......	......	1,440 0 0	60 0 0	13 5 4	13 5 4
...	...	...	......	...	......	...	......	......	...	......	...	......	...	...	...		......	......	......	......	......	......	......	......	......

STATEMENT F.

F.

Classes of people.	Total number of families.	Average. Area of holding.	Productions in maunds per acre.	Total production of each holding.	Quantity required for food.	Sale of surplus at one rupee per maund.	Average income. Total value of crops at one rupee per maund. (a)	Day-labourer. (b)	Artisan.	Total of columns (a), (b) and (c).	Average. Rent for holding.	Cost of cultivation.	Cost of food.	Cost of repair of houses, &c.
		K. G. K.	M. S. C.	M. S. C.	M. S. C.	Rs. A. P.	Rs. A. P.	Rs. A. P.	Rs. A. P.	Rs. A.	Rs. P.	Rs. A.	Rs. A.	Rs. A.
A.—Cultivators	2	5 0 0	15 0 6	118 20 0	33 20 0	85 0 0	118 8 0	......	......	118 8	27 0	......	78 8	2 8
B.—Cultivators with other sources of income.	207	1 13 3	9 0 0	41 19 0	29 30 0	11 10 0	41 8 0	38 2 0	24 6 6	104 0	14 3	1 2	67 7	3 12
C.—Artizans	76	......	......	......	......	......	......	......	127 5 0	127 5	......	......	90 15	3 2
D.—Labourers	19	......	......	......	......	......	......	63 12 0	......	63 12	......	......	52 14	1 10
E.—Beggars	27	......	......	......	......	......	......	......	......	......	......	......	......	......
Total ...	331													

W. LeB.—Reg. No. 2107C—137—14-5-88.

Expenditure. Clothing.	Expenditure. Cost of annual ceremonies, &c.	Expenditure. Total.	Amount borrowed by cultivators.	Average earnings by unskilled day labourers.	Average cost of food for each person per annum.	Average number of houses for each family with costs and value. Number of houses.	Average number of houses for each family with costs and value. Cost.	Average number of houses for each family with costs and value. Value.	Average value of clothes, &c., &c.	Average weight and value of utensils of brass, &c., possessed by each family. Weight.	Average weight and value of utensils of brass, &c., possessed by each family. Value.	Average value of ornaments possessed by each family.	Average expenditure of marriage, &c., &c.	Average cost of annual ceremonies.	Average number of persons contained in a family.	Number of persons who have no means for their maintenance.	Remarks.
Rs. A.	Rs. A.	Rs. A.	Rs. A.	Rs. A.	Rs. A.		Rs. A.	Rs. A.	Rs. A.	Md. s.	Rs. A.	Rs. A.	Rs. A.	Rs. A.			
6 0	......	114 6	10 8	......	14 4	2	3 8	15 0	6 0	3 0	3 0	30 6	100 0	(a)	5½	...	(a) Both Musulmans.
6 9	5 2	96 5	31 6	5 3	11 11	2	2 15	1 6	6 9	3 10	3 10	11 6	187 7	0 15	5½	28	
6 11	3 13	104 9	73 0	......	53 8	2	3 2	19 11	6 11	3 15	3 15	11 12	240 0	2 4	4	17	
3 13	0 13	59 0	11 9	5 5	14 0	1	1 10	4 11	5 13	0 14	0 14	0 8	200 0	.. ...	4	1	
......	......	......	......	......	......	......	......	......	......	......	......	......	......	......	1¼	27	

N. C. Sen,

Sub-divisional Officer.

CONFIDENTIAL.]

No. 109M, dated Rampore Beauleah, the 30th April 1888.

From—E. E. Lowis, Esq., c.s., Commissioner of the Rajshahye Division,
To—The Secretary to the Government of Bengal, Revenue (Agricultural) Dept.

With reference to Government circular No. 35Agri., dated 9th December 1887, I have the honour to submit my report on the condition of the lower classes of the population, after consulting selected district officers in the division.

2. My report has been delayed owing to delay in receipt of information from one or two officers who have been at pains to go into the matter thoroughly. The subject had to be enquired into carefully, and the field of enquiry was a wide one; so that it was impossible to submit anything like accurate information earlier.

3. *Dinagepore.*—The Sub-divisional Officer of Thakurgaon reports that the condition of the poorer classes of people is really deplorable, notwithstanding cheap and large quantities of land available. He has not, however, given accurate figures in support of his statement, and his estimates are not always to be trusted. He estimates the average holding of an ordinary cultivator to be 10 bigahs, yielding a produce of 30 maunds of paddy, valued at Rs. 1-12 a maund, and thinks that, though the ryot keeps the whole of his produce for home consumption, he is still in want of nearly Rs. 27 for his food alone, and that after allowing for the cost of clothes, bullocks, &c., his yearly deficit amounts to Rs. 53-14. This he has to make up by labour if he can spare the time from his agricultural pursuits. He barely gets two meals a day, and suffers from an insufficiency of food. The Collector considers that the estimate given by the Sub-divisional Officer of the average outturn, viz., 3 maunds a bigah, is obviously too low; while he has unnecessarily debited the ryot with the cost of a ploughman, &c. The general conclusions arrived at disagree from those formed by the Manager of Maldwar, a large estate in his sub-division, and from the Collector's own observation of the people. The Sub-divisional Officer, I may add, is new to the district, and does not appear to have gone very deep in his enquiries; for I observe that he does not attempt to solve the problem why it is impossible to get coolies for road or other work in Dinagepore even during the period when agricultural operations are at a standstill. This fact does not support his view of a yearly deficit to be made up by labour when the ryot can spare time.

4. The Settlement Officer of Sunkerpore also takes a somewhat gloomy view of the condition of the poorer classes of cultivators. With reference to this Mr. Marindin observes: "He seems to consider it a hardship that the women of this class should work to supplement the family earnings, and he describes with pity a meal, which consists of rice, dâl, curry and fish. It is no doubt largely due to false statements of this nature that the idea is prevalent among a certain class of philanthropists that the Indian peasantry suffer as a rule from a daily insufficiency of food. Though he takes such a low view of their condition, this officer reports that among the Mahomedans the males and females both take three meals a day, while among the Hindus the males eat three times, but the females only twice a day. The children always get four meals a day."

5. I proceed to notice briefly the information gathered regarding the four classes of rural population—cultivators, labourers, artizans, and those who subsist on charity. Information has been derived from the Manager of the Sunkerpore Estate, which represents the condition of things in the south of the district, and from the Managers of the Maldwar and Chooramon Estates, which may be said to represent the north and west of the district.

6. *Cultivators.*—The Manager of the Sunkerpore Estate reports that this class is more comfortably off than the agricultural labourers. The income of the family is supplemented by the women, who husk paddy, and sometimes by the employment in service of one or other member of the family. Six

illustrations are given, the circumstances of which are very similar. I quote the following :—

Prankrisna Kaiburta—Age 25; household seven members, father, five sons, and one daughter-in-law; working members all seven.

Sources of Income.

	Rs.		Rs.
Produce of 25 bigahs, 300 maunds, at annas 8 a maund...	50	Sale of *dahi*	60
One cart, worked for six-months brings in	30	Total ...	240
		Deduct rent ...	27
		Balance ...	213

The moveable property consists of—

	Rs.		R.
5 Bullocks	75	8 Metal plates, 6 Lotahs, 8 Brass cups	20
5 Cows	15		
1 Cart	10		
Ornaments	60		
		Total ...	180

No debts.

The ordinary food of the family is rice, dâl, fish, vegetables and *dahi*.

In another case given the ryot deals in country produce and adds Rs. 35 to his income in this way. The income and debts of the six families illustrated are as follows :—

Income. Rs.	Debts. Rs.	Income. Rs.	Debts. Rs.
126	60	64	45
213	Nil.	125	Nil.
160	41	114	20

In the illustrations given, the incomes range from Rs. 126 to Rs. 213 annually, and in all, except one case, brass utensils and silver ornaments are in use. The food is rice, dâl, fish and vegetables. In four cases the family is in debt to the following amounts :—Rs. 60, Rs. 41, Rs. 45 and Rs. 20.

Though the actual cost of living is not given in the above cases of agricultural labourers and petty cultivators, it is evident that in all, except perhaps one case, that of Kasi Boona, means are sufficient to keep the families in question above want. The exception is in the case of Kasi Boona, whose income is Rs. 64 only, and the members of the family number seven; yet even here it is stated that the allowance of food is three meals a day.

The Settlement Officer of Maldwar has made detailed enquiries in two villages and sporadic enquiries in others. The two villages selected for enquiry were Sealosh and Shagram.

In these two villages there are six families of khoodkast or settled ryots and 13 of under-ryots of Mahomedans and Hindus—no agricultural labourers, artizans or beggars. The following table shows (excluding fractions) the average resources and expenditure of these 19 families :—

	Bgs.		Mds.
Average area of each ryot's land under cultivation ...	29	Quantity kept for food and seed	99
	Mds.		Rs.
Produce in grain	129	Money value of special crops ...	12
Quantity sold	30	Income from sale of milk, &c. ...	13
	Rs.	Total money income ...	55
Money value	30		

Expenditure.

	Rs.
Rent and cost of cultivation	20
Household expenses, exclusive of grain kept for home consumption ...	22
Clothes	21
Total	63
Average number of persons in family	5

Nature of food.—Rice, choora, muri, dâl, fish and vegetables.

Quantity used daily.—Rice 5 seers, dâl 3 chittacks, fish 3 chittacks, vegetables 13 chittacks.

Number of meals taken.—Adults 3, children 4.

If the money value of the grain kept for consumption and converted into rice be calculated at the rate of Rs. 1-12 a maund, which is the average retail price throughout the year, and assuming the consumption to be 45 maunds at 5 seers per diem, the following estimates of income and expenditure would appear to be correct:—

	Rs.
76 maunds of paddy would yield 45 maunds of rice, value of 45 maunds of rice at Rs. 1-12 a maund equals	78
Income from other sources	55
Total ...	133
Expenditure.	
Cost of 45 maunds of rice at Rs. 1-12 a maund	78
Other expenses	63
Total	141

which would leave a trifling stock of paddy in the ryot's hands out of the 99 maunds *minus* 76 maunds—some 23 maunds at the end of the year. Out of the 19 families, eight are in debt to the amount of Rs. 153 as the aggregate. In five families one or more of the members are employed as servants.

Speaking generally of the condition of these 19 families, the Settlement Officer reports that the khoodkast or settled ryots are the best off. They have the pick of the lands in the village. All these families take their meals three times a day, which consists of rice, dâl, vegetables and fish. They have brass utensils and silver and gold ornaments of small value. Their houses are good and neat, made of thatching grass and bamboos. Most of them have cattle. The women do not work for wages, but help in the cultivation and household work. Except for debt principally incurred for marriage expenses, they would be in a very well-to-do condition. As far as food and clothing go, the khoodkast and under-ryots appear to live very much in the same style.

The Settlement Officer of Chooramon has made most careful and detailed enquiries into five villages which are under settlement, and has been able to give correct areas according to the survey papers. The five villages comprise 41 families. They consist of—

		Hindus.	Mahomedans.
Cultivators	29	22	7
Agricultural labourers	12	10	2
	41	41	

cultivators. The following table shows the average resources and expenditure of a family of this class:—

	Bgs.
Area of holding	21
	Mds.
Dhan and *rabi* produce (mostly the former)	114
Quantity sold	29
	Rs.
Money value	44
	Mds.
Quantity kept for home use	85
	Rs.
Money value of special crops	6
Total money income	75
Expenditure.	
Cost of cultivation	26
Cost of food and household* expenses	37
Total cost ...	63

* Excluding price of rice, as this is provided for by the produce of the cultivators' fields.

	Rs.
Average number in family	6
Naturel of food—Rice, vegetables daily, dâl, fish occasionally ...	......
	Seer.
Quantity of rice per head used daily	1
Number of meals a day—males 3, women 3, children 4.	
	Rs.
Debt	39
Brass utensils, value	8 or 9
Silver and gold ornaments, value	17

The women husk rice, weave gunny, and weed crops.

The daily diet of rice, &c., can be supplemented by fish caught in the bheels during a portion of the year, and by vegetables grown on homestead lands. Houses cost but little to repair, constructed as they are with thatching-grass and bamboos. The thatching is made from the rice straw, and nearly every ryot owns a clump of bamboos. Brass utensils are in use in most households, and cheap silver or shell ornaments are worn by the women. The necessary clothing is simple and cheap, consisting generally for the men of a *langote* or cloth one and a quarter yards long and 9 inches broad worn round the body, and a *gamcha* or cloth two yards long and one yard broad tied round the head or carried over the shoulder. Twenty-three out of the above mentioned 41 families are indebted—15 on account of marriage expenses and eight from other causes. Every male and female adult eats three meals a day, which consists of a *julpan* or early morning meal of *choora* and *muri*, or of what is left of the previous night's rice soaked in water, and two cooked meals at noon and the evening. The children have four meals—two *julpans* and two cooked meals.

7. *Agricultural labourers.*—The Manager of Sunkerpore reports that, owing to a sparse population, these are in great demand. They get in addition to wages three meals a day, and, if of the same caste as their employer, a share of his food. The women earn about Rs. 2-8 a month by husking grain for others, or by purchasing unhusked grain and selling cleaned rice in the market, the earnings from which supplement the earnings of the male members and enable the family to live comfortably. The labouring classes are mostly in debt, but do not seem much troubled by the burden, as service is given in satisfaction of debt, and payment of money is not insisted on as long as the service continues. In some cases the debt and service descends from father to son. Mr. Ricketts does not think this practice presses hardly upon those bound by this species of service. It is true the custom may be morally degrading, but on the other hand it secures the labourers a permanent employment with the certainty of sufficiency of food and clothing. Mr. Ricketts gives a typical case—

Chamba Nashya—Aged 25. household members four—himself, father, mother and wife; working members himself, father and mother. He serves on a monthly salary of Rs. 2 and daily food valued at Rs. 2-8—total Rs. 4-8 a month; approximate annual income Rs. 50. his father also serves on a monthly wage of Rs. 3 and daily food Rs. 2-8—total Rs. 5-8, and gets the same food as his employer. His master also provides him with clothes three times during the year, consisting of three *dhuties* and two *chudders*. His approximate annual income is Rs. 66. His mother husks paddy for six months in the year and thereby earns Rs. 2-8 a month, or Rs. 15 a year. The total annual income of the family thus amounts to Rs. 141. The family possesses a pair of silver bracelets and necklace valued Rs. 12, six metal utensils valued Rs. 4-8. He married three years ago at a cost of Rs. 100. He borrowed Rs. 50 at an interest of 6 annas per rupee. The money was borrowed from his employer, and the debt is being liquidated by service, except the interest which is paid in cash and amounts to Rs. 18-12 a year. The family eats three times a day. Some members of this class have small holdings and vegetable gardens, the produce of which supplement their earnings. One case is given where the labourer possesses four buffaloes, one pig, and one cart, and consumes five seers of pachwai a week, the cost of which is 10 annas. The annual income and debt of the six families in which the Manager held enquiries are :—

Income.			Debt.	Income.			Debt.
Rs.			Rs.	Rs.			Rs.
54	...	...	20	126	...	...	25
134	...	...	6	184	...	...	60
141	...	...	50	122	...	...	40

The Manager of Chooramon reports that the labourers eat *pánthábhát*, or rice left over from last night's dinner for their *julpan* or early morning meal, a cooked meal at noon, and another cooked meal at night. As a class they eat well, and are well clothed. The poorest get two meals a day, and it is but seldom that any one has to be content with one meal only.

The Settlement Officer of Maldwar has enquired into the case of seven agricultural labourers. They all have small holdings averaging four bigahs. The average produce of the holding is 23 maunds, which is kept for house consumption and the average earnings of each family Rs. 79. Besides this, the money value of other produce, such as vegetables and chillies, is calculated at Rs. 5. The cost of rent and cultivation is estimated to be Rs. 7, and the cost of living and household expenses to be Rs. 99. The following therefore would be a correct estimate of the agricultural labourer's income and expenditure :—

Income.

				Rs.
Value of paddy at Re. 1 per maund	...	...	...	23
Value of other produce	...	...	...	5
Wages of self and family	...	...	...	79
		Total	...	107

Expenditure.

Cost of cultivation	...	...	...	7
Household expenses	...	...	...	99
		Total	...	106

The agricultural labourers are paid partly in money and partly in kind; somtimes with food and lodging. The money wage is 3 annas day; when food and lodging is given it is 1 anna 3 pie. They frequently hold land. The females husk paddy and earn about Re. 1 a month. This class cannot afford brass utensils or silver ornaments. Though it would appear that they only just manage to make two ends meet, they manage to eat the same food and in the same quantities as the ordinary cultivators. They are as a class largely in debt, incurred for marriage expenses. In the case of the seven families mentioned, the debt aggregates Rs. 695 or Rs. 93 per family.

Among the 12 families of agricultural labourers, whose condition was enquired into by the Settlement Officer of Chooramon, the average area in cultivation is 2½ bigahs, the produce of which was kept for home consumption. The average wages earned by a family is Rs. 66, which is supplemented by the sale of garden crops and gives an income of Rs. 83. The cost of living for a family of six persons, exclusive of the rice consumed, comes to Rs. 48—the cost of rice at the average quantity of 3 seers a day, or 27 maunds. Of this, 9 maunds are provided by the produce of the holding and the cost of the remaining 18 maunds at Rs. 1-12 a maund comes to Rs. 31, which, plus Rs. 48, equals an expenditure of Rs. 79 against an income of Rs. 83. These agricultural labourers live in the same style as the cultivators, the only noticeable difference being in the value of their household utensils and ornaments.

8. *Artizan class.*—This class is small. Mr. Ricketts gives three illustrations of the living of this class :—

(i.) *Ram Ruttun Patni*—Age 30; members of household, himself, wife and two children; working members himself and wife. He makes bamboo baskets, tatties, &c., and his average earnings are three annas a day and approximate annual income Rs. 60: his wife earns two annas a day by husking paddy, and the total earnings of the family amount to Rs. 90. He possesses seven metal utensils, value Rs. 7, and silver ornaments, value Rs. 8; has no debts and consumes rice, dâl, fish and vegetables.

(ii.) *Rupdass blacksmith*—Himself, wife and child; working member himself; his average earnings are five annas a day, or Rs. 113 a year. He possesses five metal utensils, value Rs. 10, and silver ornaments, value Rs. 12; has no debts and lives on rice, dâl, fish and vegetables.

(iii.) *Gaya Nath Mistree, carpenter*—Himself and wife; his daily earnings are three annas and annual income Rs. 67. Besides this, he has seven bigahs of land on the *adhiaree* principle, which raises his income to Rs. 75. He has four metal utensils, value Rs. 3, and his food consists of rice, dâl, fish and vegetables. The Collector directed the Settlement Officer of Maldwar's attention to a settlement of *Tantis* (weavers) at Ranisankail, and he has furnished the following facts regarding their condition. He says, however, that he found it very difficult to arrive at a correct estimate of their earnings, so that the figures can only be taken as approximately true. There are 21 families; their aggregate annual earnings amount to Rs. 2,258, an average of Rs. 107 per family. The largest family consists of 11 members, two of ten, but the average number is five. The largest earnings are made by the families with most members in it. The family with 11 members earns Rs. 202 annually; those with ten members Rs. 182. The smallest earnings are made by a single adult male Rs. 30, and a single adult female Rs. 24. The earnings of 21 families range between Rs. 24 and Rs. 202; and the average is Rs. 107. They have no land except small garden plots round their houses. The average annual expenditure for each family is Rs. 102 in each case, a few rupees within the income. The cost of feasts is estimated to be less than one rupee per family and ornaments a little over that sum. They eat the same food as the cultivators in general. But the quantity is stated to be less, being two meals a day for each adult and three for children. The single adult female mentioned as earning Rs. 24 uses three-fourths seer of rice a day, and the single adult male earning Rs. 30 a seer of rice. The debt incurred by these weavers is appalling. Of the 21 families noted above, 18 are in debt. One debt of Rs. 150 has been incurred for trade expenses, the rest for marriage expenses: one family earning Rs. 128 owes Rs. 800; another earning Rs. 107 owes Rs. 400; another earning Rs. 132 owes Rs. 250. One family owes Rs. 14 only, and the debt of the rest varies from Rs. 20 to Rs. 100. The adult female is said to earn one-third of what the male earns. These weavers are reported to be indolent in nature and suffer from slack seasons. Their women wear shell ornaments and the use of brass utensils is limited. Though poor and in debt, it would not appear that they suffer from insufficiency of food.

9. *Class that subsists on charity.*—This class is mainly composed of Bairagees and Baishnomees among the Hindus and Fakirs among the Mahomedans. They are strong, well fed, sturdy beggars. The Collector himself visited a great portion of the district during the last cold weather, and he has nowhere seen signs of an underfed population or an instance of want of sufficient food. Hardly more than three beggars visited the Collector's camp during the three months' tour, and these showed no signs of want of nourishment. He adds:—

"As you are aware, the population does not press hardly upon the land in this district; rents are low. Rice, the staple crop, is so extensively grown that this is the largest rice-producing district in your division. The proportion of labour is so unequal to the demand that every year a large number of labourers from the west of the province visit the district for harvest work and road-making; so that, generally speaking, it may be said that the work of the district is done by imported labour. From the enquiries detailed above, it would appear that the average size of a holding varies from eight bigahs in the middle and south of the district to 20 or 29 bigahs in the west." The ordinary ryot's income in the Collector's opinion ranges between Rs. 150 to Rs. 200 per annum, and his wants being simple he is able to provide himself with sufficient food and clothing, to maintain himself in comparative comfort, and even to lay by a few rupees, if he were not burdened with marriage expenses, which run him into debt. The agricultural labourers earn enough to maintain themselves and their families much in the same style as ordinary small cultivator, but are more largely in debt. Their incomes seem to average about Rs. 100. Among the artizans the weavers are worst off, and are heavily in debt, but still they continue to buy enough food. The class that subsists entirely on charity is small, principally composed of religious mendicants. Mr. Marindin concludes—

" It would be rash to say that in a large district like this there are no individual cases of poverty and hardship, but it may be emphatically ascertained that (if the Harus, a limited case, about whom the information given is vague, are excepted) no class in this district suffers from any insufficiency of food. The enquiries have been limited as to area, but they have been made in all parts of the district, and personally from the people whose condition has been described. As far therefore as the question of food goes, the information gathered may be relied on."

10. *Rajshahye.*—This district is divided into three administrative sub-divisions, in all of which land appears to be held by ryots at an almost uniform rate of Rs. 1-4 per bigah and the quantity of land held by each ryot is calculated at bigahs 4·3 with an annual rental of Rs. 5-3 on an average, as appears from the cess papers file under Act IX of 1880. The average rate of rent stated above does not agree with what I learnt from the few personal enquiries which I made; nor does it agree with the result obtained by the officer appointed to survey and make a settlement and record of right in the Dubalhati Estate. This officer did not report direct to me, but his remarks, addressed to the Director of Agriculture, passed through me. The Collector reports that the annual value of the land on an average of produce from all sources is estimated at about Rs. 8 per bigah, exclusive of rent to landlord and expenses of cultivation. With respect to a village in the Sudder sub-division, the cess return shows the number of people holding less than 5 bigahs of land to be 35, of those holding from 5 to 10 bigahs to be 9, of those holding 10 to 20 bigahs to be 15, and of those holding 20 bigahs and upwards, who alone may in general be considered to be well off, to be 4 only out of the total population of 63 ryots. From this the percentage of the four grades of the agricultural population, which may be supposed to form more than 50 per cent. of the entire population of the district, may be roughly calculated as—

People holding	5 bigahs	55·6
Do.	5 to 10 "	14·3
Do.	10 to 20 "	23
Do.	20 and upwards	6·3
	Total ...	100

From this it will be observed that only about 6 per cent. of the agricultural class are well off, 23 per cent. seem to live from hand to mouth, relying upon their agricultural profits alone, 14 per cent. are supposed to manage to live with their families, supplementing their agricultural income with what they get by working for others, and that the greater portion seem to be unable to make both ends meet, except by denying themselves some of the necessaries of life. They cannot avoid running into debt on occasions of marriage and other social ceremonies, bad harvests, &c. The Dearah portion of the district is reported to be subject to annual inundation, which, not seldom, sweeps away the *aus* paddy, their staple crop, leaving behind very little for the cultivators to live upon.

The Sub-divisional Officer of Nattore estimates from the example of two typical villages, and also from local enquiries generally, that the average population of each agricultural village is about 250 persons and the average number of persons supported by the wages of each labourer to be three, while he estimates two families in a village, or six persons, to be dependent on charity. He calculates the average holding of each cultivator at 11 bigahs, with a rental of Rs. 16-8, the cost of cultivation at Rs. 3-8 per bigah, and the total profit to the cultivator at Rs. 15 for the 11 bigahs. The Collector considers this estimate to be much too low, and that the figures of the Cess Deputy Collector, viz., Rs. 8 as profit per bigah, are far more probable.

The Sub-divisional Officer of Nowgong made enquiries in two villages and writes as follows:—

" Like most villages of this sub-division, Chuck Dev and Chuck Mittan are villages of agriculturists, though some of their people follow a few other professions in addition to agriculture. The lands are generally of two kinds, viz., high and low lands: the soil of the former light sandy which is best suited to the cultivation of ganja and other *rabi* crops, and that of the latter stiff clay, which produces paddy and jute in abundance. In seasons of drought, when the high lands cease to be cultivated for want of moisture, the other class produces what does not prove insufficient to protect the cultivators from starvation; similarly at time of high floods, when the country is inundated, the high lands producing what preserve their owners from scarcity. The people of the villages do not, under such circumstances, entertain any apprehension of the occurrence of a famine among them."

The total population of Chuck Dev consists of 179 souls, and that of Chuck Mittan 138. The people are by caste Mahomedans, except three men who are shoe-makers. Their professions are shown below by families :—

Professions.	Chuck Dev.	Chuck Mittan.	Professions.	Chuck Dev.	Chuck Mittan.
Cultivators ...	17	15	Oil-vendors ...	3	8
Agricultural labourers ...	10	5	Coolies ...	2	1
Ganja brokers ...	2	1	Tailor ...	1	...
Stamp vendor ...	1	...	Hooka-vendor ...	1	...
Book-seller ...	1	...	Servants ...	2	...
School pundit ...	1	...	Others ...	1	...
Shoe-maker ...	1	...	Goldsmith ...	...	1

The size of the holding of two men only of Chuck Dev is above 50 and below 75 bigahs. None of the other villagers have jotes of this size. The size of the holding of three men of Chuck Mittan is above 25 and below 50 bigahs, but none of Chuck Dev have holdings of this class. Two men of the latter and three of the former have jotes to the size of above 10 and below 25 bigahs. Five men of Chuck Dev and six of Chuck Mittan have holdings above five and below 10 bigahs. The other holdings of the two villages are all below five bigahs.

11. As to the price obtained by the ryot for his produce, the poorer classes are so much in the hands of the zemindars and the mahajans that they are never able to sell at the most advantageous rate. The Collector observes that there is a consensus of opinion that within the last 20 years there has been a rise in the wages of the agricultural labourer. Formerly the rate was from one-half to two annas a day. Now it rangers from three annas to four annas a day. But this rise has been almost coincident with the rise in the prices of common food; so it does not really imply any particular amelioration in the condition of the labouring classes. The Collector does not take into consideration the fact that the labourer is fed by his employer, and besides, though wages have doubled, the price of food has not doubled.

12. The artizans are reported to be averse to work and badly off. The manufacturing classes are becoming impoverished: most indigenous manufactures have been crushed by British competition. The ancient weaving industry has been almost extinguished. The continual tendency of events has been to turn the people more and more towards agriculture and less and less to manufacture. This class of the population, however, is not always badly off, for I find that the best-to-do class of artizan, namely, the carpenter, can generally earn eight annas a day, and in the season of repairing boats from twelve annas to one rupee per day.

13. *Class that subsists on charity.*—The number of beggars is estimated by the Cess Deputy Collector at 5 per cent. of the total population and by the Sub-divisional Officer of Nattore at two families of three persons each in a village population of 250, or about 2½ per cent. The Collector thinks the truth probably lies between the two. They are chiefly Baishnavas, able-bodied and capable of work. As long as there is an ordinary sufficiency of food, they fare very well, but the moment any pressure is felt, they are the first persons who are affected by it.

14. The Collector says that food of the poorer persons holding land and the ordinary agricultural labourers is very much the same. They live generally on coarse rice and dâl and curry of vegetables. The daily expenses of a family of six persons with one child subsisting on milk has been estimated as follows by the Sub-divisional Officer of Nowgong from personal enquiries, and the Collector sees no reason to doubt its accuracy:—

Per diem.

		Rs.	A.	P.			Rs.	A.	P.
Rice, 6 seers	...	0	3	0	Tobacco	...	0	0	1½
Dâl, ⅜ seer	...	0	0	9	Spices	...	0	0	1½
Salt	...	0	0	3					
Oil*	...	0	0	3	Total	...	0	4	9
Vegetables	...	0	0	3					

Per annum.

		Rs.	A.	P.			Rs.	A.	P.
On account of above	...	106	14	0	Extraordinary for				
Cloth ...	...	8	0	0	marriage	...	25	0	0
House repairs	...	6	0	0					
					Total	...	145	14	0

To the above may be added fish, which are to be caught in every puddle for some months of the year. The people as a rule dwell in mat huts or huts with mud walls and thatched roofs, and in the selected areas taken there was only one family which had a brick-built house, and that had been only recently erected. Considering, however, the nature of the climate, the poorer classes can not in this respect be said to have any grievance.

It seems to be generally agreed that there has been a rise in the standard of comfort as regards dress. Formerly the labourer was content to wear a *langote;* now nearly every one wears a *dhuti* at least and on occasions a *piran* or coat. The use of the umbrella is also very common. The women also are better dressed.

Brass utensils are not generally used by the poorer agricultural classes. Pottery-ware is generally used.

15. In conclusion the Collector makes the following observations about the district:—

"It is almost purely agricultural, and contains very few rich men as the income-tax returns show, but a fair proportion of people well above the reach of want. The district contains generally two classes of land known as 'barinda' and the 'bhar.' The former is the high land on which only one crop, *amun*, is grown in the year, and is dependent entirely on the rainfall. The latter, comprising the greater part of the district, is generally low land, subject to inundation at least for five months in the year; and it is a fact that it is very rare to get full crops of both kinds of land in the same year. If there were such a crop, it would imply a good rainfall and also a moderate inundation. The people on the 'bhar' or lower lands get at least two crops a year, and there is such a variety that it is next to impossible all can be a failure. Besides *aus*, *amun*, and *boro* rice, mustard and pulses—and I might almost say sugarcane—grow more or less all over on the low lands. There are also in the Nowgong sub-division ganja, jute, and potatoes, to the south of the district indigo, in Nattore turmeric and in the Sudder sub-division mulberry and wheat. This implies a fairly continuous demand for agricultural labourers. Then it is a significant fact that at the time of the *amun* harvest there is an immigration of labourers from other districts, particularly to the Barindas, where the cultivators, when the crop is a good one, rarely cut their own rice." The Collector is inclined to take a gloomy view of the condition of the peasantry, but he has to admit that much of the harvest work is done by outsiders.

16. *Pubna.*—The Collector says there are hardly any agricultural labourers in the district who have no lands. The road cess and the settlement papers show that every ryot in a village has a holding, however small, of his own, though over 88 per cent. hold lands below 10 bigahs and the remainder

* They generally do not rub oil in their body.

10 bigahs and upwards. As a matter of fact, however, a ryot holding below 10 bigahs in any particular village is generally seen to occupy holdings in other villages adjoining. The poorer ryots have the privilege sanctioned by custom of planting *boro* rice in alluviated chur lands without the previous permission of the owners of them who, immediately before harvesting, send out agents to collect ticca rents from these ryots. The poorer ryots largely avail themselves of this privilege, and are better off in this district than elsewhere. They never suffer from a daily insufficiency of food, although not found to possess any permanent holding. The number of poorer cultivators may be estimated to be 75 per cent., the other 25 per cent. being well-to-do or middle-class men. Of the 75 per cent. of the poorer classes of population, 5 have no ploughs or cattle or lands except homesteads, 10 have lands from 2 to 5 bigahs with one plough and a pair of bullocks, 50 have holdings varying from 5 to 10 bigahs with similar implements and plough-cattle. Among these classes of ryots, those that have a large family to maintain generally take to *barga* cultivation in addition to cultivating their own lands. The 5 per cent. noted above maintain themselves by the wages of their labour, and those the area of whose lands is not sufficient to engage them all the year round also work for hire as labourers and rowers of boats, builders of houses, &c., by which they earn Rs. 8 to Rs. 10 a month. Boats are numerous in the district and afford ample employment, so that there is no paucity of work for the poorer classes. At Serajgunge and Baira employment is given to a large number of people in the jute trade. A cultivator owning 10 bigahs of land generally possesses a neat homestead consisting of four neat huts, one plough and two plough-cattle, his clothes and furniture being of the simplest description, *i.e.*, two strong pieces of coarse cloth for each member of his family, a pair of brass lotahs and a pair of brass plates. He takes three meals a day with half a seer of rice each time. In the morning he takes soaked rice with salt only, and at the other two a little dâl or cooked vegetable and rice. He incurs debts on occasions of marriage or other social ceremonies or for the purchase of cattle. He can hardly afford to purchase any ornament for his wife besides those made of lac which are cheap.

17. A ryot cultivating a bigah of *amun* rice has to pay on an average 12 annas as rent (cost of cultivation Rs. 3), in outturn 6 maunds per bigah on an average, which gives him one rupee per maund as the average price, besides straw for his cattle. The estimated cost of cultivation for a bigah of jute land would be about Rs. 8, including rent of land. The outturn of jute per bigah may be taken at 6 maunds, which is generally sold at from Rs. 2-8 to Rs. 3 a maund.

On the whole the poorer classes in this district, and specially in the Serajgunge sub-division, are said to be comparatively well off, and do not know what starvation means.

18. *Rungpore.*—The Collector has not made a very careful or exhaustive enquiry, and contents himself with general remarks unsupported by data of any kind. He considers that the people of the district are better off as compared with the population of any other part of Bengal. This is partly owing to the fact that the population is not sufficiently dense to render the competition for land at all keen, and partly to the fertility of the soil and to the fact that it grows such remunerative crops as jute, tobacco, and sugarcane. Moreover, the enhancement of rent has not so far as a rule been out of proportion to the increased value of the crops raised. The Collector further observes that the fact that in ordinary years no labour can be locally obtained for road-making shows the prosperous condition of the ryots here. The number of landless labourers is very small, and they are usually in regular service and fed by the ryots with whom they work. There is a complete absence of any signs of absolute poverty among the agricultural classes in this district. They have well constructed and neat houses, and a ryot usually has a couple of cows, besides a pair of bullocks. A Mahomedan ryot in addition generally has a few sheep and goats and a number of fowls about his house.

W. LeR.—Reg. No. 1737C - 137 —5-5-88.

CONFIDENTIAL.]

No. 7, dated Bhagulpore, the 2nd May 1888.

From—JOHN BEAMES, ESQ., Commissioner of the Burdwan Division and Sonthal Pergunnahs,

To—The Secretary to the Government of Bengal, Revenue Department.

IN continuation of my confidential letter No. 5, dated the 23rd ultimo, I have the honour to submit herewith the statements appended to the report from the Collector of Purneah regarding the condition of the lower classes of the people of his district. These statements were returned to the Collector for revision, and have now been resubmitted by him duly revised.

A.

Particulars of the village of Khanwah, pergunnah Dharmpur.

Serial number.	Name of head of he household.	Area of land held by him.	Bhadoi. Area.	Bhadoi. Produce per bigha.	Bhadoi. Total produce.	Other crops. Area.	Other crops. Produce per bigha.	Other crops. Total produce.	Total produce.	Home consumption for the whole year.	Balance.	Expenses for cultivation.	Balance.	Price.	Other income.	Total income.	Rent.	Balance.	Debts.	Remarks— Source of other income.
		B. C.	B. C.	M. s.	M. s.	B. C.	M. s.	B. C.	M. s.	M. s.	M. s.	M. s.	M. s.	Rs. A. P.	Rs. A. P.	Rs. A. P.	Rs. A. P.	Rs. A. P.	Rs. A. P.	
1	Gunga Munder	18 18	10 18	10 0	108 0	8 0	3 0	9 0	117 0	70 0	47 0	25 0	22 0	22 0 0	40 0 0	62 0 0	15 8 9	46 7 3	......	Sale of buffalo milk.
2	Cohabee Momin	7 10	6 0	9 0	54 0	1 10	4 0	3 0	57 0	46 0	12 0	5 0	7 0	7 0 0	25 0 0	53 0 0	8 0 9	27 0 0	6 0 0	Sale of calves and milk.
3	Shaam Momin	15 13	10 13	10 0	108 0	5 0	4 0	20 0	128 0	45 0	81 0	18 0	63 0	63 0 0	24 0 0	57 0 0	17 8 9	69 7 3	......	Ditto.
4	Behari Momin	7 0	5 0	10 0	50 0	2 0	4 0	8 0	58 0	40 0	18 0	5 0	13 0	13 0 0	18 0 0	31 0 0	6 0 9	23 0 0	......	Sale of milk.
5	Bhagboo Momin	8 4	8 0	10 0	80 0	0 4	4 0	0 33	80 33	80 0	0 33	9 33	......	......	......	......	4 0 0	......	5 0 0	
6	Manick Momin	3 4	3 4	10 0	32 0	......	......	......	32 0	17 20	14 20	1 0	13 20	13 5 0	......	15 5 0	2 8 0	11 0 0	1 0 0	
7	Ahmed Momin	7 0	7 0	6 0	42 0	......	......	......	42 0	22 0	20 0	2 0	17 0	17 0 0	......	17 0 0	9 6 0	8 0 0	3 0 0	
8	Puran Musahur	1 2	1 2	10 0	11 0	......	......	......	11 0	22 0	......	6 20	......	......	25 0 0	36 0 0	1 8 9	28 10 3	......	Wages as ploughman.
9	Mungal Musahur	3 13	3 13	10 0	38 20	......	......	......	38 20	40 0	......	1 10	......	......	35 0 0	35 0 0	3 0 9	31 15 3	......	Ditto; also wages as day labourer.
10	Thethur Musahur	0 18	0 18	10 0	9 0	......	......	......	9 0	22 0	......	9 20	......	......	21 0 0	21 0 0	1 1 9	19 14 3	......	Journeyman ploughman.
11	Tota Musahur	24 3	20 0	10 0	200 0	4 3	8 0	33 20	233 20	23 20	210 0	75 0	135 0	135 0 0	......	135 0 0	28 15 9	106 0 3	......	
12	Gopal Musahur	3 3	3 3	10 0	31 20	......	......	......	31 20	24 0	7 20	1 20	......	......	7 0 0	7 0 0	3 9 6	3 6 6	......	Sale of calves.
13	Laloo Musahur	1 8	1 8	10 0	11 20	......	......	......	11 20	55 0	......	0 20	......	......	24 0 0	24 0 0	1 6 3	22 9 9	......	Wages as ploughman.
14	Jhoti Singh	78 18	......	......	......	78 18	8 0	631 16	631 16	112 16	519 0	234 0	285 0	285 0 0	75 0 0	300 0 0	108 8 6	191 7 6	250 0 0	Sale of milk.
15	Sarinath Towaree	24 6	......	......	......	24 6	10 0	243 0	243 0	45 0	198 0	100 0	98 0	98 0 0	......	98 0 0	27 0 9	70 15 3	1,100 0 0	
16	Luchmi Pershad	38 5	5 0	5 0	25 0	29 0	7 0	203 0	228 0	50 0	178 0	70 0	108 0	108 0 0	......	108 0 0	43 1 9	64 14 3	......	

H. G. Cooke,

Collector,

Members of household.

Number		Number of members of the family.	Men.	Women.	Children.
1	Gunga Mundar	8	2	3	3
2	Chhabboo Mundar	6	2	1	3
3	Shiam Momin	6	1	3	2
4	Behari Mohim	6	2	3	1
5	Bhagloo Momin	4	2	2	......
6	Manick Momin	1	......	1	......
7	Ahmed Momin	3	1	2	......
8	Purun Musahur	3	1	1	1
9	Mangal Musahur	5	2	2	1
10	Thethur Musahur	3	1	1	1
11	Tota Musahur	3	2	1	......
12	Gopal Musahur	3	1	1	1
13	Lalon Musahur	3	1	1	1
14	Jhoti Singh	15	5	4	6
15	Susi Nath Tewari	6	2	2	2
16	Lochmi Prashad	5	1	1	3

B.

List of Kajak Musahri village.

Number of houses.	Name of head of the family.	Number of persons in the family.	Man.	Woman.	Boy.	Girl.	Permanent employment.	Other details.	Other sources of income.	Debts.
									Rs.	Rs.
1	Budhun Musahur ...	6	2	2	1	1	1	One man gets Rs. 4 per month as runner and the remaining one man and two women get Rs. 4 and Rs. 3 each respectively from Asarh to Bhado in the indigo factory, and for the other months they work as labourers to cultivators as reaper, sower and *kamaon*, for which they get three seers each. The boy tends his own cows and the girl is not fit for work.	Nil	...
2	Poonit Musahur	3	1	1	...	1	...	One man and one woman get Rs. 4 and Rs. 3 each from Asarh to Bhado; after that he digs fields at Rs. 4 a bigha, and sometimes other work as labourer.	...	...
3	Nuroo Musahur	9	3	2	3	1	...	Three men get Rs. 4 each and the two women get Rs. 3 each from Ashar to Bhado, and after that they work with the cultivators as common labourers and have two-and-a-half bighas jote in half share; three boys are not fit for work.	...	12
4	Laloo Musahur	3	1	...	1	1	...	One man gets Rs. 4 only from Asarh to Bhado, and after that he works as labourer; the children are young.	...	...
5	Shibcharan Musahur ...	2	1	1	...	...	1	One man is a runner and gets Rs. 4 per month, and his wife gets Rs. 3 from Asarh to Bhado, and after that she reaps and does other work.	...	...
6	Munger Musahur ...	5	1	1	2	1	...	One man gets Rs. 4 from Asarh to Bhado in the factory and his wife Rs. 3; after that he works as labourer and tills land, and his wife picks sheaf (*lorha*); children are young.	...	...
7	Chuttoo Musahur ...	6	2	1	...	3	...	Two men get Rs. 4 each from Asarh to Bhado and one woman Rs. 3 only; after that they work as labourer; the girls are not fit for work.	...	...
8	Dasua Musahur ...	7	1	3	1	2	...	One man gets Rs. 4 and the three women Rs. 3 each from Asarh to Bhado from the factory, and after that they work as labourer; the children are young.	...	...
9	Gujraj Musahur	10	3	2	3	2	1	One man is a runner and gets Rs. 4 per month, and the other two men and two women earn as above; the three children are young.	...	5
10	Kishna Musahur	11	3	4	2	2	1	One man is a gardener at Rs. 4 per month, and the remaining two men and four women earn as above; the children are still within their teens.	...	4
11	Bandhu Musahur	6	1	1	2	2	...	One man makes bricks at Re. 1 per thousand and the woman is labourer as above; the children are young.	...	5
12	Chatoor Musahur	5	2	2	1	...	...	One man gets Rs. 3 as ploughman from the factory and one man and two women get Rs. 4 and Rs. 3 as above, and work as labourers; the children are young.	...	6
13	Bhukhon Musahur ...	7	2	1	1	3	1	One man gets Rs. 3 as ploughman and one man and one woman get as above; the children are not fit for work.	...	...
14	Bhairo Musahur	6	1	1	3	1	1	One man is a sawyer at nine pies per cubit, and besides this he works as labourer; one woman works as above; the children are young.	...	5
15	Meota Musahur	2	1	1	...	...	...	He and his wife are labourers	...	...
16	Chetan Musahur	3	1	1	...	1	...	He is a sawyer and works as a labourer and his wife too; his girl is young.	...	...
17	Fagna Musahur	4	1	2	...	1	...	One man and two women are labourers; the girl is a mere child.	...	...
18	Cheta Musahur	7	3	2	2	...	2	Two men are ploughmen at 8 annas a month and one man and two women are labourers; the boys are not fit for work.	...	...
19	Mongot Musahur	5	1	1	3	...	...	One man and one woman are labourers; the boys do not work.	...	...
20	Tulsi Musahur	6	1	1	3	1	...	He has 5 bighas jote which he cultivates himself; the children are not fit for work.	...	...
21	Ganouri Musahur... ...	4	1	1	2	...	...	He and his wife both work as labourers and one child tends cows.	...	...

Number of houses.	Name of head of the family.	Number of persons in the family.	Man.	Woman.	Boy.	Girl.	Permanent employment.	Other details.	Other sources of income.	Debts.
									Rs.	Rs
22	Meghan Musahur	12	5	3	2	4	...	One man is a ploughman at Rs. 3 per month and one man and three woman work as above; the children do not work at all.	Nil	10
23	Doman Dufadar	14	2	2	6	4	1	One man is a dufadar at Rs. 4 a month, and one man and two women are labourers as above.	...	12
24	Tija Musahur	7	2	1	2	2	...	Two men and one woman are labourers; one boy gets five pice per diem for drying *sitti*.	...	...
25	Chattoo Musahur ...	7	2	2	2	1	...	Two men and two women are labourers; the boys are not fit for work.	...	5
26	Sohrai Musahur	3	2	1	...	...	...	One man is a ploughman at As. 8 per month; one man and one woman work as above.	...	20
27	Somar Musahur	4	1	1	1	1	...	One man and one woman earn as above, and one boy dries *sitti* at one anna per diem.	...	5
28	Sanichara Musahur ...	11	2	3	...	6	...	Two men and three women work for two months as above and after that as labourers.	...	12
29	Saki Musahur	13	4	4	3	2	1	One man is a ploughman at Rs. 3 per month, and three men and four women earn as above.	...	12
30	Akhal Musahur	6	2	2	...	2	...	Two men and two women are labourers; the girls do not work at all.	...	8
31	Sam Musahur	7	2	2	2	1	...	Two men and two women are common labourers; the children do not work.	...	6
32	Karoo Musahur	7	3	1	1	2	...	Three men and one woman work as labourers; the children do not work.	...	25
33	Bisoo Musahur	15	3	4	4	4	1	One man earns Rs. 5 as groom; the other two men and four women are labourers.	...	12
34	Nouboo Musahur	3	1	1	...	1	...	One man and one woman work as labourer; the girl is young.	...	...
35	Bhim Musahur	9	3	3	1	2	1	One man is a bearer at Rs. 6 per month, and other two men and three women work as above; the children do not work.	...	...
36	Karoo Musahur	5	1	2	...	2	...	One man works at the rate as above and two women dig fields.	...	...
37	Boherun	5	2	2	1	...	...	One man digs fields at Rs. 4 per bigha, and one man and one woman work as above.	...	...
38	Chatan	8	2	2	3	1	1	One man is employed in factory at Rs. 4 per month, and one man and two women work as above.	...	15
39	Budhon	5	1	1	...	3	1	One man is a ploughman at As. 8 per month, and one woman reaps, &c.	...	...
40	Purbhoo	4	1	1	...	2	...	One man and one woman, both of them are labourers to the cultivators.	...	...
41	Durjon	5	1	1	1	2	1	One man gets Rs. 3 per month as a cartman, and the woman earns as reaper, &c.	...	...
42	Sukan	8	1	2	3	2	...	One man and two women work as above, and has 5 bighas land and one cart.	...	...
43	Beloo	4	2	2	...	...	...	Two men and two woman are labourers and have 5 bighas land.	...	...
44	Kanhye	6	2	2	...	2	1	One man earns As. 2 daily to chop wood, and the other man and two women get as above.	...	...
45	Durhua	4	1	2	...	1	1	One man tends oxen at Rs. 3 a month and two women sow and reap as above.	...	...
46	Mongal	7	2	2	1	2	1	One man serves the rajmistry at Rs. 4 a month, and one man and two women work as above.	...	...
47	Kany	13	4	4	2	3	1	One man is a groom at Rs. 4 a month, and three men and four women are labourers.	...	...
48	Narain	6	2	1	2	1	1	One man gets Rs. 3 per month as cartman: the other is serving the rajmistry at Rs. 4, and one woman is a labourer.	...	...
49	Akal	6	1	1	3	1	1	One man is employed at Rs. 4 a month, and his wife after Aahar and Bhodo is a reaper, &c.	...	...
50	Mongar Lohar	8	2	2	2	2	1	One man is a duffadar at Rs. 4 a month, and one man and two woman are labourers.	...	...
51	Anunud Lohar	4	1	1	...	2	...	One man and one woman are labourers	...	...
52	Pursadi	10	4	4	1	1	3	Three men are ploughmen at As. 8 a month, and one man and four women have five bighas land and are labourers.	...	...
53	Newab	6	3	1	1	1	1	One man gets Rs. 6 a month at Bohara and one man works at Kajah factory, and one man and one woman are labourers (Lorha and Pusmi).	...	...
54	Ramdhani	3	1	2	...	...	...	One man and two women are labourers	...	...
55	Chhuttoo	7	2	2	...	3	2	Two men are ploughmen at As. 8 each, and the women work as Lorha and Ropa, &c.	...	...
56	Thakuri	6	1	1	1	3	1	One man is a runner at Rs. 4 a month, and his wife works as above.	...	...
57	Bipat Mochee	5	1	2	2	...	...	One man and two women are labourers to the cultivators.	...	...
58	Hurial Mochee	7	2	3	1	1	1	One man gets Rs. 3 as ploughman, and one man and two women labourers, and one woman is old.	...	...
59	Domi	12	4	5	3	...	1	One man is a ploughman at Rs. 3, and three men work at one-third of the produce (tekhri) and have five bighas jote, and five women work as above.	...	...
60	Durshim	8	1	2	3	2	...	One man ploughs land at one-third of the produce, and the two women do as above.	...	...
61	Jitan	5	1	2	2	...	...	One man and two women are labourers	...	...
62	Meghu	5	1	1	1	2	...	One man and one woman are labourers	...	...
63	Jama	5	2	2	1	...	1	One man gets 8 annas a month as ploughman and one man tills land at one-third of the produce and two women are labourers.	...	...
64	Mohan	5	1	1	...	3	...	One man and one woman work as labourers	...	...
65	Barhoo	5	1	1	1	2	...	Ditto ditto ditto	...	...
66	Bhooin	5	2	2	...	1	1	One man gets Rs. 3 as ploughman and one man and two women are labourers.	...	...
67	Somar	6	2	2	...	2	1	One man is a ploughman at 8 annas a month and one man and two women are labourers.	...	...
68	Girdhari	3	1	1	1	...	1	One man is a ploughman at Rs. 3 a month and his wife *lorha* and reaper, &c.	...	...
69	Andhoo	2	1	1	...	...	...	One man is blind and one woman lives upon beggary ...	...	...
70	Madhoo Lohar	6	2	2	...	2	1	One man is bearer at Bhawara Factory at Rs. 6 per month, and one man is too old to work, and two women are labourers.	...	...
	Total ...	464	134	126	69	105	40			

NOTE 1.—The villagers enjoy *free grazing for their cattle and pigs*. Most of the villagers own one or more cows and one or more pigs.

NOTE 2.—The 8 annas a month as wages of a ploughman is a nominal wage, for which the master is entitled to the service of the man for half of every day. The contract rests on a loan made by the master to the man. The service cannot be claimed during the indigo manufactory, i.e. from July to September. The families thus bound enjoy certain privileges above the other hired hands. Thus, where an ordinary hired labourer at harvest time makes, with the aid by his family, Rs. 3 in addition to their maintenance, a bound labourer makes as much as Rs. 5 a head. They also receive presents at festivals.

H. G. COOKE,
Collector.

C.

January.—A labourer with his family consisting of women and children work at cutting paddy. They are paid in kind, and after providing for their maintenance the savings amount in value to about two maunds per adult.

February.—The men are engaged in brick-making and still more in breaking soil on the diara lands. Lands being plentiful, cultivators break new soil every three years. This involves severe work with the *kodali*, the grass lands being hoed up to a depth of seven or eight inches in flat clods. Men are paid Rs. 4 a month for such labour. The women are engaged in gathering the mustard crop and the chilly crop; for the former they received 5 pice a day, for the latter a share in the produce.

March.—Men engaged in digging as in February. Men and women engaged in cutting the cereal crop; in this latter they are paid in kind. They maintain themselves.

April.—The same as in March.

May.—Towards the end of the month weeding indigo and paddy lands. They receive three seers of paddy per adult per diem for work on rice land, and in the case of indigo 2 annas a day for each male and 5 pice for each female.

June.—The above continues into the middle of June; just before the indigo manufacturing season begins the labourers are at their worst. They live on their savings. In the middle of June manufacturing begins, when men get Rs. 4 a month and women Rs. 3 a month.

July.—Employed on manufacturing indigo.

August.— Ditto ditto.

September.—To the middle of this month manufacturing goes on; during the second half of September they are engaged in cutting early rice; paid in kind; the whole family obtains maintenance and carry off as savings about 8 maunds a head.

October.—In this month work is slack; labourers live on the savings from their wages of June, July, August, and September, and on the supply of grain they have accumulated as reapers.

If necessary, grain can be borrowed on condition that for every 40 seers lent 50 seers are repaid at the *aghani* harvest.

November.—Work on the factory lands; pay 2 annas per man, 5 pice per woman, per diem. Towards the end of November the cutting of late rice begins, during which, being paid in kind, they maintain the whole family, and save something too as in January.

December.—*Aghani* harvest continues on the condition just stated.

In addition to the above, most families have one or more cows for which they have free pasturage. Pigs are kept by all, and are worth from Re. 1 to Rs. 5 a piece. It is said that they are kept only for private consumption, and not for sale. Pigs cost nothing to keep. They are allowed a patch of garden land, the value of which cannot be estimated. The men obtain occasional jobs as palki-bearers in the wedding season.

H. P.—Reg. No. 1914C—137—6-5-88.

CONFIDENTIAL.

No. 160GC—VII-5, dated Chittagong, the 3rd May 1888.

Memo. by—D. R. LYALL, Esq., Commissioner of the Chittagong Division.

COPY, with the enclosure, submitted to the Secretary to the Government of Bengal, Revenue Department, in continuation of this office No. 157GC—VII-5, dated 28th April 1888.

No. 990, dated Chittagong, the 30th April 1888.

From—A. MANSON, Esq., Magistrate of Chittagong,
To—The Commissioner of the Chittagong Division.

IN continuation of this office No. 855, dated the 17th instant, I have the honour to submit herewith the statistics of certain mouzas in the Ranjan Khas Mehal, and some in Satkania and Patia under Court of Wards, together with an abstract of the results in each mouza.

Result of enquiries in Raujan Khas Tehsil.

Name of Mouza.	Name of village.	MAHOMEDANS.										HINDOOS.										BUDHISTS.										Grand Total of Population.	Remarks.
			Population Classified.						Population.				Population Classified.						Population.				Population Classified.						Population.				
		Number of families.	Number of men above manual labour of any kind.	Doing any cultivation and at the same time also employing labourers or jotedars, i.e., higher sort of cultivators.	Small cultivators, i.e., those who have fixed holdings of small size, even though they may also earn something by labour.	Labourers, i.e. those who have no fixed holdings of their own, but live by labour.	Artizans, shopkeepers, boatmen, &c., who work for their living and own the implements of their trade.	Poor persons who are dependent on charity.	Males.	Females.	Total.	Number of families.	Number of men above manual labour of any kind.	Doing any cultivation and at the same time also employing labourers or jotedars, i.e., higher sort of cultivators.	Small cultivators, i.e., those who have fixed holdings of small size, even though they may also earn something by labour.	Labourers, i.e., those who have no fixed holdings of their own, but live by labour.	Artizans, shopkeepers, boatmen, &c., who work for their living and own the implements of their trade.	Poor persons who are dependent on charity.	Males.	Females.	Total.	Number of families.	Number of men above manual labour of any kind.	Doing any cultivation, and at the same time also employing labourers or jotedars, i. e. higher sort of cultivators.	Small cultivators, i.e., those who have fixed holdings of small size, even though they may also earn something by labour.	Labourers, i.e., those who have no fixed holding of their own, but live by labour.	Artizans, shopkeepers, boatmen, &c., who work for their living and own the implements of their trade.	Poor persons who are dependent on charity.	Males.	Females.	Total.		
1	2	3	4	5	6	7	8	9	10	11	12	13	14	15	16	17	18	19	20	21	22	23	24	25	26	27	28	29	30	31	32	33	34
Chikdair ...	Chikdair ...	1,294	...	108	1,294	800	...	73	1,164	1,201	2,365	403	...	279	403	694	9	33	712	705	1,417	...	...	...	......	...	...	...	...	...	...	3,782	
Sultanpore ... Chitalpara ... Kulyalenga ...	Sultanpore ...	645	44	613	645	1,836	49	94	1,697	1,584	3,281	804	19	382	804	1,875	113	43	1,646	1,890	3,236	207	...	24	27	69	...	10	72	78	150	6,667	
	Total ...	1,939	44	721	1,939	2,726	49	167	2,861	2,785	5,646	1,207	19	661	1,207	2,560	122	76	2,358	2,595	4,653	207	...	24	27	69	...	10	72	78	150	10,449	

Result of enquiries under the General Manager of the Court of Wards.

Name of Mouza.	Name of village.	3	4	5	6	7	8	9	10	11	12	13	14	15	16	17	18	19	20	21	22	23	24	25	26	27	28	29	30	31	32	33	34
Chota Chanuya ...	Chota Chanuya	277	...	1,336	109	157	...	23	846	870	1,715	21	...	53	22	......	14	2	49	41	90	...	...	...	......	...	...	...	...	...	...	1,805	
Dohazari	Dohazari ...	269	12	126	412	546	102	84	646	635	1,281	80	46	......	......	104	254	18	221	201	422	5	...	...	......	8	...	4	4	8	12	1,715	
Dolu	Dolu	172	...	375	473	90	...	24	507	455	962	......	...	......	......	......	...	...	......	......	......	...	...	...	......	...	...	...	...	...	...	968	
	Total ...	718	12	1,837	1,084	793	102	131	1,998	1,960	3,958	101	46	53	22	104	268	20	270	212	512	5	...	...	......	8	...	4	4	8	12	4,483	

A. Manson,

Magistrate.

CONFIDENTIAL.]

No. 867Agri., dated Calcutta, the 5th May 1888.

From—R. W. Collin, Esq., c.s., Offg. Director of the Dept. of Land Records and Agriculture, Bengal,

To—The Secretary to the Government of Bengal, Revenue Department.

In continuation of paragraph 6 of Mr. Finucane's letter No. 829Agri., dated the 27th ultimo, I have the honour to submit in original the report of Baboo Burhandeo Narayan, First Assistant Settlement Officer, Raj Banaili and Srinagar Ward's Estate in Bhagulpore, regarding the material condition of the lower classes of people in pergunnah Kubkhand, district Bhagulpore, where he is now engaged in settlement work.

2. The return of this report, as well as those submitted with Mr. Finucane's letter of the 27th ultimo, is requested when they are no longer required.

No. 51, dated Camp Ekar, Circle Nauhatta, the 24th April 1888.

From—Baboo Burhandeo Narayan, Assistant Settlement Officer, Raj Banaili and Srinagar Estate,

To—The Collector of Bhagulpore.

Referring to the correspondence quoted in the margin, and in compliance with the order of the settlement officer, Banaili Raj and Srinagar Estate, I have the honour to submit the following report regarding the material condition of the lower classes of people in pergunnah Kubkhand, district Bhagulpore, where I am now engaged on settlement work.

> No. , dated 23rd January 1888.
> From Director of Land Records, No. 9696—6362Agri., dated 9th December 1887.
> From Secretary to the Government of Bengal, to Director of Land Records, No. 35Agri., dated 9th December 1887.
> To all Commissioners.

2. *Villages selected for enquiry.*—I selected, as the field of my enquiries, two villages, viz. Paharpore and Asai, in which there was a sufficient variety of the people of the lower classes, and intended to prosecute my enquiries after completion of settlement in those villages to avoid the possibility of the people connecting the object of these enquiries with the settlement and being thereby led to exaggerate their poverty. The settlement of Paharpore having been finished, I have prepared the statistics for that village. I have been obliged to give up Asai, as the survey records thereof have not been received yet, and there is urgent orders to submit the report at once. The statistics for Paharpore have, however, been prepared, and the enquiries made by me personally in the village. This, I hope, fulfils the scope of enquiries contemplated in paragraph 6 of letter No. 102F., dated 27th September 1887, from the Director of the Department of land Records and Agriculture, to the Secretary to the Government of Bengal.

3. *Statistical Statement.*—The annexed statistical statement contains the name of the headman of every family in the village, information regarding his caste, number and classification of members in his family, the various sources of his income, the quantity of land held by him in the village of his residence as well as in other villages, his ostensible properties and his indebtedness. These are the distinct facts about which correct information can be given and is specially wanted by the Director in his letter quoted in the preceding paragraph. It is in respect to these conditions of things that the families differ conspicuously. Other matters are subjects only for general observation.

4. *Statistical statement how prepared.*—In preparing the statistical statement, the number of members in each family has been ascertained from the headmen of the families or their neighbours, and the area of their holdings has been taken from the *hastabood.* The statement shows a very large preponderance of boys and girls under 12 years of age over those above 12 years. The reason is that girls above 12 years get married, go to their husband's house, and are considered as women. The boys little above 12 years are stated to be of 12 years or under, and those decidedly above 12 years are returned as working men. In the last census returns boys and girls have been divided into three classes, viz. between 0 and 9, between 9 and 14 and between 14 and 19. For the Bhagulpore district there were returned 291,323 boys of the first two class, against 15,246 of the last class and 212,390 girls of the first two classes, against 1,970 of the last class, the proportion being 1 to 19 and 108 respectively. The proportion of grown-up boys and girls shown in the census returns is smaller than that shown in statistical statement of Paharpore. The proportion in that village comes to 1 against 9 as regards both sexes.

5. *Abstracts of the Statistical Statement.*—I further submit two abstract statements, the one giving the classification of population according to caste, and the other giving the classification of population according to occupation and quantity of holding.

6. *Questions raised by the Government of Bengal.*—I will now attempt to give what information I can on the broad questions of economy raised in the Bengal Government letter No. 35, dated 9th December 1887.

7. *Rate of rent.*—The rate of rent of Paharpore is Rs. 2-4. The rate of rent in other villages of the pergunnah is not higher than this, though in many villages it is lower. In some villages the rate is Rs. 2-7 or Rs. 2-8; but the ryots of those villages hold *hoonda*, or additional land, without payment of additional rent. A practice has existed in the pergunnah for a long time, of inducing ryots to accept enhancement of rate of rent by granting them the privilege of bringing waste land under cultivation without payment of additional rent for it. The rate of rent in this pergunnah compares favourably with the rates of rent in other districts where I have been. The rate of rent in Mozufferpore ranges from Rs. 2 to Rs. 10. The average rate of rent in this pergunnah is Rs. 2.

8. *Expense of cultivation.*—I confess that I feel diffident in making an estimate of the expenses of cultivation, notwithstanding the enquiries I have made. The cost must differ according to the means and disposition of each cultivator to cultivate his land highly or perfunctorily. Some delay in carrying on the agricultural operations also entails an additional expenditure. An approximate idea of ordinary expenses of cultivation for each kind of crop can be formed by analysing the various processes of cultivation and estimating the cost for each.

9. *The cost of sowing paddy broadcast.*—The most important crop in this pergunnah is paddy, which is either transplanted or sown broadcast. If the paddy has to be sown broadcast, the field is at least ploughed four times before sowing. This requires eight ploughs per bigha. The hire of a plough being one anna per plough per day, the cost of ploughing comes to eight annas per bigha. One labourer per bigha would be then required for sowing the seeds, after which the earth not broken by ploughs is turned up with spade. This requires ten labourers in the bigha, the money value of their wages being 11¼ annas at the rate at which grain is now selling. This process of breaking up earth after sowing is called *gorbahee*. After the seeds have germinated and grown about a foot, the spade is again applied for removing weeds, thinning the seedlings, and turning up earth around the seedlings left to grow. This process is locally called *tamni*. The *jeth* ryot of Paharpore exaggerated the number of labourers required for *tamni*. He stated the number to be 25 per bigha. According to the best information, it cannot be more than 10 per bigha. This process is sometimes repeated, and in making an estimate of 10 labourers per bigha an allowance has been made for the repetition. After *tamni* comes the process of weeding (*kerroni*). It is done with *khurpi*, an instrument peculiar to this country. It is a semi-oval iron blade with a wooden handle about half a foot long. The weeding requires at least 20 labourers per bigha, the money value of their wages amounting to Rs. 1-6-6. The process of weeding also is repeated if the grass again grows on the fields, and then the cost would be larger. Reaping comes the last. One-tenth of the produce is taken by the labourers employed in reaping. Threshing and winnowing also would require at least two labourers per bigha at a cost of As. 2-3. I now summarise the cost per bigha of sowing paddy broadcast—

	Rs.	A.	P.
8 Ploughs at 1 anna each	0	8	0
1 Labourer for sowing	0	1	1½
10 Do. for *garbahi*	0	11	3
10 Do. for *tamni*	0	11	3
20 Do. for weeding	1	6	6
2 Do. for { Threshing / Winnowing	0	2	3
Seeds at 1 maund per bigha	1	0	0
Total ...	4	8	4½

10. *Cost per bigha of transplanting paddy.*—When paddy has to be transplanted the field in this part of the country is tilled instead of being ploughed at first; the process is called *korni*. It requires 20 labourers per bigha, at a cost of Rs. 1-6-6, and about 15 labourers would be required for sowing seeds and transplanting them. The seedlings are transplanted after rains, when some water has collected in the field. The earth and water are then stirred up by ploughing and mudded together to make the seedlings take root. The process is called *kudwa*, from *kado* (mud). Four ploughs are ordinarily required for this purpose. Weeding takes place in those fields also in which paddy has been transplanted; but grass does not grow fast in such fields. Only five labourers at a cost of As. 5-7½ per bigha is the safest estimate for this process. Two labourers, as stated above, would be required for threshing and winnowing. The figures would then stand thus—

	Rs.	A.	P.
20 Labourers for *korni*	1	6	6
15 Ditto planting, or *ropni*	1	0	10½
4 Ploughs for *kudwa*, or mudding...	0	4	0
5 Labourers for weeding	0	5	7½
2 Ditto for threshing and winnowing	0	2	3
Seeds at 8 annas per bigha	0	8	0
Total ...	3	11	3

11. *Marua sowing.*—The staple crop in the Bhadoi season in this pergunnah is *marua*. The process of growing *marua* is simpler than that of growing paddy. The former consists of ploughing the fields and rolling the clods by *henga*, sowing the seeds, harrowing after growth of the seeds, and weeding. The agricultural experiences of the country are generally embodied in versified proverbs, and I quote one such proverb about cultivation of *marua* in the margin. The substance of it is that *marua* field should be ploughed 13 times and weeded three times before any hopes can be entertained of a good harvest. This standard of cultivation seems to be ideal, but a *marua* field is generally ploughed eight times and weeded twice, the cost being about Rs. 3 per bigha. Thus—

"Tīn kerroaī terah chās.
"Tab karó marua kedá."

	Rs.	A.	P.
16 Ploughs	1	0	0
10 Labourers per 1st weeding	0	11	3
20 Ditto for 2nd „	1	6	6
2 Ditto for threshing and winnowing	0	2	3
Seeds, 10 seers	0	2	6
Total ...	3	6	6

12. *Cost of growing rubbee.*—The soil of this pergunnah is not very well adapted for cultivation of *rubbee*, and it is not cultivated to as large an extent as other crops. The *rubbee* field is generally ploughed four to eight times, and weeded once if at all. The cost is about half the cost of cultivation of *marua* for ploughing and weeding, and one rupee per bigha for seeds.

13. *How the expenses of cultivation are met.*—The expenses estimated above are not always incurred in money. In fact this is seldom done. Some of the cultivators keep their own ploughs and bullocks, with which they plough their fields, and they exchange their use among them, when more than one plough is required on a particular day. It is a general practice for two cultivators to keep a pair of bullocks between them, the pair being used by each alternately. Each of them, however, purchases and feeds his bullocks separately. The poorer ryots who cannot afford to keep a bullock serve as ploughmen of those who keep bullocks, and plough and get the use of the plough and the bullocks in lieu of wages. One day's use is allowed for three days' service as ploughman. Then again the cultivators of lower castes with small holdings work in their own fields with women and grown-up children. The expense in their case means the money value of their own labour. Every cultivator, moreover, keeps his own seeds, and purchase of seed by him is a matter only of accident.

14. *Produce per bigha.*—It is, again, difficult to make a correct estimate of average produce per bigha of each kind of crop. The information given by the ryots of Paharpore on this point was not reliable, nor was it consistent and intelligible. One man among them, namely, Pasan Jeth ryot, was anxious to give me correct information. He had paddy in about 5 bighas this year, and the outturn was 50 maunds. This gives an average of 10 maunds per bigha, when rain is seasonable, as has been the case this year. This agrees with my own experience of other districts. In Gya I had to make appraisement in the escheated estates, and I did so after treshing and weighing a portion of the standing crops. The average in those villages in which the produce was good came to 10 maunds per bigha. The produce of best paddy land often comes to 20 maunds per bigha in good years. Another man of the village, Bhakoosh, got 275 maunds paddy in 25 bighas; but he is a headman and his lands are good. The *marua* field of Rosun yields an average of six maunds per bigha. As the yield of the *rubbee* crop in this pergunnah is generally poor, 10 maunds per bigha, including *bhadoi* and *rubbee*, is the highest estimate that can be made of the produce of *bhit* land of this pergunnah. The produce of *bhit* land in the western districts is acknowledged to be better than this.

15. *Price of staple crops.*—As statement of prices-current of staple crops is prepared and submitted by district and sub-divisional officers, they are more reliable and of more general application than the results of enquiries made in a single village. I can only mention that in Paharpore paddy sold at ten *kacha paserees* for the rupee this year.

16. *Use of straw.*—The straw of paddy is used as fodder by those cultivators who have cattle, and it is also used for thatching houses and for bedding by the poorer classes. It is occasionally sold by one cultivator to another or to cartmen for fodder.

17. *Sale of milk.*—The milk of cow is not as a rule sold here. Calves are allowed to suck. Milk of buffaloes is sold at the rate of one anna per *pucca* seer to *gawariah*, or manufacturers of *ghee*. The *gowariahs* are a different class of men from *gwallas*, or milk-men.

18. *Income from fishery and jungle produce.*—Ordinary people have no income from fishery, though the lower class men, who are not abstainers from animal food, catch fishes for home consumption. Fishery is the profession of a special caste of Mollahs. They generally take farms of fishery from the landlords. There is no jungle here; consequently there is no income from jungle produce.

19. *Wages of agricultural labourers, hire of ploughs and carts.*—My information regarding wages of agricultural labourers is positive and precise. They get half a *paseree* or 4½ *kacha* seers of coarse grain* like *marua* or paddy for a day's work. Sometimes they are fed by the employers in the morning and at noon, and then they are given only three seers in the evening. The hire

* Equal 2 seers 12 chittacks *pucca* seer.

of a plough with a pair of bullocks for a day is one anna, and that of a cart, if employed in the neighbourhood, is four annas per day. From outsiders and Government officials a higher rate is taken.

20. *Employment of Women.*—The women of the village families are as a rule employed on household work. They bring water, cleanse the house and the utensils, grind and husk grain, and cook the food; the women of the cultivators of low caste are also employed in their own fields. The women of labourers do not work for time in the fields of others except at the time of reaping. Some poor women of high and low class earn a pittance by spinning thread in a spinning-mill called *charkha*. Cotton is locally sold at three *kacha* seers for the rupee and thread at two *kacha* seers for the rupee, so that if a woman spins three seers of cotton her earning would be eight annas. I was told, and I believe rightly, that the women cannot spin more than two chittacks of cotton per day. At this rate she would earn one to two pice a day. The children collect fuel, tend cattle, and work in their own fields or for hire when sufficiently grown up.

21. *The earning of weavers.*—There are some houses of weavers in Paharpore. They do not weave cloth to sell it. They are given thread by villagers to weave it into cloth, for which they are given remuneration at a contract rate. The remuneration for cloth of particular kind and breadth is one pice per yard. One man, according to information given, can weave from three to seven yards of such cloth in a day. The weavers do not get this sort of employment throughout the year. They get the work during the four months of the cold weather when there is large demand for cloth.

22. *Blanket workers or Gaurerees.*—There are some houses of *gaurerees*, or shepherds. The shepherds of Paharpore have not got sheep of their own. They make blankets of purchased wool. One blanket, it is said, is made of three *kacha* seers of wool in three days, if one worked the whole day. The cost of wool is twelve annas, and the blanket is generally sold for Rs. 1-2. This trade thus pays at the rate of two annas a day. Blanket making seems to be more remunerative than any other employment in the village.

Barbers and Carpenters.—The barbers and carpenters get yearly allowances or *pal* from each family in the village. The carpenter gets one and a quarter maunds of grain per plough, and barber gets ten *kacha* seers per head. The carpenters of Paharpore have the custom of two other villages in the neighbourhood, viz. Asai and Chhatwan. There are 24 ploughs in Paharpore, so the two familes of carpenters in this village would get about 15 maunds each from this village alone. The carpenters and barbers are well off as a rule.

23. *Oilmen or tolees.*—The oilmen are given oil-seeds by the villagers to press out oil. For their profit they get oil-cake and one day's wages of one ordinary labourer. The oilmen as a rule present a poor appearance, and they have not much income from the profession of their caste. Some of the men of this caste follow other professions and are shopkeepers, grain-dealers and money-lenders. In the village of Paharpore, also, there is one mahajan of this caste. *Tolees*, or oilmen, are proverbially noted for stingy habits.

24. *Paucity of washermen.*—The number of washermen is comparatively small in this pergunnah. There is none in Paharpore. The reason is that the masses of the people wash their own clothes if they wash them at all.

25. There are some houses of Halwai in Paharpore. The profession of their caste is that of a confectioner, but they do not follow this profession. There is one house of *chamar* or shoe-maker. He gets the carcasses of all the animals that die in the village, and sells the hides. He also makes shoes and plays music in the marriage season. His wife acts as midwife at the time of delivery in the village families. He can make a pair of shoes in three days, which he sells for six annas, and a band of five musicians get eight annas to one rupee per day in the marriage season. The midwife gets two annas on the occasion of the birth of a female, and four annas on that of a male child.

26. *The general physique of the people.*—The general physique of the people of Paharpore and of other villages in this pergunnah, according to my observation, is somewhat inferior to that of the people of the western districts of Durbhunga and Mozufferpore. I did not, however, find any man other than sick men either emaciated or with very low physique.

27. *To what extent the labourers get employment.*—The labourers get almost daily employment during the three months of the rainy season, say from the 15th June to 15th September; they also get almost daily employment at the time of paddy harvest, that lasts for about two months from December to January. For rubbee and bhadoi harvests together, they get about one month's employment. During the remaining six months they do not get daily nor even frequent employment. The people themselves could not state the number of days during which they did not get employment. I think it will be safe to assume that they get employment for two months out of the remaining six months. This gives a total of eight months employment during the year. At the time of harvest, however, the labourers work with wife and children, and instead of getting daily wages they get as their share of the produce one-tenth of the quantity they reap. In this way they earn about double the amount of their ordinary daily wages. Setting this off against the four months of want of employment, it will be a safe and not a sanguine supposition to take for granted that able-bodied and healthy labourers as a class earn at least 4½ seers of grain by *kacha* weight per day all the year round. Four and a half *kacha* seers is equal to 2 seers and 12 chittacks of standard weight.

28. *The daily food and other expenses of the lower classes.*—The villagers, unless they be in want, take two meals, one at noon and another early at night. The lower class people

of Paharpore generally eat *marua* bread both times, because there is less of paddy land in this village. The labourers in other villages eat rice at the time of paddy harvest, and *marua* bread at the time of *marua* harvest, and they take one meal of rice and one meal of *marua* at other times. The average quantity of principal food consumed, according to the best information available, is three-quarters of *kacha* seer for men, half a seer for women, and quarter of a seer for children. The proportion may vary according to age and health of particular members of the family; but that is the general average. With the principal meal of rice or bread they take vegetables, fishes or pulse, but not more than one thing at a time. This is called *teewan*, or accompaniment of the principal food. Salt is of course invariably mixed up with *teewan*. Some very poor men go without any *teewan* at all. They catch fishes for themselves and grow vegetables in *bari*, or homestead grounds. As a rule they do not purchase vegetables or fishes. They sometimes purchase pulse. They do not purchase oil except for rubbing on the head and body occasionally. It would be a luxury if they could get some oil to cook their vegetables. The people of Paharpore said that they did not use much of spices. The spices sometimes used are turmeric, hot pepper, and coriander seeds. Most of the people eat tabocco. Fuel is not purchased, but it is picked up by women and children of the family.

How the lower classes are clothed.—In respect of cloth, the people of this part of the country are decidedly worse off than in respect of food. The clothes of both men and women of the lower classes are dirty as well as insufficient. The people of Paharpore said they spent about two rupees in the year in purchase of clothes.

29. *Brass utensils and ornaments.*—The number and kinds of brass plates and other ostensible property possessed by each family has been described in the statement annexed to this report. Almost every family has a drinking pot and a plate of brass or zinc worth one or two rupees. The three well-to-do Kunpa families of Rashim, Rasun and Dhana had one *hansoolee* or collar of silver worth Rs. 10 each. Of these Dhoraee and Rasun gave that ornament in dowry to their daughters. Rasun has got it still, and Rasun's wife has now got an armlet of Rs. 1-4. The existence of silver ornaments in other families was denied, and it was not proper to examine the ornaments on the bodies of the women. The women of Gwala caste and other cultivators whom I saw passing in the village had brass and zinc ornaments on their bodies. The girls had beads. All married women generally wear *churees* of glass or lac worth one to two annas.

30. *Marriage Expenses.*—The people of Paharpore did not spend much on marriage and other ceremonies. The well-to-do ryots spent about four rupees, and some did not spend anything at all.

31. *Indebtedness.*—The annexed statement shows that almost all the ryots in the village are in debt. Pure labourers are not in debt, because no one would lend to them. The latter class take advances to supply labourers. The reason why the cultivators are in debt is that owing to disputes about rates the rent had fallen into arrears, which the ryots have now been made to pay up by certificate process, and the soil is comparatively poor. The holding of some of the ryots has been sold up by auction, and some others have sold their cattle to pay the rent. I also observe a tendency among the men of Gwala caste to set themselves up as respectable villagers, and to abstain from working for hire if they happened to have a holding of some five bighas or more.

32. *Sufficiency or otherwise of food which the labourers get.*—I now come to the main question as to whether or not the lower class of this pergunnah get sufficient food throughout the year, both as regards quantity and quality. This fact can be ascertained with more or less approach to truth by observing the physique of the people, from their own statement, from the possession or want of property, or by fixing upon a standard of income for the subsistence of a certain number of members in a family, and then finding out what families do not come up to that standard. I have already stated above that the physique of the people of this pergunnah is a little inferior to that of the people in the western districts. This may not be necessarily due to want of food, but to a difference in climate. I am inclined to take the latter view. From enquiries made in the village, I found that out of 93 families 14 families were suffering from want of food. But this want is due to special circumstances as described in the statement, *vide* remark against Nos. 1, 5, 8, 13, 14, 17, 18, 27, 29, 31, 32, 37, 38, 40. In some cases the headmen of the families are sick. In others there are old women struggling for existence without the help of a man. The property of some others has been sold for arrears of rent. No. 8 has lost his wife, and that seems to be the reason why his household affairs are not well managed. It will appear from statistical statement that every family, as a rule, possess one or two brass utensils of the value of Rs. 1 to 2. These utensils are, however, purchased once in life or once within the time of two or three generations. The owners cling to them with tenacity, and do not part with them easily. The possession of these utensils does not necessarily show that the owners thereof are well-to-do men. The best test is the annual income in relation to the number of members in a family to be supported by that income. I have stated above that a labourer earns an average of 4½ seers of grain per day, the yearly value of this earning being Rs. 25-3. This is a safe estimate. A sanguine estimate would be five seers per day, making allowances for the earnings of his wife. It is to be remembered, however, that a part of his earning is in paddy that loses in weight when husked and turned to rice. Setting this off against the earning of the women, 4½ seers of eatable grain is the utmost that a labourer can earn. If he has a wife and two children he will consume about 3½ seers daily; one seer per day would be then left for salt, cloth, and occasional purchase of oil, *dál* and tobacco. So a labourer with a wife and two children only can live as he has been accustomed to live, from hand to mouth, but would not suffer from want of food. If he has more mouths to feed he would suffer privations, both as regards food and other necessaries

of life. If a labourer has a small holding, the net profit per bigha of this holding would amount to one-fourth of his earning as a labourer. I have made calculation thus: The produce per bigha would be 10 maunds of grain or Rs. 10 in cash; out of this he has to pay Rs. 2-4 on account of rent. The cost of cultivation, including the price of the seed, comes to about four rupees per bigha, of which three rupees represents the cost of labour. The labourer no doubt himself works in the field assisted by his wife and children; but in doing so he has often to give up other employment, and loses the wages which he would have otherwise earned. We may safely assume that his loss in this way amounts to Rs. 1-12 per bigha. The expenses of cultivation in his case would thus amount to about Rs. 5 per bigha, viz. Rs. 2-4 for rent, Rs. 1-12 loss of wages, and Re. 1 for seeds, and the net profit left would be Rs. 5 per bigha. The net produce of a bigha would thus feed one additional member of a labourer's family. Judging with this standard there is scarcely a family in the village (excluding sick men and old women) that can be said to be suffering from want of food. Among the labourers Nos. 6, 22, 23 have less income proportionately to the number of members in the family, but they come very near the standard. One man, Bansee, has seven members in his family and holds bighas 3-6, and said he did not work for hire. So he has only to pay the rent, and can save four-fifths of the produce. He is nevertheless in debt.

33. *Conclusion.*—On the whole, I am of opinion that the working classes in this pergunnah, with or without small holdings, are badly clothed, badly housed, do not enjoy any luxury of life, live from hand to mouth, but do not suffer from actual want of food in ordinary years.

Village weight and coin.—The local seer is equal in weight to Rs. 48. The *puseree* is made of nine such seers, and a maund of eight such *puserees*. The pice used is the standard pice of quarter anna.

Classification according to caste of families of Paharpore, pergunnah Kubkhand.

Number.	Caste.	Number of families.	Number of members.
1	Sheik	11	71
2	Kunjra	20	122
3	Khatwai	8	25
4	Goala	34	174
5	Halooaee	5	22
6	Tailee	4	23
7	Chamar	1	6
8	Kaith Bania	1	1
9	Hajam	1	4
10	Carpenter	2	21
11	Malah	1	4
12	Goureri	5	21
	Total ...	93	494

BURHANDEO NARAYAN,
Assistant Settlement Officer.

DATED CAMP EKAR,
The 24th April 1888.

Abstract statement showing classification of the inhabitants of Paharpore, pergunnah Kubkhand, according to profession.

Number.	Class.	Number of families.	Number of members of the families.
1	Holding 10 bighas and more and following other profession ...	2	29
2	Holding 10 bighas and more and not following other profession	3	28
3	Holding between 5 bighas and 10 bighas and following other profession	12	88
4	Holding between 5 and 10 bighas and not following other profession	4	27
5	Holding below 5 bighas and following other profession	44	227
6	Holding below 5 bighas and not following other profession	6	36
7	Pure labourers	15	47
8	Beggars	4	8
9	Shop-keepers	2	3
10	Others	1	1
	Total ...	93	494

BURHANDEO NARAYAN,
Assistant Settlement Officer.

DATED CAMP EKAR,
The 24th April 1888.

Statistical statement showing the number of members, resources of income, extent of agricultural holding, ostensible properties, and indebtedness of each family in mouzah Paharpore, pergunnah Kubkhand, district Bhagulpore.

Serial number.	Name of the head of the family.	Caste.	Number of members in the family.									Resources of income.	Extent of agricultural holding.		Brass and zinc utensils possessed by the family.	Animals possessed by the family.	Amount of debt.		Agricultural implements and other ostensible properties possessed by the family.	Remarks.
			Able-bodied men.	Old or infirm men.	Married women.	Widows.	Boys above 12 years of age.	Boys under 12 years of age.	Girls above 12 years of age.	Girls under 12 years of age.	Total number of members in the family.		Name of mouzah.	Area.			Money (in rupees).	Grain (in maunds).		
1	2	3	4	5	6	7	8	9	10	11	12	13	14	15	16	17	18	19	20	21
																	Rs. A. P.	Mds.		
1	Mossamut Daho.	Sheik ...	...	...	...	1	...	...	...	...	1	Begging ...	......	......		......	......	......	......	She is an old woman; has a stepson living separately from her. He does not earn enough to maintain her. She has no means of subsistence, so she lives on roots growing spontaneously in the paddy fields and under water; she makes bread from these roots; she also uses *bale* fruit after boiling it; she was in rags.
2	Gopal ...	Do. ...	1	...	1	...	...	1	1	...	4	1. Cultivation ... 2. Labour in the fields for hire.	Paharpore ...	2 18 5	Thali ... 1 Lota ... 1	......	......	......	Spade ... 1 Hansooa ... 1 Khurpi ... 1	Is the step-son of the foregoing woman.
3	Mittoo, son of Parun.	Do. ...	3	...	2	1	...	2	...	1	9	1. Service ... 2. Cultivation. 3. Labour in the fields for hire.	Ditto ...	2 16 0	Thalies ... 2 Lotas ... 2	Cow ... 1 Bullock ... 1	10 0 0	6	Spade ... 1 Hansoee ... 1 Khurpi ... 1	The younger brother of the family is employed as chainman in the Survey Department on Rs. 4 a month.
4	Azeem Shah...	Musulman fakir.	1	...	1	...	...	1	...	...	3	Charity ...	......	......	......	......	......	......	......	Is a professional beggar; looked healthy and sufficiently fed.
5	Heera ...	Sheik ...	...	1	1	1	1	4	...	...	8	Cultivation ...	Paharpore ...	11 6 0	Thali ... 1 Lota ... 1	Bullocks ... 2	25 0 0	5	Plough ... 1 Hanga ... 1 Khurpies 2 Hansoons 2 Spade ... 1	The head of the family. Heera being ill, it is in bad circumstances. A sum of Rs. 25 has been lately borrowed to pay rent to the landlord.
6	Mittoo, son of Dullab.	Do. ...	3	...	3	1	1	2	...	5	15	1. Service ... 2. Cultivation. 3. Labour in the fields.	Ditto ...	1 4 0	Thalies ... 2 Lotas ... 3		1 0 0	4	Spade ... 1 Hansoee ... 1 Khurpi ... 1	One member of the family is employed in the village as Burabil on Re. 1 a month.
7	Jooman ...	Kunjra ...	3	...	2	...	...	2	...	1	8	1. Cultivation ... 2. Labour in the fields. 3. Production and sale of vegetables.	Rampur ... Paharpore ...	1 18 16 2 1 3	Thalies ... 2 Lota ... 1	Cows ... 3	......	6	......	
8	Bootai, son of Hayati.	Ditto ...	1	...	...	...	...	...	1	2	4	1. Cultivation ... 2. Labour in the fields. 3. Production and sale of vegetables.	Rampur ... Paharpore ...	1 18 16 2 1 3	Lota ... 1	......	......	......	Spade ... 1 Khurpi ... 1 Hansooa ... 1	Has sublet a portion of his holding in Buial, because he cannot afford to cultivate himself. Had no full meal on the day before enquiry, as he was engaged in repairing his own house and could not work for hire.

Serial number.	Name of the head of the family.	Caste.	Number of members in the family.									Resources of income.	Extent of agricultural holding.		Brass and zinc utensils possessed by the family.	Animals possessed by the family.	Amount of debt.		Agricultural implements and other ostensible properties possessed by the family.	Remarks.
			Able-bodied men.	Old or infirm men.	Married women.	Widows.	Boys above 12 years of age.	Boys under 12 years of age.	Girls above 12 years of age.	Girls under 12 years of age.	Total number of members in the family.		Name of mouzah.	Area.			Money (in rupees).	Grain (in maunds).		
1	2	3	4	5	6	7	8	9	10	11	12	13	14	15	16	17	18	19	20	21
																	Rs. A. P.	Mds.		
9	Puhim, son of Kullur.	Kunjra ...	1	...	1	1	1	...	...	...	4	1. Cultivation ... 2. Labour in the fields. 3. Production and sale of vegetables.	Paharpore ... Rampore ... Bucoonia ... Asai ...	2 1 3 1 18 16 1 16 0 1 5 0	Lota ... 1 Bati ... 1	Bullock ... 1	......	......	Plough ... 1	
10	Dhana ...	Ditto ...	4	1	3	...	...	3	1	1	13	1. Cultivation ... 2. Production and sale of vegetables and occasional sale of milk.	Paharpore ... Bucoonia ...	6 3 10 7 6 0	Thalies ... 3 Lota ... 1	Bullocks ... 2 Goats ... 3 Cows ... 7	......	......	Plough ... 1 Spade ... 1 Khurpi ... 1 Hansoca ... 1	Condition good; sometimes borrows grain in the rainy season, but soon repays it.
11	Roson ...	Ditto ...	4	...	3	...	...	1	...	1	9	Ditto ...	Paharpore ...	6 8 10	Thalies ... 3 Lota ... 1 Bati ... 1	Bullocks ... 2 Cows ... 5	......	......	Plough ... 1 Spade ... 1 Hansoca ... 1 Khurpi ... 1	Ditto ditto.
12	Poson ...	Ditto ...	3	1	3	...	...	...	...	2	9	Ditto ...	Ditto ... Darbar ... Bucoonia ...	6 8 10 2 0 0 1 1 0	Thalies ... 3 Lota ... 1 Iron dab ... 1	Bullocks ... 2 Goat ... 1 Buffalo ... 1 Cow ... 1	......	......	Hanga ... 1 Cart ... 1 Plough ... 1 Spade ... 1 Hansoca ... 1 Khurpi ... 1	Ditto ditto.
13	Mahatali ...	Sheik ...	2	...	2	...	...	2	...	...	6	Cultivation ...	Asai ...	0 12 0	Thalies ... 3 Lota ... 1 Budhna ... 1 Baties ... 2		......	6	Spade ... 1 Khurpi ... 1 Hansoca ... 1	Mahatali and Ghogun are brothers. They held 18 bighas of land among them in Paharpore. Their holding has been lately sold for arrears of rent under the certificate process at the instance of the Srinagar Court of Wards. One oft hem, Mahatali, was able to pay the rent and might have paid it by the sale of bamboo and gachees which he possessed, but he was given false hopes of advance of money by a mahajun of a neighbouring village of Balooah, who failed him in the last hour and purchased the property himself. The brothers are without any resources now, and will have to work for hire.
14	Ghoghun ...	Do. ...	3	...	3	...	1	...	...	...	7	Ditto ...	Do. ...	0 12 0	......		......	......	Spade ... 1 Khurpi ... 1 Hansoca ... 1	
15	Bhadai, son of Karee.	Kunjra ...	3	...	1	1	...	...	...	1	6	1. Cultivation ... 2. Working for hire in the fields. 3. Production and sale of vegetables.	Paharpore ...	0 14 0	Thali ... 1 Lota ... 1	Goat ... 1	......	......	Hansoca ... 1 Khurpi ... 1	

16	Koonni ...	Ditto ...	2	...	...	...	...	...	2	1	5	1. Cultivation ... 2. Working for hire in the fields.	Ditto ...	1 10 0			......	......	Hansooa ... 1 Khurpi ... 1	
17	Gooddur ...	Ditto ...	...	1	1	...	...	2	...	1	5	1. Cultivation ... 2. Production of vegetables for sale.	Ditto ...	0 7 9			......	......	Hansooa ... 1 Khurpi ... 1	This family is not well fed; the headman of the family is suffering from dyspepsia and cannot work much. He and his wife produce some vegetables in five cottahs of land which they hold, and that is the only resources of their income.
18	Goomani, son of Sonoo.	Ditto ...	...	1	...	...	...	...	...	...	1	......		......			......	......	Hansooa ... 1 Khurpi ... 1	Was employed as chainman in the Survey Department. Is now suffering from consumption, and is helped by his uncle during his sickness.
9	Choton, son of Badar.	Ditto ...	1	...	1	...	...	1	...	...	3	1. Cultivation .. 2. Production and sale of vegetables. 3. Working for hire in the fields.	Paharpore ...	1 0 5			......	......	Hansooa ... 1 Khurpi ... 1	Does not get employment every day.
20	Ghoghon, son of Nunnoo.	Ditto ...	...	1	...	...	...	2	...	1	4	1. Cultivation ... 2. Production and sale of vegetables.	Ditto ...	5 8 5		Bullock ... 1	6 0 0	......	Plough ... 1 Spade ... 1 Hansooa ... 1 Khurpi ... 1	Employs hired labour for cultivation.
21	Oozir ...	Ditto ...	2	...	1	1	1	2	...	1	8	1. Cultivation ... 2. Working in the fields for hire. 3. Production and sale of vegetables.	Ditto ...	8 0 5	Thali ... 1 Lota ... 1	Goat ... 1	......	......	Spade ... 1 Hansooa ... 1 Khurpi ... 1	Is in debt, but the amount of debt could not be ascertained.
22	Booni ...	Ditto ...	1	—	1	...	...	2	...	2	6	Ditto ...	Ditto ...	0 14 5	Thali ... 1 Lota ... 1		......	......	Spade ... 1 Hansooa ... 1 Khurpi ... 1	
23	Fancoo ...	Ditto ...	1	...	1	...	...	2	...	1	5	1. Cultivation ... 2. Working in the fields for hire.	Ditto ...	0 10 0	......		......	......	Hansooa ... 1 Khurpi ... 1	Is a poor man; cannot live without working every day. Goes out in search of work to distant villages.
24	Sanker ...	Ditto ...	1	...	1	...	...	...	...	1	3	Daily labour ...	......	......	......		......	......	Hansooa ... 1 Khurpi ... 1	
25	Batal ...	Ditto ...	5	1	3	1	...	1	...	1	10	1. Cultivation ... 2. Production and sale of vegetables. 3. Labour in the fields for hire.	Paharpore ...	1 2 5	Thalies ... 2 Lota ... 1		......	......	Spade ... 1 Hansooa ... 1 Khurpi ... 1	Had one calf which he sold for payment of rent.
26	Suddar ...	Ditto ...	3	1	2	...	...	1	...	4	10	1. Cultivation .. 2. Production of vegetables for sale.	Paharpore ... Pertaha ...	1 18 5 3 8 0	Thalies ... 2 Lotas ... 3 Bati ... 1 Iron dab... 1	Cows ... 8 Bullock ... 1 Goat ... 1	8 0 0	......	Plough ... 1 Spade ... 1 Khurpi ... 1	
27	Mossamut Baboori.	Ditto ...	...	...	1	...	...	2	...	2	5	Working for hire in household.		......	Lota ... 1	......	......	......	......	The husband of this woman is living, but, being ill, lives in a different place with his uncle. She supports her children by working in the household of other men. She and her children live partly on roots growing spontaneously in the paddy fields and under water.
28	Goodhree, son of Poochha.	Sheik ...	1	...	1	...	...	...	...	...	2	1. Cultivation ... 2. Working for hire in the fields.	Paharpore ..	1 10 6	Lota ... 1		......	......	Hansooa ... 1 Khurpi ... 1	His small holding has been advertised for sale for arrears of rent. He mainly depends on labour for his subsistence.
29	Jhoomuck ...	Ditto ...	...	1	1	...	...	2	...	2	6	Cultivation only...	Ditto ...	1 18 10	Thali ... 1 Lota ... 1		......	......	Spade ... 1 Khurpi ... 1 Hansooas 2	Holds three bighas of land jointly with his three brothers; he cannot himself cultivate it; his brothers cultivate the land and give him his share of the produce after deducting the expenses. This family also party lives on roots.

Serial number.	Name of the head of the family.	Caste.	Number of members in the family. Able-bodied men.	Old or infirm men.	Married women.	Widows.	Boys above 12 years of age.	Boys under 12 years of age.	Girls above 12 years of age.	Girls under 12 years of age.	Total number of members in the family.	Resources of income.	Extent of agricultural holding. Name of mouzah.	Area.	Brass and zinc utensils possessed by the family.	Animals possessed by the family.	Amount of debt. Money (in rupees).	Grain (in maunds).	Agricultural implements and other ostensible properties possessed by the family.	Remarks.
1	2	3	4	5	6	7	8	9	10	11	12	13	14	15	16	17	18	19	20	21
																	Rs. A. P.	Mds.		
30	Karry	Sheik ...	3	...	3	1	...	2	...	1	10	1. Cultivation ... 2. Working for hire in the fields.	Paharpore ...	1 13 10	Thali ... 1 Lotas ... 2 Bati ... 1	Cows ... 5 Bullock ... 1	5 0 0	......	Plough ... 1 Spade ... 1 Khurpi ... 1 Hansooa ... 1	Is brother of the foregoing Jhoomuck, who has a share in the animals.
31	Mussamut Sookni.	Kunjra ...	...	...	...	1	1	1	...	1	4	Personal labour ...	......	......	......	......	......	......	......	The woman works in the household and the boy works in the fields. This family also partly lives on roots.
32	Bhorosi ...	Khatwi ...	1	...	1	...	...	...	...	1	3	1. Cultivation ... 2. Weaving ... 3. Working for hire.	Paharpore ...	0 7 5		Cows ... 2 Calves ... 2	2 8 0	1	Khurpi ... 1 Hansooa ... 1	This family also lives partly on roots. They eat leaves of plants and drink water in lotas borrowed from relatives living in the same house. The head-man looked healthy and well fed.
33	Daseo	Ditto ...	1	...	1	...	...	...	...	...	2	1. Cultivation ... 2. Working for hire.	Ditto ...	0 7 5	Thali ... 1 Lota ... 1		......	4	Khurpi ... 1 Hansooa ... 1	
34	Bideseo ...	Ditto ...	1	...	1		...	1	...	1	4	1. Cultivation ... 2. Working for hire. 3. Weaving.	Ditto ...	0 7 5	......		......	1½	Khurpi ... 1 Hansooa ... 1	
35	Dhorni ...	Ditto ...	1	...	1	1	...	...	...	...	3	Ditto ...	Ditto ...	0 7 5	Thali ... 1		2 8 0	1½	Khurpi ... 1 Hansooa ... 1	
36	Moosai ...	Ditto ...	2	...	1	...	...	...	...	1	4	1. Cultivation ... 2. Working in the fields for hire.	Ditto ...	1 0 0	Thali ... 1		5 0 0	......	Hansooa ... 1	This debt was incurred to marriage expenses.
37	Mongal, son of Kissin.	Ditto ...	...	1	...	1	...	...	...	...	2	Begging ...		......			5 0 0	......	......	The man himself is infirm; his wife has left him and gone to her father's house; he depends on the begging of his mother.
38	Khanto ...	Ditto ...	2	...	1	...	...	...	...	2	5	1. Working for hire in the field.			Thali ... 1 Lota ... 1		1 0 0	1½		
39	Mussamut Bhootka.	Ditto ...	...	...	...	1	...	1	...	...	2	Begging and working in the household.	......	......	Lota ... 1		......	......	......	Lives partly on roots; appeared in rags.
40	Runga ...	Goala ...	1	...	1	1	...	...	...	...	3	1. Cultivation ... 2. Working for hire in the fields.	Paharpore ...	0 17 0	Thali ... 1 Lota ... 1		......	8	Hansooa ... 1 Khurpi ...	Looked to be of weak physique.
41	Girdhari ...	Halwai ...	2	...	1	1	...	...	...	1	5	Ditto ...	Ditto ...	2 11 0	Thali ... 1 Lotas ... 2	......	8 0 0	......	Bhurpi ... 1 Hansooa ... 1	
42	Gopal, son of Jhonti.	Goala ...	3	...	5	1	1	2	...	2	12	Cultivation ...	Paharpore ... Aml ...	0 18 0 5 5 15	Thalis ... 2 Lotas ... 2	Bullocks ... 2	40 0 0	40	Plough ... 1 Spade ... 1 Khurpis ... 2 Hansooas ... 2	

43	Tittar Gope ...	Ditto ...	1	...	...	1	...	1	...	...	3	1. Cultivation ... 2. Working for hire in the fields.	Paharpore ...	1 0 5	Thali ... 1 Lota ... 1	Cows ... 3 Calf ... 1	......	......	Khurpi ... 1	
44	Shib Churn Teli.	Teli ...	2	...	1	1	...	...	...	...	4	1. Cultivation ... 2. Manufacture of oil. 3. Working for hire in the fields.	Ditto ...	1 0 5	Thali ... 1 Lota ... 1		......	......	Hansooa ... 1 Khurpi ... 1	Drives his oil-mill by a borrowed bullock; is well fed and is not in debt.
45	Sonahi Chamar	Chamar ...	1	...	1	...	1	2	...	1	6	1. Cultivation as under-raiyat. 2. Working for hire in the fields. 3. Manufacture of hides. 4. Music. 5. Midwifery.	Ditto ...	0 10 0	Thali ... 1 Lota ... 1		1 0 0	......	Hansooa ... 1 Khurpi ... 1	Being a Chamar by caste, gets carcasses of all the animals that die in the village. He sells, skins, and uses the flesh; he plays native music in the marriage season and occasionally prepares shoes also. The woman of the family acts as midwife at the time of delivery in the village families.
46	Jhonti, son of Jasi.	Goala ...	5	...	3	...	...	2	1	...	8	1. Cultivation ... 2. Working for hire in the fields.	Mahooa ... Bucoonia ...	0 13 0 0 10 0	Thali ... 1 Lota ... 1	Cow ... 1 Bullock ... 1	50 0 0	......	Spade ... 1 Hansooas... 2 Khurpi ... 1	His holdings of Paharpore and Chatwan have been sold up.
47	Gopal, son of Dasan.	Ditto ...	3	1	...	...	...	1	...	...	5	1. Cultivation ...	Paharpore ... Mahooa ... Bucoonia ... Chatwan ...	10 6 18 0 18 0 2 3 0 0 13 18	Thalis ... 3 Lotas ... 2	Bullocks ... 2 Calves ... 2	20 0 0	......	Plough ... 1 Spades ... 2 Hansooas ... 3 Khurpis ... 2	
48	Tittar, son of Hitram.	Ditto ...	1	...	1	1	...	...	...	1	4	Ditto ...	Paharpore ... Mahooa ... Chatwan ...	2 10 3 0 13 0 1 11 12	Thali ... 1 Lota ... 1	Bullock ... 1	8 0 0	......	Spade ... 1 Hansooa ... 1 Khurpi ... 1	
49	Phoocbha, son of Jhonti.	Ditto ...	1	...	1	1	...	...	...	1	4	1. Cultivation ... 2. Working for hire in the fields.	Paharpore ... Chatwan ... Mahooa ...	8 8 16 0 7 5 0 13 0	......		15 0 0	......	Spade ... 1 Hansooa ... 1 Khurpi ... 1	
50	Kanchan, son of Choolhai.	Ditto ...	3	...	3	1	...	2	...	2	9	Ditto ...	Paharpore ... Chatwan ...	1 6 0 0 7 0	Lota ... 1 Bati ... 1	......	......	......	Hansooas 2	Has taken advance to be paid by working in the fields.
51	Kullur, son of Hurjan.	Ditto ...	3	...	3	...	...	...	...	...	6	Ditto ...	Paharpore ... Mahooa ... Chatwan ...	2 10 3 0 13 0 0 15 16	Thali ... 1 Lota ... 1	Bullock ... 1 Goat ... 1	18 0 0	......	Spade ... 1 Hansooas 2 Khurpis ... 3	
52	Kissan Deo ...	Ditto ...	5	...	5	...	...	5	...	...	15	Cultivation ...	Paharpore ... Mahooa ... Bucoonia ... Chatwan ...	11 1 0 2 15 0 2 2 0 0 18 10	Thalis ... 4 Lotas ... 2	......	50 0 0	......	Ploughs ... 2 Hansooas 4 Spades ... 2 Hanga ... 1 Khurpis ... 4	This is a family of five brothers who have separate food but joint business.
53	Talo, son of Bholan.	Ditto ...	2	1	2	...	...	2	...	...	7	Cultivation and occasional sale of milk.	Paharpore ... Chatwan ... Mahooa ... Rampur ...	4 13 10 2 11 15 0 10 0 1 13 0	Thali ... 1 Lota ... 1	Plough bullocks 2 Cart bullocks ... 2 Cows ... 3 Buffalo ... 1	100 0 0	......	Hansooas... 2 Plough ... 1 Hanga ... 1 Spade ... 1 Khurpis ... 2 Cart ... 1	Has a better house than other raiyats.
54	Seree, son of Bholan.	Ditto ...	4	1	2	...	...	1	...	...	8	1. Cultivation ... 2. Sale of milk.	Paharpore ... Mahooa ... Bucoonia ...	4 10 0 0 10 0 0 7 0	Thalis ... 2 Lotas ... 2	Buffaloes... 4 Bullock ... 1	50 0 0	......	Plough ... 1 Spade ... 1 Hansooas 2 Khurpis ... 2	
55	Chunni, son of Boonni.	Ditto ...	1	...	1	1	...	1	...	...	4	1. Cultivation ...	Mahooa ...	1 0 0	Thali ... 1	......	......	......	......	His holding of 8 bighas in Paharpore has been sold up for arrears of rent by a certificate process at the instance of the Srinagar Court of Wards.
56	Kanchan, son of Surdyal.	Ditto ...	1	...	...	...	...	...	...	...	1	1. Labour ...	......	......	......	......	......	......	......	Holding sold up for arrears of rent as above; now depends on personal labour for subsistence.
57	Bhikha, son of Dhookha.	Ditto ...	2	...	1	1	...	2	...	...	6	1. Cultivation ... (57 and 58)	Chatwan ... Mahooa ... Bucoonia ... Asal ... Paharpore ...	1 8 10 1 0 0 2 10 0 0 5 0 6 5 10	Thalis ... 8 Lotas ... 3	Bullocks ... 2	20 0 0	......	Plough ... 1	Two brothers with separate food, but joint business.
58	Nunnoo ...	Ditto ...	1	...	1	...	...	...	...	...	2									

Serial number.	Name of the head of the family.	Caste.	Number of members in the family. Able-bodied men.	Old or infirm men.	Married women.	Widows.	Boys above 12 years of age.	Boys under 12 years of age.	Girls above 12 years of age.	Girls under 12 years of age.	Total number of members in the family.	Resources of income.	Extent of agricultural holding. Name of mouzah.	Area.	Brass and zinc utensils possessed by the family.	Animals possessed by the family.	Amount of debt. Money (in rupees).	Grain (in maunds).	Agricultural implements and other ostensible properties possessed by the family.	Remarks.
1	2	3	4	5	6	7	8	9	10	11	12	13	14	15	16	17	18	19	20	21
																	Rs. A. P.	Mds.		
59	Khantor ...	Goala ...	2	...	1	1	...	2	...	...	6	1. Cultivation ...	Paharpore ...	4 8 0	Thalis ... 2 Lota ... 1	Bullock ... 1	16 0 0	......		
60	Soncoman, son of Poochal.	Ditto ...	1	...	...	...	...	...	...	...	1	1. Cultivation ... 2. Working for hire in the fields.	Chatwan ...	0 14 0	......	......	......	8		
61	Bansi, son of Boodhui.	Ditto ...	1	...	1	2	...	3	...	...	7	1. Cultivation ...	Paharpore ... Chatwan ...	0 16 0 2 11 17	Thali ... 1 Lota ... 1	Bullock ... 1	10 0 0	......	Plough .. 1 Spade .. 1 Khurpi ... 1	
62	Bhai Lal, son of Tettar.	Ditto ...	1	...	1	...	...	2	...	...	4	Daily labour ...	......	......	......		......	......	......	
63	Mussamut Posni.	Ditto ...	...	...	...	1	...	...	...	...	1	1. Spinning ... 2. Working in the households.	......	......	......		......	......	......	
64	Mussamut Rupia.	Ditto ...	...	...	...	1	...	...	...	...	1	1. Cultivation ... 2. Working in the household.	Paharpore ...	0 13 5		......	......	......		She has sublet her small holding on Butai and depends mainly on her daily work for subsistence.
65	Rannoo, son of Jiban.	Ditto ...	2	...	2	1	...	2	...	...	7	1. Cultivation ... 2. Working for hire in the field.	Paharpore ... Mahooa ... Chatwan ...	3 15 5 1 0 0 0 17 10	Thali ... 1 Lota ... 1	Cow ... 1	......	......	Spade ... 1 Khurpi ... 1	
66	Bhai Lall and Jhoomak, son of Doollur.	Ditto ...	2	...	2	1	...	3	...	...	8	Ditto ...	Paharpore ... Mahooa ... Chatwan ...	3 8 0 0 15 0 0 10 9	Thali ... 1 Lota ... 1		......	......	Spade ... 1 Hansooa ... 1	Is in debt the amount of which could not be ascertained.
67	Mussamut Hausi.	Khatwi ...	...	...	...	1	...	...	...	...	1	1. Selling salt and tobacco.	......	......	......		......	......	......	
68	Bhorosi, son of Girdhari.	Goala ...	1	...	1	1	...	1	...	...	4	1. Cultivation ... 2. Working for hire in the fields.	Paharpore ...	3 2 0			......	......	Hansooa ... 1 Khurpi ... 1	
69	Dasan, son of Hurmohur.	Ditto ...	1	...	1	...	...	...	...	...	2	Daily labour ...	......	......			......	......		
70	Akkal	Ditto ...	1	...	1	1	...	...	...	...	3	Ditto ...	......	......		......	......	......	......	
71	Baccoo, son of Jhoomack.	Ditto ...	1	...	1	1	...	2	...	...	5	1. Cultivation ... 2. Sale of milk ...	Paharpore ... Mahooa ... Chatwan ... Asai ...	7 9 0 2 18 0 2 3 0 1 0 0	Thalis ... 3 Lotas ... 2	Bullocks ... 3 Cows ... 2 Buffaloes .. 3	40 0 0	......	Ploughs ... 2 Hanga ... 1 Khurpis ... 2 Hansooas 2 Spades ... 2	Uncle and nephew with separate food but joint business.
72	Tittur, son of Lowis.	Ditto ...	2	...	2	...	...	3	...	...	7									
73	Debi, son of Mohur.	Ditto ...	2	...	1	1	...	1	...	...	5	1. Cultivation ... 2. Working for hire in the field.	Paharpore ...	3 4 5		......	15 0 0	......	Hansooas 2 Khurpis ... 2	Brothers with separate food but joint business.
74	Kanchan ...	Ditto ...	1	...	1	...	...	1	...	...	3									

75	Ram, son of Hanooman.	Hajam ...	1	1	1	1	...	...	...	...	4	1. Cultivation ... 2. Shaving.	Paharpore ...	0 10 0	Thali ... 1 Lota ... 1	Bullock ... 1 Cow ... 1	......	......	Plough ... 1 Spade ... 1 Khurpi ... 1 Hansoca ... 1	In good condition ; free from deb
76	Girdhari, son of Jiban.	Carpenter		1	8	...	...	6	...	1	16	1. Cultivation ... 2. Carpentry.	Paharpore ... Chatwan ... Mahooa ... Asai ...	8 0 0 1 12 0 0 18 0 1 16 0	Thalis ... 4 Lotas ... 2	Cows ... 2 Bullocks ... 3	10 0 0	......	Ploughs ... 2 Hanga ... 1 Spades ... 2 Hansoocas 4 Khurpis ... 4 Bedahni ... 1	In good condition.
77	Bachi, son of Jibun.	Ditto ...	1	1	2	...	...	1	...	...	5	Ditto ...	Paharpore ... Asai ...	2 5 5 0 18 0	Thali ... 1 Lota ... 1	Bullocks ... 2 Cow ... 1	......	......	Plough ... 1 Spade ... 1 Hansoca ... 1 Khurpi ... 1	Ditto.
78	Boonni, son of Choolhai.	Goala ...	1	...	1	...	...	2	...	...	4	Daily labou ...	......	......	......		......	......	......	
79	Samfud, son of Gouri.	Ditto ...	2	...	...	1	...	...	...	...	3	Ditto ...	......	......	......		......	......	......	Holds no land except a little bares near his house ; could not marry on account of poverty ; earns [enough to maintain himself and his mother.
80	Badan, son of Tiluk.	Halwai ...	2	...	3	...	...	...	...	...	5	Ditto ...	......	......	Lota ... 1	Cow ... 1	2 0 0	......	......	
81	Hanooman, son of Baijoo.	Ditto ...	1	...	1	...	2	...	...	...	4	Ditto ...	......	......	Thali ... 1 Lota ... 1	Cow ... 1	......	......	......	
82	Peari, son of Rubbi.	Ditto ...	1	...	1	...	...	...	...	1	3	Ditto ...	......	......	......	......	......	......	......	
83	Doman, son of Chandi.	Teli ...	2	...	1	...	...	1	...	2	6	1. Cultivation as under-raiyat. 2. Manufacture of oil.	Paharpore ...	0 1 5	Thalis ... 2 Lota ... 1	Bullocks ... 2 Cow ... 1	......	......	Plough ... 1 Spade ... 1 Khurpi ... 1 Hansoca ... 1	
84	Tittur, son of Moosai.	Mollah ...	2	...	1	1	...	...	...	...	4	1. Cultivation as under-rayat. 2. Fishery. 3. Working for hire in the field.	Ditto ...	0 2 0	Thali ... 1 Lota ... 1	......	10 0 0	......	Net ... 1 Hansoca ... 1 Khurpi ... 1	
85	Lalee	Garori ...	1	...	1	...	...	...	...	1	3	1. Cultivation ... 2. Manufacture of blanket.	Rampore ...	0 10 0	Thali ... 1 Lota ... 1		10 0 0	......	Hansoca ... 1 Khurpi ... 1	
86	Mongal, son of Dookhan.	Ditto ...	1	...	1	1	...	1	...	...	4	1. Cultivation ... 2. Working for hire in the fields.	Paharpore ...	0 13 0	Thali ... 1		8 0 0	......	Hansoca ... 1	
87	Mussamut Roonia.	Ditto ...	...	...	...	1	...	1	...	...	2	1. Sale of salt and tobacco.	......	......	......	......	......	......	......	
88	Genessee ...	Ditto ...	2	1	1	...	1	2	...	3	10	1. Cultivation ... 2. Manufacture of blanket.	Paharpore ... Rampore ...	2 19 0 2 5 0	Thalis ... 3 Lotas ... 3	Bullock ... 1 Cow ... 1	55 0 0	15	Plough ... 1 Spade ... 1 Hansoocas 2 Khurpis ... 2	
89	Bachhi, son of Bootau.	Halwai ...	2	...	1	1	...	3	...	...	7	1. Cultivation ...	Paharpore ... Asai ... Bacoonia ...	2 3 0 1 11 0 1 5 0	Thalis ... 2 Lotas ... 2	Bullocks ... 2	10 0 0	......	Plough ... 1 Spades ... 2 Hansoocas 2 Khurpis ... 2	
90	Bachhi, son of Kanhai.	Goala ...	2	...	2	1	...	1	...	...	6	1. Cultivation ... 2. Working for hire in the fields.	Paharpore ... Chatwan ...	0 6 0 0 16 0	Thali ... 1	Bullock ... 1 Cow ... 1	8 0 0	......	Spade ... 1 Hansoca ... 1 Khurpi ... 1	
91	Mongal ...	Teli ...	3	...	1	...	...	4	...	...	8	1. Cultivation ... 2. Oil-making. 3. Money-lending.	Bucoonia .. Kedlie ... Paharpore ...	2 13 0 2 10 0 0 9 17	Thalis ... 3 Lotas ... 2	Bullocks ... 4 Cows ... 2	......	......	Cart ... 1 Plough ... 1 Hansoca ... 1 Khurpi ... 1	Well-to-do.
92	Jhoomack ...	Do. ...	2	...	2	...	...	1	...	...	5	1. Cultivation ... 2. Oil-making. ...	Paharpore ...	0 9 17	Thali ... 1 Lota ... 1	Bullocks ... 2 Goat ... 1	......	......	Spade ... 1 Hansoca ... 1 Khurpi ... 1	
93	Mussamut Dookhia.	Gurari ...	...	...	...	1	...	1	...	...	2	Daily labour ...	......	......	......	......	......	......	......	The boy works in the field and the mother in the households of the village.
	Total ...	......	144	17	118	43	11	104	6	54	494	......		280 8 7	167	119	611 0 0	85½	233	

CAMP EKAR, The 24th April 1888.

BURHANDEO NARAYAN,
Assistant Settlement Officer.

H. P.—Reg. No. 22530—137—16-5-88

CONFIDENTIAL]

No. 8, dated Bhagulpore, the 5th May 1888.

From—J. BEAMES, ESQ., Commissioner of the Bhagulpore Division and Sonthal Pergunnahs,

To—The Secretary to the Govt. of Bengal, Revenue Department.

IN continuation of my confidential letter No. 7 of the 2nd instant, I have the honour to submit herewith copy of a report received from the Collector of Monghyr regarding the condition of the lower classes of the people of his district.

No. 273R, dated Monghyr, the 3rd May 1888.

From—HERBERT MOSLEY, Esq., Collector of Monghyr,

To—The Commissioner of the Bhagulpore Division.

WITH reference to your confidential letter No. 1 of the 19th December 1887, I have the honour to inform you that I have had careful enquiries made in the following villages, viz.—

Mohanpur and Indruk	...	... In Monghyr thana.
Tikapur and Belha	...	... „ Gogri „
Billo and Dakra	...	... „ Shekpura „
Bilori ...	...	... „ Sekundra.
Mahana ... Ulao ... Gurdaspore ...	...	... „ Beguserai.

2. The information obtained is embodied in the two statements with remarks attached. I think these will give all that is required, and I have thought it will be more convenient to give it in this form than in the shape of a more or less discursive report.

3. In the lengthy return No. 2 it will be seen that crops are not sold to any extent. Money is borrowed from mahajans for seed and other expenses and for rent, when it is paid in cash, and the mahajan takes payment in grain, taking care that the rate of valuation shall be well in his favour; that is to say, he takes his interest and makes a second profit on the sale of grain at a good deal over the valuation on which he received it.

Remarks on Table I.

IN all these villages and in many more I visited in the far interior, I find people living in thatched sheds with mud walls.

There are unskilled artizans in almost all of these villages; they mend ploughs and are paid in kind; their women only work in the field during cutting season when crops are harvested, and earn Rs. 2 to Rs. 3 worth in grains for each crop.

There are very few weavers in these villages, and those that are found appear to me very poor; their earning by profession is very uncertain, so they labour also in the field; women, without exception, wear coarse country cloths, but males prefer *markin*, being cheaper at the market; hence the number of weavers is apparently decreasing.

H. MOSLEY,

Collector.

Remarks on Table No. 2.

4. *Indruk.*—In this village the agricultural outturn is not supplemented in any other way. The straw is used for feeding for cattle.

5. Agricultural labourers are paid in grain, the value of which amounts to two annas a day. These labourers are villagers with houses of their own.

6. No artizans live in this village; the cultivators depend mostly for one meal upon different preparation of indian-corn, such as "bread" "*chatu*;" the latter they eat with a little salt and *merrich*; they earn a sufficient livelihood. They keep it in stock for consumption for all the year round; in the evening they use other produce according to the season of the year. During ceremonies, such as marriage or Sradh, they eat rice. Each family possesses silver ornaments, *hansli*, *bank* and *kara*, made of brass; a pair of brass *karas* is worth about eight annas. Silver ornaments are of the value of Rs. 10 to Rs. 20, which the women wear on ceremonial occasions.

Marriage expenses are said never to exceed Rs. 300.

Mohanpur.—The people derive no income from jungle produce, by selling fish, and in any other way than from agriculture or labour. The houses are thatched. Agricultural labourers are paid in grain, two seers *basi* each per day, which is nearly two annas a day.

Unskilled artizans get at the same rate in kind, and in cases where they are pressed hard their women go to work in the field during cutting season. They eat chiefly *makai* and other crops which they keep in store, but scarcely eat rice, excepting on occasions of ceremony. They feel no want of food. Each family, excepting three or four, has silver ornaments of the value of Rs. 25. Small debts are incurred for payment of rent and interest to mahajans. Rs. 25 to Rs. 50 are spent for Sradh, but larger amounts are required for marriages which, however, in no case exceed Rs. 200 to Rs. 300.

The same remarks apply in the case of *Tikapur* cultivators, but the people of *Mahana* are free from debt. Their outturn is not supplemented in any other way. They, like others, use their straw for cattle and for repairs of thatched houses. The people do not feel want, but depend for one meal upon season vegetables such as *sakurkund* (sweet-potato). Many take rice as well at 7 P.M. The majority use brass utensils and the rest drink from earthen pots.

All live in low thatched houses, many of which are not in good order but want repairs. They wear coarse country cloths and possess three or four silver ornaments of the value of Rs. 10 to Rs. 15 for each family. They lavish money in marriage ceremonies, when they freely indulge in rice, as well as at the time when near and dear relatives are invited during social ceremonies. They spend in marriages about Rs. 200 to Rs. 300, often supplementing their cash by borrowing.

Some were found in Olao and Gurdaspore, who seem to feel a want of proper nourishment. The people in these two villages and Belba are more or less indebted.

There are few weavers in these villages, and their professional earnings are very uncertain. Some say it amounts to two annas a day, which, being insufficient, they go to work in the field.

The cultivators of Gurdaspore and Olao depend for one meal every day upon *sakurkund* and other vegetables, like their neighbours of Mohana. They eat at night bread and boiled flour of indian-corn, and other season produce as *komie*, *kerao*, &c.; they all live in thatched houses which they repair with straw. Their grain outturn is not supplemented in other ways. The cattle eat the straw.

About fifty families use pottery, the rest possess brass utensils and silver ornaments, viz. *Husli*, *Baju*, of the value varying Rs. 15 to Rs. 20 for each family. Most of them expend Rs. 100 to Rs. 150 during marriage ceremonies, but in other social observances they spend Rs. 15 to Rs. 30. For this they incur debt.

Regarding the cultivators of the remaining three villages, Bilori, Billo and Dakra, very few are indebted, and even that is on account of marriage ceremonies. They eat rice during day and bread of *makai* and wheat, &c., at night. They all live in thatched houses which are repaired with straw. The females wear country cloths, but the males proper fine *markin*.

Each family has a sufficient quantity of brass utensils. All possess silver ornaments of more or less value, and in a few cases the value of the ornaments of a family amounts to Rs. 50. They spend Rs. 200 to Rs. 300 in marriages, but they are moderate in other ceremonies.

H. MOSLEY,
Collector.

TABLE No. 1.—Vide *page 2 of Mr. Finucane's letter.*

NAME OF VILLAGE.	Total population.	Actual number of families dependent on charity.	Actual number of families dependent on wages of labour.	Average number of persons whom each labourer's wage has to support.	The number dependent on wages plus profits of small holdings.	How far such wages and profits are sufficient to supply the daily food requirements of the number of persons dependent upon them.	REMARKS.
1. Mohanpur ...	1,358	1	148	5	38 families with 275 persons.	The earning is sufficient to meet the daily food.	They wear mostly coarse cloths which they keep very dirty; they say they cannot provide for washerman's wage out of income. They all use brass utensils, and live in thatched houses with mud walls. 126 men are indebted.
2. Indruk	1,126	1	92	7	52 families with 154 persons.	Sufficient, but 50 men are indebted.	(2 to 4). Though some are indebted they get sufficient food and are not in want. Most of them use brass utensils, each family possessing only a lotah and a thali.
3. Tikapur ...	5,018	1	319	7	151 families with 1,092 persons.	Sufficient, about 100 are indebted.	
4. Belha ...	1,177	10	491	4	137 families with 992 persons.	Sufficient, about 50 are indebted.	
5. Billo ...	920	2	64	2	67 families with 332 persons.	Sufficient	(5 to 7). Only five persons in Belori are indebted, the people are not in want of food, but very miserable in their habitations. Most of them live in mere huts.
6. Dakra ...	902	...	89	5	11 families with 61 persons.	Ditto ...	
7. Belori ...	1,156	6	65	5	24 families with 139 persons.	Ditto ...	
8. Mahana ...	886	1	37	7	22 families with 150 persons.	Ditto ...	(8 to 10). It is said people scarcely get rice to eat, and depend for one meal daily upon boiled *sakurkund* and other season vegetables. Many of them are indebted and use pottery. I have come across many who are thin and apparently seem to feel a want of due nourishment.
9. Ulao ...	1,763	3	101	6	160 families with 993 persons.	Ditto	
10. Gurdaspur ...	1,539	13	69	5	74 families with 218 persons.	Ditto about 50 indebted.	

H. MOSLEY,
Collector.

TABLE No. 2.—*Vide Government of Bengal No. 35, dated 9th December 1887.*

1	2	3	4	5	6	7	8	9
Village.	CULTIVATORS.	Area of holding.	Produce obtained.	The price for which that part of it not consumed for subsistence is sold.	Rent.	Expenses for cultivation.	The extent to which they are indebted.	REMARKS.
		B. K. C. D.	Mds. s. c. k.		Rs. A. P.	Rs. A. P.	Rs. A. P.	
Indruk	Bhaslu Rai	35 0 0 0	300 0 0 0	...	96 0 0	105 0 0	35 0 0	Debt on account of social ceremonies.
	Kheman Dhanuk	14 0 0 0	70 0 0 0	...	42 0 0	43 0 0	40 0 0	
	Musudun Dhanuk	5 0 0 0	25 0 0 0	...	15 0 0	15 0 0	15 0 0	
	Chamoo Dhanuk	7 0 0 0	35 0 0 0	...	21 0 0	21 0 0	22 0 0	
	Hulas Gope	7 0 0 0	42 0 0 0	...	35 0 0	21 0 0	10 0 0	
	Nakat Dhanuk	7 0 0 0	35 0 0 0	...	28 0 0	21 0 0	60 0 0	
	Mohur Gope	13 0 0 0	91 0 0 0	...	9 8 0	40 0 0	45 0 0	
	Lungroo Gope	5 10 0 0	34 0 0 0	...	17 0 0	25 8 0	18 8 0	
	Beni Rai	21 0 0 0	165 0 0 0	...	60 0 0	33 0 0	300 0 0	Debt on account of marriage ceremony.
	Gokul Rai	10 0 0 0	50 0 0 0	...	50 0 0	30 0 0	150 0 0	Ditto.
	Net Lal Rai	7 0 0 0	28 0 0 0	...	14 0 0	21 0 0	75 0 0	
	Kallar Rai	9 0 0 0	45 0 0 0	...	27 0 0	27 0 0	25 0 0	
	Durshan Rai	5 0 0 0	30 0 0 0	...	25 0 0	15 0 0	125 0 0	Ditto.
	Rajaram Rai	12 0 0 0	60 0 0 0	...	55 0 0	36 0 0	100 0 0	Ditto.
	Kanhia Rai	10 0 0 0	56 0 0 0	...	40 0 0	30 0 0	200 0 0	Ditto.
	Sorman Rai	15 5 0 0	103 0 0 0	...	90 0 0	54 0 0	200 0 0	Ditto.
	Sukul Rai	12 0 0 0	60 0 0 0	...	42 0 0	36 0 0	50 0 0	
	Bhaku Rai	12 0 0 0	60 0 0 0	...	42 0 0	36 0 0	125 0 0	
	Ram Rai	3 0 0 0	12 0 0 0	...	6 0 0	6 0 0	70 0 0	
	Sahebram Rai	6 0 0 0	36 0 0 0	...	30 0 0	18 0 0	100 0 0	
	Beloo Rai, son of Chetru Rai.	7 0 0 0	42 0 0 0	...	35 0 0	21 0 0	125 0 0	
	Tota Rai	15 0 0 0	67 0 0 0	...	60 0 0	45 0 0	200 0 0	
	Mohur Rai	4 0 0 0	20 0 0 0	...	16 0 0	12 0 0	40 0 0	
	Badlu Rai	7 0 0 0	21 0 0 0	...	14 0 0	21 0 0	10 0 0	
	Darias Rai, son of Bhuput Rai.	5 7 0 0	25 0 0 0	...	17 0 0	15 0 0	30 0 0	
	Jeebun Rai	3 0 0 0	15 0 0 0	...	15 0 0	9 0 0	22 0 0	
	Kehar Rai	5 10 0 0	27 0 0 0	...	7 9 0	16 6 0	56 0 0	
	Pheka Rai	6 0 0 0	35 0 0 0	...	20 0 0	18 0 0	35 0 0	
	Sahebram Rai	11 0 0 0	68 0 0 0	...	55 0 0	33 0 0	60 0 0	
	Sirdar Rai	5 10 0 0	8 0 0 0	...	15 8 0	4 8 0	30 0 0	
	Uma Rai	18 5 0 0	34 0 0 0	...	23 7 0	18 0 0	100 0 0	Ditto.
	Hira Rai	9 12 0 0	27 0 0 0	...	14 10 6	28 0 0	180 0 0	Ditto.
	Pucha Rai	40 0 0 0	200 0 0 0	...	160 0 0	120 0 0	50 0 0	
	Meghu Rai	15 0 0 0	75 0 0 0	...	60 0 0	45 0 0	100 0 0	Ditto.
	Chunder Rai	38 0 0 0	200 0 0 0	...	133 0 0	108 0 0	125 0 0	Ditto.
	Kali Rai	12 0 0 0	60 0 0 0	...	44 0 0	36 0 0	150 0 0	Ditto.
	Ramrup Rai	5 0 0 0	25 0 0 0	...	25 0 0	15 0 0	200 0 0	Ditto.
	Baikumar Rai	60 0 0 0	300 0 0 0	...	150 0 0	180 0 0	150 0 0	Ditto.
	Musan Rai, son of Saina Rai.	70 0 0 0	300 0 0 0	...	210 0 0	210 0 0	600 0 0	Ditto.
	Bhuglu Pottack	12 0 0 0	60 0 0 0	...	36 0 0	36 0 0	10 0 0	
	Bansi Rai	36 0 0 0	135 0 0 0	...	150 0 0	90 0 0	200 0 0	Ditto.
	Hansraj Rai	4 0 0 0	20 0 0 0	...	12 0 0	12 0 0	50 0 0	
	Juri Rai	15 0 0 0	75 0 0 0	...	50 0 0	45 0 0	300 0 0	For social ceremonies.
	Bhoopun Rai	15 0 0 0	96 0 0 0	...	60 0 0	45 0 0	50 0 0	Ditto.
	Toral Rai	21 0 0 0	126 0 0 0	...	80 0 0	33 0 0	100 0 0	Ditto.
	Tallu Rai	24 0 0 0	120 0 0 0	...	96 0 0	75 0 0	300 0 0	Ditto.
	Chinban Rai	18 0 0 0	90 0 0 0	...	72 0 0	54 0 0	300 0 0	Ditto.
	Hardhar Rai	25 0 0 0	125 0 0 0	...	75 0 0	75 0 0	400 0 0	Ditto.
	Pardip Rai	18 0 0 0	108 0 0 0	...	90 0 0	54 0 0	200 0 0	Ditto.
	Gheena Rai	24 0 0 0	116 0 0 0	...	96 0 0	72 0 0	300 0 0	Ditto.
	Nathan Sahu	1 0 0 0	10 0 0 0	...	5 0 0	3 0 0	......	
	Ram Rai	30 0 0 0	220 0 0 0	...	80 0 0	60 0 0	......	
2. Mohanpur	Rajha Hajjam	4 0 0 0	16 0 0 0	...	12 0 0	8 0 0	75 0 0	
	Ghaba Hajjam	7 0 0 0	28 0 0 0	...	21 0 0	14 0 0	10 0 0	
	Luchmi Hajjam	4 0 0 0	16 0 0 0	...	12 0 0	8 0 0	5 0 0	
	Chamari Gope	4 0 0 0	16 0 0 0	...	12 0 0	8 0 0	16 0 0	
	Narain Gope	3 0 0 0	6 0 0 0	...	9 0 0	6 0 0	45 0 0	
	Gandhu Gope	5 0 0 0	20 0 0 0	...	15 0 0	10 0 0	75 0 0	Debt incurred on account of marriage.
	Lurka Gope	5 0 0 0	20 0 0 0	...	16 0 0	10 0 0	15 0 0	
	Meghu Rai	2 0 0 0	8 0 0 0	...	6 0 0	4 0 0	80 0 0	
	Sabhan Gope	2 11 0 0	10 0 0 0	...	7 0 0	5 0 0	25 0 0	
	Munghar, son of Gharjar	2 0 0 0	8 0 0 0	...	6 0 0	4 0 0	100 0 0	Ditto.
	Bhairo Moondi	6 0 0 0	24 0 0 0	...	18 0 0	12 0 0	65 0 0	Ditto.
	Bhola Moondi	10 0 0 0	40 0 0 0	...	30 0 0	20 0 0	150 0 0	Ditto.
	Dumri Lal	4 0 0 0	16 0 0 0	...	12 0 0	8 0 0	5 0 0	
	Sukaria Dhanuk	5 0 0 0	20 0 0 0	...	15 0 0	10 0 0	20 0 0	
	Bhuttoo Dhanuk	4 0 0 0	16 0 0 0	...	12 0 0	8 0 0	10 0 0	
	Gann Gope	3 0 0 0	12 0 0 0	...	9 0 0	6 0 0	25 0 0	
	Bhupat Teli	2 0 0 0	8 0 0 0	...	6 0 0	4 0 0	4 0 0	
	Khiran Gope	2 0 0 0	9 0 0 0	...	6 0 0	4 0 0	25 0 0	
	Umrao Gossain	1 0 0 0	5 0 0 0	...	3 0 0	2 8 0	42 0 0	For marriage ceremony.
	Raghu Gope	7 0 0 0	34 0 0 0	...	27 0 0	16 0 0	25 0 0	Ditto.
	Narain Gope	7 0 0 0	34 0 0 0	...	27 0 0	16 0 0	50 0 0	Ditto.
	Haso Rai	3 0 0 0	11 0 0 0	...	9 0 0	5 0 0	52 0 0	Ditto.
	Bidia Rai	2 10 0 0	10 0 0 0	...	9 0 0	5 0 0	30 0 0	Ditto.
	Jhukri Gope	1 0 0 0	5 0 0 0	...	3 8 0	2 8 0	25 0 0	Ditto.
	Meghur Moondi	5 0 0 0	15 0 0 0	...	17 0 0	11 0 0	20 0 0	Ditto.
	Etwari Gope	4 0 0 0	16 0 0 0	...	13 0 0	9 0 0	35 0 0	Ditto.
	Tekan Gope	10 0 0 0	40 0 0 0	...	30 0 0	21 0 0	15 0 0	
	Bhola Gope	8 0 0 0	42 0 0 0	...	25 0 0	17 0 0	10 0 0	
	Bhola Moondi	11 0 0 0	44 0 0 0	...	35 0 0	23 0 0	20 0 0	
	Dukha Moondi	2 0 0 0	7 0 0 0	...	7 0 0	5 0 0	25 0 0	
	Khandi Singh	1 0 0 0	4 0 0 0	...	3 0 0	3 0 0	10 0 0	
	Bundhu Momin	7 0 0 0	34 0 0 0	...	21 0 0	16 0 0	15 0 0	
	Methru Chamar	25 0 0 0	100 0 0 0	...	80 0 0	50 0 0	250 0 0	Ditto.
	Bhusi Chamar	12 0 0 0	42 0 0 0	...	36 0 0	26 0 0	70 0 0	Ditto.
	Pultal Manjhi	14 0 0 0	54 0 0 0	...	45 0 0	30 0 0	35 0 0	For Sradh.
	Pokhun Pasban	9 0 0 0	45 0 0 0	...	30 0 0	22 8 0	12 0 0	
	Ramdyal Pasban	4 0 0 0	14 0 0 0	...	14 0 0	8 0 0	15 0 0	
	Shibdyal Kurmi	2 0 0 0	7 0 0 0	...	7 0 0	4 0 0	5 0 0	
	Sankar Hajjan	3 0 0 0	9 0 0 0	...	9 0 0	6 0 0	10 0 0	

1	2	3				4				5	6			7			8			9
Village.	CULTIVATORS.	Area of holding.				Produce obtained.				The price for which that part of it not consumed for subsistence is sold.	Rent.			Expenses for cultivation.			The extent to which they are indebted.			REMARKS.
		B.	K.	C.	D.	Mds.	S.	C.	K.		Rs.	A.	P.	Rs.	A.	P.	Rs.	A.	P.	
8. Tikarampur.	Jhonti Dhobi	1	10	12	0	8	0	0	0	...	1	8	6	8	0	0	20	0	0	
	Ramdyal Sahukandu ...	6	2	9	0	30	0	0	0	...	9	8	3	15	0	0	10	0	0	
	Aghore Mandal Keot ...	3	0	16	0	15	0	0	0	...	7	3	6	6	0	0	10	0	0	
	Bhoju Mandal Keot ...	5	5	15	0	26	0	0	0	...	9	7	6	10	0	0	15	0	0	
	Ajach Mandal Keot ...	3	0	0	0	10	0	0	0	...	8	3	0	4	0	0	......			
	Sobran Mandar Keot ...	11	11	17	0	70	0	0	0	...	20	12	0	28	0	0	50	0	0	
	Mami Mandar Keot ...	9	5	12	0	45	0	0	0	...	11	10	9	15	0	0	......			
	Panchoo Mandar ...	15	17	19	0	80	0	0	0	...	29	2	0	32	0	3	45	0	0	
	Budri Mandar	8	9	17	0	41	0	0	0	...	16	9	9	16	0	0	......			
	Tirbhuan Mandar	17	7	11	0	90	0	0	0	...	31	2	3	54	0	0	50	0	0	
	Pran Mandar	19	5	4	0	100	0	0	0	...	30	6	8	40	0	0	38	0	0	
	Bulaki Mistry	14	15	6	0	72	0	0	0	...	23	11	5	29	0	0	......			
	Pubbi Hajjam	4	5	1	0	50	0	0	0	...	7	8	9	20	0	0	......			
	Mewa Sahu	7	2	12	0	25	10	0	0	...	16	5	3	14	0	0	......			
	Durga Hajjam	1	17	18	0	10	0	0	0	...	4	3	3	4	0	0	20	0	0	
	Saitan Mandar	12	1	6	0	20	0	5	0	...	22	11	6	8	0	0	25	0	0	
	Kirpa Mandar	26	14	13	0	130	0	0	0	...	54	5	9	53	0	0	15	0	0	
	Haman Mandar	3	15	0	0	15	20	0	0	...	6	10	9	8	0	0	10	0	0	
	Leela Sahu Kundu ...	1	10	8	0	7	0	0	0	...	3	1	3	8	0	0	5	0	0	
	Daljit Mandar	8	15	18	0	31	0	0	0	...	3	1	5	13	0	0	9	0	0	
	Kheman Mandar ...	2	1	12	0	5	0	0	0	...	2	4	3	4	0	0	......			
	Kheman Mandar (2nd) ...	2	19	17	0	15	0	0	0	...	4	12	6	6	0	0	......			
	Seeta Mandar	13	3	13	0	10	0	0	0	...	19	0	6	18	0	0	......			
	Ram Mahton Dhanuk ...	42	18	9	0	225	0	0	0	...	51	9	9	54	0	0	100	0	0	
	Bunai Hajjam	0	19	4	0	3	0	0	0	...	1	13	3	1	8	0	......			
	Inder Mahton	20	11	9	0	103	0	0	0	...	40	8	6	40	0	0	......			
	Fakir Mahton	8	10	10	0	3	0	0	0	...	5	4	6	1	4	0	......			
	Khanlar Mahton	3	7	0	0	11	0	0	0	...	5	8	8	4	8	0	......			
	Raman Mandar	3	18	9	0	13	0	0	0	...	7	5	6	6	0	0	......			
	Chhabu Mandar	10	15	0	0	46	0	0	0	...	17	14	5	21	0	0	......			
	Shyam Pasban	2	14	6	0	3	0	0	0	...	8	12	6	4	0	0	......			
	Lachmah Pasban	10	8	14	0	9	0	0	0	...	18	3	3	6	0	0	......			
	Panchu Mandar	3	19	9	0	11	34	0	0	...	9	7	11	7	14	0	50	0	0	
	Masudam Mandar	2	10	0	0	6	1	0	0	...	4	0	1	4	0	0	250	0	0	
	Makhan Mandar	2	10	0	0	6	1	0	0	...	4	1	0	4	0	0	100	0	0	
	Pairi Baita	2	0	0	0	6	0	0	0	...	3	12	0	3	12	0	25	0	0	
	Sita Baita	2	0	0	0	5	0	0	0	...	3	12	0	4	0	0	......			
	Bharosi Teli	4	0	0	0	16	0	0	0	...	6	8	0	8	0	0	......			
	Kanchan Mandar	4	0	0	0	16	0	0	0	...	6	8	0	8	0	0	......			
	Mussamut Jibia	2	10	0	0	10	0	0	0	...	3	12	0	5	0	0	......			
	Garbhu Pasdar	2	10	0	0	10	0	0	0	...	3	12	0	5	0	0	25	0	0	
	Bhatu Mandar	2	10	0	0	7	10	0	0	...	5	5	4	5	0	0	25	0	0	
	Badri Mandar	10	0	0	0	60	0	0	0	...	15	0	0	20	0	0	30	0	0	
	Sarwan Mandar	10	0	8	0	60	0	0	0	...	15	0	0	20	0	0	......			
	Kaleswar Mandar	8	10	0	0	37	0	0	0	...	12	12	0	17	0	0	100	0	0	
	Dular Mandar	8	0	0	0	30	0	0	0	...	9	13	0	10	0	0	54	0	0	
	Kanhia Mandar	6	12	10	0	19	35	0	0	...	16	4	0	13	3	0	25	0	0	
	Masudan Mandar	5	1	0	0	15	8	0	0	...	9	13	2	10	1	0	100	0	0	
	Bhadoi Mandar	5	0	0	0	15	0	0	0	...	9	0	0	10	0	0	50	0	0	
	Sona Mandar	1	16	1	10	5	17	0	0	...	4	10	6	3	9	0	45	0	0	
	Girdhari Mandar	1	18	0	0	5	35	0	0	...	4	10	0	3	9	0	......			
	Tota Mandar	1	3	8	0	3	18	0	0	...	2	12	9	2	4	0	......			
	Mussamut Sanichari ...	1	3	8	0	3	18	0	0	...	2	12	9	2	4	0	......			
	Ganes Tanti	0	10	0	0	3	0	0	0	...	0	12	0	1	0	0	10	0	0	
	Bhukhan Mandar	2	10	0	0	15	0	0	0	...	3	12	0	5	0	0	55	0	0	
	Kali Mandar	5	9	19	0	15	10	0	0	...	13	9	9	11	0	0	55	0	0	
	Radha Mandar	5	9	19	0	20	0	0	0	...	15	0	0	11	0	0	50	0	0	
	Chamru Mandar	6	10	0	0	33	0	0	0	...	18	0	0	13	0	0	......			
	Beraspat Hajjam	2	15	17	0	8	16	0	0	...	5	10	9	5	10	0	30	0	0	
	Bhagiu Mandar	2	15	17	0	8	16	0	0	...	5	10	9	5	10	0	25	0	0	
	Lachumen Beldar	2	6	16	0	7	2	0	0	...	4	3	9	4	9	0	25	0	0	
	Paquir Mandar	12	19	7	0	39	0	0	0	...	21	14	3	25	14	0	350	0	0	
	Gopal Mandar	4	17	12	0	14	22	0	0	...	9	16	9	9	21	0	48	0	0	
	Shumram Mandar	16	16	10	0	50	16	0	0	...	33	5	4	33	0	0	500	0	0	
	Ram Lal Gope	4	10	0	0	20	0	0	0	...	11	8	7	8	0	0	50	0	0	For marriage.
	Bhadai Mahton	4	17	0	0	20	0	0	0	...	13	5	0	6	0	0	30	0	0	Ditto.
	Bhadai Mahton	3	0	0	0	9	0	0	0	...	3	11	9	6	0	0	25	0	0	
	Kheman Gope	4	0	0	0	20	0	0	0	...	8	0	0	8	0	0	25	0	0	
	Bulaki Gope	3	0	0	0	9	0	0	0	...	5	11	9	6	0	0	25	0	0	
	Bansi Gope	7	18	0	0	35	0	0	0	...	15	6	0	14	0	0	100	0	0	Ditto.
	Raja Gope	21	13	0	0	63	0	0	0	...	31	13	6	42	0	0	125	0	0	Ditto.
	Bhikhari Mahton	61	7	15	0	183	0	0	0	...	65	18	0	188	0	0	30	0	0	Ditto.
	Jhakri Gope	7	13	0	0	35	0	0	0	...	15	7	0	14	0	0	25	0	0	Ditto.
	Gopal Mahton	13	0	0	0	65	0	0	0	...	27	10	0	26	0	0	10	0	0	Ditto.
	Sita Gope	26	7	6	0	130	0	0	0	...	41	18	7	61	0	0	50	0	0	Ditto.
	Kamal Gope	10	0	0	0	60	0	0	0	...	22	0	0	20	0	0	20	0	0	
	Sukhan Gope	12	0	3	0	60	0	0	0	...	26	4	0	33	0	0	......			
	Bhatu Gope	18	0	0	0	80	0	0	0	...	23	12	0	30	0	0	25	0	0	
	Bhatu Gope Kalan ...	18	0	0	0	108	0	0	0	...	23	13	0	36	0	0	50	0	0	
	Chander Gope	20	12	0	0	100	0	0	0	...	30	14	0	40	0	0	100	0	0	
	Chon Gope	21	6	0	0	126	0	0	0	...	6	5	0	42	0	0	50	0	0	
	Adhi Gope	21	6	0	0	126	0	0	0	...	6	0	0	45	0	0	50	0	0	
	Shib Charan Gope	14	0	0	0	70	0	0	0	...	28	0	0	28	0	0	30	0	0	
	Meghu Gope	14	0	0	0	70	0	0	0	...	28	8	0	28	0	0	25	0	0	
	Kali Gope	7	12	4	0	35	0	0	0	...	8	6	0	14	8	0	10	0	0	
	Nehari Gope	7	12	4	0	35	0	0	0	...	8	8	0	15	0	0	15	0	0	
	Mokund Gope	22	8	2	0	66	0	0	0	...	22	5	0	44	0	0	125	0	0	
	Hiraman Gope	10	6	1	0	100	0	0	0	...	53	5	0	40	0	0	......			
	Sirwan Gope	6	16	1	0	80	0	0	0	...	13	11	0	12	0	0	20	0	0	
	Rup Chand Gope	8	8	1	0	40	0	0	0	...	18	6	0	16	0	0	30	0	0	
	Mamheb Gope	43	1	4	0	66	0	0	0	...	26	3	0	24	0	0	200	0	0	
	Shiboo Gope	32	1	6	0	192	0	0	0	...	20	0	0	50	0	0	20	0	0	
	Leela Gope	10	0	0	0	60	0	0	0	...	18	0	0	20	0	0	15	0	0	
	Jugroo Gope	10	0	0	0	60	0	0	0	...	18	0	0	20	0	0	15	0	0	
	Shambhu Gope	14	0	0	0	70	0	0	0	...	28	0	0	28	0	0	30	0	0	
	Tuna Gope	10	0	0	0	60	0	0	0	...	15	0	0	20	0	0	15	0	0	
	Bunsi Gope	8	10	0	0	51	0	0	0	...	12	12	0	17	0	0	25	0	0	
	Isser Gope	8	10	0	0	51	0	0	0	...	12	12	0	17	0	0	25	0	0	
	Birj Lal Gope	4	0	0	0	24	0	0	0	...	6	0	0	8	0	0	10	0	0	
	Retu Gope	4	0	0	0	24	0	0	0	...	6	0	0	8	0	0	5	0	0	
	Persad Gope	4	10	0	0	27	0	0	0	...	6	12	0	9	0	0	9	0	0	
	Sobhan Gope	3	0	0	0	30	0	0	0	...	7	8	0	10	0	0	......			
	Gurdyal Gope	10	10	0	0	63	0	0	0	...	13	12	0	21	0	0	......			

1	2	3	4	5	6	7	8	9
Village.	Cultivators.	Area of holdings.	Produce obtained.	The price for which that part of it not consumed for subsistence is sold.	Rent.	Expenses for cultivation.	The extent to which they are indebted.	Remarks.
		B. K. C. D.	Mds. S. C. K.		Rs. A. P.	Rs. A. P.	Rs. A. P.	
	Balkiman Gope	10 10 0 0	63 0 0 0	...	15 12 0	21 0 0	......	
	Mungul Gope	5 5 0 0	60 0 0 0	...	12 6 0	16 4 0	10 0 0	
	Phuddi Gope	8 0 2 0	48 0 0 0	...	12 0 0	16 0 0	8 0 0	
	Taral Gope	21 8 0 0	63 0 0 0	...	36 12 0	42 0 0	50 0 0	
	Pulinkdhari Gope	21 6 1 0	61 0 0 0	...	36 11 0	42 0 0	40 0 0	
	Kanchan Gope	22 4 4 0	66 0 0 0	...	16 15 0	44 0 0	100 0 0	
	Shyam Gope	7 12 4 0	35 0 0 0	...	6 6 0	14 0 0	......	
	Lalji Gope	7 12 4 0	35 0 0 0	...	8 6 0	14 0 0	......	
	Bhairo Rai	25 2 0 0	100 0 0 0	...	33 2 0	50 0 0	......	
	Bairam Rai	14 2 2 0	70 0 0 0	...	22 8 0	28 0 0	50 0 0	
	Gunput Rai	10 1 1 0	44 0 0 0	...	27 0 0	22 0 0	10 0 0	
	Dharai Rai	16 1 1 0	96 0 0 0	...	27 0 0	32 0 0	20 0 0	
	Darbari Rai	18 1 4 0	80 0 0 0	...	33 8 0	36 0 0	25 0 0	
	Chundi Rai	6 4 0 0	30 0 0 0	...	13 9 0	12 0 0	......	
	Shibdyal Gope	5 0 0 0	25 0 0 0	...	7 6 0	10 0 0	......	
	Mosaheb Gope	5 0 0 0	25 0 0 0	...	7 6 0	10 0 0	......	
	Hiraman Gope	47 1 2 0	235 0 0 0	...	105 4 0	84 0 0	200 0 0	
	Hanaman Gope	5 14 0 0	25 0 0 0	...	15 5 6	10 0 0	20 0 0	
	Poorun Gope	5 14 0 0	25 0 0 0	...	15 5 6	10 0 0	20 0 0	
	Radhe Gope	21 2 5 0	63 0 0 0	...	31 12 0	42 0 0	250 0 0	
	Bhoobun Gope	16 0 0 0	96 0 0 0	...	25 9 0	12 0 0	......	
	Mundroo Gope	16 1 0 0	96 0 0 0	...	28 9 0	18 0 0	......	
	Kunbia Gope	8 2 1 0	48 0 0 0	...	18 6 0	16 0 0	......	
	Bansi Gope	11 1 3 0	55 0 0 0	...	11 1 0	22 0 0	......	
	Chaudun Gope	7 3 3 0	36 0 0 0	...	15 8 0	14 0 0	......	
	Rawan Gope	13 12 2 0	65 0 0 0	...	35 10 0	27 0 0	10 0 0	
	Wife of Chamman Gope ...	13 12 2 0	65 0 0 0	...	35 10 0	27 0 0	20 0 0	
	Toolsi Gope	4 12 2 0	27 0 0 0	...	13 5 0	9 0 0	......	
	Gurbhu Gope	13 0 4 0	78 0 0 0	...	18 5 0	26 0 0	10 0 0	
	Girdhari Gope	11 1 3 0	55 0 0 0	...	11 1 0	23 0 0	18 0 0	
	Hirya Lal Gope	11 0 0 0	55 0 0 0	...	11 0 0	22 0 0	......	
	Mawji Gope	7 4 0 0	42 0 0 0	...	16 15 0	14 0 0	......	
	Chuttur Gope	26 1 5 0	156 0 0 0	...	14 12 0	52 0 0	100 0 0	
	Lahai Gope	26 1 5 0	156 0 0 0	...	14 12 0	52 0 0	125 0 0	
	Dowlut Gope	13 0 0 0	78 0 0 0	...	27 0 1	26 0 0	25 0 0	
	Ghanshyam Gope	13 0 0 0	78 0 0 0	...	27 0 1	26 0 0	30 0 0	
	Ram Gope	10 0 0 0	60 0 0 0	...	15 0 0	20 0 0	45 0 0	
	Khajo Gope	10 10 0 0	63 0 0 0	...	15 12 0	20 0 0	80 0 0	
	Ram Lal Gope	4 8 0 0	20 0 0 0	...	11 8 0	4 8 0	60 0 0	
	Badri Gope	4 8 0 0	20 0 0 0	...	11 8 0	4 8 0	10 0 0	
	Masudan Gope	5 0 0 0	25 0 0 0	...	13 5 0	10 0 0	......	
	Madhu Gope	5 0 0 0	25 0 0 0	...	13 5 0	10 0 0	......	
	Ram Gope	5 10 0 0	27 20 0 0	...	13 12 0	11 0 0	......	
	Hira Gope	12 0 0 0	55 0 0 0	...	33 6 0	26 0 0	125 0 0	For marriage.
	Hira Kandoo	12 0 0 0	65 0 0 0	...	33 6 0	26 0 0	......	
	Wife of Roop Chand ...	10 0 0 0	60 0 0 0	...	14 0 0	20 0 0	......	
4. Mahana ...	Bhadai Kandoo	4 12 2 0	28 0 0 0	...	12 5 8	9 0 0	......	
	Barhma Singh	15 0 0 0	75 0 0 0	...	16 0 0	30 0 0	......	
	Bodhi Singh	15 0 0 0	60 0 0 0	...	12 0 0	24 0 0	......	
	Tejoo Singh	12 0 0 0	60 0 0 0	...	12 0 0	21 0 0	......	
	Sheik Ibrahim Hossein ...	11 0 0 0	55 0 0 0	...	11 0 0	16 8 0	......	
	Musammut Foocho Kumri	4 0 0 0	20 0 0 0	...	4 0 0	6 0 0	......	
	Sheik Mahomed Ali ...	8 0 0 0	40 0 0 0	...	9 0 0	12 0 0	......	
	Bhagwan Dutt	3 0 0 0	15 0 0 0	...	4 8 0	6 0 0	......	
	Jeebraj Kandoo	1 10 0 0	7 20 0 0	...	6 0 0	1 8 0	......	
	Ram Lal Kahar	1 0 0 0	5 0 0 0	...	5 0 0	1 8 0	......	
	Ram Lal Rai	2 0 0 0	10 0 0 0	...	2 0 0	3 8 0	......	
	Samodha Kumri	2 0 0 0	10 0 0 0	...	2 0 0	3 0 0	......	
	Goodur Rai	5 0 0 0	25 0 0 0	...	5 0 0	9 8 0	......	
	Ram Bharosa Rai	0 13 0 0	3 20 0 0	...	1 5 0	1 0 0	......	
	Burhma Rai	1 2 0 0	5 0 0 0	...	3 3 0	3 0 0	......	
	Juggoo	0 5 0 0	1 20 0 0	...	1 0 0	0 6 0	......	
	Bhichook Rai	1 10 0 0	7 20 0 0	...	1 8 0	1 8 0	......	
	Khubhal Rai	7 0 0 0	35 0 0 0	...	1 12 0	7 0 0	......	
	Bundi Rai	5 0 0 0	25 0 0 0	...	5 0 0	6 4 0	......	
	Musammut Jhaw Kumari...	4 0 0 0	20 0 0 0	...	4 0 0	6 12 0	......	
	Bunsi Sahoo	0 10 0 0	3 20 0 0	...	1 8 0	1 0 0	......	
	Batoran Kandoo	1 0 0 0	5 0 0 0	...	3 0 0	3 0 0	6 0 0	
5. Gurdaspur	Bhugwan Dutt Jha ...	1 5 0 0	6 10 0 0	...	3 0 0	4 0 0	......	
	Kali Singh	10 0 0 0	50 0 0 0	...	23 0 0	21 0 0	50 0 0	
	Bhinak Singh	4 0 0 0	24 0 0 0	...	10 0 0	9 0 0	200 0 0	These debts are incurred chiefly for marriage ceremony.
	Khatar Singh	7 0 0 0	28 0 0 0	...	13 0 0	15 0 0	325 0 0	
	Dahoo Singh	16 0 0 0	96 0 0 0	...	56 0 0	35 0 0	300 0 0	
	Andhi Singh	11 0 0 0	66 0 0 0	...	30 0 0	23 0 0	200 0 0	
	Mukhu Singh	6 0 0 0	30 0 0 0	...	18 0 0	12 0 0	120 0 0	
	Sadho Singh	3 0 0 0	15 0 0 0	...	7 8 0	6 0 0	75 0 0	
	Bhagbati Singh	13 0 0 0	52 0 0 0	...	87 8 0	26 0 0	300 0 0	
	Bhika Singh	1 15 0 0	14 0 0 0	...	4 8 0	4 0 0	45 0 0	
	Gobind Singh	15 0 0 0	39 0 0 0	...	37 8 0	35 0 0	425 0 0	
	Natho Singh	50 0 0 0	250 0 0 0	...	150 0 0	125 0 0	1,000 0 0	
	Beda Singh	8 0 0 0	45 0 0 0	...	23 0 0	15 0 0	400 0 0	
	Simbi Singh	2 0 0 0	11 0 0 0	...	6 8 0	4 0 0	50 0 0	
	Tookroo Singh	1 10 0 0	8 10 0 0	...	4 8 0	3 0 0	30 0 0	
	Bankhandi Singh	3 0 0 0	18 0 0 0	...	9 0 0	7 8 0	100 0 0	
	Hiraman Singh	10 0 0 0	45 0 0 0	...	20 0 0	15 0 0	250 0 0	
	Gooraon Singh	5 0 0 0	25 0 0 0	...	11 4 0	10 0 0	150 0 0	
	Bansi Singh	15 0 0 0	60 0 0 0	...	45 0 0	22 8 0	250 0 0	
	Geeha Singh	7 0 0 0	28 0 0 0	...	14 0 0	10 8 0	......	
	Ruttoo Singh	100 0 0 0	500 0 0 0	...	250 0 0	150 0 0	60 0 0	
	Gunni Singh	20 0 0 0	125 0 0 0	...	40 0 0	40 0 0	10 0 0	
	Sardhari Singh	20 0 0 0	125 0 0 0	...	40 0 0	40 0 0	......	
	Soobi Singh	50 0 0 0	200 0 0 0	...	100 0 0	75 0 0	75 0 0	
	Golam Singh	50 0 0 0	200 0 0 0	...	100 0 0	75 0 0	75 0 0	
	Keshri Singh	25 0 0 0	100 0 0 0	...	50 0 0	37 8 0	300 0 0	
	Jhandoo Singh	30 0 0 0	150 0 0 0	...	75 0 0	45 0 0	......	
	Bansi Singh	10 0 0 0	50 0 0 0	...	25 0 0	15 0 0	50 0 0	
	Neem Narain Singh ...	5 0 0 0	25 0 0 0	...	10 0 0	7 8 0	200 0 0	
	Pooroo Singh	10 0 0 0	40 0 0 0	...	20 0 0	15 0 0	100 0 0	
	Jubraj Singh	35 0 0 0	175 0 0 0	...	105 0 0	52 8 0	......	
	Thana Singh	15 0 0 0	75 0 0 0	...	22 8 0	30 0 0	......	
	Phaku Singh	18 0 0 0	108 0 0 0	...	54 0 0	36 0 0	......	
	Buto Singh	10 0 0 0	40 0 0 0	...	15 0 0	15 0 0	......	
	Beni Singh	12 0 0 0	72 0 0 0	...	30 0 0	24 0 0	......	

1	2	3	4	5	6	7	8	9
Village.	Cultivators.	Area of holdings.	Produce obtained.	The price for which that part of it not consumed for subsistence is sold.	Rent.	Expenses for cultivation.	The extent to which they are indebted.	Remarks.
		B. K. C. D.	Mds. S. C. K.		Rs. A. P.	Rs. A. P.	Rs. A. P.	
5. Gurdarpur—*contd.*	Mithoo Singh	7 0 0 0	31 20 0 0	...	10 8 0	18 0 0	30 0 0	
	Behari Singh	3 0 0 0	15 0 0 0	...	6 0 0	6 0 0	25 0 0	
	Bhairab Singh	9 0 0 0	45 0 0 0	...	27 0 0	13 8 0	......	
	Sookhal Singh	5 0 0 0	25 0 0 0	...	10 0 0	10 0 0	......	
	Tara Singh	7 0 0 0	35 0 0 0	...	17 8 0	10 8 0	25 0 0	
	Fakir Singh	12 0 0 0	60 0 0 0	...	36 0 0	18 0 0	100 0 0	
	Mala Singh	9 0 0 0	45 0 0 0	...	22 8 0	13 8 0	......	
	Chhodi Singh	3 0 0 0	15 0 0 0	...	9 0 0	6 0 0	50 0 0	
	Kanhea Singh	11 0 0 0	44 0 0 0	...	22 0 0	16 8 0	......	
	Bhikhi Singh	16 0 0 0	80 0 0 0	...	32 0 0	24 0 0	......	
	Paroo Singh	2 0 0 0	10 0 0 0	...	5 0 0	3 0 0	20 0 0	
	Hardyal Singh	1 0 0 0	5 0 0 0	...	3 0 0	1 8 0	10 0 0	
	Akin Kandoo	0 10 0 0	2 20 0 0	...	1 8 0	0 12 0	5 0 0	
	Mala Kandoo	0 10 0 0	2 20 0 0	...	1 8 0	0 12 0	3 0 0	
	Jhoomuk Singh	10 0 0 0	40 0 0 0	...	20 0 0	15 0 0	50 0 0	
	Ram Lal Singh	13 0 0 0	65 0 0 0	...	26 0 0	26 0 0	......	
	Noni Singh	2 0 0 0	10 0 0 0	...	4 0 9	3 0 0	20 0 0	
	Bhuttoo Kahar	0 10 0 0	3 0 0 0	...	1 8 0	0 12 0	......	
	Choonni Kahar	0 5 0 0	1 20 0 0	...	0 12 0	0 6 0	5 0 0	
	Ghamandi Kandoo	0 10 0 0	2 20 0 0	...	1 8 0	0 12 0	......	
	Mithoo Pasban	2 0 0 0	10 0 0 0	...	4 0 0	3 0 0	......	
	Sookhum Pasban	1 0 0 0	5 0 0 0	...	3 0 0	1 8 0	......	
	Leela Dhanuk	1 10 0 0	7 20 0 0	...	3 12 0	2 4 0	......	
	Gurdyal Dhanuk	0 15 0 0	3 30 0 0	...	2 4 0	1 0 0	......	
	Bank Barhi	0 10 0 0	3 0 0 0	...	1 8 0	0 12 0	......	
	Ponchain Dhanuk	1 0 0 0	5 0 0 0	...	2 0 0	1 8 0	6 0 0	
	Purdeep Singh	2 8 0 0	10 0 0 0	...	4 0 0	3 0 0	25 0 0	
	Bissoo Singh	5 0 0 0	25 0 0 0	...	10 0 0	7 8 0	......	
	Dougal Singh	5 0 0 0	25 0 0 0	...	10 0 0	7 8 0	......	
	Khamajit Singh	3 0 0 0	13 0 0 0	...	6 0 0	4 8 0	25 0 0	
	Ranjeet Singh	10 0 0 0	45 0 0 0	...	30 0 0	18 0 0	......	
	Dariao Singh	5 0 0 0	22 20 0 0	...	10 0 0	7 8 0	50 0 0	
	Ram Prosad Singh	4 0 0 0	16 0 0 0	...	6 0 0	6 0 0	22 0 0	
	Bodh Singh	2 0 0 0	10 0 0 0	...	4 0 0	3 0 0	15 0 0	
	Karam Rai	1 0 0 0	5 0 0 0	...	2 0 0	1 8 0	20 0 0	
	Lughoo Rai	3 0 0 0	12 0 0 0	...	7 8 0	4 8 0	25 0 0	
	Gunput Singh	1 0 0 0	4 0 0 0	...	2 0 0	1 8 0	5 0 0	
	Nowrungi Singh	1 0 0 0	4 0 0 0	...	2 0 0	1 8 0	5 0 0	
	Ramroop Singh	0 10 0 0	2 0 0 0	...	1 0 0	0 12 0	50 0 0	
	Gendha Singh	4 0 0 0	20 0 0 0	...	8 0 0	6 0 0	50 0 0	
6. Ulao ...	Gondur Chowdhry	1 19 16 0	9 35 0 0	...	7 7 10	3 10 0	......	
	Sukhu Chowdhry	1 19 16 0	9 35 0 0	...	7 7 10	3 10 0	......	
	Bhumi Chowdhry	2 0 0 0	10 0 0 0	...	8 0 0	4 0 0	......	
	Chamroo Chowdhry	2 0 0 0	10 0 0 0	...	8 0 0	4 0 0	......	
	Ram Chowdhry	3 13 15 0	17 20 0 0	...	14 12 0	6 8 0	......	
	Bairam Chowdhry	9 3 8 0	46 10 0 0	...	35 10 0	18 4 0	25 0 0	
	Haman Chowdhry	9 0 0 0	46 0 0 0	...	36 0 0	18 0 0	10 0 0	
	Gopal Chowdhry	0 15 18 0	4 15 0 0	...	3 3 9	1 14 6	......	
	Raghubar Chowdhry	3 3 12 0	15 14 10 0	...	12 12 0	6 3 3	9 0 0	
	Barhma Chowdhry	3 3 12 0	15 14 10 0	...	12 12 0	6 3 3	......	
	Kulloo Chowdhry	4 15 0 0	23 34 0 0	...	19 0 0	8 13 0	16 0 0	
	Kambi Chowdhry	4 15 0 0	23 34 0 0	...	19 0 0	8 12 0	25 0 0	
	Sarabai Chowdhry	3 10 0 0	17 20 0 0	...	14 8 0	6 8 0	......	
	Raineshar Chowdhry	3 18 17 0	18 35 0 0	...	15 1 0	6 13 0	8 0 0	
	Dukhea Rai	4 9 0 0	23 0 0 0	...	19 0 0	8 4 0	10 0 0	
	Mussamut, wife of Raja Ram.	4 9 0 0	23 0 0 0	...	19 0 0	8 4 0	19 0 0	
	Bunsi Kumhar	3 9 10 0	17 10 0 0	...	3 14 10	6 10 0	25 0 0	
	Nowrunji Dhanuk	3 9 10 0	17 10 0 0	...	3 14 10	6 10 0	30 0 0	
	Gondur Banihar	1 5 9 0	6 5 0 0	...	5 1 10	2 4 3	......	
	Jhugroo Teli	1 0 0 0	6 0 0 0	...	5 0 0	2 0 0	......	
	Amrit Teli	1 0 0 0	6 0 0 0	...	5 0 0	2 0 0	......	
	Dulloo Mehter	7 1 16 0	28 10 0 0	...	27 8 9	14 2 0	70 0 0	
	Jhummun Mehter	0 13 19 0	8 15 0 0	...	2 12 0	1 8 0	......	
	Summun Mehter	1 2 0 0	12 4 0 0	...	4 6 7	2 2 0	......	
	Madhu Mahton	1 2 0 0	12 4 0 0	...	4 6 7	2 2 0	......	
	Kari Dhanuk	3 10 0 0	17 20 0 0	...	14 3 0	6 8 0	......	
	Chanchal Dhanuk	1 0 0 0	7 0 0 0	...	4 0 0	2 0 0	......	
	Hansraj Kahar	1 0 0 0	7 0 0 0	...	4 0 0	3 0 0	......	
	Champman Dhanuk	1 10 0 0	10 0 0 0	...	6 0 0	3 4 0	25 0 0	
	Gopal Kandoo	0 17 5 0	9 15 0 0	...	3 7 10	1 11 6	......	
	Taleb Ali	0 17 5 0	9 15 0 0	...	3 7 10	1 11 6	......	
	Hera Sahoo Kandoo	6 9 5 0	64 5 0 0	...	25 13 9	12 11 3	60 0 0	
	Dyal Sahoo Kandoo	6 9 5 0	64 5 0 0	...	25 13 9	12 11 3	50 0 0	
	Poran Sahoo Kandoo	1 8 9 0	12 35 0 0	...	5 11 0	2 9 6	......	
	Goojai Chowdhry	4 19 0 0	44 36 0 0	...	19 14 0	8 14 0	100 0 0	
	Kanhea Chowdhry	4 19 0 0	44 36 0 0	...	19 14 0	8 14 0	200 0 0	
	Jhaman Rai	2 18 4 0	24 8 12 0	...	11 10 5	5 6 0	50 0 0	
	Behari Rai	2 18 4 0	24 8 12 0	...	11 10 5	5 6 0	50 0 0	
	Bhuttoo Rai	2 5 10 0	10 6 6 0	...	8 11 7	2 4 6	50 0 0	
	Kunni Rai	2 3 10 0	10 6 6 0	...	8 11 7	2 4 6	35 0 0	
	Roopun Tanti	0 10 0 0	3 0 0 0	...	2 0 0	1 4 0	......	
	Sonoo Rai	0 5 0 0	2 20 0 0	...	1 0 3	0 8 0	......	
	Ghogun Tanti	4 4 1 0	43 2 0 0	...	12 0 0	8 4 0	10 0 0	
	Bhoottoo Tanti	4 4 1 0	43 2 0 0	...	12 0 0	8 4 0	15 0 0	
	Bija Tanti	2 0 0 0	14 0 0 0	...	6 0 0	4 0 0	......	
	Mussamut Bhuttoo Tanti	2 0 0 0	14 0 0 0	...	6 0 0	4 0 0	......	
	Mussamut Rawan Tanti	4 11 19 0	44 6 0 0	...	18 5 12	8 11 0	25 0 0	
	Omrao Pasi	4 11 19 0	44 6 0 0	...	18 5 12	8 11 0	20 0 0	
	Luchman Hajjam	1 2 1 0	4 2 2 0	...	4 6 10	2 2 0	......	
	Sobrun Hajjam	0 18 18 0	3 15 12 0	...	3 12 10	1 14 6	......	
	Dukhia Missar	0 18 18 0	3 15 12 0	...	3 12 10	1 14 6	......	
	Jhonti Rai	0 17 0 0	3 14 8 0	...	2 10 1	1 13 0	......	
	Mowli Mian	0 10 0 0	3 0 0 0	...	2 0 0	1 0 0	......	
	Tengur Koonjra	1 0 0 0	6 0 0 0	...	4 0 0	2 0 0	......	
	Aklu Koonjra	13 15 0 0	55 0 0 0	...	15 2 7	26 12 0	28 0 0	
	Kanhea Teli	13 15 0 0	55 0 0 0	...	15 2 7	24 12 0	30 0 0	
	Saheb Kunjra	0 13 16 0	3 10 0 0	...	2 12 7	1 3 6	......	
	Bhairo Kunjra	0 13 16 0	3 10 0 0	...	3 12 7	1 3 6	......	
	Bhuta Kunjra	0 15 15 0	3 15 0 0	...	1 2 7	1 5 6	......	
	Tengur Kunjra	0 10 11 0	2 6 0 0	...	2 1 0	1 2 0	......	
	Madhu Kunjra	0 9 0 0	1 35 0 0	...	1 12 9	14 8 0	......	

1	2	3	4	5	6	7	8	9
Village.	Cultivators.	Area of holdings.	Produce obtained.	The price for which that part of it not consumed for subsistence is sold.	Rent.	Expenses for cultivation.	The extent to which they are indebted.	Remarks.
		B. K. C. D.	Mds. S. C. K.		Rs. A. P.	Rs. A. P.	Rs. A. P.	
	Meghu Kunjra	2 9 0 0	9 35 0 0	...	9 12 15	4 15 6	......	
	Bhadai Kunjra	2 9 0 0	9 36 0 0	...	9 12 15	4 15 6	......	
	Jhoomuk Kunjra	1 0 0 0	6 0 0 0	...	4 0 0	2 0 0	......	
	Fakeera Kunjra	5 8 15 0	21 38 0 0	...	21 12 0	10 9 6	50 0 0	
	Bharosi Kunjra	4 4 0 0	34 24 0 0	...	12 0 17	8 4 0	50 0 0	
	Kunhu Kunjra	0 8 4 0	2 35 0 0	...	2 10 10	1 2 0	......	
	Sukul Nunjra	0 14 2 0	4 8 0 0	...	3 13 0	1 8 6	......	
	Handi Kunjra	0 14 2 0	4 8 0 0	...	2 12 0	1 8 6	......	
	Raju Kunjra	1 0 0 0	6 0 0 0	...	4 0 0	2 0 0	10 0 0	
	Bunsi Kunjra	17 14 7 0	10 3 6 0	...	70 14 6	34 15 0	100 0 0	
	Rupun Kunjra	17 14 7 0	103 6 0 0	...	70 14 0	34 15 0	100 0 0	
	Bhugia Kunjra	0 19 16 0	5 35 0 0	...	3 15 7	1 15 6	......	
	Kalu Teli	0 10 0 0	3 0 0 0	...	2 0 0	1 0 0	......	
	Kamal Kandu	0 18 18 0	5 36 0 0	...	3 12 7	1 15 9	......	
	KanhiaKandu	0 18 18 0	5 36 0 0	...	3 12 7	1 15 9	......	
	Bodhu Kandu	0 18 18 0	5 36 0 0	...	3 12 7	1 15 9	......	
	Lalit Missir	1 9 8 0	9 0 0 0	...	5 0 0	2 15 0	10 0 0	
	Aklu Missir	1 9 8 0	9 0 0 0	...	5 14 0	2 15 0	15 0 0	
	Bhikha Rai	2 15 4 0	16 20 0 0	...	11 1 0	4 15 0	20 0 0	
	Bhatoo Missir	0 19 2 0	5 15 0 0	...	3 13 0	1 15 6	......	
	Buttoo Barhi	0 10 0 0	3 0 0 0	...	2 0 0	1 0 0	......	
	Mussamut, wife of Molha-kandu.	1 10 0 0	9 0 0 0	...	6 0 0	3 0 0	15 0 0	
	Durga Kandu	1 10 0 0	9 0 0 0	...	6 0 0	3 0 0	7 0 0	
	Dielan Kandu	1 0 0 0	6 0 0 0	...	4 0 0	2 0 0	......	
	Gudru Kandu	1 0 0 0	6 0 0 0	...	4 0 0	2 0 0	......	
	Meghu Jolaha	0 10 0 0	3 0 0 0	...	2 0 0	1 0 0	......	
	Leela Raikalan	1 11 0 0	9 10 0 0	...	6 5 0	2 12 0	......	
	Karela Jalaha	0 10 0 0	3 0 0 0	...	2 0 0	1 0 0	......	
	Rupan Rai	6 9 19 0	38 35 0 0	...	25 15 12	12 10 6	25 0 0	
	Bala Rai	6 9 19 0	38 35 0 0	...	25 13 12	12 10 6	25 0 0	
	Uma Rai	2 10 0 0	13 0 0 0	...	11 0 0	5 0 0	......	
	Luku Rai	2 10 0 0	13 0 0 0	...	11 0 0	5 0 0	......	
	Naku Missir	0 10 0 0	3 0 0 0	...	2 0 0	1 0 0	25 0 0	
	Lala Rai Khurd	2 8 12 0	19 0 0 0	...	13 10 18	7 0 0	10 0 0	
	Dukha Barai	3 10 0 0	19 0 0 0	...	13 12 0	7 0 0	15 0 0	
	Gopal Barai	3 10 0 0	19 0 0 0	...	13 12 0	7 0 0	100 0 0	
	Jhajha Dhanuk	1 16 14 0	12 12 0 0	...	6 2 0	3 4 0	20 0 0	
	Bhuggu Kahar	1 10 14 0	12 12 0 0	...	6 2 0	3 4 0	20 0 0	
	Pucha Kumhar	0 10 0 0	3 0 0 0	...	2 0 0	1 0 0	......	
	Leela Missir	1 0 0 0	6 0 0 0	...	4 0 0	2 0 0	......	
	Bodhu Missir	1 0 0 0	6 0 0 0	...	4 0 0	2 0 0	......	
	Bishun Dutt Missir ...	4 18 9 0	36 15 0 0	...	19 11 0	9 12 0	25 0 0	
	Balam Rai	4 4 7 0	35 10 0 0	...	18 14 0	8 4 0	30 0 0	
	Behari Kandu	0 19 16 0	26 16 0 0	...	3 15 7	6 9 0	......	
	Jeetun Kandu	0 19 16 0	26 15 0 0	...	3 15 7	6 9 0	......	
	Bharosi Dosadh	3 9 7 0	26 15 0 0	...	13 14 0	6 9 6	20 0 0	
	Sonichar Dosadh	3 9 7 0	26 15 0 0	...	13 14 0	6 9 6	20 0 0	
	Saman Dosadh	3 0 0 0	19 20 0 0	...	13 0 0	6 0 0	......	
	Jagi Dosadh	2 1 0 0	16 2 0 0	...	11 3 0	4 1 0	......	
	Bansi Chowkidar	2 1 0 0	16 2 0 0	...	11 3 0	4 1 0	......	
	Choolhai Dosadh	2 0 0 0	12 0 0 0	...	11 0 0	4 0 0	10 0 0	
	Luchman Dosadh ...	2 0 0 0	12 0 0 0	...	11 0 0	6 0 0	10 0 0	
	Jhukri Dosadh	1 10 0 0	9 0 0 0	...	6 0 0	3 0 0	......	
	Bhikhari Dosadh	1 10 0 0	9 0 0 0	...	6 0 0	3 0 0	......	
	Luchman Missir	4 4 0 0	25 10 0 0	...	16 14 0	8 4 0	50 0 0	
	Shital Mian	3 0 0 0	12 0 0 0	...	11 0 0	4 0 0	25 0 0	
	Pahalwan Tanti	2 17 2 0	22 24 0 0	...	11 8 15	5 14 6	10 0 0	
	Jhaman Khanr	2 17 2 0	22 24 0 0	...	11 8 15	5 14½ 0	9 0 0	
	Bhichuk Dhanuk ...	1 10 14 0	12 12 0 0	...	6 2 0	3 4 0	20 0 0	
	Hira Dhanuk ...	1 10 0 0	9 0 0 0	...	6 0 0	3 0 0	20 0 0	
	Bikno Dhanuk	1 10 0 0	9 0 0 0	...	6 0 0	3 0 0	30 0 0	
	Kallar Dhanuk	1 18 0 0	14 5 0 0	...	0 6 0	2 12 6	28 0 0	
	Bhichhuk Dhanuk ...	0 15 8 0	7 5 0 0	...	3 1 0	1 12 6	......	
	Nuthoo Dhanuk	0 15 5 0	7 5 0 0	...	3 1 0	1 12 6	......	
	Luchman Dhanuk ...	0 10 0 0	3 0 0 0	...	2 0 0	1 0 0	......	
	Karu Kahar	0 10 0 0	3 0 0 0	...	2 0 0	1 0 0	......	
	Tatal Kahar	1 0 0 0	6 0 0 0	...	4 0 0	2 0 0	......	
	Bhanja Ram Kahar ...	1 10 15 0	12 10 0 0	...	6 2 7	3 0 6	......	
	Bhuku Kahar	1 10 15 0	12 10 0 0	...	6 2 7	3 0 6	......	
	Sanichia Dhanuk	1 0 0 0	6 0 0 0	...	4 0 0	2 0 0	......	
	Shib Charan Dhanuk ...	1 10 0 0	9 0 0 0	...	6 0 0	3 0 0	5 0 0	
	Boodhun Dhanuk ...	1 10 0 0	9 0 0 0	...	6 0 0	3 0 0	10 0 0	
	Hanuman Dhanuk ...	0 10 0 0	3 0 0 0	...	2 0 0	1 0 0	......	
	Sonu Kahar	1 5 8 0	10 5 0 0	...	5 1 5	2 2 6	......	
	Bhuttoo Kahar	1 5 8 0	10 5 0 0	...	5 1 5	2 2 6	5 0 0	
	Bhagu Teli	0 10 0 0	3 0 0 0	...	2 0 0	1 0 0	......	
	Shyam Dhanuk	1 0 0 0	6 0 0 0	...	4 0 0	2 0 0	......	
	Nanhu Dhanuk	1 0 0 0	6 0 0 0	...	4 0 0	2 0 0	......	
	Ram Sahai Dhanuk ...	0 10 0 0	3 0 0 0	...	2 0 0	1 0 0	......	
	Siboo Kanda	0 19 16 0	7 27 0 0	...	3 14 7	1 14 6	......	
	Mussamut, wife of Tosul Dhanuk.	1 5 8 0	10 5 0 0	...	5 1 14	2 4 0	......	
	Bhuttoo Dhanuk	1 5 8 0	10 5 0 0	...	5 1 4	2 4 0	......	
	Ram Lal Dhanuk	0 18 18 0	9 35 0 0	...	3 12 7	1 12 0	......	
	Gyan Dhanuk	2 7 3 0	18 10 0 0	...	9 10 9	4 10 6	30 0 0	
	Janki Dhanuk	2 7 3 0	18 10 0 0	...	9 10 9	4 10 6	50 0 0	
	Bidesi Kahar	1 10 0 0	9 0 0 0	...	6 0 0	3 0 0	......	
	Teja Kahar	1 10 0 0	9 0 0 0	...	6 0 0	3 0 0	......	
	Pirengi Kahar	0 19 16 0	7 27 0 0	...	3 15 7	1 14 6	......	
	Nangru Kahar	0 19 16 0	7 27 0 0	...	3 15 7	1 14 6	......	
	Mussamut Ram Tahal Kahar	0 10 0 0	3 0 0 0	...	2 0 0	1 0 0	......	
	Bulloo Rai	4 17 8 0	25 27 12 0	...	19 7 10	9 6 8	48 0 0	
	Sokhi Rai	4 0 0 0	24 0 0 0	...	16 0 0	8 0 0	30 0 0	
	Gondur Rai	10 14 14 0	83 10 0 0	...	42 10 0	21 6 8	25 0 0	
	Kamlapat Rai	1 18 0 0	11 6 0 0	...	7 9 10	3 6 8	10 0 0	
	Jhakri Rai	1 18 0 0	11 6 0 0	...	7 9 10	3 6½ 0	10 0 0	
	Ram Sahai Mali	1 10 0 0	9 0 0 0	...	6 0 0	3 0 0	......	
	Gossain Basdeb Das ...	2 0 0 0	12 0 0 0	...	8 0 0	4 0 0	......	
7. Betha ...	Sheik Sona	7 18 0 0	38 0 0 0	...	15 7 0	15 8 0	50 0 0	
	Sheik Bhikha	1 13 0 0	8 10 0 0	...	2 9 6	5 13 0	......	
	Shaik Hossein	1 13 0 0	8 10 0 0	...	2 9 6	5 13 0	......	

1	2	3	4	5	6	7	8	9
Village.	Cultivators.	Area of holdings.	Produce obtained.	The price for which that part of it not consumed for subsistence is sold.	Rent.	Expenses for cultivation.	The extent to which they are indebted.	Remarks.
		B. K. C. D.	Mds. S. C. K.		Rs. A. P.	Rs. A. P.	Rs. A. P.	
7. Belha—*contd.*	Sheik Dahu	1 12 0 0	8 10 0 0	...	3 11 0	8 12 0	......	
	Mussamut Amiran ...	10 2 0 0	60 0 0 0	...	19 9 0	20 0 0	10 0 0	
	Sheik Behari	2 0 0 0	12 0 0 0	...	4 6 0	4 0 0	......	
	" Musai	0 16 0 0	4 20 0 0	...	1 6 10	1 16 0	......	
	" Nathu	6 11 0 0	39 10 0 0	...	23 1 0	13 9 0	25 0 0	
	" Khoda Buksh ...	1 10 0 0	8 10 0 0	...	3 0 0	3 18 0	......	
	" Hiru	5 3 0 0	30 0 0 0	...	10 5 0	11 0 0	......	
	" Palroo	10 12 0 0	63 20 0 0	...	18 8 0	13 4 0	50 0 0	
	Chamru Momin Banihari	4 0 0 0	24 0 0 0	...	8 0 0	8 0 0	......	
	Sheik Umaid	9 14 0 0	59 0 0 0	...	19 6 0	19 4 0	20 0 0	
	" Mumheb	6 12 0 0	40 0 0 0	...	13 3 0	13 0 0	......	
	" Meher	43 13 0 0	261 20 0 0	...	26 11 0	87 0 0	100 0 0	
	" Janu	1 9 0 0	9 0 0 0	...	2 14 0	3 0 0	......	
	" Ali Baksh	1 0 0 0	6 0 0 0	...	2 0 0	2 0 0	......	
	" Molhan	1 8 0 0	9 0 0 0	...	3 0 0	3 0 0	......	
	Mussamut Dahu	6 7 0 0	39 0 0 0	...	10 11 6	13 0 0	......	
	Sheik Mangal	1 19 0 0	11 0 0 0	...	3 13 0	3 12 0	......	
	" Raham Ali	1 19 0 0	11 0 0 0	...	3 13 0	3 12 0	......	
	" Bhuttoo	2 0 0 0	12 0 0 0	...	4 6 6	4 0 0	......	
	Tiloki Fakir	4 0 0 0	24 0 0 0	...	12 0 0	8 0 0	......	
	Madan Dhunia	1 8 0 0	9 0 0 0	...	3 0 0	3 0 0	......	
	Kanchan Kumhar	16 15 0 0	100 0 0 0	...	29 8 0	34 0 0	50 0 0	
	Thakuri Kundu	1 5 0 0	8 0 0 0	...	2 8 6	3 0 0	......	
	Bhichhuk Kundu	1 5 0 0	9 0 0 0	...	2 8 6	3 0 0	......	
	Soban Kundu	3 0 0 0	18 0 0 0	...	6 0 0	6 0 0	......	
	Sitaram Sahu	1 5 0 0	9 0 0 0	...	2 8 0	3 0 0	......	
	Luchman Gope	1 0 0 0	6 0 0 0	...	2 0 0	2 0 0	......	
	Makhun Gope	0 9 0 0	5 0 0 0	...	0 14 6	1 8 0	......	
	Akhal Gope	0 9 0 0	5 0 0 0	...	0 14 6	1 8 0	......	
	Durga Sahu	4 16 0 0	29 0 0 0	...	9 9 6	9 0 0	29 0 0	
	Jhonti Mahton	29 1 0 0	174 0 0 0	...	48 1 10	58 0 0	50 0 0	
	Ghogbu Mahton	7 17 0 0	46 0 0 0	...	15 7 0	25 0 0	100 0 0	
	Pucha Mahton	14 10 0 0	87 0 0 0	...	28 8 0	29 0 0	50 0 0	
	Gopal Mahton	14 10 0 0	87 0 0 0	...	28 8 0	29 0 0	15 0 0	
	Gopal Mahton	24 10 0 0	147 0 0 0	...	18 5 0	49 0 0	50 0 0	
	Madhu Mahton	20 0 0 0	120 0 0 0	...	40 0 0	40 0 0	25 0 0	
	Banai Mahton	4 16 0 0	29 0 0 0	...	9 10 3	10 0 0	......	
	Narsing Sahu Teli ...	15 18 0 0	95 0 0 0	...	32 6 3	31 8 0	......	
	Durbari Sahu	15 18 0 0	95 0 0 0	...	32 6 3	31 8 0	......	
	Tengar Mahton	1 11 0 0	9 0 0 0	...	3 1 3	3 0 0	......	
	Domun Mahton	8 11 0 0	51 0 0 0	...	16 3 6	17 0 0	16 0 0	
	Jhoomuk Mahton	13 1 0 0	82 0 0 0	...	25 11 0	27 6 0	45 0 0	
	Musaheb Mahton	8 3 0 0	49 0 0 0	...	16 2 0	16 2 0	......	
	Hanuman Mahton... ...	5 0 0 0	70 0 0 0	...	10 0 0	10 0 0	......	
	Bhanja Lal Mahton ...	4 0 0 0	24 0 0	...	8 0 0	8 0 0	......	
	Bhikan Mahton	8 3 0 0	49 0 0 0	...	16 2 0	16 2 0	15 0 0	
	Ram Lal Mahton	7 0 0 0	42 0 0 0	...	14 0 0	14 0 0	15 0 0	
	Ashman Mahton	2 8 0 0	14 0 0 0	...	3 12 3	4 12 0	......	
	Dhowtal Mahton	2 8 0 0	14 0 0 0	...	3 12 3	4 12 0	......	
	Chulhai Mahton	4 15 0 0	28 10 0 0	...	8 9 8	7 14 0	16 0 0	
	Bhagwan Mahton	3 2 0 0	18 15 0 0	...	5 5 0	6 2 0	......	
	Dhunraj Mahton	3 0 0 0	18 0 0 0	...	6 0 0	6 0 0	......	
	Ram Lal Mahton	0 14 0 0	5 0 0 0	...	0 11 3	1 8 0	......	
	Behari Mahton	0 14 0 0	5 0 0 0	...	0 11 3	1 8 0	......	
	Murat Mahton	3 0 0 0	18 0 0 0	...	6 0 0	6 0 0	......	
	Bansi Mahton	4 0 0 0	24 0 0 0	...	8 0 0	8 0 0	......	
	Thakru Dhobi	0 10 0 0	3 0 0 0	...	0 8 0	1 0 0	......	
		1 8 0 0	8 0 0 0	...	3 0 0	2 12 0	......	
	Peer Bakhsh	1 0 0 0	6 0 0 0	...	2 0 0	2 0 0	......	
	Mangal Sahu Kalwar ...	0 10 0 0	3 0 0 0	...	0 8 0	1 0 0	......	
	Gopal Kundu	10 0 0 0	60 0 0 0	...	20 0 0	20 0 0	85 0 0	
	Bilo Teli	5 0 0 0	30 0 0 0	...	10 0 0	10 0 0	......	
	Gouri Laheri	2 0 0 0	12 0 0 0	...	4 0 0	4 0 0	......	
	Jhullu Sahu	13 8 0 0	80 0 0 0	...	27 4 6	26 12 0	26 0 0	
	Etwari Sahu	13 8 0 0	80 0 0 0	...	27 4 6	26 12 0	10 0 0	
	Akal Sahu	5 6 0 0	30 20 0 0	...	10 9 1	10 5 0	......	
	Amir Mian	5 6 0 0	30 20 0 0	...	10 9 1	10 5 0	......	
	Bansi Khunjra	3 0 0 0	18 0 0 0	...	9 0 0	6 0 0	......	
	Syam Mahton	1 0 0 0	6 0 0 0	...	2 0 0	2 0 0	......	
	Pursi Mahton	1 0 0 0	6 0 0 0	...	2 0 0	3 0 0	......	
	Bhakhun Sahu Teli ...	5 0 0 0	30 0 0 0	...	10 0 0	10 0 0	10 0 0	
	Sona Mahton	1 6 0 0	8 0 0 0	...	4 8 0	2 12 0	......	
	Dharam Mahton	1 6 0 0	8 0 0 0	...	4 8 0	2 12 0	......	
	Jhamak Osta	0 5 0 0	3 0 0 0	...	0 9 2	0 12 0	......	
	Budhu Sahu	1 0 0 0	6 0 0 0	...	2 0 0	2 0 0	......	
	Talebar Mahton	1 8 0 0	8 0 0 0	...	3 0 0	2 12 0	......	
	Sobhan Mahton	1 8 0 0	8 0 0 0	...	3 0 0	2 12 0	......	
	Juar Mahton	1 8 0 0	8 0 0 0	...	3 0 0	2 12 0	......	
	Biku Mahton	4 9 0 0	26 0 0 0	...	8 12 6	9 0 0	9 0 0	
	Jhukree Mahton	4 9 0 0	26 0 0 0	...	8 12 6	9 0 0	19 0 0	
	Gokul Mahton	24 0 0 0	144 0 0 0	...	48 0 0	48 0 0	48 0 0	
	Lalju Kandu	3 10 0 0	21 0 0 0	...	7 0 0	7 0 0	16 0 0	
	Ramdhan Sahu	2 0 0 0	12 0 0 0	...	4 0 0	4 0 0	......	
	Amrit Mahton	1 10 0 0	9 0 0 0	...	3 0 0	3 0 0	......	
	Puran Mahton	1 10 0 0	9 0 0 0	...	3 0 0	3 0 0	......	
	Ram Mahton	1 10 0 0	9 0 0 0	...	3 0 0	3 0 0	......	
	Bandhu Mahton	10 0 0 0	60 0 0 0	...	30 0 0	20 0 0	......	
	Nowrungi Mahton... ...	5 0 0 0	30 0 0 0	...	10 0 0	10 0 0	......	
	Radhe Mahton	5 0 0 0	30 0 0 0	...	10 0 0	10 0 0	......	
	Bhasi Mahton	5 0 0 0	30 0 0 0	...	10 0 0	10 0 0	......	
	Khedan Mistry	1 10 0 0	9 0 0 0	...	3 0 0	3 0 0	......	
	Mohur Mistry	2 0 0 0	12 0 0 0	...	4 0 0	4 0 0	......	
	Amrit Mahton	2 0 0 0	12 0 0 0	...	4 0 0	4 0 0	......	
	Sakru Sahu	1 20 0 0	9 0 0 0	...	3 0 0	3 0 0	......	
	Musai Sahu	1 0 0 0	6 0 0 0	...	2 0 0	2 0 0	......	
	Pucha Sahu	1 0 0 0	6 0 0 0	...	2 0 0	2 0 0	......	
	Santu Sahu	0 13 0 0	3 20 0 0	...	0 15 9	1 6 0	......	
	Kali Sahu	0 13 0 0	3 20 0 0	...	0 15 9	1 6 0	......	
	Gopal Sahu	4 18 0 0	28 0 0 0	...	9 13 0	9 8 0	65 0 0	
	Parus Sahu	4 18 0 0	28 0 0 0	...	9 13 0	9 8 0	10 0 0	
	Dowlut Sahu	4 0 0 0	24 0 0 0	...	8 0 0	8 0 0	25 0 0	

1	2	3	4	5	6	7	8	9
Village.	CULTIVATORS.	Area of holdings.	Produce obtained.	The price for which that part of it not consumed for subsistence is sold.	Rent.	Expenses for cultivation.	The extent to which they are indebted.	REMARKS.
		B. K. C. D.	Mds. s. c. k.		Rs. A. P.	Rs. A. P.	Rs. A. P.	
7. Belha—*concld.*	Laljee Mahton	1 10 0 0	9 0 0 0	...	3 0 0	3 0 0	......	
	Tilak Mahton	1 10 0 0	9 0 0 0	...	3 0 0	3 0 0	......	
	Bulaki Mahton	1 10 0 0	9 0 0 0	...	3 0 0	3 0 0	......	
	Sukan Mahton	3 0 0 0	18 0 0 0	...	6 0 0	6 0 0	......	
	Modi Mahton	3 0 0 0	18 0 0 0	...	6 0 0	6 0 0	......	
	Namedhari Mahton ...	5 0 0 0	30 0 0 0	...	10 0 0	10 0 0	......	
	Ramdhan Mahton ...	5 10 0 0	33 0 0 0	...	11 0 0	11 0 0	25 0 0	
	Bhuttoo Sootiar	0 5 0 0	30 0 0 0	...	0 8 0	10 0 0	......	
	Krishnu Shah	0 10 0 0	3 0 0 0	...	1 0 0	1 0 0	......	
	Firangi Shah	0 10 0 0	3 0 0 0	...	1 0 0	1 0 0	......	
	Budhu Shah	0 10 0 0	3 0 0 0	...	1 0 0	1 0 0	......	
	Lotun Tanti	0 10 0 0	3 0 0 0	...	1 8 0	1 0 0	......	
	Modhi Tanti	1 0 0 0	6 0 0 0	...	3 0 0	2 0 0	......	
	Pheku Tanti	1 0 0 0	6 0 0 0	...	2 0 0	2 0 0	......	
	Mughu Tanti	1 10 0 0	9 0 0 0	...	3 0 0	3 0 0	20 0 0	
	Laljee Tanti	0 15 0 0	4 20 0 0	...	1 8 0	1 8 0	......	
	Chethru Tanti	0 15 0 0	4 20 0 0	...	1 8 0	1 8 0	......	
	Pheku Tanti	0 15 0 0	4 20 0 0	...	1 8 0	1 8 0	......	
	Bhola Chamar	0 10 0 0	3 0 0 0	...	1 0 0	1 0 0	......	
	Jhunmak Chamar	0 10 0 0	3 0 0 0	...	1 0 0	1 0 0	......	
	Nathu Sahu	2 0 0 0	12 0 0 0	...	4 0 0	4 0 0	10 0 0	
	Bhattu Gope	1 8 0 0	8 0 0 0	...	3 0 0	3 12 3	......	
	Jhakri Kandu	1 8 0 0	8 0 0 0	...	3 0 0	2 12 3	......	
	Jhonti Malee	0 10 0 0	3 0 0 0	...	1 8 0	1 0 0	......	
	Shyam Sahu	0 4 0 0	1 10 0 0	...	0 5 10	0 4 0	......	
	Gunee Sutiar	0 4 0 0	1 10 0 0	...	0 5 10	0 4 0	......	
	Khantar Hajjam	0 18 0 0	5 0 0 0	...	0 10 0	1 12 0	......	
	Dukha Mandar	29 13 0 0	177 20 0 0	...	29 8 0	59 6 0	100 0 0	For marriage ceremonies.
	Purai Mandar	29 0 0 0	174 0 0 0	...	29 0 0	58 0 0	50 0 0	
	Makun Mahton	29 0 0 0	174 0 0 0	...	29 0 0	58 0 0	10 0 0	
	Musan Tiar	3 15 0 0	22 20 0 0	...	7 8 0	7 8 0	25 0 0	
	Debi Mandar	3 15 0 0	22 20 0 0	...	7 8 0	7 8 0	20 0 0	
	Kali Sutiar	3 15 0 0	22 20 0 0	...	7 8 0	7 8 0	......	
	Raj Kumar Mandar ...	9 5 0 0	55 20 0 0	...	10 5 6	18 8 0	10 0 0	
	Musummat Asia	9 5 0 0	55 20 0 0	...	10 5 6	18 8 0	10 0 0	
	Sukan Mandar	2 0 0 0	12 0 0 0	...	4 0 0	4 0 0	......	
	Bundi Mandar	2 0 0 0	12 0 0 0	...	4 0 0	4 0 0	......	
	Mathan Duhiar	4 10 0 0	27 0 0 0	...	10 1 0	9 0 0	......	
	Gudar Duhiar	8 10 0 0	51 0 0 0	...	17 0 0	17 0 0	......	
	Gopal Mandar	24 10 0 0	147 0 0 0	...	18 5 0	49 6 0	50 0 0	
	Chetan Mandar	20 0 0 0	120 0 0 0	...	30 0 0	40 0 0	45 0 0	
	Lala Mandar	15 0 0 0	90 0 0 0	...	28 8 0	34 0 0	10 0 0	
	Shyam Mandar	10 0 0 0	60 0 0 0	...	20 0 0	20 0 0	20 0 0	
	Budhu Hajjam	0 5 0 0	1 20 0 0	...	0 6 0	0 8 0	......	
	Mansul Sahu	1 10 0 0	9 0 0 0	...	3 0 0	3 0 0	......	
	Chulhai Sahu	1 10 0 0	9 0 0 0	...	3 0 0	3 0 0	......	
	Pach Kowri Sahu	1 10 0 0	9 0 0 0	...	3 0 0	3 0 0	......	
	Bansi Sahu	1 10 0 0	9 0 0 0	...	3 0 0	3 0 0	......	
	Bisu Kalal	1 10 0 0	9 0 0 0	...	3 0 0	3 0 0	......	
	Kaji	1 8 0 0	8 0 0 0	...	3 0 0	2 12 0	......	
	Soman Chowkidar ...	3 0 0 0	18 0 0 0	...	6 0 0	6 0 0	10 0 0	
8. Bilori ...	Abdulla Khan	0 4 0 0	1 0 0 0	...	0 14 0	0 6 0	......	
	Bhuttoo Molajada ...	1 2 5 0	6 0 0 0	...	0 7 3	2 3 0	......	
	Kasim Momin	1 5 0 0	11 0 0 0	...	3 9 3	4 8 0	15 0 0	
	Fakeera Momin	1 2 0 0	10 20 0 0	...	0 11 5	4 3 0	......	
	Amir Momin	1 15 0 0	12 0 0 0	...	0 9 9	3 8 0	......	
	Gangu Momin	1 6 0 0	8 0 0 0	...	2 3 6	2 8 0	......	
	Kasim Khan	0 6 0 0	1 8 0 0	...	2 14 1	0 9 0	......	
	Roshun Momin	0 4 0 0	1 0 0 0	...	1 5 5	0 6 0	......	
	Mamuam Momin	0 6 0 0	1 8 0 0	...	1 2 3	0 9 0	......	
	Mannu Kahar	3 10 0 0	25 0 0 0	...	1 3 6	7 0 0	30 0 0	
	Jhonti Kahar	1 10 0 0	7 0 0 0	...	5 5 6	3 0 0	25 0 0	
	Manjhi Kahar	3 10 0 0	19 0 0 0	...	1 0 6	6 0 0	......	
	Musammut Dokhan Hajjam	1 15 0 0	11 0 0 0	...	3 15 3	3 8 0	......	
	Bhattu Tanti	4 0 0 0	28 0 0 0	...	11 11 3	8 0 0	......	
	Tilak Dhobi	6 2 0 0	42 0 0 0	...	15 1 9	12 0 0	......	
	Ajhori	2 12 10 0	17 0 0 0	...	7 6 3	5 3 0	20 0 0	
	Nulich Dosadh	1 10 0 0	10 20 0 0	...	5 0 0	3 0 0	......	
	Guhan Dosadh	8 14 0 0	59 0 0 0	...	19 10 9	17 0 0	......	
	Dhroop Dosadh	2 5 10 0	15 20 0 0	...	6 4 9	4 8 0	......	
	Budhu Dosadh	2 8 0 0	17 20 0 0	...	6 5 9	4 12 0	......	
	Sibcharn Dosadh	0 18 0 0	5 0 0 0	...	1 6 6	0 14 0	......	
	Jeeb Lall Pasi	5 10 0 0	35 0 0 0	...	31 13 6	11 0 0	......	
	Jhalu Pasi	6 18 0 0	41 0 0 0	...	26 5 6	12 14 0	......	
	Mahadeo Kumar	0 10 0 0	3 0 0 0	...	2 0 0	1 0 0	15 0 0	
		area	rent		produce	expense	debt	
9. Billo ...	Faka Koeri	8 5 0 0	5 6 17 0	...	16 0 0	7 0 0	10 0 0	
	Meghu Koeri	4 9 0 0	5 12 3 0	...	20 0 0	9 0 0	......	
	Bundhu Koeri	5 10 0 0	1 2 6 0	...	1 2 0	0 10 0	......	
	Mohun Koeri	2 6 0 0	2 14 4 0	...	11 15 0	5 0 0	......	
	Sukun Koeri	5 13 0 0	10 5 14 0	...	27 20 0	15 0 0	25 0 0	For marriage.
	Sukar Koeri	5 8 0 0	7 6 4 0	...	27 20 0	15 0 0	25 0 0	Ditto.
	Akal Koeri	31 11 0 0	40 9 0 0	...	155 0 0	62 0 0	50 0 0	Ditto.
	Degan Koeri	0 9 0 0	2 2 6 0	...	1 17 0	0 14 0	......	
	Goha Koeri	2 5 0 0	1 12 10 0	...	11 20 0	4 8 0	......	
	Andhar Koeri	2 5 0 0	1 12 10 0	...	11 20 0	4 8 0	......	
	Jicha Koeri	1 11 0 0	6 1 2 0	...	5 0 0	3 4 0	......	
	Meghon Koeri	6 17 0 0	7 2 10 0	...	33 20 0	13 8 0	......	
	Mungra Koeri	4 5 0 0	6 9 6 0	...	17 5 0	9 6 0	......	
	Jhukri Kandu	4 7 0 0	11 2 0 0	...	13 10 0	9 6 0	......	
	Chetu Kandu	8 0 0 0	2 3 9 0	...	1 13 0	1 0 0	......	
	Chamman Kandu	1 17 0 0	8 0 0 0	...	8 20 0	3 8 0	......	
	Ramdi Chamar	28 15 0 0	28 13 17 0	...	143 20 0	67 0 0	20 0 0	
	Latar Chamar	6 6 0 0	6 6 7 0	...	24 0 0	13 0 0	......	
	Gunee Chamar	3 5 0 0	4 2 10 0	...	13 0 0	6 0 0	......	
	Becha Chamar	10 1 0 0	9 7 0 0	...	50 0 0	20 0 0	20 0 0	
	Jeeb Lal Chamar	9 5 0 0	11 8 4 0	...	46 4 0	19 0 0	......	
	Bhoju Chamar	0 4 0 0	0 8 0 0	...	1 0 0	0 8 0	......	
	Dahu Tawa	2 1 0 0	1 12 4 0	...	10 0 0	4 0 0	......	
	Ghola Sonar	0 4 0 0	0 1 13 0	...	1 0 0	0 8 0	......	
	Damri Pasi	2 7 0 0	5 5 19 0	...	14 10 0	4 8 0	......	
	Bahari Pasi	1 14 0 0	3 6 6 0	...	0 6 7	4 2 0	......	

1	2	3	4	5	6	7	8	9
Village.	CULTIVATORS.	Area of holdings.	Produce obtained.	The price for which that part of it not consumed for subsistence is sold.	Rent.	Expenses for cultivation.	The extent to which they are indebted.	REMARKS.
		B. K. C. D.	MDS. S. C. K.		RS. A. P.	RS. A. P.	RS. A. P.	
9. Billo—*contd.*	Balaki Pasi	0 15 0 0	2 14 14 0	...	0 4 0	1 13 0	......	
	Bandhu Noniar	0 8 0 0	1 4 9 0	...	1 14 0	1 0 0	......	
	Teja Hazaree	6 8 0 0	15 4 3 0	...	21 13 0	15 0 0	7 0 0	
	Hardyal Hazaree	6 8 0 0	15 4 3 0	...	21 13 0	15 0 0	13 0 0	
	Sama Kahar	9 9 0 0	11 11 0 0	...	47 0 0	18 8 0	20 0 0	
	Dulwa Dhanuk	4 8 0 0	8 4 0 0	...	16 8 0	9 0 0	25 0 0	
	Hanuman Dhanuk ...	24 0 0 0	22 0 3 0	...	120 0 0	48 0 0	30 0 0	
	Rewa Kahar	5 4 0 0	8 8 3 0	...	12 8 0	7 8 0	18 0 0	
	Chintaman Kahar	5 0 0 0	8 0 0 0	...	15 0 0	6 0 0	......	
					M.			
	Himmat Garezi	2 8 0 0	3 9 14 0	...	12 35 0	5 0 0	......	
	Bodhu Gareri	2 16 0 0	11 5 5 0	...	9 0 0	7 4 0	......	
	Chamman Gareri	46 6 0 0	86 8 2 0	...	184 0 0	103 8 0	20 0 0	
	Chunderman Gope ...	2 16 0 0	11 8 6 0	...	9 0 9	7 4 0	10 0 0	
			Rent.					
	Raja Ram Gope	2 10 0 0	6 1 9 0	...	10 0 0	6 9 0	......	
	Manjhine Gope	2 13 0 0	7 14 9 0	...	11 8 0	5 12 0	......	
	Durshun Gope	2 13 0 0	7 14 9 0	...	11 8 0	5 12 0	......	
	Fool Singh Gope	2 4 0 0	2 15 7 0	...	11 20 0	5 0 0	......	
	Cheetun Gope	4 15 0 0	10 5 1 0	...	19 0 0	10 6 0	20 0 0	
	Bihasput Gope	3 12 0 0	10 9 7 0	...	14 8 0	2 9 0	......	
	Bigu Gope	9 10 10 0	16 8 2 0	...	33 8 0	24 0 0	......	
	Raju Gope	9 10 10 0	16 8 2 0	...	33 5 0	24 0 0	......	
	Gheena Gope	2 4 0 0	3 9 0 0	...	13 0 0	5 0 0	......	
	Pakhar Gope	3 11 0 0	8 9 0 0	...	13 0 0	5 0 0	......	
					M			
	Chulhan Gope	3 4 0 0	4 4 2 0	...	16 20 0	6 8 0	......	
					M			
	Degan Gope	4 18 0 0	6 2 11 0	...	23 0 0	9 0 0	......	
	Soukun Gope	0 4 10 0	1 4 0 0	...	0 16 0	0 7 0	......	
					M			
	Jhakrun Gope	19 6 0 0	25 10 3 0	...	96 0 0	39 0 0	......	
					M	Expense.		
	Teka Gope	19 17 0 0	16 1 10 0	...	53 0 0	21 0 0	......	
	Doman Gope	5 2 0 0	6 9 1 0	...	26 0 0	10 0 0	......	
	Jeetun Gope	0 15 5 0	2 10 4 0	...	4 0 0	1 12 0	......	
	Jungla Gope	0 15 5 0	2 10 4 0	...	4 0 0	1 12 0	......	
	Bhattu Gope	9 7 10 0	23 6 0 0	...	38 0 0	20 4 0	......	
	Rewat Gope	10 17 10 0	25 8 3 0	...	38 10 0	24 12 0	......	
	Himmat Dosadh	12 0 0 0	11 4 0 0	...	32 0 0	26 0 0	......	
	Jib Lall	4 0 0 0	4 9 11 0	...	24 0 0	8 0 0	......	
	Jangu Dosadh	13 15 0 0	16 4 17 0	...	65 0 0	28 0 0	......	
	Chuni Dosadh	7 8 0 0	0 12 3 0	...	35 0 0	14 0 0	......	
	Sanwan Dosadh	0 10 0 0	1 4 0 0	...	3 0 0	1 0 0	......	
	Bhikhari Dosadh	0 18 0 0	1 10 11 0	...	4 0 0	2 0 0	......	
	Uttim Dosadh	4 10 0 0	5 7 4 0	...	25 0 0	9 0 0	......	
	Bansi Dosadh	3 11 0 0	8 5 13 0	...	12½ 0 0	5 0 0	......	
		Area.	Produce.		Rent.	Expense.		
10. Dakra ...	Chulpan Gope	34 4 18 0	136 35 0 0	...	29 10 9	68 0 0	50 0 0	(Extent of debt for a marriage.
	Somur Gope	5 5 0 0	17 10 0 0	...	6 10 0	10 4 0	......	
	Sukun Gope	10 16 0 0	38 0 0 0	...	13 11 9	21 0 0	......	
	Chhukowri Singh	1 0 0 0	5 0 0 0	...	1 8 3	2 0 0	......	
	Andhi Dosadh	18 3 5 0	70 0 0 0	...	14 2 6	38 0 0	......	
	Dhansar Dosadh	7 12 0 0	30 15 0 0	...	7 12 0	16 0 0	......	
	Gurram Dosadh	9 4 12 0	22 0 0 0	...	8 9 9	23 0 0	......	
	Fool Chund Dosadh ...	14 18 11 0	48 15 0 0	...	20 4 3	29 4 0	......	
	Behari Sonar	8 7 10 0	40 0 0 0	...	11 11 3	17 0 0	......	
	Anbachh Burhi	9 4 8 0	45 0 0 0	...	16 13 3	19 0 0	......	
	Musru Burhi	4 10 4 0	18 0 0 0	...	6 9 4	9 0 0	......	

HERBERT MOSLEY,

Collector.

H. P.—Reg. No. 2480C—137 · 17-5-88.

CONFIDENTIAL.]

CONDITION OF THE MASSES.

No. 1M.A, dated Calcutta, the 17th May 1888.

From—A. Smith, Esq., Commissioner of the Presidency Division,
To—The Secretary to the Government of Bengal, Revenue Department.

With reference to your circular No. 35Agri., dated the 9th December last, and enclosures, I have the honour, after consulting the District Officers in this Division, to submit the following report regarding the condition of the lower classes of the population.

2. I regret the delay in the submission of this report; the reports from Nuddea and the 24-Pergunnahs were received only on the 10th and 12th April respectively. Further information had to be called for from Nuddea, which reached this office only on the 20th ultimo.

3. Owing to shortness of time the enquiries were restricted to limited areas, and the district reports could not be prepared as carefully and completely as the subject deserves. The information collected is not symmetrical, so that it is necessary to present it district by district.

4. The enquiries have been made in several typical villages in the manner suggested by Mr. Finucane.

5. For the purposes of the present enquiry the poorer classes have been divided into four classes, viz. cultivators, agricultural labourers, artizans, and those who subsist on charity—as suggested in paragraph 3 of your circular under reply. The Collector of the 24-Pergunnahs has, however, divided them into seven orders, viz. non-labouring classes, cultivators, labourers, artizans, beggars, fishermen, shop-keepers and traders.

6. The Collector of Nuddea observes that the above classification is simple enough; but until more definite instructions as to the practical application of this classification are given, the results arrived at, he is afraid, will be as diverse and as various as the number of officers consulted. The difficulties which meet the enquiring officers at the outset are that there is no distinct boundary to each class. A large body of the cultivators work as labourers both on their own lands and on the lands of others. Labourers have their jotes. Artizans work as common labourers, and also largely supplement their labour by farming on a small scale. Persons subsisting on charity do not so subsist all the year round. I agree in these remarks.

7. The Collector of Jessore has put in class I the cultivators with 10 bighas and upwards, and those with less than 10 bighas, but with enough to live on without working for daily wages; fishermen and those having some other calling being placed in class II. In class III have been included labourers and those with small means, and in class IV indigent people.

8. In Khoolna, under the head of cultivators, come all those who live by actual cultivation of the land. Agricultural labourers include all those whose chief means of subsistence is wages for work in cultivation. By artizans is understood all those who live mainly by the exercise of any trade or pursuit involving manual labour.

9. I have already observed that the enquiries have been made in several typical villages; of these the Collector of the 24-Pergunnahs has selected two from which the information is most complete, viz. Kamrabad in the Sudder sub-division and Dolchita in the Bussirhat sub-division. In the former the enquiries were made by the Sudder Sub-deputy Collector; in the latter by the Deputy Collector of Bussirhat. Similar enquiries have been made by the Sub-divisional Officers of Baraset and Diamond Harbour, and by the manager of the estate of the minor Baroda Prosad Rai Chowdhery, in three other villages within their respective jurisdictions; but the information given by these officers is of too general a character for such a detailed analysis as the Collector proposes to make. So far, however, as their reports go, they accord generally with the information obtained in respect of the two selected villages.

10. The inhabitants of the two selected villages comprise the following classes :—

Village.	Non-labouring classes.		Cultivators.		Labourers.		Artisans.		Beggars.		Fishermen.		Shop-keepers and traders.	
	Number of families.	Persons.	Number of families.	Persons.	Number of families.	Persons.	Number of families.	Persons.	Number of families.	Persons.	Number of families.	Persons.	Number of families.	Persons.
Kamrabad, Suddar sub-division.	28	Men ... 47 Women 53 Boys ... 45 Girls ... 24	33	Men ... 67 Women 71 Boys ... 52 Girls ... 27	16	Men ... 18 Women 22 Boys ... 15 Girls ... 12	11	Men ... 17 Women 19 Boys ... 19 Girls ... 6	3	Males ... 2 Females 4	...	......	...	.....
Dolchita, Bussirhat sub-division.	67	Men ... 83 Women 111 Boys ... 83 Girls ... 68	125	Men ... 208 Women 243 Boys ... 165 Girls ... 112	129	Men ... 143 Women 166 Boys ... 93 Girls ... 56	26	Men ... 31 Women 43 Boys ... 15 Girls ... 24	7	Men ... 4 Women 6 Boys ... 4 Girls ... 2	34	Men ... 53 Women 48 Boys ... 32 Girls ... 19	24	Men ... [illegible] Women [illegible] Boys ... [illegible] Girls ... [illegible]
Total ...	95	514	158	931	145	525	37	174	10	22	34	152	24	[illegible]
Average number of persons in each family	5·3		5·9		3·6		4·7		2·2		4·4		4·3	

I.—NON-LABOURING CLASS (INCLUDING CULTIVATORS WHO CULTIVATE THEIR LANDS BY MEANS OF HIRED LABOUR).

11. A notice of this class is not, strictly speaking, required by the Government orders ; but as the information has been collected, it may as well be recorded. Of the 95 families in Kamrabad and Dolchita, 81 families, comprising 456 persons, are in comfortable condition ; while 14 families, numbering 58 persons, are in straitened circumstances. The well-to-do families thus average 5·6 persons in each family, the others averaging only 4 persons to each family. This is what might have been expected. Those in indifferent circumstances belong to the decayed class of *bhodrolok*, who will not accept labourer's work, and will not stoop to beg openly. Extravagance, litigation and apathy have combined to reduce them to a condition which, whatever their faults may be, must excite our sympathy. Many of them practically subsist on the charity of their better-to-do kinsfolk and caste-fellows, removed only by the less ostentatious manner of giving and receiving alms from the class of professional beggars. The well-to-do non-labouring classes in the two sample villages hold lands either as petty landlords or as tenure-holders, and derive their means from cultivating the whole or part of their lands by hired labour and subletting the rest, if any ; from money-lending, services under Government or private employers, or some other more or less remunerative occupation.

II.—CULTIVATORS WHO CULTIVATE THEIR LANDS THEMSELVES WITHOUT HIRED LABOUR.

12. The 158 families of cultivators in the two selected villages hold between them 358 bighas of homestead and 1,892 bighas of ordinary arable lands. They pay Rs. 2,925 rent and Rs. 267 chowkidari tax and cesses. Thus, on an average, each family consists of 5·9 or say 6 persons and holds about 14 bighas at an initial cost of Rs. 20 per annum.

13. Of the 158 families of cultivators, as many as 116 were found to be in debt. Thirty-one families owe sums from Rs. 25 downwards, 35 owe from Rs. 26 to Rs. 50, 30 from Rs. 51 to Rs. 100, 9 from Rs. 101 to Rs. 150, 4 from Rs. 151 to Rs. 200, and 7 owe from Rs. 200 to Rs. 400. The debts amount in all to Rs. 8,387 or Rs. 53 per family, taking all 158 families. Taking indebted families only, each one's debt amounts to Rs. 72, or nearly the selling value of one year's crop. It does not, however, follow from this that the cultivating class is generally steeped in penury. There is scarcely a person among them with any credit who will not make use of it to its full extent, and it is quite possible that some of the remaining 42 families are not in debt, because they have not sufficient credit to justify the *mahajan* allowing them advances.

14. It is found that all of the 158 families are fully provided with the necessary agricultural implements and bullocks. They also, without a single exception, have the requisite brass and pewter utensils for cooking and other

domestic purposes, none of them being reduced to the use of earthen vessels. The women of 91 out of the 125 Dolchita families have silver ornaments and some few of them small gold ornaments, ranging in value from Rs. 10 to Rs. 30. The women of the remaining 34 families wear pewter and shell-lac ornaments. The women of most of the 33 Kamrabad families have also silver and a few of them gold ornaments.

III.—AGRICULTURAL LABOURERS.

15. The 145 families of labourers in the two selected villages hold between them 220 bighas of homestead lands for which they pay Rs. 575 rent, cesses and chowkidari-tax included. Their annual earnings are estimated at Rs. 7,297, or about Rs. 53 to each family of two to three adults and one child. This is in addition to what they make from the small plots of homestead lands which most of them hold. Deducting rent, &c., from their earnings, each family of three to four persons, one of whom is a child, would have Rs. 46 on which to live, besides the garden produce of its homestead plot of 1½ bighas. It is difficult, however, to ascertain with any degree of accuracy what the average earnings of day-labourers amount to in the year. The reports also do not show how many of the 145 families in the two selected villages hold homestead lands and how many have no lands at all. The Sub-divisional Officer of Baraset states that in the village of Nowpara, which he selected for the enquiry, out of 96 families of labourers, 59 have small holdings, while 37 families subsist upon labour alone. The rate of labour he lays at from 4 annas to 5 annas 3 pies per diem, and he stated that some labourers earn from Rs. 70 to Rs. 100 per annum. Mr. Forbes thinks that the Sub-divisional Officer of Baraset has possibly over-estimated the earnings of ordinary labour, but that the Deputy Collector of Bussirhat and the Sub-Deputy Collector have under-estimated them. The Sub-divisional Officer of Diamond Harbour states that the rate of unskilled labour is 3 to 4 annas a day and for skilled labour, such as that of a thatcher, 4 to 5 annas.

16. In the sub-divisions of Baraset and Bussirhat there appears to be little or no emigration or immigration of labourers, which seems to point to the fact that while there is no demand for outside labour, there is still sufficient employment to keep the resident labourers at their houses. In the large rice-producing tracts of the Diamond Harbour sub-division, the case is different. There labour is at certain times of the year in great demand, and not only do the resident labourers find sufficient employment, but labour has also to be imported, large batches of coolies coming from Midnapore and Orissa, and even so far as from Chota Nagpore, during the harvesting season. In this respect the rural parts of the Sudder sub-division resemble Bussirhat and Baraset rather than Diamond Harbour, except towards Canning and the Joynagar thana, where outside labour is annually required to assist in cutting the crops.

17. Of the 145 labouring families in the two selected villages, 95 are in debt to the extent of Rs. 3,990, or Rs. 42 per family, while 50 are free from debt. As with ordinary cultivators, so also in the case of labourers, these debts are contracted and wiped off in whole or part year by year. During the three or four harvest months in ordinary years, the circumstances of both classes are fairly easy, and the mahajan's account is settled so far as means and inclination permit. During the remaining months those who run through their stocks owing to bad seasons or extravagance have to turn to him again and borrow, as they also occasionally do when they are in need of marriage and *Shrad* expenses, and their credit justifies the loan.

18. With both classes (cultivators and labourers) good seasons go to balance bad seasons in the matter of the mahajan's bill. During times of scarcity heavier debts are incurred which are paid off in years of plenty. In ordinary years balance of accounts is fairly maintained. It is in the nature of a native of the lower classes, and for that matter often of higher classes as well, to accept advances whenever he can get them. Indebtedness seldom means starvation, but usually quite the reverse.

19. All but six of the 145 families of agricultural labourers in the two selected villages have brass vessels for domestic use. The other six have only

earthen utensils. In about five out of every eight families, the women have cheap silver ornaments, the women of the other families wearing pewter and brass anklets and bangles. On the whole the condition of the agricultural labourer in this district does not appear to differ very much from that of the poorest of the ryots who cultivate their own lands. Each has equally to practise thrift, and although the cultivator can offer better security, yet his superior credit is apt to lead him further into debt, whilst he has always good season or bad season to meet the landlord's rent.

20. The foregoing remarks as regards both cultivators and labourers apply principally to the northern, western, and central portions of the 24-Pergunnahs district in which the two selected villages lie. The circumstances of these people in the southern portion, including the Diamond Harbour sub-division with its large rice-producing tracts, are, comparatively speaking, more favourable. The last census returns go to show this ; for while there was a decrease in population in the Barrackpore, Dum-Dum, and Baraset sub-divisions, and in the home thana of the Sudder sub-division, there was a large increase in the Diamond Harbour sub-division and in the southern and eastern parts of the Bussirhat and Sudder sub-divisions, in which directions the rice cultivation is year by year extending. The conclusions drawn by the Sub-divisional Officer of Diamond Harbour are that the cultivators in his sub-division are generally in a prosperous condition, while as regards the labourers he says—

"They are well off for the first three months after the harvesting season, but experience some difficulty during the next nine months, though not to the extent of actual insufficiency of food, for they have the means of supplying their wants from the mahajan's stock, which appears to be sufficient to carry them on from one harvest to another. I speak of ordinary good years, and my enquiries have led me to believe that this sub-division always enjoys ordinary good years. In bad years the proper classes have labour within easy reach out of their homes, and therefore stand little chance of actual suffering."

IV.—ARTIZANS.

21. There are 37 families of artizans of all kinds in the two selected villages. They number four and seven members in each family. Between them they hold 133 bighas of land (or between three and four bighas per family) for which they pay Rs. 263 rent, cesses, &c. Their estimated earnings from their different trades aggregate Rs. 2,957, leaving, after deducting rent, &c., Rs. 2,694, or Rs. 73 per family net earnings, besides the whole of the produce of their holdings. Twenty families are in debt to the amount of Rs. 1,369, or Rs. 93 each, the remaining 17 being free from debt. In most of them the women have silver ornaments, and they all possess brass utensils.

22. The artizans, as a class, are doubtless better off than agricultural labourers, and in many instances their condition is better than that of cultivators who cultivate their own lands. But there are extreme cases of poverty among them, such as that of weavers, seldom to be met with among the other classes. The only help for these people is to seek work in factories either in place of or to supplement their home manufactures. This is what they appear to be doing, and the Sub-divisional Officer of Baraset gives an example of two out of three weaver families in Nowpara, who have sent two of their members to work in a jute factory where they are each earning the very respectable pay of Rs. 10 per mensem.

23. In the suburban and municipal areas extending some 40 miles along the bank of the Hooghly, north and south of Calcutta, a large number of hands, estimated at from 40,000 to 50,000, are employed in the various jute and cotton presses and mills, brick, shell-lac, sugar and other factories, in oil and rice mills, and in the Government gun-foundry, small-arms and ammunition works, and other industries. The labour is partly indigenous and partly imported, and as regards both scale of wages and regularity of payment the work people are certainly in a better position than agricultural labourers, and are probably as well off as most other artizans.

24. *Fishermen.*—The Government orders do not specially refer to this class. It is, however, numerically speaking, an important one in a district like

the 24-Pergunnahs, intersected with numerous *khals* and *jhils*, and requires some notice. In one of the selected villages there are no persons of this caste. In the other there are 34 families each averaging four to five persons. In other words, each family finds food for one person more than a labourer's family, and for one person less than an ordinary cultivator's family. Like agricultural labourers, these people usually hold small plots of homestead lands. In the village of Dolchitta, the 34 families hold between them 29 bighas. Their annual earnings from their trade are estimated at Rs. 2,584, which, after deducting Rs. 74 rent and taxes, leaves an income of Rs. 74 per family, besides the produce of its small plot of land. Twenty-two of these families owe debts to the sum of Rs. 1,232, or Rs. 56 each, the remaining 12 being free from debt. The women of 18 families wear simple silver ornaments; those of 16 pewter and shell-lac.

25. These people have an advantage over agricultural labourers in being able to supply themselves with a material portion of their food-supply. On the whole their means appear to fall between those of the labouring and cultivating classes.

Beggars.—The number of beggars—persons openly living on charity—in the two selected villages is 24, or one per cent. of total population. Their indigence is indicated by the smallness of their families, averaging only from two to three persons. In the village of Nowpara, in the Baraset sub-division, there are eight families, numbering only 12 persons. Probably one per cent. may be taken as the general proportion of beggars to total population in the northern and western parts of the district. In the large rice tracts to the south and east they do not appear to be so numerous. The Sub-divisional Officer of Diamond Harbour says:—

"The number of persons living upon charity is very small indeed. There is one class of persons, viz. the Boirageos, who receive alms; but the number of this class is very small in this sub-division, and many of them even hold lands."

27. Mr. Forbes has made the following general remarks:—

"The general conclusions to which the result of the enquiries points are that while the upper classes of cultivators, holding directly from the zemindar, are in easy and independent circumstances, the under-tenants, though paying comparatively high rates of rent, are still able with ordinary care to provide themselves with a sufficiency of food and clothing and other necessaries; that the demand for labour is equal to, and at certain seasons more than equal to, the indigenous supply, and persons in search of work can usually find it within easy reach of their homes; and that there is no cause for anxiety under any ordinary circumstances, such as have obtained for many years past, as regards any class of the labouring population suffering from an insufficiency of food-supply."

28. The following is the result of the enquiries made by the Collector of Nuddea in different parts of his district. He has denominated the villages in which the enquiries have been made alphabetically:—

Group I.	Families.	Population.
Village A	200	1,391

This population is divided as follows:—

44	Families of cultivators	numbering	403 persons.
56	„ of labourers	„	334 „
27	„ of weavers	„	210 „
22	„ of tailors	„ ...	175 „
15	„ of carpenters	„	105 „
13	„ of beggars	„	39 „
7	„ of domestic servants	„	35 „
2	„ of shop-keepers	„	4 „
7	„ of potters	„	69 „
3	„ of jotedars	„	14 „
2	„ of Mussulmans	„	6 „

29. The village of which the above analysis is given is a village of considerable prosperity. Of the 44 families of cultivators, four families sell vegetables, having small garden plots, but no oxen or plough. Of the

remaining 40, 18 have their own small farms or holdings, and 22 hold lands on the *burga* system, giving half produce of the land they cultivate to the holders and occupiers; practically they are little better than labourers on the co-operative system. Of these 40 families, 25 have one plough, eight have two ploughs, two have three ploughs, three have four ploughs, one family has five ploughs, and one has no plough. Each plough necessitates the possession of two yoke of oxen. In the family having five ploughs there are twenty-one members, the family pays Rs. 130-6 rent, and holds 100 bighas of land. The family having no plough numbers 12 members, pays rent to the extent of Rs. 6-8, and holds four bighas of land. Of the three families each having four ploughs, one family, consisting of 15 members, holds 12 bighas of land of their own at a yearly rent of Rs. 12, and 36 bighas which is cultivated on the *burga* system. A second family of 23 members holds 60 bighas of land at Rs. 67-12; they hold no *burga* land. The third family, consisting of 17 members, holds four bighas at Rs. 4 per annum, and 44 bighas on the *burga* system. Of the two families having three ploughs each, one family, consisting of 20 members, holds three bighas of land at a rent of Rs. 3, and 33 bighas of *burga* land; the second consisting of 24 members holds 12 bighas at a rent of Rs. 19 and 24 bighas on the *burga* system. It does not appear that the number of members in a family much affects its prosperity; the prosperity of a family appears to be regulated by the number of ploughs it can afford to keep in work.

30. Of the families having two ploughs each, it will suffice to say that they consists of families of from 12 to 6 members each; that they hold from 20 to 24 bighas of land chiefly on the *burga* system. Three families of them hold jama land to the extent of 6 bighas and 12 bighas respectively.

31. Of the families having one plough, the number of members appears to be from 4 to 10, and the land they hold from 10 to 12 bighas. The land is generally held on the *burga* system. It appears from the above that the majority of the cultivators have no land of their own, and hold 10 or 12 bighas of *burga* land only. This shows that the occupants of these lands have ceased to cultivate. Taking the case of one family of cultivators consisting of four persons, their circumstances are as follow:—

	Rs. A. P.
Rent	13 8 0
	Bgs.
Land ...	12
	No.
Cattle	4
Aus paddy	4
Aman	5
	Bish.
Produce	6
	Rs. A. P.
Value	60 0 0
	Bgs.
Land producing *kalas* ...	2
	No.
Matar	10
	Rs. A. P.
Value of both	24 0 0
Expenses of cultivating paddy	6 0 0
Total or gross value of produce	84 0 0
Net income	64 8 0

32. Taking another case, the number of persons in family being 8, rent Rs. 19-5; land 16 bighas; cattle three heads; *aus* paddy six bighas, *aman* six bighas; produce six bishes; value Rs. 60; land producing peas 12; value of crop Rs. 24; cost of cultivation Rs. 6; gross value Rs. 84; income Rs. 58-11. This family also serves and earns by that means Rs. 60 per annum.

33. Of the 58 families of labourers, three families only hold land. One family of 10 members holds 20 bighas at Rs. 27, a second family of six persons holds four bighas at Rs. 6, and a third family, consisting of six persons, holds three bighas at Rs. 38. Daily wages when work is to be had on 3 annas. The remaining 58 families subsist by day labour only. They get work for nine months in the year. In the harvest time each labourer is reported to be able to earn as much paddy in lieu of wages as will last him for three months; he is thus provided for during his idle season. All the cultivators in this village are said to be more or less indebted. The causes are various and need not be discussed. Both cultivators and labourers are more or less the slaves of mahajan's and the so-called *bhodrolok*.

34. The remaining population of the village consists of well-to-do people with whom this report has nothing to do. Coming to artizans and beggars, the weavers have lands which they let out and have in their own possession; their manufactures are exported; they are well-to-do. Tailors, carpenters and potters are also all well-to-do. The number of families dependent on the charity of others was 13 only. They are chiefly destitute females or old childless persons. In bad seasons these people are badly off. Every year makes their condition worse, as the struggle for life in the other classes grows harder. It is to this class, viz. that of destitute paupers, the attention of Government should be first directed.

35. *Village B.*—Two hundred and twenty-six families, 997 souls. Of these 77 families are actual cultivators, 63 families have one plough each, and 14 two ploughs each.

36. Taking the case of a family of 15 persons having two ploughs, their circumstances are as follow :—

		Rs. A. P.	
Rent	... ...	37 8 0	
		Bgs.	
Land	... ...	30	
Aus	... ...	28	112 maunds yield.
Aman	... ...	28	56 ditto.
		Rs. A. P.	
Value of *rabi* crops	... ...	30 0 0	
Turmeric	... ...	25 0 0	
Sugarcane	... ...	40 0 0	
		No.	
Cows	... ...	3	
Plough cattle	... ...	8	
		Rs. A. P.	
Value of paddy	... ...	168 0 0	
Total income	.. ..	263 0 0	
Net income	... ...	225 8 0	

37. This family appears to be more prosperous than most such families, but it has been taken without special selection. The members of it do not labour and they are not indebted. Taking the case of another family of four persons having one plough, their circumstances are as follow :—

		Rs. A. P.	
Rent	... ...	18 12 0	
		Bgs.	
Land	... ...	15	
Aus	... ...	13	yield 52 maunds.
Aman	... ...	13	" 26 "
		Rs. A. P.	
Value of *rabi*	... ...	15 0 0	
Value of turmeric	... ...	25 0 0	
Value of sugarcane	... ...	45 0 0	
		No.	
Cows	... ...	2	
Plough cattle	... ...	4	
		Rs. A. P.	
Gross income	... ...	163 0 0	
Deducting for labour and rent	...	96 4 0	only.

38. This family also is not indebted. The number of families living on charity in village B is 16, numbering 32 persons; they are supported uncomplainingly by the rest of the population in good seasons; in bad seasons they have to manage for themselves, more or less getting relief from the Government or the general public. All the artizans of the village are prosperous; they are chiefly weavers, tailors, carpenters, and thatchers. They find work as well beyond as in the village precincts. It is impossible to ascertain with any degree of accuracy what their earnings are. Suffice it to say that they find their handicraft more profitable than cultivation, for though most of these families have land, they let it. Thatchers and house-builders earn easily Rs. 7-8 per mensem. Labourers are not badly off or generally indebted in this village.

39. *Village C.*—In this village there are 133 families and a population of 656 persons distributed as follows:—

38 families of cultivators.	10 families of weavers.
12 ditto of labourers.	3 ditto of beggars.

The remaining 70 families are not accounted for, because they are not included in any of the above classes, being petty landlords, tailors, clerks, &c.

40. There are four families of cultivators paying each Rs. 20 per annum rent, and one other family paying Rs. 27. These five families appear to be pretty well off, but the remaining families having one plough only are badly off. The rents paid by them average Rs. 9. Labourers and weavers are not well-to-do.

41. Generally with reference to the neighbourhood in which the villages A, B, and C of group 1 are situated, the Bengali peasant's condition has improved vastly within the last 30 years owing to the increased cultivation of jute, turmeric, sugarcane, and winter crops. Families of six persons and over with one plough and 10 or 12 bighas of land are generally indebted and have to pay from 25 to 37½ per cent. interest for advances. Beggars and paupers do not in ordinary years extend one per centum of the population.

42. *Group* 2.—Villages D, E, and F are situated in the south of the district. These three villages are purely agricultural, with population as follows:—

				Families.
D—Thana Chaydah	...	...	..	75
E— Ditto	...	...	...	100
F—Thana Harinhatta	...	...	...	128

Division of the population.

				D.	E.	F.
				75	100	128
Cultivator	...	...	...	44	60	72
Agricultural labourers	...	...	...	22	30	36
Artisans	...	...	...	...	1	2
Beggars	...	...	...	1	...	2
Others	...	...	...	8	9	16

Area of holdings.

D.	Bgs.	Bgs.	E.	Bgs.	Bgs.	F.	Bgs.	Bgs.
3 ryots have	70		10 ryots have	60		5 ryots have	80	
13 ditto	40		15 ditto	30 to	33	18 ditto	60 to	80
15 ditto	20 to	25	15 ditto	15 ,,	20	12 ditto	30 ,,	40
14 ditto	10 ,,	15	20 ditto	10 ,,	15	25 ditto	20 ,,	25
						12 ditto	10 ,,	15

Those who have less than 10 bighas are not considered in these and other villages as "cultivators," but as labourers, though they cultivate their land by hired ploughs, and thus supplement their wages of labour by the produce of their small holdings.

43. Proportion of the various crops of the different holdings—

In D.—The ryot with holding of 70 bighas cultivates—

	Bgs.		Bgs.
Aus	20	Tobacco	10
Aman	30	Jute	5

and has to give 5 bighas to his hired labourers as part of their wages.

Ryot with 40 bighas cultivates—

	Bgs.		Bgs.
Aus	10	Jute	4
Aman	20	Tobacco	6

Ryot with 20 bighas cultivates—

	Bgs.		Bgs.
Aus	7	Jute	2
Aman	8	Tobacco	3

Ryot with 10 to 15 bighas cultivates 3 or 4 with *aus*, 3 or 4 with *aman*, and 1 or 2 bighas with tobacco and jute each.

In F.—The ryot with a holding of 80 bighas appropriates 13 bighas to tobacco, 28 to *aus*, 35 to *aman*, and allows 3 or 4 bighas to remain uncultivated to recruit.

A ryot with 55 to 60 bighas devotes 10 bighas to tobacco, 20 to *aus*, 26 to *aman*.

A holding of 35 to 40 bighas will be cultivated with tobacco 6 or 7 bighas, *aus* 16, and the rest with *aman*.

Holdings of 20 to 25 bighas will have—

4 bighas tobacco. | 10 bighas *aman*.
8 ditto *aus*.

Holdings of 15 bighas will have—

2 bighas tobacco. | 8 bighas *aman*.
5 ditto *aus*.

Holdings of 10 bighas will have—

4 or 5 bighas *aus*. 5 or 6 bighas *aman*.

The whole or nearly the whole of the *aus* land will produce a second or *rabi* crop.

44. Produce obtained per bigha—

	D.	E.	F.
	Mds.	Mds.	Mds.
Aus	10½	8½	8
Aman	11	10½	10½
Tobacco	4½	...	4
Jute	5	6	...
Oilseeds	(Not grown here.)		2½
Pulses	2	2	2

45. The figures for produce given above represent a good average out-turn. In good fields and favourable seasons as much as 12 maunds of paddy, 6 maunds of tobacco, 8 maunds of jute, 3 maunds of oilseeds, and 3 maunds of pulses, such as peas, musur, mug, &c., are produced. Besides the paddy obtained from *aus* and *aman* fields, the cultivator gets one khan or 1,280 bundles of straw, valued at Rs. 3 or Rs. 3-8. The pulse stalks are used as fodder and the mustard and linseed stalks as fuel.

46. Rate of rent per bigha—

	D.			E.			F.		
	Rs.	A.	P.	Rs.	A.	P.	R.	A.	P.
Aman	1	8	0	1	12	0	1	8	0
Aus	1	12	0	2	0	0	1	0	0
Tobacco	2	0	0	......			2	0	0

The above are the prevailing rates, but holders of old jotes pay in the lump a smaller sum than new ryots.

47. The cost of cultivating, including rent per bigha, is—

	D.			E.			F.		
	Rs.	A.	P.	Rs.	A.	P.	Rs.	A.	P.
Aus	7	0	0	7	0	0	6	0	0
Aman	6	0	0	5	8	0	5	4	0
Tobacco	15	0	0	......			17	0	0
Jute	7	0	0	7	0	0	......		

Oilseeds, Pulses.—No cost is incurred for raising these second crops. The land (*aus* land) has to be ploughed after the rains, whether a second crop is raised or not, and the cost of this plough is taken into account in calculating the cost of *aus*. The price of seed, which is very small, and the cost of reaping, are the only expenditure to be deducted from the value of the produce. The second crop is wholly a profit.

48. The profit from each bigha of *aus* is—

	D.	E.	F.
	Rs.	Rs.	Rs.
From paddy	3½	1½	1
" straw	3½	3½	3½
Second.			
Crop of pulses	3	3	3½
Of oilseeds	7	7	7

In the first two villages oilseeds are not produced to any extent evidently because the soil is not fit for them. The above calculation is based upon the supposition that paddy sells at Re. 1 per maund, and pulses at Re. 1-8, and mustard and linseed at Rs. 3-8 per maund. If the prices are higher, as they frequently are, the profit is large.

Of *aman* (at Re 1 per maund)—

	D.	E.	F.
	Rs.	Rs.	Rs.
From paddy	5	5	5½
" straw	3½	3½	3½

Of tobacco Rs. 21 at Rs. 8 a maund, 23 (at Rs. 10 per maund).
Of jute D, Rs. 13 (at Rs. 4 per maund), Rs. 17E (at Rs. 4 per maund).

Taking an account of the agricultural operations of a ryot with a holding of bighas 70 in village D, we get a profit of Rs. 140 from paddy and straw of 20 bighas of *aus*.

	Rs.
From pulses	60
" amun paddy and straw of 30 bighas	255
" 10 bighas of tobacco	210
" 5 bighas of jute	65
Total ...	730

The ryot with a small holding of 10 to 15 bighas will have a profit of Rs. 144.

49. From the information given above the profits of ryots of other class of this and the other villages named can easily be obtained.

50. The cost of cultivation has been calculated on the supposition that the cultivator or the members of his family do nothing, and that everything is done by hired ploughs and labour. As a matter of fact, however, the greater portion of the cost of cultivation is earned by the cultivator, and his brothers, sons or nephews. Servants have to be employed by holders of such big jotes as 70 or 80 bighas, even if there are several adult male members in the family. But as stated above a greater portion of the amount shown as cost of cultivation remains in the cultivator's family.

51. It is now necessary to ascertain the expense the ryots of different classes have to incur for maintenance, as until that is done the price of surplus produce not required for consumption cannot be ascertained.

In D it is reported that each of the three ryots holding 70 bighas has 15 to 18 members in the family; ryots with a holding of 40 bighas 9 persons in the family; ryots with a holding of 25 bighas usually have 5 or 6 persons; those with a holding of 10 or 15 bighas, 4 or 5.

Most of the labourers have three or four persons to support.

A substantial ryot reported that the consumption required for his family amounted to 200 maunds of paddy and 10 maunds of *dál*. He has to buy salt Rs. 12, oil Rs. 40, spices Rs. 12, fish and vegetables about Rs. 24, cloth Rs. 60, and to spend Rs. 50 in repairing the house. Taking Re. 1 as the price of paddy, and Rs. 1-8 as the price of *dál*, the total expenditure comes to Rs. 413. It has been shown that the profit of this ryot is Rs. 730. He has to spend some money almost every year in buying one or two bullocks. The expenditure for marriages and other social ceremonies is incurred occasionally.

52. The second class of ryots or men with 40 bighas consume about 100 maunds of paddy, and other articles in proportion.

Third class	...	...	...	70 maunds.
Fourth "	...	...	...	60 "
Labourers	...	...	...	50 "

The ryot with 70 bighas has 20 bighas of *aus*, and this at the rate of 10½ maunds would yield 210 maunds of paddy. He has 30 bighas under *aman*, and the produce is 11 maunds per bigha, or 330 maunds the whole. He has therefore 540 maunds, of which he requires 200 maunds for domestic consumption. He can sell or lend 340 maunds. He gets about 40 maunds of pulses and he consumes 10 maunds. He can and does sell 30 maunds. He sells the whole of his jute and his tobacco. The straw is used in feeding his cattle, but the surplus, if any, is sold or used in thatching his house :—

The price of the surplus grain and other articles not required for domestic use is therefore—

						Rs.
Paddy	...	...	...	...	...	340
Pulses	...	...	...	...	...	45
Tobacco	...	...	...	...	...	360
Jute	...	...	...	...	...	100
				Total	...	845

From the sale proceeds of these articles he has to pay the rent, wages of servants, and day-labourers, and for the articles of consumption, cloth, &c., which he has to buy, as well as to meet the outlay on repairs of house, replacing dead or useless bullocks, and other extraordinary expenditure. Ryots of this class do not usually sell the paddy, but keep it in hand and lend it at interest.

53. Taking the case of the third class, that is, a ryot with 20 or 25 bighas, we find that he cultivates 8 bighas of *aus* and 8 of *aman*, and gets 84 maunds and 88 maunds respectively, or 172 maunds on the whole; he consumes 70 maunds, and there is a surplus of 102 maunds. He gets—

						Rs.
From tobacco	...	...	...	...	...	108
" pulses	...	...	...	...	...	24
" jute, or altogether		...	...	...	...	40
				Total	...	274

54. The Collector has already allowed the quantity of rice he will consume, and deducting from the sale proceeds Rs. 274, the other expenditure for consumption, cloth, and repairs at one-third of the first class ryot, or Rs. 71, there remains a sum of Rs. 203 for payment of rent, cost of cultivation, and extraordinary expenditure. There is apparently no need to borrow, but as a matter of fact ryots of this class, and even those of a higher class, have to

borrow every year. The fact is, having been compelled to borrow in a bad year, or on account of a social ceremony or marriage, they find it difficult to extricate themselves from the debt of the mahajan with its heavy rate of interest. This brings me to the next subject for enquiry, viz. the extent of debt. I should commence by saying that debt is contracted only by cultivators and not by labourers ; in fact landless labourers, or poor cultivators, with very small jotes, are unable to borrow. If people of this class require a lump sum of money, they engage to serve some well-to-do cultivator for a certain term, and get the requisite advance.

55. In D, where there are 44 actual cultivators, 3 do not borrow, but can afford to lend money and paddy to their neighbours ; 9 have no necessity to borrow ; 15 are too poor to get credit, and 17 families borrow. That is about 38 per cent. of the cultivators borrow. Some of these 17 ryots borrow food for one month, some for 3 months and a few for 5 months. These borrow paddy in May or June and repay in August or September with 37½ per cent. interest in kind for the few months interveneing between the taking of the loan and the repayment. Many ryots have to borrow money for a short time for payment of rent, and these debts are contracted at the rate of 24 or 30 per cent. per annum. These are in the nature of temporary accommodations contracted when the crops are ready, but have not been actually sold. With a view to sell the crop to the best advantage, but at the same time to meet the pressing demand of the landlord, this money debt is contracted, but repaid within a short time. Money debts for marriages and other social ceremonies are contracted occasionally, that is, twice or thrice during the lifetime of a man. But many make wrong starts with a debt contracted for their marriages either by themselves or their fathers, and remain handicapped with it all their lives. To this must be added the debt they are obliged to incur in bad seasons, and the high rate of interest. In spite of this, owing to the removal of restrictions on the cultivation of lucrative crops, the opening out of the country by rail and other roads, and the numerous other advantages brought about by the English rule, the material condition of the ryots and of all classes connected with agriculture has greatly improved and is improving every day. Ryots with 25, 20, 15 bighas or less usually borrow. We have seen that they require about 50 or 60 maunds of paddy a year. The largest borrower therefore does not borrow more than 20 or 25 maunds of paddy, the value of which is as many rupees. It is admitted by all the ryots that the wife of the poorest ryot has more than that amount in silver and gold on her person, and if the ryot felt the burden of the debt very heavily he could at once pay off by selling the jewels. The debt is kept on partly from habit and partly, it is said, to keep up a connection with the mahajan whose assistance may be needed when crops have seriously failed, and when there is a litigation. The mahajan is an institution which the ryots think it worth while to support even at the sacrifice of a certain quantity of paddy in the shape of interest. The mahajan himself occasionally oppresses his debtors, but protects him from the oppression of the zemindar or others, and saves him from starvation in seasons of scarcity.

56. In E, where there are 60 cultivators, 30 do not borrow and the remaining 30 borrow to the following extent :—15 borrow paddy for five months' consumption, 12 borrow paddy for three months' consumption, three borrow for a month or less. The rate of interest is 25 or 37½ per cent. according as the ryot is solvent or poor. The poorer and the less punctual debtors have to pay the higher rate of interest.

Wages given to labourers of different classes in the several villages where enquiry was made are—

57. In D, an able-bodied agricultural servant gets Rs. 6-8 per month. He gets also 1 bigha or 25 cottahs of land from the employer. The servant pays the rent, but all the cost of cultivation has to be borne by the employer. A sum of Rs. 12 will have to be advanced to him, and be recovered in 12 monthly instalments of Re. 1. If the servant happens to be a resident of another village than that of his employer, he will get Rs. 3 a month as salary, and also food, cloth and land as mentioned above.

A juvenile labourer of less than 17, but capable of doing half as much work as an adult able-bodied man, gets Rs. 2 as salary, food, cloth and one bigha of land.

A rakhal or cowherd gets Re. 1-4, food, cloth and half a bigha of land.

Day-labourers receive 3 annas 3 pie or 4 annas per day according to the season. The higher rate is paid during pressure of agricultural operations such as transplanting, harvesting, &c.

58. In E, an adult agricultural servants gets Rs. 5 monthly, a little oil and some food every day, and one dhoti and one gamoha a year, and a bigha of land under the same condition as stated in the case of D.

Juvenile labourers get Rs. 2½ and one meal, as well as a bigha of land.

Rakhals yet 6 to 12 annas, 2 meals, cloth, and 10 cottahs of land.

Wages for the day 3 annas 3 pie to 4 annas.

59. In E 3 annas 3 pie a day is given to day-labourers; servants get food, Rs. 3 salary, and one cloth in winter; land is not usually given. One class of servants employed for a short time in making bales of tobacco gets one meal and Rs. 4-8 per month.

The custom of paying in kind does not prevail to any great extent, though, if the servant or labourer asks for paddy, or if the employer has no ready cash, paddy is given.

60. Many of the labourers have small plots of land. The distinction between small cultivators and labourers lies in this, that a man who has a plough and oxen is called a *chasa* or cultivator, and he that has no plough or oxen for tilling his small holding is known as a *mojoor* or labourer. It is rare to find a man or even a widow without some land. The greater part of the paddy required for consumption is obtained by most labourers from their own fields. But even those who have no land get enough for their maintenance, and there is no such thing at present as living upon insufficient food. We will take the case of a labourer without any land, and four members in the family, viz. the man, his wife and two children, one a boy and the other a girl. He will require daily two seers of rice or a maund and a half a month. He will not buy cleaned rice from the bazar, but paddy in the village, which his wife will boil, dry and husk. In his case a maund of cleaned rice will cost Rs. 1-4, or at Rs. 1-8 for 60 seers he will have to pay Rs. 2-4. His salt, oil, dâl, and spices will not cost him more than six pies a day; but even if we allow it at the rate of one anna a day, his total expenditure will come to Rs. 4-2. He gets, as has been shown, Rs. 5 to Rs. 6½ a month and about 10 maunds of paddy from the land he got from his employer. If he gets Rs. 5 he saves 14 annas a month or Rs. 10-8 a year, and another Rs. 10, the value of paddy. He has to buy at most Rs. 7 worth of cloth, for it is admitted even by well-to-do ryots that for ordinary wear the men require cloth worth Rs. 2, females Rs. 3, and children Re. 1. The Collector has taken a bad case, but still there is no starvation nor even more stinting than that observed amongst the cultivating class. If the son of this labourer is five years old, he is no longer a burden upon the father. He not only earns his own bread as a cow-keeper, but actually assists the family; for he gets yearly from Rs. 4½ to Rs. 15 food, and half a bigha of land, or say five maunds of paddy. A female child does not earn anything but she brings at her marriage about Rs. 100 to Rs. 200 to the father, and is useful to the mother as soon as she learns to work. If this man has a cow, it is a source of some gain and supplies all the fuel required by the family, for only cow-dung cakes are burnt. Male children, whether of the agriculturist or of the labourer, begin to earn or become useful from the 5th year, and women and female children do all the household work, as well as husking the paddy and making cow-dung cakes. Agricultural labourers are fully employed, and at times the want of more labourers is felt. There is a slack season, but it is of short duration, and those who work as day-labourers make up for this by charging higher wages in the busy season. On the average they earn six rupees a month. That the agricultural labourers are fully employed is evident from the circumstance that they cannot be induced to work on the roads. Whenever a road has to be repaired in the south of this district, the contractor has to import up-countrymen for the work.

61. There are no weavers in the villages in which this enquiry was made, and no other artizans except two or three blacksmiths or kamars. There can be no doubt that weavers have been reduced to great poverty in many parts of the country. As regards other artizans, such as goldsmiths, carpenters, braziers, potters, &c., they are very well off and never earn less than

Rs. 12 or Rs. 15 a month. Blacksmiths who reside in rural villages also earn as much. Each kamar makes about a 100 ploughs a year. For making these ploughs and repairing them and other agricultural implements he gets from Rs. 100 to Rs. 150 a year. The making and repairing of these tools takes about 100 days, and the remaining 265 days he employs himself in making knives, *daws*, *kodalies*, &c., which he sells at fairs or bazars. An indifferent blacksmith or carpenter will not consent to work as a servant for less than Rs. 12 a month, and if he works on his own account he earns much more. Artizans residing in rural villages have, like other ryots, lands for cultivation.

62. The number of idle persons who subsist on charity is much less now than it was a few years back. Such people are rare in agricultural communities, though a few professional beggars, chiefly Boisnabs, can be seen in towns and urban parts. There are about 300 families in the three villages in which this enquiry was made, and the population must be at least 1,500 at the rate of 5 per house, and in this population there are three beggars.

63. Cultivators and labourers, like the rest of the population, live chiefly upon rice and dâl. They also eat a quantity of *sag* or vegetables chiefly grown in their own homesteads, and fish occasionally. Everyone gets a sufficient quantity. The houses are mud-walled (not well ventilated) and grass-thatched huts, of which there are two to eight or nine in each house according to the circumstance and the need of the family. There is great improvement in the dress of the classes under consideration. In fact in the matter of raiment there is very little distinction between a successful agriculturist and a well-to-do man of the higher class. Even the poorer classes of men or women wear the same machine-made dhotis and cloths which are worn by the *bhodrolok* classes. Cheap shawls, allowan woollen wrappers, are common enough in the villages, and there are very few labourers even who have not got a pair of shoes or an umbrella for fairs or attending courts. For ordinary wear the ryot has four dhotis and one or two gamchas which cost him about Rs. 2 a year. His wife costs him about Rs. 3 for her four saries, and the children each about Re. 1. But every one spends another few rupees for holiday clothes and clothes for the winter.

64. There is also great improvement in the matter of utensils. The chief pottery is confined to the handis or cooking pots which are used by the rich and the poor alike. It is admitted by the ryots that the earthenware sanki off which Mahomedan ryots used to eat are no longer to be seen, and both Hindus and Mahomedans use the brass or bell-metal thalis, cups, &c., in the same way as the superior classes. A ryot with a holding of 70 or 80 bighas has at least two brass gharas or ghailas, three badnas, if a Mahomedan, or three gharus if a Hindu, nine or ten thalis, five or six cups (or batis), four ghatis and lotas, and three tumblers. Even a poor man of the labouring class has at least two thalis, two or three batis, one garu, one ghara. Those who used to take food for the labourers in the fields in earthen pots 20 years ago now carry it on huge bell-metal cups, and that the wife of the same man whose mother wore jewellery worth Rs. 20 or Rs. 25 is wearing trinkets valued at Rs. 100 or Rs. 125. The marriage expenses of Mahomedans and the very low caste Hindus is about Rs. 50. But Hindus of other castes, such as goalas, satgopes chasadhopas, &c., have to spend about Rs. 300 in the marriage of their sons, but they get in return as much in the marriage of their daughter. There is no minimum limit to the expenditure for other social ceremonies, and a man may expend as little or as much as he can afford in the *Sradh* of his father or mother. But owing to improvement in taste and in the idea of comfor, these ceremonies cost more than they used to do before. People in bad health and of inferior physique are frequently met with in all parts and among all classes of people. But this state of things is not due to want of nourishment, but climatic influence.

65. It will be seen from the above that, in the centre of the district, 50 per cent. of the population are cultivators and 25 per cent. agricultural labourers; one per cent. artizans; beggars and helpless people, 5 per cent. The holdings of cultivators vary from 10 to 150 bighas. The produce obtained from a bigha is rather less than four maunds of rice. The return from ten bighas of rice land is about Rs. 43 for grain and straw. The cost of

labour, rent, &c., is Rs. 31. On the same land the cultivator will also have a winter crop, which will bring him in a profit of about Rs. 32; thus 10 bighas of land will, after paying for labour the usual rates, bring in a net profit of about Rs. 44.

66. Day labour varies from 2 to 3 annas. Work can always be found during nine months of the year.

67. Artizans generally supplement their handicraft by cultivation. Carpenters, blacksmiths and weavers are said to earn Rs. 7½ per mensem.

68. All the industrious classes are said to have advanced in prosperity in the last 30 years. They spend more money on their household luxuries, such as brass vessels and ornaments for their wives and children. They also spend more money on social and religious ceremonies. There is of course much misery in a thickly-populated country like this; but it is confined to two classes—those who cannot work and those who will not work.

69. In the west of the district, the following diagram will give an idea of the produce of an average holding of 30 bighas:—

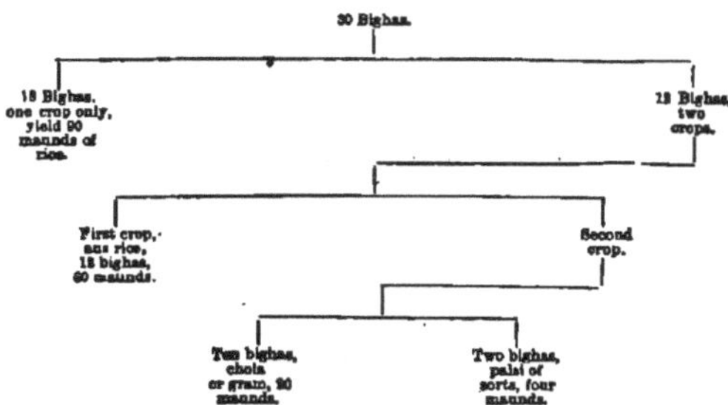

The total produce is 150 maunds of rice, or Rs. 150, and 24 maunds of pulses, &c., Rs. 36: total Rs. 186. The net profits, after paying for labour, will be about Rs. 92. A large portion of the wages of labour will be received by the cultivator and the adults of his family. In the west of the district, land is poor and plentiful, and the paupers and beggars are few. The population is sparse and purely agricultural. Artizans are carpenters and backsmiths; they all earn over Rs. 10 per mensem.

70. The wages of agricultural labourers are high in this district. For nine months in the year an adult male, at ordinary work, can earn from Rs. 5 to Rs. 6 per mensem; during harvest time he can earn more, and undoubtedly does so. When they are paid in kind, it is said that an adult labourer earns enough paddy to keep him during the three slack months. Boys also earn something from Rs. 6 to Rs. 8 per annum. The women of these parts do not work in the fields; they attend markets and buy and sell vegetables and produce.

71. With reference to artizans in agricultural villages, they are extremely well off; they always hold land; they have no difficulty in finding work; the chief difficulty is to get them to work when there is work to be done. Their women and female children are not employed in out-door labour; their chief occupation is husking paddy, fetching water and attending markets.

72. The helpless people in this district varies from 5 to 1 per cent. of the population. The fact, hovever, is that in times of scarcity their numbers are largely increased by helpless women, aged and widows, old men and other infirm persons, who are usually maintained by their families in times of plenty. In every family there are helpless people who are tolerated in times of plenty, but cast adrift as soon as scarcity or famine appears.

73. With reference to paragraph 8 of the Government Circular, the Civil Surgeon was consulted, and the following is the substance of the note put by

him. The following is a tabular statement of the persons admitted to the jail in 1887 who gained and lost weight during incarceration :—

Statement showing the number of persons who gained or lost in weight, arranged according to classes, in the Nuddea Jail during the year 1887.

Classes.	Gained in weight.		Lost in weight.		Stationary.		Total of each class.
	Total.	Percentage to admission.	Total.	Percentage to admission.	Total.	Percentage to admission.	
Cultivators	155	68·58	29	12·83	42	18·59	226
Agricultural labourers ...	94	69·11	18	13·23	24	17 66	136
Artizans	9	40·90	4	18·18	9	40·92	22
Those subsisting on charity	12	85·71	2	14·29	......	......	14

Statement showing the number of persons gained or lost in weight in the Nuddea Jail during the year 1887.

Year.	Gained.		Lost.		Stationary.	
	Total.	Percentage gained to admitted.	Total.	Percentage lost to admitted.	Total.	Percentage of stationary to admitted.
1887	383	63·20	122	20·13	101	16·65

74. These figures show that among those subsisting on charity, 85·71 per cent. gained weight during the imprisonment. Among agricultural labourers and cultivators 69·11 and 68·58 respectively gained, while only 12·83 and 13·23 respectively lost. Among artizans 49·90 gained, 40·92 remained stationary, while 18·18 lost in weight.

75. The conditions which would in jail tend to cause gain in weight are—

1. Sufficiency of good.
2. Sufficiency of clothing.
3. Lighter and more sedentary labour than that usual in the free state, while conditions tending to cause loss are—

1. Anxiety and change in mode of life.
2. Deprivation of society of friends and of comforts.
3. Regular work.

76. It seems probable that persons belonging to the class subsisting on charity are presumably more or less idle in habits, and would feel the unfavourable effects of regular work, and this is the class which shows the greatest gain in weight.

77. Similar reasoning may be applied to the other classes noted. It will be observed that the figures in the table quite support presumptions which abstract reasoning on the subject might lead to.

78. Thus among artizans, whose habits are probably least changed by incarceration, 40·92 did not gain, 18·10 lost, and 40·90 only gained. Among cultivators, 68·58 gained, 18·59 were stationary, 12·83 lost; while among agricultural labourers (less favourably situated as regards freedom from want) 69·11 against 17·66 neither gained nor lost, 13·23 lost. Among those subsisting on charity (the class most open to privation) 85·71 gained and 14·29 lost.

79. There is no emigration from this district. If work is slack the labouring classes go where they can find it and return to their homes again.

80. The Collector of Jessore states that during his late tour he paid special attention to the condition of the agricultural classes, but did not see his way to make any elaborate calculation about areas of holdings and outturn per bigha so as to try and gauge the amount of their sustenance. He has

had, however, statistics prepared, under his immediate superintendence, of nine large villages situated in different parts of the district, which is annexed below—

Names of villages.			Total number of houses examined.	First class with 10 bighas or more.	Second class with less than 10 bighas but having either a substantial holding or other good means of livelihood.	Third class having two bighas, but generally dependent on labour.	Fourth class in indigent circumstances.
Pahbellah, station Chowgatcha	...	...	49	6	12	28	3
Chanchra, station Kaligunge	...	...	129	16	38	72	3
Kanchunnagore ...	...	...	87	6	23	58	......
Durgapore, station Sarail	...	...	83	20	30	30	3
Jugurnathpore, station Narail	...	...	68	20	20	14	14
Alpokia, station Monorampore	...	...	80	11	26	43	......
Unui, station Bongong ...	...	...	64	9	11	41	3
Kaloopole, station Bongong	...	...	105	35	18	48	4
Vekutia, station Kotwali	...	...	133	33	54	31	16
Total		...	798	155	232	365	46

81. Out of 798 homesteads examined, 155 belong to class I, 232 to class II, 365 to class III, and 46 to class IV. But the latter included professional beggars. The true number was about 20, there being two or three really poor householders in a village. It will be seen that half of the people are in the first two classes. The houses of the first class are well built and well stocked with cattle and poultry. Each homestead is composed of four houses often with little out-offices, and the agricultural implements and produce lying about are proofs of the possession of some substance. Men of this class generally have under-tenants and others in various degrees of dependence on them, and where they have date-tree cultivation, they are extremely well off, as is demonstrated by the clothes they wear, and the air of comfort about their houses. These men are certainly not as a rule in debt, but are often money-lenders. This class comprises the numerous lakirajdars, who are mostly Hindus of good caste, and still more numerous gantidars, who are of all castes and many are Mahomedans. Class II are fairly well off, but many are in embarrassed circumstances. They represent the poor respectables of the agricultural world. Class III includes all the low caste people, such as moochies, who as labourers find work suitable to their position. The high rate of the wages they command suggests that they must be well off, and the well-fed appearance of themselves and their children satisfactorily proves it.

82. The prosperity of the agricultural classes of this district is also secured by the various extra crops such as chillies, tobacco, turmeric, sugarcane, &c., and then there are many men other than the cultivators with shares in such crops. On this ground too no statistics that merely dealt with areas of holdings and amount of rent paid would give any true conception of the condition of the peasantry. The weavers also of these parts are fairly numerous and gain a comfortable competence.

83. The Collector of Khulna states that the south of this district is different, and its social conditions, from the north. In the north the condition and circumstances of the agricultural classes more or less resemble that of the Jessore and Backergunge districts, while in the south the great clearings of the Sunderbuns tracts have their own marked features. As a rule rent is lower, the area of holdings is larger, and as a consequence the agricultural classes are better off in the south than in the north. On the other hand in the south they have only their own winter rice crop and no cold-weather crops, and but few fruit trees. The cultivation is easier in the south, but necessitates the construction of embankments and in many cases the transport of the plough cattle by water to the land, as many ryots living in the northern parts of the district have lands in the Sunderbun tract, or "abad" as it is locally called. Life in those parts being one of some hardship, the population is found to consist almost entirely of cultivators and labourers of the latter class. There are much fewer

residents than would be requisite, but for the custom of a large annual immigration of daily labourers from the north at the end of December to reap the amun crop all over the district; but particularly in the bils and Sunderbun tracts the custom of letting land on the *burga* system at a rent of half the crop is common. This custom makes it very difficult to collect correct statistics of the area each ryot cultivates. All the people of these lower classes sleep on mats on the floor, on a rug made of their old worn-out clothes stitched together, and a similar rug for a covering. Some have a coarse mosquito net. Pillows are usual. They all mostly grow some vegetables near their *baries* for home consumption. The adults take two and children three meals a day, consisting of rice, dal, vegetables, fish, chillies, huldi and salt. They all consume tobacco, pan and supari. The habit of living as a joint-family results in there being often two or three families in one household. The prosperity or otherwise of the group so formed will depend, of course, on the relative number of productive and unproductive individuals which form it. The excessive expense incurred by the marriage of a male member of a family involves the family in debt for years, and unless this expense is to some extent met by the "pan" received for females when given in marriage, it becomes a serious drain on the family resources. In fact but for this the majority of the poorer classes would be much better off and able to live without feeling the pressure of poverty as long as crops and prices remained normal. Besides the heavy sums thus incurred as debts, there is the ruinous interest at from 6 to 9 annas per rupee per annum to be paid on them until the principal is wiped off. The duty of supporting the widow and other helpless members of the family adds to the burden falling on the productive members. Poor as they are, their marriages cost them from Rs. 56 to Rs. 200. The Hindoos of these classes use earthen *kulsis* for carrying water and *handis* for cooking, but Mussulmans use earthen pots largely for other domestic purposes.

84. As regards, firstly, the class of cultivators, this term includes persons who can barely manage to support themselves and dependents, and all the intermediate grades of the class up to those who are very well to do and far removed from want of any kind.

85. It would seem that a cultivator with a family consisting of himself, wife and two or three children can furnish himself and them sufficiently with the necessaries of life from the produce of holding of 15 bighas; any holding larger in area will of course make him so much the better off. Of 247 holdings in two villages in the Chandkhali khas mehal towards the south of the district, it was found that there were—

Of 10 bighas and under	62
10 to 20 bighas	47
20 to 30 "	27
30 to 40 "	13
40 to 50 "	19
Of over 50 "	79

and the average for the whole 247 was 58 bighas.

86. Of 891 holdings in the Syedpore Trust Estate, in the north of the district, there were found to be—

Of 10 bighas and under	673
10 to 20 bighas	102
20 to 30 "	43
30 to 40 "	25
40 to 50 "	7
Over 50 "	41

and the average for the whole was 16 bighas.

87. In the south, land is to be had cheaper and more readily than in the north, and hence the larger average area in the former part. The average of 100 holdings taken from the road cess returns for an estate in Morrelgunge thana was $17\frac{1}{4}$ bighas, and of 100 holdings taken from the same returns of several estates in the Khulna and Bagirhat sub-divisions was a little over $6\frac{1}{2}$ bighas. Taking 13 maunds of paddy, value Rs. 11, as the average outturn of a bigha of average rice land, and the cost of cultivation as Rs. 3-8 with

Rs. 1-8 as rent, total Rs. 5, there remains Rs. 6 per bigha as net profit, and for 15 bighas Rs. 90. The straw will be eaten by the plough-cattle or left to rot on the field. The cost of living for the ryot, his wife and three children, will be—

	Rs.
Rice value	36
Other supplies	30
Clothes	10
Other expenses	4
To pay off debts	10
Total ...	90

Of the total of 1,138 holdings in, the Chandkhali and Syedpore mehals above noticed, it will be seen that 735, or nearly 65 per cent., consist of holdings of 10 bighas and under; and Mr. Waller thence infers that some 50 per cent. about were not in a position to procure the necessaries of life in sufficiency. Apart from other possible errors of calculation, the value of the labour, though a fair deduction in estimating the profits of the farm, cannot be properly taken off in calculating, the tenants' means of living. The value of the labour is 15 × $3\frac{1}{2}$=Rs. 52-8. The bulk of this probably goes to the tenant himself.

88. The meals consist of rice, dâl and some chillies, and coarse vegetables, and on hât day fish; but few partake of milk. If there is a cow and the children do not take the milk, it is sold for four pice a seer. A Mahomedan may make a couple of rupees a year by the sale of eggs. Some of the poorer ryots make Rs. 5 or so a year by making and selling a coarse kind of mat called "nal." This and household work are the only employments their women have. The children may earn eight annas to Rs. $1\frac{1}{2}$ a month as cattle herds.

89. The rent does does not appear to press unduly or deteriously on the mass of the cultivators. These mostly hold at rates which cannot be easily or much enhanced; but where new tenants engage for land now, higher rates are demanded. The custom of paying the whole year's rent between December and March after the amun is cut and harvested is convenient to the cultivators and seems to result in their more promptly discharging their obligation to their landlords. In the Sunderbuns in many places it is the custom to have the rent paid before the crop is disposed of. This is where the tenant comes from a distance. As to indebtedness among the holders of the 247 holdings in Chandkhali, it appears that of those holding 10 bighas and under, 79 per cent. were in debt on the average Rs. 28 per household, and of those holding 10 to 20 bighas, 86 per cent. owed on the average Rs. 44 per household, and of those holding over 20 bighas and upwards 84 per cent. were in debt to the amount of Rs. 136 on the average. A considerable amount of this debt in the case of those holding the larger area was borrowed to meet the cost of cultivation, and the greater part for the expenses of marriage. Here is an example of a badly off cultivator of the *Pod* caste in the southern parts. He and his brother-in-law are living in union. His brother-in-law came last July from another part, as he could not get land there to cultivate:—K. M. has a wife and mother and the brother-in-law a wife and three young children to support. He cultivates some 10 bighas *burga*, and he got 12 solies (=25 maunds) of paddy as his half of the crop. He used all the rice he got for home consumption except Rs. 12 worth which he sold in the hât and then borrowed 1 *solie* to be repaid by $1\frac{1}{2}$ *solies*. He has to borrow from 1 to 2 *solies* in this way yearly, repaying it in Magh or Falgoon to keep himself; he owns one bullock and two cows, which eat the straw. One of these he bought last year with Rs. 11 borrowed at 4 annas per rupee. He also got eight *solies* chatan rice in *Agrabagan*, of which he sold $2\frac{1}{2}$ to buy clothes with, consumed some, and has some still in store. The *bari*, in which are his huts, belongs to his maternal aunt, a widow. He earned Re. 1 by working eight days at two annas a day at making an embankment in Pos. During the months *Ashin* to *Pos* he cuts *malia* reeds, and he and the women weave mats (*madur*). Some 2, value 5 annas, are sold at weekly hâts, which brings in some four or five rupees in the season. They catch fish themselves during the greater part of the

year, and when then the bils are closed they buy it in the hât. He cuts his own fuel gratis. When the cows give milk they consume it themselves. He has one hut and his brother-in-law another. He has a brass ghoti, two brass batis and a brass ghara (this he got at his marriage), and four bell-metal thalis. His wife's ornaments are worth about Rs. 12. These he bought when he married her seven years ago. He paid his father-in-law Rs. 100 for his wife. He raised this by giving his sister in marriage for Rs. 90, and borrowing Rs. 40 which he paid off in three years. Clothes for himself yearly cost Rs. 2¼ and for each child Re. 1. His mother's *Sradh* would cost Rs. 2 or 3. He and his brother-in-law with two ploughs cultivate the 10 bighas, the jotdar, of whom he holds, supplying one bullock.

90. There is another similar case:—C. M. is a Musulman ryot, also of the southern part. He holds two bighas at Rs. 3 rent and four bighas *burga*. From this he might get 16 solies of paddy in all. He owns 3 bullocks and a cow; such cattle are worth about Rs. 8 each. He earns about Rs. 10 a year by making and selling "nal" mats. He consumes about 2½ seers of rice a day and spends two annas at each weekly hât. He owns eight metal utensils, value Rs. 7. His wife's ornaments are worth Rs. 14. He borrowed and spent Rs. 150 at his marriage, of which he has paid off all but Rs. 25, which bears interest at 4 annas per rupee. He paid off the debt from the proceeds of cultivation and labour.

91. As to agricultural labourers, there are very few of these who have not also a bit of land. Their wages vary from Rs. 2 to Rs. 3½ a month with three meals. When hired by the day they get 2½ to 4 annas and their mid-day meal. Their expenses and mode of living are much the same as in the case of the poorer class of cultivators. Their women sometimes earn a little by husking rice at home for others. In the Sunderbuns at rice-reaping time the labourers get one bundle for every 10 or 11 they cut. A diligent man can earn so much as 18 maunds of paddy in this way in the season. The demand for agricultural labour in this district is greater than the supply, and work is to be had at all seasons. The labourers do not seem to have suffered in physique for want of sufficient nourishment.

92. Many cultivators from the northern parts of the district, after reaping their own rice crop which matures earlier than that of the southern parts, go to the Sunderbun tracts and earn wages as reapers of the rice crop there. The children also can earn something as herd boys. In the south they mostly get fuel for nothing and can fish free except while the bils are closed. In the north they have to buy fuel and fish as a rule. There is also the employment of wood-cutting in the Sunderbuns, and of cutting the leaves called *golpatta* for use as thatch.

93. Of the labourers in the Chandkhali khas mehal, 46 per cent. were found to be in debt on an average to the extent of Rs. 38 per family. Also of four families of fishermen half were in debt to the amount of Rs. 14 per household. The following numbers of agricultural labourers were found in villages in—

Name of Thana.	Total population.	Labourers.
Magura	393	15
Kaligunge	101	25
Bagirhat	1,090	None.
Ditto	775	35
Ditto	202	8
Ditto	778	133
Paikgacha	227	57
Chanduria	101	31
Chandkhali	585	92
Khulna	860	300
Ditto	437	100
Ditto	100	None.
	5,609	786

giving about 14 per cent of the population. There are fewer labourers in Bagirhat than in the rest of the district. The following is an example of an agricultural labourer in the southern parts:—M.S. is a Mussulman and has a mother, wife and six children to support. He holds 1½ bighas of paddy land at Rs. 3 rent. He gets about 6 *solies* (10 seers = one *soli*) of rice from this land. During eight months he works as a daily labourer at 4 annas a day for rice cutting and 3 annas for other work. This man says that he could cultivate 15 bighas if he could get it, but he cannot, and now the zemindars ask Rs. 2 and middlemen up to Rs. 4 rent per bigha. He is old and broken, but he says a hale young man might earn Rs. 5 or Rs.6 a month by daily labour. He has some 20 *supari* trees, the best of the nuts of which he sells, and uses the residue, which is sufficient for 10 months' consumption.

94. He owes Rs. 15 on a bond at 6 annas per rupee interest since Baisak last, and in Kartic he borrowed 12 palis (20 seers = 1 pali) at 50 per cent. interest, which he has to do every year, repaying in Falgoon and Chait. He says if he had 10 or 12 bighas of land he would support his family without running into debt; but there are too many for him to support single-handed, and an old man as he is. He paid Rs. 125 when he gave his son in marriage, and last year received Rs. 51 for his daughter on her marriage at the age of 10.

95. He owns eight metal vessels. He catches fish for himself. He spends 6 or 7 annas twice a week on articles for home, consumption. This man aged about 50 or 60, says that, since his marriage, marriage expenses have increased for those of his class from Rs. 45 to Rs. 125.

96. The outcome seems to be that an agricultural labourer earning Rs. 5 a month is about as well off as a cultivator with a holding of 10 bighas.

97. In the artizan class, the Collector has included goldsmiths, carpenters, blacksmiths, weavers, barbers, washermen, potters, oil-makers, and gharamis.

98. With the following results; all these classes usually also hold some land.

99. The artizans whose condition has been enquired into were not the best off of their class. The following are the accounts of their condition given by themselves:—

100. B. K., a goldsmith, a man of about 50, and has only himself and his wife to support since he separated from his two brothers about 30 years ago on account of a quarrel. He works daily at home at his trade. He is helped by a boy, a relation, whom he boards as his remuneration. He gets 6 pice per *bhari* of silver, and Re. 1-8 to Rs. 1-12 per *bhari* of gold worked up. By this he can earn about Rs. 5 monthly. He has an occupancy right in 10 bighas of rice land in a *bil* some three miles off. He pays rent at Re. 1 a bigha. He gets about Rs. 25 worth of rice from his land, which is half the crop, as he lets it out "barga." This supplies him all the rice needed for home consumption, and leaves Rs. 4 or 5 worth for sale. He has also two bighas homestead land held at Rs. 4-12, on which grow mangoes, jacks, tamarinds, bamboos, suparies, and cocoanuts, all of which he consumes except about Re. 1 or Re. 1½ value of supari, which he sells. He has one cow which produces 1½ seers of milk a day, which is consumed at home. He spends about 3 annas per week on things bought at the hât. He spends his entire income, but was not in debt till last year, when he had to borrow Rs. 20, as he was laid up for seven months with fever. On this debt he has to pay 6 annas per rupee per annum. He says that men of his trade have not earned so much as they used the last 10 years, as *Chandals* and *Jogis* have begun to work as goldsmiths. He has three huts, one to live in, one a cow-house, and one to work in. Furniture consists of one large wooden box and a taktaposh. His metal vessels are—of brass, a kalsi, a garu, and two ghotis; of bell-metal, three thalis, three ghotis, and four batis. His wife's gold and silver ornaments are worth about Rs. 15. Religious ceremonies cost about Rs. 3 a year.

101. This man is fairly well of, getting about Rs. 60 a year by his trade, and Rs. 25 from his land, and about Re. 1 from sale of fruit, while he has only himself and his wife to keep.

102. R.T. is an oilman. The family consists of 17, including father, mother, five sons, three sons' wives, four sons' children. The father is old and sickly. He and two grown-up brothers work at their trade during four months of the year, and during the remaining eight at cultivation. They have seven

bighas of their own and hold 10 more *barga*, which they till themselves. This land produces rice valuing Rs. 88, which is consumed at home. No other crop is grown on his land. His land only produces eleven-fifteenths of the rice needed for home consumption. There are bamboos, supari, cocoanut, and mangoe trees on his homestead, the fruits being all consumed by the family. They have nine houses, three to dwell in and other six for other domestic purposes, which they repair themselves. His stock in trade consists of one oil-press made by themselves at a cost of Rs. 10. A press lasts two years. The four cattle who turn the press are also available for the plough. They buy mustard-oil seeds at Rs. 5 a maund: this produces some 20 seers of oil, value 5½ rupees. He also buys oil at Rs. 10 and sells it at Rs. 11 a maund. He and his two brothers sell some 30 seers of oil every hât day, or some 80 maunds a year. His furniture consists of one large and two smaller wooden boxes and a taktaposh. He has four brass and 32 bell-metal vessels. The women's ornaments are worth about Rs. 120. They are not and have never been in debt. They might save some Rs. 90 a year if they did their best. Clothing costs for each—

	Rs.	A.	P.
Woman	6	0	0
Man	2	4	0
Child	1	8	0

Religious ceremonies cost about Rs. 3-8 a year, and entertaining relations Rs. 4 or Rs. 5. They spent Rs. 80 last year on the marriage of two of their sisters, and received Rs. 350 as *pân* for the two. The marriage of a brother would come to between Rs. 400 and Rs. 450, the *pân* amounting to over Rs. 200. His father's *Sradh* would cost some Rs. 50.

103. Here three men support 14 unproductive persons. Their income is about Rs. 80 from their trade and Rs. 90 from land=Rs. 170 in all. The men admitted that they might save Rs. 90 a year by an effort.

104. J.P. is a potter. His family consists of self, wife, and seven children, the eldest of whom is 15. He works at his trade, helped by his eldess son. He works at his trade about eight months, and on some land he holdt some four months of the year. The favourable season for his trade is from Agrahayan to Falgoon. At other times operations are liable to be interfered with by the weather. He can only make *kalsis*. Of these he can make some 16 in a day, which sell at 1 to 1½ pice a piece. During the rainy season he cannot make more than eight a day. Fuel for baking the pots comes to some Rs. 6 a month. He sells his ware at the hât himself. His wife sometimes helps at moulding small pots. His other children only herd his cattle, of which he has five, three being plough cattle. He and his wife have two and the children three meals a day. His five bighas of rice land held at Rs. 10 rent provides enough rice for home consumption for six or seven months in a good and four or five months in a less favourable year. For the remaining months rice comes to Rs. 3 a month. He spends weekly on hât days 12 to 14 annas on articles of consumption other than rice. The half seer of milk his cow gives daily is consumed at home. He tills his own land. He owes Rs. 150 at nine annas per rupee per annum interest since last year, when he borrowed it for his son's marriage. He has not yet paid off any portion of the principal, as he was laid up sick for four or five months. He says he never had more than Rs. 15 in hand at a time. His wife's ornaments of silver are of some Rs. 20 value. He expects to pay off his debt in some four years, and then will borrow again to marry another son. He will get Rs. 80 to Rs. 100 for each of his girls when he marries them. He has five boys and two girls. The only other produce of his land (he has one bigha of homestead also held at Rs. 2 rent) is the fruit of two mangoe trees. He has three brass and three bell-metal vessels. He has six huts, two for living in, one for cooking, one cowshed, one dhenki shed and one work-room.

105. Here the father and a son of 15 have to support themselves and seven others. His statement of his income from his trade seems to be understated, as according to it his income from his trade would not be over Rs. 10 less Rs. 6 for fuel = Rs. 4 net a month, while he spends 12 to 14 annas each hât = 13 annas × 104 or Rs. 84½ a year, and has to buy about Rs. 18 worth of rice during the year; so that he must make on an average about Rs. 9 a month, net by his trade to pay his way.

106. G. G. is a gharami. His family consists of self (an oldish man), four nephews, and their three wives and six children. The three nephews work as gharamis during the season, *i.e.* Magh and Falgoon, and earn five annas a day each. During some three-and-a-half months these three work as agricultural labourers or in houses at 2½ annas a day and the midday meal. They only get work about 15 days in the month. The three women earn nothing. He has 21 bighas of land, of which only 5½ are cultivable with rice, held at a rent of Rs. 29. He gets enough rice from this for home consumption. The land produces nothing else but a few cocoanuts and bamboos which are consumed at home. Of his four nephews, one is idle and dissipated, and one gets Rs. 2 a month as a carpenter's apprentice. Of the 21 bighas, one homestead is held at four annas rent. His family consumes three seers of rice a day. He has two cows, and sells the milk; by these he gets 6 pice a day during four months of the year. He has four brass and six bell-metal vessels. His furniture consists of two tuktaposhes. He at present owes Rs. 250 at an interest of three pice per rupee per month. He has mortgaged 6½ bighas of land and pawned all the silver ornaments, value Rs. 40. He says he raised Rs. 10 only on these, and has to pay two pice per month per rupee interest. He was much better off till five or six years ago, when he gave up a boat trade in rice and nuts, when there was a lot of work on houses, when Khulna become a sudder station. In 1883 he had Rs. 200 made out of contracts, which went on his nephew's marriage. The marriage of the one nephew remaining to be married will cost Rs. 80 as *pân* and Rs. 100 as expenses. He spends annas 6 a year on religious rites. He has eight huts. Sometimes adults have to go with one meal one day in the seven owing to want.

107. This family might be fairly comfortable if the men were more laborious. They evidently are idle and content to live from hand to mouth rather than work a little harder. Three men have to support 11 persons, which, as their land is not productive and they are in debt, would require diligence.

108. M.K. is a blacksmith. His family consists of self, three brothers, and two sisters-in-law. He left home last year to come and work in a large bazar with a relation. Two brothers work as blacksmiths at home, and one is still too young. They make *dhaos*, reeping, hooks, kodalis, small knives, &c. A smith could earn Rs. 10 a month if he could find a sale for all he could make. He and his relation here buy a maund of iron each month at from Rs. 3 to Rs. 5½ a maund, and Rs. 2 charcoal. They make their own tools, which cost about Rs. 6 to provide new. The two earn about Rs. 7 a month net profit between them. Their joint board comes to Rs. 3½ to Rs. 4 a month, and he pays Re. 1 a year as rent for a hut to live in. He cannot afford to buy milk. The two save about Rs. 2 a month each. They have sent home Rs. 25 each during the year nearly past. He says he left home for economy's sake, as he has not to entertain any one, and so saves Rs. 1½ monthly.

109. They have at home 4 bighas of land, including their homestead, of which two produce rice and the rest mustard-seed. They let the land out *burga* last year. They got 3½ salis rice, value Rs. 14, and Rs. 7 worth of sarsha. The rent is Rs. 2 a bigha. All this and the fruit of three trees are consumed at home. They have two dwelling and one cook house. The women's ornaments are worth Rs. 13. The rice from their lands was enough for eight months, and they had to buy rice for the remaining four at a cost of some Rs. 2-8 a month. Every *hât* day they spend annas 7 or annas 8 on other articles than rice. They now owe Rs. 225 borrowed for expense of the eldest brother's marriage. Another brother was married four years ago at a cost of over Rs. 200, some of which was in hand and some had to be borrowed. They also incurred a debt of Rs. 50 during the last three years, owing to illness and cost of medical attendance on one of the family.

110. According to this the trade of a village blacksmith is not a thriving one, as, even if diligent at his work, he cannot make over Rs. 4 a month for want of a market.

111. G.M. is a carpenter, with a family to support consisting of himself, wife, three girls, a nephew and a widowed sister-in-law. He works mostly out at jobs in houses. He occasionally makes a box at home. He cannot make ploughs or wheels. He works at his trade about 15 days in the month. This is the usual practice. He can earn about Rs. 10 a month. He is paid by the job, and not by the day. His tools, when new, do not cost quite Rs. 5, and with annas 10 or annas 12 a year for repairs will last three years. He has 8½ bighas of land, held at a rent of Rs. 8 or Rs. 9 a year. This includes his homestead, which produces thatch grass and fruits, of which he sells some Rs. 5 or Rs. 6 a year. He has to buy 30 seers of paddy every five days at a cost of annas 7½, equal to Rs. 2-13 a month, and spends annas 5 or 6 each hât day on other articles, equal to Rs. 3. He has one dwelling house, one cook and one cow-shed. He has one wooden box, two brass and five bell-metal vessels. He owes at present Rs. 30 at an interest of 2 pice per rupee per month, which was incurred for the cost of his father's *Sradh* two years ago. Before that, some five years ago, he had to borrow Rs. 40 for his brother's marriage. This he paid off in three years. This man has six persons to support, but his income is Rs. 125 a year, and so he may be considered pretty well off.

112. M.P. is a barber with a family of 13, consisting of himself, wife and child, two fathers' brothers and their wives and one widowed aunt, two mother's sisters, both widows, two cousins, one male and one female. He works daily at his trade and attends some 120 persons monthly and serves some 30 households besides. He gets from annas 2 to 8 a month from the better off and annas 8 to a rupee a year from the less well-to-do. This brings him about Rs. 5 a month: his women only do household work. He holds 20 bighas of land at one rupee a bigha and some 2 bighas chakran land. Two of the other males till this; one is too old to work. Only 16 bighas are under cultivation and rest lying fallow. He gets about Rs. 100 worth of rice from his land, of which he sells some Rs. 15 worth and consumes the rest. On 2 bighas homestead he has fruit trees, bamboos and thatch grass, all of which are consumed at home. Besides his wages, he gets presents, such as a piece of cloth or the like when he attends a marriage.

113. He was not in debt till the last two years, when, one of the working males having died, he had to borrow Rs. 60 for current expenses. His expenditure each hât day is some annas 12; on religious and social rites some Rs. 30 a year; on repairs to houses Rs. 20. He has nine houses, three boxes and a taktaposh, 14 brass and 36 bell-metal vessels and gold and silver ornaments, value Rs. 80.

114. P.N. is a weaver with only himself and his wife to support. He works and his wife helps at the weaving. In a month he can weave 18 *gamchas*, 12 large and 16 small *dhooties*, the sale of which brings him some Rs. 9 monthly, which less Rs. 5-8 cost of thread leaves Rs. 3-8 net profit. A loom lasts a life-time and costs about Rs. 3-12 to make. He holds only 1½ bighas homestead at an annual rent of Rs. 2-12, producing fruits and bamboos. By sale of cocoa and supari nuts he makes Rs. 6 or Rs. 7 a year, and consumes all the rest. He has no cattle. Excepting his *gamchas*, he has to buy the clothes he and his wife wear at a cost of Rs. 4-8, as he can make coarse clothing fit for cultivators. He has to buy 1½ seers of rice a day, and every hât spends 4 or 5 pice on other articles. He owns three houses, a wooden box, taktaposh, five brass and eight bell-metal vessels, and gold and silver ornaments value Rs. 90.

115. His mahajan supplies him with the thread for weaving on credit and repays as soon as he realizes the value of the clothes made of it. In this way he owes the mahajan some Rs. 12 at present; but no interest is charged, a running account being kept. He does not sell European *thans* as others do. He would be better off if he could get some land and let it out *burga*.

116. He says there are some 30 families of the *Tanti* caste, all of whom, except 2 or 3, work as weavers, but many of them have land and money also. He says that there is still sufficient demand for coarse clothes, but that whereas 40 years ago a dhoti of five haths was worth 5 to 5½ annas, it now sells for only 4 annas.

117. R.D. is a washerman. He has four persons to support. He gets an annual fee of Rs. 1½ to Rs. 2 from some five persons, and washes for others

at 1 pice per piece, and earns in all about Rs. 5 a month. He holds six bighas of land, which supplies enough rice for six months' consumption. For the remaining six months the rice he has to buy costs about Rs. 3 a month. He buys an umbrella and shoes perhaps once a year. The other articles besides rice cost him about Rs. 2 a month. His father's *Sradh* some seven years ago cost Rs. 50, which he borrowed at 12 per cent., and he still owes some of this.

118. Of the nine artizan families mentioned above, seven are in debt to the extent of Rs. 85 on the average. The debts were incurred mainly to meet marriage expenses, and partly on account of sickness and consequent loss of income.

119. As to the class who subsists on charity, excluding those, such as old people and widows whose relations support them in their households, there are those who have to support themselves by begging alms. These may be divided into those who are strong and well enough to work, but have taken to living by begging from choice as a profession, and those have no available means of subsistence.

120. S.D. is a specimen of the former and S. of the latter. S.D. and his wife both beg daily, and pick up four or five seers of rice a day, of which they consume what they require and sell the rest. They spend about 1 anna at each hât. They eat two meals a day, consisting of rice, dâl, vegetables, fish and chillies. They have two huts, in one of which they live. They have one brass *ghoti* and a *thal* and a *bati* of bell-metal. The woman's silver ornaments are worth Rs. 3. S. is an old woman. She begs daily, and picks up from 1½ to 2 seers of rice a day. She also receives 2 or 3 pieces of clothing in charity in the year. She sells any rice she does not want for her food, and spends about 2 pice each *hât*. She lives in the house of a *Baishtab*, who lets her live there gratis. She takes two meals a day, consisting of rice, dâl, and vegetables. She has one brass *ghoti* and silver bangles worth Rs. 3.

121. The following figure shows the number of this class found in villages in the following thanas :—

Thana.	Population.	Beggars.
Magura	393	5
Kaligunge	101	5
Bagirhat	1,090	25
Ditto	202	25
Paikgacha	227	10
Chandurea	101	2
Beniari	738	5
Khulna	860	10
Ditto	437	7
	4,149	94

or a little over 2 per cent. Of these 94, about 37 were of the idle and the rest of the helpless class.

122. The Collector of Moorshedabad reports that for the purposes of the present enquiry the district of Moorshedabad may be divided into two tracts into which it naturally falls, viz. the Barh and the Bagri.*

* More properly the Bagri and Kalantar, the land towards Beldanga and Patkabari being called the Kalantar.

123. In the Barh tract, which extends from north to south along the whole of the west frontier of the district, and of which the Bhagirathi forms the approximate eastern boundary, the land is *ek-fasla*, yielding only one main crop—the *aman* rice—in the year. This crop is sown in May and transplanted in June and July and reaped in the latter end of November or December. A small quantity of winter crops, such as gram, linseed, and wheat, are now grown by the cultivators, who have been taught, by the experience of the drought of 1883, 1884 and 1885, the danger of depending on a single crop. In some of the large *bhils* also winter crops have of late years taken the place of *bora dhan*. Sugarcane is also generally grown in every village.

124. In the Barh the average rate of rent paid by the actual cultivator is about Rs. 6 an acre. The best rice land is Rs. 3-8 per bigha. But grazing lands are often as lowly rented as 6 annas or 8 annas a bigha. For thaching

grass Re. 1 a bigha is the highest rate. It will be noticed that these rates are somewhat higher than those quoted in Hunter's Statistical Account of Bengal; but the Collector is inclined to think that the rates there given were too low, although no doubt land may be found at lower rates than those the Collector has quoted. The land immediately to the west of the Bhagirathi lets at lower rates, and lands where early rice (*aus*) and *rabli* is grown let at 12 annas to Re. 1-4 a bigha. But for the best *aman* rice land, which yields 10 maunds of dhan per bigha, the rate is never less than Rs. 3 and sometimes Rs. 4. The amount of lands which can be properly tilled with one plough varies from 12 to 16 bighas, and this fact operates materially upon the average size of holdings, as the class of cultivators who can afford to keep one plough are largely in the majority.

125. In the village of Mobarackpur, thana Kaligunge, there are 50 families cultivating 800 bighas of land. Of these one family has 200 bighas, one 100 bighas, and two families 60 bighas each. The remaining 380 bighas are divided among 46 families giving an average of about 8 bighas for each family. But the holdings are by no means equally divided. Some of the 46 families hold only three or four bighas of land, and have no plough of their own. Two or three only have more than one plough. There are 18 agricultural labourers in this village, none of whom hold any land. There are nine families of *kalus* oil millers), eight of whom have small holdings and grow *dhan* for their own consumption, while at the same time following their profession. There is only one shop in this village where salt, oil, and condiments are sold. The shopkeeper last year took 2 bighas of land. There is one iron smith who mends the village ploughs and gets for every plough in the village 4 to 5 *aris* of *dhan*, an *ari* being about five seers. This man works for other villages also, and his income may be roughly estimated at from 50 to 60 maunds of *dhan*, which would give him from 30 to 40 maunds of rice as his yearly wage. It was calculated that this man's family consumed about 2 maunds of rice a month, which would leave him from 11 to 16 maunds of rice to sell or exchange for other necessaries. The plough mending is his main occupation, but no doubt his income was supplemented to a certain extent by other odd jobs, such as repair of *daos*, spades, &c. This man was said to be a fair specimen of his class. Of course in a bad year his income would be extremely precarious. The village barber holds 12 bighas of land which he gives in *burga*, that is, let out for payment in kind of half the produce. There is one weaver in the village: he has four bighas of land. There are three carpenters who hold no lands. The weaver gets about 2 or 3 annas a day for his trade.

126. A season of scarcity and high prices would affect him seriously, as the price of the common country cloth he manufactures would not rise with the price of rice, the demand being less in a season of agricultural depression when the cultivators cannot afford new cloths. In this village there is only one man affected with leprosy and one old woman nearly blind, who lives solely on charity. This village suffered much from the failure of crops in 1885. At present the people appear happy and contented.

127. The following facts have been collected regarding the village Momenabad, thana Kaligunge, Lalbagh:—There are 33 houses with a population of about 150—all Mahomedans, and all either agriculturists or labourers. There are about 54 working male members in the 33 families, of whom seven have no land and subsist by labour. The labourers mostly get money wages varying from Rs. 10 to Rs. 28 a year, as well as food and clothing for themselves. In some cases they get the *dhan* of one or two bighas of land given them, for which, however, they have to pay rent, cultivation expenses being borne by their master.

128. The agricultural holdings are small, averaging about 12 bighas. The villagers here said that for five consecutive years they have very poor crops. In 1884-85 the area cultivated was also below the normal. The wages of labour consequently fell to six pice or eight pice a day in addition to the midday meal, which represented about an anna. In 1886-87 the whole of the cultivated area was utilized, and there was a bumper crop, sending wages at once to annas 3 and even higher. *Gharamis* who used to get annas 4 a day now gets annas 6. *Aman dhan* is the only crop grown. For the past two

years the average yield per bigha has been seven maunds. For three years before that it was three to four maunds. The cost of cultivation per bigha in this village this year has been about Rs. 3. The rents vary from about Rs. 1-4 to Rs. 3-8, but the average is Rs. 2 a bigha.

129. In this village nearly every family was in debt more or less; six families only said they had no debts. The gomasta of the village, who held 40 bighas of land, owed Rs. 200 to his mahajan; but he had married three daughters in the previous year, and spent Rs. 275 on the ceremonies. The average debt of each family was Rs. 5 or Rs. 6. When food is plentiful, *i.e.* when times are good, the whole of the agricultural population eat four times a day. Each grown-up male consumes 1¼ to 1½ seers of rice a day.

130. On an average each full-grown male has to support two other persons, viz. the average number in the family is three, and in families of more than three members there are, as a rule, at least two adults able to labour. The women of the labouring classes of Hindus work in the fields, wherever work is required. Mohamedan women never work in the fields, but husk rice and do other work which can be done at home or in private houses. Children of this class also commence to earn something towards their own support at the age of nine years.

131. The percentage of labourers to agriculturists in the Rarh tract is much smaller than in the Bagri and Kalantar to the east of the river, and may be roughly estimated at 12 to 15 per cent., including those labourers who hold not more than three bighas of land. In prosperous years this class has little to complain of; for a full harvest not only calls for all available labour to cut and store it, but it encourages the agriculturist to extend his operation and sow more land with surplus seed. But the labouring class is not provident, and what they get they spend as it comes. In famine years the labourers in the Rarh always suffer severely.

132. The village of Chandra Sikarmati contains, as nearly as could be ascertained, 25 families of Mussulmans, 15 of Bagdis, seven of Telis, one Mali, and one Bairagi—in all 49 families. The Bagdis, with the exception of two families of chowkidars, who have some lands, are all labourers, and support themselves by work and catching and selling fish. Two or three of them act as palki-bearers. These people are very poor. Their huts were found to contain nothing of value, and it is said to be more than probable that except in times of great plenty they are insufficiently fed, that is to say, their general health and physique would benefit by a more generous diet. The Mahomedans, with two exceptions, have all lands. One Baboo Sheik, who is too old to work hard, has six minor children and no land. He has no home of his own, and lives in other peoples' houses. His eldest son works as a cowherd and gets his food and clothing and a salary of one rupee per annum. The others live by what labour they can procure and are able to do. Another Mahomedan is a leper and unable to work. He has a wife and three little boys, one of whom is a cowherd. His wife works as a labourer, which is rare among Mahomedan women, and must be held as a sign of real indigence. These last two families are said to be insufficiently fed, and no doubt such is the case. Both the Mali and Bairagi have a little land, but supplement their income, the former by the manufacture of sola articles, and the latter by begging. The extent of holdings on land in this village is said to vary from 2 to 10 bighas. The village is a poor one and there are no wealthy residents; but there must be some holdings of considerably larger extent than 10 bighas. The wages of agricultural labour paid in this village are 2 annas a day in cash, or 1 anna cash and the day's food. The richer residents of the locality live in the neighbouring village of Batur in the same *panchayet* circle. Batur is a much larger village, but from enquiries there, it appears that there are only two families which did not get sufficient food.

133. In another village named Kanduri in the same part of the country, there were about 200 families, about half being Hindus and half Mahomedans, of which two families only were found in indigent circumstances and badly fed, owing in both cases to the age of some members and the infirmities of others.

134. The fact is that the natives of the country, both Hindus and Mahomedans, though by custom and religion exceedingly charitable, are not actively so. The recipients of charity must come to their doors to be fed.

The result is that the sturdy beggar prospers while the sick and infirm, who are beggars not by choice but from necessity, are often left to starve unpitied, and their condition does not awake any active feeling of sympathy among their neighbours.

135. Village Augarpur, in mouzah Bharatpore, is purely a Mahomedan village containing about 110 families, of which four families are entirely dependent on charity. One of these families consist of an old man and his wife. They have their adult sons, who have separated and set up on their own account, but are said to be unable to materially assist their parents, having as much as they can do to support their own families. Cases of this kind point to the existence of a very narrow margin between the average condition of the small agriculturist and indigence.

136. In Mouzah Chaitanpur, thana Asanpur, on the west bank of the Bhagirathi, there are at present 108 families with a population of about 370 men. Two-thirds are Hindus and one-third Mahomedans. In 22 of these families, the head of the family is a woman, and the earnings of the women form the support of the family. Fourty-one families have no land, and live on labour alone. There are nine weaver families with nine working members, and mason families with four working members. There are three widows who subsist on alms.

137. Of the 108 families in this village, 90 are more or less in debt, the united debt aggregating about Rs. 1,000. Some families were found to owe as much as Rs. 200. Others as little as Rs. 2. About 150 persons of both sexes sell here jungly produce and fuel, and about half of them also work on the fields during the crop season.

138. Although situated on the west bank of the Bhagirathi, mouza Chaitanpur resembles the *Bagri* tract rather than the Rarh, as regards its natural features. The land yields two crops in the year, and the conditions of husbandry are therefore more similar to those on the east bank of the river. It may be generally assumed that, while in seasons of favourable harvest the cultivators of the Rarh tract are better off than their neighbours to the east, any deficiency of rainfall tells on them much more severely. It is true that the *Bagri* lands within the embankment suffer almost equally with the Rarh from deficient rainfall; but these lands give two crops, and it is rarely that both of them fail entirely. Outside the embankment, the *Bagri* crop suffers from inundation; but the rich harvest which follows the subsidence of the river amply repays the cultivators for previous losses, and accordingly, as might be expected, the general condition of the *Bagri* ryots is better than that of the cultivators of the Rarh.

139. The Bagri and Kalantar tracts also abound with mangoe, jack, and other fruit trees, which materially conduce to the general prosperity of the inhabitants, and it is interspersed all over with jheels and rivers which afford a plentiful supply of fish. As a rule the cultivators to the east of the Bhagirathi and those in tracts near Jungipore on its western bank are better off, taking one year with another, than those in the Rarh tracts.

140. The following statistics have been obtained from the Ward's office of the Cossimbazar Estate:—The average holding of a Moorshedabad ryot, as far as this estate is concerned, is about 15 bighas, out of which one bigha is generally mulberry land. The cost of cultivating a bigha of land may be estimated at Rs. 4-6. The average outturn of a bigha of paddy is 6 maunds 10 seers in the Bagri tract, which, at one maund per rupee, gives Rs. 6-4. The price of straw is about Re. 1. The cost of cultivation is calculated as if the cultivator used hired labour entirely, but he does not do so. He works for his neighbour and his neighbour works for him, and ploughs are lent and borrowed mutually. Seed also is generally kept over or borrowed, and its cost is not an outlay prior to harvest. The family of a ryot consists on an average of five members, say two adults, two women and one child; the father and his wife, a grown-up son, with a girl-wife and an infant child. This is a full average, probably too high. Allowing for deduction on account of the cultivator's own labour and seed, the net profit per bigha is Rs. 4-12, which for 14 bighas is Rs. 66-8. The net profit of a bigha of mulberry is Rs. 32, which gives a total of Rs. 98-8 net profit for 15 bighas, and this for one crop only. But the cultivator and his family line on the rice they grow. The amount of rice consumed by a family such as that stated is almost 4½

seers a day, or 3 maunds 15 seers a month, that is to say, nearly 40 maunds a year. Taking 40 maunds of rice as representing 60 maunds of paddy, it follows that the rice cost them Rs. 60 a year. Other condiments may be estimated at Rs. 18, or in all Rs. 78 for cost of food, calculated on a very liberal scale, which leaves Rs. 20 for clothes or luxuries. In lands yielding two crops, about Rs. 28 more may be added as the net profit of the second crop, on 14 bighas, which leaves him Rs. 48 after feeding himself and his family.

141. So much for the cultivators who, as a class, are very well off in this district, on the Bagri tracts at all events.

142. The agricultural labourers, *i.e.* those who live principally or entirely by labour, may be roughly estimated at about 30 per cent. of the agricultural population on the Bagri tract. The usual rate of wages is two annas a day and *jalpani* and tobacco. But this year three annas and even four annas were paid, as the bumper crop created demand for labour.

143. Artizans in the Bagri tract are more plentiful and are a more important class than in the Rarh. Those employed in the silk filatures get from Rs. 3 to Rs. 6 a month. The skilled artizans in silk command much higher wages, and skilled mistries in silk filatures are paid as high as Rs. 50 per month. Common country carpenters also are numerous and find work in boat-making and mending and making boxes for packing silk and indigo, &c. They are paid 4 annas to 6 annas a day. Weavers of common country cloth are said to earn 4 annas a day.

144. The present year is undoubtedly one of exceptional prosperity due to last year's and this year's good crops. But in an average year the percentage of inhabitants who can be called insufficiently fed on the Bagri tracts is exceedingly small.

145. The number of beggars in the Bagri tract, specially near the large towns, is much larger than on the west of the river Bhagirathi. The widely-famed but often misplaced charity of the Maharani Surnomoye has much to answer for in this respect.

146. It is very difficult to estimate accurately, or even approximately, the number, with reference to population, of professional beggars, and for statistical purposes the difficulties are enhanced by the well-known fact that many of these beggars are in no way entirely dependent on the alms they receive; that many of them have accumulated savings and hold lands and are in no danger of starvation; even if in a year of famine the gates of charity are closed but as far as the enquiries have gone, they tend to show that among the lower classes of the purely, agricultural tracts in every village of, say, 100 houses, there are in the Rarh tract at least two or three individuals who are driven to subsist on charity by infirmity, and probably some ten or a dozen more whose means of livelihood are so small that in a year of scarcity they would be in serious difficulties.

147. To summarize briefly the result of the above enquiries, it may be said that in the Rarh tract the proportion of labourers to agriculturists may be roughly estimated at from 10 per cent. in some places to 15 per cent. in others. In the Bagri and Kalantar tracts the proportion of labourers is estimated at 30 per cent. The number of intermediate holders who cultivate their own lands through their servants is much greater to the east of the district; consequently there is greater demand for labour, and the labourers are not only more plentiful, but better off. Add to this that most of the lands in the Bagri and Kalantar tracts yield two crops, and it will be seen that the condition of the agricultual labourer in these parts is probably as good as in any part of Bengal.

148. In the Rarh tract it is different. Here the holdings are smaller, the ryots mostly cultivate their own lands, and the extent of their holdings is limited by their command of labour within their own families, or rather these families have in the course of time accommodated themselves to the requirement of the holding.

149. As regards the number subsisting on charity, the result of enquiry seems to show that in every considerable village of, say, 100 houses, there are three or four persons at least who are unable to earn their own livelihood and are supported by their neighbours. But in a year of abundant crop, such as

the last two, it is almost certain that nearly every one in the district has enough food not only to support life, but to satisfy hunger and maintain health.

150. As, however, the lower classes by nature are improvident, it is certain that in a year of drought and scarcity from 10 to 15 per cent. at least of the agricultural population in the Barh will suffer difficulty in procuring sufficient food, the number being capable of enhancement in proportion to the severity of visitation.

151. In the Bagri and Kalantar tracts a year of partial failure of crops should not affect the labouring class seriously, as the large factories create a demand for labour even at the worst of times, and all that would happen as a rule would be that the rates of labour would fall to subsistence rates. Where there is no demand for labour, there is little to do, and a man who has not to work hard can live and keep his health on half of what he would require if doing a full day's work.

H. P.—Reg. No. 2858C—127—23-5-23.

CONFIDENTIAL.]

CONDITION OF THE MASSES.

No. 202GC—VII-5, dated Chittagong, the 14th May 1888.

Memo. by—D. R. LYALL, Esq., Commissioner of the Chittagong Division.

COPY, with enclosures, submitted to the Secretary to the Government of Bengal, Revenue Department, in continuation of this office No. 157GC—VII-5, dated 3rd May 1888.

No. 49T, dated Chittagong, the 8th May 1888.

From—BABOO HARIPADA GHOSE, Tehsildar, Town Khasmahal, Chittagong,

To—The Magistrate of Chittagong.

WITH reference to your letter No. 125, dated 16th January 1888, I have the honour to enclose herewith my census report in the vernacular, together with an English statement, and beg to make the following general observations on the condition of the lower class of people in Chittagong:—

The Mahomedan cultivators in Chittagong are, generally speaking, prosperous. Their land is fertile, the Government rent is not excessive, and the nature of cultivation is simple, consequently less costly. The heaven is always kind to them, and sends down profuse rain in the season. With the increase of sailing vessels in the Chittagong port, and there being easy water communication throughout the district, the trade in rice is very brisk. Rice is always sold in Chittagong at very high rates. This shows that the prospect of the agriculturists has materially changed from those days when the produce was great and consumption was less.

As soon as the cultivation season is over, the lower class generally go to British Burmah to find out services. They work there from *Magh* to *Choitro*, and generally return with money. They are never extravagant, and always frugal, and know no luxury. Their food is simple; a dish of dry fish and hot chillies is more than enough. Milk is a delicacy unknown to many, and fowls' meat, used in the advent of an honoured guest in the house, costs nothing, as they breed fowls, and no house is without them.

The Mahomedans generally use an "langat' when at home. It is a piece of rag measuring about 2ft by 9 inches. When out some of them, especially those that travel in Burmah for gain, use a *longee* and English shirt, a white cap, and a kerchief. These costing but Rs. 5 in all, give them a respectable appearance. The women are most dirtily and cheaply clothed.

The lower class has no metallic plates, as the similar Hindoos must have as a rule. Re. 1 for earthen plates, pots, &c., may be estimated for the year.

The bedding consists of a heap of dirty rags.

Their ornaments are simple and of silver weighing about 10 to 20 tolas, in a family. A few may be found to have the luxury of a gold "bolok" or nose-ring. It would not be out of the way to say that the people attach so much importance to this piece of ornament that half of the country ballads is addressed to the ring or to the fair owner.

They get a supply of their building materials, such as bamboos, sun-grass and cane, from the hills. Where the hills are near they go in number and take away the building materials and fuels without any taxes. In certain places something has to be paid to the local zemindars. Where there is no hill, the people are rather unfortunate, for they have to purchase such things. The very appearance of the houses will show whether the building materials were purchased or collected. Where money is to be expended, there the houses are generally very poor in appearance and substance. Repairs are only given to them when they are woefully leaky.

The people are contented, and feel very happy when they can hoard a little. Their hard savings remain buried in the ground, and are spent only to fill up the pockets of their pleaders when they have occasion to come to the courts. Had they been as prudent as they were in other respects, the agricultural class in Chittagong would have been the richest in comparison with the same class in other districts of India.

They are miser beyond measure. They very niggardly pay their physicians. When hope of life is extinct, it is then that they loosen their purse string. There would not be so much havoc from cholera had the people been paying to their phycisians.

The following census report books in the vernacular are sent herewith:—

For mouza Potenga	....	...	... 6 for six classes.
" Mohora	...	...	... 6 for ditto.
" Knaish	...	...	... 5 for five classes.

Kindly acknowledge the receipt of the above.

No. 1060, dated Chittagong, the 10th May 1888.

Memo. by—A. MANSON, Esq., Magistrate of Chittagong.

COPY, with copy of enclosure, submitted to the Commissioner of Chittagong, in continuation of this office No. 990, dated 30th April 1888, with the vernacular papers in original.

Number of men above manual labour of any kind.
Doing any cultivation, and at the same time also employing labourers or jotedars *i.e.* higher sort of cultivators.
Small cultivators, *i.e.* those who have fixed holding of small size, even though they may also earn something by labour.
Labourers, *i.e.* those who have not fixed holdings of their own, but live by labour.
Artisans, shop-keepers, boatmen, &c., who work for their living, and own the implements of their trade.
Poor persons who are dependent on charity.
Males.
Females.
Total.
Number of families.
Number of men above manual labour of any kind.
Doing any cultivation, and at the same time also employing labourers or jotedars, *i.e.* higher sort of cultivators.
Small cultivators, *i.e.* those who have fixed holdings of small size, even though they may also earn something by labour.
Labourers, *i.e.* those who have no fixed holdings of their own, but live by labour.
Artisans, shop-keepers, boatmen, &c., who work for their living, and own the implements of their trade.
Poor persons who are dependent on charity.

CONFIDENTIAL.]

CONDITION OF THE MASSES.

No. 712LR, dated Dacca, the 18th May 1888.

From—W. R. Larminie, Esq., c.s., Commissioner of the Dacca Division,

To—The Secretary to the Government of Bengal, Revenue Department.

With reference to your Circular No. 35Agri., dated 9th December 1887, I have the honour to submit the following report.

2. The time allowed for the collection of the information asked for is much too short to admit of any accurate statistical details being furnished by the district officers whom I have consulted, and they all disclaim any approach to any such accuracy being possible.

3. It will be seen, however, that the circumstances of Eastern Bengal are as such that no very detailed information seems necessary.

4. My own personal experience, which has been derived from such visits as were possible during a period of three years to almost every part of the division, has led me to the conclusion that, looking to their needs, the peasantry of Eastern Bengal are about the most prosperous in the world. There is a higher degree of average comfort, and less marked poverty than I have seen anywhere else. The people are, as a rule, well clothed, sufficiently fed, and comfortably housed. Wages are comparatively high, and labour is so scarce that the indigenous supply is not sufficient. Even the criminal population, as reported by Dr. Crombie, displays none of that squalid poverty which is to be found elsewhere. The district officers agree in the main with the views I have expressed above.

5. I shall now proceed to discuss more in detail the questions raised in the correspondence above referred to. The Collector of Dacca denies the possibility of finding such sample villages as would justify general conclusions. He says that circumstances vary so much that no statistics of any value could be derived from such partial enquiries, and to construct theories on such imperfect data would be like building a pyramid on its apex.

6. However, from the more detailed enquiries made by his Sub-divisional Officers and from his own general knowledge of the district, he has come to the conclusion that there is no such distress anywhere as would lead to an insufficiency of food. The cultivators are all well off, and have become more prosperous of late years in consequence of the extended cultivation of jute. Agricultural labourers are also well to do. They generally have a small holding of their own, by the cultivation of which they supplement their earnings. They also, with but few exceptions, engage in fishing when not otherwise occupied.

7. Artizans generally are prosperous, with the exception of some weavers who, when working for others, just earn a livelihood, and are generally in debt. The total number of weavers is under 20,000 out of a population of over two millions.

8. Beggars are not very numerous, and manage to support themselves in tolerable comfort.

9. The conclusions of the Collector of Mymensingh vary but little from those come to by the Collector of Dacca. He reports, however, that laboures are generally paid Rs. 4 or Rs. 5 per mensem with food and sometimes with food and lodging. These are, as far as my experience goes, high wages compared with those earned in other parts of Bengal. The weavers and potters are also said to be less prosperous than they were. The Collector reports that there has never been in Mymensingh any such failure of crops as led to any serious distress.

10. The Collector of Fureedpore has given more detailed information, the chief items of which are as follows. Cultivators earn from Rs. 9 to Rs. 20 a month, labourers from Rs. 4 to Rs. 9, some of these supplementing their earnings by fishing, &c. Artizans generally earn sufficient for their livelihood, but weavers are sometimes a little pushed. Indebtedness is common, but the liabilities are generally incurred for marriages and other religious ceremonies. Widows are generally cared for by their relations, and beggars here,

as elsewhere, manage to live fairly well. The northern and southern portions of the district of Furreedpore are the most prosperous. The intermediate portion, which chiefly consists of swamps, contains a less well-to-do population but nowhere is there any danger of any serious distress.

11. The Collector of Backergunge quite scouts the idea of any possible distress. He calculates that each cultivator holds about nine acres yielding annually about 117 maunds of cleaned and husked rice. Allowing eight members to each family, he calculates that from the sale of rice alone there would be, after paying rent and providing clothes, salt, oil, &c., an annual profit of Rs. 20 to which would be added the value of pulses, betelnuts, &c.—All further details in regard to the district of Backergunge, are given in the copy (herewith submitted) of the Collector's report, which is not in my opinion, in any way too highly coloured.

12. I have to apologize for the delay in forwarding this report, but I did not receive the required information from the Collector of Dacca till the 15th instant.

No. 151LR, dated Burisal, the 20th April 1888.

From—H. SAVAGE, ESQ., Offg. Collector of Backergunge,
To—The Commissioner of the Dacca Division.

WITH reference to your memorendum No. 2766LR, dated the 17th December 1887 forwarding a copy of Circular No. 35Agri. of 9th December 1887, I have the honour to submit the following report.

2. The frequent assertion quoted by Sir E. Buck in his Circular No. 44F—8-1, dated 17th August last, that "the greater proportion of the population of India suffer from a daily insufficiency of food" can never have been made by the most irresponsible agitator concerning the people of Eastern Bengal, and least of all concerning the population of Backergunge, and I think it unnecessary to make any extended report on the subject.

3. I will therefore but briefly comment on the condition of the four classes, cultivators, agricultural labourers, artizans, and those who subsist on charity.

(*A*) *Cultivators.*—The census returns of 1881 shew a total of 13,71,629, or two-thirds of the whole population, under this class, and it may be added nine-tenths of the remaining one-third are-tenure holders or land-holders supported directly by this class.

4. The average number of inhabitants of each house in the district was found to be 8·45, and it may therefore be calculated that the number of separate houses occupied by a number of holdings held by cultivators are in round numbers of 160,000, for it is a peculiarity of the inhabitants of the district that each villager ordinarily selects as a site for his house "the spot which appears most eligible in relation to his agricultural pursuits," and thus each house of a cultivator stood on his holding.

5. These 160,000 holdings cover the 2,235 square miles of cultivated land estimated to be in the district, so that each holding is on an average close on nine acres.

6. The average produce of paddy per acre is found to be 26 maunds in this district, which will produce 13 maunds of rice, so that if each cultivator performed the whole of his own agricultural labour himself he and his family would get 117 maunds of rice a year.

7. If each member of the family of eight use ½ a seer rice a day (a more than ample allowance) the yearly consumption would be 36 maunds leaving 81 maunds worth (at Rs. 2 a maund), Rs. 162, to pay rent and purchase other necessaries and luxuries.

8. The average rent and cesses for each holding come to about Rs. 45 and a large allowance for each family on account of clothes, salt, oil, &c., will be Rs. 8 per month, or Rs. 96 a year, so that at the end of the year the cultivator will have at least Rs. 20 to spare, and that without taking into account the value of the straw or of the pulses grown in the cold weather, or of the valuable crop of betel-nuts from the palms with which every house is surrounded.

9. Pratically, indeed, the cultivators of this district are so well off that they never do perform the whole of their agricultural operations themselves. They plough and they sow, but very seldom do they reap. Thousands of labourers come at the time of harvest from all the surrounding districts, particularly Furreedpore and Noakhally, and nearly the whole of the crops of the district are reaped by them, while the local cultivators idle away their time.

10. The Backergunge cultivator, with all his opportunity of doing so, very seldom, however, becomes a rich man. He spends his surplus money on marriages, *mélas*, and most of all on his darling luxury, litigation, and, on the authority of a well-known local zemindar. I may add that the ryot who in harvest time with his valuable crops around him will scarcely wet his feet even to go to his fields and look after the reaper, will, by the sowing season, be ready to borrow money at cent per cent.

11. As a further proof that no cultivator in the district is really in want, I may state that I have never heard of one who does not actually cook food twice a day.

12 (*b*). Agricultural labourers in the district are very few, as may be inferred from the fact of the large immigration of labourers at harvest time. The few there are (50,000, at the outside) get four to six annas a day without food or Rs. 3 or Rs. 4 with food per month during the time for ploughing and sowing, and one-fifth of the produce for harvesting.

13. This one-fifth of the produce is what the immigrant labourers get for harvesting, and is a further proof of the good condition of the cultivators.

14. A labourer with a family of eight will ordinarily with those of the family able to work earn not far short of a rupee a day, and if he be a thrifty man will soon become a cultivator on his own account.

15 (*c*). *Artisans.*—Gold and silver-smiths, blacksmiths, carpenters, potters, and braziers are well off in the district, as may be expected from the condition of their principal clients, the cultivators. Weavers who are but few in number, find their occupation almost gone, and for the most part have become cultivators or labourers.

16 (*d*). Beggars are very few in number (it is estimated not more than 2,000 in all) and are nearly all old prostitutes who have turned Baishnavies, and who, as a rule, find begging a trade so profitable that, on their death they leave generally a very handsome legacy to their gurus.

17. To sum up, it must to any unprejudiced observer be clear that Backergunge is in a most prosperous condition, and that whatever may be the case in other parts of India, British rule has been an unmixed blessing to this part of Bengal, if indeed safety of person and security of property be considered a blessing.

18. Backergunge for two centuries before the battle of Plassey was overrun and devastated by bands of Portuguese and Mug pirates, and the early British officials found it one-half jungle and the other half inhabited only by the outcastes of more peaceable parts of the country, and a comparison of the state of the country then and now cannot but impress the most unjust critic with the advantages of British rule.

J. H. B.—Reg. No. 2666C—137—23-5-86.

CONFIDENTIAL.]

CONDITION OF THE MASSES.

No. 3617, dated Calcutta, the 20th May 1888.

From—A. S. LETHBRIDGE, Esq., M.D., Inspector-General of Jails, Bengal,

To—The Secretary to the Government of Bengal, Revenue Department.

I HAVE the honour to submit the following report on the physical condition of persons of the poorer classes admitted into the jails of the Lower Provinces, called for in your endorsement No. 3696—653Agri. of 9th December last.

Circular No. 44F—6-1, dated the 17th August 1887.
Circular No. 35E—6-2, dated the 21st March 1888.

2. On receipt of the circulars cited in the margin, copies were sent to the Superintendents of Central and District Jails, who were asked to report on the question, and to support their opinions, if possible, by figures and weights; also to note distinctly the caste and calling of the prisoners referred to in their remarks.

3. In accordance with the wishes of Government expressed in Circular No. 31Agri., the discretion of the Superintendents was not fettered as to the manner in which facts were to be ascertained. They were allowed to adopt their own methods of investigation, and to form their opinions on information collected in the most convenient and suitable manner for the purpose. The majority of them have responded to this request by submitting the conclusions at which they have arrived from facts and figures obtained from the jail registers and from an examination of the prisoners in their jails. The result, I regret to say, is unsatisfactory; no definite conclusion can be arrived at from these reports.

*Dr. Meadows, Mozufferpore.
" McLeod, Gya.
" Russell, Saron.
" Cobb, Monghyr.
" Stewart, Cuttack.
" Swaine, Lohardugga.
" Polden, Chittagong.
" Cameron, Rajshahye.
" Russell, Nuddea.
" Dott, Rungpore.

†Dr. O'Brien, Burdwan.
" Crawford, Backergunge.
Captain Power, Darjeeling.
Surgeon Wilson, Jessore.
Mr. Payne, Dacca.
Dr. Bose, Furreedpore.
" Mookerjee, Dinagepore.
" Sanders, Moorshedabad.
" Moorhead, Hazaribagh.
Mr. Sevenoaks, Midnapore.

‡Mr. Larymore, Alipore.
" Leonard, Bhagulpore.
" Donaldson, Presidency.
" Beadon, Buxar.
Dr. Purves, Patna.
" Bovil, Chumparun.
" Gregg, Hooghly.
" Basu, Mymensingh.

4. Ten* Superintendents named in the margin have concluded that the poorer classes admitted into their jails are underfed in their homes. Ten† Superintendents have arrived at diametrically opposite conclusions. Eight‡ Superintendents offer no opinion as to whether the poorer classes of criminals are insufficiently fed in their homes, on the grounds that the evidence is insufficient. An analysis of the figures submitted in the reports shows that in all 3,857 typical cases were chosen for examination. Some of these prisoners were actually in jail when the enquiry was made, while the facts regarding the remainder were obtained from the jail registers. In the hope of arriving at a definite conclusion, some Superintendents have adopted the method of taking the admission weights of a number of the classes indicated in the circular and comparing them with a standard based on the admission weights of a number of prisoners of the better classes. Another method used was to take the weights on admission of a number of these prisoners and to compare those weights with present weights, and then to show in the form of a percentage the gain or loss.

In some instances the physical condition of the poorer classes on admission was sought for in the admission registers. The health of 2,881 prisoners was ascertained in this manner, and as in every case the proportion of healthy admissions was greater than either the indifferently healthy or unhealthy, it was used as evidence in favour of the theory that the prisoners in question were sufficiently fed in their homes. Some Superintendents report a deterioration in the physical condition generally of the prisoners they are now receiving as compared with previous years, and support their observation with figures. This is notably the case in the Rungpore district, and Mr. Leonard at Bhagulpore alludes to the falling off in the physique of his prisoners. In the Presidency Jail also the standard of health is becoming lower, and the proportion of prisoners received in bad and indifferent health is higher than in former years. But it is difficult to decide from the statistics which the Department can furnish whether this deterioration is due to increased poverty of the masses or climatic causes resulting in a greater prevalence of malaria in certain districts. Of the ten Superintendents who think that the poorer classes suffer from a daily insufficiency of food, those of the Cuttack, Chittagong, Rajshahye, Nuddea, and Rungpore jails have, in my opinion, arrived at this conclusion on insufficient data. On the other hand, there is no doubt that the Superintendents of the other jails in this list are in a great measure correct in supposing that the poorer classes of their districts have a great struggle for existence.

5. Besides the methods of inquiries above detailed, Mr. Larymore, of the Alipore Jail, who has had great experience of native life and character, has taken the statements of some prisoners of the classes indicated in the circulars, and as they may be of use in this enquiry, I enclose these statements for reference. The prisoners who gave their testimony were all specially selected as men who, in jail, have acquired a character for independence and straightforward dealing.

6. The well known fact that prisoners gain in weight after admission into jail is not a reliable indication that the poorer classes are insufficiently fed in their homes. This gain, although it may be more marked in the case of poorer classes, is not confined to one class of prisoners, but is shared by all. From the time the Police begin to take up the case of an under-trial prisoner until he is finally disposed of by the sentencing court, he experiences a period of deep anxiety and often distress, during which there must be considerable loss of weight. I am disposed on this account to think that the indication which the admission weights seem to give of defective nutrition is in a measure incorrect, and that the normal physical condition is not reached until the convict recovers his ordinary mental and bodily condition some time after admission. The comparison of the admission weights of the poorer classes with a standard taken from the admission weights of prisoners of the better classes is one which does not recommend itself to me. There are racial characteristics, caste distinction, physical developments due to special labour, and other influences at work which are quite sufficient to account for differences in weight without seeking for an explanation in the style of living of the different classes.

7. The conclusion forced upon me from the materials I have gathered, and my own conviction, is that a jail is not the field from which any reliable information can be obtained as to the condition of the poorer inhabitants of the agricultural districts of Bengal. There is no foundation for the formation of even general conclusions, and I doubt if criminal statistics in any shape or form can be of real value in guaging the normal and permanent condition of the masses. The life led by habitual prisoners when at large is well known to be opposed to all the laws of health: then as regards those who have never been in jail before, and whose imprisonment is to them the greatest misfortune that could befall them, the worry, anxiety, expense and possibly oppression to which, before actual conviction, they have been subjected, cannot fail to prey upon their minds, affect their health, reduce their weight, and give them the appearance of persons who in free life have suffered from insufficiency of food. It is in my opinion only through the Magistrates or other similar agency that a knowledge of the condition of the poorer classes must be sought for. Having for ten years paid a yearly visit to nearly every district in Bengal, His Honour the Lieutenant-Governor may wish to have my opinion as to general condition of the poor classes in Bengal. The only parts of the province in which there need be an anxiety on this score are Behar and Chota Nagpore. In Behar the districts of Mozufferpore and Sarun and parts of Durbhunga and Chumparun are the worst, and there is almost constant insufficiency of food among those who earn their living by daily labour. The main cause of this distress is the extreme density of the population of these districts. In consequence of the almost total absence of the worst forms of malarial diseases in these districts, there is a rapid tendency to increase in population. The only remedy for this evil is emigration. Much has been done in improving the road and railway communications between these districts and those where there is a scarcity of labour; but more might be done in encouraging emigration by offering cheap facilities for travelling by the new railway about to be opened through Purneah to Northern Bengal. The poverty in Chota Nagpore is due mainly to the unproductive nature of the soil. The extraordinary demand for labourers from Chota Nagpore in the tea industry has to a certain extent remedied the tendency to excessive poverty. The people themselves have also adopted a system of annual emigration at certain seasons to the rice-producing tracts of Bengal, which in a great measure obviates extreme hardship and daily insufficiency of food.

Serial number.	Jail register number.	Names of prisoners.	Religion or caste.	Native of—	Period of sentence.	Date of sentence.	Crime.	Weight on admission to jail.	Last weight.	Health on admission.	How many times in hospital and for what disease.	How employed in jail.	REMARKS.
		Cultivator.			Y. M. D.			lbs.	lbs.				
1	3140	Bhim Luskar	Hindoo, Pode	24-Pergunnahs ...	7 0 0	12th August 1886	Sections 149 and 304.	116	130	Indifferent ...	28th August 1886 to 28th August 1886 for diarrhoea; 15th February 1887 to 27th February 1887 for ague; and 6th March 1887 to 18th March 1887 chicken-pox.	Weaving, No. 7 yard.	
2	6490	Dinu Sardar	Ditto ...	Diamond Harbour	1 0 0	29th June 1887	Section 110 ...	108	110	Good	Nil.	Ditto ditto.	
3	6091	Satoo Bagdi	Hindoo, Bagdi	24-Pergunnahs ...	3 0 0	10th November "	Do. 148 ...	110	110	Do.	25th November 1887 to 2nd December 1887 for dysentery.	Ditto ditto.	
4	5516	Jomir Bag	Musulman ...	Ditto ...	2 0 0	9th September 1887.	Do. 147 ...	129	124	Do.	23rd March 1888 to 26th March 1888 for diarrhoea.	Ditto ditto.	
5	5364	Sadoolah Shaik ...	Ditto ...	Khulna, Jessore ...	3 0 0	15th April 1887	Do. 148 ...	135	143	Do.	Nil.	Ditto ditto.	
6	6814	Kullimuddin	Ditto ...	Noakholly ...	1 0 0	19th December "	Do. 457 ...	104	106	Do.	Nil.	Ditto ditto.	
7	6494	Abdool Hakeem ...	Ditto ...	Ditto ...	1 0 0	19th September 1887.	Do. 417 ...	100	112	Indifferent ...	Nil.	Ditto ditto.	
8	6307	Lalon Ghose	Hindoo, Gowala	Hooghly ...	1 0 0	28th October 1887	......	110	116	Do. ...	Nil.	Weaving, No. 9 yard.	
9	6539	Nondo Dhopa	Do., Dhopa	Purulia	1 0 0	12th " "	Section 457 ...	104	107	Good	Nil.	Ditto ditto.	
10	2060	Bhojo Hurry Bagdi ...	Do., Bagdi	Hooghly	7 0 0	5th June "	Dacoity, section 395.	93	96	Do.	30th June 1885 to 8th July 1885 for fever; 26th August 1886 to 29th August 1886 for ague; 30th January 1887 to 13th February 1887 for chicken-pox.	Workshop carpenter.	
11	1496	Kedar Kaiburto ...	Do., Kaiburto.	24-Pergunnahs ...	7 0 0	5th " 1885	Do. do. ...	134	131	Do.	10th November 1886 to 28th January 1887 for chicken-pox.	Ditto turner.	
12	2424	Gopinath Dass ...	Ditto ...	Ditto ...	7 0 0	22nd April 1886	Do. do. ...	122	120	Do.	26th January 1887 to 14th February 1887 for chicken-pox.	Ditto carpenter.	
13	2084	Ijootoolah	Musulman ...	Sylhet	Life.	29th July 1882	Do. 304 ...	...	141	......	22nd March 1884 to 26th March 1884 for ague.	Ditto ditto.	
14	1878	Ainuddy	Ditto ...	24-Pergunnahs ...	"	9th February 1884	Do. 304 ...	...	129	......	1st March 1884 to 10th March 1884 for chicken-pox; 23rd April 1884 to 28th April 1884 for ague; 15th October 1884 to 20th October 1884 for ague; 6th August 1885 to 21st October 1885 for contused wounds; 8th March 1886 to 12th March 1886 for diarrhoea; and 28th November 1886 to 1st January 1887 for ague.	Ditto blacksmith.	
15	905	Arshadally	Ditto ...	Barrisal	10 0 0	6th June 1886	Do. 304 ...	110	120	Good	15th July 1885 to 22nd July 1885 for dysentery, and 27th January 1887 to 10th February 1887 for chicken-pox.	Ditto ditto.	
16	5779	Sabhong Rai	Hindoo ...	Hill Tipperah ...	6 0 0	22nd " 1887	Do. 395 ...	122	130	Do.	14th October 1887 to 21st October 1887 for scabies.	Jute mill.	
17	5780	Ram Doyal	Do.	Ditto ...	6 0 0	Ditto ditto	Do. 395 ...	126	123	Do.	Nil.	Ditto.	
18	1163	Behari Rout	Do., Rout	Beerbhoom ...	7 0 0	25th January 1887	Do. 395 ...	104	110	Indifferent ...	19th November 1887 to 23rd November 1887 for bronchitis, and 8th February 1888 to 22nd February 1888 for chicken-pox.	Ditto.	
19	1164	Tegu Rout	Ditto ...	Ditto	7 0 0	Ditto ditto	Do. 395 ...	106	118	Do ...	Nil.	Ditto.	
20	1784	Pulin Manjhi	Hindoo, Rajbungshi.	Moorshedabad ...	10 0 0	19th September 1885.	Do. 394 ...	114	130	Good	14th August 1886 to 21st August 1886 for ague; 17th November 1886 to 29th November 1886 for dysentery; and 5th January 1887 to 27th February 1887 for dysentery.	Ditto.	
21	4638	Rai Chagan Kapali ...	Hindoo, Hapali	Jessore	3 0 0	24th December 1886.	Do. 211 ...	111	125	Indifferent ...	25th April 1887 to 2nd May 1887 for spleen; 8th June 1887 to 16th June 1887 for spleen; 12th September 1887 to 9th October 1887 for bronchitis; and 12th March 1888 to 30th March 1888 for chicken-pox.	Ditto.	
22	3166	Fatick Sardar	Do., Kowrah	24-Pergunnahs ...	5 0 0	12th August 1886	Do. 149 and 304.	107	128	Do. ...	27th November 1886 to 9th December 1886 for bronchitis, and 24th January 1887 to 14th February 1887 for chicken-pox.	Ditto.	
23	3169	Bhooban Pundit ...	Ditto ...	Ditto	7 0 0	Ditto ditto	Do. do. ...	98	106	Do. ...	3rd February 1887 to 23rd February 1887 for chicken-pox.	Ditto.	
24	5880	Rostom Khan	Musulman ...	Jessore	10 0 0	13th April 1887	Do. 304 ...	100	105	Do. ...	15th February 1888 to 6th March 1888 for chicken-pox.	Ditto.	
25	3967	Belait Ally	Ditto ...	Chittagong ...	3 6 0	27th January "	Do. 149 and 326.	107	115	Good	Nil.	Ditto.	
26	5877	Asdmuddy	Ditto ...	Jessore	5 0 0	28th June "	Section 325 ...	103	104	Do.	2nd February 1888 to 22nd February 1888 for chicken-pox.	Ditto.	
27	3561	Deraj Mondul	Ditto ...	24-Pergunnahs ...	8 0 0	1st October 1886	Do. 376 and 511.	124	130	Indifferent ...	12th November 1887 to 18th November 1887 for ague, and 14th December 1887 to 17th December 1887 for diarrhoea.	Ditto.	
28	3694	Ameer Ally	Ditto ...	Chittagong ...	5 0 0	26th July "	Section 326 ...	105	129	Do. ...	3rd March 1887 to 9th March 1887 for chicken-pox, and 5th May 1887 to 10th May 1887 for ague.	Ditto.	

Serial number.	Jail register number.	Names of prisoners.	Religion or caste.	Native of—	Period of sentence.	Date of sentence.	Crime.	Weight on admission to jail.	Last weight.	Health on admission.	How many times in hospital and for what disease.	How employed in jail.	REMARKS.
		Agricultural Labourer.			Y. M. D.			lbs.	lbs.				
29	5645	Bhola Nath Sardar ...	Hindoo, Howrah	Diamond Harbour	8 0 0	30th June 1884	House-breaking, section 457.	108	108	Good	Nil.	Weaving, No 9 yard.	
30	2753	Haroo Bagdi	Hindoo, Bagdi	Bankoorah ...	7 0 0	9th „ 1886	Dacoity ...	92	100	Indifferent ...	17th June 1886 to 22nd June 1886 for ague; 24th February 1887 to 4th March 1887 for ague; and from 6th April 1887 to 23rd July 1887 for conjunctivitis.	Ditto ditto.	
31	6082	Kassimuddy	Musulman ...	Barrisal	8 0 0	28th July 1887	Theft, section 380.	112	110	Bad	2nd December 1884 to 6th December 1884 for diarrhœa, and from 8th January 1888 to 20th February 1888 for debility.	Ditto, No. 7 ditto.	
32	6263	Kristo Chungo ...	Hindoo, Chandal.	Ditto ...	8 6 0	25th August „	Sections 324 and 326.	105	109	Good	18th February 1888 to 23rd February 1888 for ague.	Ditto, No. 9 ditto.	
33	6069	Hurry Dhon	Chakma Hill tribe.	Chittagong ...	1 3 0	24th June „	Section 457 ...	104	106	Indifferent ...	5th November 1887 to 9th November 1887 for ague.	Ditto, No. 9 ditto.	
34	634	Kherodhur Sardar ...	Hindoo, Pode	24-Pergunnahs ...	7 0 0	16th April 1884	Do. 395 ...	105	107	Good	11th October 1884 to 14th October 1884 for ague; 22nd January 1886 to 28th January 1886 for ague; 4th March 1886 to 10th March 1886 for lymphangitis; and 29th December 1886 to 14th January 1887 for chicken-pox.	Workshop blacksmith.	
35	3914	Baikanto Sardar ..	Do., Kowrah.	Ditto	7 0 0	9th December 1886.	Do. 304 ...	108	113	Do.	27th January 1887 to 15th February 1887 for chicken-pox; 6th March 1887 to 11th March 1887 for ague; and from 4th August 1887 to 9th August 1887 for ague.	Ditto ditto.	
36	793	Poran Bagdi	Hindoo, Bagdi	Ditto ...	10 0 0	21st August 1885	Do. 304 ...	114	125	Indifferent ...	9th July 1886 to 20th July 1886 for contused wounds and boil, and 18th October 1886 to 4th December 1886 for ottorrhœa.	Ditto ditto.	
37	1955	Romjan Shaik ...	Musulman ...	Moorshedabad ...	5 0 0	24th November 1885.	Do. 395 ...	115	115	Good	14th April 1886 to 6th May 1886 for condyloma, and 1st August 1886 to 11th August 1886 for hemicrania.	Ditto rivetman.	
38	1782	Julmi Shaik	Ditto ...	Ditto ...	7 0 0	17th July 1886 ...	Sections 147 and 304.	119	132	Do.	Nil.	Ditto carpenter.	
39	1957	Anaruddy Shaik ..	Ditto ...	Ditto ...	5 0 0	24th November 1886.	Section 395 ...	114	130	Do.	6th September 1886 to 12th September 1886 for ague; 13th February 1887 to 23rd February 1887 for chicken-pox; and 19th September 1887 to 26th September 1887 for asthma.	Ditto latheman.	
40	4898	Bolaki Shaik	Ditto ...	Furreedpore ...	7 0 0	8th June 1887 ...	Do. 304 ...	108	117	Indifferent ...	1st November 1886 to 4th November 1886 for dysentery; 4th March 1888 to 21st March 1888 for chicken-pox.	Jute mill.	
41	7973	Jinoo Shaik	Ditto ...	Moorshedabad ...	7 0 0	23rd November 1887.	Do. 395 ...	118	133	Ditto ...	20th March 1884 to 6th April 1884 for diarrhœa; 7th July 1884 to 11th August 1884 for debility; 14th December 1884 to 21st December 1884 for diarrhœa; 3rd August 1885 to 12th August 1885 for measles, and 18th April 1887 to 27th April 1887 for bronchitis.	Ditto.	
42	6503	Derastullah	Ditto ...	Barrisal	4 0 0	26th September 1887.	Do. 457 ...	106	101	Good	Nil.	Ditto.	
43	2734	Sreemonto Baroi ...	Hindoo, Kalburto.	24-Pergunnahs ...	8 0 0	7th June 1886 ...	Do. 395 ...	120	135	Do.	10th July 1886 to 13th July 1886 for diarrhœa, and 12th February 1887 to 25th February 1887 for chicken-pox.	Ditto.	
44	5041	Bhootnath Deria ...	Hindoo, Chandal.	Ooloobariah, Hooghly.	1 6 20	22nd February 1887.	Do. 380 ...	96	110	Indifferent ...	6th March 1888 to 16th March 1888 for chicken-pox.	Ditto.	
45	4880	Ishan Chundra Bera...	Hindoo, Kalburto.	Howrah, Hooghly	10 0 0	10th September 1886.	Do. 304 ...	98	110	Good	14th March 1888 to 2nd April 1888 for chicken-pox.	Ditto.	
46	2703	Sukra Rajwar ...	Hindoo, Rajwar.	Burdwan ...	5 0 0	17th December 1886.	Do. 395 ...	94	118	Bad	Nil.	Ditto.	
47	6546	Sreeram Bouri ...	Hindoo, Bowri	Manbhoom ...	8 0 0	18th October 1887	Do. 376 ...	118	128	Indifferent ...	Nil.	Ditto.	

		Artisan.													Profession or calling.
48	5871	Sonal Karikar ...	Musulman ...	Jessore	2	0	0	18th June 1887 ...	Sections 457 and 380.	100	123	Good	Nil.	Weaving, No. 7 yard...	Cloth-weaver ...
49	6496	Bhogowan Mondul ...	Ditto ...	Barrisal	1	0	0	29th October 1887	Section 325 ...	116	118	Do.	Nil.	Ditto ...	Carpenter ...
50	6373	Abbash haik ...	Ditto ...	24-Pergunnahs ...	3	0	0	28th December 1887.	Do. 147 ...	126	125	Indifferent ...	Nil.	Workshop carpenter	Ditto and jailor.
51	5919	Nagorullah	Ditto ...	Barrisal	5	6	0	19th January 1884	Sections 324 and 304.	120	137	Good	Nil.	Ditto ditto ...	Boat builder ...
52	6363	Atab Shaik	Ditto ...	24-Pregunnahs ...	0	6	0	31st December 1887.	Section 379 ...	110	130	Do.	Nil.	Ditto viceman ...	Viceman ...
53	4462	Mohendra Lal Seal ...	Hindoo, Bhaskar.	Dum-Dum ...	1	10	15	1st March 1887 ...	Do. 406 ...	128	131	Do.	Nil.	Ditto ditto ...	Watchmaker, &c.
54	3536	Jogendra Chundra Dam.	Hindoo Boistom.	24-Pergunnahs ...	2	0	0	25th September 1886.	Do. 457 ...	98	106	Indifferent ...	8th January 1887 to 28th January 1887 for chicken-pox.	Ditto ditto ...	Type-maker ...
55	4167	Hira Lal Pal	Hindoo Kumar	Nuddea	7	0	0	9th September 1886.	Do. 325 ...	103	115	Bad	18th February 1887 to 7th March 1887 for lichen; 13th May 1887 to 6th June 1887, ague; and 20th July 1887 to 8th August 1887, ague.	Ditto latheman ...	Potter ... ...
56	1892	Abdool Hakim ...	Musulman ...	Dum-Dum ...	5	0	0	8th February 1886.	Do. 325 ...	94	100	Indifferent ...	6th June 1887 to 22nd July 1887 for bronchitis	Mason	Mason ... ...
57	7353	Kasem Mondul ...	Ditto ...	Barrackpore ...	9	0	0	10th December 1883.	Do. 395 ...	115	121	Do. ...	21st April 1884 to 30th April 1884 for fever; 17th March 1885 to 9th April 1885 for diarrhoea.	Do.	Do. ... ...
58	4406	Poresh Shaik ...	Ditto ...	24-Pergunnahs ...	10	0	0	26th February 1887.	Do. 304 ..	108	118	Good	Nil.	Do.	Do. ... ...
59	2364	Kaloo Shaik ...	Ditto ...	Ditto ...	7	0	0	3rd May 1886 ...	Do. 304 ...	109	108	Do.	28th January 1887 to 30th January 1887 for ague.	Jute mill	Do. ... ...
60	6678	Attiar Rohoman ...	Ditto ...	Ditto ...	2	0	0	4th February 1888.	Do. 379 ...	104	106	Indifferent ...	Nil.	Ditto	Tailor ... ...
61	4841	Gokool Chamar ...	Hindoo, Chamar.	Howrah	1	0	0	14th April 1887 ...	Do. 429 ...	118	125	Good	Nil.	Ditto	Shoemaker ...
62	5960	Joggesher Moochy ...	Hindoo, Moochy.	Bassirhat ...	1	0	0	14th October 1887	Do. 380 ...	100	107	Do.	9th March 1888 to 31st March 1888 for chicken-pox.	Ditto	Basket worker ...
		Beggars.													
63	980	Chittra Narain Boiragi.	Hindoo, Boiragi.	Diamond Harbour	7	0	0	9th September 1885.	Do. 395 ...	116	119	Indifferent ...	2nd August 1886 to 15th August 1886 for gum-boil; 3rd April 1887 to 9th April 1887 inflamed foot; 1st February 1887 to 5th February 1887 for ague; 9th February 1887 to 24th February 1887 loss in weight.	Weaving, No. 7 yard.	
64	4637	Kaimullah Shaik ...	Musulman ...	Jessore	3	0	0	2nd November 1886.	Do. 326 ...	112	113	Good	8th August 1887 to 18th August 1887 for ague; 15th October 1887 to 21st October 1887 for bronchitis; and 18th February 1888 to 14th March 1888 for bronchitis.	Jute mill.	
65	6377	Khokan Dass Boiragi	Hindoo, Boiragi.	Kastea, Nuddea...	0	6	0	17th December 1887.	Sections 147 and 323.	89	96	Do.	Nil.	Ditto.	
66	6468	Behari Boiragi ...	Ditto ...	24-Pergunnahs ...	1	0	0	5th January 1888	Section 380 ...	96	100	Indifferent ...	10th February 1888 to 28th February 1888 for chicken-pox.	Ditto.	

ALIPORE JAIL,
The 13th April 1888.

A. D. LARYMORE,
Superintendent, Alipore Jail.

C. E. G.—Reg. No. 3027C—137—26-5-88.

Confidential.]

No. 351R, dated Ranchi, the 31st May 1888.

From—C. C. STEVENS, ESQ., C.S., Commissioner of the Chota Nagpore Division,
To—The Secretary to the Government of Bengal, Revenue Department.

IN reply to your circular No. 35Agri., dated 9th December 1887, calling for a report on the subject of the condition of the lower classes, I have the honour to submit the following observations. I regret that there has been some delay in collecting information. Even now I am not in a position to submit a thoroughly satisfactory report.

2. In the immense area covered by the Chota Nagpore Division there is, as might be expected, a great variety of local conditions. There are also strongly marked differences of race, and the gradations from little more than savagery to orderly and civilized institutions are many. It is therefore not easy, if indeed it is possible at all, to lay down general deductions which shall at the same time be accurate in regard to particular instances.

3. As the local officers have been left very much to themselves to determine the method and means of conducting their enquiries, their reports have varied greatly in their nature and scope. Some officers, perhaps, have not altogether complied with the injunction to avoid ostentatious or formal enquiries, while others have generally avoided details. On account of these diversities of form in the reports, as well as the local varieties to which I have already alluded, it will be most convenient for me to consider the several districts singly, and to forward in original the reports which have been submitted to me.

4. I begin with the district of Manbhoom, which is, upon the whole, the most advanced in the division. On the east it borders on the Sonthal Pergunnahs and the regulation districts of Burdwan and Bankoora, and this portion is materially affected by the coal-fields, the works on which give abundant and lucrative employment. The southern and part of the western tracts are wild and primitive, while most of the remainder is under cultivation and is fairly well populated. The District Officer selected for his enquiries nine villages, situated in different parts of his charge, which, he thought, would, in size, population, wealth and occupations, be fairly representative of the district. He drew up a set of questions, which were put to each ryot in the presence of every other ryot in the village, and the results were tabulated in a statement which accompanied Mr. Baker's report. That gentleman claims for this that the statistics present "a tolerably complete and, as far as they go, absolutely accurate picture of the condition of all classes" in the nine villages. The care and industry expended on the statement must be acknowledged, but Mr. Baker himself, later on in his report, has impugned its "absolute accuracy" in some important particulars.

5. Regarding the population and its distribution into the four classes of cultivators, agricultural labourers, artizans, and dependents on charity, Mr. Baker summarizes his statistics in the following way:—

"The nine villages visited contain 550 separate households, with a gross population of 3,362 souls. The females exceed the males in the proportion of 51 to 49. The population includes 1,010 adult males, 1,081 adult females, and 1,271 children under 12 years of age. The number of earning members is 1,192, or rather more than 35 per cent. of the whole population.

"The distribution of the people among the four main classes described in the Government circular is as follows:—

	No. of families.	Percentage.
"Cultivators	277	50·4
Agricultural labourers	157	28·5
Artizans	100	18·2
Dependent on charity	16	2·9

"In other words, one-half live by agriculture, rather more than one-fourth by agricultural labour, less than one-fifth by some form of trade or handicraft, and the small residue are dependent on charity."

But this division into the four classes is not sharply defined, for only 148 families, or 53 per cent., confined themselves to agriculture, while 42 also earn money as labourers, and 87 add to the profits of their cultivation by trade or handicraft. Again, 43 families of labourers and 36 of artizans, or 27 and 36 per cent., respectively, hold small parcels of land for which they pay less than Rs. 5 rent.

6. In Manbhoom, as in the greater part of the division, measurement of lands by a definite standard is as yet unknown, and consequently it has been impossible to supply information as to the areas of holdings. The value of the crops raised by the cultivating class, including miscellaneous receipts from straw, jungle produce, &c., is stated to be Rs. 18,033, but I cannot help doubting whether this is not below the truth, for on looking into the details of the villages, I find in the case of Pairachuli, which contains more than the usual proportion of pure cultivators, the value of the produce is only Rs. 30·5 per family; while in Chainpur, which has a smaller proportion of such persons, the value is over Rs. 120·2 per family. The average of Rs. 65·28 gross income per family obtained by the Deputy Commissioner is probably, I think, too low. He estimates the whole cost of cultivation at a little more than half the gross value of the crop. Taking into account the income from labour, trade, &c., he finds the income of each family, subsisting entirely or mainly by cultivation, to be about Rs. 48. This is rather too low if, as I think, the value of the produce is taken at too low a figure.

7. I can scarcely abbreviate the following account given by Mr. Baker of the agricultural labourers:—

"Turning now to the agricultural labourers, we find that in 157 households there are 355 earning members, of whom 240 are males and 115 are females. In other words, in this class there is one working woman for every two working men. It is satisfactory to find that more than three-fourths of these labourers usually obtain employment for the greater part of the year, thus:—

"Number employed for less than three months in the year ..	43
" " " more than three and less than six months ..	49
" " " more than six months	263
Total ..	355

"The earnings of these 355 labourers during the year amount to 2,785 maunds of paddy, valued at Rs. 1,740, together with Rs. 2,122* in cash. Their total earnings thus amount to rather less than Rs. 11 per head per annum. The total income of an average family of this class from all sources is—

* Of this, however, Rs. 1,340 were earned by labourers in mouzah Debiana, most of whom are miners, and not agricultural labourers.

	Rs.
From labour	24·6
" cultivation (net)	4·48
" miscellaneous	·73
Total ..	29·81"

I am inclined to think that these estimates of income are too low.

8. I may also quote at length the following account of the artizans:—

"The information collected regarding the third class, or artizans, is meagre. The people were usually unable to give any reliable account of their gross expenses, and the figures given by them of their net earnings are probably not very reliable. I noticed a general tendency to understate these, and I have no doubt that the figures obtained are materially less favourable than the real truth. No attempt has been made to distinguish the various handicrafts. The total income of the 100 families belonging to this class, and the average income of each family, are as follows:—

	Total income.	Average income.
	Rs.	Rs.
"From trade	2,688	26·88
" cultivation (net)	441	4·41
" miscellaneous	377	3·77
Total ..	3,506	35·06"

In this instance it will be observed that the income is admittedly understated.

9. Although the average receipts of each of the three classes of cultivators, labourers, and artizans are probably greater than they are reported to be, I see no reason to doubt that the Deputy Commissioner has rightly concluded that those classes stand in order of income as follows—First cultivators, second artizans, third labourers; and I am not prepared to question the relative ratios of income per family arrived at, viz. Rs. 48, Rs. 35·06, and Rs. 29·81 respectively.

10. As might be expected, the cultivators have far the largest proportion of livestock. The average value of livestock per family of the three classes are thus estimated:—

	Rs.
Cultivators	50
Artizans	9
Labourers	7

11. In the matter of indebtedness, the following are the conclusions arrived at—

Class.	Proportion in debt.	Average indebtedness per family.
	Per cent.	Rs.
Cultivators	75	54
Artizans	61	13
Labourers	55	10
Dependent on charity ..	*Nil*	*Nil*

The Deputy Commissioner remarks that "these figures go some way to prove that the extent and degree of indebtedness depend much less on the probable necessity of the borrower than on the security he is able to offer," and he points out the general coincidence between the amount of debt and the value of the livestock. I quite think that this coincidence is not accidental, and have reason to believe that Mr. Baker's remark is of general application.

12. The following figures show the number of families said to be never without two meals a day:—

Cultivators	240	families out of	277
Labourers	121	ditto	157
Artizans	76	ditto	100
Beggars	14	ditto	16

Mr. Baker, however, thinks that the real number of families which always secure two meals a day is less than those figures show. He says that "it seems to have been made a point of honour to deny any deficiency in the matter of daily food." I am inclined, however, to think that the very same reason which would lead the ryots to understate their income would lead them to exaggerate, rather than to minimize, the general hardship of their condition.

13. The Deputy Commissioner has drawn up the following table, containing certain facts bearing upon this enquiry:—

Number of Families.	Cultivators.	Labourers.	Artizans.	Beggars.
Using brass utensils	276	121	92	12
Average weight of brass utensils per family (seers)	15	1·6	4·6	2·4
Quantity of salt used per family per annum (seers)	56	25	35	22
Quantity of food-grains required for one year's consumption per family (maunds)	42	19	25	10

He has also attempted to divide the several classes into—(1) those who are well-to-do, (2) those who have sufficient, and (3) those who have not sufficient. I am, however, unable to attach any value to the results obtained. Mr. Baker himself shows that no credit is given for the produce of homestead lands, such as chillies, tobacco, potatoes, &c., or for the value of milk and *ghee*; and, further, no credit is given for jungle fruits, leaves and roots, which are much used for food in the wilder parts of the district. For information as to the extent to which these products supplement the ordinary cultivated crops, I would refer to a paper by Mr. V. Ball of the Geological Survey, quoted in paragraphs 47-53 of the Statistical Account of Hazaribagh.

14. The general conclusions arrived at are the following:—

(1) "Rather less than two-thirds of the householders are in debt, debt being most common, and a long way most heavy in amount among the cultivators.

(2) "Among the cultivating classes the standard of living is fairly high, though a considerable number—perhaps one-fourth—fail to maintain it permanently.

(3) "Among the labouring classes there is a section, under one-fifth, which is well-to-do, but the majority have to put up with a standard of living which is barely half as high as that common among the cultivators.

(4) "Artizans, though better off than the labourers, are still behind the cultivating classes in comfort.

(5) "The number of families wholly dependent on charity is almost ·2 per cent. of the whole."

With these views I concur upon the whole, though I am of opinion that the true position of affairs is somewhat better than the Deputy Commissioner takes it to be.

15. The Singbhoom district may be regarded as divided into two main portions—Dhalbhoom on the east and the Kolhan on the west. Besides these tracts, the Deputy Commissioner has under his charge the sequestrated Political State of Porahat, and one or two other less important areas. It also completely envelopes the States of Seraikella and Kharsawan. Dhalbhoom and the Kolhan differ materially in their political conditions, as well as in the races which inhabit them. Dhalbhoom is subject to the jurisdiction of the High Court and the Judicial Commissioner; it is permanently settled, and generally is on the same footing as the neighbouring district of Manbhoom, by which it is bounded on the east, and which it much more nearly resembles in all its conditions than it does the Kolhan. The Dhalbhoom estate was formerly managed by the Court of Wards, but was taken over by the late Rajah, four or five years ago, on his coming of age. About a year and a half ago, as, by his dissipation and mismanagement, he had reduced the property to the verge of insolvency, charge of it was assumed by the Deputy Commissioner under the Encumbered Estates Act. The death of the Rajah a few months afterwards made no difference in the condition of the estate, which is still being managed under the supervision of the Deputy Commissioner. The information submitted regarding Dhalbhoom is given on the authority of the Manager, but the Deputy Commissioner regards that officer's conclusions as less satisfactory than the facts would probably justify. His own impressions, derived (it is true) from a short tour in the tract, led him to believe that "the people were fairly prosperous." "I saw" (he says) "no indications of want anywhere, and though I did receive complaints against the excessiveness of the land assessment and the operation of the income tax, I saw nothing to raise even a suspicion that the people were half-starved or poverty-stricken. On the contrary, I was very greatly surprised to find them looking so well nourished, so well clothed, and so comfortably housed, considering the manner in which the estate had been mismanaged during the previous three years of the late Rajah-zemindar." I am not in a position to speak from my own personal observations, since I have not been able to visit Dhalbhoom.

16. The Manager's enquiries were made by selected tehsildars in two groups, each comprising five typical villages, and in one large village which was considered to be particularly prosperous. The statistics are given in four tables, which, however, are far less elaborate than those submitted from

Manbhoom, and I am obliged to say that I have no great confidence in them. In form A are shown the average area of each ryot's holding, the average gross and net incomes of each ryot, and the average net profits available for maintenance of each person; but with the exception that in one group of five villages the average area of the holding is 12 bighas and in the other group it is 11, the remaining figures are identical in the two groups. The conclusion drawn is that the amount available for the support of each person is but Rs. 6-11-6, which is enough for four months only. But the produce is taken at only from 4 to 4½ maunds of *dhan* per bigha. This seems an extraordinarily low rate, and I should question whether the actual yield is not as much of cleaned rice as there is said to be of *dhan*. The miscellaneous sources of income, too, are no doubt understated. In statement No. I corresponding statistics have been given for one large village, Mondah. These are somewhat more favourable, though still, I suspect, below the truth. The average area of the ryot's holding is 16½ bighas, the produce is 5½ maunds of *dhan* per bigha, and the net profit of the family is Rs. 41-7; the average available for each ryot's sustenance is Rs. 7, which is said to be only enough to last for four months.

17. According to statement II, the average annual income of each labourer's family in the village of Mondah is Rs. 44-4, or Rs. 2-13 more than that of each agriculturist's family, which is very unlikely. Statement III also appears to me to be open to much doubt.

18. I would discard the statistics entirely, and consider that more information is to be obtained from the verbal remarks of the Manager, which are founded on his own experience and that of others, besides the statistics. These are to the following effect:—

"The condition of the people engaged exclusively in agriculture may be said to vary directly according to the area of land cultivated by each family. The larger the size of the ryot's holding, the greater is the margin of profits available for the maintenance of his family; and as the number of persons dependent on a well-to-do ryot cultivating a large holding is not larger, in proportion to his profits, than the number dependent on a poorer ryot cultivating a smaller holding, the former are far better off than the latter as to finding a living from the profits of the ryot's holdings. The caste or tribal conditions of the ryots have often an important bearing on their condition in life. A Sonthal or Bhoomij, as a rule, supplements the profits of his cultivation by the income he derives from the sale of fowls, swine or other small cattle, such as goats and sheep; but an orthodox Hindu ryot, a Gowala or Rajput, or Teli, for instance, has religious or social prejudices against the rearing even of the less objectionable cattle, such as sheep and goats, for the purpose of sale. The former can eke out his means of subsistence by living upon the flesh of the fowls and cattle he rears, but the latter would depend chiefly on the income he derives from the sale of such cattle as he may rear without prejudice to his own caste, and this he can do only where there is a ready market for them. In rural tracts, remote from towns, where there are no markets for the sale of livestock, the Hindu ryot has scarcely any inducement to rear it on any large scale.

"It would appear from the reports received by me that about one-half the agriculturists are in a chronic state of indebtedness to their mahajans. My own enquiries, however, tend to show that this proportion is rather below the mark, and that about ten-sixteenths of this class are hopelessly indebted. It is a common saying in the pergunnah that the *chashis* (agriculturists) cultivate their lands for their mahajans."

It will be noticed that the proportion of agriculturists in debt corresponds nearly with that ascertained in Manbhoom.

19. The Manager goes on to say as follows:—"The mainstay of the ryots is the winter rice crop of December. After payment of rents and cesses by the sale of a portion of the crop, and returning the loan of grain previously taken from the mahajan with the usual addition of one-half of the advance, the portion of the produce left for the maintenance of the ryots and their families enable them as a rule to live upon it for only four months, namely from Aghran to Falgoon (December to March). With Chyte commences the strain. The ryot again resorts to the mahajan for an advance of grain, and lives upon

the advance, supplemented (in the case of poorer ryots) by *mohua* flowers and *kenda* fruits, till Bhadro, when the harvesting of the *bhadoi* crops, viz. *aus dhan* or early rice, *makoyi*, *marooa*, &c., relieves the pressure, and enables him to hold out till the next Kartik. The interval between Chyte and Bhadro is usually the hardest time for the bulk of the ryots, and during this period they can seldom afford to eat two full meals of grain a day."

From this it would seem that the ryots are usually able to clear off their debts each year, and to start again with fresh loans. In reference to the difficulties experienced by the ryots in tiding over the time between the middle of the hot weather and the rains, I need not again quote Mr. Ball's remarks on the use of jungle produce. I think it very probable that during this period many of the ryots do not get two meals of *grain* per diem, but that they are able to support life without great privation by other food.

20. The condition of the agricultural labourers is thus described:—

"On the whole, this class is better off than the poorer agriculturists. Even the poorest of the latter cannot do without the help of his *krishan* or *moolia*, and though himself pinched by want of a sufficiency of food, he takes care to keep his *krishan* on and in good humour. Indeed, the life of a poor ryot is a life of constant self-denial, endured with a philosophic contentment. My enquiries show that about a tenth of the number of the agricultural labourers cultivate small holdings of an average size of 2 bighas each, in addition to their working in the fields of their employers. These holdings are locally called *dahina* lands, and are cultivated with implements and cattle borrowed from their employers. It will be seen from statement No. II that the yearly earnings of a family of agricultural labourers amount to Rs. 44-4 in the case of the small minority who cultivate *dahina* lands, and Rs. 38-4 in the case of those who do not cultivate any land. The net amount of profits available for the support of a person of this class has been estimated at Rs. 11 and Rs. 12-8 respectively in the two cases above mentioned, and this is just sufficient to maintain him for seven or eight months in the year. Those who depend upon the labourer's wages for support usually find a hard time of it after the harvesting of the winter rice crops, when they have no work to do in the fields. At this time they go to the jungle and find a living by selling fuel. Then, also, the children and the less able-bodied of the poorer members of this class usually betake themselves to begging, and are called *kangalies* or poor people, as distinct from the class of professional beggars."

I can scarcely think that the labourers are really better off than the agriculturists.

21. The artizans, again, are said to be still better off than the labourers. I will again quote the Manager's report:—

"I have little to say regarding this class. Its chief subdivisions are carpenters, lohars or iron-smiths, oil-pressers, and weavers. They are very unequally distributed in the villages. The carpenters and lohars are usually found in the larger villages, inhabited by well-to-do men. In the best cultivated taraf the number of artizans found in a group of five villages is 50, while in an average taraf the number is 35. Numerically, the oil-pressers preponderate all over the pergunnah. The weavers form a minority. Here they do not find their occupation gone, nor suffer from any exceptional degree of poverty. They manufacture coarse cloths for the use of the lower classes of the population, who prefer them to the more finished, but less durable, products of foreign mills. The average monthly earnings of each person of this class may be estimated at Rs. 4-8 or Rs. 5.

"The carpenters and the lohars usually find difficulty in obtaining work during the four months of the year from September to December. The lohars have sometimes a bad reputation, and in a season of high prices are not unfrequently found implicated in petty crimes. The general condition of the artizan class, excepting perhaps the lohars, is slightly better than that of the agricultural labourers."

The Deputy Commissioner has submitted a paper on the artizans, drawn up by the Deputy Inspector of Schools, who has been in the district for some years. He gives a more favourable account of them than the Manager does, and it would appear that the artizans have no difficulty in obtaining a livelihood, but some of them spend too much in drink.

22. The Manager then deals with the classes subsisting on charity :—

"The number of such persons found in each of the two groups dealt with was found to be 45 and 50 respectively. The average number of each village may be estimated at 8. This class may be subdivided into two principal sections, viz. (1) professional beggars, (2) persons whom physical infirmities or high prices of food have compelled to live on the bounty of others. The professional beggars are as a rule well off. They are mostly itinerant singers and *sadhoos* or religious mendicants, and the daily doles of grain and money they collect enable them to live even in some comfort. The members of the other section are often very badly off. Being usually of the lowest castes and classes of population connected with crime, they are more despised than pitied, and the small daily doles of grain they receive hardly suffice to keep their body and soul together. They are left to perish miserably of want in the case of protracted illness."

23. Regarding the condition of the Kolhan there is nothing but good to be said. The Kols are the direct tenants of Government, and are managed through mandas or heads of villages, and mankis or heads of groups of villages. The settlement now in force is for 30 years, and the Government rents are realized with the utmost regularity. The Deputy Commissioner took the holdings of 20 ryots at random, and found that on the average each was a little less than 12 acres.

The Deputy Commissioner gives the following account of this part of his district :—

"From enquiries made by me, I learnt that the average yield of an acre of rice land is 25 maunds and 30 seers, and that the average value of the produce per acre is Rs. 17, *i.e.*, at the rate of $1\frac{1}{2}$ maunds per rupee.

"From the above figures it will be found, then, that a ryot receives from his rice lands alone on an average Rs. 204 per annum. This by itself is no mean income, and when you add to it the profits derived from the crops sown on the uplands, such as oilseeds, pulses, millets, &c., and take into account the large quantity of edible fruits, flowers, and roots the forests provide free of cost, I think I may safely say that the agriculturist in the Kolhan is a prosperous man. These remarks apply to all classes who inhabit the Kolhan, but with greater force to the aboriginal tribes, who, in addition to large and productive tenures and a light assessment, enjoy the privilege of brewing their own ale without taxation.

"Money not being very plentiful in the Kolhan, it is not easy to compute what proportion of their produce the ryots convert into hard cash. Here barter is the custom. The clothes they wear, their livestock, consisting of pigs, sheep, goats, pigeons, &c., and even plough cattle, are acquired by barter.

"Beyond lots of good food, the people indulge in few luxuries. Their rice-beer, to which they are very partial, they brew themselves; they grow their own tobacco; their clothing, scanty by choice and not of necessity, is spun in the village, and is preferred by them to imported goods; they despise gold and silver, and prefer ornaments made of brass and bell-metal. Their houses are substantially built, and bear the appearance of being proof against sun, wind and rain, and they are gradually substituting metal for earthen utensils.

"Marriage expenses here are limited and within the means of the people. Amongst the Kols the price of a wife is limited to ten heads of cattle and one pair of oxen. One cow and Rs. 7 in cash is received as an equivalent, and this scale is becoming gradually adopted by the other castes also."

I do not feel sure that the profits of the ryots are quite so large as the Deputy Commissioner finds them to be, but it is not possible for any one to go into the Kolhan without seeing that the people are in a prosperous and happy condition.

24. The conditions of Porahat are something like those of the Kolhan. The ryots hold directly under Government, being represented by the village headmen; the settlement is for 20 years, and they pay a rent of Rs. 1-14-6 per acre, which is just double of that collected in the Kolhan. The Deputy Commissioner took the holdings of 20 ryots at random, and found that their rice lands (which alone are assessed) were on the average a little less than 6 acres. He estimates the produce of paddy at $30\frac{1}{4}$ maunds per acre, and

the value at 1½ maunds per rupee. This last seems to be rather a high rate—at least for past years—but the construction of the Bengal-Nagpore Railway right through the State will doubtless have the effect of raising the price of produce in the future. The Deputy Commissioner estimates the value of the produce of a ryot's rice land at Rs. 130 per annum, which is much below his estimate for the Kolhan, but he understands that the produce of the uplands is far greater, and the Porahat ryot is nearly, if not quite, as prosperous as the ryot of the Kolhan.

25. In regard to the state of agricultural labourers in the Kolhan and Porahat, Mr. Renny offers the following observations:—"From information furnished to me, I estimate the agricultural labourers to muster 20 per cent. of the population in the Kolhan and 30 per cent. in Porahat. In the former estate the rate of remuneration is 3 seers of *dhan* and three pots of rice-beer per diem, and in the latter 4 seers of *dhan* and one pice in cash. This remuneration is paid generally during nine months of the year, and during the remaining three months the labourer finds no difficulty in supporting himself, as there is always employment to be found in road-making, reservoir construction, and under the Forest Department. To show that the labourer is not in want and can look after himself, I will here mention what I was told by the District Engineer in charge of the Singbhoom division of the Bengal-Nagpore Railway, now under construction. He said that, until he entered the Government estate of Porahat, he had no difficulty about labour, but that immediately he entered that estate he found that the people would not look at his rates. I have been told the same thing over and over again by the European and native contractors working on the line. The railway before entering Porahat passes through the Political States of Kharsawan and Seraikella, and the permanently-settled zemindaries of the Manbhoom district. The circumstance related above shows therefore that the people in Porahat are more independent than those in the neighbouring Political States and in the native zemindaries, and from this I argue that they are better to do and more prosperous."

26. Respecting the classes dependent on charity, the Deputy Commissioner is not in possession of much information, but he believes them to be few in number and to be well looked after.

27. The following remarks by Dr. Manook, who has been many years in the district, are quoted in *extenso*:—

"The cultivators, that is those who live upon the produce of their land, are the best off. Among the Kols of this class specially the men are well nourished and physically strong; the women sleek and well-dressed, and the children well fed and taken care of. Their houses are of better class, their clothes made of better stuff, and their household utensils of brass and metal. This class supplements its income from cultivation by rearing cocoons, and this aids them in paying their rents and putting by something for the purchase of cattle and other necessary articles. Next to these come the artizans, the weavers, brass-workers and blacksmiths, who form the majority of the artizan class in the district. The physical condition of this class is also good. The brass-workers are the best off among them, for their handicraft fetches high value. Next the weavers, who can easily earn one to three rupees a week. The village blacksmith class is somewhat poorer, but he is not poverty-stricken. He earns sufficient to keep himself in physically good condition for his hard work.

"Of the labouring classes, the purely agricultural labourer is the worst off, but not so badly off as to affect his physical conditions for want of food. He is poor, his house is small, and it is among his class that the brass and metal utensils have not replaced the earthenware vessels, and whose clothing is of the scantiest. This class of labourers, in the south-west of the district, in the jungle pirs of the Kolhan, Rengrapir, Lotapir, Relapir, and parts of Sarandapir, are perhaps worse off than their bretheren in other parts of the district owing to limited cultivation in these parts, and their physical condition would indicate that they are not often well fed."

The tracts mentioned in the last part of these remarks have, however, been visited lately by the Deputy Commissioner, who has not found any indications of the poor condition mentioned by Dr. Manook.

28. The next district to be dealt with is Lohardugga. This district is divided into two tracts, which are sufficiently distinct to require separate

treatment, viz. Chota Nagpore Proper (which comprises the Ranchi plateau and the pergunnahs between the plateau and Manbhoom) and Palamow. The former of these tracts is mainly inhabited by the aboriginal tribes from which the supply of labour for the tea districts is principally drawn, while in the latter, as we pass northwards, the conditions gradually shade (as one might say) into those of South Behar. I regret that the Deputy Commissioner, Colonel Lillingston, has not favoured me with a single remark embodying the results of his own experience, or even collated and summarized the information obtained for him by his subordinates, but has simply forwarded it to me as it stands.

29. In the tract comprising Chota Nagpore Proper enquiries have been made in one village by Deputy Collector Baboo Girindra Chandra Banerjee, in one by the Canoongoe, and in five by Mr. Slack, late Settlement Officer. Mr. Slack considers that his position as Settlement Officer, enquiring into the condition of villages under settlement, was not favourable for the acquisition of perfectly trustworthy information on these social subjects, since it was to the interest of his informants to understate their profits and to make their condition appear as bad as possible. Again, he could get no accurate idea of food bought or of the cost of living, since the people themselves had none. As he was prosecuting his enquiries he was occasionally asked by a ryot whether he took him to be a mahajan and a keeper of accounts. Mr. Slack's investigations included 206 families and 1,311 people, of whom 379 were adult men, 368 were women, 321 boys and 243 girls. The village inspected by the Deputy Collector contained about 60 families and 300 individuals. The particulars of that seen by the Canoongoe are far from clear, since he gives the total population as 200, but estimates the number of families living on the wages of labour alone at 60. Probably the figures given for population mean families and not individuals. If we take it so, all the special enquiries taken together relate to 7 villages, 466 families, and about 2,700 persons.

30. Mr. Slack has not ventured to estimate the average holding of a ryot, because the ryots of the villages which he enquired into held lands in other villages in which there is no standard of measurement. The Canoongoe takes the average at 2 powas of low land, and the Deputy Collector at 3 or 4 powas, this low land in each case being supplemented by an indefinite quantity of high land. The powa varies greatly not only in different villages, but even in the same, so that nothing better than a guess is attainable. The holding may perhaps be taken at from 4 to 8 acres.

31. I am not prepared to trust the details of the quantity of produce or the cost of cultivation given in the reports of the two native officers. The Deputy Collector's estimate of the cost of cultivation gives a total much exceeding the gross value of the produce, and that of the Canoongoe appears sometimes to include and sometimes to exclude the price of the labour of the ryot and his family. Mr. Slack has not attempted to give statistics on this point.

32. The figures collected by Mr. Slack allow for an average of not more than from 2 chittacks to half a seer of rice per diem for each adult, but, as he points out, this is plainly much too low, since in the great majority of instances the people have at least two full meals in the day. At the same time it must be remembered that rice is not the sole food available. Considerable assistance is obtained from the maize and other crops of the rains, and in the hot weather from *mahua* and other products, and in all seasons from *sags* and other vegetables. Mr. Slack found that out of 206 families, 179 have at least two meals a day invariably, while only five are said to have but one meal, and that merely for part of the year. The Deputy Collector found in his village, out of 60 families, two or three "were well off," six or seven "suffering from a daily insufficiency of food," and the rest "living from hand-to-mouth, but apparently obtaining sufficient." A gentleman, whose business leads him into close connection with the people, and who takes an intelligent interest in them, tells me that it is very rare that a family has not two meals a day. In the neighbourhood of Ranchi he does not think that the food is to any great extent eked out by resort to jungle produce. The Sub-Manager of the encumbered estates, however, does consider that the poorer ryots have some difficulty in getting on during the latter part of the hot weather, and it is certain that at that time of the year labour is most easily procurable. None of these three officers found any beggars.

33. The amount of indebtedness varies much in different villages, but on the whole is less, as regards both the number of the debtors and the amount of the debts, than might perhaps have been expected. In the village visited by the Canoongoe he found no bhuinhar or rent-paying ryot in debt, though in adjoining villages 60 per cent. were said to be so. The Deputy Collector says that "few" of the ryots in his village are in debt. Collecting the figures given in Mr. Slack's report, I find the following results:—Of 129 cultivators, 50 were in debt, owing in the aggregate Rs. 601 in cash and 32½ maunds of *dhan*. Of 76 labourers and artizans, 25 were in debt, and owed in all Rs. 137 in cash and 3 maunds of *dhan*. The rates of interest were from 25 per cent. to 50 per cent., and the money was generally borrowed to pay rent, but sometimes to provide the means for social ceremonies, and occasionally for food. The amount of indebtedness is so small that it is obvious that the debts are not allowed to accumulate as a rule. In reference to the country near Ranchi, the gentleman whom I have already mentioned is of opinion that debt is common, especially among those who have good security to give.

34. Earthen vessels are used for cooking, but the food is often eaten from metal vessels.

Mr. Slack's report contains no estimate of the proportion; the Deputy Collector says that metal utensils are to be found in almost every house in the village inspected by him, while in the Canoongoe's village it is said that about 20 per cent. of the people have culinary or other utensils of metal.

35. I have not much information regarding ornaments. They are for the most part made of lead, or of brass or other metal. They are worn in considerable quantities, but their intrinsic value is small.

36. The cost of social ceremonies varies much. In mouzah Parandih Mr. Slack found that in 15 families the expenses attending a marriage were about Rs. 6, and *sradh* about Rs. 2; while the remaining six families spent from Rs. 10 to Rs. 70 and from Rs. 8 to Rs. 50 on these ceremonies respectively. In Bishahatu a boy's marriage costs Rs. 20, a girl's Rs. 10, and a funeral ceremony Rs. 10. In another village a marriage costs from Rs. 12 to Rs. 20, and a funeral from Rs. 2-4 to Rs. 5. In another a boy's marriage costs from Rs. 5 to Rs. 100, a girl's from Rs. 5 to Rs. 50, and a funeral ceremony from Rs. 8 to Rs. 40. In the village of Lota, among the agriculturists a marriage costs Rs. 15 and a funeral Rs. 4. In some places and among some castes the bridegroom pays the father of the bride from Rs. 5 to Rs. 12. The Canoongoe estimated the marriage expenses at Rs. 15 and the funeral expenses at Rs. 5 in the village seen by him: the chief item in the latter is for *banoya* or rice-beer.

37. Emigration exercises a powerful influence over the tract now under consideration. The people, particularly Uraoons and Mundas, are highly valued both in the tea districts and elsewhere as labourers. They do not object to travelling long distances, and for very many years there has been much spontaneous emigration for miscellaneous labour. In the present day the emigration to the tea districts is far the most important. Emigration to the Dooars is neither assisted nor regulated by law. It is managed by means of garden-sirdars who come down, recruit their friends and neighbours, and take them to the gardens, where no contract is entered into, and the labourers can leave when they like. Such emigrants generally return to their homes, and frequently go back several times to work in the gardens. The annual number of those so returning has been estimated by a very competent person at 10,000 per annum, including women and children, and the savings brought back at a lakh of rupees. Under the Assam system the proceedings are less healthy and satisfactory. Coolies proceeding to Assam are bound by contracts for three or five years, and these contracts may be entered into either locally or after arrival in Assam. A cooly who has been bound by contract has a definite money value; consequently there is a great temptation to abuses in recruiting. On the other hand, a man who has served five years in a tea garden is much more useful than a new recruit. Therefore the planters are able to offer inducements of a legitimate kind to such coolies to remain in the garden, and sometimes it is to be feared that the temptation to resort to illegitimate means of persuasion is not altogether resisted. However this may be, the result is that emigration to Assam is more permanent than to the Dooars, and probably less money comes back to Chota Nagpore. Still large sums are remitted to

relatives or brought back by returning emigrants, and it must be allowed that whatever abuses exist, whether in recruiting or in the gardens, emigration is of great service. It relieves the pressure on the land (and such pressure exists in some localities), it brings money into the district, and it assists in keeping in check the rapacity of landlords and money-lenders. The annual emigration is estimated at 25,000 persons.

38. Employment in the local tea gardens and in other service also materially helps the lower classes. Labour is exceedingly cheap, though it is becoming dearer. It is both common and convenient for one or more members of the family while residing at home to take work outside. My own garden coolies, most of whom are paid Rs. 2-8 per mensem, thus live at home, and when there is a pressure of work on their own fields it is not easy to make them regular in their attendance. Much of the rent, I am informed, of the villages near Ranchi and other centres is paid with money thus gained in service.

39. Mr. Ainslie, the Subdivisional Officer of Palamow, made minute enquiries into the conditions of 129 families living in their villages. As to the general state of his subdivision, he says that "it is wholly untrue that the greater proportion of the population suffer from a daily insufficiency of food. It is a fact that at certain seasons of the year a small proportion of the population have not sufficient food, but the proportion of the population that so suffers entirely depends as to whether the harvests are good or bad, and on the price of food-grains. In a year of scarcity in the subdivision a good deal depends on the *mohua* crop, for *mohua* is extensively used as food by the lower classes of the population, especially when food-grain is dear. During my tour in the last three months I have been through those parts of the subdivision where there are a large majority of the poorer classes, and I have not discovered any widespread poverty or distress of a chronic character."

40. The very elaborate statement compiled by the Canoongoe will be submitted with this letter. It is to be regretted that neither the Subdivisional Officer nor the Deputy Commissioner had a summary made, or indicated the points in which the information given may be taken as strictly accurate, and those in which merely guesses have been made. I have not now time to prepare a summary, but there are a few points which call for remarks. I do not regard the details of expenditure as very trustworthy; they seem to be mere estimates, and in some instances the amount considerably exceeds the apparent income. It will be observed that the entries in column 37 are on an uniform scale. For each seer of food consumed at an average meal it is estimated that 15 maunds per annum will be eaten; but 15 maunds is equal to 600 seers: consequently on 235 days in the year two meals per diem, and on the remaining 130 only one meal, are estimated for. This is the scale throughout for the Brahmin, who hires labour for the cultivation of his land, for the ticcadar of the village, and for the old woman and children unable to work, and all supported by a poor widow: the average cost per maund of the food is the same in all instances. Other items also are clearly estimates applied to particular cases, and not the ascertained facts of those particular cases.

41. In other matters, such as the number of persons in each family, the quantity of land, the numbers of cattle and of metal utensils, the figures are probably correct; and possibly the estimates of the produce may be sufficiently careful, but these cannot be checked.

42. I find none of the 129 families living on charity, though some of the Brahmins who are ashamed to dig are not ashamed to beg, and in certain families there are persons unable to work.

43. In one village, which contains 27 families, no fewer than 20, being all the cultivators, are in debt. The amounts vary from Rs. 3 to Rs. 40 in cash, and 7½ maunds of grain and Rs. 25 in cash and 18 maunds of grain. The total debts amount to Rs. 388-4 in cash and 122 maunds of grain, or an average of Rs. 19-7 and 6 maunds of grain for each family. In another village, out of 57 families, 18 cultivators owe Rs. 957, three keepers of sheep owe Rs. 65, and two others owe Rs. 35. Of the cultivators, two owe Rs. 200 each and one owes Rs. 150; the remaining 15 owe Rs. 407, or Rs. 27 each. This is an excellent illustration of Mr. Baker's suggestions that the amount of debt

depends less on the necessity of the borrower than on the security which he is able to offer.

In the third village 14 cultivators out of 21 cultivators had debts to the total amount of Rs. 999-4. Of this sum Rs. 400 was owed by a cow-keeper, who, besides his cultivation, had 33 head of cattle, and Rs. 200 was owed by a man who borrowed it to lend out again on mortgage. Of 45 persons not holding lands, nine owed Rs. 593-8; but of this Rs. 400 was due from one man, a cow-keeper, possessing 23 head of cattle.

44. In the first village 21 families out of 27 possessed two or more metal utensils; all the 19 cultivators had them.

In the second village 26 out of 28 cultivating families possessed such utensils, varying in number from 2 to 16 or 18. Out of 29 landless families, 18 had each two metal utensils, and one had one only. In the third village 20 out of 21 cultivating families had metal utensils, usually from two to four in number, but in one case 15. Of the remaining 24 families, 15 had from two to four such utensils and four had only one each.

45. Upon the whole, looking to the number of cattle and metal utensils, and also the quantity of land held, I am disposed to think that the cultivators are decidedly well off. Of the labourers, however, there are probably some who in ordinary years find it difficult to support themselves at times, and in bad seasons are likely to suffer.

46. In Hazaribagh the tracts in the extreme east are very greatly affected by the coal mines and railway, which of course bring them in large profits and afford the means of disposing of surplus produce. Respecting this part of the district the information supplied to me is exceedingly meagre, but happily it is the portion regarding which least anxiety need be felt. In two villages regarding which some enquiries were made by the Manager of Dhunwar estate, Mr. Tweedie, no beggars were found, but in one small one examined by the Giridih Subdivisional Officer's orders two were discovered. Mr. Jarbo's investigation comprised only 21 houses with a population of 157. Only one family depended solely on cultivation; the rest obtained their livelihood partly as labourers or as artizans, but of these most hold but a little land—not more than 2 or 3 bighas (local bighas, each equal to 2 standard bighas) to each family.

It is said that the income from both cultivation and the second source is scarcely sufficient to provide two full meals a day, the houses are thatched with straw, and if enclosed at all are merely surrounded with brushwood. The ryots provide themselves with clothes sometimes by taking loans, and sometimes by starving themselves in their food and eating jungle fruits. The artizan is better off, has generally a tiled house with a mud wall, and can procure clothes without starving himself. This is the whole of the information given by Mr. Jarbo, who has evidently taken very little trouble in the matter.

47. The remainder of the Hazaribagh district resembles more nearly the tracts by which it is bounded, viz. Manbhoom on the south, Chota Nagpore Proper on the south-west, and Palamow on the west and north-west. The District Officer, Colonel Garbett, has himself collected certain figures in five villages, but he has not favoured me with those general impressions of the conditions of the district which his tours must have enabled him to form. In three of the five villages he considered the physical condition of the people to be fair and thought them sufficiently fed. In another the physical condition was generally good, and most of the labourers seemed sufficiently fed. During the slack season many of the labourers in this village betake themselves to the Giridih collieries, and can find employment throughout the year. In the remaining village he thought the physical condition of the people good and believed them to be sufficiently fed.

48. In none of the five villages did Colonel Garbett find any family dependent on charity. On the subject of indebtedness, and on several others, I do not see that any enquiries have been made.

49. In the five villages there are 127 families of cultivators and 34 of "non-cultivators," by which latter term I understand persons who do not in any way combine cultivation with their other source of income, whatever it may be. The total population was 901, of whom no fewer than 617 are said to be adults. I cannot but think that there is some error here.

50. So far as the cultivators are concerned, the five villages scarcely represent a fair average of the district, since four of them grow poppy, which is a very profitable crop. The average gross produce of each cultivating family in those four villages is valued at Rs. 48, Rs. 83, Rs. 140, and Rs. 149 respectively, without counting *mohua* and other fruits. However, the gross produce of the other village in which there is no poppy is estimated at no less than Rs. 84½ for each of the cultivating families. I have not seen much of the rural portions of the Hazaribagh district, but if Colonel Garbett's figures are correct, I should be disposed to think that the condition of the agriculturalist in those five villages is better than the average.

51. The following are the rates of wages :—

Unskilled labour.

Each man per diem	3	seers grain or	1 anna 6 pies
Woman	2	ditto	1 anna
Child about 7 ..	1½ to 2	ditto	9 pies to 1 anna
Carpenters and blacksmiths			2 annas 6 pies to 3 annas

per diem (part being generally taken in grain), and a maund of grain per annum for each plough in the village.

In one village two families of potters were found. They were said to be fully employed, and the average earnings were estimated at 3 annas per diem.

52. The following table gives the result of Colonel Garbett's enquiries as to cattle :—

	Buffaloes.	Bullocks.	Goats.	Sheep, &c.
369 pure agriculturists own ..	55	325	71	....
80 artizans and traders ..	8	97	7	....
144 pure labourers ..	*Nil*	12	8	....
308 labourers who also cultivate	14	122	45	....
901 ryots in all own ..	77	556	131	....

The figures in the first column represent population—not number of families, of which there are 161 in all.

53. The foregoing paragraphs will have shown that, on the whole, the District Officers have not followed the orders of Government with sufficient care, and that there are not a few points which have escaped attention. If it is the desire of Government to pursue these investigations further, I should advise the circulation of a full set of questions, which must be answered by all officers. In this division it is peculiarly difficult to arrive at an accurate general conclusion from the consideration of a limited area.

54. The following, however, may be taken as the opinion which I have formed on certain points. The number of persons living on charity only is very small indeed. The great majority of the people are sure of two meals at least in the day in an ordinary season, and of the remainder most, if not all, are sure of two meals a day in an ordinary year, with the exception of the latter part of the hot weather. Rice is not by any means the only food, though it is the most important article. It is largely supplemented by vegetables, maize, and other crops grown in the rains, by *mohua*, and in a large portion of the division by numerous jungle products. Further, there is some fish, though not much in comparison with Lower Bengal, and animal food, both wild and tame, is occasionally procurable. There are few, if any, animals which are not accepted as food by some caste or tribe. Emigration has been of great advantage, especially to Chota Nagpore Proper; it has been the means of relieving the pressure which exists in some places on the land; it has brought much money into the division, and has afforded to some extent a check on the rapacity of money-lenders and landlords. Probably at least half the cultivators are in debt, but the amount of debt is generally small. It is usually incurred for the purpose of paying rent or performing some social ceremony. In some places seed-grain is borrowed; in others each ryot saves his own. The cultivators as a class are better off than the village artizans or mere labourers, but in towns the artizans are very well paid. The artizans and labourers are far less in debt than the cultivators, because they have less to offer as security. The rates of wages are certainly rising. In the parts most inhabited by aboriginals they are still very low, and often the wages of one or two members of the family are

regarded merely as supplementing the general resources. The effect of European enterprize in the matter of tea cultivation, the collection of tussar cocoons, and other produce has been to throw large sums of money into the country, and the construction of the Bengal-Nagpore Railway, now in progress, and the feeder roads will have the same result. Upon the whole, though beyond any doubt there are very many poor people in the division, whose livelihood, especially when there are partial failures of crops, is precarious, there seems to be no doubt that the great majority are not ordinarily severely pressed. The physique of different classes and castes and tribes varies very much, but generally speaking it is fairly good.

55. I have seen all the Native States of which the supervision rests with me, but have had no opportunity of making minute and systematic enquiries regarding the condition of the people. Probably such enquiries would be distasteful and alarming to the Chiefs. The population of the States is quite as varied, if indeed it is not more so, as that of the British districts. The least civilized of all are the Kharwars. Those of Jushpore are only beginning to eat rice and salt, and have hitherto subsisted on jungle roots, fruits and leaves, with very little in the way of cultivated crops: their physique is excellent. Mr. Ainslie, the Subdivisional Officer of Palamow, has made enquiries regarding Sirgoojah, and thinks the condition of the people is much the same as it is in Palamow. On the other hand, the inhabitants of the States bordering on and enclosed in Singbhoom are considered by the local officers to be less prosperous than those of the British districts. My own opinion is that, on the whole, the inhabitants of the States are nearly as well fed and clothed as those of the British districts, but their houses are certainly not so good. This probably arises from their being less secure and more autocratically governed. I have been told—I can hardly say with what truth—that in the Tributary States generally it is very difficult for a subject to grow rich. The people of Gangpore seem to me to be generally better off than others. Many of them wear gold ornaments, and seem to have a comparatively high standard of living. I do not think that there is very much emigration either from or to the States. The Rajahs are fully alive to the importance of attracting population, and grant lands on very easy terms. The Rajah of Jushpore told me last year that a good many people from Burway (a wild and backward zemindari in the west of Lohardugga) have come into his State to avoid exactions from the family of the Rajah of Burway. On the other hand, the Rajah of Gangpore complained to me that he was much cheated by immigrants from the Lohardugga district, who took lands from him and cleared them and occupied them only during the period when little or no rent was being levied. The Chiefs are all anxious to receive new-comers and to prevent the emigration of their own people.

W. J.—Reg. No. 81T—60 & 65—26-6-88.

Confidential.]

No. 286G, dated Bankipore, the 2nd June 1888.

From—JOHN BOXWELL, ESQ., Offg. Commissioner of the Patna Division,
To—The Secretary to the Government of Bengal, Revenue Department.

I HAVE the honour to submit the report on the condition of the lower orders of the population of this division, called for in your circular No. 35Agri. of the 9th December last.

2. I have now before me special reports only from five districts, but I have materials for reporting on the condition of the other two.

3. The final opinion will be arrived at in two ways—by general considerations based on large figures, corresponding to the outside boundary of a surveyed area; and by results of careful examination of small selected areas, corresponding to the internal detailed survey. If the results of the two methods agree, or rather in proportion to the agreement of the two methods, will be the value of the conclusion.

4. As there will be a good deal of arguing on what must be, as well as of statement of what is, I will explain some of the basis of the argument. Comparison of population and area yields a good conclusion about plentiousness of food only when the area grows its own food. A town is a perfect case at one end of the scale. As a town grows no part of its own food, density of town population is completely irrelevant. A mouzah which grows all its own food is a perfect case at the other end. Then the ratio of acres to population is a direct index to average comfort. Another consideration brings us a step closer, even than average comfort, in the required direction. Food-grains are not worked up into anything except food, and rich men eat little more than poor men; that is, a man's wealth is not measured by the quantity of food he eats, and the difference in quantity between just enough to live on and plenty is not very great. Therefore we may be sure that the food which is not exported is spread over the area which grows it in return for labour.

5. Another elementary point is worth insisting on. It is sometimes said of a particular area that the people pay their rent with rice and live on *marwa* and the poor grains. This is only true as far as the whole area exports rice. Whether rice is sold to pay rent or not, all the rice which is not exported out of the area under consideration is spread as food over that area.

6. The result of this dull, but necessary, arguing is that we must first ascertain whether the area under consideration imports food or not. If it imports food on a large scale, we may at once give up all idea of arriving at any knowledge of the condition of the poorer classes from a comparison of area and population. If, on the other hand, it does not import food to any considerable extent, then this comparison of area and population is one of our surest methods of reaching a right conclusion.

7. We then come down to such particulars as the average outturn per acre, and the quantity of food necessary to keep a family in health. And finally we examine our selected areas for individual facts.

8. The districts of the division fall into the following scale:—

In Shahabad	..	1	acre represents	·7	souls.
" Gya	..	1	" "	·7	"
" Chumparun	..	1	" "	·76	"
" Patna	..	1	" "	·91	"
" Durbhunga	..	1	" "	1·2	"
" Mozufferpore	..	1	" "	1·3	"
" Sarun	..	1	" "	1·36	"

Tirhoot and Sarun form an area of very dense population—more than a soul to an acre. Of the remaining four districts. Patna is the most dense, and Shahabad is the least, in the division. Mr. Quinn declares the lower classes in Patna to be very poor. Mr. Power says the corresponding people are fairly comfortable. That there are two persons less on every 10 acres in Shahabad is probably part of the cause.

9. For various reasons I am inclined to think Mr. Quinn's judgment about the Patna district exceptionally good. I have had much correspondence and some controversy with Mr. Grierson about the condition of the people of Gya. I am prepared to admit, or rather assert, that, though the population is not dense, still the people are badly off. The hills and jungle necessarily reduce the density figure of the district, leaving the population quite dense enough in parts, with poor soil and not very much help from canals. But when Mr. Grierson asserts that the ordinary ryot, in ordinary years, cannot support himself from his land, but has to supplement by *borrowing*, I think he attempts to establish an impossible case.

10. This leads up to a very important subject,—the indebtedness of the poor cultivators. I shall go back to interesting remarks made and quoted by Mr. Quinn, but I think a misconception should be got rid of. General indebtedness of a poor agricultural community is not like, and is much less bad than, the common indebtedness of an extravagant man. It means nothing more than that in the tight season—that is, the season of ploughing and sowing—the mahajan advances what he recovers with interest in the harvest. The strange notion that borrowing makes a permanent addition to a cultivator's income, and the common view that a peasantry in debt is on its way to ruin, seem to be equally wrong and almost equally paradoxical. In a low state of civilization people are unable to do their own saving. Their mahajans do it for them, and make them pay well for it; but in an ordinary year the produce of the soil, including of course pasture and jungle, supports the cultivator, the labourer, the mahajan, and the landlord. It will be interesting to inquire why Gya and Shahabad, the districts of least density, should be represented as one the best off and the other the worst off in the division.

11. In discussions of this kind we are surrounded with dangers, and therefore our reasoning should be as much as possible cumulative, so as to neutralize the fallacies that impend everywhere. The food produce per acre is one of the most difficult and uncertain parts. As has been pointed out, an error of a maund per acre would make all the difference between comfort and misery. Even the quantity of food necessary to keep a man in health is uncertain, because it varies with the character of the food and of the man.

12. With these cautions, I may go on to assume two-thirds of a seer of food required for each man, woman, and child each day, and 10 maunds of food per acre the annual outturn. About this estimate I can only say that it is made by the best judges, I know, who still are quite aware of its uncertainty. The population of the division is about a soul to an acre of cultivated land. A family is taken to consist of two adults and three children. According to the estimate, we want from each acre 244 maunds for food and we get 400, or a surplus of over 60 per cent. for everything.

13. Leaving generalities and coming to particular enquiries, I begin with Patna. Mr. Quinn confined his attention to the rural population. Among them he says of artizans and beggars :—

"As regards artizans outside the town, this class are to a considerable extent holders of land; those living entirely by the practice of handicrafts being probably not more than 4 or 5 per cent. of the population. I cannot furnish a detailed account of the mode of life of this class, but they are said to be generally better off than the petty cultivators or labourers. The artizans, who are also holders of land, are reported to be a prosperous body. The proportion of the village population who subsist entirely on charity is very small."

14. Coming on to the agricultural class, he gives this table for a small selected area :—

Population.	Total area.	Cultivated area.	Average rent per bigha.	Average area of holding.	Petty ryots on 6 bighas or less.	Labourers.
			Rs. A.	Bgs.		
2,708	3,392	2,706	3 8	8	634	460

The average size of holding is correct from actual inquiry. Deducting the 460 labourers, with their families, the comparison of holding to population gives as the average number in family 6·6. This is close enough to ascertained facts to be taken as correct. Here the petty cultivators and labourers form that poorer class about whom we are enquiring, and are about 40 per cent. of the whole. About them Mr. Quinn says:—

"The condition of these people can only be described as one of extreme poverty and indebtedness, those only being free from debt whom the mahajan will not trust."

15. In another place Mr. Quinn takes the result of very careful inquiry in two villages and finds the average product Rs. 12 per bigha, and the average cost, exclusive of the cultivator's labour, Rs. 6; so that, including the wages of his own labour, on which he is living at the time, the ryot makes the value of Rs. 6 out of a bigha. A previous estimate gave 8 maunds of food as the outturn. This gives 26 seers per rupee, the mofussil price of food, and this is admitted to be about right. As before, a family of five wants 1,220 seers of food in the year. A bigha yields to the ryot only 4 maunds. The other half goes in rent, seed, hire of bullocks, and the like. At 4 maunds a bigha it takes 7 bighas to yield 1,220 seers. Therefore, a holding of less than 7 bighas will not support a family unaided. But 40 per cent. of the people have holdings of 4 bighas or less. Therefore, they must eke out a subsistence by labour for others, and such additions as will be mentioned afterwards.

16. I have had much controversy about the quantity of food required for a family. The Behar jail rules give a labouring prisoner 1 seer 4½ chittacks of good food. The Famine Code gives 14 chittacks as sufficient for an able-bodied labourer. Most people whom I have consulted say that the labourers in the villages want much more than this. As the food they get is coarse and poor, it is likely they want more of it; but when it is said that the more comfortable cultivators can do with much less food than their own labourers, I begin to doubt the local criticism of the official estimates.

17. The end of Mr. Quinn's report is very well condensed from the papers of the inquiries he ordered. I quote in full:—

"It follows that, in order to support life at all, these small cultivators must work for others as well as themselves. The Manager, whose remarks I extract below, calculates that a man and his wife, who work for others besides cultivating their own land, may earn about Rs. 12 per annum, including the proceeds from collecting and selling cow-dung. He also estimates the cost of supporting a family of two adults and two children at Rs. 33. The total earnings of a ryot with a holding of 4 bighas would thus be about Rs. 36, and the cost of maintenance Rs. 33, leaving a margin of Rs. 3; but the average area of petty holdings is less than 4 bighas, and the result is that most ryots of this class cannot afford to take a full supply of food.

"Their fare is of the very coarsest, consisting to a great extent of *khesari dál*, and the quantity is insufficient during a considerable part of the year. They can only take one full meal instead of two. They are badly housed, and in the cold weather insufficiently clothed.

"The condition of those who support themselves entirely by labour is rather worse than that of the better class of petty cultivators. They are almost always paid in kind, the usual allowance of a grown man being 2 to 2½ seers of the coarsest and cheapest grain, value about 1¼ annas. Women receive about half this rate, but their employment is less regular. Ordinarily, male labourers do not find employment for more than eight months of the year.

"A wage of 1¼ annas per day would be about Rs. 2-6 per mensem; but taking an average of Rs. 2 per mensem throughout the year, the annual earnings of an adult would be about Rs. 24; his wife's earnings might be Rs. 6, total Rs. 30, which is not enough to give two adults and two children a full supply of the coarsest food, with sufficient clothing and a hut to shelter them. The Subdivisional Officer of Behar estimates the earnings of a labourer at 2 annas per diem, or Rs. 4 per mensem; but even this rate, which I think an over-estimate, would only yield Rs. 32 for the eight months during which labour is generally to be had.

"The conclusion to be drawn is that of the agricultural population a large proportion, say 40 per cent., are insufficiently fed, to say nothing of clothing and housing. They have enough food to support life and to enable them to work, but they have to undergo long fasts, having for a considerable part of the year to satisfy themselves with one full meal in the day."

18. Durbhunga and Mozufferpore, East and West Tirhoot, having very much in common, and being dealt with separately, ought to furnish a good basis for comparison. Both District Officers are quite new to the districts, and are reporting on materials collected by other men. Mr. D'Oyly does not quite endorse the opinion of Mr. Samuells, and there is no doubt that when they differ, Mr. D'Oyly is right. Mr. Bolton's is a well-reasoned paper.

19. In the density scale Durbhunga comes just under Mozufferpore, but has less indigo and opium, and a little more jungle. The idea given by the two reports is that the Durbhunga people are rather the worse off.

Having opinions of my own about Durbhunga, I can say that, wherever they touch the same subject with Mr. Bolton, they completely corroborate his. Where I do not support his views by means of knowledge of my own, I can see that his view is both probably right and well argued. I condense his report here. Tajpore has most kinds of lands, and is best able to resist bad seasons. Madhubani is most exclusively rice-bearing, and least able to resist. The Sadar is intermediate in character, as well as geographically. Improvement of communications diminishes reserve stocks. "The well-being of the population must be held to rest entirely on the results of each year's harvests." The percentage (60) of ryots holding less than 4 bighas, ascertained by inquiry in the selected Tajpore villages, may be accepted for the whole district. I now quote :—

"There is no doubt that the bulk of the cultivating population are occupiers of small holdings, and it is very probable that the holdings of 2 bighas or less are more numerous than those of between 2 and 4 bighas. A small holding may, however, be sufficient by itself for the entire maintenance of its tenant and his family, if the lands are suitable for the most renumerative crops, such as tobacco, sugarcane and opium, and the smallness of the holding is not therefore always evidence of the tenant's poverty. Still, as a very general rule, the tenants of small holdings of less than 4 bighas are badly off, and it is necessary, where their families are of the usual size, that they should supplement cultivation by labour. This labour they obtain generally by assisting the more independent tenants in the cultivation of their holdings or harvesting of their crops, or by temporarily emigrating into neighbouring districts to help in gathering in the harvests."

Again—"*Marwa* cakes or Indian-corn in the day and rice at night form the ordinary diet of most classes, and they are able to supplement or replace one or other of these at certain seasons with vegetables, sweet potatoes or other roots, and fish, which is fairly cheap. As regards rents, they are, I have no doubt, generally high, and the tenants are much harassed by the incessant efforts of the landlords to enhance them."

20. Mr. Bolton estimates half the whole number of agricultural labourers to hold some land. The others are mostly "*Ján*"; called elsewhere "*Kamia.*" They are serfs, never likely to rise into any higher position, but then helped over bad times by their masters, who do not like to lose them. The remarks about indebtedness may be considered in connection with the other reports. Artizans are declared to be better off than the lowest class of cultivators. People who subsist on charity are very few. Mr. Samuells "tried to form some conclusion by general inquiries in villages, but it is almost impossible," in his opinion, "to get at the truth in this way." "The general reply," he adds, "is that every man eats according to his *liakat.*" I cannot understand this, especially as Mr. Quinn and Mr. Grierson have obtained their most valuable information from inquiries in villages. Mr. D'Oyly is thus thrown very much on his own resources for making the Mozufferpore estimate.

21. Mr. Grierson's Gya report came in last night. I have read it once through. It is far the most elaborate, and also the most gloomy of all. It will be impossible to do justice to it in the few hours that remain before post time. As I have not yet got the Sarun report, the district about which I know least, I shall have to submit a supplementary report. I am still receiving communications from the districts in answer to my comments. It is quite clear that a divisional report ought to be more useful and more correct than even a very good district report, but for this end the district reports should be collated at leisure, and the District Officers questioned on all obscurities. There has been little time for this. About the Gya report, I say what I said of Mr. Grierson's former report of the same nature. I know myself that he

is somewhere about right, and that much of the new light he has thrown on the subject is true and good. He does not seem to know or care how far his critic agrees with him, and he does not seem to be startled at strange results. With so much reservation, I can say he proves the poorer people in Gya to be very poor, and to be insufficiently fed. Just now I will use his report chiefly to help to explain the other district reports. I return to Mozufferpore. The local bigha varies, but the average is not far from an acre. The information about size is vague, but a very large proportion of the holdings is said to be very small. Tirhoot, and especially Mozufferpore, is noted for the very large number of very small maliks.

22. As was to be expected, the greatest differences are found in the estimate of outturn per acre. No doubt the average outturn does differ greatly in different places, but in our ignorance I think we colour. The Mozufferpore average produce of *dhan* per acre is put down as high as 17 maunds, and *rabi* and *bhadoi* at 12 maunds, while the price is said to be about a rupee a maund.

23. Mr. D'Oyly proves against Mr. Samuells that wages of labour have increased. He says—"A labourer will get from 4 to 5 seers of *dhan* (unhusked rice) a day. For cutting crops labourers get one bundle in every 16 bundles cut. Labourers have work nearly all the year round where there are indigo factories. From the middle of September to the middle of February indigo preparations are going on, and in December and January the rice crop is cut. In April and May indigo is weeded; in July *bhadoi* crop is weeded; in August and September the *bhadoi* crop is cut. These agricultural labourers generally have small holdings of their own, and many keep goats. Baboo Nandanlal, zemindar, tells me that formerly labourers used to get 4 seers of *dhan* or 5 seers of *makai* (Indian-corn) a day; now they get the same quantity, and, over and above this, they also get each two *rotis* or cakes of half a seer each, made either of barley or *makai* or *marwa*. Money wages for labour were formerly 4 pice a day; now they are up to 2 annas." He adds a remark to the effect that Tirhoot pays its labourers a good deal better than Gya. Seetamarhi appears to be worse off in all respects than the rest of Mozufferpore, just as Madhubani is worse off than the rest of Durbhunga.

24. The condition of artizans is treated very shortly, and people who subsist on charity are declared to be very few. Artizans appear, as in other places, to be better off than the lowest class of cultivators. In Mozufferpore, about the indigo factories, this is true also of the labourers.

25. It is very clear to me from the reports that Mozufferpore occupies an intermediate position in every respect between Durbhunga and Chumparun, to which district I come next. I have an excellent report from Mr. Henry, and only by this last post I have had a second letter from him with explanation of details.

26. By this report Chumparun is better off than any district in the division; better even than Shahabad. And yet some of the facts are hard to reconcile with this. "Sixty per cent. of the population either have no holding or cultivate holdings of 2 acres or less"; and again "the average holding of cultivated land of a family in the district is only 4½ acres."

27. I have had much controversy and discussion about the quantity of food necessary for a family, and necessary for an able-bodied, working man. The men who take gloomy views demand for the poor labourers and cultivators a quantity of food larger not only than the official allowance, but also than the jail allowance and the quantity thought sufficient by the more comfortable cultivators. Then reasons are urged on both sides. Prisoners, well-to-do cultivators, labourers on official allowance, eat more wholesome and nourishing food, and therefore want less: on the other hand, prisoners cooped up in a dismal jail and kept to penal labour would pine away unless they got excellent nourishment.

Mr. Henry's calculation is of this kind. The population (1,721,608) contains 350,000 families of two adults and three children. The family food is 5½lb a day, or 25 maunds a year; or for the whole district 8,750,000 maunds. The 1,300,000 cultivated acres at 14 maunds an acre give 18,200,000 maunds, or more than double the food required. The most probable weak point in this argument is the outturn per acre. As so much of the food is rice, I am not sure that a sufficient allowance has been made for the difference between husked and unhusked grain.

28. But now I come to the peculiar feature of Chumparun. Mr. Henry writes:—"From the treasury figures of the last three years it appears that the following amounts were paid out to cultivators as the price of the opium delivered at the two sub-agencies of Motihari and Burharwa:—

			Rs.
In 1885-86	..	..	23,79,670
„ 1886-87	..	..	23,60,500
„ 1887-88	..	..	22,57,900

the area under poppy in these years being about 62,000 acres; and on this land the cultivators also grew a crop of maize. Some deduction must be made for the value of the Nepal opium, which may be put down at 500 maunds, valued at 3 lakhs of rupees, reducing the total to 20 lakhs of rupees, in round numbers, as the amount given to cultivators during each of the past three years in payment for their opium.

At present there are about 75,000 acres under indigo, a large proportion of which is grown on what is known as the *khuski* system, the rate of remuneration paid being about Rs. 15 the acre, giving a total of a little over 11 lakhs of rupees paid to the cultivators for the use of their land and for their labour in cultivating the indigo plant. To this sum must be added the cost of labour employed in the manufacture and carting of the plant, which will not be less than 7 lakhs of rupees, making the total 18 lakhs of rupees. I have not succeeded in obtaining exact figures, and in my estimate have therefore been careful to put down the sum as low as seems reasonable. Messrs. Dear & Co. carry on an extensive business in timber taken from the Nepal and Ramnuggur jungles, and the portion of their yearly outlay, which represents the cost of carting and sawing, may be put down at 2 lakhs of rupees. This is also a low estimate."

29. With respect to labour, I quote—"With the exception of persons belonging to superior castes, Brahmans, Babhans, Rajputs and Kaisths, all members of the cultivator's family work in the field, and some members engage themselves for daily labour, the wages earned being—

		A.	P.				
Adult males	..	2	0	a day	or 3	seers	of grain.
„ women	..	1	6	„	or 2-8	„	„
Boys above 12	..	1	0	„	or 2	„	„

Ordinarily they are paid in grain. Labourers employed by cultivators on field work get two meals. Before commencing work they eat some parched grained or boiled sweet potato: this meal is known as *panpiai*.

"At midday they eat bread or cake made of the flour of the cheapest grain procurable in the market, adults receiving half a seer and boys less, the amount allowed being as much as a person can eat. This meal is known as *kalewa*.

"At night all classes have a regularly cooked meal, consisting of boiled rice, vegetables, fish; or bread, *dâl*, and vegetables, according to their means and tastes.

"Persons of all classes are said to get a sufficiency of food in ordinary years." And again—"The majority of the cultivating class, including the landless labourers, take three meals. In the early morning they eat *bhunja* or parched grain, usually *makai* or gram, cooked sweet potatoes, or some of the rice which may have remained over from the preceding night. At noon they ordinarily eat bread made from different grains, according to the season, and also *sathu* or coarse flour. At night they have a regularly cooked meal of rice and vegetables, or rice and *dâl*, or occasionally fish with bread or *dâl* and vegetables.

"The nature of the food is coarse, but from all accounts a sufficiency is obtained."

30. Durbhunga and Chumparun discuss the question of comparative comfort of the cultivators in Nepal and India. Durbhunga gives it in favour of Nepal; Chumparun of India. According to native views, they ought to be happier in Nepal, because they pay lower rent and no regular taxes or cesses; need not be clean or orderly; are in fact let very much alone, subject to sudden requisitions when occasion demands. According to our notions, they ought to like being given roads and bridges, and doctors, and magistrates and police, and put up with regular taxation. I cannot answer the question decisively.

31. Shahabad is another district that claims to be well off. This position is subject to the strongest attack. No one disputes that the lower classes in Patna, Gya, and Durbhunga, and also Mozufferpore, are badly off. No one doubts that Chumparun is exceptionally well off; whereas I have heard much arguments against the prosperity of Shahabad. The jungles of the Kaimur hills bring the density of the population of the cultivated parts up to 84 per acre. The canal system makes the food-supply much more steady. Without attempting to estimate the outturn per acre, Mr. Power assumes that "in all years there will be considerably more food produced than is absolutely necessary for the consumption of all the people, including the non-agricultural population." He then sets himself to consider the distribution. He begins with the landless labourers, whom he thus describes:—"This report, however, chiefly concerns itself with the landless labourers, who undoubtedly are the lowest in the social scale. They consist of the lowest castes—*Kurmis*, *Dosadhs*, *Chamars* and *Jolahas*, and some *Baniahs*. They are known by the general term of *Kamia*. Theirs is the minimum standard of comfort in the district. They are really serfs, and are entirely dependent upon their masters, the maliks and superior cultivators. They are looked upon by their masters as their chattels, and obey them implicitly. In most places they are paid daily in kind, at the rate of 4 seers of rice or *sathu*, according as which is most plentiful, in the hard working season and 3 in the slack time. They are not allowed to go to another master. They are not allowed to work for anyone else without permission. Their food is served out to them by their masters twice a day. Just as much as they eat is supplied to them for a midday meal, and the rest of the grain is given at night. As the average daily consumption of an adult individual is one seer of rice per diem (Macdonnell's Food-grains, section I, paragraph 36, and paragraph 239 of Mr. Deputy Collector M. S. D. H. Ahmed's special report to Government, 1874), there is a surplus. With this surplus clothes such as are worn, the furniture of the hut made by the labourer, tobacco, earthen pots, and a few other necessaries are bought. The wives of all these *Kamias* work and receive a smaller allowance than the male usually. Children at 12 begin to get an extra allowance, if not before. Besides *dál* and salt no other condiments are given, but sometimes vegetables are bartered in exchange for grain. The fiction is usually kept up that the labourer is in his master's debt for grain, &c., advanced when he was ill or was not working, or for some marriage or other festival, but the usual allowance of grain given daily is never cut, even though the *Kamia* is refractory. He is then punished by personal chastisement. It seems to be intuitively known to their masters that to stint their allowance of grain would drive these labourers to flight."

Having thus found that the lowest class has sufficient food, Mr. Power takes it for granted that all other classes have more than enough.

32. I find that I cannot now handle the reports properly. They are too full of matter to be adequately treated in a short time, and, as already explained, the Sarun report has not come yet; while the Gya report, very long and very closely argued, only came last night. I must therefore submit a supplementary report myself, and will now be content with a very slight summary. Durbhunga and Patna, which are Nos. 4 and 5 in increasing poverty are Nos. 5 and 4 in increasing density of population. Chumparun and Shahabad, which are Nos. 1 and 2 in prosperity are Nos. 3 and 1 in increasing density. This looks as if the reports were well founded. But Gya, which is only second in density, is worst of the six, and probably will be worst of the seven, in poverty; and I know that the report is in the main right. Therefore we must not trust too much to the calculations from density.

This very important and melancholy fact seems proved, that a very large number of people in Patna and Gya, about 40 per cent. of a population of over 3,880,000, are insufficiently fed. I have little doubt that the same kind of thing is true in Durbhunga to a less degree, and that Mozufferpore, Shahabad and Chumparun will be found to be better off. I know less of Sarun than of any of the districts. Most likely it will come high up in the scale of prosperity. As I have been compelled to take time for a second report, I think it better to end this abruptly without appearance of completeness.

W. J.—Reg. No. 527—60—18-6-88.

Confidential.]

No. 20PT, dated Camp Pooree, the 3rd June 1888.

From—C. F. Worsley, Esq., Offg. Commissioner of the Orissa Division,
To—The Secretary to the Government of Bengal, Revenue Department.

With reference to your circular No. 35Agri., dated 9th December 1887, and enclosures, I have the honour to submit the first instalment of a report on the condition of the lower classes of the population in this division.

2. In submitting their reports to my office the Collectors have laboured under great disadvantages, being all of them new to their respective districts, and having received nothing in the way of notes from their immediate predecessors. The consequence is that, though in some instances information collected by subordinate officers has been forwarded for my use, it is impossible for me to speak with much authority on the subject, inasmuch as the Collectors themselves have pleaded ignorance of their districts as a reason for making no comments.

3. In Cuttack district, three villages, situated within the Government estate of Banki, which is now under settlement, were selected for the purposes of enquiry. The investigation was conducted by the Sub-Deputy Collector, now acting as Settlement Officer, and the results have been recorded in the form of answers to certain questions proposed by the Collector, who has sent on the answers to me with the following brief memorandum:—"I have, of course, no personal knowledge of the condition of the agricultural classes here, such as a cold weather tour would enable me to obtain, and I have no notes left to guide me to an opinion. From limited opportunities I have had, derived chiefly from my visit to the Aul estate, I consider the people I have seen to be a well-to-do peasantry, but it is impossible for me to generalize on an experience so very limited."

4. Under these circumstances, and because the Banki estate cannot be regarded as a typical estate of Cuttack, I consider that it would be useless on the present occasion to transcribe a variety of facts and figures. In two out of the three selected villages there are no lands for cultivation, and the inhabitants hold lands in various adjoining villages. The number of beggars and of others who subsist on charity are reported to be very small. The condition of the agricultural labourers and small cultivators seems fair. They live in mud-built huts, own cattle, and have of late years replaced earthen pots by brass utensils. Their food consists as a rule of rice and *sag*, and occasionally of other vegetables; and though some at times are not fully fed during half of the year (October to March), they all get two sufficient meals a day. The physique of the people is described as good.

5. Mr. Allen's report of Pooree district, which is based partly on what he has himself seen during four or five weeks of extensive tours, and partly on information obtained from Mr. Taylor, the experienced Subdivisional Officer of Khorda, and others, is as follows:—

"I have the honour to report that I have not as yet had time to make the detailed enquiries in typical villages, as suggested in Mr. Finucane's No. 100T of the 27th September, or to compile figures showing the number of persons in the district who hold land sufficient for the support of their families, or of those who, holding insufficient land for subsistence, supplement the proceeds of cultivation by working as labourers, fishing, manufacturing salt, or other occupations. In fact, having been for so short a time in charge of the district, I am not as yet in a position to give any very precise or detailed information on the very difficult and important subject under report. I hope hereafter to submit something of more practical value than can be done at present, but in the meantime I beg to submit a few notes as a first instalment of what I have myself seen in a hurried tour over a considerable part of the district, or gathered from Mr. Taylor and others, who have had a longer acquaintance with the people of this district than myself.

"My own idea, from what I have seen in places supposed to be now in a distressed state, owing to a more or less complete failure of the main crops for three years, is that the lower classes of the population are at least as well off as those of the better parts of Behar. I have now traversed a great part of the district, and nowhere have I seen any signs of serious distress. Everywhere the people, men and women, seemed fairly nourished, and the children were fat and healthy looking. Another thing which shows that the people are generally pretty well-to-do is the fact that, even amongst the lowest classes, such as, sweepers, *bouries*, *pans* and *savars*, very few women or children will do earthwork on roads, tanks, or embankments. The poorer women will husk rice, plant or weed paddy, and pick or sell firewood, but they will not join in any work which associates them with strange men, and a very great many will do no work out of their own houses or those of their immediate neighbours. Except a few professional mendicants on the road to Pooree, I hardly saw a single beggar, and this again is evidence of the generally good material condition of the lower classes.

"I am assured by Mr. Taylor that, with the exception of the educated classes, the Ooriya ryot never makes any show of wealth, and that it is impossible to judge from a man's costume, house, or surroundings whether he is rich or poor. Mr. Taylor cited two out of many cases personally known to him, where really wealthy contractors, one of the cultivator and one of the writer-caste, wear the common coating *dhuti* and *chudder* of the country, and live in ordinary mud hovels, not a whit better than their next-door neighbours, whom he knows to be mere paupers.

"The Pooree district is almost entirely an agricultural tract, and the great bulk of the population are cultivators themselves; either occupancy ryots, or sub-ryots holding more or less land. The proportion is small of those who subsist entirely by labour or by work as potters, blacksmiths, carpenters or weavers, as in Pooree almost all artizans and traders combine agriculture with their other means of subsistence.

"The total area of arable land in the district is probably about 800,000 acres. The total population may be estimated at 900,000. Taking 100 to represent the four orders of the poorer classes, I should estimate that 80 per cent. were cultivators, or men who combine agriculture with other things; 15 per cent. purely agricultural labourers, with no land of their own; 4 per cent. artizans, with no lands; 1 per cent. beggars, &c.

"Of persons who subsist on charity, *i.e.*, of *bond fide* beggars, there are very few indeed. In Khorda, where a detailed settlement has been recently made, dancers, musicians, beggars and others together only form 0·15 of the population; and taking the whole district, including the town of Pooree, where beggars naturally congregate, I do not think that 1 per cent. of the population subsist merely by begging. Of course in a district like Pooree there are many who are called mendicants, Brahmins and Bairagees, but these are not generally paupers, and they mostly hold arable lands, from which they get half share of the crop as rent.

"Rents are low in Pooree as compared with Bengal and Behar districts. In Khorda, where the rents have lately been enhanced, the average per acre all over is only Re. 0-8-10$\frac{7}{20}$ per acre, while the average rent on cultivated and occupied area is only Rs. 1-9-5$\frac{12}{20}$. The highest rate per acre for first class two-cropped rice land being only Rs. 3-12 per acre; and out of a total of 150,000 acres of rice land in Khorda, only 532·243 acres have been assessed in the first class. The old settlement rates in the Pooree district are somewhat higher than the rates now assessed in Khorda, and zemindars of course take higher rents again from all ryots who do not hold the old settlement pottahs. It is impossible at present to give an average of rates per acre now actually paid by the cultivators to zemindars in Pooree, but that average will certainly not exceed Rs. 5 per acre.

"Average outturn of the principal crop (rice) is estimated at 14 maunds, or about 10$\frac{1}{4}$ cwt. per acre, and the average price of paddy exceeds Rs. 6 per *bharan* of 8 maunds, or 12 annas per maund, which gives Rs. 10-8 per acre for grain, and the value of the straw averages Rs. 2 per acre.

"Prices of food-grain, as will be seen by the weekly returns, are low as compared with the Bengal districts. The people have, besides their crop, fishing in lakes, rivers and tanks, and along the coast on the sea; plying boats and bullock carts, quarrying and carriage of stone, lime and forest produce, mangoes and other fruits, of which the mango in ordinary seasons form a material item of the food-supply. The manufacture of salt also affords employment to the poorer classes living near the Chilka Lake and Devi river, and there is always a good deal of work on provincial and district roads and embankments, and works of khas mehal improvements. In fact, I believe the supply of labour all over the district equals the demand, and there is no necessity for going long distances to search for work, even in bad years.

"In the neighbouring district of Ganjam, in Madras, the material condition of the poorer classes is much the same as in Pooree, and so in the Native Tributary States of Ranpur, Nayagarh, Khandpara, which adjoin this district.

"The principal crop (paddy) is more than sufficient, even in bad years, for local consumption, and large quantities of grain are exported to Cuttack and Ganjam, and *viâ* Pooree to coast ports, Ceylon and the Mauritius. Amounts not less than 100,000 tons of paddy, and probably a good deal more, are annually exported.

"The people appear to me to be of fairly good physique, and though not very robust, they are fairly active and strong. This is also Mr. Taylor's opinion, but the medical officer in charge of the district considers that 'they are weak, but active, and their general physique is stunted.'

"The jail statistics show that, notwithstanding the good food and light, regular work, only 58 per cent. during the past year (a year of comparative scarcity) gained weight during their confinement. This is one of the facts which leads Dr. Sandel to believe that the people are as a rule insufficiently fed.

"Wages of unskilled labour vary, according to demand, from 6 pice to 3 annas a day for adult males, from 4 to 6 pice for women, and for children according to size. For skilled work, as for brick-layers, stone-cutters, black-smiths, carpenters and palki-bearers, the wage is from 4 to 8 annas a day. Wages of labour is often paid in kind, especially for agricultural labour, and the system of agricultural bond servants is also prevalent throughout the district. These men are said to get 2½ seers of paddy per day, and occasionally a piece of cloth and a portion of their marriage expenses. They pay no rent for their homesteads, where they grow vegetables and keep poultry. On the whole, they fare better than ordinary labourers.

"The Ooriya prefers mud huts to pucca, and there is a general idea that a house with mud walls and thatched is healthier than a masonry building; and many families, though they could well afford to build and live in pucca houses, prefer to live in mud ones, thinking that it is unlucky to build a masonry house. This applies even to most of the Gurjhat Chiefs.

"In Orissa villages the houses are almost always built on each side of fairly wide streets with a back ground or garden. Ventilation is generally better than in Behar, and the houses, though unfurnished, are neater and cleaner. The clothing of the poorer classes is somewhat scanty, consisting generally of a common *dhuti* and *chudder*. For bedding and coverlet in the cold season a soft, thick matting, made of grass, called *henso*, is used. As there is very little cold weather in Orissa, no great amount of clothing is necessary, but still the poorer classes must be considered as insufficiently clad. This is also Dr. Sandel's opinion.

"For ornaments the poorer classes use a great deal of brass, bell-metal, and pewter; delicate women often having a weight of 8 or 10 seers on their arms. Gold nose-rings and silver ornaments are occasionally seen on women even of the agricultural classes.

"Brass *gurrahs* and other household cups and plates are used by all but mere beggars. The cooking is done almost entirely in earthen pots, even by the well-to-do.

"There are enormous numbers of cows and bullocks in the district, but owing to want of good pasture the cows give but little milk. Of buffaloes there are also a good number. These get better fed, as they can thrive on the plants in the jungles and graze in swamps, which are inaccessible to cows. In the jungly part of the district there are large herds of goats, which afford a good supply of flesh and milk.

"Fish, prawns, crabs, and shell-fish are caught in enormous quantities in the Chilka Lake, and carried long distances for sale at the hâts, as the lower classes seem to prefer them when full flavoured. Besides these, large quantities of fish are dried with or without salt, and prawns are preserved and exported largely to Burmah for the preparation of *napee*.

"On the whole, I am of opinion that the lower classes in this district are not under-fed, though many of the very poorest live in fact from hand-to-mouth. I am, I think, borne out in this view by the fact that, though the principal crop (rice) has entirely or partially failed for the last three years over a good deal of the district, there is still nowhere any signs of actual starvation or serious distress; and though two small *quasi*-relief works were lately opened in two of the worst parts of the district, and ordinary rates of wages were given, the number of persons applying for work was so few that these works have to be completed by contractors on the usual terms. Nothing ever occurs in the way of emigration in Pooree, and nothing to speak of in the way of annual migration in quest of work to neighbouring districts. Even this year the people of the worst tracts, which bordered the district of Ganjam, have only crossed the border in very limited numbers, and that only because they were attracted by rates of wages higher than they could command in the neighbourhood of their homes.

"When paddy fails, *mandia*, *kulthi*, and other crops supply food for those who cannot afford to buy grain in the local markets. Fish and various kinds of sea-weed, which grow wild about the Chilka Lake, are also freely utilized, and in the forest tracts the poorest classes will collect roots and herbs, which, boiled in rice-liquor, supplement a purely grain diet. That the nutrient ratio of their food is deficient according to European notions must be admitted, but the Ooriya appears to thrive on a diet wanting in albumenoids, which would be fatal to a European constitution.

"Indebtedness is said to be pretty general, but, so far as I can make out, the poorer agriculturists are not worse off in this respect than in other parts of Bengal, and one of the main causes of debt—the expenses of marriage and other social ceremonies—is in Pooree comparatively low.

"In conclusion, I ought perhaps, as we have been directed to consult Civil Surgeons, to quote the opinion of Dr. Sandel, though it is opposed to what I have recorded above. He considers 'that the poorer classes of this district are not properly fed and clad. They barely subsist on coarse rice and a spinnage curry, cooked without oil. As a rule, they do not have more than one meal a day, and very often food once cooked lasts for two days. He concludes his brief report by observing that the determining causes that lead to the misery and poverty of the Ooriyas here can be set aright by a proper organization of their general surroundings.'"

6. From what I saw of Pooree district during two short tours in September and October 1887, and from what I have seen and learnt during my present three weeks' residence in the district, I am disposed to endorse the views recorded by Mr. Allen.

7. The Collector of Balasore has forwarded copies of reports received from Dr. Zorab, Superintendent of the Balasore Jail, and from Deputy Collector Baboo Prankristo Roy, with the remark that, "being new to the district and to the Ooriya race, he is unable to express any opinion worth recording." Dr. Zorab's report, which is based upon 15 years' local experience, describes a most prosperous state of things. He writes:—

"I have been in the district since June 1873, close upon 16 years now, and notice very many changes, one and all of which indicate material progress in the condition of the agricultural classes and the district at large. The exports have increased very much indeed, and there is always a very brisk exportation going on within the last few years, whereas in the early years of my stay here only a few native sloops would carry away all that the port had stored.

"The importations have vastly increased. In the place of a few native sloops bringing in goods in the early years of my stay here, we have now not only weekly steamers pouring in goods, we have now additional supplies by the canal route. The town itself shows great increase in trade. Shops have multiplied for all kinds of stores. In the place of one or two cloth godowns, we have now strings of godowns hanging out linen and woollen materials to attract customers. Grain and store shops have increased. Sweetmeat shops have largely increased. All round us the town shows every sign of prosperity.

Out in the district I see also signs of progress. Our very dâk bearers, who used to be very sparely clad, now go gaily along materially adding to the weight by piling umbrellas and warm covering on the burden they carry. Wages of labourers in the early years was 6 pice male, and 4, or even 3, pice a day per woman. It has now risen to 12 pice and 7 pice respectively. Carpenters and masons are getting pretty nearly double the old rates, and the smallest vigilance in exacting the full number of hours leads to instant desertion. Cart-hire has risen from 2 to 4 annas a day, and the number of carts risen from 50 to over 200. In the early years almost all goods were brought on pack-bullocks, whereas now cart traffic preponderates.

"As regards the main point at issue, I distinctly remember overhearing conversation amongst the domestics as to the poverty and inability to obtain two good meals daily in early years. Latterly I have never heard any such talk. On the contrary, the diffidence they betray as to the retaining of their appointments is in marked contrast with the anxiety they showed to please, so as not to lose their posts. In my mind there is not the smallest doubt that of later years there has been great prosperity in the land."

8. The Deputy Collector's report is also very favourable, and may conveniently be quoted here:—

"In dealing with the subject mentioned above, the first thing I would notice is, that this district, on the whole, may very properly be classed as agricultural, because the principal means of subsistence of most of its people is agriculture. Calculating on the figures obtained in respect of some of the estates now under settlement and partition, it has been found that 98 per cent. of the ryots are cultivators, and only 2 per cent. nonculturists. It is remarkable that in six estates now under settlement only two ryots out of 507 were found as not having cultivated lands. Again, of the artizans and cultivators, which form 98 per cent. of the total population, more than half are dependents on the profits derived from agriculture alone. Hence the total population of this district may more conveniently be divided into two orders instead of four, as suggested in paragraph 3 of the Government letter, viz.—(*i*) cultivators and (*ii*) those who subsist on charity. The cultivators, again, may be subdivided into three classes—(1) those who have no other occupation but cultivation, (2) cultivators who occasionally work as agricultural or unskilled labourers, and (3) cultivators who are also artizans or traders by profession. Although in the village in which I made personal enquiries as to occupation, &c., of the residents, I did not meet with a single ryot who has not at least an acre of land to cultivate, from my own observations in other parts of the district, enlightened by the opinion of officers of much large experience, and tested, so far as possible, by the figures of the last census, the proportion of the population included in each of these classes mentioned above is estimated as follows:—

Persons having no other occupation than agriculture ..	40	per cent.
Persons dependent on wages of unskilled labour and profits of small holdings	45	"
Persons dependent on skilled labour and profits of trade, &c. ..	10	"
Persons dependent on charity, including the blind, lame, leprous, and otherwise disabled	5	"

"Compiling figures from some of the road cess returns, six estates under settlement and one large estate under partition, I find the average area of a ryot's holding to be about 3 acres, and the average annual rent payable therefor Rs. 3-6. On sorting these ryots according to the area of their holdings, it is found that the proportion of ryots holding 3 acres or less is 70 per cent. of the total number. Here it should be observed that the area of the ryots depending solely on agriculture varies from 7 to 15 acres, according to the number of bullocks they keep. A ryot keeping a pair of bullocks generally possesses 7 or 8 acres of land, and such a ryot can easily maintain a family consisting of seven or eight members, according to the popular idea of a *mân* or acre per head for subsistence. About 20 per cent. of the ryots occupying larger holdings are supposed to live much more comfortably than the others; to lay by something in the shape of grain, ornaments, utensils, &c.; and also to be more liberal than others in expenses on account of marriages, &c. Of the ryots holding 3 acres or less,

Area of ryots' holdings.

most part have some other occupation besides cultivation, such as fishermen, potters, braziers, blacksmiths, carpenters, manufacturers of salt, masons, washermen, barbers, oilmen, tailors, drummers, basket-makers, confectioners, milkmen, sweepers, sundies; and other people of the lowest order, such as Kandras, Doms, &c., having small quantities of land to cultivate, supplement their small profits derived from their small holdings by the earnings or wages they get by carrying on their respective professions. The ryots of the cultivator class holding land less than 3 acres supplement their agricultural profits by the wages they get as agricultural labourers, *i.e.*, by assisting their fellow-ryots having more lands than what they can themselves cultivate. Thus, according to the existing arrangement, which has grown naturally by the observance of the social rules and customs for centuries past, very few people in the district, excepting those who become helpless under extraordinary circumstances, suffer to any appreciable extent from a daily insufficiency of food in a year of good or average harvest.

Produce per acre.

"The produce (paddy being the staple food of this district) per acre in a year of average harvest ranges according to the fertility of the soil from 2 to 6 *ponties* per acre. The average rate of produce per acre is estimated by experienced local men to be 3½ *ponties*, or 12 maunds 10 seers per acre. To this may be added the straw produce at the rate of 3 *pans* per acre, the value of which is Re. 1-8.

Expenses of cultivation, including rent.

"The average rate of rent per acre obtained from the figures respecting certain estates mentioned is Rs. 1-3-3 per acre. As most of the people in this district, and almost all of the lower classes of the population, cultivate their lands by their own plough and own hands, the expenses of cultivation are but nominal in most cases; hence the expenses of cultivation, including the rent, may be safely estimated at Re. 1-6 per acre.

The price for which the produce not consumed can be sold.

"The price of paddy sold within the district varies at times from 10 to 14 annas per maund. So the average price per maund may be estimated at 12 annas, but it is to be remembered, as stated above, that only the ryots of the regular cultivator class, who hold land 7 acres or more, and the mahajans or paddy-lenders can have surplus paddy to dispose of. The other ryots having smaller holdings also occasionally sell a portion of their produce for the purpose of paying rent and buying cloths and other necessaries, but these people generally have to borrow paddy again from their mahajans towards the middle or close of the year, according to the want of each. The paddy-lenders generally take 25 per cent. on the quantity lent as interest after each harvest. In this way there are numerous ryots who are personally indebted from generation to generation, the amount of their debt increasing or decreasing temporarily according as their harvest is bad or good. It is a matter of regret that such ryots should ever remain indebted, and can hardly expect to improve their condition, even if they have successive good years, because the mahajan, who always brings forward a heavy balance against them, including interest and compound interest, no way affected by the law of limitation, takes the benefit of the exceptionally good year; while the poor ryot, by the sweat of whose brow the produce is obtained, remains poor as ever, living from hand-to-mouth. Nowadays in the interior of the district one may meet here and there men and women of the cultivator class exulting in petty luxuries, such as coloured woollen and linen clothes, shoes, umbrellas, and bulky ornaments of various metals and shapes; but the fact which deserves to be reiterated here is that the enjoyers of these luxuries are none but those cultivators who, having surplus produce, get the advantage of better prices at better markets in these days of extensive exportations, and also those hereditary mahajans who feed themselves fat on the produce of other's toil.

Extent of indebtedness of the cultivators.

"In the village of Sumbulpur, in which I made careful enquiries on this and other points, 7 out of 16 ryots were found indebted, and their debts were said to vary from Rs. 10 to Rs. 50. Most of these debts were said to have been incurred on account of marriages and other social ceremonies, and the area of the holdings of these debtors ranges from 3 to 8 *máns*. Including the debtors in paddy, I think nearly one-third of the ryots are indebted more or less.

"The wages of agricultural labourers are known to be various in the different parts of the district. In some places such labourers, called *Báramásiás*, are kept and maintained throughout the year, and the rate of their wages is as follows:—

Wages of agricultural labourers.

"A loan of Rs. 5 is given to the labourer without interest, one *mán* of land is given for his own cultivation rent-free, and besides he is to get a piece of *gámchhá* (napkin) and 5 seers of paddy daily.

"Another class of labourers are allowed fooding and clothing, besides pay of Rs. 9 to Rs. 18 per annum, according to their age and working power per annum. The ticca labourers, who work by days, get at places close to the town at the rate of 3 to 4 annas per diem, and in mofussil at the rate of 2 annas to 2 annas 3 pie or 6 to 8 seers of paddy per diem.

"As mentioned above, most of the artizans of this district supplement their earning from their professions by incomes derived from the cultivation of small holdings. In the village visited by me I met with four weavers, of whom two cultivate a *mán* of land each, and the other two 12 *máns* each. Each of these weavers has got a *taut* (weaving machine), and they admitted before me that each of them can on an average earn Rs. 5 a month by weaving clothes. Under the circumstances, I think in Orissa, where the conservative character of the Ooriyas still induces them to use country-made clothes to a larger extent, the weavers *are* better off than their caste-fellows in other parts of the province. I need hardly mention here that the females of the weaver class help the males a great deal by preparing and setting thread for the machine, &c. The artizan classes of which the females work with the males in their own profession are the tailors, shoemakers, weavers, oilmen, washermen, workers of lac ornaments, makers of bamboo baskets, &c. The prevailing rates of wages paid to the different classes of labourers in this district are shown in a statement given below:—

Condition of the artizans.

Description of Labourers.	Skilled.		Unskilled.		Remarks.
	From	To	From	To	
	Rs. A. P.	Rs. A. P.	Rs. A. P.	Rs. A. P.	
Carpenters ...	0 5 0	0 6 0	0 4 0	0 4 6	Approximate daily wages.
Blacksmiths	0 4 0	0 5 0	0 3 6	0 4 0	
Tailors ...	0 6 0	......	0 3 0	0 4 0	
Weavers ...	0 6 0	0 6 0	0 4 0	0 5 0	
Shoemakers	0 4 0	0 5 0	0 3 0	0 4 0	
Brassware-makers	0 4 0	0 5 0	0 3 0	0 4 0	
Thatchers ...	0 3 0	0 3 6	0 2 0	0 2 6	
Oilmen	0 3 0	0 3 6	0 2 0	0 2 6	
Bricklayers ..	0 4 0	0 5 0	0 2 6	0 3 0	
Washermen	0 4 0	0 4 6	0 3 0	0 3 6	
Workers of lac ornaments	0 4 0	0 5 0	0 3 0	0 3 6	
Lime-workers	0 3 0	0 3 6	0 2 6	0 3 0	
Makers of bamboo, cane baskets	0 2 0	0 2 6	0 1 6	0 2 0	
Coolies ...	0 2 6	0 3 0	......	......	
Masons ...	0 6 0	......	0 5 0	0 6 0	

"The agricultural labourers in the mofussil cannot find employment throughout the year, though they remain fully employed in the season of cultivation. In previous years the manufacture of salt used to provide employment to thousands of men for three to four months in a year, when their services were not very much wanted for the purpose of cultivation. The abolition of many such manufactories of late has of course rendered such labourers out of employ, and these men will no doubt suffer materially on this account.

"The number of persons subsisting on charity, such as lame, blind, leprous or otherwise disabled and helpless, may be estimated at 2 per cent. of the whole population.

Persons subsisting on charity.

"From my own observations of the nature of food, drink, dress, ornaments and habitations, &c., of the people of Orissa, extending over a period of nine years, I can say that the condition of the people of the lower classes at present is much better than in previous years, and that the change that is gradually taking place is decidedly for the better. As regards sufficiency of food, I may say that, if there be people in this district really suffering from a daily insufficiency of food, their number is not greater than what is to be always found even in prosperous countries under special circumstances.

Condition of the people in general.

" I need not fear of understating their number if I say that the proportion of such persons to the whole population is not more than 2 to 3 per cent.

" The condition of the population in British territory is much better than that of the population of the contiguous Tributary States of Nilgiri and Mourbhunj. The migration of people (non-criminals) from British territory to the Tributary States is never heard of; while numerous ryots of Mourbhunj are known to have migrated to pergunnahs Fatiabad, Gurpada, Jamkunda, and Nampo. The causes of this migration are probably better soil, better climate, better administration, and security of the ryot's right of occupancy to the land, &c."

9. I regret exceedingly that I am compelled to submit this report in such an unsatisfactory shape.

W. J.—Reg. No. 56T—225—25-6-88.

CONFIDENTIAL.]

No. 13RG, dated Burdwan, the 6th June 1888.

Memo. by—E. V. WESTMACOTT, ESQ., Offg. Commissioner of the Burdwan Division.

COPY of the following forwarded to the Secretary to the Government of Bengal, Revenue Department, in continuation of this office No. 7RG of the 16th April last.

No. 205G, dated Suri, the 30th May 1888.

From—C. J. S. FAUDLER, ESQ., Officiating Collector of Beerbhoom,
To—The Commissioner of the Burdwan Division.

I HAVE the honour to resubmit the report on the condition of the rural population in this district.

For the purpose of this enquiry, four villages, viz. Dholla, Durgapore, Beleya, and Gangmuri, were selected as typical of the various parts of the district, and a canoongoe was deputed to prepare lists of the inhabitants of each, containing detailed information as to the profession, property, liabilities, and means of livelihood of each individual.

Population classified.

NAME OF VILLAGE.	Number of families in census return.	Number of population in census return.	Number of families in existence.	Number of population in existence.	Male.	Female.	Children.	Number of persons each man has to support.	REMARKS.
Dholla	(a)93	336	(a)84	316	96	107	113	3	(a) The difference is due to the ravages of malarious fever.
Durgapore	(b)162	619	(b)140	440	146	144	150	3	(b) Twelve families have migrated to Rampore Hât, as they had no means of subsistence.
Beleya	68	871	179	674	206	243	225	3	
Gangmuri	(c)203	904	(c)186	746	249	235	262	3	(c) At Gangmuri 600 persons died of malarious fever.

The bulk of the information collected is shown in a series of tables annexed to this report, of which Nos I to XIII show figures for each village, and Nos. XIV to XVIII show figures for each individual in Dholla village. Appendices I to IV show the income and expenditure of selected individuals of each class as stated by themselves. The inhabitants have been divided into five classes, viz., cultivators, agricultural labourers, common labourers, artizans, and mendicants. *Primâ facie* it would not appear that the people should be as a body badly off; the cultivators, as a rule, have fairly large holdings and small families; the labourers get good wages when there is any work to be had, and will not work for low wages at any time. Still, when the income and expenditure is to be estimated in figures, it is found that in almost every case the expenditure turns the scale—and this though the last two years have been prosperous, the rice harvest of 1886 having been 14 annas and that of 1887 12 annas. The estimates now submitted are based upon the statements of the people themselves, and these cannot of course be relied upon implicitly. With the best intentions, a ryot who keeps no accounts cannot be expected to remember his exact profits from his cultivation, and much less can a labourer remember how many annas he has earned, what his children have brought in, or how much his wife has made by picking up sticks. The probability therefore is that the people are better off than the tables would induce us to suppose. The excise and trade returns, and all similar external gauges, indicate a very great increase in comfort among the people during the last two years. Of the poorer cultivators and labouring classes, however, it does not appear that they have been able to do much more than live even in these good years, and there can be no doubt that they have no reserve to fall back upon in bad years. The Dholla returns show that the majority are in debt (even including the ryots with large holdings) in spite of the bumper rice harvest of 1887. They have not yet recovered from the bad seasons of 1884 and 1885; marriages, funerals, and festivals help to keep them back.

Cultivators.—About one-third of the families are cultivators. The average holding is 6 acres in Gangmuri, 4½ in Durgapore, and 5¼ in Dholla and Beleya.

Of the 30 families of cultivators in Dholla, only three hold less than 10 bigahs and eight others from 10 to 13. Families average no more than two adults and one child. The cost of living is estimated as follows for a cultivator :—

For one adult.

	S. CH.		As.	P.
Cooked rice and *muri* twice a day	0 15	=	0	7½
Salt, oil, sauce, &c....			0	4½
			1	0

	Rs.	A.	P.
i.e., yearly	22	13	0
Cloth, three pairs, at Rs. 1-4 ...	3	12	0
Two chuddars	1	4	0
Two napkins	0	3	0
Miscellaneous expenses	2	0	0
Total ...	30	0	0

A child costs half as much only.

The produce of an acre of land and its cost of cultivation is shown in Table IX. From this it would appear that from one acre a ryot can clear about Rs. 6-12 only ; so that it would require about 11 acres for the support of a man, his wife, and child. Of the 30 cultivator families in Dholla, there is only one who has this quantity of land. The estimated cost of cultivation, however, does not take into consideration the fact that a great deal of the work done by the family—the manure, seeds, and much of the labour—is not paid for. It is impossible to estimate this saving, which varies in each case. As a rule, however, the cultivator does not pay ready money for labour, but he employs labourers by the year, who work his land under his supervision. At the time of harvest, these labourers are given one-third of the produce, minus the advances they have received. Thus, supposing the produce of an acre to be worth Rs. 21, the labourer gets Rs. 7, the zemindar about Rs. 4, and miscellaneous expenses for seed, repairs, &c., Re. 1, and the cultivator Rs. 9—thus the average holding of 5 acres gives Rs. 45. But the cost of living of the cultivator—father, mother, and one child—has been estimated at Rs. 75. The balance of Rs. 30 is made from the *rubbee* crop, sugarcane, vegetables, and other petty sources of income. The poorest cultivators can no doubt live on less than Rs. 30. The cost of living of the wife is probably never so much as Rs. 30, except in rich families.

Table VII shows the total income from their land of all the cultivators in the four villages, which does not quite cover their cost of living. They have, however, additional sources of income in their garden produce, ducks and fowls, hire of carts at seasons, fish from their tanks, fruit and fuel. These sources of income cannot be estimated with any degree of accuracy for the mass, as they vary for each individual. In no case are they of any substantial value, though they help to make both ends meet.

Table XIV gives the details of property and income as far as they could be collected for each of the cultivators in Dholla. The actual income and expenditure of one ryot from each village according to their own statements has also been recorded, and is given in the appendices. As to their possession, the detailed table for Dholla shows that there is no dirth of bullocks ; many of the cultivators have a cow. Brass utensils are in general use, but these articles last a long time, and the annual expenditure on them is small. In the four villages only Rs. 30 were spent last year. It was not found possible to ascertain what quantity of silver and gold ornaments were in the possession of the cultivators. Besides their own living, the cultivators have to provide themselves with houses and tools and to spend money on marriages, funerals, and festivals. The houses are poor thatched edifices, which cost but little, and last a long time with petty annual repairs. To set himself up in tools, including plough and cart, a cultivator has to spend about Rs. 16-8 shown in the margin. When once they are bought, they are kept in order by the village artizans for a fixed yearly contribution. For a good pair of bullocks, the average price is Rs. 40. As to the cost of marriages, funerals, and festivals it varies indefinitely according to the means of the individual ; such expenditure is rarely done except on borrowed money, the rich man hampering himself considerably, the poor man a little.

	Rs.	A.
Nangalor plough	0	4
Ish (ईश)	0	2
Jowal (yoke)	0	2
Fal (फाल)	0	6
Spade	1	0
Rope	0	4
Palan	2	0
Cart	12	4
Total ...	16	8

Eighteen of the 30 cultivator families in Dholla are in debt, the total debt amounting to Rs. 1,093. The indebted are not by any means the smaller landholders in every case. Marriages and extravagances, as well as the bad crop in 1884, account for the indebtedness. In the four villages taken, 30 per cent. of the cultivators are in debt, the average indebtedness being Rs. 150, or about two years' net income.

Agricultural labourers.—There is in this district a large class of agricultural labourers who are regular permanent servants as described above. The cultivators take them on by the year to do the bulk of the work of cultivation under their own supervision, and pay them one-third of the produce. During the year before the crop ripens, these labourers live upon advances of grains given by the cultivators, which are deducted with 25 per cent. interest from the labourer's share, as will be seen from the Statement No. XV. Few of the labourers are free from debt. They are assisted by their women and children in the work, being mostly low caste men. They depend upon the cultivators who advance them what they require. They eke out their livelihood by other employments as shown in the table. One specimen case from each village has been taken, and his income and expenditure recorded as accurately as he could give it (*vide* Appendices Nos. I to IV). The cost of living of an agricultural labourer is estimated at Rs 24. It is noticeable that in Dholla their families average five persons each, against the cultivator's three. In Gangmuri 50 per cent. of the agricultural labourers hold lands of their own, on an average of 2½ acres; but in the other villages they do not. Even in Gangmuri 40 per cent. of them are indebted for advance of grain to the cultivators.

Non-agricultural labourers.—This is a class which works chiefly at house-building, carrying, and other miscellaneous odd jobs; they also work in the fields, when there is any unusual demand for labour for any agricultural process. As a rule, they are paid from 2 annas a day to 2½ annas. The labourers in Dholla have stated their daily wages in most cases at 2 annas 6 pie, and estimate that they have been in employment for nine months of the year and upwards. As it was shown that the cost of living in the case of a cultivator was only Rs. 30 a year, the labourers upon their showing have not been badly off. On the other hand the four specimen labourers, whose income and expenditure have been recorded in detail, show in each case a heavy deficit. This shows how hopeless it is to get an accurate estimate of the financial position of people who live from hand to mouth and keep no accounts. It is impossible to feel certain that we are correct within 50 per cent. The fact, however, is undoubted, that labour in this district cannot be got under 2 annas a day per head, and often not for that; so that it does not appear that the labourers are at present in distress.

The artisans—Generally have fixed clientele; each of their customers calls them in for any job for which they are wanted, and pays them a fixed quantity of grain a year, generally 30 seers or a maund of paddy. In Dholla they have from 25 to 30 customers each; besides this, they generally have a little land; they are in much the same position as the cultivators. About 50 per cent. of them are more or less in debt. At Beleya there are a number of artizans who, up till the last few years, made a very good living out of corn-smelting. This industry has died out, and the corn-smelters now earn their living as cultivators and labourers.

Mendicants.—There are not many of these. Such as there are are mostly old people, past work from age or disease. They are supported by chance charity.

W. LeB.—Reg. No. 3768C—137—9-6-88.

on by the year to do the bulk of the work of cultivation under their own supervision, and pay them one-third of the produce. During the year before the crop ripens, these labourers live upon advances of grains given by the cultivators, which are deducted with 25 per cent. interest from the labourer's share, as will be seen from the Statement No. XV. Few of the labourers are free from debt. They are assisted by their women and children in the work, being mostly low caste men. They depend upon the cultivators who advance them what they require. They eke out their livelihood by other employments as shown in the table. One specimen case from each village has been taken, and his income and expenditure recorded as accurately as he could give it (*vide* Appendices Nos. I to IV). The cost of living of an agricultural labourer is estimated at Rs 24. It is noticeable that in Dholla their families average five persons each, against the cultivator's three. In Gangmuri 50 per cent. of the agricultural labourers hold lands of their own, on an average of 2½ acres; but in the other villages they do not. Even in Gängmuri 40 per cent. of them are indebted for advance of grain to the cultivators.

Non-agricultural labourers.—This is a class which works chiefly at house-building, carrying, and other miscellaneous odd jobs; they also work in the fields, when there is any unusual demand for labour for any agricultural process. As a rule, they are paid from 2 annas a day to 2½ annas. The labourers in Dholla have stated their daily wages in most cases at 2 annas 6 pie, and estimate that they have been in employment for nine months of the year and upwards. As it was shown that the cost of living in the case of a cultivator was only Rs. 30 a year, the labourers upon their showing have not been badly off. On the other hand the four specimen labourers, whose income and expenditure have been recorded in detail, show in each case a heavy deficit. This shows how hopeless it is to get an accurate estimate of the financial position of people who live from hand to mouth and keep no accounts. It is impossible to feel certain that we are correct within 50 per cent. The fact, however, is undoubted, that labour in this district cannot be got under 2 annas a day per head, and often not for that; so that it does not appear that the labourers are at present in distress.

The artisans—Generally have fixed clientele; each of their customers calls them in for any job for which they are wanted, and pays them a fixed quantity of grain a year, generally 30 seers or a maund of paddy. In Dholla they have from 25 to 30 customers each; besides this, they generally have a little land; they are in much the same position as the cultivators. About 50 per cent. of them are more or less in debt. At Beleya there are a number of artizans who, up till the last few years, made a very good living out of corn-smelting. This industry has died out, and the corn-smelters now earn their living as cultivators and labourers.

Mendicants.—There are not many of these. Such as there are are mostly old people, past work from age or disease. They are supported by chance charity.

W. LeB.—Reg. No. 3768C—137—9-6-88.